INTERNATIONAL TRADE
AND THE
TOKYO ROUND
NEGOTIATION

INTERNATIONAL TRADE
AND THE
TOKYO ROUND
NEGOTIATION

• • •

GILBERT R. WINHAM

PRINCETON UNIVERSITY PRESS
Princeton, New Jersey

ALL RIGHTS RESERVED
Library of Congress Cataloging in Publication Data
will be found on the last printed page of this book
ISBN 0-691-07725-8 (cloth)
0-691-02243-7 (pbk.)

This book has been composed in Linotron Sabon

Clothbound editions of Princeton University Press books are
printed on acid-free paper, and binding materials are
chosen for strength and durability.
Paperbacks, although satisfactory for personal collections,
are not usually suitable for library rebinding

Printed in the United States of America by
Princeton University Press
Princeton, New Jersey

This book is dedicated to my parents

ALFRED RATHBONE WINHAM
1909–1980

MARGERY RANKIN (POST) WINHAM
1912–1984

CONTENTS

Preface   ix

Abbreviations and Acronyms   xiii

Introduction   3

1 The Tokyo Round and the Political Economy of
   International Trade   15

2 Background: Creating the Capacity to Negotiate   58

3 The Negotiation Launched, 1973–1974: Issues before the
   Tokyo Round   91

4 Early Phase, 1974–1977: Resolution of the Problem in
   Agriculture   128

5 Middle Phase, 1977–1978: The Bonn Summit Run-up   168

6 End Phase, 1978–1979: Completion of the Codes   212

7 End Phase, 1978–1979: Tariffs, Wine Gallons, and Other
   Matters   256

8 Internal Decisionmaking in the Major Participants   306

9 Explanation of Process and Results   350

10 Conclusion: The Future of the World Trading System   402

Appendix A   The Tokyo Declaration   413

Appendix B   Summary of Six "Code" Agreements Negotiated
at the Tokyo Round   417

Selected Bibliography   425

Index   439

PREFACE

International negotiation has become the primary mechanism by which industrial nations make trade policy. The trend in this direction started with the U.S. Reciprocal Trade Agreements Act of 1934. It was reaffirmed by the establishment of GATT in 1947, and it has continued through a succession of negotiations both under and outside GATT auspices. The Tokyo Round negotiation of 1973–79 was the seventh and largest of a postwar series of GATT multilateral negotiations. This book is a political history of that negotiation.

In writing a history about a discrete event, I felt obliged to report by what process that event had come about and to analyze the substantive impact it might have had on the environment in which it occurred. This book tackles both these tasks: readers can judge for themselves to what extent it has succeeded. But in carrying out these tasks, I could not help but wonder whether what from hindsight seems so clearly to be a trend toward international negotiation would indeed continue to be a trend into the future. The past half-century has seen a growth of collective decisionmaking in international trade, and the Tokyo Round was part of that development; it will be fascinating to find out if the Tokyo Round continued that trend or if it was a turning point toward a more individualistic and nationalistic style of trade policymaking. Questions such as these were clearly beyond this book, but at least they did motivate the effort to understand contemporary trade negotiation and its meaning for the international economic system. For the ultimate answers, one must wait—impatiently—for the future to unfold.

The data gathered for this book consisted mainly of personal interviews, government documents, and secondary sources. Numerous confidential interviews were conducted with government officials and international civil servants who participated in the Tokyo Round. These sources cannot be identified, although in many cases the richness of the ideas discussed in interviews surely warranted attribution. I am delighted to take this opportunity to thank my interviewees for the generous and unreciprocated concession of their time. I hope they will feel compensated with the knowledge that this book will be a lasting record of their accomplishments.

Portions of this manuscript have been published elsewhere. The material on Canada in chapter 8 draws on an article entitled "Bureaucratic

Politics and Canadian Trade Negotiation," *International Journal* 34 (1978–79); the material on the United States in the same chapter comes in part from a piece called "Robert Strauss, the MTN and the Control of Faction," *Journal of World Trade Law* 14 (1980). The discussion of the wine-gallon case comes largely from an article entitled "The U.S. Winegallon Concession: How the Biggest Chip in the Tokyo Round Was Negotiated," *International Journal* 36 (1981). I am grateful to these journals for the rights to reprint.

This book was begun in 1979–80. It represents an effort that has stretched out over a long six years, a fact which leaves me with a feeling more of mild embarrassment than of prodigious achievement. Much help was received along the way. A Rockefeller Fellowship in International Relations, held at Harvard University's Center for International Affairs, enabled me to begin research. Much of the writing was done thanks to a Leave Fellowship from the Social Sciences and Humanities Research Council of Canada, which was held at Dalhousie University's Centre for Foreign Policy Studies. I would like to thank both these granting agencies for their financial support, and my colleagues at both these institutions for their intellectual support and stimulation. Further intellectual stimulation was taken from my frequent involvement with GATT's Commercial Policy Course, which is a training program designed for government officers coming from developing countries. It would be hard to find a more rewarding opportunity in which to teach, and to learn, than that afforded by this course.

Several people have read all or parts of the manuscript and have proffered criticism. These include I. M. Destler, Jeffrey Hart, Robert Keohane, Charles Lipson, and Bruce Wilson. I wish to record my thanks to these people, and particularly to Messrs. Destler and Keohane, who, as assessors for Princeton University Press, went beyond the call of duty in making extended helpful suggestions for redrafting. Most of the criticism I received I acted upon; but lest anyone assume that with this statement I am seeking to evade my responsibilities as an author, let me hasten to embrace academic convention with the assertion that the errors remaining with the text are indeed of my own making.

Special thanks are due to Eileen LeVine, who typed portions of the manuscript, and particularly to Doris Boyle, who typed and managed the preparation of the final manuscript. Mrs. Boyle is as professional a person as I have ever met, and working up to her standards was an experience any author could benefit from. I acknowledge with gratitude assistance provided by Geoffrey Martin and Nina Winham in the important chores of preparing the bibliography, appendixes and index.

Finally, I would like to thank my wife, Linda Joyce (Tanner) Winham, for being a supportive companion, whose indifference to the finer points of foreign trade policy was a stabilizing influence throughout this endeavor.

Halifax, Nova Scotia
December 1985

ABBREVIATIONS AND ACRONYMS

ACTN	Advisory Committee for Trade Negotiations
AIA	American Importers Association
APAC	Agricultural Policy Advisory Committee
ASP	American Selling Price
AVE	*Ad Valorem* Equivalent
BDV	Brussels Definition of Value
BISD	Basic Instruments and Selected Documents (GATT)
BTN	Brussels Tariff Nomenclature
CAP	Common Agricultural Policy
CBC	Canadian Broadcasting Corporation
CCC	Customs Cooperation Council
CCTN	Canadian coordinator for trade negotiations
COREPER	Committee of Permanent Representatives
CTTC	Canadian Trade and Tariffs Committee
DEA	Department of External Affairs
DISC	Domestic international sales corporation
EC	European Community
ECE	Economic Commission for Europe
EEC	European Economic Community
EFTA	European Free Trade Association
GATT	General Agreement on Tariffs and Trade
GSP	Generalized system of preferences
IBM	International Business Machines Corporation
IMF	International Monetary Fund
IPAC	Industrial Policy Advisory Committee
IPC	Integrated Program for Commodities
ISAC	Industry Sector Advisory Committee
ISAR	Industry Sector Advisory Report
ISO	International Standards Organization
ITC	International Trade Commission *or* Department of Industry, Trade, and Commerce
ITO	International Trade Organization
IWC	International Wheat Council
LDC	Less-developed country (or developing country)
LDP	Liberal Democratic party
LPAC	Labor Policy Advisory Committee

xiii

LTA	Long-Term Arrangement on Cotton Textiles
MAF	Ministry of Agriculture and Forestry
MFA	Multifibre Arrangement *or* Ministry of Foreign Affairs
MFN	Most-favored nation
MITI	Ministry of International Trade and Industry
MTN	Multilateral trade negotiation
NTB	Nontariff barrier
NTM	Nontariff measure
NTT	Nippon Telephone and Telegraph Company
OECD	Organization for Economic Cooperation and Development
OEEC	Organization for European Economic Cooperation
OMA	Orderly marketing arrangement
OMB	Office of Management and Budget
OPEC	Organization of Petroleum Exporting Countries
QR	Quantitative restriction
RTA	Reciprocal Trade Agreements Act
s and d	Special and differential treatment
SAC	Sector advisory committee
SALT	Strategic Arms Limitation Talks
SDR	Special drawing right
SIC	Standard Industrial Classification
SITC	Standard International Trade Classification
STR	Special trade representative
TEA	Trade Expansion Act
TNC	Trade Negotiation Committee *or* Transnational corporation
TNCC	Trade Negotiations Coordinating Committee
TPSC	Trade Policy Staff Committee
UNCLOS	United Nations Conference on the Law of the Sea
UNCTAD	United Nations Conference on Trade and Development
USTR	United States trade representative
VER	Voluntary export restraint

INTERNATIONAL TRADE
AND THE
TOKYO ROUND
NEGOTIATION

INTRODUCTION

An argument can be made that the postwar system of international economic cooperation narrowly averted a crisis of major proportions in the early 1970s. One aspect of this crisis occurred on August 15, 1971, when the U.S. government suspended the convertibility of the dollar into gold. This action precipitated the breakdown of the fixed exchange system negotiated in the Bretton Woods Agreement of 1944. The U.S. action represented a sudden devaluation of the leading international currency against gold, and it led to a period of great uncertainty as the major world currencies sought an equilibrium rate against the U.S. dollar. Forty years earlier, on September 21, 1931, a similar devaluation of the leading international currency—the British pound—plunged the world into a fundamental monetary disequilibrium in which various governments engaged in competitive devaluations against gold in an effort to correct payments imbalances and to generate domestic employment through increased exports. The period of financial instability lasted about five years, and at the end currencies held roughly the same relative position they had had in 1931. All that resulted was a general revaluation of gold, accomplished at considerable cost to the international economy.[1]

A second aspect of the crisis of the early 1970s occurred in the trading system. Despite the successful conclusion of the Kennedy Round of trade negotiations in 1967, a cumulation of disparate policy actions by major trading nations had by 1970 created a profound threat to the liberal trading regime forged in the GATT agreement of 1947. The European Community (EC)[2] extended its area of preferential treatment to African and European nations, thereby threatening the fundamental GATT principle of nondiscrimination; and it deepened its protection of European agriculture, which brought it foursquare into conflict with

---

[1] Kindleberger, *World in Depression*.

[2] There is often some confusion about the term European Community (EC). Prior to July 1967, there were three Communities: the European Coal and Steel Community (ECSC), established in the Paris Treaty of 1952; the European Economic Community (EEC, or Common Market); and the European Atomic Energy Community (Euratom), the last two established in the Treaty of Rome of 1958. These Communities had separate executives and councils of ministers. In 1967 the three Communities merged, and now have a single executive (i.e., Commission), one Council of Ministers, a European Parliament, and a Court of Justice.

3

U.S. export interests. For its part, the United States negotiated a series of "voluntary" quantitative restrictions with its trading partners, and it narrowly avoided having Congress pass in 1970 a protectionist bill (the Mills bill) that would have mandated quotas on textiles and shoes, and would have made further quantitative restrictions probable in other import-competing industries through a loosening of escape-clause procedures. Such a sharp escalation of protectionism by a major trading nation would undoubtedly have led to retaliation by America's trading partners, with the resulting possibility of a rapidly spiraling downturn in world trade. History has recorded just such a downturn in the events that preceded and followed passage by the U.S. Congress of the extremely protectionist Smoot-Hawley tariff of 1930. As recalled by Secretary of State Cordell Hull: "When I came into the State Department [in 1933] I found in the files no fewer than thirty-four formal and emphatic diplomatic protests presented by as many nations, following the passage of the Smoot-Hawley high tariff Act. Nor had their protests been confined to words . . . they retaliated in kind."[3] In the wake of this retaliation, which commenced even while the Smoot-Hawley bill was in preparation, world trade declined over the years 1929–34 by 66 percent. The decline in U.S. trade was an even higher 75 percent, from $9.5 billion in 1929 to $2.2 billion in 1934.[4]

The international economic system of the early 1970s, unlike that of the 1930s, managed to survive both a monetary and a trade crisis. It went on to adjust to major instabilities produced by the oil shocks of 1973 and 1979, and to persistent recession and inflation through much of the decade. Without a doubt, successful passage through this crisis was necessary to insure that international economic relationships would not break down in the severe recession that commenced in the late 1970s. However, like any crisis narrowly averted, the crisis of the early 1970s passed from public attention once the immediate danger was over. Had the system faltered, the breakdown would have been exhaustively analyzed by scholars and commentators alike. In this sense, regrettably, failure teaches a more enduring lesson than success, and studying system failures is a more exciting occupation than dissecting successes. Yet careful attention should be given to complicated systems when they work well (if not necessarily as planned), for the obvious reason that we want to be able to copy success in the future. In part, this is what this book is designed to do.

The crisis of the early 1970s was most sharply focused in the mon-

---

[3] *Memoires*, p. 355.
[4] Tasca, *Reciprocal Trade Policy*, 4.

etary system. Pressure began to build on the fixed-rate IMF system during the mid-1960s, and several major currencies, notably the pound sterling and the French franc, underwent major devaluations with attendant disruption of international financial markets. There were several reasons for these difficulties. First, inflation commenced in the Western industrialized nations in the mid-1960s, led by the U.S. government's attempt to finance major social reforms and the Vietnamese war without an increase in taxes. Inflation affected nations differently, and in turn caused currencies to become overvalued or undervalued in relation to each other. In a fixed exchange system, domestic inflation thus became translated into a problem of external payments, and governments found themselves unable to manage the often conflicting policy requirements of the domestic and international economy. A second cause of difficulties in the IMF system was the reserve role of the U.S. dollar. As a reserve currency with a par value specified in gold and against which other currencies were valued, the U.S. dollar could not fluctuate against all other currencies, which effectively denied to the U.S. government the policy tool of a currency devaluation which was instrumental in providing flexibility in the system. The fact that this system provided unique advantages to the United States, which will be addressed later, only served to extend a structurally flawed system longer than might otherwise have been the case. Finally, the IMF fixed-exchange system was particularly vulnerable to speculative movements of short-term capital. Governments were obliged to support the dollar value of their currencies, and when payments difficulties developed, it was all too predictable in which direction any movement would likely go. This created a situation rife for speculation, which was compounded by the growing amounts of money available for international transfer. As a result of increasingly disruptive speculation, problems of short-run stability came to dominate policymaking in international monetary affairs, at the cost of addressing longer-run problems of fundamental equilibrium between national economies.

The postwar monetary system of par values and dollar convertibility ended in August 1971 when the United States unilaterally suspended the dollar's convertibility into gold. This action was followed by a four-month period of great uncertainty in international financial markets. In December 1971, in what became known as the Smithsonian agreement, the dollar was formally devalued in terms of most currencies. The Smithsonian realignment lasted little over one year, and, after another brief crisis, the United States announced a further 10 percent devaluation of the dollar in February 1973. The month following the second devaluation, all major currencies began a managed float, which completed the shift from the old IMF system. The initial move to floating rates was pragmatic and defensive, and ostensibly intended to head off speculation, but it was quickly apparent that the new arrangements were a necessary reform. Diplomatic efforts were made in 1976 to reform the system through collective policy, which culminated in a January meeting in Jamaica of the IMF board of governors, but in the end these efforts only succeeded in ratifying the system of managed floating that was already well established in practice.[5]

Reform of the monetary system constituted the first step out of the crisis of the early 1970s. The second step was the overhaul of the international trade system, accomplished in the Tokyo Round of trade negotiations. It was not by accident that reform in the monetary system preceded reform in international trade. It is widely assumed that a sound payments system is essential to maintain a high level of international trade, and that efforts to liberalize trade are very problematic in times of monetary disarray. Furthermore, there are reasons why moving from a par-value system to a managed float would in itself facilitate reform in international trade. No matter how stable a system of fixed exchange rates might be, it requires trade policy to be conducted with an eye on the effects that changing trading balances will have on a nation's balance of payments. As a result, trade liberalization must be defended on the grounds that it will promote sufficient exports to maintain an equilibrium on payments. In a system of floating currencies, the link between trade balances and the system of payments is made principally through the value of currencies and not in the level of a nation's financial reserves. In practice, the politics of exchange rates are less volatile than the politics surrounding the issue of balance of payments. Thus the successful reform of the monetary system created both stability and greater flexibility in national payments, and together these advanced the prospect for reform in trade relations.

The respective reforms in the international monetary and international trade systems presented problems of a different order. The difficulties in the monetary system were principally difficulties of the system itself. It was less a matter that national monetary policies were in direct conflict than it was that the old system was unable to handle the inevitable divergencies of national policies that occur in any system. There was a growing awareness that the system itself had to change to allow greater flexibility for national actors within it, and the task was how to

[5] An insider's account of these developments is provided in de Vries, "Jamaica." See also the excellent review article by Haberler, "International Monetary System." For a more extended treatment, see Solomon, *International Monetary System*, and Odell, *U.S. International Monetary Policy*.

change it without creating on the one hand a crisis of confidence that could lead to breakdown, or on the other hand destructive quarrels over monetary sovereignty. On the trade side, however, the problem was not so much with the system as with an accumulation of injurious policy actions taken by various nations against the interests of others. The basic structure and rules of the international trading system were sound, and indeed they were not fundamentally altered during the negotiations of the 1970s. Rather the task of reform was to negotiate methods to make the old rules apply more fairly, and to devise more modern means of protectionism, before a pattern of retaliation set in that could unravel the whole fabric of the trading system so patiently constructed after World War II. In sum, the difficulties of the monetary system had a flavor of inevitability about them. By contrast, the problems of the trade system were man-made.

The methods of reform of the two systems were also different. In monetary relations, it is possible to fall back on the currency market to manage the system. Thus the system has a natural regulator, which many theorists have defended as the preferred mechanism for maintaining an equilibrium in international payments.[6] Furthermore, monetary policy affects a national economy undifferentially,[7] in the sense that when an exchange rate changes, it changes for all parties within the given economy. As a result, monetary policies are unlikely to stimulate strong activities on the part of special-interest groups, which by their nature are attracted to the prospect of differential gain or loss. Neither of the two preceding conditions of monetary relations exists in international trade relations. International trade constitutes a vast system of diverse economic relations between nations, and national trade policies, unlike monetary policies, are bureaucratically complex and often inconsistent. No natural regulator exists as a practical political possibility in the international trade system. Moreover, since trade policy actions normally affect only parts of an economy instead of the whole, they are a natural magnet for pressure from special interests. The result is that regulation, or control, or management—whatever name it is given—is very much more complex in international trade than in monetary relations. These inherent differences were reflected in the reforms of the two systems that followed in the wake of the crisis of the early 1970s. Reform of the monetary system, as finally represented in the acceptance of the status quo at Jamaica in 1976, was essentially a move-

[6] See, for example, the congressional testimony of Friedman, reprinted in article form as "Using the Free Market."

[7] The differing impact of trade and monetary policy on a national economy is usefully analyzed in Curzon and Curzon, "Management of Trade Relations," esp. 164.

ment toward simplicity. Reform in the trade system, as represented in the volumes of agreements produced by the Tokyo Round of trade negotiations, was a movement toward complexity.[8]

The Tokyo Round was conducted from 1973 to 1979. It was not a good time to negotiate trade agreements. In the first place, conditions in the international economy were far from propitious. The worldwide inflation begun in the 1960s continued into the early 1970s and then increased explosively after 1973 in the wake of the quadrupling of oil prices by the OPEC nations. There followed in 1975 in the industrialized countries the deepest recession of the postwar period. The combination of unprecedented inflation and recession brought severe pressures on governments to maintain liberal trade policies, and especially made it difficult to develop new initiatives to reduce protectionism. In addition, concern for energy management became an obsession of nearly all governments, which diverted attention from problems in trade relations. The problems of inflation, recession, and energy shortage abated slightly after 1975, but they continued to create an environment of great uncertainty in which a policy of trade reform seemed out of place.

A second problem affecting the negotiation was structural, namely the declining stature of the United States in the international economy and the corresponding rise of the European Community. Without commenting on the principle of hegemony in general, it is certainly the case that American hegemony was a liberalizing force in the early postwar economic system. On trade matters specifically, the United States often defined the nature of the debate with the Europeans, but the quid pro quo was that tangible benefits of trade liberalization flowed disproportionately toward Europe. This informal modus operandi had broken down by the mid-1970s. In 1971, the United States suffered its first trade deficit in this century, and in 1973 Britain, Ireland, and Denmark joined the EC, making it the largest trading entity in the world. These changes altered the agenda of international commercial negotiations, and insured that the bargaining itself would be conducted along the more difficult lines of equality between major actors. Further complicating the structure of the negotiations was the presence of the developing countries with their collective demand for special and differential treatment within the GATT procedures. Not only were these countries prepared to dispute the substantive distribution of benefits from any

---

[8] The Tokyo Round results would seem to be consistent with the observation by Cooper, *Economics of Interdependence*, 153, that "A well known proposition in the theory of economic policy requires that the number of policy instruments be at least as great as the number of objectives (target variables) if all objectives are to be achieved."

trade negotiation, but they also brought a fundamental challenge to the long-established GATT philosophy of nondiscrimination.

A third problem was the series of specific trade problems that had accumulated in commercial relations since the 1960s. Heading the list were the longstanding disputes between the United States and the EC over agricultural trade, and the extension of preferential trading relations by the Community. The former had been the basis for unresolved demands by the United States in the Kennedy Round, while the latter was a new policy thrust which appeared to American officials as a threat to the nondiscriminatory commercial relations of GATT. Other trade measures were less controversial on an individual basis, but in the aggregate were coming to be recognized as a fundamental threat to a bilateral trade regime.[9] These included negotiated agreements, usually reached between large importing countries and smaller exporting nations, to limit the volumes of certain lines of exports. Such agreements evaded the GATT prohibition against quantitative restrictions because they were "voluntary," but they nevertheless constituted a cynical abuse of the clear intention of the General Agreement. Other policy measures bore less directly on international trade, but nevertheless had important trade-distorting effects. For example, domestic subsidies to industry and agriculture affected the interests of trading partners both in the subsidizing country's market and in third countries. Similarly, customs procedures and safety and other standards often impacted unfavorably, whether through accident or intent, on foreign trade relations. Taken together, these restrictions were known as nontariff measures (NTM's), and they represented a major unfinished task left over from the trade-liberalizing efforts of the Kennedy Round in the 1960s.

The Tokyo Round of the 1970s, or the Multilateral Trade Negotiation (MTN), as it was also called, completed a major overhaul of the international trade system. Previous trade negotiations within GATT had dealt almost exclusively with tariffs,[10] and while they made an important contribution to the postwar liberal commercial regime, they did not penetrate very deep into the legal fabric of protectionism in the various GATT member states. By comparison, the Tokyo Round went further into the diverse mechanics of trade restrictions, and in the process trod more closely on the sovereign rights of national jurisdiction than any trade negotiations had previously attempted. The negotiated codes

[9] For example, Bergsten, "U.S. Trade Policy," 619, suggests that the restrictive impact of various U.S. protectionist measures passed after 1962 was "undoubtedly greater than the liberalizing effect of our tariff cuts in the Kennedy Round."

[10] The antidumping code negotiated at the Kennedy Round was an important exception, and will be examined later.

of the Tokyo Round effectively amounted to a constitutional reform of the General Agreement of 1947,[11] which itself had been a document produced in response to a great crisis and breakdown in the international trading system. That the Tokyo Round was able to address issues like subsidies that had been unresolved since the creation of GATT demonstrates further that the negotiation was an extraordinary response to extraordinary circumstances.

The Tokyo Round was the main focus of policymaking in the international trade system of the 1970s. Trade policy can cover a bewildering number of subjects, ranging from tariffs and quantitative restrictions, export controls and licensing schemes, to investment or export incentives, foreign assistance programs, technical barriers to trade, and customs procedures. The Tokyo Round engaged most of these subjects in one way or another. For some countries, such as, for example, the United States, the Tokyo Round effectively subsumed trade policy within the process of negotiation, much as American foreign policy toward the Soviet Union in the past has become subsumed in the SALT negotiating process. A great deal was at stake in the Tokyo Round negotiation, and had the negotiation failed, there would have been an enormous loss of momentum in the effort to maintain the machinery of collective policymaking in international trade.

Of course the negotiation did not fail, and certainly not in the technical sense, in that a wide-ranging agreement was indeed signed by a substantial number of the participating countries. However, like many acts of a legislature where the purpose of legislation is *not* to decide,[12] the Tokyo Round did not settle controversial issues of international trade policy so much as it provided ground rules and a mechanism for settling such issues in the future. Thus even several years after its formal conclusion, it is still too early to determine the precise effect of some of the settlements reached at the negotiation.

At the time of its conclusion, the Tokyo Round was widely considered to be successful in economic terms. It did reduce tariffs and some other nontariff measures directly, and it resolved some trade disputes with the result that fewer restrictions will be applied in the future. However, there was criticism from some quarters that the agreements did not go far enough, and that in some cases protectionism was advanced rather than driven back. This is not a new problem in trade policymaking. Legislation regulating economic intercourse is often a result

---

[11] The constitutional nature of the Tokyo Round has been suggested by one of the leading scholars of the GATT. See Jackson, "GATT-MTN System."

[12] Cf. Bauer et al., *American Business*, 79: "But the one thing that in a democracy the parliament must not do is to settle controversial issues."

of many conflicting compromises, as was recognized by Daniel Webster when he said of the tariff of 1824, "It exposes both those who support and those who oppose the measure to very unjust and injurious misapprehensions."[13] The same was true of the results of the Tokyo Round. The Tokyo Round was predominantly a liberal undertaking, but it made compromises with protectionist forces, and in so doing tended to shift the ground from an argument between liberalism and protectionism to one of the management of the international trade system. The emphasis at the Tokyo Round was on fair trade, not free trade, and the various governments accepted that the notion of fair trade included certain elements of protectionism. Fair trade represented an amalgam of American and European ideas on trade policy, which had long escaped the policy of consensus within GATT. The main concern of fair trade was the openness of the international economic system, understood in relative rather than absolute terms. The Tokyo Round was not a victory for doctrinaire free trade, but rather for responsible international management in a field where reasonable people have been deeply divided throughout history. In GATT and elsewhere, one can still encounter statements tilting at the generalized "forces of protectionism" (for which the "forces of evil" might be substituted with equal precision), but this occurs less frequently today than it once did. To a large degree, the Tokyo Round changed the nature of the debate, as well as changing the content of the international economic management of the system.

The Tokyo Round was also considered successful in political terms. The main political task facing the Tokyo Round was to create a collective decision-making system for international trade. The major impediment to this task was the hegemonic leadership of the United States, which had served the postwar international economic system very well, but which was an inappropriate arrangement for the 1970s and beyond. The Tokyo Round completed the transition, begun in August 1971, from a hegemonic economic system to one principally managed by a US/EC partnership. It was an enormous structural change in international political-economic relations, and it was successful because it engendered confidence in the system itself. In the monetary area, confidence after 1971 was maintained by creating a smooth-working market system for clearing international payments. In the trade area, confidence was maintained through the appearance of joint US/EC leadership and by the very fact of nations reaching agreement at the Tokyo Round to provide multilateral management of trade relations.

[13] "Speech," 317.

The Tokyo Round underscored the extent to which multilateral negotiation has become the point of departure for managing the international trade system. Multilateral negotiations are not new in international trade, but in the GATT system since 1947 they have been limited mainly to the negotiation of tariffs, and they have been constrained by the preponderant position of the United States. In contrast with past GATT negotiations, the Tokyo Round was a rulemaking exercise of major proportions. Furthermore, in comparison with multilateral negotiations in most other areas of international politics, the agreements at this negotiation constituted guidelines that reach further into the nation-state and impact more deeply on individual human behavior than is normally the case in international agreements. In this sense, trade relations have the capacity to raise issues of diplomacy and international rulemaking before they are faced elsewhere, and this is not a new phenomenon. In his thorough study of intertribal diplomacy, Numelin describes trade, along with war, as one of the great "promoters" of diplomacy among primitive tribes.[14] In the modern day, trade continues to be, along with problems of security, an engine in the development of modern diplomacy. The various code negotiations of the Tokyo Round were a case in point, and arguably they were the most advanced, in terms of bureaucratic complexity, of any multilateral negotiations occurring today. These negotiations handled issues of great technical complexity, which is now becoming true of many areas of international negotiation, but the greatest complexity lay in integrating the conflicting trade legislation of many nations into a coordinated set of international rules. In their efforts to mesh the rulemaking apparatus of different countries into a single structure, the Tokyo Round negotiators faced problems that will likely become commonplace in the future as nations cope with the implications of an increasingly interdependent world.

An important purpose of this book will be to examine multilateral negotiation as a management process in the context of the Tokyo Round negotiation, where management was a plausible goal of the parties involved. There is some urgency to this task. One would expect that problems of interdependence will become more acute in the international system in the future. However, it is improbable that international government can be developed to manage such problems, at least in the short run. The international system will probably have to rely on a

[14] *Beginnings of Diplomacy*, chs. 9 and 10. A more recent statement of the same theme comes from Schelling, "National Security Considerations": "Aside from war, trade is the most important relationship countries have with each other."

form of ad hoc negotiation procedures to manage international problems for some time to come. It is desirable that more thought be given
to negotiation as a process for political and economic control, simply
because there are not many processes available to the international
community for managing a growing interdependence.

In studying political events, whether they are international negotiations or acts of national legislatures, an argument can be made that the
process of policymaking is more important than the substance of policy. This is an argument E. E. Schattschneider advanced in his classic
study of the Smoot-Hawley tariff of 1930.[15] The task Schattschneider
set himself was to understand a policy that was written largely by the
interest groups of the day, and that was widely regarded by responsible
opinion at the time and subsequently as being a profound mistake.
Schattschneider's task was to be accomplished through an analysis of
the process by which the tariff was made. In the author's words:

> If it is true that demands largely determine public policy, it follows
> that policies can be explained in terms of the processes by which
> pressures are shaped and modified. . . . By what process did the
> few become so dominant that their demands could not be denied?
> In answering these questions we shall be able to make progress to-
> ward an understanding of the policy itself.[16]

History of course vindicated Schattschneider's choice of research priorities. Shortly after the passage of the Smoot-Hawley tariff, Congress itself recognized the limitation of the legislative process of setting tariff
rates, and it passed the Reciprocal Trade Agreements Act of 1934
which transferred this power to the executive branch. The United
States and other trading nations then began the long road back to a
more responsible tariff policy through the process of international negotiation, which was a different process from unilateral legislation, and
which produced a significantly different outcome.

Schattschneider's book on the Smoot-Hawley tariff was a study of
the closing down of the international trade system of the 1930s. The
analysis of the Tokyo Round presented here is a study of efforts to open
up this system in the late 1970s and beyond. The former policy was a
unilateral action, and it could be done practically in one stroke; the latter policy was a multilateral endeavor, and it will take time. The process behind the major policy instrument in each case—the Smoot-Hawley tariff and the Tokyo Round accords—provides an understanding of

[15] *Politics.*
[16] Ibid., 5.

the meaning of these instruments themselves. What is substantively important about the Tokyo Round is its impact on international trade, but this substance is not fully intelligible in the absence of an understanding of how the agreements came about. The political interests that had to be dealt with in the formation of the Tokyo Round are still there to be dealt with in its application. Thus a book that is a history of a trade negotiation should, it is hoped, be useful in understanding what impact that negotiation will have on the international trade system.

· I ·

THE TOKYO ROUND AND THE POLITICAL ECONOMY
OF INTERNATIONAL TRADE

INTRODUCTION

The GATT trade negotiation called the Tokyo Round was concluded in Geneva in April 1979. Officially it began at a ministerial trade conference in September 1973 in Tokyo, from which it derived its name. Unofficially the negotiations started earlier than that. At the close of the Kennedy Round in 1967, the GATT secretariat, led by Sir Eric Wyndham-White, sought to convince the major trading nations to extend trade liberalization into the nontariff area, which had been largely overlooked at the Kennedy Round. This early effort was unsuccessful, but by the early 1970s chaos in the international monetary system resurrected fears of trade protectionism and made national governments more receptive to new initiatives in international trade policy. A new attempt at liberalization became a formal goal of the major trading nations as they drafted the 1971 Smithsonian agreement that made sweeping changes in monetary relations.

The negotiations started slowly, with most of the early period devoted to gathering and classifying enormous amounts of trade data, particularly regarding the nontariff measures applied by the various trading nations. One factor which slowed work in the early period was that legislation authorizing the U.S. president to negotiate was not in place until the Trade Act of 1974, signed on January 3, 1975, after a difficult passage through the U.S. Congress. Further delays were caused by the U.S. election of 1976, and it was not until 1977 that the United States had a top-level team in place to conduct the negotiation. After 1977, events moved quickly. An impasse between the United States and the European Community (EC) over agriculture was overcome, and a timetable was set for completion of the negotiation. By January 1978, comprehensive offers of trade concessions were tabled by the major industrial nations, and direct bargaining began. The inevitable snags and political difficulties were met and overcome, most notably a last-minute dispute involving the U.S. Congress and the EC over export subsidies and countervailing duties, a dispute which threatened to unravel the emerging agreement. The final settlement was included in a procès-verbal signed in April 1979. It was initialed by the major industrialized

15

nations and some developing nations, subject to subsequent ratification by governments through national legislative processes.

The agreement reached at the Tokyo Round, or the multilateral trade negotiation (MTN), as it is also called, is generally regarded as being the most comprehensive and far-reaching results achieved in trade negotiations since the creation of the General Agreement on Tariffs and Trade (GATT) in 1947. The results fall in three categories: six codes (plus a sectoral code for trade in aircraft) dealing with nontariff measures; tariff reductions; and a series of revisions of GATT articles primarily of interest to developing nations. The codes update and expand the trade law of the GATT, and are the most important part of the Tokyo Round accord. They cover respectively customs valuation, import licensing, technical standards for products, subsidies and countervailing measures, government procurement, and antidumping. Negotiations on a safeguards code failed.

The general thrust of the code negotiations was to increase the openness, certainty, and nonarbitrariness of the rules governing international trade, with the expectation that such trade would be facilitated. In some areas the negotiation was accomplished without appreciable controversy. For example, in codes on customs valuation, import licensing, and standards, nations proceeded from the widely shared philosophy that government regulations in these areas should not be used to provide protection for domestic producers, either through design or otherwise. In other areas, agreement was more problematic. The attempted code on safeguards encountered a determined insistence by European Communities on the right to apply safeguards selectively, which was resisted by the developing nations, which would be the primary targets of this tactic. The disagreement was not resolved and no general agreement was reached on this code. Also, the code on subsidies/countervail triggered deeply held disagreement between the United States and the EEC over the appropriateness of agricultural export subsidies in modern government practice, but in the end this disagreement was reconciled and the code was signed.

The most important aspect of the codes was the extent to which they constituted a beginning—and not a final step—toward a more open international economy. The codes contained provisions for consultation and dispute-settlement procedures that allow aggrieved exporting nations to raise claims within the appropriate GATT mechanisms. These procedures will accomplish two things: they will reduce the sovereignty, and hence the right to arbitrary action, that importing nations have traditionally exercised in the nontariff aspects of international trade; and they will increase the propsects that the trade regulations of foreign nations will be explicit, justifiable, and hence more certain for exporters. In international trade, one nation's sovereignty is another nation's uncertainty. In many cases, it is uncertainty, even more than absolute levels of protection, that deters international exchanges. As one Canadian official said about the European Community's variable-subsidy program in agriculture (which also could have been said about the lack of a systematic injury test in U.S. countervail legislation), ". . . what we *really* want is to get a handle on their system."

The Tokyo Round codes tended to change GATT rules from statements of broad principle to more detailed regulations relating to domestic and international procedures. They are expected to reduce trade protectionism, but they would probably be oversold if assessed only on this criterion. For example, the subsidy/countervail code was loosely written; it left considerable scope to countries employing subsidies, and commensurate scope regarding the definition of injury to countries applying countervailing duties. It is improbable that the code will change governmental practice substantially in the short run. Similarly, the customs valuation code eliminated the American Selling Price (ASP), which had been an unresolved problem in the Kennedy Round, but the protection offered by the ASP was maintained through increased tariffs. In both examples, the codes served as an attempt to increase the orderliness, and possibly the fairness, of international trading arrangements, but not necessarily to reduce protectionism. Even selective safeguards, which had they been agreed would have contravened the traditional GATT norm of nondiscrimination, could have been viewed as a mechanism to promote orderly trade, for they would have provided protection at the point of disturbance without affecting general trade patterns.

The Tokyo Round results also included a major agreement on tariff reductions. To put these results in perspective, tariff negotiations were the main item of business in the six multilateral negotiations that were held under GATT auspices through the Kennedy Round of 1967. Tariffs were not the major focus of this negotiation, yet the average reductions of about 35 percent of industrial nations' tariffs achieved at the Tokyo Round were very comparable to the reductions of the Kennedy Round. The reductions covered more than $100 billion of imports, and will be phased in over an eight-year period which began in 1980.

The major controversy in the tariff negotiation was to arrive at a tariff-cutting formula for manufactured products. A similar controversy had occurred in the Kennedy Round, at which time nations settled on a linear approach supported mainly by the United States. In the Tokyo Round, proponents of a tariff-harmonizing formula carried the day, and nations agreed to table offers according to a compromise "Swiss" formula that generally required tariff cuts to be proportional to the size of the tariff. The final bargaining produced a number of exceptions to the general formula, particularly in industries where imports are already high. For example, in the United States, where the average tariff cut was 31 percent, the duties for leather imports were reduced by only 4 percent; for apparel, 15 percent; for automobiles, 16 percent; and tariffs on footwear and color televisions were exempted from any cuts whatsoever. Similar exceptions were made by other trading nations as well.

A third result of the Tokyo Round was a series of revisions to the GATT articles, known as the "framework" agreement. Negotiations on this subject were initiated by Brazil, and were carried on in a separate negotiating group formed in November 1976. The framework agreement came in five parts, and covered subjects such as safeguard actions for development purposes (or infant industry measures), trade measures taken to correct payment deficits, export controls, and deviations from most-favored-nation (MFN) procedures for developing countries. One far-reaching accord in the framework package was the Understanding regarding Notification, Consultation, Dispute Settlement, and Surveillance. This agreement required GATT members to notify trading partners of the trade measures they adopt, and it should help provide early warning for all countries. It was a further step in the direction of improving the GATT machinery to handle trade disputes.

The Tokyo Round produced only modest results in agriculture, which was of course an area of particular concern to the United States. The United States received some tariff concessions from other countries on high-profile products like citrus fruits, tobacco, and rice, and an agreement was struck to establish a consultative council to improve international trade policy in agriculture. However, it was clear after this negotiation that America's major trading partners, mainly Japan and the EC, were unwilling for reasons of economic security and domestic politics to expand significantly their foreign imports of agricultural products. Particularly in the case of the EC, this is a matter of conscious social policy. European governments have sought to avoid the rationalization of agriculture on the scale that has occurred in the United States, with its consequent outmigration of surplus farm labor to urban areas. Increasing foreign trade would simply be another way to rationalize European agriculture, with the added disadvantage from the European viewpoint that the benefits would flow disproportionately to American farmers. The EC was simply unwilling to allow trade to exact a social cost it has already declined to pay.

The Tokyo Round in Historical Perspective

How does one put the Tokyo Round into a proper perspective? This is indeed one of the more difficult tasks for analysts writing on a single case study in international relations. The Tokyo Round was a unique event, but it had historical precedents and it was connected with other events in the international economic system. In terms of time, and depending on the distance one moves from the subject, the Tokyo Round could be seen simply as growing out of the unfinished business remaining from the Kennedy Round of the 1960s; or it could represent an extension of multilateral efforts to liberalize trade under the regime established by the General Agreement on Tariffs and Trade of 1947; or, from even greater distance, it could be viewed as a continuation of a trend from the reciprocal trade agreements of the 1930s to remove important economic decisions from the domain of unilateral national decisions in favor of negotiated agreements at the international level. In terms of space, the Tokyo Round could be approached restrictively as involving only the system of international trade legislation within the GATT; or it might be more broadly analyzed in its relation to the sum of political/economic relations of the major trading nations during the past decade. What follows is a brief attempt to place the Tokyo Round in its proper perspective, beginning with the meaning it had for international institutions in the 1970s and moving backwards in successive steps to determine its place in the historical development of international commercial relations.

The GATT Perspective

A first perspective concerns the relationship of the Tokyo Round to the GATT, and the impact that the trade negotiation had on the international organization that sponsored it. GATT itself is an unusual institution in international affairs. What is now known as the General Agreement was originally a set of trading rules appended to the results of a tariff negotiation concluded in 1947 among twenty-three countries.[1] The rules were designed to prevent the various tariff concessions from being undercut by other nontariff measures, and they were expected to be incorporated into the framework of the nascent International Trade Organization (ITO), the treaty for which was signed in March 1948. The U.S. Congress subsequently refused to ratify the ITO charter and the organization never came into being. In its place, GATT has gradually grown to take on some of the functions, as well as the organizational

[1] See Dam, *The GATT*, 12–13.

presence, originally intended for the ITO. As one might expect, the unusual origins of GATT have lent to it an air of impermanence and pragmatism, which have ironically been a source of strength in an international system where law ultimately rests on the consent of the governed.

The objectives of the GATT, as stated in its preamble, were twofold: first, to achieve a "substantial reduction of tariffs and other barriers to trade," and, second, to secure the "elimination of discriminatory treatment in international commerce." Beyond this, other goals were contained in the General Agreement, which have been usefully summarized by Gerard and Victoria Curzon.[2] The Curzons write of the four "pillars" of the GATT, which, in addition to the two objectives already mentioned, include the norm of reciprocity and the achievement of an international trade order. The latter makes reference to the various GATT articles that lay down ground rules for situations where nations must rescind concessions already given, or in general must take actions that prejudice the trading interests of other contracting parties.

The means for carrying out the first objective of reduction of trade barriers was to be multilateral negotiations, which the contracting parties might sponsor "from time to time" (Article 27 bis). Under this provision, GATT has sponsored seven negotiations since its inception, including the Tokyo Round, and it has accomplished a dramatic reduction in tariff protection among industrialized countries. For example, U.S. tariffs on dutiable nonagricultural products averaged about 25 percent in 1946, but they were less than 12 percent prior to the Kennedy Round, and they will fall to about 6 percent when the Tokyo Round cuts are fully phased in. Comparable reductions in duties have been made by other nations. However, other than removing some discriminatory quotas, GATT had achieved less success in reducing nontariff measures prior to the Tokyo Round.

With regard to GATT's second objective, nondiscrimination, as well as its other goals, the means for achieving these aims lay in the various commitments contained in the thirty-eight articles of the General Agreement.[3] For example, some articles specified that customs procedures, licensing arrangements, and government fees or taxes should be applied in a nondiscriminatory manner, and in a way that they do not themselves become barriers to international trade. Certain practices were banned outright in the GATT, such as export subsidies and quan-

---

[2] "Management of Trade Relations." Another helpful summary of the principles of the GATT regime is found in Finlayson and Zacher, "The GATT."

[3] The figure thirty-eight includes Part IV of the Agreement, added in 1966.

titative restrictions (with some exceptions). Furthermore, the GATT provided a series of mechanisms for nations that were experiencing difficulties from import competition, ranging from antidumping and countervailing procedures to an escape clause for industries threatened with serious injury. It would be accurate to say that, prior to the Tokyo Round, GATT had been far more successful in carrying out its goal of tariff reductions, which was based on negotiation, than its other goals, which were based on the GATT code of conduct and backed up by quasi-judicial procedures. In terms of substance, the Tokyo Round was intended to address some of the less successful areas of the GATT regime, and particularly specific nontariff measures. In terms of procedure, the Tokyo Round represented an attempt to apply the method of multilateral negotiation that worked well on tariff reductions to the other less tractable goals of the GATT.

As an organization, GATT needed the Tokyo Round. The changes of the 1960s and early 1970s had brought considerable pressure for organizational adaptations. For one thing, a rapid growth in membership brought new demands on the organization's legal norms. The GATT was orginally signed by twenty-three nations, and by the late 1960s this figure had more than doubled (at present there are eighty-nine signatories). An even larger number of nations have participated in trade negotiations held under GATT auspices. Many of the new signatories and participants in GATT were developing nations, which sought to use the organization to gain preferential trading arrangements consistent with their development needs. Such demands conflicted with the trading interests of the industrialized nations that had originated the GATT, and thus a fundamental change was established that continues to be central to the politics of the organization. Another source of pressure on GATT has come ironically from success, and not failure, in the domain over which it exercises some jurisdiction. From the late 1940s to the beginning of the Tokyo Round, the value of world production grew by an annual average of about 5 percent. International trade grew at an even faster 7 percent. Such rapid growth created pressures for adjustment and led national governments to resort to protectionism to insulate their economies against these changes. Also the increase in trade included changes in the nature of trade, generated largely by the operations of transnational corporations, which created new problems in trade management for national governments. In sum, then, GATT found itself in an economic environment by the early 1970s that was far removed from the environment faced at its inception. The changes of the intervening decades of the 1950s and 1960s posed a major test of relevance for GATT.

GATT is the main international organization in the trade field, but it is not without its competitors. On one side, it faces UNCTAD, which the developing countries view as a far more sympathetic forum for their particular interests in international trade. On the other side is the OECD, which lacks a specific mandate in international trade, but which has nevertheless advanced cooperation among the industrialized countries on a number of issues that impinge closely on trade relations. Either organization could have assumed parts of the task of making the international trade machinery relevant to the economic realities of the 1970s. To meet this competition, GATT had to demonstrate a capacity to adapt to changing circumstances, which is a prerequisite for survival in any institution. The Tokyo Round was essential in adapting the GATT to the new realities of international trade, and hence this perspective is an important part of evaluating the results of the negotiation.

The 1970s Perspective

A second and somewhat broader perspective on the Tokyo Round flows from the political/economic bargaining that attended the monetary crisis of the early 1970s. As mentioned earlier, there were inevitable causes for crisis in the monetary system, such as the inability of the system to contain the effects of speculation or differing national rates of inflation. In addition to these difficulties, there were political disputes between the United States and its European allies over the benefits that accrued from the system. These disputes were far-ranging, and in the process of settling them a linkage was established between monetary policy and trade policy that enhanced the political prospects for a major trade negotiation during the 1970s.

The major dispute in the old IMF system centered on the role of the U.S. dollar. The IMF system of fixed rates had provided that national monetary reserves would be held in the form of gold, currencies, and drawing rights on the IMF itself. The U.S. dollar was identified as a key currency for reserve purposes, although initially it was not a major element in national reserves. However, by the late 1950s the United States had begun to run a large balance-of-payments deficit. This had the effect of providing surpluses for other countries, and hence created much-needed additional liquidity for the whole system. Initially the U.S. deficit was welcomed on both sides of the Atlantic. For the United States, an increase in dollar holdings abroad, which could be converted to gold under the IMF rules, was tolerable because of the enormous gold reserves in that country. For the Europeans, the U.S. deficit relieved the "dollar shortage" of the early 1950s and substantially eased payments pressures against the United States and other countries.

The IMF system had differing advantages and disadvantages for both the United States and other IMF members. These became increasingly pronounced as the U.S. deficit continued into the 1960s, fueled by inflation within the United States itself. For the European and other nations whose currencies were pegged to the U.S. dollar, an advantage was that they could take unilateral action to adjust the par value of their currencies to correct serious imbalances in their payments positions. A disadvantage was that an increasing proportion of national reserves became held in U.S. dollars, which became more problematic as the U.S. deficit worsened. For the United States, whose dollar was pegged to gold, there was no way to devalue its currency against other national currencies without at the same time taking the much more important action of changing the reserve value of gold. The United States therefore could not take the action available to other nations to reverse its balance-of-payments deficit. On the positive side, however, the system removed the need for American authorities to exercise the same discipline over balance-of-payments deficits as other countries, for as long as other nations were willing to hold dollars there was little cost to the gold reserves of the United States. Furthermore, there were foreign-policy advantages, as outlined below, that accrued to the United States from its payments deficit. It was the latter that were particularly opposed by America's European allies, and especially France.

It is important to recognize that the main factor in the U.S. deficit during the 1960s was not the balance of international trade. Indeed the United States did not suffer a trade deficit until 1971. Rather the main aspects of the deficit, particularly as seen from European eyes, were the payments required to maintain U.S. military forces outside the United States, which escalated sharply after 1965 because of the war in Vietnam, and the payments resulting from direct investments by U.S. corporations in foreign countries, especially in Europe. In both cases, critics of the United States felt they were being required by the monetary system to underwrite unpopular American policies. In the case of foreign investment, the argument was made especially by the French that the system placed few restraints on American corporations to export capital (as occurred in other countries during balance-of-payments difficulties), and as a result American firms continued to be able to purchase valuable European assets with dollars that were suspected of being increasingly overvalued.[4] The limiting aspect of the system was

[4] For further elaboration of this point, see Aron, *The Imperial Republic*, and Gilpin, *U.S. Power*.

the willingness of the European and other nations to hold U.S. dollars as national reserves. After 1965, European central banks were increasingly reluctant to hold U.S. dollars and made substantial drawings on U.S. gold reserves. The U.S. payments position improved during 1968 and 1969, but the effect was transitory. In 1970 the United States suffered a record payments deficit of $9.8 billion, which worsened to $31.2 billion in the first three quarters of 1971.[5] Moreover it was clear that 1971 would produce the first deficit on merchandise trade the United States had suffered in this century. In the face of this economic adversity, the Nixon administration announced on August 15, 1971, the suspension of convertibility of the dollar into gold for foreign central banks, a temporary 10 percent surcharge on dutiable imports, and a wage-price freeze.

The brief résumé above demonstrates that there was ample opportunity for the United States and the European nations to disagree over the operation of the international monetary system. Essentially, the Americans felt the Europeans (and the Japanese) should take more responsibility for making the system work by holding dollars and by appreciating their currencies against the U.S. dollar. The Europeans felt the United States should make greater efforts to stem its rate of inflation, which would have a positive effect on U.S. trade balances. This political background became important in the bargaining that followed the U.S. actions of August 1971. The import surcharge levied by the United States in 1971 was entirely consistent with actions other nations had taken during balance-of-payments difficulties. What was new, and shocking to the Europeans, was the U.S. demand that an improvement of $13 billion would be needed in its balance of payments before the surcharge could be lifted. Apart from its magnitude, this demand presented two major difficulties for America's allies. First, the means spelled out by the Americans for meeting the $13 billion came largely in the trade area, and represented demands on the institutions and procedures of the European Common Market. Not only did this appear to present an unprecedented linkage between trade and monetary matters in economic negotiations, but it also appeared to be an obvious attempt by the United States to use its position in the monetary system to gain trade advantages. Second, the U.S. demand appeared to place the burden of adjustment entirely on America's trading partners. This gave the impression of a dramatic turnabout in the attitude the United States had adopted toward the international economic system since World War II. This impression was heightened by the posture taken by the

[5] U.S. Government, *Economic Report*, 150.

Nixon administration, that it was in no hurry to lift the surcharge or otherwise end the period of tension it had created.

Negotiations over monetary and trade arrangements continued over the fall of 1971. On the trade side, American negotiators pressed home the argument that U.S. imports had risen dramatically over the 1960s, thus fueling expansion abroad, but that restrictive practices in foreign countries had prevented a corresponding rise in U.S. exports. Practices that were singled out included the EC's Common Agricultural Policy (CAP), which severely restricted U.S. agricultural exports to Europe, and the efforts to achieve a free-trade area between the EC and the European Free Trade Association (EFTA), which would have the effect of extending the preferential area of the EC with deleterious results for U.S. trade. On the monetary side, the United States pressed for a devaluation of the dollar and a realignment of other currencies, which in any case was in progress through market forces following the declaration of dollar inconvertibility. The negotiations were difficult and were compounded by the nationalistic style of Secretary of the Treasury John Connolly, which appeared calculated to leave America's trading partners uncertain over how far the United States might go to achieve its goals.

As is often the case with difficult negotiations, a settlement if it comes at all is reached at the highest levels. In the monetary negotiations of 1971, the resolution occurred in a meeting in early December between President Georges Pompidou of France and Chancellor Willy Brandt of West Germany, and a subsequent meeting between Pompidou and President Richard Nixon. At the first meeting a satisfactory relationship was worked out between the French franc and the German mark, which would allow the Germans flexibility to appreciate the mark against the U.S. dollar.[6] In the second meeting, the parties agreed to work towad a realignment of currencies through the devaluation of the dollar and a revaluation of some other currencies. Implicit in the agreement was the U.S. commitment to drop the import surcharge of 10 percent. The United States dropped its demand for a $13 billion adjustment in its balance of payments without receiving any tangible concession, save for a commitment by the French president to prepare a mandate with other EC countries for an "imminent opening of negotiations with the United States . . . in the area of trade."[7] The agree-

[6] Shonfield, "International Economic Relations," 84. Shonfield, perhaps taking a European view, indicates that the Brandt-Pompidou meeting was "the crucial act in the conclusion of the drama."

[7] The quotation is taken from the communiqué from the meeting, cited in Solomon,

ments from these meetings were subsequently confirmed in the well-known meeting of the finance ministers of the Group of Ten at the Smithsonian Institution on December 16–17, 1971. The actions that flowed from the Smithsonian meeting included a devaluation of the U.S. dollar from $35 to $38 per ounce of gold, the termination of the surcharge, and a fresh initiative toward a multilateral trade negotiation.

The confrontation that ended with the Smithsonian agreement has been described by Andrew Shonfield as a "key event" in the story of postwar international economic relations.[8] If so, the event must be understood (as Shonfield does understand it) more in subjective than objective terms. The United States received a 10 percent revaluation of major surplus currencies against the dollar, but it was a figure that was insufficient by itself to turn around the U.S. payments deficit. The United States did not fulfill its demands in the trade area, other than to receive a gesture from the Europeans to negotiate further. The question arises whether, from the standpoint of the benefits exchanged, the incident could be described as a key event, and whether it warranted the strongarm tactics the Americans applied in the circumstances. The answer to the second question prejudges the first. Shonfield has criticized the American tactics on the grounds that they were unnecessary and ultimately unproductive. This judgment would be resisted by most American experts, who found the policy of the surcharge necessary to establish U.S. credibility and seriousness of purpose in the negotiations.[9] There obviously is no answer to this question, but what is clear is that the confrontation changed the nature of postwar economic debate between the United States and the Europeans, and that its results were more important in terms of political process than economic substance.

The confrontation broke up the mental habits of the fixed exchange system, as Shonfield has argued, but it did more than that. It also broke up assumptions on both sides of the Atlantic about U.S. hegemony in the postwar international economy. The United States had lost power to control events in the international economy by 1970, but this was a fact that had not yet been reflected in the economic diplomacy of the Western nations. The confrontation that ended with the Smithsonian agreement started a process of adjustment toward a political/economic equality between the United States and Europe which was continued in

---

International Monetary System, 205. Solomon, perhaps taking an American view, has not even mentioned the earlier Brandt-Pompidou meeting.

[8] Shonfield, "International Economic Relations," 85.

[9] For a summary of experts' views, see Robert B. Semple, Jr., "Import Surcharge Ended by Nixon," *New York Times*, December 21, 1971, 53.

the trade negotiation that followed it. Not only did the diplomatic events in the monetary system precipitate a negotiation on trade, but they also ensured that that negotiation would be conducted on a more bipolar basis than was previously the case with multilateral commercial negotiations.

The Postwar Perspective

A third perspective on the Tokyo Round is the entire postwar period from 1945 through the conclusion of the negotiation in 1979. The main characteristic of this period was the ascendancy and then incipient decline of the United States in world political/economic relations. The role of the United States in the world economic system was an important variable which shaped both the agenda and the subsequent negotiations of the Tokyo Round.

The ascendancy of the United States in the early postwar period was immediately evident in the play of international policymaking. Through the Truman Declaration of 1947, the United States took over leadership of the Western alliance. The United States enjoyed a preponderant position in the formation of the postwar international organizations, which was clearly evidenced when the ITO collapsed without U.S. ratification and support. Reconstruction aid to Europe through the Marshall Plan further demonstrated the economic strength of the United States in the Western system. In addition, U.S. economic ascendancy could be demonstrated by figures representing three important areas of the international economic system, namely international monetary payments, trade, and foreign investment. In 1947, the United States held about 70 percent of the monetary gold stock of the world. Even a decade later, this figure had not dropped below 59 percent of the world's stock.[10] There was an acute shortage of U.S. dollars over this period, and the dollar itself began to serve as a reserve currency for international payments. Regarding trade, by 1950 the United States accounted for nearly 17 percent of world trade, and its share was about one and one-half times the share of the next leading nation (Great Britain).[11] Through the decade of the 1950s the United States increased its preponderance in world trade. By 1960, U.S. trade was 20 percent of overall world trade, over twice as large as that of the next leading nation (Great Britain), and roughly equal to the combined total of the three leading European economies, namely Great Britain, France, and

[10] Cooper, *Economics of Interdependence*, 41.
[11] Krasner, "State Power," 334.

27

West Germany. Finally, with regard to foreign investment, the United States went from an initial accumulated stock of foreign investment of $7 billion in 1946 to over $100 billion in 1973.[12] The latter figure represented fully 51 percent of total world foreign investment in that year. The second ranking nation in foreign investment in 1973 was the United Kingdom with 13.5 percent, or about one-quarter of the U.S. total. In sum, all of the major indicators of international economic performance demonstrate that the United States was in a unique position of leadership in the first two decades of the postwar period.

During the 1960s, the position of the United States began to change, and this change was reflected in the statistics in all areas of the economic system. The role of the U.S. dollar in the international monetary system has already been mentioned. As for gold, which is often used as a primitive indicator of economic strength, the persistent payments deficit of the United States over the 1950s gradually translated into a loss of gold reserves by the U.S. Treasury. In 1947, the gold reserves of the United States were $22.8 billion, which climbed to a postwar high of $24.5 billion in 1949.[13] U.S. gold reserves remained above $20 billion through 1958, and then fell to about $13 billion in the mid-1960s. By 1971, when the U.S. government declared the U.S. dollar no longer convertible into gold at the IMF rate of $35 per ounce, the U.S. gold stock had fallen to $10.2 billion, approximately one-half of what it had been at the end of World War II.

Regarding trade, the export surplus of the United States dissipated through the 1960s and turned to a deficit in 1971. Krasner's figures show that by 1972 the United States had lost its commanding trade position; in that year its trade was only approximately 20 percent larger than its next nearest competitor, West Germany. Even more important was the establishment of the European Community and its effect on U.S. leadership in world trade. When the EEC was created in 1958, it and the United States accounted for roughly the same volume of international trade. Since then, however, thanks to economic growth in Europe and to the growth in membership of the EC itself, the trade volume controlled by the EC has surpassed that of the United States. For example, in 1973 when the Tokyo Round began, U.S. exports of $68 billion were approximately 13 percent of world trade, and were dwarfed by the combined exports of EC members of $205 billion. In terms of external trade alone, the EC accounted for over $93 billion in exports,

[12] U.N. Commission, *Transnational Corporations*, 236.
[13] U.S. Senate, *International Financial Crisis*, 200.

over one-third larger than U.S. exports.[14] Finally, with regard to foreign investment, the 1970s still saw the United States in a preponderant position in the world economic system, but a downward trend had begun in the mid-1960s. In 1967, the United States accounted for nearly 54 percent of the total world stock of direct investment, with the United Kingdom a distant second with 17 percent.[15] By 1976, the U.S. share had dropped to less than 48 percent, a reduction of about 6 percent. The British also experienced a comparable decrease. The major increases over this period were experienced by Germany and Japan, whose shares went respectively from about 3 percent to 7 percent and about 1 percent to nearly 7 percent. Other substantial increases were posted by Switzerland and the Netherlands. Taken in all, the same indicators that demonstrate U.S. ascendancy in the postwar world economy through the mid-1960s also demonstrate that that ascendancy had become greatly diminished by the mid-1970s.

What was the nature of the Western economic system that prevailed after World War II? Obviously it was a system where the objective economic power of the United States created an inevitable leadership role for that nation. However, U.S. leadership rested easily on the other Western nations because the interests and capabilities of the leader fitted the mood and needs of the followers. The security dictates of the early cold war with the Soviets made the United States more willing to lead and the Europeans more willing to follow than otherwise might have been the case. On the American side, security concerns helped motivate the U.S. government (especially Congress) to extend reconstruction aid to Europe and to become deeply involved with the problems of dismantling intra-European economic autarchy. For the Europeans, security reasons ultimately led them to support the primacy of the United States and its currency in the monetary system, and as well to accept politically a level of American foreign investment that would probably have been objectionable under less-strained international conditions. Even factors which later came to create problems in U.S.-European relations seemed to promote U.S. leadership in the 1950s, such as a payments deficit that provided foreign exchange for European central banks, and the provision of managerial talent that accompanied U.S. direct investment. In short, the United States dominated the system, but it was a domination that was borne easily by the major subordinate nations within the arrangement.

Any system in which one nation is dominant is likely to reflect the

[14] International Monetary Fund, *Directory*, part A, 2, 6.
[15] U.N. Commission, *Transnational Corporations*, 236.

values of that nation. The trade system set up under the GATT after 1947 was no exception, for it incorporated many of the ideas for post-war trading relations generated in the U.S. government during the war. It is useful to examine some of these values, since they were affected by the later shift in the economic position of the United States and the European countries, and as a result became an important factor in the Tokyo Round. In examining values, particularly as these affect a negotiation, a distinction should be made between the values and the interests of parties. Interests are driven by objective factors, whereas values spring from the practice of governments and reflect the political and organizational principles of the society they reflect. The distinction between the two can be seen in the trade in agricultural products, which has been a historically divisive issue between the United States and Europe. Objective factors such as comparative advantage have clearly motivated U.S. diplomats in past negotiations to demand increased access for American agricultural exports in European markets. In addition, however, U.S. demands have been motivated by disputes over the political management of agricultural trade, and particularly over the extent of government interference with free market forces. The latter dispute is a question of values, and as the United States and Europe became more equivalent in economic strength such disputes took on greater significance.

One American value that became influential in the early GATT trade regime concerned the relationship between government and the economy. Americans historically have tended to be more suspicious of the role of government in economic life than their European counterparts, and the importance of this value has been reinforced by the independent role of Congress in the American federal government. One example of the effect of this value in international relations is the Marshall Plan, for Congress required this important foreign-policy program to be administered by a "business-oriented" bureaucracy independent of the U.S. State Department. In addition to being suspicious of government, American leaders attached enormous political importance to the achievement of economic growth. One reason for this, as Charles Maier has noted, is that economic growth had historically been a way Americans had solved internal problems of political conflict.[16] It was only natural that American leaders approached the international system from a perspective that effectively put primacy on economic as opposed to political relations. Economic growth was the main objective, and international trade was viewed as a major vehicle to accomplish

[16] "Politics of Productivity."

30

growth. These views translated into a liberal position on international trade, which is reflected in the aims of the GATT preamble of reducing tariffs and other barriers to trade. On balance, the Americans adopted a much more liberal position respecting trade than their European counterparts, particularly on the matter of nontariff measures.[17] From the European standpoint, trade liberalization seemed a remote prospect given the circumstances facing the European economies immediately after the war. For the Americans, however, trade liberalization was an attractive goal in ideological terms, and it was consistent with national interest, since the United States was favorably positioned to benefit from freer trade. On this matter, the preeminent position of the United States in the early postwar system was the decisive factor.

A second American value that shaped the GATT was that of multilateralism, which became embodied in the MFN procedures of Article 1 that guaranteed nondiscrimination between contracting parties. For the Americans, this value was part and parcel of the thrust toward reducing trade restrictions, and U.S. delegations took a doctrinaire position on this matter during the formative period of GATT.[18] The Europeans were far less supportive of this value, fearing that their weaker economies would be unable to withstand the strain of multilateral trade liberalization. Furthermore, the Europeans were more sympathetic to a regional approach to the reconstruction of world trade. These conflicting views created a serious strain in the preparatory negotiations for the GATT, along the lines neatly summarized by Gerard Curzon: "To put the matter simply, the GATT for the Americans was Article 1; for the Europeans it was Articles 12 and 24."[19]

The genesis of the U.S. multilateral approach could be traced to an economic philosophy of freer trade, but it also had roots in a more general American view of world politics. From the nineteenth century onwards, the United States has opposed the institution of spheres of influence in Europe and the Far East. As but one example of this, the United States pursued an "Open Door" policy in the Far East, a policy which had little substance and made little sense in international politics, but

[17] The U.S. position was not wholly consistent, however. As Dam, *The GATT*, 14, has noted, the U.S. Department of Agriculture insisted on exception to the rule against quantitation restrictions in order to protect the domestic price system in the United States.

[18] See, generally, Gardner, *Sterling-Dollar Diplomacy.*

[19] "Crisis in Trading System," 36. The articles referred to are as follows: Article 1, General Most-Favored-Nation Treatment; Article 12, Restrictions to Safeguard the Balance of Payments; and Article 24, Territorial Application in Frontier Traffic—Customs Unions and Free-Trade Areas.

which was immensely popular in American domestic politics.[20] Similarly, in the negotiations with the Soviets at the close of World War II, the Americans resisted proposals advanced by the Soviet leadership to establish de facto spheres of influence on the European continent. Thus the support for multilateralism in trading relations was an extension of a more general political attitude about how the postwar world should be organized. This attitude unfortunately ran headlong into important economic and political interests of the European countries. For example, the Continental powers under the influence of Jean Monnet were leaning toward a European approach toward economic revitalization, while the British sought to maintain the sterling area and the system of imperial preferences. To make matters worse, the United States was far from consistent in its pursuit of multilateralism in trade relations. At the same time as the United States was militating for nondiscriminatory treatment in the GATT negotiations it was demanding that the European nations draw up a multilateral reconstruction plan as a condition for receiving Marshall aid from the United States. Futhermore, the United States later welcomed with enthusiasm the moves to establish a Common Market among six former European belligerents in World War II. The upshot was that because of their importance to the United States the principles of multilateralism and nondiscrimination were prominent in the commitments of the GATT, but from the outset they were principles flawed by controversy and inconsistency.

A third value pressed on the GATT by American trade officials concerned the means for implementing the trade-liberalizing objectives of the General Agreement. The United States took the view that what was needed was a code of international trade law that would clearly set out the obligations nations had toward each other's commercial activities. Enforcement of this law would be carried out through GATT dispute-settlement procedures. The code approach formulated by the United States proved unacceptable to many of the original signatories of the GATT largely because the substance of the code was unacceptable. The United States had in the main sought to ban nontariff measures outright, and to set up a process whereby tariffs would be reduced over time through negotiation. However, as previously mentioned, other countries, including the major European nations, wanted to retain the freedom to continue restrictions. Whether the opposition to trade liberalism was based on economic philosophy or on the particular circumstances that followed the war is an interesting question, but it is essentially irrelevant to the political resolution of the problem. The

[20] Kennan, *American Diplomacy*, ch. 2.

Europeans were wary of a code approach to international trade and sought instead to preserve their right to administrative discretion. They preferred to build a postwar trading system on practice rather than pronouncement. The irony of the situation is that the United States, a common-law country where customary practice is influential, took a code approach to international trade law; whereas the European nations, where (except for Great Britain) code law is more the norm, took an approach to international trade based more on custom and empirical practice.

The result of the different approaches taken by the United States and its allies is that the GATT was an awkward compromise from the very outset. The U.S. approach prevailed in that the GATT did come to embody a set of trade rules supported by a dispute-settlement procedure. However, the rules were weakened by many exceptions, some which were initiated by the United States itself, and in the end the exceptions gravely weakened the legitimacy of the overall effort. Indeed it was exceptions to the trading rules that helped turn the U.S. Congress against the ITO, which would have incorporated the GATT rules in its framework.[21] As for the dispute-settlement process in the GATT, it was invoked frequently during the 1950s, but its operation only seemed to confirm the realist, or perhaps cynical, belief by many GATT members that international judicial processes were unable to modify substantially the economic practices of sovereign states, and particularly those of the more powerful states. The use of the dispute-settlement procedures waned after the 1950s, concurrently, interestingly, with the relative economic decline of the nation that had most strongly supported them. In sum, the value of establishing a code of trade law remained a goal within the GATT, but as trade practices became more diverse during the 1960s there appeared to be a growing disparity between the GATT articles and the forms of protectionism actually practiced by the contracting parties.

The most visible and important part of GATT has been the trade negotiations it has sponsored since 1947, not the GATT code of conduct. However, even these negotiations were not very successful until fairly recently. After 1947, the GATT sponsored negotiations in 1949 (Annecy), 1951 (Torquay), 1956 (Geneva), and 1960–61 (the Dillon Round). These negotiations took up some important institutional matters, such as the accession of new members, but they did not make sig-

[21] It should be noted that the GATT survived U.S. politics because, unlike the ITO, it was an executive agreement and hence U.S. participation did not have to be approved by Congress. From the origin of the GATT, the U.S. Congress was hostile to it.

nificant progress in liberalizing trade. One reason is that the European countries relied heavily on nontariff measures through the mid-1950s and hence any tariff concessions given during GATT negotiations were not meaningful in trade terms.[22] Furthermore European recovery from the war did not occur as quickly as expected, as evidenced by the fact that European currencies were not made fully convertible until 1958, which made it difficult for these nations to increase their exposure to international competition. The Kennedy Round of 1963–67 emerged as the first significant negotiation in GATT after the initial negotiaton. It led to an average tariff reduction among the participants of about 35 percent, in sharp contrast to a reduction of less than 10 percent on a much smaller trade volume in the Dillon Round that preceded it. The Kennedy Round was, moreover, the first GATT negotiation at which the nations of the EC participated as a single unit, which created the impression in both the United States and Europe that the Kennedy Round was "the first major negotiation of a common interest across the Atlantic in which neither side was more equal than the other."[23] In retrospect, it is interesting to note the historical correlation between a successful outcome in trade negotiation and the increasing equality of the major actors in those negotiations, for it is a trend which continued through the Kennedy Round and on into the Tokyo Round of the 1970s.

The Kennedy Round will be the subject of further discussion in Chapter 2. Suffice it to say at this point that the Kennedy Round was an important turning point in the postwar economic relations between the United States and Europe, and in the development of GATT itself. As Bauer, Pool, and Dexter have argued, the United States made a fundamental decision in initiating the Kennedy Round to meet the potential threat of a unified Europe through liberal rather than isolationist policies.[24] This move entailed the risk of opening U.S. industry to the competitive pressures of a resurgent Europe, but the alternative might have been to counter European regionalism with a form of regionalism in return. This would have had serious consequences for GATT as an institution, and for the concept of multilateralism in international trading relations. Instead, the Kennedy Round was successfully negotiated, and its success was a positive factor in the political integration of the Atlantic community. Moreover, in economic terms, it has been established that the negotiations prevented one-third to one-half of the diversions from U.S.-European trade that might have occurred from European in-

---

[22] Curzon has labeled the European reductions "false concessions" as opposed to real ones given by the United States ("Crisis in Trading System," 37).

[23] Preeg, *Traders and Diplomats*, 262.

[24] *American Business*, 76.

tegration.[25] In short, the Kennedy Round ensured the continued vitality of the multilateral approach, and of GATT as well. It set the stage for the Tokyo Round, which was an even more direct attempt to revitalize the basic structure of GATT itself.

The Longer-Run Perspective

A fourth perspective on the Tokyo Round has its roots in the Great Depression of the 1930s, and even further back in history in the international political economy since the mid-1800s. First, however, the depression. The United States emerged from World War I as the largest trading nation in the world. It was therefore to be expected that domestic events affecting the trade capabilities of the United States would have wide impact on commercial relations in the international system. Such was the case with two events of the early 1930s; the Smoot-Hawley tariff of 1930 and the Reciprocal Trade Agreements Act of 1934. The first was the culmination of a trend toward protectionism that had begun in the late nineteenth century. The second was the beginning of a trend toward liberalism which was interrupted by World War II but then continued to the present. These two events of the 1930s marked the major watershed in international commercial policy in this century. They were a more important watershed than World War II (although the latter is more frequently referred to) because they were economic events originating in the world economic system, rather than being the economic results of a cataclysm in the international political system. Both events had a profound impact on the economic milieu in which the Tokyo Round took place.

There is no one answer in economic literature as to what caused the depression of the 1930s, nor is it even known whether the causes were primarily real or monetary, or national or international in their origin. What is generally agreed, however, is that the breakdown of the international economic system undoubtedly deepened the depression within national economies, and it is understood that that breakdown was associated with several failed attempts to negotiate a more cooperative approach in the international regime. Two such attempts stand out. The first was the World Economic Conference of 1927, and particularly the Conference on Import and Export Prohibitions and Restrictions which it sponsored in the same year. Both conferences aimed at countering the trend toward increased tariffs that was occurring in all countries during the 1920s. The initial results of the negotiations were

---

[25] Preeg, *Traders and Diplomats*, 220.

favorable. A tariff truce was agreed upon, and a code of international behavior was established that regulated the use of quantitative restrictions and other trade prohibitions. However, nothing came from this initiative. The code failed by one nation to receive the eighteen signatures needed to bring it into force, which precipitated withdrawals by other nations, thus killing the treaty.[26] As for the tariff truce, it was effectively ended when the newly elected administration of Herbert Hoover in the United States commenced congressional hearings that led to the Smoot-Hawley tariff, amid the pledge to increase tariffs for farmers suffering from falling prices.

The second attempt to negotiate a cooperative international approach came at the World Economic Conference of 1933, where the United States was represented by the newly elected administration of Franklin D. Roosevelt. The main issue at the second conference involved monetary and not trade policy, and particularly turned on an effort by the European nations to secure the commitment of the United States to an international currency-stabilization plan. Such a plan ran counter to the determination of the Roosevelt administration to inflate domestic prices and to reduce the dependence of the domestic economy on international currency exchanges. As Roosevelt himself put it in a widely publicized message during the conference, "The sound internal economic situation of a nation is a greater factor in its well-being than the price of its currency."[27] The U.S. position contributed to the collapse of the conference, and in its wake nations engaged in a period of competitive exchange-rate devaluations through the mid-1930s. As Charles Kindleberger has commented on this episode: "The Democratic Administration . . . had little interest in or knowledge of the world economy. . . . It would not be for three years that the administration felt a responsibility for the operation of the international economic system."[28]

In between the world economic conferences of 1927 and 1933 came the Smoot-Hawley tariff of 1930. This legislation raised U.S. duties to historic levels and increased the scope of tariff coverage as well, although the precise extent of the coverage was incalculable in the aggregate.[29] The Smoot-Hawley Act was not a dramatic turnaround in pro-

---

[26] Shonfield, "International Economic Relations," 45.

[27] Quoted in Kindleberger, World in Depression, 220.

[28] Ibid., 231.

[29] Schattschneider, Politics, 17, reports that the Smoot-Hawley tariff made extensive use of "basket clauses," of which the following might be an example: "all raw or unmanufactured articles not enumerated or provided for." The U.S. Tariff Commission reported that the effect of basket clauses in one product area (chemicals) could be to extend cov-

tectionism, since all major trading nations were protectionistic at that time. Rather, it represented a new level in the long movement by nations toward closing off their economies to foreign imports. In this of course it succeeded, for in the wake of the Smoot-Hawley tariff and the retaliation which it precipitated, world trade fell by about two-thirds by the mid-1930s. The breakdown of trade after 1930 was alarming to Western governments, but even more alarming was the process that had led to that breakdown. The Smoot-Hawley Act was written in congressional committees that were essentially unable to master the detail that had become inherent in any major tariff legislation. Because of this, and because of the general sympathy toward protectionism created by the depression, Congress essentially extended protection to all those groups that demanded it. The spectacle created was that of a gross excess of the democratic process and of a loss of control over the economy by both the U.S. president and the congressional leadership.[30]

The Smoot-Hawley process had been watched closely by other governments, and they moved quickly to retaliate. Perhaps the most significant of foreign reactions was the abolition by Great Britain of its historic policy of free trade in 1931, and its negotiation of the Ottawa agreements of 1932 which created a tariff preferential area in the British Commonwealth. Ironically this preferential arrangement which was precipitated by U.S. actions later became a stumbling block for the efforts of a new generation of American leaders to promote nondiscrimination in international trade. At home, there was also a sharp reaction to the Smoot-Hawley Act. The breakdown of trade took its toll on public sympathy toward protectionism. The tariff became an issue in the presidential election of 1932, and was attacked by Roosevelt as contributing to the depression. Following his election, Roosevelt appointed in Secretary of State Cordell Hull a man who was committed to the view that free trade was an essential ingredient in world prosperity, and an even more important ingredient in international peace and stability.[31] Hull organized the State Department and Tariff Commis-

---

erage from a single unit containing 20 specific items to around 1,500 chemicals that would be dutiable under the act. As for tariff rates, Tasca has cited research by Wallace and Fay in *Weltwirtschaftliches Archiv* (July 1936) estimating that the Smoot-Hawley Act raised U.S. duties by 12 percent over the already high levels of the Fordney-McCumber tariff of 1922. Tasca judges that this estimate is too low (*Reciprocal Trade Policy*, 191).

[30] On the theme of control, Schattschneider, *Politics*, 292–93, concluded his book: ". . . the forces brought to bear on democratic government are now wholly beyond conscious control. The subject is, therefore, one of the greatest in modern politics. To manage pressures is to govern; to let pressures run wild is to abdicate."

[31] As Hull, *Memoires*, 81, himself put it; "But toward 1916 I embraced the philosophy

sion to begin working with Congress to prepare new tariff legislation. The legislation was delayed through 1933 because of the greater priority attached to emergency domestic programs, and during that year Hull suffered a personal defeat in the events of the World Economic Conference in London. In the following year, the legislation was enacted under the title Reciprocal Trade Agreements Act (RTA) of 1934. It was a victory for Hull, who remembers it in the following terms: "My fight of many long years for the reciprocal trade policy and the lowering of trade barriers was won. To say I was delighted is a bald understatement."[32]

The RTA of 1934 produced a revolution in U.S. and even international trade policy, which is perhaps a curious statement to make about a law that was essentially only an amendment to the Smoot-Hawley Act. The central element of the RTA was that it empowered the president to lower (or raise) tariffs up to 50 percent from Smoot-Hawley levels in the course of trade negotiations with other countries. From the standpoint of American politics, the RTA transferred tariff-setting policy to the presidency, which could organize itself bureaucratically for the task, and away from the Congress, which had ultimately proven incapable of managing the tariff or of discriminating between the many appeals brought by constituents for protection. This transfer substantially increased the control the government exercised over trade policy, and it has been an essential part of the U.S. trade-policy structure ever since 1934. From the standpoint of international politics, the RTA was revolutionary in that it implicitly accepted that setting tariff rates could no longer be a unilateral policy by a nation-state, but was rather a bilateral matter to be settled through negotiation. This action eventually changed over half a century of international commercial policy, but it was not the first time that nations had recognized the importance of diplomacy in achieving trade liberalization. In the previous century, the French free-trade movement led by Michel Chevalier had sought to convince French manufacturers and the government of Louis Napoleon to follow the British example of free trade established in the 1846 repeal of the protectionist Corn Laws. This met with little success until the opportunity arose to incorporate the subject in a commercial and political negotiation with Great Britain. The result was the Anglo-

---

I carried throughout my twelve years as Secretary of State, into numerous speeches and statements addressed to this country and to the world. From then on, to me, unhampered trade dovetailed with peace; high tariffs, trade barriers, and unfair economic competition, with war."
[32] Ibid., 357.

French (Cobden-Chevalier) treaty of 1860, which was instrumental in the later opening of the French market to British manufacturers.[33]

The U.S. government pursued reciprocal trade agreements with other countries as far as economic circumstances after 1934 would allow. By 1939, the United States had concluded twenty-one agreements which made reductions in about a thousand duties. All agreements were made on an MFN (i.e., nondiscriminatory) basis, which slowed the process of negotiation but extended more widely the impact of the agreements. The process was effectively arrested during the war, even though some additional eleven agreements were reached during the hostilities. The bilateral agreements reached under the RTA program were in the main successful in increasing the flow of international trade, but perhaps the greatest value of the program was that it provided a corpus of experience in trade liberalization that became integrated into the GATT after the war. The act of reaching bilateral agreements gave governments the opportunity to create mechanisms for liberalizing trade, which was demonstrated by the fact that most of the GATT articles drawn up in 1947 were taken from various agreements reached during the previous decade under the RTA system. For example, the escape clause that became written into Article 19 of the GATT was drawn from an agreement reached with Mexico in 1942, and was in turn representative of similar escape clauses the United States had insisted be included in all its agreements.[34] Incorporation of these clauses and other mechanisms into the GATT required that essentially bilateral procedures be adapted for a multilateral venue, but this posed little problem even in the tariff area, where parties exchanged benefits on a precise quid pro quo basis.

The reciprocal trade program was concurrent with a sea-change in U.S. and world public opinion respecting protectionism and free trade. Nowhere can this be better observed than by contrasting the climate of opinion that existed during the passage of the Smoot-Hawley tariff in 1930 against the climate existing in 1953–54 when the Republican party under Dwight Eisenhower reversed its historic policy of protectionism by extending the RTA of 1934. Both events have been the subject of major analytical works on trade policy, namely by Schattschneider and by Bauer, Pool, and Dexter. Analyzing the first event, Schattschneider describes the policy as taking place in an environment favorable to protectionism, and within a legislative system that encouraged protectionist pressure groups to press their demands vigorously

[33] Condliffe, *Commerce*, 222–23.
[34] Jackson, *World Trade*, 553–54.

on the Congressmen who made the policy. In the second event, the authors describe the environment of public opinion as on balance supportive of free trade, and they find (surprisingly) that there was relatively little effective political pressure on the legislators, particularly from the more powerful economic interests in the country. What appeared to change was the principle of free trade versus protectionism, or, more precisely, the expectations that people held as to which principle was just and would ordinarily prevail as a general rule. This change was important for international trade policy, and will be discussed further in Chapter 9.

The period which encompasses 1934 to the present had its antecedents in history which provide additional perspective on the analysis of events around the Tokyo Round. The early 1930s ended a period of global protectionism which had begun in Europe during the great depression of 1783–1896. Protectionism started in this period as a straightforward response to hard times. Owing to a series of rapid technological improvements in the mid-1850s, the comparative advantage in grain growing shifted decisively to the New World, with the result that grain prices fell sharply in European markets. At the same time, a slump occurred in industrial production, which continued for over two decades in the form of low prices and low return on capital for manufactured products. International competition became severe, and in all countries there were strong pressures for protection against imports. One by one, national governments succumbed to the pressures, reversing a period of relatively free trade which extended back to the 1820s. Austria-Hungary raised tariffs in 1876, and Italy followed in 1878. In 1879, Germany shifted to a protectionist policy and so, because of its size in the European economy and its philosophy of nationalism and mercantilism, set a protectionist tone for the overall system. France responded to German protectionism with restrictions of its own. Britain, the Low Countries, and Switzerland, however, resisted the move toward higher tariffs. By the end of the century, Britain was the only major nation practicing free trade. In the New World, the United States had remained avowedly protectionist throughout the nineteenth century, and had avoided the midcentury movement toward free trade due largely to the effects of the Civil War. In sum, the depression that began in the 1870s also triggered a sixty-year period of protectionism. Nationalism and war after the turn of the century exacerbated the protectionist trend that was already well established as a response to the economic conditions of the late nineteenth century. It was not until the international system had gone through a major war and was mired in another depression that any successful move to reverse protectionism would be made.

Prior to the period of protectionism which commenced during the 1870s, the European system enjoyed a brief period liberal commercial exchange, which flowed from the apparent triumph around midcentury of the doctrine of free trade.[35] This period was initiated by Great Britain. As Condliffe has noted, the Napoleonic Wars left Britain in relation to Europe in approximately the same position in which World War II had left the United States.[36] The wars had left British manufacturing capabilities unscathed, and following the wars Britain's economic strength enabled it to become the leading creditor country in the world. Britain provided aid and loans to European nations and had large exports of foreign investment, mostly to the United States and British colonies in Asia. Trade with the United States and the colonies was substantial, but trade with Europe was hampered by high tariffs on the Continent and by the protectionist Corn Laws in Britain which restricted imports of grain from European countries. Efforts by British statesmen to promote liberalism in Europe were met with demands that Britain herself rescind duties on grain.

A campaign for free trade began among British merchants in the second quarter of the nineteenth century. The campaign was part of a broader effort of political reform in British society, and its eventual success resulted in part from the political realignment wrought by the Reform Act of 1832. The campaign was ably led by Richard Cobden, who demonstrated, as Cordell Hull did a century later, the importance of pragmatic political leadership in promoting the ideal of free trade. Britain repealed the Corn Laws in 1846 and followed up this action with a series of administrative and diplomatic measures over the next two decades that put free trade into practice. Included in these measures was the negotiation in 1860 of the Cobden-Chevalier commercial treaty with France, which was equally important in improving political and economic relations between the two countries. The Cobden-Chevalier treaty initiated a period of relatively free trade with France, and it stimulated a series of similar trade-liberalizing treaties between the various nations in Europe. In sum, it would be accurate to say that the midcentury period of free trade originated in the domestic politics of Great Britain and spread to the nations of Europe through the mechanism of

---

[35] As F. W. Taussig noted in his presidential address to the American Economic Association in 1904, "Forty years ago, the doctrine of free trade seemed to be triumphant, alike in the judgments of thinkers and in the policy of the leading countries" ("The Present Position of the Doctrine of Free Trade," in *Free Trade*, 1).

[36] *Commerce*, 203.

international commercial treaties. The European commitment to free trade, however, was considerably less enduring than the British, and it turned around quickly in the face of depression after 1870. For the British, free trade remained essentially the commercial policy of the nation until well after World War I.

In the sweep of history, then, from the mid-1800s to the present, how would one situate and describe the Tokyo Round? It would represent a continuation of the trend toward the regulation of international commerce through international negotiations instead of unilateral national legislation, which had occurred in various international commercial agreements and in the Cobden-Chevalier treaty of 1860, and then received a setback in the depression, war, and failed international conferences over the period from 1870 to 1930. In terms of size, the Tokyo Round was quite simply the largest commercial negotiation ever held. In terms of substance, it was the most profound commercial negotiation since the early postwar conferences that constructed the GATT and the abortive ITO, and its agenda ranked in scope, although not in aspiration, with the World Economic Conference sponsored by the League in 1927. The Tokyo Round occurred during a period of trade liberalism which had its roots in the reciprocal trade agreements program of the mid-1930s, and which continued through a hiatus of global warfare to the present. How long this period will endure is of great practical concern for the economic well-being of the international community. This is a question that the successful conclusion of the Tokyo Round negotiation may have some bearing upon.

THE TOKYO ROUND IN THEORETICAL PERSPECTIVE

The Tokyo Round was a case of a single multilateral negotiation in a liberal trading regime that has extended roughly from 1934 to the present. Not only is it useful to situate this case in a historical perspective, it is also useful to analyze it in the context of the theory of political economy, that is, the theory of the relationship between economics and politics.[37] One focus of concern in that body of theory has been the nature of the international trading regime, and the conditions which create change in that regime.[38] Much of what has been written on that sub-

[37] For a useful discussion of this theory, see ch. 1 ("The Nature of Political Economy") in Gilpin, *U.S. Power*.

[38] The Webster's definition of regime is "a mode of rule or management" (or "a form of government"), which clearly is adequate to describe the modern GATT system. Other definitions can be found in the theoretical literature. For example, Robert Keohane has defined regimes as "patterns of regularized cooperative behavior in world politics," while

ject is relevant to an analysis of the Tokyo Round, and in turn a study of the Tokyo Round may contribute to a theoretical understanding of the contemporary GATT regime.

The main issue at stake in assessing the nature of any particular international trade regime is the extent to which it is open or closed (i.e., liberal or protectionist). At the extremes, this presents little problem of judgment. For example, distinguishing between the trade regime of the 1930s and that of the 1970s on the basis of liberalism is straightforward, just as it is also easy to distinguish between the extremes of democratic and totalitarian forms of government. What are much more problematic are the comparisons made between essentially similar systems. It would be difficult, and probably pointless, to try to determine whether Canada or the United States is the more democratic, and in the same vein it is difficult to substantiate the argument that trading relations of the 1970s were more or less liberal than those of the 1960s. As systems become more similar, the indicators of liberalism (or democracy) tend to become unclear.

Depending on what factors one takes into account, the judgments reached about any given comparisons can vary widely. For example, the trade relations of the 1970s were more liberal than those of the 1960s from the standpoint of a lower aggregate level of tariffs, but they were less liberal in the greater incidence of bilateral export-restraint agreements (VER's). The problem is that free or unrestricted trade, like democracy, is a value that exists nowhere in pure form, but is found only in approximate terms in real systems. Consequently, there will always be differences between individuals over which features of any particular regime should be selected as representative of the regime, and as well there will be differences over the meaning of terms like liberalism or protectionism as generally applied to trading relationships. As a result, theories about the nature and changes of international economic regimes can be expected to fall considerably short of scientific precision.

A further problem in evaluating the liberalism of the GATT trading regime is whether one chooses government policy as the main measure of liberalism or emphasizes objective indicators such as trade flows. Policy, which would seem to be more directly related to the meaning of

---

Oran Young views them as "social institutions around which actor expectations converge in a given area of international relations." The last two definitions emphasize that in international relations the existence of national sovereignty normally dictates that modes of rule or management will be based on the continuing consent of the ruled. This is certainly true for cooperative regimes like the GATT. For further discussion, see Keohane, "Hegemonic Stability," 133, and Young, "International Regimes."

liberalism, is indeed inconsistent. On the one hand, the GATT contracting parties maintain an unequivocal commitment to liberal trade policy as a general approach, while on the other hand they have maintained or increased protectionism in problematic sectors such as textiles, steel, and consumer electronics. The result, as several theorists have noted, has been to create a contradictory regime of international trade policy.[39] At the level of trade flows, however, a conclusion about the nature of the regime would seem quite unambiguous, since world trade has grown by an annual average of about seven percent over the postwar period. The problem with this indicator, however, is that there is no assured linkage between the policies of government and resulting trade flows, except in the negative sense that severe restrictions can definitely lead to lower trade flows. The probability is that trade has increased as much because of generally buoyant postwar conditions as because of the specific policy actions of trading nations. Consequently, trade flows themselves may be a dubious measure of the liberality of the system.

From another perspective, however, it is clear that the purpose of liberal trade policy is to increase international trade flows, and therefore an increasing level of trade might indicate that whatever policies had been pursued were at least not detrimental. Certainly this assumption would seem appropriate in comparing the present to the early 1930s, where the true measure of protectionism was seen in the rapidly falling trade flows between nations. Thus it is difficult to get an overall measure of the liberalism of the contemporary GATT regime. One must proceed by judgment, and it would seem that the judgment of most observers is that the GATT continues to be in essence a liberal trading regime. On this point, the conclusion reached in Charles Lipson's study of the contemporary GATT regime seems essentially accurate:

> Finally, despite some overall weakening of the regime, there are many areas in which liberalization continues. The GATT remains an important multilateral forum, as the Tokyo Round showed. The nontariff codes negotiated there should help reduce or control a number of trade barriers such as discriminatory government procurement. Tariffs continue to be reduced and are no longer a serious obstacle for most manufacturers. Beyond these specific achievements, the Tokyo Round's success indicates that the major trading powers still support a relatively open trading order despite protectionist pressures and a difficult economic environment.[40]

[39] See, for example, Burenstam Linder, "International Economic Disorder."
[40] "Transformation of Trade," 452.

The problems faced in evaluating GATT liberalism also exist in assessing the results of a major negotiation like the Tokyo Round. Did the Tokyo Round increase or decrease the liberality of contemporary trading relations? Most observers would assume the former, if for no other reason than that the stated goal of national governments at the Tokyo Round was to increase the openness of the trading system. However, some analysts have reached the opposite conclusion, as evidenced in the following assessment by Canada's chief negotiator at the Tokyo Round: "An overall look at the Tokyo Round shows that it sanctioned a significant movement toward greater reliance on systems of 'contingent' protection and on related discretionary trade-regulating mechanisms and away from tariff-based systems."[41] Thus there is disagreement over the nature of the Tokyo Round much as there is over the nature of GATT itself, which makes any analysis of the effects of the Tokyo Round on GATT problematic at best. What will be done in the following chapters is to analyze the impact of the Tokyo Round on GATT in describing the process whereby the Tokyo Round agreements were negotiated. For the moment, however, it is useful to outline several theories that have been advanced to explain the conditions that lead to liberalism or protectionism in trading regimes. These theories provide some background in assessing the results of the Tokyo Round negotiation.

Impact of Hegemonic Stability

The most prominent history of regime change in the literature of political economy is the theory of hegemonic stability. Briefly, this theory states that cooperative international regimes occur in historical periods when economic capabilities are unequally distributed among nations; in other words, during periods of hegemonic dominance by a leading nation. The theory essentially has its origin in the work of Charles Kindleberger on the 1929 depression. Kindleberger attributes the depth and severity of this depression to the fact that no nation was able to provide the leadership needed to stimulate recovery. In his words:

The world economic system was unstable unless some country stabilized it, as Britain had done in the nineteenth century and up to 1913. In 1929, the British couldn't and the United States wouldn't. When every country turned to protect its national private interest,

[41] Grey, *Trade Policy*, 20.

the world public interest went down the drain, and with it the private interests of all.[42]

Specifically, Kindleberger argued that Great Britain and the United States failed to provide economic leadership in three particulars: (i) by not maintaing an open market for distressed exports; (ii) by not providing countercyclical, long-term investment; and (iii) by not acting as a lender of last resort in financial crises. This theory of stability probably places more emphasis on monetary mechanisms than on trade relations, although it is clear that Kindleberger regarded U.S. trade cutbacks inspired by the Smoot-Hawley tariff as a major contributing factor in the depression. Furthermore, the theory is one of crisis behavior, and there is no certainty that the factors which promote stability in crisis are also those which avoid crisis in the first place. Nevertheless the theory of stability elaborated by Kindleberger is compelling in its assertion that hegemonic leadership is necessary to maintain an open international economic system, and it is a point of departure in examining the sources of liberalism in world trading relations.

Other analysts have carried this theory some distance further. For example, Robert Gilpin's study of the trade and investment regimes created under British hegemony in the nineteenth century and American hegemony in the twentieth assumes that a liberal order cannot be created without the support of the most powerful state(s) in the system.[43] This idea is not exactly the same as saying that powerful states necessarily create liberal orders, but it is clear from Gilpin's historical account that this in fact occurred under British and then American hegemony. Another analyst who has tackled this problem is Stephen Krasner, who has explicitly linked the imbalance of economic power to a liberal trading order. As the author puts it, "The most important conclusion of this theoretical analysis is that a hegemonic distribution of potential economic power is likely to result in an open trading structure."[44] Krasner's method in reaching this conclusion was to divide the history of world trade relations into separate periods and to assess the openness of each period by quantitative indicators such as the average height of tariffs, or the proportion of trade flows in aggregate world production. This method substantiated his hypothesis, and also suggested that changes in the openness of the trading system tended to

---

[42] *World in Depression*, 292.

[43] Gilpin, *U.S. Power*, 85, states, ". . . a liberal international economy cannot come into existence and be maintained unless it has behind it the most powerful state(s) in the system."

[44] "State Power," 318. For a further statement of the theory, see his "Tokyo Round."

come about in response to economic crisis. A third approach to the question of hegemonic stability has been taken by Robert Keohane, who has explored this hypothesis while analyzing recent regime structures in the areas of trade in manufactured goods, monetary relations, and the petroleum trade.[45] Keohane finds that there have been fewer changes in power resources or in the nature of the regime in the area of trade than in money or oil, and hence he suggests that the hegemonic stability theory is not disconfirmed. However, he notes that this theory explains those changes that have occurred in trade relations rather less well than in the other regimes, largely because trade changes (especially protectionistic policies) are particularistic in nature and occur at the same time nations collectively are undertaking liberal policies. Keohane has concluded that "Most major forces affecting the trade regime have little to do with the decline of U.S. power," and he suggests that an adequate explanation of the trade regime would require an analysis of domestic actors and patterns in the various trading nations.[46] As we shall see shortly, this argument is consistent with another set of theories for explaining the nature of trading regimes.

The strengths of the theory of hegemonic stability lie in its clarity and in its apparently correct interpretation of the fairly brief periods of British and then American ascendancy in international economic relations. It is true that at the peak of their economic power, Britain and the United States appeared to be successful in promoting a liberal trade regime. It is further true that a closing of the regime was coincident with the loss of British power, although a similar occurrence in the case of the recent loss of U.S. power seems nowhere near as clear-cut. The difficulty with the theory is that it rests essentially on two cases, and therefore any relationship between hegemonic nation-states and the trade regime may depend more on which countries are the hegemons than on any inherent connection between power and regime. A further problem is that the theory is a blunt one, especially when applied to the international trade regime, and it seems better able to account for change measured in decades than change measured in years. This may account for some of the difficulties of Keohane and Lipson in establishing a clear connection between declining U.S. economic power in the 1970s and changes in the international trade regime.

Despite these difficulties, however, the theory of hegemonic stability is the most developed of the various explanations of open trading sys-

[45] "Hegemonic Stability."
[46] Ibid., 152. As Keohane has further noted, "Protectionism is largely a grass roots phenomenon."

tems, and as such it is a useful guide for an analysis of the Tokyo Round. It is clear on the facts that American economic hegemony has been declining since the late 1960s and the theory would therefore predict a certain closing of the liberal trading system established under the GATT umbrella. One would expect this closing to become apparent in a major international negotiation over trade, most likely in the form of difficulties or disagreements in the negotiation that would impede the possibilities of establishing a cooperative (or liberal) policy. If, however, the negotiation is seen to proceed on the basis of cooperation toward essentially liberal solutions, there may be some grounds for reassessing the theory of hegemonic stability. In this manner, one might expect the Tokyo Round to serve as a limited test of the theory.

Impact of Group Processes

A second theory to explain the presence of a liberal or cooperative regime in international trade deals with domestic political processes within trading nations. Again, the genesis of this theory is found in the work of Charles Kindleberger, specifically in an article written in 1951 which explained the response of several European nations to the sudden decline in the price of wheat during the depression of the 1870s.[47] As Kindleberger reconstructs the situation, developments in technology in agriculture and transportation during the middle of the nineteenth century, particularly in the United States, were passed on to European consumers in the 1870s in the form of rapidly falling prices for wheat and rye. This created a common crisis among agricultural producers throughout Europe, but the response of the various European governments differed. Britain, under the influence of the rising manufacturing class, did nothing, and therefore completed the breakup of agriculture as a political and economic power in the country. In Germany and France, where agriculture was more prominent in the domestic sociopolitical order, protection against cheap imported grains became the preferred policy, thus beginning a pattern of agricultural protectionism that continues today. Protection was also undertaken in Italy, but there an increase of tariffs on grains was slowed by resistance from the industrialist class, and the problem became resolved by the emigration of large numbers of the Italian peasantry to the New World. Only in Denmark was the response consistent with classical economic theory. There, under the leadership of commercial agricultural institutions, agriculture underwent a revolution and the country shifted from

[47] "Group Behavior."

48

an inefficient import-competing grain production to a more efficient dairy farming. In sum, Kindleberger notes that the different national responses to a single economic stimulus depended a great deal on domestic politics in each national society. In each country the willingness of important groups to accept a verdict of the marketplace and their relative power position in society were factors that lay behind the economic policies chosen by the government. As Kindleberger notes of this case, "The decisive factors do not appear to lie in the field of economics at all but in that of society."[48]

A modern application of Kindleberger's theory would be the argument that trade policy is a result of internal politics as well as being a reaction to external circumstances, such as the policies of other nations. This of course is not a proposition that would surprise contemporary trade analysts. Analyses of GATT trade negotiations, for example, commonly refer to the constraints placed on government's ability to pursue liberal policies by those domestic groups that see their interests hurt by those policies. Where the group-behavior theory may be helpful, however, is in pointing to particular phenomena in the domestic structure, or particular governmental procedures or values, that systematically lead to a more liberal (or illiberal) commercial policy. An example of such a structural phenomenon, noted by Lawrence Krause and C. Fred Bergsten, is the tendency of organized labor in the United States to be disproportionately represented by the less-technology-intensive and competitive industries in that country.[49] The result of this wholly internal group process has been to help turn a major economic constituency in the United States against a liberal trade policy. As for governmental procedures or values, the work of Peter J. Katzenstein on comparative economic policies of industrial nations has emphasized the importance of the domestic structure over the logic of international relations themselves.[50] Of particular concern in Katzenstein's approach are the domestic attitudes toward the role government is expected to play in the economy. Where countries differ sharply on such attitudes, there can be commensurate differences in commercial policies: in France, for instance, where a greater tolerance for government involvement than would be acceptable in the United States leads also to a reliance on economic tools (such as subsidies or export promotion) that are anathema to American policymakers. Such attitudes become very important in negotiations over commercial policy, and, as Katzenstein

[48] Ibid., 42.
[49] Bergsten, "U.S. Trade Policy," 635. See also Krause, "Trade Policy."
[50] For example, "International Relations.," See also his "Conclusion."

himself points out, they become important especially in periods when the external balance of power becomes more equal between the major actors in the international economy.

The group-process theory is not likely to develop the conceptual clarity of the theory of hegemonic stability, because the variables it points to are very dissimilar and are not easily subsumed into a general explanation of international commercial policy. When writing in 1951, Kindleberger noted that there was no satisfactory theory of group behavior to explain national commercial policies, and the situation appears no better today. Such as it is, the theory seems better suited as a guide to certain important factors that affect the nature of trading regimes than as a general statement of the relationship between independent and dependent variables. In the study of the Tokyo Round which follows, the theory will serve as a reminder of factors not to be overlooked rather than as a hypothesis to be proved or disproved. The task will be to describe the negotiation and examine to what extent internal processes as opposed to other factors appeared to account for the essential dimensions of the external agreement.

Impact of Trade Structures

A third theory, or group of theories, to account for a liberal trade regime deals with the effects of trade structure (i.e., the types of products traded) on the regime. Generally, there are two branches of theory of interest here. The first concerns the phenomenon of intra-industry trade, or the simultaneous export and import by countries of products within the same industry. The second concerns the effect on international trade of direct overseas investment by multinational firms.

The main economic theory of international trade is that of comparative advantage, which states roughly that each nation will specialize in and export its least-cost products, based ultimately on its relative endowment of the factors of production. This theory has a prima facie plausibility for trade in primary products where resource endowments frequently dictate production possibilities. However, the theory has become increasingly inaccurate as a predictor of contemporary patterns of trade in manufactured products. Between 1960 and 1970, the proportion of manufactured products in total world trade has risen from about 50 percent to 60 percent, and it averaged in the high 50s for the decade of the 1970s.[51] As noted by Shonfield, these figures are highly significant in that they represent a breaking of a historic link between

[51] GATT, *International Trade*, 1971, 1980/81.

manufactures and primary products which in the past had effectively limited the growth of trade in manufactures to the amount of increase in the production and trade of primary goods.[52] This interpretation is consistent with the rapid growth of world trade that has occurred over the past two decades. A further aspect of this argument is that the growth of world trade has occurred disproportionately among the industrialized nations, and particularly in those manufactured products which these nations export and import simultaneously, such as automobiles, chemicals, and consumer electronics. Recent research on such intra-industry trade has estimated that it comprises over one-half of OECD trade in manufactures, and that it has steadily increased as a proportion of total trade during the postwar period.[53] Explaining intra-industry trade is difficult, since, according to the model of comparative advantage, one would expect nations facing severe competition from foreign imports to relocate production to other areas of the economy. Such interindustry specialization has not occurred, however. Instead, through product differentiation, competition and trade between the industrialized nations have occurred in the same industries.

Theory to explain intra-industry trade has been advanced by Staffan Burenstam Linder and others. Burenstam Linder has shown that trade in manufactures is essentially an extension of a nation's domestic activity across national frontiers, and that consequently products that are exported tend to be products that are already manufactured for domestic consumption.[54] From this, it follows that nations with most similar demand structures (as determined by per capita income levels) will make the best trading partners. This theory neatly explains the phenomenon noted by Richard Cooper and others of the increasing amount of trade and economic integration between industrialized nations, especially the United States and the European Community;[55] and the theory also has important implications for theorists concerned with the pattern of economic adjustment to international trade. For our purposes, however, it is important to note that intra-industry trade, and the concurrent phenomenon of increasing trade in manufactures between industrialized nations, is apparently related to an increasing lib-

[52] "International Economic Relations," 106.

[53] See, for example, Grubel and Lloyd, *Intra-Industry Trade*. It should be noted that estimates of the proportion of intra-industry trade are dependent on the level of aggregation used in measuring trade flows, and hence are subject to some disagreement. For further research on this subject, see Giersch (ed.) *Intra-Industry Trade*.

[54] *Essay on Trade*, 86–99.

[55] Cooper, *Economics of Interdependence*. See esp. ch. 3, "Increased Sensitivity of Foreign Trade."

eralism of the trade regime; and for two reasons. The first is that industries involved in intra-industry trade have been dynamic and adaptive institutions and have had a liberal orientation toward international trade. Hence, the more predominant these industries become in international trade the more likely are governments in the industrialized nations to take a liberal stance on trade policy. Second, it is easier to negotiate trade concessions on intra-industry trade, since the tradeoffs involved in such negotiations can be made in the same industry, thus assuring that the same industry that would suffer a loss through a trade concession might also be in a position to receive a compensating benefit. In this sense, it could be said that intra-industry trade and the GATT process of achieving trade liberalization through reciprocal concessions are mutually reinforcing.[56]

A rather different branch of theory which relates trade structure to the trade regime deals with the effects of direct international investment. Since World War II, trade patterns have been increasingly influenced by the investment activities of multinational corporations, particularly American corporations. The essential motivation behind these activities, as noted by Robert Gilpin and others, is the maximization of corporate growth and the suppression of foreign (and domestic) competition.[57] The process that has led to such investment has been convincingly explained by Raymond Vernon's product-cycle hypothesis.[58] Briefly, Vernon's argument is that during the postwar period the United States presented unique market incentives for certain high-income, labor-saving products. Such products were developed in the United States and subsequently exported to other countries. As the product becomes standardized, lower labor costs abroad make it possible to service foreign markets more efficiently through setting up production facilities abroad than through foreign exports. If such a possibility exists for one firm, it exists for others as well, and as a result foreign investment becomes an imperative in order to meet the threat of real or potential competition.[59] Thus the process of market competition between large, mainly American, firms has led to an enormous outpouring of

[56] See Lipson, "Transformation of Trade," 445. For further argument that GATT negotiations favor intra-industry over interindustry specialization, see Hufbauer and Chilas, "Specialization."

[57] See Gilpin, U.S. Power, 135. See also a similar analysis presented in Galbraith, New Industrial State.

[58] "International Investment."

[59] Vernon states, "Any threat to the established position of an enterprise is a powerful galvanizing force to action; in fact, if I interpret the empirical work correctly, threat in general is a more reliable stimulus to action than opportunity is likely to be" (ibid., 200).

foreign investment in the postwar period, which by 1971 had produced a value of international production (i.e., the worldwide production of branch plants) amounting to $330 billion, greater than the value of world exports in the same year (some $310 billion).[60] There is a lively argument over whether the process that generated this level of international investment is unique or whether it will continue in the future. Vernon's product-cycle theory suggests that the conditions that gave rise to U.S. overseas investment were coincidental and temporary, but Andrew Shonfield has countered with the argument that the multinational corporation provides profound marketing and production advantages, and is the most efficient institutional structure for achieving worldwide division of labor in innovative industries. As Shonfield states, "That would suggest that the 1960's, far from being the climax of a once-and-for-all advance of the multinational corporation, on the lines of Vernon's argument, may in fact have been the prelude to a more profound process of internationalizing international production."[61]

Regardless of which argument is correct, the existing levels of international investment have already had a profound impact on international trade patterns. One important effect has been to raise questions about the assumption classical trade theory makes that international trade occurs between disinterested parties. A growing portion of international trade is carried out between parent firms and their subsidiaries in foreign countries, an exchange that is known as intrafirm trade. The importance of such exchanges in U.S. trade was noticed at the time of the Williams Commission report in 1971, specifically in a minority statement tabled by union leaders I. W. Abel and Floyd E. Smith.

> Intra-corporate transactions clearly are not competitive despite the Report's implications to the contrary, because subsidiaries do not compete effectively with parent firms. As much as half of what is reported as "U.S." trade is now represented by intra-corporate transactions between U.S. based multinational companies, their foreign subsidiaries, and their foreign affiliates in both industrial and developing countries.[62]

More research by Gerald Helleiner has confirmed the assertion made by Abel and Smith concerning the proportion of related-party exchanges in overall U.S. trade flows.[63] The implication of such intrafirm

---

[60] Shonfield, "International Economic Relations," 115.

[61] Ibid., 120.

[62] U.S. Government, *United States International Economic Policy*, 341.

[63] *Intra-Firm Trade*. Helleiner states: "In 1977, fully 48.4 percent of the value of total U.S. imports originated with exporters who were related by ownership to the importing

trade is that the prices set on goods being traded across national boundaries often do not conform to real values, but rather are artificial prices (i.e., "transfer prices") which are manipulated to minimize the corporation's exposure to tariffs and other taxes applied by different governments. Intrafirm trade raises important definitional problems about international trade, and it creates difficulties in administering national trade policies. However, from the standpoint of the trade regime, its existence probably creates a bias toward trade liberalism, because the transnational firms engaged in such trade have an interest in reducing the national barriers that apply to the intrafirm flow of goods and services. From the perspective of a transnational firm, national tariffs or other trade barriers act as an additional tax on internal transfers; and the less they exist, the better.

The approach of this study will be to analyze situations where the structure of trade affected negotiations at the Tokyo Round, and where this factor might offer a better explanation of the results than other factors we have considered. Prima facie, there were several areas where the objective structure of trade seemed to be an important if not determining factor in the flow of negotiation. One such area was the relations between developed and developing countries. Another was in certain code negotiations, such as the customs valuation code which dealt with the issue of the transaction price of traded goods, or the subsidies/countervail code which tackled the problem of defining "related parties" in international commerce. Finally, the question of intrafirm trade and transfer pricing was at the root of the tension between the Europeans and the Americans over the basic purpose of the negotiation itself. An attitude that underlies European commercial policy, especially that of the French, is that most transactions in international trade are manipulated to some degree, and hence it is unrealistic to speak of trade flows as responding to free market forces. This argument provides a justification for government intervention, and it amounts to an attack on the basic raison d'être of trade liberalization within the GATT. This attitude was sharply at odds with the view taken by American negotiators, and it was a sore point that underlay much of the negotiation on subsidies and other forms of government incentives.

Impact of Liberal Values

A fourth theory to account for the presence of a liberal trade regime is simply the existence of liberal values in the commercial policies of the

---

firms" (p. 29). By "related," Helleiner means 5 percent or more of the voting stock of a subsidiary owned by the parent company.

major trading nations. This explanation, which is perhaps too self-evident to warrant the term theory, posits that Western governments in the postwar period saw freer trade to be in their own national interest, and they worked at cooperative solutions mainly through GATT to ensure that those interests were realized. The liberal-values explanation is a variant of the sort of social-psychological theory used by David McClelland to explain the rise (and fall) of the economic power of various nations. In McClelland's rather memorable words, "What each generation wanted above all, it got."[64] In the same vein, the liberal-values explanation would hold that the kind of trading system the Western nations wanted in their own interests, and in which they were willing to invest considerable diplomatic effort to achieve, they were in the last analysis able to achieve. The explanation risks being self-evident and even circular, but the risk of not exploring it may be to assume that explanations of economic behavior must possess a certain degree of obscurity before they can be considered valid. What is left for the analyst in the liberal-values explanation is to show empirically that liberal values have indeed been sought by trading governments in the postwar period, and that these values were plausible values given the other interests of these nation-states.

The liberal-values explanation has been examined by several writers. At a general level, Gerard and Victoria Curzon have advanced two competing interpretations to explain the nature of the postwar trading system.[65] One is that the system essentially flowed from the interests industrialized nations have had in liberal trade and exchange policies; the second is that the system resulted from the imposition of a U.S. preference for free trade which the European nations were too weak to resist. The Curzons label the first the liberal-trade hypothesis; and the second was the oligopolistic model, which ultimately derived from the Bismarckian notion that free trade is an aggressive self-serving policy of the strong. It should be obvious that, except for differences in terminology, the oligopolistic model of the Curzons bears some similarities to the hegemonic-stability model of Kindleberger and others.

The analysis presented by the Curzons defends the view that shared liberal values have been the major determinant of the postwar system. As they put it, ". . . *historically* speaking it is a fact that European governments pursued freer trade policies after the war not because the United States forced them to, but because they genuinely believed that, on the whole, their economies would benefit thereby."[66] Liberal values

[64] *Achieving Society*, 437.
[65] "Management of Trade Relations."
[66] Ibid., 195 (emphasis in original).

were characteristic of all the major nations in the system, and where there was protectionist backsliding, it was as likely to come from some high-cost, labor-intensive industries in the United States as from the European nations. The Curzons did admit to some qualifications to this argument. For example, they cite Jacob Viner's well-known generalization that large nations trade for political reasons and small nations trade for economic reasons as accounting for some of the sense of responsibility the United States has demonstrated in international economic affairs, but in the main they argue that these affairs have been conducted with a singular absence of political pressuring. Their examination yields the conclusion that "All the evidence suggests that the dominant-country, oligopolistic model of trade relations does not account for postwar trade cooperation (or monetary cooperation, for that matter) as well as the liberal trade hypotheses."[67]

Other analysts have also used the liberal-trade hypothesis to explain the essential features of the postwar trade system. One approach has been taken by John Ruggie in an article that argues that a basic compromise was reached after World War II between liberal free-trade orthodoxy, found mainly in the United States, and an older order located mainly in Europe that was hostile toward freer international trade and monetary relations.[68] According to this theory, a compromise was struck which favored on the one hand the multilateralism that was being advanced under the Reciprocal Trade Agreements program, while on the other it sought to ensure stability through continued domestic intervention in international trade and monetary flows. Ruggie speaks of this compromise as creating a system of "embedded liberalism," in which nations seek "to devise a form of multilateralism that is compatible with the requirements of domestic stability."[69] Yet another theory of trade liberalism has been presented by Andrew Shonfield.[70] Shonfield has argued that the distribution of economic power changed fundamentally after World War II, resulting in an exceptional gain for the United States. The United States had a national ideology which favored a liberal and open international system, and while this ideology was not completely consistent in practice, it nevertheless motivated U.S. behavior in the main.[71] The United States received substantial support for this position among the British, who found liberalism appealing in principle and in practice found following the American lead a ne-

---

[67] Ibid., 200.

[68] "International Regimes."

[69] Ibid., 399.

[70] "International Economic Relations."

[71] Shonfield has summed up U.S. ideology in the following terms: "The ideal, in a word, is that of a liberal judicial order applied to the international system" (ibid., 95).

cessity which nevertheless did not impose undue strain. Germany and Japan were also willing to follow the American model of international economic liberalism, which became an integral part of the program of postwar reconstruction in those countries. Only France, in Shonfield's view, pursued a more "normal" policy of economic nationalism, and while this produced strains within the Western alliance, it was contained within the operations of the collective economic organizations created at the end of World War II.

To sum up, both Ruggie and Shonfield have argued that particular political arrangements after World War II ensured that liberal principles would prevail in the international economy of the West. Where Ruggie sees this as a conscious political choice, Shonfield views it as an unplanned result of a particular constellation of political and economic power. Both seem to use the existence of liberal values, or the desire to achieve such values, as the main determinant of the international economic system. This approach provides a good guideline from which to examine the Tokyo Round. In the analysis that follows, the data will be examined to assess whether economic liberalism was used as a self-evident rationale by the major participating nations, and whether this rationale genuinely appeared to motivate national behavior. In other words, the analysis will concern itself with the question of whether liberal values appeared to be an independent factor underlying the Tokyo Round negotiation, and not just a byproduct of a particular (e.g., hegemonic) distribution of economic power.

THE Tokyo Round was a turning point in the history of trade relations under the GATT. With success in reducing national tariffs, the GATT members had achieved about all that could be achieved with this particular form of cooperative economic decisionmaking. The Tokyo Round committed GATT members to a renewed attack on a form of trade restrictions, namely nontariff barriers, which GATT had hitherto had little success in controlling. This new commitment could be viewed as an important change in the GATT regime; and certainly it has been viewed as a constitutional reform of the GATT mandate. The preceding section had reviewed several theories in the political-economy literature that bear on the creation and change of international economic regimes, which may be useful in understanding what occurred at the Tokyo Round and what significance it may hold for the international trading system. What remains is to analyze the circumstances of the Tokyo Round, making use of the theory where it advances an explanation of the meaning of this particular negotiation; or, conversely, assessing whether the developments of the Tokyo Round necessitate a reformation of the received theory.

· 2 ·

BACKGROUND: CREATING THE
CAPACITY TO NEGOTIATE

Large negotiations like the Tokyo Round often appear as discrete phenomena in the flow of political events. They get initiated with a fanfare that assures the attention of the policy community, and develop an internal force that preempts national policymaking in the subjects covered by the negotiation. They necessarily widen political discussion. The visibility of large negotiations undoubtedly has some political advantage for the participants. It imparts urgency to the issues being dealt with, and it increases the authority of the process itself. It enhances the legitimacy of the results. But it can also obscure the fact that negotiations are embedded in a broader policy process, and that the issues taken up in large negotiations have a long, and often problematical, history in that process. Negotiations often bring together policymakers and bureaucrats for another cut at problems they have confronted in other arenas throughout their careers. In this sense, international negotiation is simply policymaking by another means.

The context from which the Tokyo Round emerged was one of rapid change in the pattern of world trade, together with ferment within the policy structures dealing with trade. It was both an unsettled and a creative period in the history of trade relations. The obvious point of departure for the Tokyo Round was the Kennedy Round of trade negotiations, completed in June 1967. By its success as a tariff negotiation, the Kennedy Round promoted the viewpoint that large-scale negotiation was an effective mechanism for liberalizing the international trading regime. By its failures, notably in the areas of agriculture and nontariff measures, the Kennedy Round left a legacy of unfinished business which structured the agenda for subsequent negotiation. In some cases, such as the American Selling Price (ASP) issue, the legacy was one of misunderstanding and political discord which heightened the political pressure on Tokyo Round negotiators.

World trade grew sharply in the period immediately following the Kennedy Round. This influenced the attitudes of both exporting and import-competing interests, and paradoxically encouraged both to support a new round of multilateral negotiations. For the latter, rising trade increased pressures in domestic markets. This inspired a sharp increase in protectionist pressures throughout the industrial world, beyond that which might have been expected to follow the conclusion of a trade-liberalizing negotiation. For the former, rising trade increased the importance of the international trade system, while at the same time making that system appear increasingly fragile. Increased trade flows created greater demands on the payments mechanism, and in turn increased the pressure which led to the fundamental restructuring of the international monetary system after 1971. Then, too, the protectionism stimulated by the growth of trade precipitated a series of disputes between the major trading nations which heightened the danger that government actions taken under the pressure of protectionist sentiment in one country would become the rationale for protectionist acts in other nations.[1] In sum, the late 1960s was a period when international trade, and more broadly the international economy, were of great concern to many countries. Governments responded by striking commissions or study groups to assess the future direction of international trade and other economic relations.[2] From this earlier examination of the issues came many of the positions that were later negotiated in the Tokyo Round.

Finally, parallel developments were occurring within GATT that encouraged a movement toward a major trade negotiation. One of the recurring problems of large-scale negotiations is to develop an information base that will allow parties to determine what the issues are and to develop mechanisms that will give them the capacity to address those issues systematically and completely. This was especially true in the area of nontariff measures (NTM's), which are so numerous, diverse, and complicated as to defy any simple comprehension of what the problem is. In the Kennedy Round, the complexity of these barriers, as well as the lack of negotiating mandates to tackle them, insured that negotiation would make little headway in this area. Following the Kennedy Round, GATT members, with the assistance of the GATT secretariat, began compiling an inventory of NTM's which provided both data and a structure for the code negotiations of the Tokyo Round. The technical work of this period flowed smoothly into the preparations for the Tokyo Round; it linked the bureaucratic activities of the GATT secretariat into the subsequent negotiating activities of national delegations so closely that in some areas it would be difficult to distinguish the

---

[1] This fear is summed up in the expression "trade war." See, for example, Malmgren, "Coming Trade Wars?"

[2] One of the most prominent of such commissions was the Commission on International Trade and Investment Policy ("Williams Commission"), appointed by President Richard M. Nixon. Cited as U.S. Government, *United States International Economic Policy*.

one from the other. The preparatory technical work increased the capacity of nations to negotiate NTMS, and with this increased capacity to negotiate came an increased will to take action.

KENNEDY ROUND: 1963–1967

The Kennedy Round of trade negotiations was conducted in Geneva among eighty-two nations from May 1963 to June 1967. It was the sixth round of multilateral negotiations held under the auspices of GATT since its creation in 1947. The Kennedy Round resulted in an agreement to make the most significant and widespread tariff reductions that have been achieved in GATT negotiations. The negotiation also produced an antidumping code to help standardize national policies in this area, as well as an international grains agreement which established price ranges for wheat and provided for multilateral sharing of food aid to developing countries.

The economic results of the Kennedy Round were substantial. Because there are different means to assess the value of tariff reductions, each with some measure of uncertainty and bias, it is not possible to generate a single definitive assessment of the results. However, when approximate general averaging procedures are used, it is probable that the major participants made reductions of about 35 percent on nonagricultural tariff rates, and that the trade covered by these reductions represented about 80 percent of the dutiable trade of the industrialized countries.[3] By comparison, the average reduction in the Dillon Round concluded in 1961 was about 10 percent for the United States and the European Economic Community (EEC). At the most successful negotiation prior to the Kennedy Round, namely at Geneva in 1947, the United States reduced tariffs by about 20 percent on average on all dutiable imports.

The results on agricultural trade were less impressive in the Kennedy Round. On both trade coverage and tariff reduction, concessions were less extensive in agriculture than on industrial trade. For example, data compiled by Preeg indicate that total dutiable agricultural trade (other than grains) of industrial countries was $1.65 billion, on which duty reductions were made on $861.9 million, or 52 percent.[4] The average tariff reduction on dutiable imports was approximately 20 percent. These figures demonstrate that some progress was made at the Ken-

[3] See Preeg, *Traders and Diplomats*, esp. ch. 13 and Appendix A; and Evans, *Kennedy Round*, ch. 15.
[4] *Traders and Diplomats*, 252.

nedy Round in lowering qualitative barriers to agricultural trade, despite assertions in the United States (the principal demandeur of agricultural concessions) that the negotiation was fruitless. However, results in agriculture cannot be adequately assessed by tariff reductions, since the major restrictions on trade are nontariff measures such as quotas, licensing requirements, health standards, and variable levies. These measures were not effectively addressed in the Kennedy Round.

Apart from the economic results of the Kennedy Round, there were important political results that flowed from the successful completion of this major negotiation. Trade liberalization in GATT has been a continuing struggle between liberalizing and protectionist forces. Those favoring liberalism have used negotiation, and especially multilateral negotiation, as the principal means to free trade from government restrictions. Those favoring protectionism have been more ascendant, and more effective, between major trade negotiations. Protectionist actions that might have been applied in another period are often postponed during a negotiation in order not to prejudice the outcome of the negotiation. This increases the salience of the negotiation over time because there are increasingly more policy issues riding on the outcome, and in turn puts more pressure on the negotiators to reach an acceptable settlement.

The Kennedy Round took on enormous importance as a symbol as it went along. It became a test of the national will of the major participants to continue the postwar trend toward trade liberalization. Even more important, it was a test of the willingness of nations to avoid a breakdown that would have led to increased protectionism. The main reason the Kennedy Round succeeded is that governments feared what the implications of failure might mean for the international economic system, and because they wanted to avoid blame for causing such implications. In a strict sense, of course, it is clear that a deadlock in the Kennedy Round would have meant only that nations did not agree to reduce tariffs; this would have had no necessary consequences for increased protectionism. However, the situation did not get framed in such terms. The political reality was that nations felt under great pressure to avoid a breakdown of a dialogue that had extended five years and of a settlement that would help structure trading relations in the foreseeable future. Against these general concerns, the positions delegations took on individual tariffs or products ultimately became less important. Thus the main political result of the Kennedy Round was the achievement of the agreement itself, especially since the agreement was significant in trade terms.

Kennedy Round Negotiating Methods

The principal negotiating methods employed at the Kennedy Round could be classified as formal and informal. The former have received considerable attention in the literature on international trade policy. The fundamental method of the Kennedy Round, as of all GATT negotiation, was the most-favored-nation (MFN) principle, which in practice meant that tariff reductions extended to one nation (usually the principal supplier of the product in question) would be equally available to all nations. A second basic method was the principle of reciprocity, that is, the means negotiating partners use to evaluate any exchange of concessions. Reciprocity is not easily defined: any general definition of the term (such as "fair exchange of concessions") runs the risk of being self-evident, while any specific definition cannot be advanced without taking a position on the substance of a negotiation. Despite the absence of definition, however, one can observe that the principle of reciprocity is a determinant of bargaining behavior. It leads negotiators to develop certain procedures and measures for evaluating the progress of a negotiation which often are uniquely related to the substance of the negotiation but which may not have any rationale other than to facilitate an exchange of concessions. For example, the measures that have evolved employing the variables "duty reduction" and "volume of imports" to assess the value of tariff concessions no doubt make trade bargaining easier, but they do not make much sense in economic terms.[5]

One of the distinguishing formal mechanisms developed in the Kennedy Round was the linear-cut approach to tariff reductions. Negotiations prior to the Kennedy Round typically proceeded on the basis of bilateral exchanges of request-and-offer lists which described the products under consideration, the present rate of duty, and the requested (or offered) rate of duty. Where concessions were granted, these would be "multilateralized" through the operation of the MFN principle, and consequently nations preparing to extend concessions would engage in negotiations with all those nations likely to benefit from the concession. This method of negotiation was tedious, and it required any general settlement to be built piecemeal from the bottom up. In the Kennedy Round, nations agreed in principle to offer initially a "substantial linear tariff reduction" (i.e., across-the-board reduction) on industrial products, from which a "bare minimum of exceptions" could be made

---

[5] Evans, *Kennedy Round*, 23. Evans's chapter "Reciprocity" is an excellent discussion of the subject.

subject to negotiation.[6] This procedure got more on the table at the outset, and insured that the main thrust of the negotiation would be on exceptions rather than on the initial offer. It was assumed—and this was
subsequently confirmed—that this procedure would lead to a larger
settlement than could be achieved through item-by-item bargaining.

The linear approach was an aggregating mechanism that brought
forward at once many items for consideration for tariff reductions.
This mechanism reduced the complexity of decisionmaking for those
who wanted to propose tariff reductions, while at the same time shifting the burden of initiation to those who wanted to retain trade restrictions. As an approach to the liberalization of trade, it was an excellent
improvement over previous practices. It was, however, a very controversial mechanism. The linear approach sharply advantaged nations
that started with higher tariffs at the outset, and nations, like the United
States, whose tariff structure ranged from very high to very low duties.
On the other hand, participants like the EC that had lower duties or a
more uniform tariff structure were disadvantaged and hence resisted
the full implications of the linear approach. The result was that on
products where significant disparities existed between the tariffs of different nations, no general rule was agreed to or applied at the Kennedy
Round. This reduced the effectiveness of the linear approach as a specific negotiating method, but it did not negate the usefulness of general,
or formula, approaches to trade negotiation. In the subsequent Tokyo
Round, the general approach was continued in the guise of a harmonization formula which solved the principal difficulties participants
had experienced with the linear approach of the Kennedy Round.

Agreement on a linear approach at the Kennedy Round, however
tenuous the agreement may have been in practice, nevertheless seemed
to get the negotiating process under way. The next step after agreement
on the negotiating rules was the tabling of exceptions lists, which together with the hypothetical 50 percent linear offer, constituted each
nation's completed offer. This was a difficult step from the standpoint
of national decisionmaking, and was not completed until the early
months of 1965, over eighteen months after the negotiation was initiated. Once offers were completed, negotiations were quickly engaged
on a bilateral and multilateral basis. Some of the negotiation was chan-
nelled into sector groups, such as chemicals, steel, and pulp and paper,
where negotiations took up broader issues of structure of the industry

---

[6] This language is taken from the text adopted at the GATT ministerial meeting of May
21, 1963: GATT Press Release 794, May 29, 1963. One year later, nations participating
in the Kennedy Round adopted 50 percent as a working hypothesis for the substantial
linear reduction.

as well as specific exchanges of tariff concessions. As the negotiation wore on, each nation attempted to achieve a balance in its position by increasing its concessions where necessary, or by withdrawing offers tabled on an *ad referendum* basis for which compensating benefits were not judged forthcoming.[7] At the end of the negotiation, a large and somewhat unstable package deal took shape, in which negotiators faced a series of simultaneous problems: first, a multilateral problem created by the MFN principle which made negotiating positions interlocking; second, a bilateral problem created by the need to improve the offers of selected countries; and finally, a unilateral problem dictated by the obligation to decide to accept settlement on the basis of last stated offers (assuming the last stated offers of other nations constituted adequate reciprocity). That this concluding process was not entirely a tidy one, especially when conducted under the deadline pressures associated with the Kennedy Round, could be seen in the following journalist's report filed shortly after the conclusion of the negotiation:

> Deep and very widely shared satisfaction over settling the major Kennedy Round controversies is alternating here with genuine ignorance as to what the settlements may mean in detail. At this stage even senior officials in the various delegations have not yet broached the task of analyzing the precise contents of the agreements reached.
>
> It is not just a matter of detailed information remaining unpublished until the accord has been formally signed a few weeks hence. The hasty deals reached by top negotiators in the frantic final hours often have not been translated into actual texts, nor sometimes even communicated to those on the next steps of the hierarchy.[8]

In addition to formal methods, several informal negotiating practices evolved by trial and error out of the Kennedy Round experience. One concerned the relationship between the parties to the negotiation, and it underscored the limitations of multilateral negotiation. The Kennedy Round was a multilateral negotiation, but participants quickly found that meaningful concessions usually could be given only between the principal supplier of individual goods and the major importers. Multilateral negotiations were useful for exchanges of information and for

---

[7] An *ad referendum* agreement is an unbinding agreement contingent on settlement of issues to be negotiated subsequently.

[8] H. Peter Dreyer, "Tariff Talks Package Gets Mixed Reaction," *Journal of Commerce* (New York), May 1967, 1.

general discussions of structural problems of trade and production in different industries, but they did not facilitate specific discussions of reciprocity (or quid pro quo) that were a necessary part of the exchange of concessions. Consequently, what was a multilateral negotiation in name became a large, complicated series of bilateral (or plurilateral) negotiations in fact. The main action of the negotiation often occurred away from the multilateral chambers.

The importance of a nation in the negotiation at the Kennedy Round was in proportion to the size of its economy. The larger a nation's trade, the more incentive it had to make demands of other nations on its exports, and the more it had to offer (assuming the presence of trade restrictions) on its imports from other countries. This put a large burden on the negotiating capabilities of delegations from large countries. The structure of the situation maximized the amount large nations had to accomplish in order for a substantial agreement to build up, and it minimized the amount smaller nations could do in the negotiation. Negotiating teams accommodated to these realities by initiating major deals in small groups of the most significant trading nations,[9] and then attempting to sell the deal (and secure compensating concessions) to smaller countries that had an interest in the products in question. This informal negotiating mechanism was successful at the Kennedy Round, and it is likely that the realities of trade relations would not have permitted any departure from these procedures—however, it is undeniable that these methods created negotiating difficulties between delegations from large nations, who often felt overextended, and delegations from small nations, who often felt left out of the negotiation. Furthermore, this artifact of the negotiation process exacerbated the already strained relations between the developed nations (several of which were large countries as well) and the less-developed nations (which were uniformly small nations in trade terms).

A second informal method concerned relations between negotiating delegations and the GATT secretariat. The subject material that delegations negotiated at the Kennedy Round was both extremely voluminous and technical. Both of these aspects tended to increase the importance of the GATT secretariat: the first, because it created a need for information handling (i.e., storage, retrieval, and dissemination), which was largely filled by the GATT bureaucracy and support service; and the second, because it created a need for expertise that had been developed in the GATT professional staff. As a result, portions of the

[9] The small group in the Kennedy Round that included the United States, the EEC, the United Kingdom, and variously Canada and Japan became known as the "bridge club."

secretariat staff became closely involved with the actual negotiation of the Kennedy Round. Meetings occurred frequently at the technical level between senior GATT staffers and senior bureaucrats and representatives of national governments. Some of these meetings became a permanent part of the negotiation, with a fairly fixed national representation (depending on the subject under discussion) and with a fairly fixed individual representation. Thus below the level of the political negotiation was operating a technical level of information exchange and, in many cases, decisionmaking as well. Initiatives at these meetings would vary, but often GATT experts took initiatives and kept the work moving.

A third informal method involved the procedures for reaching tradeoffs in the negotiation, particularly in the final phase as nations put together a package settlement. It is normal in trade negotiations, as in any negotiations, to make tradeoffs between benefits one hopes to gain against items one is able to give up. Normally negotiators try to make such tradeoffs over similar products, or within product sectors, since it is politically advantageous to be able to demonstrate that each sector realized compensating gains for any losses it might have suffered. Consequently negotiators have evolved the practice of trying to make sectors "self-balancing"; that is, attempting to seek concessions in those areas where they will be expected to make concessions. Against this political desideratum is the economic reality that sectoral trade is often not balanced between any two countries, and consequently the areas in which a nation seeks concessions may not be the same areas where other nations seek concessions from it. The result was that nations negotiated within sectors as far as possible at the Kennedy Round, but were forced by the end of the negotiation into considerations of tradeoffs between sectors. Thus factors inherent in the negotiation of international trade tended toward an increasing politicization of the process as it moved toward a conclusion.

Several major delegations at the Kennedy Round followed a strategy of bringing in more senior individuals at the end to conclude the negotiation. This increased the ability of the participants to take decisions that would be politically controversial in the respective capitals. It also helped negotiating teams to change "set"; that is, to shift from the routine procedures of interdelegation bargaining that had been pursued previously in the negotiation to procedures that permitted general overarching restatements of the remaining issues. New faces tend to bring new ideas to difficult problems, and when the new faces are senior government officials they have considerable scope to resolve deadlocked issues. At the Kennedy Round, there was some suggestion that major delegations kept senior people at home and away from the negotiation until late in the game. This helped delegations to avoid becoming psychologically committed to single interpretations of difficult problems, and it created the flexibility and freedom needed to conclude the eventual settlement.

Kennedy Round: An Evaluation

The Kennedy Round was a valuable learning experience for nations in the techniques of multilateral negotiation, and the problems encountered in this negotiation gave national policymakers some idea of what to expect in the Tokyo Round. By comparison with the latter, the Kennedy Round was a very contentious negotiation. This stemmed from two factors. First, the Kennedy Round was predominately a tariff negotiation, and negotiating tariff changes is a distributive matter in the sense that wages are a distributive matter in a union negotiation. It is well known that distributive negotiations can lead to extended haggling about small changes in substance. This style was evidenced, for example, in the long discussions over the exceptions lists tabled by the participants. Then, too, tariffs are the most politically prominent of the various instruments of national trade policy. They are an easily understood, and aggregated, measure of protectionism, and hence changes in tariff levels are open to criticism from sources that might not be as concerned about changes in other forms of protection. Thus the subject material of the Kennedy Round helped to increase the heat of the negotiation. At the end, the Kennedy Round was concluded only after a lengthy and dramatic session under deadline pressure: the expiration of the U.S. delegation's authority to negotiate. Without this deadline, and without a very interventionist style of mediation by the GATT secretary general, Sir Eric Wyndham-White, it is doubtful whether a general settlement could have been achieved.

One of the major controversial issues of the Kennedy Round was the ASP system of customs valuation. Briefly, this system provided for the assessment of duty on a foreign product based on the value of "like or similar" goods produced domestically. The ASP applied to very few American imports, principally benzenoid chemicals and several other unrelated products.[10] However, on those products on which it applied, the results were indeed onerous for exporters. For one thing, the ASP could result in prohibitively high tariffs through the simple expedient of the domestic industry overpricing the item the foreign product was

[10] See Dam, *The GATT*, 191.

67

similar to. This might then relieve competitive pressure on a range of functionally related products. Alternatively, the domestic industry might commence production of an import-competing item, which could result in a dramatic change in the duty applied. The EC regarded the ASP as illegal under GATT Article 7 on customs valuation, and that, plus the uncertainty that ASP procedures created for European exporters, led to a strong demand for its revocation. On the other hand, the American negotiators had not been authorized by Congress to change the ASP, nor was there any chance that such authority would be forthcoming. The issue produced the most serious, and potentially fatal, deadlock of the negotiation.

The dispute was settled by an agreement in the chemical sector which provided for a substantial reduction in European tariffs conditional on the subsequent repeal by Congress of the ASP. The agreement later faltered on the refusal of Congress to change the ASP system. This issue was perhaps one of the most important areas of carryover from the Kennedy Round to the Tokyo Round. For one thing, the ASP itself became a symbolically important issue for the Europeans, no doubt because its procedures created such arbitrary advantages for domestic manufacturers that it seemed flatly inconsistent with the philosophy of trade liberalism that supposedly motivated the negotiation. It is obvious that the ASP made a considerable impact on the European Community, for its abolition was one of the main political demands to be included in the instructions for EC negotiators at the Tokyo Round, and for which the Europeans would be willing later to rewrite the valuation procedures of the Brussels Definition of Value system.

An even broader significance of the ASP was that it raised the question of the rights of arbitrary action in international trade, which came to be important in the Tokyo Round in the emphasis on "fair trade" as well as freer trade. Apart from the code on antidumping, the ASP was the only major nontariff measure (NTM) negotiated at the Kennedy Round. It demonstrated for the participating nations that NTM's raise different issues in international trade than do tariffs; namely the right of an importing state to force the costs of adjustment, and the resulting uncertainty, onto the producers in the exporting state. Many NTM's, such as the U.S. countervail procedures, EC variable levies in agriculture, and Canadian customs valuation procedures, share this characteristic of creating uncertainty for exporters. By comparison, tariffs are a much more stable form of protection and hence are not as disruptive of the efforts of exporters to plan for production, investment, and so forth. The ASP issue helped to highlight the importance of including

NTM's in any future effort to liberalize trade through international negotiations.

Despite the major focus on tariffs at the Kennedy Round, one significant result was achieved in the NTM area in the negotiation of an antidumping code. Antidumping practices of trading nations are aimed at protecting domestic producers from goods being unloaded at less than fair market prices, but the practices themselves can often be a deterrent to foreign trade. Need for a code originated in complaints against the United States over the length of time of antidumping procedures, while the United States lodged complaints against Canada over the lack of a test of injury in Canadian practice, and against other countries, particularly the Europeans, for the lack of open and impartial procedures for assessing dumping. The code was negotiated separately from the main tariff negotiation at the Kennedy Round, and it was agreed upon with surprisingly little difficulty. It had considerable effect in structuring the common antidumping regulations that were being developed by the EEC during the Kennedy Round,[11] and it led to the adoption by Canada of an injury requirement in its legislation. For its part, the United States agreed to an expedited antidumping procedure as well as a change in the practice of withholding appraisement during antidumping investigations (which had increased uncertainty for the foreign exporter). However, opposition was raised in Congress to the antidumping code, which was negotiated without an explicit mandate from Congress, and a bill was subsequently passed prohibiting the United States Tariff Commission from implementing the code. The experience with the antidumping code probably improved the chances for negotiating NTM's in the Tokyo Round. It underscored for American negotiators the importance of securing an adequate initial negotiating mandate from Congress, and of keeping leading congressmen on board the positions as they developed in the negotiation. Also, of course, the code was a useful preliminary skirmish for the kind of legislative negotiation that characterized the code negotiations of the Tokyo Round. Such legislative negotiation was dissimilar in many respects to bargaining over tariff changes.

One of the important results of the Kennedy Round that was later to affect the style of the Tokyo Round was the emergence of the EEC as a single negotiating unit. The Kennedy Round marked the first time the Europe of the Six had negotiated externally with other nations. This

[11] A U.S. government report stated that "One of the most important benefits of the code to the United States will be the adoption by other countries of fair and open procedures along the lines of present United States practices" (U.S. Government, *1964–1967 Trade Conference*, vol. 1, pt. 1, 165).

was not easily achieved, and indeed internal disagreement in the Six stalled the Kennedy Round for two years. Integration accelerated in the EEC after the Kennedy Round, and the inclusion of new members, notably the United Kingdom, brought the combined economies of the enlarged EEC to a level equal with that of the United States. The EEC entered the Tokyo Round as an economic superpower with considerable negotiating experience accumulated in the Commission of the EC. The structure of the negotiation shifted from the more unipolar one of the Kennedy Round to a bipolar configuration in the Tokyo Round. In practice, this meant that most issues would be worked out first by the two major participants, after which other nations would be included in the discussions.

Developments in International Trade, 1967–1973

Following the Kennedy Round, strong arguments were made in favor of launching immediately into a follow-up negotiation to capitalize on the momentum of the Kennedy Round. This plea, made especially by the GATT secretary general, Sir Eric Wyndham-White, was received unenthusiastically by the GATT members. The timing was simply inopportune. Pressure for increased protection had risen in the major Kennedy Round participants during the mid-1960s to the point where the successful completion of the Kennedy Round was doubtful, let alone the commencement of a new negotiation. The initiative in GATT eventually bore fruit in that the technical planning that commenced in GATT late in 1967 proved vital to the Tokyo Round negotiation, but the GATT leadership failed to generate the political will needed for a new negotiation to get under way.

The demonstrations of renewed protectionism were nowhere clearer than in the United States. Before the Kennedy Round was completed, the Senate had passed a resolution opposing any changes in the ASP. This action was subsequently followed by a series of bills that would have imposed quotas on a wide range of U.S. imports. Voluminous hearings on trade-related bills were held by the House Ways and Means Committee in mid-1968, and the general tenor of the testimony was sharply in favor of restrictive action. Despite strong pressure, the committee did not report out any of the restrictive legislation before it, on the grounds that if it was approved the demands for additional protection from other interests would have become uncontrollable. Included in the bills not brought forward was the ASP repeal, and hence this concession negotiated at the Kennedy Round became a dead letter, along with the matching concessions on the European side, notably deep cuts in the chemicals sector and a general acceleration of the phasing-in period for European tariff cuts.

Although the call for a new negotiation fell on deaf ears in 1967, it was soon clear that events in the late 1960s were seriously endangering the world trading system, and that some action would be necessary to accommodate to new forces while preserving the essentials of the GATT system. These concerns eventually led to a new negotiation. Negotiation is motivated by a combination of fear and opportunity. In this case, the fear stemmed from the fact that governments were increasingly initiating forms of protection that were outside the framework of GATT rules. The opportunity came from the fact that the constituents of trade policy recognized the danger to a trading system they had a stake in, and supported government action to safeguard that system.

The difficulties GATT faced were raised most visibly in textiles, which interestingly is an agent of change in the modern world economy just as it was an agent of change at the beginning of the industrial revolution. Textiles are a labor-intensive product which can be produced at great advantage in low-wage countries. By the 1950s, Japan had developed a strong capability in the manufacture of textiles and sought to export in increasingly large amounts to industrialized Western countries. More recently, these policies have been followed by other newly industrializing nations, notably Korea and Taiwan. The sharp increase in textile exports put enormous pressure on textile producers in North America and Europe, which caused political concern in part because of the large numbers employed in the industry. The pressure for action was not easy to accommodate within the escape-clause provisions of the GATT, because the prices of foreign textile imports were so low that such mechanisms were ineffective.[12]

Turmoil in the textile market had led to the conclusion of a Long-Term Arrangement on Cotton Textiles (LTA) in 1962. The centerpiece of the LTA was the concept of "market disruption," which was understood as any sudden large flow of very low-priced imports from one or more trading partners.[13] Under the LTA, exporters agreed to avoid disruptive trade through the means of self-imposed voluntary quotas, while importers bound themselves to accept a growing amount of cotton textiles from exporters. Of the two concepts "market disruption" and "voluntary quotas," the latter came to have greater use in the trade policy of the industrialized nations. For example, the United States subsequently initiated agreements, called voluntary export restraints (or

---

[12] See Hudec, *GATT Legal System*, 212. Also see Article 19 of the General Agreement.
[13] For a useful discussion of market disruption, see Jackson, *World Trade*, ch. 23.

VER's), with exporters of meat, steel, and wool and synthetic textiles, and on each occasion used a threat of more stringent legislation to secure the compliance of foreign governments. Ostensibly such agreements were intended to avoid situations of market disruption, but this was increasingly interpreted in such a loose way as to include any significant increase in imports.

The use of VER's was both an evasion of GATT obligations and a direct confrontation with those obligations. The evasion occurred in that importing nations could deny that they had abridged their obligations under the GATT on the grounds that the restrictive agreements were voluntary and hence not prejudicial to exporting nations. Whether this dubious argument was valid was of little consequence, however, since it was clear that nations resorting to VER's considered these procedures to be outside the scope of GATT inquiries. The confrontation created between the VER's and GATT obligations occurred in that the former were contrary to the GATT prohibition on quantitative restrictions. The historic thrust of the General Agreement in the postwar period has been to encourage nations to forgo a reliance on quantitative restrictions on trade in favor of tariffs, which were a "fairer" form of protection and more consistent with underlying market forces. The development of VER's constituted a threat to this philosophy, and it raised questions about the relevance of the GATT system as a means to regulate future international trade.

The worry over VER's led to a broader concern that a major overhaul of the GATT system was needed and that a more restricted approach would not suffice. This concern stemmed largely from the increasing use of nontariff measures and the interchangeability of these measures one for another. Nontariff measures greatly diversified the potential for protectionism, and that diversity made it difficult for national trade-policy officials to get a complete picture of the barriers faced by their own exporters. A frequent complaint of domestic producers in the period after the Kennedy Round was that foreign governments had set up a complicated (and often not obvious) array of measures to restrict trade, while on the other hand their own governments took a less restrictive approach to trade. This put pressure on governments to increase the use of restrictive measures in order to promote, through reciprocal punishment, the concept of fair trade. This was not a successful method of handling the problem, and likely could not be, since the domestic producer harmed on the one side bore no necessary relationship to the foreign exporter harmed on the other. It was obvious a broader approach to the problem was needed.

Another problem was that where NTM's are concerned, trade protectionism can take many forms, and protection that is prevented by international agreement in one form can easily be applied in another form. For example, changes in valuation procedures can easily negate the effects of reducing tariffs, and health standards and technical barriers can protect domestic producers as effectively as quotas. These factors underscored the need for a general approach to the problem of nontariff restrictions, since any attempt to deal with issues on a piecemeal basis would simply mean that national governments would develop surrogates for any forms of protection that became prohibited. Indeed this concern materialized over the antidumping code, which many nations claimed was incomplete because it did not deal adequately with the related issue of countervailing duties.

The opportunities for a new trade negotiation came in a series of reports that demonstrated that the management of the international trading system went well beyond the capabilities of individual national governments. These reports gave ample excuse for agencies sympathetic to new initiatives to begin planning for a follow-up to the Kennedy Round.

The first indications of concern came as a result of two initiatives made by President Lyndon Johnson as the Kennedy Round was drawing to a conclusion. First, Johnson appointed a Public Advisory Committee on Trade Policy, composed of leading trade unionists and members of the business community. Second, the president instructed the special representative for trade negotiations, William R. Roth, to conduct a study of future U.S. trade policy, in concert with the aforementioned committee and other officials, to ensure that the Kennedy Round "did not mark the end of the drive toward trade liberalization."[14] The result of these initiatives was a report that emphasized the changing nature of the international trading system and the need to develop the capacity of foreign-trade policy to adapt to these changes. The report stressed the continuing liberal orientation of the United States in international trade, but it noted that U.S. exports were still encumbered by restrictions of other countries despite the progress made in the Kennedy Round. Since many of these remaining restrictions, both tariffs and nontariff measures, were legal under the GATT, the only way they were likely to be removed was through negotiation.

The report outlined briefly some of the types of nontariff measures that nations applied, and suggested that these might be negotiated in terms of codes of uniform practice to be established among trading nations. This, however, was a tentative proposal, since it was admitted

[14] U.S. Government, *Future Trade Policy*, i.

that NTM's were complex and a method for negotiating them would probably have to evolve out of a further analysis of the problem. The real force of the report, however, was to stress the urgency of laying the groundwork for another negotiation as soon as possible: namely ". . . the complexity of a future general trade negotiation requires that serious preparatory study begin now."[15] The report urged that further study of the feasibility of a general negotiation be taken within the U.S. government, and that the United States initiate discussion in GATT to outline an approach to such a negotiation.

The momentum in the United States toward a rethinking of trade policy was continued by the Nixon administration. In May 1970, President Richard Nixon established a Commission on International Trade and Investment Policy, drawn widely from the business, labor, and academic communities across the country and chaired by Albert L. Williams of IBM. The Williams Commission, as it was subsequently called, met over the ensuing year with approximately one hundred officials and experts, and produced a report in July 1971. The tone of the entire report was evidenced in the first paragraph: "The world has changed radically from the one we knew after World War II. We believe it is imperative that the United States, in its own interest, bring its international trade and investment policies into line with the new realities."[16]

The report went on to speak of a crisis of confidence growing within the United States over the operation of the international economic system. Foremost among the causes of this crisis was the increased pressure of imports in American markets, along with a perceived decreasing ability of the United States to capitalize on its comparative trade advantages because of foreign restrictions. The crisis had produced mounting pressures in the United States for import restrictions, growing demands for retaliation against restrictive measures abroad, and a prevailing sentiment that other nations were not doing their fair share in helping with the persistent deficit in the United States balance of payments. The report summed up the problem in the following words: "The core of the present difficulty is the fact that government policies and practices, and international arrangements for collective decisionmaking, have not kept abreast of the high degree of international economic interaction which has been achieved since World War II."[17]

The report outlined a program for action designed to maximize the contribution of international trade and investment to the United States

---

[15] Ibid., 19.
[16] U.S. Government, *United States International Economic Policy*, 1.
[17] Ibid., 6.

economy. Included in this program were suggestions on how to strengthen the domestic economy, but the gist of the program was a call for international negotiations to deal with problems of international payments and trade. The proposal for trade negotiations was spelled out in considerable detail. They were to be comprehensive in scope, to include both tariff and nontariff restrictions on trade, and to be based on overall rather than sectoral reciprocity. After some analysis of GATT's weaknesses, notably in liberalizing agricultural trade, the report proposed that GATT should remain at the center of any negotiating effort, and furthermore that issues be approached not as a renegotiation of the GATT agreement itself, but as a series of codes that would update and tighten existing GATT obligations. Without such an effort, the commission foresaw that additional distortions would probably arise in international trade as governments sought to intervene to protect their constituents in an increasingly unfair trading system.

The proposals for a new multilateral trade negotiation of the Williams Commission received an international endorsement in an OECD study published the following year. The report was the product of a study group organized in 1971 on a recommendation of the OECD Council of Ministers. The group was chaired by Jean Rey, former Kennedy Round negotiator and president of the European Commission, and included eleven prominent individuals from different OECD nations who acted in their personal capacities rather than as representatives of national governments. The mandate of the group was to analyze trade and related problems in a longer-term perspective and to suggest ways in which such problems might be dealt with.

The Rey group, like the Williams Commission before it, noted the rapid changes occurring in the international economic system, and emphasized the effects such changes had on the institutions of international trade. The report stated: ". . . the rapid rate of development of our societies has profound effects on traditional frameworks and structures, necessitating constant re-appraisal not only of mechanisms but of policy objectives themselves."[18] The task was one "of strengthening the existing frameworks, adopting them to the present situation and opening up new paths for multilateral co-operation."[19]

The Rey report called for a major effort to liberalize trade further through international negotiation. Such an effort would have to be comprehensive and deal not only with tariffs but, more important, with nontariff measures, which as the former were reduced had become the

[18] OECD, *Policy Perspectives*, 15.
[19] Ibid.

chief obstacles to trade in some areas. The report examined some of the difficulties involved in negotiating NTM's, particularly the problem of achieving reciprocity and the burden of accumulating and analyzing the large amount of information that would be required to negotiate NTM's successfully. Like the Williams Commission, the Rey group assumed that NTM's would be removed in the context of negotiations over codes of good behavior. That would serve as a guide for national legislation with respect to trade policy. The important element was for governments to be able to reach agreement on the principles that would be applied to international trade; once these were established, it was likely that specific measures or recommendations could be settled. One such principle the group recommended was that NTM's should not be adopted as a part of government trade policy: "Non-tariff measures must not be used as an instrument of trade policy, in other words as a means of granting disguised protection or giving domestic producers an advantage over foreign competitors."[20] The principle later became an operating guideline in the code negotiations of the Tokyo Round.

DEVELOPMENTS IN THE EUROPEAN COMMUNITY PRIOR TO 1973

The Kennedy Round had become toward its conclusion a negotiation between a few major participants, principally the United States, the EC, the United Kingdom, and Japan. Events following the Kennedy Round moved in a direction to reduce further the principal actors in any subsequent negotiation. In the early 1960s, Britain reversed an historic policy and applied for membership in the EC. This initiative was quashed by President Charles de Gaulle of France in a celebrated press conference in January 1963, but continued efforts by the British and their European allies, along with a change of government in France, made the prospect of British accession much more likely by the end of the decade. Enlargement of the EC would mean that world trade in the 1970s would be dominated more completely by the two major actors (namely the United States and the EC) than was the case in the 1960s. Since negotiation usually reflects the pattern of real forces, this would mean that the Tokyo Round would become a more bilateral affair than even the Kennedy Round had been. It was evident by the late 1960s that action would have to be forthcoming from the two major economic powers within GATT for any multilateral negotiation to materialize in the 1970s.

The United States and the EC both have a large and complex internal system for producing economic policy. To participate in a major inter-

<hr>

[20] Ibid.

national negotiation, each system needed a set of instructions, the drawing up of which was a complicated process in its own right. In the United States, these instructions came from the U.S. Congress in the form of the Trade Act of 1974, which did not give American negotiators a complete mandate to negotiate until 1975. The instructions for the EC were authorized by the Council of Ministers; they were formed largely as a follow-up to the Smithsonian agreement of 1971 and were in place well before the Tokyo Round Declaration of 1973 which initiated the Tokyo Round. The instructions for the EC negotiators were caught up in a period of upheaval and change in the development of the EC as an institution, which influenced what the EC sought from the negotiation. It is useful to review these developments.

The Kennedy Round had been a major step in the integration of Europe. This trade negotiation had been proposed by the United States as part of President John F. Kennedy's Grand Design for a North Atlantic partnership. A further American motivation was the fear that European integration would close traditional markets to U.S. exporters. From either perspective, the American initiative put pressure on the EC, particularly since its six original members were committed to an outward-looking, liberal posture in international trade. The Kennedy Round was a major test of the internal cohesiveness of the EC. Since 1958, when the Treaty of Rome established the Common Market, the EC had been working out a common approach to agriculture, which subsequently became one of the most prominent areas of joint policy-making of the EC. The Kennedy Round forced the pace of EC decisions on agriculture because of the need to agree on a common pricing structure before negotiating with the United States. An important step in this direction was taken in a meeting of the Council of Ministers in December 1964 when the Germans agreed to a common price on cereals. However, subsequent discussions over the arrangements for financing a common agricultural policy reached deadlock. This deadlock was hardened by a French boycott of EC institutions in protest against the provisions of the Treaty of Rome that would have permitted decisions in the Council of Ministers to be reached on a majority basis after January 1, 1966. These internal disagreements were largely resolved by early 1966, but the cost had been that the EC was incapable of serious external negotiation for over two years of the Kennedy Round. The year 1966 was spent largely in building a bureaucratic machine in the EC Commission capable of representing the diverse interests of the Community.[21] By January 1967, with only six months remaining in

[21] A fuller account of this process can be found in Coombes, *Politics and Bureaucracy*, esp. 191–216.

the American delegation's authority to negotiate, the EC was finally able to engage in a serious exchange of proposals with the United States and other countries.

Settlement of the Kennedy Round raised issues of national conflict within the EC. The Germans had important concerns in the bargaining over industrial tariffs, and they were eager to see the negotiations concluded successfully. The French had fewer interests directly at stake in the Kennedy Round, and had mainly used the negotiation as a gauge to induce the Germans to accept the evolving EC policy on agriculture. For its part, the EC Commission supported both the German and the French positions, and for equally sound bureaucratic reasons, since both the external trade negotiations and the internal agricultural policy tended to expand the competence of the Commission itself. The major trade-offs between the Germans and French were reached prior to and during the crisis of 1965, after which it was clear the Germans would participate in a common policy on agriculture and the French would not prevent EC participation in the Kennedy Round. However, France continued to be the most reluctant member of the EC to conclude the Kennedy Round, and it took advantage of the negotiation to probe weaknesses in the American position. One such example was the EC demand for the removal of the American Selling Price on chemicals, which was a customs valuation procedure that the Europeans claimed was inconsistent with GATT obligations. The ASP had been the subject of a last-minute, but ultimately unsuccessful, compromise in the Kennedy Round, and it returned to the forefront in the Tokyo Round as one of the early political demands of the EC on the United States.

Following the Kennedy Round, the EC became absorbed in internal matters. Further agreement was reached on the financial arrangements for the common agricultural policy at a meeting of heads of government in December 1969. Progress was made on greater unification of monetary policy, and in February 1970 the governors of the central banks of the Six signed an accord establishing short-term monetary support within the EC. Relations with the developing countries associated with the EC, namely the Associated African and Malagasy States and the East African Community, were deepened. Most important, formal negotiations for the accession of four European nations—the United Kingdom, Ireland, Denmark, and Norway—were opened in June 1970. In this context, the EC was decidedly not interested in undertaking a further external negotiation. It took American pressure, and particularly the actions of August 1971, to force the problems of North Atlantic trade onto the EC agenda. In the Smithsonian agreement of December 1971, the EC accepted a new round of multilateral trade negotiations as part of a solution to the growing crisis in international trade and monetary relations. This agreement was quickly followed up in February 1972 with a joint declaration between the United States and the Community to commence preparations for a trade negotiation, a declaration which underscored the relationship between the Smithsonian agreement on monetary relations and a Tokyo Round dealing with international trade.[22]

The EC reached an important turning point in the Paris summit conference of the heads of government in October 1972. This meeting included three new member states,[23] and it reaffirmed the Community's intention to achieve economic and monetary union. The conference defined new initiatives for the Community in regional, social, and industrial policies and other areas, and it called on the Commission to draw up the appropriate plans of action. International trade was included in this mandate. The conference communiqué emphasized the importance of international trade and of maintaining a "constructive dialogue" with the United States, Japan, and Canada on trade matters. It stated, "In this context the Community attaches major importance to the multilateral negotiations in the context of GATT, in which it will participate in accordance with its earlier statement."[24] The communiqué called upon Community institutions to decide on a global approach to the negotiation prior to July 1973, in the expectation that a negotiation could be concluded by 1975. To this end, the EC Commission submitted a document to the Council of Ministers in April–May 1973, which became known as the EC's Overall Approach to the forthcoming negotiation.[25] After approval by the Council in June 1973, it formed the basic general instructions from which EC negotiators operated at the start of the Tokyo Round.

[22] The EC Commission recorded this event as follows: "Early in the year, the outstanding event in relations between the United States and the Community was the conclusion, on 11 February 1972, of an agreement in the trade field which, in a way, constituted the commercial aspect of the monetary regulation of 18 December in the framework of the Smithsonian Institute agreements. It comprises, on the one hand, a joint declaration by which the two parties undertake to begin, in 1973, far-reaching multilateral negotiations in GATT, and on the other hand, an exchange of letters concerning reciprocal commercial commitments" (Commission of the European Communities [hereafter cited as Commission], *Sixth General Report*, 200).

[23] These states were Denmark, Ireland, and the United Kingdom, which joined the EC formally on January 1, 1973. Norway declined to join, after a referendum in September 1972 went against accession.

[24] Commission, *Sixth General Report*, 14.

[25] The complete title of the document is found in the bibliography under Commission, "Development."

The Overall Approach reviewed the EC's role in international trade and went on to take a position on some of the issues that would likely be raised at a forthcoming negotiation. At the general level, the document affirmed the conviction—no doubt in response to previous U.S. criticism—that the establishment of the EC had caused a vast expansion of trade throughout the world. It criticized, however, the universal GATT system, which it saw as "blocked by the limitations inherent in the fact that a great many small and medium sized partners were confronted by a much stronger one." The EC argued that this commercial inequality had itself caused nations to form regional free-trade areas and customs unions. The documents took note of previous efforts to liberalize international trade, such as the Kennedy Round, and it claimed that the EC emerged from these talks with the lowest customs tariffs of all the major GATT trading partners. The Overall Approach was unequivocal in its support for trade liberalization, and it argued clearly in support of the hypothesis that trade liberalization and trade expansion produced rising levels of employment and standards of living.[26]

While it supported a new negotiation to liberalize trade, the Overall Approach cautioned that improvements in trading relations would be fruitless unless stability could be returned to international monetary relations. The document rejected outright the notion that defects in the monetary system could be rectified by measures taken in the commercial field, which was a direct response to suggestions by American officials to the contrary. The strong position of the EC on monetary relations was inspired by the French government. In an internal document which had reviewed the prospects for a new negotiation, there were listed a series of "conditions préalables," of which the first dealt with a longstanding demand of the French on U.S. monetary policy, namely:

> La première de ces conditions, déjà évoquée ci-dessus, est évidemment le rétablissement d'un système monétaire international stable à l'égard duquel les Etats-Unis auraient les mêmes obligations que leurs partenaires. Faute d'y parvenir préalablement à l'ouverture de la négociation commerciale, il devra être clairement précisé que l'application des accords intervenus dans le cadre de cette négociation restera suspendue jusqu'au règlement effectif du problème monétaire.[27]

[26] For example, "This vast movement of liberalization and almost uninterrupted economic expansion within the Community have made possible a remarkable expansion of its international trade. This in turn has provided the basis for a high and stable level of employment and the rise in the standard of living of recent years" (ibid., 5).

[27] Government of France, *Prochaines Négociations*, 5.

The Council's document argued that liberalization of commercial exchanges could easily be undone by manipulated changes in exchange rates, and it went on to propose a series of measures designed to protect against a further reduction of the American dollar, such as an automatic system of important surcharges and export-tax relief keyed to the rate of the U.S. currency. Once the system was in place, the Community would withdraw it only if the United States would agree prior to the negotiation not to increase protectionism or affect the prices of its products through future monetary measures.[28] This was clearly a position which if pursued would have made negotiation impossible, but it demonstrated the importance for the prospects of the Tokyo Round of reaching an enduring settlement in monetary affairs.

The Overall Approach reviewed the different subject areas of the forthcoming negotiation. The argument was terse, and the document concentrated on areas where the EC would likely be defending a position against foreign countries, especially the United States, in the upcoming negotiation. On industrial tariffs, the document recommended a formula approach to the negotiation designed to level off the differences in the tariff structures of different nations. This was a continuation of the Kennedy Round debate where the EC had proposed tariff harmonization in lieu of the linear cuts proposed by the Americans.[29] The Overall Approach also rejected the total elimination of tariffs as being an unrealistic goal, which again put the EC at odds with a U.S. goal previously expressed in the report of the Williams Commission. On a less-controversial note, the EC document called for reciprocity in industrial tariff-cutting to be reached in "each individual field" rather than concessions in one area being balanced against those in another. As explained in chapter 1, this practice had become customary in GATT negotiations, even though it had the effect of limiting the potential for tradeoffs in the exchange of concessions.

Regarding nontariff measures, the Overall Approach moved cautiously, perhaps reflecting the lack of negotiating experience nations

[28] For example, "La Communauté ne pourrait renoncer à ces mesures que si le Gouvernement des Etats-Unis proclamait, avant l'ouverture de la négociation, sa décision de ne pas relever, sous quelque forme que ce soit, son niveau actuel de protection et de ne pas affecter la compétitivité de ses produits par des manipulations monétaires" (ibid., 8).

[29] The document candidly outlined a major concern of the EC in pursuing a harmonization approach, namely to preserve its future bargaining position on tariffs vis-à-vis the United States: "This [i.e., harmonization] is the only approach which would make it possible to avoid a situation in which, following further reductions of customs tariffs, some would be so low that certain countries would have little hope of subsequently obtaining reductions in the higher customs duties which others would still be maintaining" (Commission, "Development," 7).

had in this area. Certainly there was less evidence of entrenched positions or of obvious efforts to prepare a position against the commercial practices of another nation. The EC document noted the need to address NTM's case by case, and it explored various mechanisms, such as notification procedures or the use of interpretive notes to the GATT, that would be useful in negotiating a reduction in these trade barriers. The document stated that the solutions to specific types of NTM's might require a conditional MFN approach if all nations did not accept the solution, and while this went against the usual American support for the principle of nondiscrimination, it was an approach that gained wide acceptance in the subsequent NTM negotiations. The only area of sharp conflict that was evident in the section on NTM's was the statement calling for all nations to cease to benefit from the explanation provided by the Protocol of Provisional Acceptance. This protocol was the mechanism under which the United States had defended the ASP in the Kennedy Round, and the reference to the protocol gave early warning on what would become a major demand of the EC in the subsequent negotiation.[30]

The Overall Approach reserved its firmest position for the area of agriculture. Recognizing agriculture as a source of past and probable future conflict with the United States, the document stated simply that the "principle of the Common Agricultural Policy should not be called into question in dealing with this sector." It also went on to describe agriculture as having "fundamental and specific characteristics," owing to the universal existence of farm-support policies in agricultural trading nations and the inherent instability of world markets for agricultural products. The Overall Approach proposed two different approaches for a negotiation on agriculture. One was to negotiate "international arrangements" (i.e., commodity agreements) for certain products that would specify price ranges and adjustments of supply, and the other was to adopt codes of conduct covering export practices. Significantly the latter proposal, which might have been used by the United States to restrict the use of EC export subsidies, was dropped from the final ver-

[30] The Protocol of Provisional Acceptance of 1947 had enabled nations whose existing legislation was in one way or another inconsistent with the obligations of the General Agreement to join the GATT. The ASP, erected in 1922, was an example of such legislation. Since 1947, most nations have brought their domestic legislation in line with the agreement, which was ostensibly the intention of the protocol. In the Kennedy Round, the U.S. negotiators had argued that the EC should compensate the United States for the removal of the ASP. This angered EC negotiators, who felt that the United States was in violation of GATT by retaining the ASP at all. For further information, see Dam, *The GATT*, 342.

sion of the Overall Approach as approved by the Council of Ministers in June 1973.[31]

A final area of some importance covered by the Overall Approach was relations with the developing countries. At the level of principle, the document had no difficulty in affirming the need "to take particular account in these negotiations of the interests of developing countries." However, the text also revealed certain problems that might be encountered in achieving this goal in practice. First, the text commented on helping to expand developing countries' trade without detriment to the advantages enjoyed by those nations which had concluded special preferential arrangements with the EC. This indicated that the EC's approach to the developing countries would be circumscribed by the EC's associational agreements (from which EC exports also derive preferential treatment), which would therefore reduce the capacity of the EC to make new initiatives in an external negotiation. Other areas where principle and practice risked parting company were evident in the EC's position on generalized tariff preferences, and on specific preferences for processed agricultural products from developing countries. On the former, the Overall Approach noted the need for agreement with the United States on a "comparable scheme" to effect improvements in general preferences; this agreement had been difficult to achieve in the past. On the latter, it is well known that domestic procedures in developed countries have been extremely resistant to extending benefits to processed imports from developing countries. This is especially true of important commodities such as sugar, where sugar-beet producers in temperate climates compete directly with the tropical sugar-cane producers in developing countries. Finally, on the matter of safeguards, which is an issue in GATT that mainly affects trade relations between developed and developing countries, the Overall Approach proposed that changes in the GATT procedures on safeguards should provide for their use "in a selective fashion."[32] This point was to prove unacceptable to the developing countries at the Tokyo Round, and indeed led to a blockage in the negotiation on the safeguards code.

With the approval of the Overall Approach in June 1973, the EC was ready to commence negotiation in the Tokyo Round. The process of mobilizing a position for the negotiation had been a long one, but, in

[31] See Golt, *GATT Negotiations*, 28.

[32] For a description of the safeguards issue, see ch. 3. It should be noted that the final document approved by the Council of Ministers in June 1973 dropped any reference to the selective application of safeguards, but spoke only of establishing a "better practical application of the Safeguard Clause" (i.e., Article 19 of GATT). In fact, however, selectivity became a principal concern of the EC in the subsequent negotiation.

comparison with what happened the United States, which was not ready to negotiate until 1975, the process was relatively expeditious. The internal negotiation was also complex, owing partly to the complexity of the subject matter of the Tokyo Round, and partly to the increasing complexity of the institutions of the EC itself. It is a truism that the larger and more complicated a political system becomes internally, the more difficulty it will experience in mounting an external negotiation. This has long been true of the United States, and it is increasingly the case with the EC. Formulating the Overall Approach required consultation with many different interests within the Community, but it was a relatively open bureaucratic process that in the end produced a public statement of desiderata governing EC participation in the negotiation. The entire process was much removed from the secrecy that is normally assumed to be part of diplomatic activities.

Following the enlargement of the EC, it was evident that a bipolar arrangement existed in the sphere of commercial relations. It was equally evident that for the Tokyo Round to succeed, it would need the commitment of both commercial superpowers. Ironically the EC produced tangible evidence of this commitment more easily than the United States, which had initiated the negotiation. The reason was that the internal bureaucratic/diplomatic process of the EC proved on this occasion to be more efficient than the legislative process of the United States. A further reason is that in order to expand its own competence, the Commission of the EC wanted the negotiation more than did the U.S. Congress, and consequently it was motivated to ensure that the process of consultation moved efficiently. Finally, the process of drawing up the American negotiating authority, which was to be accomplished in the passage of the U.S. Trade Act, was delayed for over eighteen months by the wrangle over the section that would have provided MFN status for the Soviet Union. Because of this unforeseen problem, U.S. negotiators did not have congressional authority to negotiate until early in 1975. This incident completely derailed the timetable for the negotiation set by the EC, and it resurrected memories of the Kennedy Round, when extraneous internal issues in the EC had forced a lengthy delay in a GATT trade negotiation.

PREPARATIONS IN GATT: CREATING THE CAPACITY TO NEGOTIATE

For any negotiation to conclude successfully, the nations participating must feel an agreement is needed from the standpoint of their national interest. Such a need was demonstrated early in the preparation that led to the Tokyo Round. However, a second factor is needed for successful negotiation, and that is the capacity to address the questions that will be raised in the negotiation. Normally it is assumed that national governments know how to handle those issues they wish to take up in international negotiations, and that the most important factor is the national will to negotiate (i.e., make hard choices) over those issues. This viewpoint tends to ignore the fact that the issues nations negotiate today are often complex and increasingly technical, and that to negotiate and make decisions on such issues requires enormous preparatory work. Not only is such work required to familiarize national representatives or international civil servants with the subject matter of the negotiation, although that is undoubtedly important. Such work is also needed to create the very subject matter of the negotiation, or at least to arrange the material in a manner that renders it negotiable.

The question of the capacity to negotiate was nowhere better observed than in the handling of nontariff measures (NTM's) within the GATT. Unlike tariffs, NTM's were often individually different from one another, and as well their effects were often felt principally in bilateral trade relationships rather than in multilateral relationships. As a result, NTM's presented negotiators with an enormous diversity, which in the Kennedy Round had made it difficult for nations to seek out multilateral agreements to reduce them. In some cases, negotiators clearly had no mandate to consider removal of NTM's, but one reason for this was that NTM practices were so varied that national governments had little confidence that actions they could take would successfully address the problem. In such an environment, nations could always assume that they were unfairly disadvantaged by the NTM's of other nations, and that the uncertainty of the overall system worked to their disadvantage. Thus it became recognized among the contracting parties to the GATT that it would be necessary to generate and organize a vast amount of information about NTM's before they could be successfully negotiated.

In November 1967, immediately after the Kennedy Round, the twenty-fourth session of the contracting parties met and assessed the past and future work of GATT. It was recognized that no comprehensive negotiation could reasonably be expected in the near future, but the members nevertheless agreed to initiate a program of work that would enhance the prospects at a later date. Specifically the parties authorized the creation of a Committee on Trade in Industrial Products to explore possibilities for further progress on trade liberalization. Second, the parties commissioned an "objective analysis" of the tariff situation that would result when all Kennedy Round concessions had been implemented. Finally, the GATT secretariat was called upon to draw up an inventory of nontariff measures affecting the trade of members. A preliminary edition of this inventory was to be completed by the following summer, after which appropriate machinery was to be set up to deal with problems identified in the inventory.[33]

The analysis of tariffs was conducted by the GATT secretariat, and later became known as the Tariff Study. By the time the Tokyo Round started, this study had assembled on computer tapes the tariff data for most of the developed countries in GATT. This represented a breakthrough from the procedures of the Kennedy Round, and it required a sustained technical effort to develop consistent categories for reporting different national tariff structures. The Tariff Study eventually provided a complete and accurate record of the various national tariffs in force, no mean feat in itself, but it also permitted rapid analysis of changes in individual tariffs on the overall tariff structure of a nation. The Tariff Study, and the computerized procedures that flowed from it, eventually gave Tokyo Round negotiators a much clearer and more rapid view of the concessions or other changes they might make during the negotiating process.[34]

The major focus of the GATT program of work was on NTM's. The initial task was to arrive at some understanding of the outside parameters of the problem. To do this, GATT members relied on the process of notification, a method commonly used in GATT procedures to increase the amount of information available to contracting parties. In previous exchanges, the normal procedure for notification had obliged the country applying a restriction to provide information about that restriction to the international body. This was a convenient procedure for matters such as tariffs, which are obvious measures of protectionism and therefore do not involve difficult questions of definition. But NTM's are often designed for purposes other than protectionism and might restrict trade only co-incidentally to achieving other purposes; hence it was difficult for nations applying an NTM to label it as such. In constructing the NTM inventory, the contracting parties undertook to have the exporting country notify GATT which measures were maintained by other (importing) countries that constituted in some way a restriction to its exports. Importing countries maintaining the measure were then allowed to reply to the complaint.

[33] GATT, *Basic Instruments and Selected Documents* (BISD), Seventeenth Supplement, 1970, 115.

[34] The Tariff Study created a form of common language, of which Ray has written: "If nothing else, the great merit of a 'common language' is that it makes international negotiations a good deal easier; otherwise there is no way of comparing notes, or much time is wasted in making these notes comparable" ("Internationalization of Economic Analysis," 406).

This procedure demonstrated the seriousness and good intent with which GATT members approached the NTM problem, for the accumulation of information itself is a political act. Especially when information is gathered in the context of adversarial procedures, it can have consequences for national policy at a later stage. The result of GATT's NTM initiative was that by 1969 an inventory of some eight hundred notifications had been constructed. The inventory showed prominently the country maintaining the measure, the identification of notifying countries, a description of the measure in question, and a summary of the factual aspects of the measure as well as the positions of the parties involved.

The next step in the process was to organize the material. The notifications were initially placed in five main groups:

(i) government participation in trade,
(ii) customs and administrative entry procedures,
(iii) standards involving imports and domestic goods,
(iv) specific limitations on imports and exports such as quantitative restrictions, and
(v) restraints on imports and exports by the price mechanism.

These categories eventually served as a basis for organizing the efforts of GATT members, for the documentation flowing from the NTM effort became broken down into parts 1 to 5, and working groups were established to deal with each of the five groups of measures. In some cases, notably on customs procedures and standards, the early organization was maintained throughout the subsequent negotiation, and codes evolved from this effort. In other cases, the material went through further transformation as nations sought out those areas that were negotiable, and discarded others, such as quantitative restrictions, where little agreement could be reached.

Another means to organize the material was to compare the measures notified with the legal requirements of the General Agreement. In some cases, notifications concerned situations that some parties felt were covered by the existing rules of the GATT, and where what was needed was a more diligent observance of international requirements. An example of this category was procedures for subsides and countervailing duties. It was expected that this category would be difficult to deal with, since the issues had been the source of longstanding differences within GATT. The probable approach to this category would be the development of interpretive codes that would avoid the legal problem of amending the GATT outright but would create greater uniformity in the application of GATT procedures.

A second category was notifications that went beyond the provisions of the General Agreement. These cases reflected changes that had occurred in international trade since World War II, for which the GATT rules were simply inadequate. The most obvious examples were notifications concerning the trade-distorting impact of government procurement policies, a result of the increasing role of government in the economy. The procedure adopted for this category was to seek new rules to augment the General Agreement.

The two categories above concerned issues of multilateral concern. Beyond these cases was a third category of situations of principally bilateral concern, which nevertheless might be important because of the volume of trade at stake. It was expected that such cases would be taken up by the countries involved. Where these bilateral cases became a subject of multilateral concern was in the extent to which they opened up questions about more effective machinery for consultation or dispute settlement. The latter subject itself became an issue as the Tokyo Round gathered momentum.

To sum up, it was commonly agreed at the start of the Tokyo Round that the negotiation would have to handle NTM's. However, negotiating NTM's was problematic in that they were largely undefinable, numerous, often concealed, and incomparable, and that their effects were unknown precisely but generally thought to be pernicious. Negotiators had to achieve an intellectual understanding of these measures before they could negotiate their removal. In general terms, the task was to gather data about NTM's; to list, categorize, and structure that data into workable groups and subgroups; to relate the new data to existing GATT trade rules and obligations; and finally to create a negotiating structure that was congruent to the structure found in the data. From this process, negotiable definitions of NTM's gradually emerged.

The means for handling NTM's were not arcane, but instead were ordinary methods of GATT administrative practice, namely the notification process, the compilation of the NTM inventory, and the subsequent breakdown of that inventory into negotiable categories. The key was the generation and structuring of information. Essentially this was a bureaucratic act, and in an environment of ignorance, uncertainty, and complexity it was a creative act as well. There is an argument that bureaucracy is an uncreative force in political life and that creativity is the work of individual minds operating outside the normal organization of government.[35] This may be true for some situations. However, when

[35] For example, Kissinger has argued that "every creative act is lonely." See *American Foreign Policy*, 19.

88

the greatest impediments to political action are ignorance, uncertainty, and complexity, the establishment of a bureaucratic process to generate and structure information may be the most creative step that can be taken to address the problem.

What occurred in the early phase of the Tokyo Round bears some analogy to Galbraith's illuminating discussion of the modern industrial technostructure.[36] That Galbraith was writing about the business world and not international diplomacy only demonstrates how much the two have become alike. Galbraith's concern was to analyze corporate planning and techniques of market control, and he identified the generation and manipulation of information as essential to this task. The capacity to generate information was in turn dependent on group processes, not individual creativity, and it was deeply influenced by the hierarchical structure of bureaucratic organization. In the case of the modern corporation, information generation ultimately assisted the corporation to control its external economic environment. In the case of the Tokyo Round trade negotiation, information generation served a similar function in that it promoted greater international control over important areas of international trade. In this sense, international negotiation can take on a management function in contemporary international relations.[37]

There was little use of sophisticated information-processing technology in connection with the negotiation of NTM's, although elsewhere in the Tokyo Round (specifically in the tariff negotiation) computers were used to help generate the aggregate results of individual changes of position. In the future, one might expect a greater use of computer technology, such as the measurement of the amount of world trade affected by different NTM's, which is not possible now because of inconsistent definitions and measurements. In other negotiations, such as the Conference on the Law of the Sea (UNCLOS), computers have been used to provide information for the negotiation and to help in reaching an agreement. Specifically, in the seabed negotiation, a computer model was designed which demonstrated the relationship between important variables (such as cost and profit) in seabed mining operations.[38] This model generated politically acceptable information on a subject in which parties to a negotiation were previously arguing in ignorance. While this model was more complicated, it essentially served the same function as the NTM inventory in the Tokyo Round. Thus in both the

[36] New Industrial State, esp. ch. 6, "The Technostructure."

[37] For further analysis of this point, see Winham, "Negotiation."

[38] The model was developed by a team from M.I.T. led by Professor J. D. Nyhart, and is described in Sebenius, Law of the Sea.

simple techniques of the Tokyo Round and the more sophisticated technology used in the UNCLOS, one sees important advances in the capacity to negotiate the complicated problems of the international system.

THE movement toward negotiation in the Tokyo Round was gradual, as it is in most large-scale negotiations. The parties must become convinced that the negotiation is needed, and that it will be in their interests to pursue. This conviction must be generated at the highest political levels in the capitals of the major participants. The existence of, and the later reports from, teams like the Williams Commission and the Rey group indicated that such a conviction was gaining momentum in the United States and the European Communities.

As well as needing political momentum, large-scale negotiation requires that a technical base be built, for on complex issues like trade the determination to negotiate cannot be far separated from the capacity to negotiate. Developing the technical base occurred at the lower levels in government, and especially in the interaction between national delegates and the secretariat at GATT. Essentially the technical work entailed the selection, collection, and organization of data, but in some cases, such as the highly technical area of standards, the work had progressed as far as the drafting of *ad referendum* solutions to selected problems. Thus by the time of the Tokyo Declaration in 1973, at which point most history books would record the commencement of the Tokyo Round, the political decisionmaking and the technical support work were already moving in a direction that would ensure negotiation could be undertaken.

· 3 ·

THE NEGOTIATION LAUNCHED, 1973–1974:
ISSUES BEFORE THE TOKYO ROUND

The Tokyo Round had its official beginning, and took its name from, a GATT ministerial meeting held in Tokyo on September 12–14, 1973. This meeting was attended by representatives of 102 nations, including both members and nonmembers of GATT, and at its conclusion the participants unanimously adopted the Tokyo Declaration which launched the multilateral trade negotiation. The aim of the negotiation was stated in the broadest terms possible: to "achieve the expansion and ever-greater liberalization of world trade and improvement in the standard of living and welfare of the people of the world" and to "secure additional benefits for the international trade of developing countries."[1]

The Tokyo Declaration was a heavily negotiated document. In its general wording, one can easily miss the enormous importance of this endeavor. The Tokyo Declaration was significant because it defined trade relations in the early 1970s as a negotiable problem. This created a presumption that something could be done to improve the difficulties in the international trading system. The declaration structured the exercise of trade policy for the participating nations in terms of both process and substance. It accomplished the first by setting up the mechanism of negotiation, which, when used by governments as a tool of policymaking, tends to preempt unilateral policymaking to ensure that international concerns will become more important in national decisions than would otherwise be the case. It accomplished the second because negotiation is a form of policymaking that is predisposed toward compromise; by agreeing to initiate a major negotiation, nations were accepting the probability that certain strongly held policies would have to be modified in the direction of their partners' demands. Particularly in the area of nontariff measures, the agreement to begin a negotiation was a significant accomplishment in its own right, and one which would expose some areas of domestic jurisdiction to international scrutiny for the first time.

The Tokyo Declaration also created a presumption that something

[1] GATT, "The Tokyo Declaration: Declaration Issued at the End of the Ministerial Meeting Held in Tokyo, 12–14 September 1973." The entire declaration is reproduced in Appendix A.

91

would be done about the state of international trade in the early 1970s. Negotiation is traditionally a mechanism for conflict resolution, but multilateral negotiation in GATT has become more than that: it is an investment in international decisionmaking. A trade negotiation like the Tokyo Round is an enormous affair and extremely costly in terms of the time and attention of government officials. Once entered into, it is difficult to end without some form of agreement being reached, since the time and effort expended create a kind of "sunk cost" for governments that can be justified only through achieving a negotiated settlement. Embarking on the Tokyo Round was therefore an important political decision in itself, for it indicated that the participating governments were disposed to let the momentum of the negotiation process exert force in the direction of change in the international trade regime.

THE TOKYO DECLARATION

The call for multilateral economic negotiation had been one of the major recommendations of the report of the Williams Commission tabled in July 1971.[2] This report had called for a broad approach to negotiation that would encompass subjects ranging from monetary questions dealing with balance-of-payments adjustments to trade matters involving tariff and nontariff restrictions. The breadth of the recommendation, and the urgency with which it was put, left no doubt that an influential segment of American opinion would support an international trade negotiation. The report itself concluded in the following words:

> These problems will not wait. Several times during the past few years, situations developed in which unilateral actions by one or another major trading nation could have precipitated an international crisis. We believe no time should be lost in getting these negotiations underway.[3]

Subsequent events quickly underscored the commission's recommendations. On August 15, 1971, the United States suspended the dollar-gold convertibility that had been the keystone of the Bretton Woods monetary regime. This act created the crisis atmosphere that the Williams Commission had predicted. Subsequent negotiations between the major economic powers helped to stabilize monetary relations and to ease the immediate crisis. In the aftermath of this crisis, there developed an increasing awareness of the need to institute a wide-ranging negoti-

[2] U.S. Government, *United States International Economic Policy.*
[3] Ibid., 307.

ation on trade matters, to be conducted under GATT auspices. On the European side, this awareness was given formal expression in a declaration of the EC Council of Ministers in December 1971: "The Community is ready . . . to take part in overall negotiations on the basis of mutual advantage and reciprocity and requires an effort from all participants."[4]

In February 1972, following intensive bilateral discussions, the United States initiated declarations respectively with the Commission of the European Community and the government of Japan "to initiate and actively support multilateral and comprehensive negotiations in the framework of GATT beginning in 1973."[5] These declarations stimulated an immediate positive response from the GATT membership. The GATT Council agreed in a meeting in March 1972 on the principle of initiating a multilateral negotiation the following year, and it subsequently constituted a preparatory committee to lay the groundwork for the opening of the negotiation. The Preparatory Committee met extensively in the first half of 1973, and completed a report and draft declaration for the ministerial meeting in Tokyo in September 1973.[6]

The committee's draft hammered out a common approach to the negotiation, save for two important issues. One concerned the difference between the EC and the United States over the link between trade and monetary relations. Principally at the insistence of the French, the EC took the position that negotiation on trade issues was contingent on an equitable revision of the monetary system, and particularly one that would remove the advantage accruing to the U.S. dollar by virtue of its role as a key currency. The United States opposed this formulation and insisted instead that negotiations should proceed independently on trade matters, without prejudice to simultaneous efforts elsewhere to improve international monetary arrangements. The force of precedent favored the American position; too, events in monetary relations, notably the movement during 1972–73 toward flexible exchange rates, made it less likely that any major overhaul of the monetary system would be possible. Consequently the EC agreed at the Tokyo meeting to proceed with a trade negotiation and to incorporate its concern for monetary negotiations in a nonbinding recommendation contained in paragraph 7 of the Tokyo Declaration (see Appendix A), although the French had made clear their intention of insisting on effective monetary

[4] Cited in Golt, *GATT Negotiations*, Appendix B, "The 'Overall Approach' to Trade of the European Community," 59.

[5] GATT, *Tokyo Round*, 4.

[6] The report is contained in the following document: GATT, *Report of the Preparatory Committee for Trade Negotiations*, MIN(73)W/2, August 7, 1973.

changes as a condition to concluding a trade negotiation.[7] In the end, events overtook this potential dispute. The quadrupling of oil prices in late 1973, and the later inflation and stagnation that occurred in the Western economies, removed all possibility that a formal monetary system resembling the Bretton Woods agreement would be constructed during the 1970s.

A second issue saved for ministerial decision in Tokyo concerned the special treatment to be accorded to the least developed countries as opposed to other developing nations. This question raised the difficult issue of whether all developing countries, which have enjoyed special status in GATT procedures since the addition of Part IV to the General Agreement in 1964,[8] are equally deserving of this status for the purpose of exchanging trade concessions. The industrialized members of GATT took the position that a distinction should be made for levels of development among the less-developed countries, while the backers of the Group of 77, sensing that such a distinction might be used to deny them preferential treatment, strongly resisted the attempt to develop a relative notion of development. The industrialized countries succeeded in introducing a concern for "the particular situation and problems of the least developed among the developing countries" into paragraph 6 of the Tokyo Declaration, and hence insured that this question would be raised in the substantive negotiations that were to follow. But this did not settle the question by any means, and the developing countries continued to resist in the various code negotiations the implications of "graduation," as the issue came to be known. Insertion of the issue in the Tokyo Declaration proved to be the opening shot in what became a long and tedious battle.

The Tokyo Declaration was a cautious and heavily negotiated text. Its drafters had a tendency to get agreement on wording through the expedient of including in the text the positions of both sides in any dispute. This technique outlined the problems the negotiation would face, while leaving solutions to subsequent bargaining. This created a framework for the negotiation and helped to identify the priority items. It advanced the process by providing a guideline to initiate and evaluate progress in the negotiation. If this technique had any drawbacks, it was that it disguised much of the disagreement, which in turn promoted frustration later in the negotiation.

One example of the papering over of difficult issues was apparent in

[7] This intention was specified in an internal document that outlined, among other things, the conditions the EC should set in the forthcoming negotiation. See quotation in ch. 2, p. 80.

[8] Dam, *The GATT*, 236–41.

the treatment of agriculture in the Tokyo Declaration. The United States and the EC have long held irreconcilable views on agriculture which are consistent with their role as exporting and importing countries respectively. U.S. negotiators have usually attempted to have agricultural and industrial products treated identically in trade negotiations, in an effort to increase the prospects for liberalization in the agricultural sector. The EC, on the other hand, has insisted on the separate treatment of agriculture in order to deflect American demands for liberalization of European agricultural policies. This issue received extended discussion in the Kennedy Round, but the position of the Community negotiators was unshakable. Agricultural products were exempted from the linear-cut procedures applied in the industrial sectors, and in general the extent of liberalization was much less in agriculture than in other areas.

The negotiations on the Tokyo Declaration resurrected the old lines of division between the Americans and Europeans. The passage of time had not attenuated the differences between the two sides; in fact, it had created reasons for both sides to be more insistent. On the American side, there was the perception, largely correct, that U.S. agricultural interests had not gained much from the Kennedy Round, which intensified the demand for a more favorable outcome at the Tokyo Round. The Europeans, however, had even more to defend, since by the early 1970s the Common Agricultural Policy (CAP) of the EC was firmly in place and, although it was openly protectionist, it was nevertheless one of the most successful policies of the Community. It was clear in the Preparatory Committee that the issue could not be settled head-on, and thus the Tokyo Declaration effectively deferred the dispute through the use of wording that accommmodated the divergent positions. For the Americans, the declaration stated in paragraph 4 that the negotiations "shall cover . . . both industrial and agricultural products," a formula which was consistent with equal treatment of both sectors. For the Europeans, the document stated that the negotiations "should take account of the special characteristics and problems in this sector." Each side maintained its own definition of the issue, and as a result the divergent views of the United States and EC were projected downward into the subsequent negotiations at the working level, where, as it turned out, they created major problems for the overall progress of the talks.

A second example of facilitative language in the Tokyo Declaration arose in the context of relations between the developed and less-developed nations. One issue over which these two groups had long contended is to what degree reciprocity would be a criterion for exchanges of trade concessions. On the one hand, the developed countries preferred to start from the formal premise of reciprocity, which has historically been a cornerstone of GATT negotiation, and to make exceptions where appropriate for exchanges between unequal partners. On the other hand, the less-developed countries have sought to weaken the principle of reciprocity and thereby greatly to reduce the expectation that concessions extended by developed nations would create any commitment for compensation on the part of the recipient. In GATT negotiations, these alternative positions became a practical matter of who paid whom for concessions received, but the underlying issue went to a much more fundamental difference about the nature of underdevelopment in the international system.

The developed countries sought to incorporate the developing countries into a diplomatic system that was a creature of the former's economic needs and bargaining style. They assumed that underdevelopment was an economic question, related mainly to levels of industrialization, and that it was an inherently temporary state. They further assumed that nations were ultimately individual actors within GATT and that the status of each nation at GATT negotiations was conveyed by a general acceptance of the rules of the General Agreement and a willingness to bargain in good faith and to exchange concessions. From this general approach, the notion that exceptions might be made for developing nations was an accepted deviation from the overall expectation of reciprocity.

The developing countries started from the premise that underdevelopment, even more than individual nationhood, was the most profound determinant of their identity. They sought to create a status of underdevelopment, and to seek involvement with GATT on what appeared to be permanently preferential grounds. They focused on the perpetuating and unchanging aspects of their underdevelopment, and they were keenly aware of how economic disadvantages led to disadvantages in other aspects of international life. Implicit in the status of underdevelopment was their belief that economic benefits were owed them by right rather than by mutual exchange, and they approached bargaining in GATT more as an exercise in collective development planning and less as a search for individual quid pro quo. From this perspective, the notion that the developing nations should be absolved from expectations of reciprocity in GATT negotiations was a cardinal tenet.

The argument over reciprocity between the developed and less-developed countries was an old question by the time the Tokyo Declaration was negotiated, and the participants in the Preparatory Committee worked out a formula that succeeded in bridging this difference. For the developed countries, the declaration noted that the negotiations were to be conducted according to the principles of "mutual advantage, mutual commitment and overall reciprocity" and "consistently with the provisions of the General Agreement relating to such negotiations." However, the declaration immediately qualified these principles with the following statement: "The developed countries do not expect reciprocity for commitments made by them in the negotiations to reduce or remove tariff and other barriers to the trade of developing countries."[9] As with the dispute on agriculture between the United States and the EEC, the Tokyo Declaration managed to include widely divergent viewpoints on the issue of reciprocity between developing and less-developed countries. The declaration met the diplomatic needs of the moment, for it provided an adequate political basis on which to get the negotiation started. However, there was no doubt that the issue of reciprocity, and the even thornier problem of graduation, would be one of the major controversial themes of the negotiation.

On a less controversial note, the Tokyo Declaration established the machinery for the prosecution of the negotiation. Under paragraph 10, a Trade Negotiation Committee (TNC) was created, consisting of all countries participating in the Tokyo Round, and chaired by the Director General of GATT, Mr. Olivier Long. The task of the TNC was to establish appropriate plans and negotiating procedures, and to exercise overall supervision over the negotiation. The TNC was not intended to be a forum for negotiation itself, since its large size precluded any working interaction. The TNC met regularly throughout the negotiation to receive formal reports of the subordinate bodies it created, and in this manner monitored the pace and substance of the negotiation.

The TNC went to work immediately following the Tokyo ministerial meeting of September 1973. In February 1974, the TNC created six specialized subcommittees which conformed to the six negotiating areas outlined in paragraph 3 of the Tokyo Declaration. They were:

Group 3(a) Negotiations on *tariffs*;
Group 3(b) Reduction or elimination of *nontariff measures*; or their trade-distorting effects;
Group 3(c) Examination of the *sector* approach as a complementary negotiating technique;
Group 3(d) Examination of the *multilateral safeguards* system;
Group 3(e) Negotiations on *agriculture*; and
Group 3(f) Negotiations on *tropical products*.

[9] GATT, "Tokyo Declaration," paragraph 5. See Appendix A.

The TNC additionally laid down a program of work which assigned specific tasks to these groups, with the exception of Groups 3(c) and 3(d), which were not activated until the following October. These tasks were specific in nature, and designed to continue work already begun and to complete the initial preparations for the negotiation. For example, Group 3(b) was assigned to complete documentation and basic data on nontariff measures assembled in the context of an earlier GATT program of work of 1967, to continue the study of a possible code regarding countervailing duties, and to begin work on packaging and labeling.[10] Similarly Group 3(a) was tasked to complete documentation on tariffs, and to determine the base year or years for the collection of statistics as well as the unit of account to be used in the negotiation.

The creation of negotiating groups and the assignment of specific tasks reflects an interaction between substance and organization in the negotiation process that appears obvious after the fact, but which at the time was the subject of considerable planning and discussion. The Tokyo Round negotiation was conducted in a subject area that is at once immense, technical, and extremely complicated. As previously discussed, one major objective of the preparatory period of the negotiation was to build up an information base so that national representatives could understand the problems over which they would have to make decisions. One aspect of this preparation was for nations to agree on the general priorities of the negotiation; this was accomplished in the Tokyo Declaration. Another was to create organizational machinery at the working level, for where such machinery is not created and used there is less likelihood that the relevant areas will receive the attention needed to support decisionmaking at a later stage. Implicit in the organizational effort was the need to define operational tasks. In a large negotiation, nothing gets done unless formal tasks are assigned to specific individuals or groups, and with deadlines attached.

The tendency in the early phase of the negotiation was to include as much as possible for examination by the working groups. Thus, for example, Group 3(b) was assigned work on export restrictions even though there was little prospect for substantial movement in that area. As time went on and the work took on greater focus, the decisions respecting tasking and the establishment of working groups became important because they determined the direction of the overall negotiation. Where these decisions became controversial, the controversy would often be over what initiatives were being taken rather than over

---

[10] TNC, "Programme of Work Adopted by the Committee on 7 February 1974," GATT docs., MTN/2, February 11, 1974.

what substantive decisions were being taken. In any large negotiation like the Tokyo Round, the shape of the final outcome is a product of the organization of the early stages, and as a result nations invest considerable effort in negotiating over the preparatory and data-gathering phases.

Following the February 1974 meeting of the TNC, work began in four of the six new subcommittees. Each operational group held a series of meetings through the early months of 1974, and submitted progress reports at the July 1974 meeting of the TNC. The TNC received these reports and assigned additional tasks to be completed by the TNC meeting in October 1974. In this bureaucratic manner, the participating nations moved step by step through the preparatory phase of the negotiation.

As an example of the work at this stage of the negotiation, one can consider the operation of Group 3(b). In a meeting of March 4–7, 1974, this group updated the inventory of nontariff measures that was already well developed, and reassessed the categories into which the measures were grouped in the light of their usefulness in future negotiation.[11] Regarding import documentation, it assessed the work being done by the Economic Commission for Europe (ECE) and the Customs Cooperation Council, and it commissioned the GATT secretariat to prepare progress reports on this work in preparation for further consideration within the Tokyo Round. In other areas, such as embargoes or export restraints, the group decided it would be difficult to examine the issues further "without entering into negotiations proper,"[12] and thus the issue was postponed pending receipt from the secretariat of a document synthesizing the various suggestions made in the area. The operations of Group 3(b), and of the other groups, were characterized by a maximum use of the GATT secretariat to provide historical, interpretive, and technical information to support the negotiation; and the tendency to divorce data-gathering from negotiation as much as possible, in order to build up a common information base on which to proceed.

The structure of the working groups underwent two changes during 1974, one nominal and the other significant, after which they remained substantially unchanged throughout the negotiation. These changes were confirmed in a meeting of the TNC in February 1975. The nominal change was to move away from the titles established by reference to the Tokyo Declaration (e.g., Group 3[b]) in favor of assigning titles that

[11] "Group 3(b)—Meeting of March 1974," GATT docs., MTN/3B/7, March 12, 1974.
[12] Ibid., 3.

described the work of the group (e.g., Nontariff Measures Group).[13] The other change was to further subcategorize the Nontariff Measures Group and the Agriculture Group into subgroups, which became the basic GATT negotiating units in these areas, and to which GATT secretariat officials were assigned for support and technical services. The subgroups were as follows:[14]

Group: Nontariff Measures
Subgroups: (i)   Quantitative Restrictions
            (ii) Technical Barriers to Trade
            (iii) Customs Matters
            (iv) Subsidies and Countervailing Duties
            (v) Government Procurement (added in July 1976)
Group: Agriculture
Subgroups: (i)   Grains
            (ii) Meat
            (iii) Dairy Products

A final organizational change was the addition of a seventh group, called the Framework Group, to the original six groups drawn up from paragraph 6 of the Tokyo Declaration. This group was established in November 1976 under the chairmanship of the director general of GATT to respond to requests of the less-developed countries that the Tokyo Round examine the overall legal structure of trade relations within GATT. The group was tasked to consider "improvements in the international framework for the conduct of world trade which might be desirable in the light of progress in the negotiations."[15] Negotiations in this group eventually produced an "enabling clause" which introduced differential and more-favorable treatment as an integral, instead of temporary, part of the GATT system.

ISSUES BEFORE THE TOKYO ROUND, 1973–1974: AD REFERENDUM TEXTS

The greatest problems in the early period of the Tokyo Round were procedural. The reason for this is that the Tokyo Declaration had not

[13] The six renamed groups were as follows: Tariffs, Nontariff Measures, Sector, Safeguards, Agriculture, and Tropical Products. The name change was reflected in GATT documentation. For example, the document series from the 3(a) group which started with MTN/3A/1 ended around 1974–75 and was replaced with the series MTN/TAR/1. Similar changes occurred in the other groups.

[14] GATT, *Tokyo Round*, 9.

[15] Ibid.

achieved a common approach to some of the most difficult issues facing the negotiation. The declaration had included quite varied interpretations of important matters such as the procedures for negotiating tariff reductions, the relations between developed and less-developed countries, and the overall approach to agricultural protectionism; and it was assumed these matters would be thrashed out when the negotiation got under way. However, what had been difficult in the preparatory phase of the negotiation proved to be no less insurmountable once the negotiation had begun. Procedural issues, particularly the issue of agriculture, prevented any definitive progress from being made for the first four years of the Tokyo Round.

Despite the lack of overall progress, the early period of the Tokyo Round was fruitful in that it opened up a large range of areas for formal negotiation. Some of these areas were fairly well advanced from previous meetings in GATT, and were already the subject of partially negotiated texts, lists of principles, or *ad referendum* agreements. These included technical barriers to trade (more commonly known as standards), customs valuation, import licensing, and quantitative restrictions. Several other areas also had a history of past negotiation in GATT, but since (along with quantitative restrictions) they were among the more controversial issues, the early negotiation left the Tokyo Round negotiators with much less to build upon. These were: subsidies and countervailing duties, tropical products, and multilateral safeguards. In all seven areas, the early negotiation built up a technical and informational base for negotiation and identified the main lines of disagreement among the participants.

Standards

Product standards are specifications that lay down "some or all of the properties of a product in terms of quality, purity, nutritional value, performance, dimensions, or other characteristics."[16] Such specifications include, where appropriate, testing methods, regulations concerning safety or durability, and procedures for packaging, marking, and labeling products. Standards are adopted through actions of either government agencies or private organizations: they ensure minimum levels of control over products offered on the market, and particularly ensure that such products function as intended and that they do not jeopardize other important concerns, such as human health, environ-

[16] "Definitions: Working Paper by the Secretariat," GATT docs., MTN/NTM/W/14, June 26, 1975, 5.

mental quality, or industrial safety. Standards obviously are essential in modern industrial society, and the more society relies on the products of high technology the more important standards will be in regulating the productive process.

Standards have been adopted largely by domestic organizations with a view to establishing specifications that apply principally within national jurisdictions. Historically, they have not been for the most part intended to restrict trade; indeed the organizations promulgating standards have tended to be more oblivious of international trade than aware of the trade-distorting effects standards could produce. Nevertheless the process of generating standards and certifying products has complicated and inhibited trade in numerous ways. For example, standards might be developed quickly, with an eye mainly on domestic processes, leaving foreign producers insufficient time or even insufficient capacity to adjust. Or regulations promulgating standards might be exceptionally complicated or uncertain, which would more likely damage foreign producers operating at a greater distance from the market. A common problem was the tendency to draw up regulations in terms of a known local design rather than by performance, which meant foreign products with different designs, but perhaps the same function, would automatically be disqualified. Finally, access to testing systems, particularly when such systems existed only within an importing country, created additional and often insurmountable burdens for exporters.

The concern for standards is a relatively recent phenomenon in GATT history. The General Agreement makes no specific reference to standards,[17] although it could be argued that it covers standards in a general way. For example, Article 3 recognizes that internal "laws, regulations and requirements . . . should not be applied to imported or domestic products so as to afford protection to domestic productions."[18] However, this provision was clearly insufficiently detailed to handle international trade in the 1960s and 1970s. Even as the Kennedy Round closed, there was a growing recognition that technical barriers to trade would be an important subject to any new negotiation.

The impetus to negotiation in the post–Kennedy Round period came from three factors. First was the recognition that of the 900 notifications in the GATT nontariff measure (NTM) Inventory, some 150 notifi-

[17] Nor is there any reference to standards in Jackson's authoritative treatise on GATT, namely *World Trade*.
[18] *GATT*, Article 3. Two other articles (11 and 20) refer to standards or measures necessary to protect health, but both in the context of permissible exceptions to GATT provisions.

cations were in the standards area. This led to standards being included as one section in the five-section breakdown of the inventory. The discovery of the prevalence of standards-related issues was one of the major surprises of the NTM inventory. Indeed uncovering this subject area was a substantial confirmation of the value of the inventorying process. Not only did the inventory produce a comprehensive set of data where only scattered bits of evidence were available previously, but also it encouraged officials to think in terms of a general problem rather than about isolated and unconnected examples. The next step was to think through what GATT documents routinely refer to as the "techniques and modalities" of fashioning a general policy for a general problem. The fact that standards is an unemotional, and generally little known, problem in international trade meant that much of the latter work could be accomplished at the expert level in GATT, without much interference from political forces in the member countries.

A second impetus came from the United States. U.S. interest in GATT work on standards was quickened by the action of Britain, France, and Germany in concluding a tripartite agreement (CENEL Agreement) for the harmonization and certification of electronic components. This agreement made it difficult for producers outside the three countries to get their products certified, and hence had potential adverse trade effects for nonparticipants in the agreement. Since this scheme was expected to be the first of several similar standardization arrangements designed to increase the integration of European economies, it seemed imperative for the United States to widen the standard-setting and certification process beyond the European Community. A corollary concern of the United States was to open up the European process to U.S. surveillance and possible participation. It was a longstanding belief in the United States that certification procedures were more open and accessible to nationals and foreigners alike in America than in Europe, and U.S. officials saw in the standards negotiations in GATT a means for moving European practices in the direction of greater transparency. Ultimately this took the form of a U.S. demand for membership and participation in regional certification systems in Europe, a demand which the European nations successfully resisted in the subsequent negotiation.

A third impetus came from the Europeans. Trade officials in the larger European nations had long held the view that the United States was considerably less willing to adopt international standards than the Europeans themselves. Negotiations of standards in GATT gave them a forum from which to press on the United States standards and certification procedures that had a European origin. This was important for reasons both internal and external to the European Community. Regarding the latter, the Economic Commission for Europe was involved with the problem of standards in trade between Eastern and Western Europe, and there was a desire to extend common standards to a wider arena. As for internal trade, the Commission of the European Communities was itself becoming involved in the promulgation of standards, even though at the time of the Tokyo Round its efforts were minor in the context of the thousands of standards under national or private jurisdiction.[19] The Commission was keenly interested to have the United States accept its standards, since it would increase the authority of the Commission with member states in this increasingly important area.

The work on standards advanced very quickly in the preparatory phase of the Tokyo Round. By the time of the ministerial meeting of 1973, a draft code had been prepared in a reasonably advanced form. Above all, the draft code introduced a concern for international trade into the standard-setting and certification processes of participating countries. In particular, the code would encourage signatories to participate in setting standards in international organizations on as wide a basis as possible, and to pursue international, as opposed to regional, certification arrangements for assuring conformity to standards. The draft code spelled out certain rules that should be followed by national standards bodies so as not to create trade impediments (e.g., "adherents shall specify mandatory standards in terms of performance rather than detailed design").[20] The exchange of technical information was also emphasized in the draft code, and several provisions spelled out requirements for adequate notice of proposed new standards, for full publication, and for time for comment by affected parties. Finally, the draft code provided for a GATT committee for preventing technical barriers to trade, which had the power to investigate complaints about the implementation of the code and to recommend remedial actions to the parties. In case of serious violations of the code, the committee was empowered to refer the question to the GATT contracting parties for appropriate action.

The standards code was nearly completed by the time of the Tokyo Declaration. Some nations, notably the United States, were interested in implementing the code separately from other aspects of the Tokyo

[19] At the time of the conclusion of the Tokyo Round, the EC had adopted approximately 150 industrial and 50 agricultural standards, each promulgated by an EC directive (personal interview).

[20] "Standards; Packaging and Labelling; Marks of Origin: Background Note by the Secretariat," GATT docs., MTN/NTM/W/5, April 21, 1975, 13.

Round. This plan was quashed by the European Community, which felt the draft code provided insufficient reciprocity for European interests. With the Tokyo Declaration, the negotiations on standards effectively went back to the beginning, since it was necessary for those nations already committed to the code to persuade others to accept it without substantial change. Fortunately all participants of the Tokyo Round were willing to accept the draft code as a negotiating text, which structured the subsequent negotiation into bargaining sessions over incremental changes in the basic text.

The period 1973–75 thus constituted a hiatus in the negotiations over technical barriers to trade. The standards committee made little progress on the basic text in this period, but it did succeed in adding to the draft code some provisions related to marks of origin, packaging, and labeling. One of the main tasks of the negotiators in this area was to educate, repeatedly, the nations that newly joined the negotiation on technical barriers. The second main task, particularly for U.S. and EC negotiators, was to present the viewpoints of their respective governments on the issue of the participation of federal governments in the standards code. The position of the EC, rejected by the United States, was one of concern over whether federal governments had sufficient control over subsidiary governments to be able to participate fully in the obligations outlined in the draft code. This issue proved to be one of the most troublesome areas in the subsequent negotiation of the standards code.

Customs Valuation

Customs valuation refers to the practice of establishing a monetary value on imported goods. Such a value lies at the basis of a tariff system of trade protection. If tariff duties are *ad valorem*, i.e., a percentage of value, then the means of establishing the value of a good will have a bearing on the amount of duty paid. Clearly, valuation procedures have the potential to be used for protective purposes. Import values are normally established by customs officers at the point of entry in the importing country, prior to the calculation of tariff duties. If the value (i.e., price) of the goods in question is raised above the transaction price, or a "fair" market price, then the valuation process may have acted as a surrogate for higher tariffs on the goods.

Customs valuation and customs procedures more generally have been subjects of agreements between nations for much of the twentieth century. In 1923, an International Conference on Customs Formalities produced an International Convention relating to the Simplification of

Customs Formalities which advanced international law on customs beyond that attained in the GATT more than two decades later.[21] Many of its provisions were intended to reduce inefficiencies, uncertainties, and protectionist tendencies that existed mainly in the administration of customs procedures. The General Agreement itself took up the issue of customs valuation in Article 7, where the basic legal requirement was stated as follows:

> The value for customs purposes of imported merchandise should be based on the actual value of the imported merchandise on which duty is assessed, or of like merchandise, and should not be based on the value of merchandise of national origin or on arbitrary or fictitious values.[22]

Subsequent paragraphs went on to define actual value as the price the merchandise would have fetched under "fully competitive conditions." The problem with this information, of course, is that it leaves a great deal of discretion to customs officials in importing countries to define "fully competitive conditions." As a result, the actual value of merchandise tends to become whatever officials say it is.

In an effort to achieve greater standardization in customs matters, thirteen European governments formed in 1947 a European Customs Union Study Group. The work of this group led to three conventions which were signed in Brussels in 1950. One established the "Brussels Tariff Nomenclature" system for classifying tariffs, which by 1970 had been adopted by all important trading nations in GATT except the United States and Canada. The second, the Brussels Convention on Valuation, set up procedures for customs valuation that became known as the Brussels Definition of Value (BDV). These procedures have had steadily widening acceptance among trading nations, and by 1970 had been adopted by most important trading nations of GATT, with the exception of the United States, Canada, Switzerland, India, and Brazil. The third convention established the Customs Cooperation Council (CCC), which was an international organization designed to administer the agreement and to insure uniform application of the customs practices of the signatories.

The pressure to negotiate customs valuation issues in the post–Kennedy Round period came largely from the European Community. It was driven above all by the feeling that uniformity of customs practices

---

[21] Jackson, *World Trade*, 441. Jackson notes that GATT was intended to include a larger number and wider variety of nations, and that hence it was understandable that its provisions on customs matters might be less stringent.

[22] *GATT*, Article 7, paragraph 26.

was a worthwhile goal in trading relations and that the most obvious and reasonable way to attain this was for all nations to adopt the initiatives launched by the Europeans themselves. This argument was given added impetus by the efforts the CCC nations had made to accommodate BDV procedures to nonsignatories. For example, in June 1974 the CCC adopted a recommendation that amended the convention on valuation to allow nations that operate a valuation system based on f.o.b. values (such as the United States) to apply the BDV, which is based on c.i.f. values.[23]

Apart from the sentiment for universality, the European Community had specific objectives in the area of customs valuation. The most important of these was the removal of the American Selling Price (ASP) method of customs valuation which had been such a bone of contention in the Kennedy Round. The ASP, it will be recalled, established the value of foreign goods in reference to "like or similar" goods produced domestically, which is a flat contravention of Article 7 of the GATT. The ASP is not a legal violation of the GATT because, in the Protocol of Provisional Acceptance whereby the United States and other nations acceded to the GATT, practices already in existence were exempted from the requirements of the General Agreement. Since the ASP (and the Final List method of valuation, another U.S. practice objected to by the Europeans) predated the GATT, American negotiators have held that the United States is under no legal or moral obligation to alter these customs procedures. European negotiators, on the other hand, felt that the General Agreement constitutes requirements that all nations are obliged eventually to accept, and they resented the notion that the United States was permanently exempted from the provisions of Article 7. Thus the Europeans resented the ASP because of its inconsistency with the GATT even more than its actual impact on trade, and this resentment was exacerbated by the fact that the EC had negotiated an end of the ASP in the Kennedy Round, only to have that agreement nullified by the failure of Congress to implement the action.

The position of the United States on customs valuation was one of calculated indifference. This resulted from both symbolic and practical aspects of the situation. Regarding the first, U.S. negotiators had long been accustomed to taking the lead on most issues in GATT negotiations, which carries with it a certain psychological burden of taking the initiative to the other party. On customs valuation, this burden was clearly on the EC side, and U.S. officials, undoubtedly enjoying the sight

[23] "Customs Matters: Communication from the CCC," GATT docs., MTN/NTM/W/ 17, August 1975, 10.

of the other side being told to "get something" in the negotiation, were in no hurry to end the moment. On the second, the United States was under less pressure from exporters than was the Community to negotiate changes on matters involving customs. Although the effects of the ASP were not widespread, it did produce some very high tariff duties on specific products, which led European firms to lobby the Commission to get the American practice dropped. American exporters did not face equivalent problems in their trade with Europe, although there were some complaints about the practice of European customs officials of "uplifting" values in the transactions between American multinational companies and their European subsidiaries. American negotiators consequently enjoyed some respite from domestic pressure on this issue.

In the period following the Kennedy Round, customs valuation was one of the areas isolated for discussion and possible negotiation. Customs-related issues were frequently "notified" in the NTM inventory, and a working group was established to explore this subject further. By 1970, this group had worked out an *ad referendum* text containing draft principles and interpretive notes to make for greater uniformity in the application of Article 7 of the General Agreement. The text itself was a very modest achievement indeed. It did not addresss the question of uniform application of BDV, or specific problems such as ASP. The interpretive notes did outline a procedure for determining the "actual value" of merchandise, which was based initially on the actual selling price or the probable selling price under competitive conditions. Further procedures were spelled out for situations where value could not be determined by these methods.[24] Even though these notes represented some improvement in the degree of uniformity of national practice, the text was still so minimal that customs officers would be little constrained in their decisions on valuation. This plus the fact that some nations did not consider the texts fully acceptable meant that very little had been achieved in this area.[25]

The result was that nations went into the Tokyo Round with very little accomplished on customs valuation despite the existence of an *ad referendum* text on the subject. The overriding U.S. position was that

[24] Specifically, the text referred to a "nearly ascertainable equivalent" value, which would take into account variables such as conditions of production (including wage rates) in the supplier country ("Customs Matters: Background Note by the Secretariat," GATT docs., MTN/NTM/W/7, April 29, 1975, 14).

[25] For example, the Canadian delegation to the working group did not consider the draft text to be the simplest or most effective solution to valuation problems, while the United States felt its support would depend on obtaining some "balance of advantage" in this area (*ibid.*, 18).

if it was going to be asked to adopt a new customs system like BVD (which certainly would have entailed dropping ASP and the Final List provisions in U.S. customs law), then the Europeans must be willing to offer some important concessions. This argument upset the Europeans, who felt they should not have to "pay" the United States to adopt procedures that were already legally required by the GATT. Some indication of potential change in the U.S. attitude came in March 1973, when the U.S. Tariff Commission recommended to the Senate Finance Committee that the United States adopt an international customs valuation system. However, this attitude had not affected the U.S. position within GATT; it continued to oppose any fundamental shift in valuation practices.

Import Licensing

Import licenses are a legal permission given to an importer by his government authorities to import merchandise from foreign suppliers. Import licenses are most frequently used to administer quantitative restrictions, particularly quotas. In the case of quotas, importers apply for licenses and receive these up to the permitted level of importation, after which no further licenses are issued. For other trade restrictions, such as health standards, licenses will be issued only for merchandise that complies with the regulations in question.

Many countries maintain licensing procedures as a condition of importation even though the licenses are issued automatically and are not related to any accompanying trade restriction. The rationale for such procedures is that they are necessary for statistical and surveillance purposes. However, they can create barriers to trade above and beyond the restrictions they might have been designed to administer. For example, in the NTM inventory there were frequent notifications of trade problems that were traced to the operation of licensing systems rather than to the content of restrictive trade practices. Some of the problems that were raised were uncertainty over whether licenses would be issued, delays involved in processing applications, and bias in favor of one importer over another.

The main problem in this subject area came over the question of automatic licensing. The United States had long taken the view that automatic licensing deterred trade by burdening it with unnecessary red tape and should therefore be abolished. The United States proposed that the only useful function that automatic systems provided—namely collection of statistics—could better be achieved through other methods. However, the countries with automatic systems—principally the developing countries—flatly resisted this position. Their resistance came from several concerns. First, dropping automatic licensing would have required them to change their bureaucratic procedures; they encountered resistance from those agencies whose task it was to administer import licenses. Second, there was considerable support for the surveillance aspect of automatic licensing procedures, particularly in some countries where many economic activities require the permission of government authorities. Finally, the issue tended to get bound up in the more general question of quantitative restrictions, to which licensing procedures are often related. Developing countries were more sympathetic overall to the use of quantitative restrictions than the United States, and they were reluctant to dismantle the administrative procedures whereby such restrictions might be implemented.

In the preparatory work for the Tokyo Round, GATT participants had by June 1972 developed two *ad referendum* texts on import licensing: one on automatic import licensing, and the other on licensing to administer import restrictions. Neither document had gone very far to reconcile the basic difference on automatic licensing, although there was a fair measure of agreement on other issues. For example, the former code limited the amount of documentation that could be required in the application process, and placed certain restrictions on the procedures for handling applications, such as a turnaround time of five working days or less and a prohibition against refusing licenses for minor errors in documentation. However, the issue of automatic licensing was effectively square-bracketed in the text. The developing countries proposed what was known as Alternative I: "Automatic licensing, where required, shall not be used to restrict imports." Alternative II, proposed by the United States, stated simply, "No automatic licensing shall be required for the importation of goods after———."[26] Because of the failure to get agreement on this point, the overall code had little chance of winning general approval.

The second code contained a series of provisions designed to apply when a licensing system is used to administer quotas or other import restrictions. The emphasis in these provisions was on the timely publication of information by the importing government, and on the development of licensing practices that would ensure timely and reasonable treatment for importers. For example, government authorities would be required to publish "all useful information concerning formalities

[26] "Quantitative Restrictions (Including Import Prohibitions and So-Called Voluntary Restraints) and Import Licensing Procedures: Note by the Secretariat," GATT docs., MTN/NTM/W/2, April 3, 1975, 15.

for filing applications for licenses,"[27] and, where licensing was done in conjunction with fixed quotas, all information relevant to the quotas was required to be available as well. The latter provision was significant because it would eliminate the obvious abuses of the secret quota. Regarding the treatment of importers, the draft code would require that the processing of applications be "as short as possible" and that applicants should be given the reason for refusal of requests, along with the right to appeal.

The right of appeal constituted a significant step in increasing the openness and fairness of licensing procedures, and in some countries would have necessitated a change in established practice. Perhaps as an indicator that impartiality in import licensing was not internationally established, it can be noted that the most contentious section of the draft code concerned discrimination in licensing practices. Article 1, which was square-bracketed to indicate lack of consensus, read as follows: "Licensing systems to administer import restrictions shall not be designed nor operated in such a manner as to prohibit imports from certain sources or discriminate between sources of imports."[28] The disagreement on this article demonstrated, as did the dispute over automatic licensing more generally, that many trading nations were unwilling to forgo licensing procedures as an instrument of trade policy.

The establishment of the draft codes in 1972 represented a high-water mark in GATT work on import licensing, and there was little follow-up immediately before or after the Tokyo Declaration in 1973. In 1975, import licensing was folded into the work on quantitative restrictions, and a subgroup was established to carry on the negotiation in this area. This action effectively reduced the importance of import licensing. In comparison with quantitative restrictions, import licensing was viewed more as a nuisance than as a barrier to trade, and most of the subsequent discussion focused, albeit unproductively, on the former. It was not until mid-1978, when U.S. views on automatic import licensing had moderated, that the Tokyo Round participants were able to pick up the existing draft codes on import licensing and complete an agreement.

Quantitative Restrictions (QR's)

Quantitative restrictions are probably the most troublesome area in modern GATT relations. Ironically this area is also one where GATT has

[27] Ibid., 18.
[28] Ibid., 17.

111

posted its most impressive achievements. The negotiations leading to the General Agreement in 1947 were dominated by discussions of QR's, as nations sought to construct a legal system that would dismantle the quota systems that were established in the 1930s and which continued in place throughout World War II. The subsequent activity in the early years of GATT focused on the removal of quotas, and, along with the complementary work done in the Organization for European Economic Cooperation (OEEC), these efforts were largely successful in removing the quotas on industrial products applied by the developed nations. The problem today is principally in agriculture, where quotas continue to be prevalent, and in the different approaches taken on the use of quotas by the developed and less-developed members of GATT.

The position of the General Agreement on QR's is one of flat opposition, with very few exceptions. Article 11 states that "No prohibitions or restrictions other than duties, taxes or other charges, whether made effective through quotas, import or export licenses or other measures, shall be instituted or maintained by any contracting party." The major exception to this provision was for balance-of-payments reasons, which created a legal relationship between QR's and monetary instability. As European currencies regained convertibility in the 1950s, it was expected that the rationale for, and the use of, QR's would be discontinued. For the most part, this is what occurred, particularly on industrial products. However, in the agricultural area, nations found that domestic producers had become so dependent on existing quotas that it was politically impossible to remove them. These QR's became known as "residual" restrictions. Such restrictions were blatantly inconsistent with Article 11, although a technical argument could be made that they were "legal" under the Protocol of Provisional Application, which made allowances for domestic regulations in force before the General Agreement was signed. Furthermore these restrictions were very numerous. In the early 1960s, GATT made an effort to inventory the residual restrictions maintained by members. The list ran to over one hundred pages, and nearly all of the major trading nations, including the United States and the present EC nations, had a large number of entries.[29]

The opposition to QR's is largely based on their unfavorable effects on the free flow of international trade. More than tariffs, which affect trade indirectly through price, QR's directly affect the quantity of goods that can be exchanged, and consequently they have greater capacity to seal off a national economy from the international market. QR's thus represent a complete break from the concept of market exchanges, and

[29] Dam, *The GATT*, 165.

therefore act as a disincentive to increased economic efficiency, either for the protected domestic producer or his foreign counterpart. A second effect of QR's on trade is achieved through their administration. Unlike tariffs, which are a relatively open and unchanging (in the short run) form of protection, QR's can be administered in a way that allows maximum capacity for manipulation by the authorities in the importing country. Quotas can be openly published or secret, and can be rapidly adjusted to meet the needs of the domestic market. Hence the uncertainty that is created for exporters exacerbates the breakdown in trade beyond that caused by the quota itself.

The opposition to QR's in GATT has on occasion approached the status of a crusade, particularly on the part of U.S. negotiators.[30] Certainly it is true, as was noted by one GATT staffer, that ". . . if what you see the GATT doing is Good, then QR's are Bad!"[31] But the problem is that free trade is not seen as an unqualified benefit by any member of GATT. The European nations have defended the use of QR's as a necessary instrument of agricultural (and social) policy since the mid-1950s, and have made extensive use of QR's in the CAP of the EC. For their part, the developing countries have insisted on the right to use QR's as a necessary part of their development programs. A further problem is that virtually all GATT members, including the United States, are badly compromised on the issue of QR's. For example, the United States maintains a number of restrictions under the Agricultural Adjustment Act, which weakens its case against the European nations. Furthermore the United States has made use in recent years of voluntary export restraints (VER's) on products like textiles, steel, and meat. Since VER's operate like quotas, and certainly have been negotiated under the threat of legislated quotas, the United States has badly compromised its argument against the use of quotas by the developing countries. The result of the inconsistent positions taken by the United States and other countries is that the GATT itself is badly compromised in the area of QR's. As legal scholar Kenneth Dam has noted, ". . . the conclusion is inescapable that the developments in [the QR] area, more than in any other, have served to undermine the legalistic approach of the draftsmen of the General Agreement."[32]

Because of their continuing importance in international trade and GATT diplomacy, it was obvious that QR's would be included as a subject for negotiation in the Tokyo Round. The early phase of the work

[30] For example, Jackson, *World Trade*, 309, has quoted a U.S. negotiator at one of the preparatory sessions leading up to the GATT as follows: "Of all the forms of restrictionism ever devised by the mind of man, the Quantitative Restriction is the worst."
[31] Personal interview.
[32] Dam, *The GATT*, 166.

consisted mainly in codifying the extensive documentation that had been collected in GATT. Quantitative restrictions touched a number of different areas of GATT activities, and as a result information on them was gathered from sources as disparate as a GATT-produced "Study of Textiles" (GATT doc. 43797), reports from a Joint Working Group on Import Restrictions, various background notes by the secretariat, and, of course, the inventory of NTM's. In March 1973, Working Group #4 of the Committee on Trade in Industrial Products attempted to narrow the differences on QR's and to produce some documentation that might serve as a basis for subsequent multilateral negotiation. The result was two draft texts of possible solutions for the elimination of QR's.

The first text was proposed by the developing countries, and was directed exclusively at the developed countries. The text called for an overall gradual liberalization and elimination of QR's, as well as of export restraints (i.e., VER's), to be undertaken during the course of the Tokyo Round. The countries participating in this action were identified as follows: "Each individual developed contracting party shall contribute according to the relative importance of its quantitative restrictions of all types."[33] The text further prohibited any new QR's, and called upon parties to carry out progressive quota increases on products now embargoed or affected by export restraints. No mention was made of any action to be taken by developing countries.

The second text was put forward by the United States. It made a distinction between legal and illegal QR's, and proposed that nations maintaining the latter eliminate them outright at the beginning of the negotiation or pay compensation to other GATT members. The former would be subject to negotiation in the Tokyo Round, and the purpose of the negotiation would be to devise an "overall plan for the elimination of QR's . . . inconsistent with the General Agreement but legal under waivers or protocols of accession."[34]

The two texts indicate how far apart nations were on the subject of QR's. Not only was there a division on basic issues such as the distinction between legal and illegal QR's and on the obligations of developing countries in the QR area, but there was also serious disagreement on other important aspects of the problem. Some of these disagreements

[33] "Synthesis of Suggestions for Extending Differential Treatment to Developing Countries in the Field of Quantitative Restrictions: Note by the Secretariat," GATT docs., MTN/3B/15, May 27, 1974, 10.

[34] Ibid., 10. It should be noted that few nations accepted the distinction made by the United States between legal and illegal QR's, which was candidly admitted in a U.S. document summarizing the MTN: "Most other countries do not want to make any distinction between legal and illegal restrictions on the grounds that whether legal or not, they restrict trade" (U.S. House of Representatives, *Background and Status*, 32).

were definitional. For example, was the variable levy maintained by the EC in its Common Agricultural Policy a QR, or, as the EC negotiators insisted, did it fall outside the scope of the consultations on QR's? A similar definitional problem involved VER's: Were VER's to be considered as QR's, or, as the developing countries contended, should they rather be taken up in the negotiations on safeguards and escape-clause actions? Other questions concerned whether QR's could be applied in a discriminatory manner (which they clearly had been in the past); and whether textiles, on which there are previously existing international agreements, should be included in the negotiation on QR's. None of these questions were resolved in the preparatory work and early negotiation of the Tokyo Round, and the effort at negotiation itself only seemed to highlight, and possibly to exacerbate, the longstanding divisions between GATT members.

By 1975, it was becoming apparent that there was little likelihood that a multilateral code-type agreement would emerge from the negotiations on QR's. Consequently, a proposal was circulated by the Canadian delegation to proceed on the basis of specific (i.e., bilateral) requests and offers, and to monitor multilaterally the progress of the negotiation.[35] This proposal was not greeted enthusiastically by the developing countries, which, because of their weaker position in negotiating individually with developed nations, preferred a multilateral approach over a bilateral one. However, there was little alternative, for a multilateral solution was impossible and events were inevitably moving in the direction of bilateral negotiations. After 1975, multilateral discussion of QR's became increasingly a pro forma exercise, while substantive negotiation tended to be done in bilateral contacts between individual countries. Despite the change in venue, the Tokyo Round never did accomplish a significant reduction in QR's. As the official GATT summary of the negotiation noted, "At the conclusion of the Negotiations it was evident that the offers made in response to these [bilateral] requests would leave a large body of [quantitative] restrictions still intact."[36]

ISSUES BEFORE THE TOKYO ROUND, 1973–1974: NON-TEXT NEGOTIATION

In addition to the four areas above where *ad referendum* agreements had been drafted, the early period of the Tokyo Round took up several contentious issues that had been long before the GATT. These included

[35] "Proposal by the Canadian Delegation to the Sub-Group: 'Quantitative Restrictions,' " GATT docs., MTN/NTM/W/6, April 21, 1975.
[36] GATT, *Tokyo Round*, 87.

subsidies and countervailing duties, multilateral safeguards, and tropical products. The first two involved legal interpretations of members' obligations under the General Agreement, and were in a sense fundamental constitutional questions for the GATT trading system. The last dealt with products principally of concern to developing countries, the treatment of which got bound up in the broader issue of the relations between developed and developing countries within GATT.

Subsidies and Countervailing Duties

Subsidies have been one of the most controversial instruments of commercial policy throughout the life of GATT. Countervailing duties, used by some nations to offset the trade effects of subsidies, have been no less controversial than subsidies. Because the use of subsidies by GATT members was widespread, and rapidly increasing, in the years prior to the Tokyo Round, there could be no doubt that the trade negotiation would have to tackle these two subjects. And since the prospects of stagflation in the industrialized countries, already apparent in the early years of the Tokyo Round, promised even greater reliance on subsidies by major trading countries, it was imperative that the negotiation make some progress in this area.

The main difficulty with negotiating subsidies and countervailing duties in GATT has been knowing where to begin. Subsidies are generally understood to be a government-sponsored incentive to industry, but they are not defined with any precision in the GATT. The original provision of the General Agreement on subsidies was Article 16, which simply required any member maintaining a subsidy that had trade effects to notify GATT and to discuss with other interested parties the possibility of limiting the subsidization. On countervailing duties, the GATT was more specific. In Article 6, which is entitled Antidumping and Countervailing Duties, a countervailing duty is defined as a "special duty levied for the purpose of offsetting any bounty or subsidy bestowed . . . [on] . . . any merchandise." Although this definition is clear, the General Agreement was nowhere as specific about the application of countervailing duties, and the comparison with antidumping duties is instructive. Dumping, or the exportation of products at less than normal market value, was generally agreed to be unacceptable in commercial relations, and therefore GATT signatories readily acknowledged in Article 6 that antidumping duties should be used to "offset or prevent" dumping. No similar acknowledgement was provided for countervailing duties, undoubtedly because GATT members were deeply divided over the legitimacy of subsidization practices. Article 6 simply defined countervailing duties and specified certain restrictions on their use,[37] but beyond this offered little guidance for application or further negotiation.

The difficulty of negotiating subsidies and countervailing duties can be seen in the Michelin case involving Canada and the United States. In 1970, the federal government of Canada and the provincial government of Nova Scotia offered a package of incentives to the Michelin Company of France to locate a tire manufacturing plant in Nova Scotia. Included in these incentives were subsidies from the federal Department of Regional Economic Expansion, designed to offset the cost of locating a world-scale manufacturing plant in an economically underdeveloped region some distance from major markets. Some portion of the tires produced at this plant were subsequently exported to the United States, where authorities sought to apply countervailing duties to offset the federal subsidy granted to Michelin. The ensuing clash between the Canadian and United States governments underscored the dilemma of trying to create international rules in this policy area. The Canadian government insisted on its right to use subsidies to promote regional expansion, and pointed out that countervailing duties would undermine a legitimate domestic policy of a trading partner. The United States government took the position that the subsidy created an unfair cost advantage for Michelin tires, which were competing in the American market with tires of American firms not enjoying similar government assistance. The issue, which has cost the Michelin plant about $9 million since the countervailing duty was imposed in 1973, clearly demonstrates that the subsidies area raised difficult problems of commercial policy.[38]

The main issue in GATT negotiations on countervailing duties has been the role of an injury test in deciding when such duties are appropriate. Some nations, principally the United States, have domestic legislation that permits countervailing actions without a prior determination of whether a foreign subsidy has caused material injury to domestic firms. Such legislation is inconsistent with Article 6, but since it was in effect before the United States entered GATT, it is generally considered legal under the terms of the Protocol of Provisional Application. The lack of an injury test in United States legislation has been the

---

[37] Two important restrictions were that the countervailing duty may not exceed the subsidy determined to have been granted, and that the duty may not be levied unless the subsidy granted causes or threatens to cause material injury to an established domestic industry in the importing country.

[38] Jennifer Grass, "Michelin Gets Help as the Competition Howls," *Financial Post*, June 4, 1980.

source of bitter criticism from America's trading partners, partly on the symbolic ground that the United States has avoided one of the important legal obligations of the GATT, and partly because the lack of an injury test has left the United States government free to countervail without demonstrable economic justification. The United States has generally refused to negotiate the issue, on the ground that subsidies are the prior question and should therefore be dealt with first. As a result of this standoff, GATT has made little progress over the years in refining the rules of countervailing duties as they applied to subsidies. Considerable progress was made however in further defining the notion of material injury in countervail actions over dumping, in connection with the Antidumping code negotiated at the Kennedy Round. The procedures included in the code bore an obvious similarity to countervailing in subsidy cases, and they served as a useful analogy in the later negotiation over subsidies in the Tokyo Round.

Unlike countervailing duties, subsidies have been a continuing subject of GATT activity, with the result that important additions have been made to Article 16. In 1955, a review session of the contracting parties added additional provisions to Article 16 (now known as Section B), which dealt with export subsidies. Specifically, Section B stipulated that parties should "seek to avoid the use of subsidies on their export of primary products" and that in cases where subsidies were used they should not be applied in a manner that gave the subsidizing country "more than an equitable share of world export trade in that product." For nonprimary products, Section B required parties to cease any export subsidy on a product "which resulted in the sale of such product for export at a price lower than the comparable price charged for the like product in the domestic market." Section B did not specify any firm date for implementation, and hence a subsequent declaration was signed in 1960 which provided a method for joint implementation by developed countries.[39] The declaration also listed eight practices that were to be banned, including, for example, currency retention schemes that involve a bonus on exports, remission of direct taxes, and subsidized insurance or credit for purposes of export. In a legal area where definitions are especially difficult to achieve, the list provided a desirable concreteness to GATT policymaking on subsidies.

The activity in GATT since 1947 clarified the areas of disagreement on subsidies and countervailing duties, and it produced an advance in

[39] The declaration was signed by sixteen developed GATT nations, including the EC members and the United States. See "Subsidies and Countervailing Duties: Note by the Secretariat," GATT docs., MTN/3B/21, September 30, 1974, 3.

members' legal obligations to one another. The 1960 declaration demonstrated that there was little disagreement in GATT that developed countries should not make use of export subsidies on trade in nonprimary products. However, movement from this formula in any direction caused difficulties. The obligations of developing countries regarding subsidies were unclear, although there was a general tendency to treat them more permissively on matters of subsidies. Regarding the nature of the subsidy, the clear agreement to prohibit export subsidies evaporated entirely when the subsidy under consideration served domestic purposes other than the stimulation of exports. Such subsidies were known as domestic (or production) subsidies,[40] and nations were generally unwilling to have these instruments of domestic economic policy subjected to international regulation within GATT. Finally, the 1960 declaration on nonprimary products most clearly did not apply to agricultural products. For most nations, particularly the Europeans, agricultural subsidies were an essential part of national economic management and were not a negotiable issue within the GATT. Their use was widespread and growing, and the only international discipline to which they were subject was the obligation in Article 16(B) that recommended against the use of agricultural export subsidies to gain a more-than-equitable share of world export trade.

In the preparatory work for the Tokyo Round, there was little doubt that subsidies and countervailing duties would be a major issue in the upcoming negotiation. The NTM inventory recorded a substantial number of notifications in this area, which made the issue even more unavoidable. The positions of the major trading nations were essentially unchanged, however, with the result that the work from the preparatory sessions of the Tokyo Round through the first two years of the negotiation itself was wholly unproductive. Most participants, especially the EC, pressed the United States to incorporate the material-injury provision called for by Article 6 in U.S. countervailing legislation. The U.S. response was that subsidies were a prior issue, and that an agreement that provided discipline on the use of subsidies would itself settle the problem of countervail procedures.[41] There the matter rested. The ini-

[40] The aforementioned case of the Michelin plant is arguably an example of a domestic subsidy.

[41] The U.S. position was summarized in the following excerpt: "The United States has underscored the point that emphasis on CVD's [i.e., countervailing duties] is misdirected, since subsidies, not CVD's are the basic problem. Subsidies are serious trade distortions that must precede countervail action. Therefore, why should the onus be on the countervailer rather than on the subsidizer? Logic suggests that a satisfactory solution on subsidies should largely resolve the countervail issue. In any event, the United States has made

tial negotiations in the Tokyo Round perpetuated a deadlock that was inherent in the GATT itself. The increased exposure of members to the problem produced some technical work that proved useful in later negotiation,[42] but it did little to settle basic differences.

Multilateral Safeguards

The issue of safeguards goes to the roots of GATT as an instrument for regulating and expanding international trade. One of the major goals of the original contracting parties was to provide stable conditions of access to the markets of the respective member states. The assumption underlying the General Agreement was that once QR's were substantially eliminated through outright prohibition, the main instrument for protecting domestic markets would be *ad valorem* customs duties. Thus the task of providing stable market access would be achieved by a gradual reduction and binding of duties through multilateral negotiations. It was recognized that this process would need to have safety-value procedures to allow nations experiencing unforeseen economic difficulties to backtrack on the negotiated commitments made to their trading partners. Such procedures were generally called safeguards, and their use was defended by those most committed to the concept of free trade. On the one hand, it was held that the existence of safeguards encouraged nations to go further in negotiations to liberalize trade than they otherwise might have gone. On the other hand, it was generally agreed that safeguards increased the flexibility and resilience of the international trade regime overall, and reduced prospects that a disturbance in one part of the system might cause nations to back away from the entire process of trade liberalization.

There are numerous safeguarding provisions in the General Agreement of one sort or another. These range from a general requirement for members to consult on matters arising from the agreement (Article 22) to an enumeration of specific circumstances that might permit a member to maintain trade barriers, such as balance-of-payments difficulties (Article 11) or national-security concerns (Article 21). However, the major safeguarding provision of the GATT is Article 19, which permits GATT members to reimpose barriers on the general grounds that domestic producers are suffering serious injury from foreign imports.

---

clear that there can be no clear resolution of the CVD problem except in the context of a satisfactory settlement of the problem of subsidies on both industrial and agricultural products." (U.S. House of Representatives, *Background and Status*, 27).

[42] For example, the 1960 list of prohibited export subsidies was expanded in committee work, but it was illustrative only and not binding on GATT members.

This article has been the basis for most safeguarding actions through-out the history of GATT, and it was the focus of the safeguards negoti-ation in the Tokyo Round.

Article 19 gives nations the right to take emergency action to apply protective measures, but outlines the circumstances in which such ac-tions are justified. Specifically a nation must show that the product on which the action is being taken is being imported in increasing quan-tities such as to cause or threaten serious injury to domestic producers of competitive products. Article 19 also specifies that the increased im-ports must arise as a result of both "unforeseen developments" and ex-isting obligations incurred under the GATT agreement, but the latter provision has never been a significant constraint on nations resorting to safeguarding actions.[43] However, the provisions for assessing in-creased imports, and injury therefrom, have been incorporated into na-tional administrative procedures for trade management, and in some countries such as the United States, Canada, and Australia, they have a basis in statutory law as well. In the case of the United States, safe-guarding actions are currently provided for in Article 201 of the Trade Agreements Act of 1979, which empowers a United States governmen-tal regulatory agency (the United States International Trade Commis-sion) to recommend import restrictions to the president in cases where it deems increased imports have been the cause of injury to domestic producers.[44] Normally, actions of the ITC would be preceded by public hearings, in which both exporters and importers would be expected to present their case. In other jurisdictions, safeguarding procedures are a matter for administrative discretion. For example, Article 226 of the Treaty of Rome provides for safeguarding procedures during the tran-sition period in the formation of the EEC. The article did not contain the concept of injury, although it did elaborate a notion of "serious diffi-culties," and it left the action that might be taken entirely with the Commission. Thus the specific procedures for applying Article 19 have differed from one GATT member to the next.

Safeguarding actions have been taken frequently in the history of GATT. By the start of the Tokyo Round negotiations, GATT records re-vealed that there had been sixty-four actions by fourteen GATT mem-

---

[43] "Group 3(d)—Safeguards: Factual Note by the Secretariat," GATT docs., MTN/3D/1, August 23, 1974, 3.

[44] It should be noted that the concept of safeguarding actions in U.S. trade legislation predated the GATT, and that the incorporation of these procedures in the GATT was largely a result of the insistence of U.S. negotiators. For further information, see Jackson, *World Trade*, ch. 23, "The Escape Clause and Market Disruption (Article XIX)."

bers.[45] By far, most (i.e., forty-four) of these actions were undertaken by three states, namely the United States, Australia, and Canada. The fact that the heaviest users of Article 19 procedures are also "statutory" states suggests a relationship between the openness with which safeguards provisions are promulgated and the frequency with which they are used. This point has been the subject of some controversy within GATT. On the one hand, the statutory nations have advanced the argument that open safeguards procedures provide greater fairness for importers and exporters alike, and further insure that administrative actions which effectively function as safeguards get labeled as such; on the other hand, nonstatutory nations have held that open procedures encourage the evasion of GATT obligations by making it more difficult for governments to deflect quietly the protectionist pressures that arise within their constituencies. At base, this controversy is a reflection of different styles of government, and it became an issue in one way or another in several of the code negotiations at the Tokyo Round, including the negotiation over safeguards.

One point that was not controversial about the operation of Article 19 was the expectation that safeguarding actions would be taken on a nondiscriminatory basis. While this is not explicit in the text of Article 19, it was nevertheless clearly the intention of the drafters of the GATT, and GATT practice has been wholly consistent with this interpretation. Since 1947, Article 19 actions have taken the form of increases in bound tariffs in about two-thirds of the cases and the imposition of QR's in the other third, but in every case the action has affected equally the trade of all exporting countries. At the time of Japan's accession to GATT in 1955, some members sought to retain certain discriminatory QR's against Japanese exports, and it was suggested that an additional clause should be inserted in Article 19 to permit safeguards on other than an MFN basis. The rationale for this position was that if nations were required to apply on an MFN basis those restrictions they currently had (or might have) in force against Japan, it would lead to a general increase in trade protectionism. In the end no changes were made to Article 19, but rather nations avoided the problem by invoking Article 35, which permitted existing GATT members to suspend MFN obligations against new members. This affair was significant because it raised the issue of the selective (i.e., discriminatory) application of safeguarding procedures against particular nations that are thought to be causing a trade problem. It was on this issue that the negotiation on the safeguards code at the Tokyo Round ultimately foundered.[46]

[45] "Group 3(d)—Safeguards" (note 43 above), Annex C, 17-23.

[46] Another historical precedent bearing on the notion of selectivity was the concept of

By the time the Tokyo Round was launched in the early 1970s, it had been apparent for some time that Article 19 was not accomplishing the purposes for which it had been intended. The major cause of instability in the trading world tended to come from rapid increases in exports in particular industries, such as textiles and steel, and from particular countries, such as Japan and the newly industrializing countries such as Taiwan and Korea. The dilemma for importing nations was that not to act risked severe dislocation in domestic markets, while action (presumably nondiscriminatory) under Article 19 would disrupt the trade of third countries that were not the cause of the problem. To avoid this dilemma, importing nations like the United States began to conclude bilateral agreements with selected exporting nations with the intention of limiting exports of certain products. These agreements, known as VER's, have been typically struck between nations of dissimilar bargaining power, and accepted by exporting nations in order to forestall the imposition of more stringent import controls. VER's have been common in the textile sector between importers like the United States and the European Community and smaller exporters such as Japan, Korea, Taiwan, and Hong Kong. Other highly visible examples of VER's have been the agreements between the United States and Japan, and Canada and Japan, which restricted automobile exports from the latter to an agreed annual quota. Many VER's have been negotiated openly with notification being made to GATT, although there has been widespread suspicion that other efforts at trade restrictions have not been made public knowledge.[47] In either case, however, these agreements have been outside the GATT framework, and their existence has demonstrated that the safeguards provisions of the GATT were not adequate for the trade-adjustment problems of the 1970s.[48]

"market disruption," which was examined by a working party and subsequently defined by the GATT contracting parties in 1960 as being, inter alia, "a sharp . . . increase of imports of particular products from particular sources" (BISD, Ninth Supplement, 1962, 26). Some GATT members sought to incorporate in general GATT procedures defense mechanisms against market disruption. Such mechanisms would of necessity have been selective and discriminatory, and their inclusion was successfully resisted and the attempt abandoned. However, market disruption was subsequently incorporated in international trade treaty law in the Arrangement regarding International Trade in Textiles which came into being on January 1, 1974.

[47] For example, V. Curzon Price notes that VER's can be constituted by a simple exchange of letters between a trade minister from a developed (presumably strong) country and one from a developing (presumably weak) country. In this exchange, the former notes that imports have become a problem, and requests that export growth be kept within "reasonable" bounds in order to avoid the application of more stringent import controls; the latter merely acknowledges the request of the former. The question is: Is this an agreement, or is it not? See Price, "Surplus Capacity," 310.

[48] Besides VER's, there were two other types of trade-restricting agreements that grew

It was apparent to the framers of the Tokyo Declaration that safeguards would be a major issue in the upcoming negotiation. In the first place, it would be necessary to improve the safeguards mechanisms of the GATT in order to remove the incentive for nations to make restrictive bilateral agreements that were themselves endangering the GATT role in the international trade system. Secondly, an improved safeguards mechanism would be needed to encourage nations to liberalize trade in the Tokyo Round negotiations. This had been the old GATT rationale for Article 19 and it appeared to be even more valid in the period when successive GATT-inspired negotiations had reduced tariffs to a very low level and hence left national economies very much exposed to one another. Finally, the issue of safeguards was very high on the agenda of Third World nations; they bore the brunt of the bilateral procedures and sought to get safeguards incorporated into the multilateral, presumably nondiscriminatory, framework of the GATT.

The negotiation on safeguards was begun with a decision by the Trade Negotiations Committee in July 1974 that Group 3(d) should commence technical and analytical work with the goal of isolating the major problems to be faced in substantive negotiations. In response to this decision, the GATT secretariat prepared two lengthy factual notes on safeguards provisions of the GATT agreement,[49] and the political issues involved were thoroughly aired the following October in a formal meeting of Group 3(d). It was quickly determined that the major problems facing the group were whether safeguards measures could be applied on a discriminatory basis, what conditions constituted market disruption and serious injury, and what provisions would be made for international and/or GATT surveillance of safeguards measures. National positions at the October 1974 meeting were tentative, but they revealed a considerable divergence on some of the major issues, such as the selective application of safeguards. Following the 1974 meeting, very little substantive negotiation on safeguards took place until 1978, although there were meetings of Group 3(d) in 1975 and 1976, and several proposals were submitted by some developing countries over this period. It is probable that, apart from the historic difficulty with the safeguards area, the slowness of the negotiation on this subject was due to the general impasse that occurred at the Tokyo Round until mid-

---

up during the 1970s, one between national governments in importing countries and industry in the exporting country, and the other between industries in exporting and importing countries. Generally these agreements are known as orderly marketing arrangements (OMA's). They have been used in product areas such as steel and color televisions.

[49] See "Group 3(d)—Safeguards for Maintenance of Access: Factual Note by the Secretariat," GATT docs., MTN/3D/2, August 30, 1974.

1977, and a perception on the part of the participants that the safeguards negotiation ought not to proceed faster than other areas in the negotiation. At bottom, safeguards are a restrictive action, and it was successfully argued that nations should make progress on the liberalizing aspects of the Tokyo Round before they negotiated measures that might reduce the scope of that liberalization. As with other areas of the Tokyo Round, the early negotiation mainly served to build the factual basis on which participants would later begin the process of exchanging proposals.

Tropical Products

One of the major objectives of the developing countries at the Tokyo Round was to improve access in developed-country markets for their exports of tropical products, principally agricultural products. Some effort had been made toward achieving this objective in the Kennedy Round, but that negotiation did not produce very significant concessions for developing countries. In the interval between the Kennedy and Tokyo rounds, the developing countries maintained the pressure in this product area, with the result that the GATT secretariat was called upon to produce a series of studies on trade in tropical products. These studies compiled basic data on production, trade flows, prices, and export receipts on a number of the principal tropical products, such as bananas, tea, and cocoa. The studies also provided detailed background information at the tariff-line-item level on measures in developed countries that affected access for tropical products, including barriers such as post–Kennedy Round tariff levels, and a wide variety of NTM's. These studies were augmented by continued discussion over the 1967–73 period in the Trade and Development Committee of GATT and in the smaller Special Group on Trade in Tropical Products. By the time the Tokyo Round was launched, a "solid basis for negotiations" had been established through the ordinary activities of GATT.[50]

The Tokyo Declaration of 1973 designated tropical products as a special and priority sector, and underscored its importance by delegating one of the six TNC groups to pursue the negotiations in this area. With the secretariat studies to guide it, Group "Tropical Products" quickly identified the main problems faced by exporters. Historically the tropical-products sector has been a difficult area of trade relations, in part because the products are predominantly agricultural, which itself is an area least receptive to trade liberalization, and in part because

[50] GATT, *Tokyo Round*, 37.

many tropical products are import-competing or are themselves produced in temperate-zone countries. Consequently importing countries have maintained a wide variety of protective devices which came under the scrutiny of Group "Tropical Products." One such device was the tariff on processed products, and particularly the maintenance of ascending tariff duties depending on the degree of processing, which generally impeded the establishment of processing industries in less-developed countries. Another problem was the maintenance of preferential trading arrangements in which some developing countries received more favorable treatment than others not party to such agreements. Finally, QR's, internal taxes, health standards, and other types of nontariff barriers have been employed by developed nations against developing nations' exports of tropical products.[51]

After identifying the main problems of exporting nations, Group "Tropical Products" turned to the question of negotiating procedures. The developing nations generally pressed for a multilateral approach, which was a position they had taken earlier without success in the Kennedy Round. Various multilateral techniques for handling tropical products were proposed. One was to treat tropical products as a single sector, and to negotiate across-the-board reductions in tariffs and other forms of protection. Another method might concentrate on eliminating tariff escalation based on degree of processing. Another proposal was to negotiate stabilization arrangements for particular tropical products, which had the added advantage that it could protect exporters against extreme price fluctuations as well as providing increased market access for their products. Despite the pressure from the developing countries, however, it was quickly obvious that multilateral techniques on tropical products were not acceptable to the developed nations. These countries contended that some tropical products were being dealt with in the agricultural negotiations in the Tokyo Round, and that some multilateral techniques, such as price stabilization schemes, were better left to international forums other than GATT negotiations. The impasse on negotiating approach meant that the only method for proceeding would be through bilateral requests and offers on specific products. This method was adopted by Group "Tropical Products" in its meetings of April and June of 1975.[52] The group drew up guidelines for the negotiation of tropical products, and invited developing countries to submit initial request lists for concessions from importing na-

[51] For further information, see U.S. House of Representatives, *Background and Status*, 49–52.

[52] "Meeting of July 1975: Statement by the Chairman of Group 'Tropical Products,'" GATT docs., MTN/W/16, July 16, 1975.

tions. It was assumed the group would be kept informed of the progress of the negotiations, and would explore any subjects that subsequently might appear to be amenable to multilateral solutions.

Adoption of request-and-offer procedures expedited the negotiation on tropical products, and by July 1975 some twenty-five developing countries had submitted their initial lists. These lists ended up containing requests not only on tropical products, but also on a broad range of products including agriculture, raw materials and minerals, and semi-manufactures; in effect, they represented "shopping lists" of concessions developing countries sought from developed nations. The lists, plus the technical work long since completed by the GATT secretariat, set the stage for productive negotiations in Group "Tropical Products" during the difficult 1975–77 period of the Tokyo Round. In some cases, particularly on tropical products such as coffee, tea, spices, and cocoa products, MFN concessions and GSP contributions were extended in 1977 on a nonreciprocal basis by developed countries.[53] These constituted in effect the first tangible results from the Tokyo Round. Requests that were not responded to after 1977 were left for further bilateral negotiations or were incorporated into other areas of the Tokyo Round, such as the negotiations on tariffs and on agriculture. Group "Tropical Products" continued to meet occasionally after 1977 to review the progress of developing-country interests, but it did not have a central role in the negotiations between developed and developing countries.

By the end of 1974, the Tokyo Round was successfully launched and there were a series of concrete and important issues before the negotiation. Other issues were added in the 1975–77 period, demonstrating the sense of momentum produced by the negotiation and its capacity to embrace issues that might otherwise have been dealt with in other arenas. In most cases, considerable preliminary work had been done on the issues before the Tokyo Round. The issues themselves were by varying degrees divisive in the community of trading nations; however, all were negotiable, in the sense that nations had a reasonable prospect of reaching agreement on them. Above all, the issues constituted a realistic and meaningful agenda for an international economic negotiation. Such cannot always be said of multilateral economic negotiations, and on this point comparisons will be made between the Tokyo Round and the negotiation in UNCTAD of the Integrated Program for Commodities (IPC) in chapter 9 of this book.

[53] GATT, Tokyo Round, 156. The abbreviation GSP refers to the Generalized System of Preferences; for further information, see "The Framework Group" in ch. 4 below.

· 4 ·

EARLY PHASE, 1974–1977:
RESOLUTION OF THE PROBLEM IN AGRICULTURE

It is characteristic of large multilateral negotiations to move in spasms, with large spaces of time sandwiched between periods of useful activity. When a large negotiation is moving forward, it is a ponderous affair, with a long succession of meetings that gradually chip away at the subject matter of the exercise. The process can take on a machinelike quality, lurching along seemingly under the force of its own momentum. Yet the process is surprisingly delicate, and the mechanism of common endeavor which sustains it can easily be upset. When the negotiation has become stalled, it takes uncommon effort to pick up the pieces and reestablish the momentum.

This description would fit the Tokyo Round. It had taken a major effort at the political and technical level to launch the Tokyo Round. This effort had carried through the Tokyo Declaration of 1973 and into the bureaucratic planning for the negotiation. Then nothing happened: the process seemingly ground to a halt. There are several things that can cause a negotiation to become unhinged, and most seemed to befall the Tokyo Round during the years from 1974 to mid-1977. A negotiation can falter if the environment in which it is conducted is unpropitious. Such happened to the Tokyo Round in the Yom Kippur War of October 1973, which led to the Arab oil boycott and the subsequent rapid quadrupling of oil prices. To say this diverted attention from an international trade negotiation would be an exercise in understatement. Another problem that can derail an international negotiation is internal politics in a crucial country. In the Tokyo Round, internal disagreement over the Nixon-Ford trade bill insured that the U.S. administration would have no negotiating authority until 1975, and then one year later the attention of that administration became too diverted by presidential electoral politics to focus on a trade negotiation in Geneva. And finally, a negotiation can run into the most commonplace of difficulties, namely a blockage among the important parties as to the substantive issues before the negotiation. This took place in the Tokyo Round in the dispute over agricultural trade between the United States and the EC. The dispute was longstanding and profound. Like many serious substantive disputes in negotiation, it took on the guise of a pro-

128

cedural conflict and therefore created a wider blockage than its substantive importance warranted.

To sum up, the period 1974 to mid-1977 constituted down-time for the trade negotiation. Some work got done, but it was mainly technical work, especially the gathering and collating of data. Two new issues were introduced to the negotiation, namely government procurement and a package of legal modifications to the GATT that became known as the framework agreement, which were of special concern to the developing countries. Regular meetings were held over 1974–77 in some areas of the negotiation, such as the subgroups on grains and dairy products, but only minor matters were taken up. There was no progress on any major issue until after the breakthrough of mid-1977.

THE U.S. TRADE ACT OF 1974

International negotiations are typically conducted by a diplomatic instrument, but they proceed on instructions from a sovereign. In the EC, the Commission was delegated to conduct the Tokyo Round, but it depended on a grant of authority from the Council of Ministers, and it reported back to them. In the United States, on the matter of foreign trade the Constitution prescribes that the U.S. Congress is sovereign. Since the Reciprocal Trade Agreements Act (RTA) of 1934, the traditional U.S. approach to trade negotiation has been for Congress to extend a legislated grant of authority to the executive, specifying the substantive limits and the time period for the negotiation.

In the Kennedy Round negotiation, Congress granted a negotiating authority for five years to the Kennedy administration in the Trade Expansion Act (TEA) of 1962. At the outset, the trade negotiation had figured prominently in President John F. Kennedy's Grand Design for a close partnership between North America and Western Europe.[1] The negotiation was an important political initiative, and it had important economic results, because in reducing tariffs among the industrialized countries it reduced the divisiveness caused by the advance of European integration in the EC. However, from the standpoint of the mechanics

---

[1] President Kennedy made the political goals of his trade policy clear in introducing the trade legislation to Congress. "The success of our foreign policy depends in large measure upon the success of our foreign trade, and our maintenance of Western political unity depends in equally large measure upon the degree of Western economic unity. An integrated Western Europe, joined in trading partnership with the United States, will further shift the world balance of power to the side of freedom" ("Special Message to the Congress on Foreign Trade Policy," included as Appendix B in Preeg, *Traders and Diplomats*, 285–86).

of GATT negotiations, the Kennedy Round was an ordinary exercise. It was primarily a tariff negotiation and, if it differed from past negotiation in GATT, the difference was more in degree than in kind. It was also an ordinary exercise from the standpoint of U.S. legislative processes. The TEA of 1962 was significant because of its deep tariff-cutting authority, but the mechanism was entirely consistent with the history of American participation in trade negotiations. The act did not give the administration authority to conclude agreements on nontariff forms of protectionism that already by the mid-1960s were becoming increasingly prominent in international trading relations.

In the Tokyo Round, it was clear from the outset that it would be necessary to negotiate on nontariff measures (NTM's). This was problematic for the U.S. system from several perspectives. First, there was a problem of legislative process. The RTA/GATT procedures had dealt mainly with tariffs, and Congress had come to accept the practice of delegating (within limits) its tariff-setting powers to the executive. However, NTM's went into areas of Congress's mandate to regulate commerce other than tariff policy, and they often involved matters—such as product standards—that had little to do with international trade in their origin. The problem was that it would likely take a far-reaching grant of authority from the Congress to the president for the latter to carry out a meaningful negotiation with other countries on NTM's. This was a rerun of the same issue that had faced the Congress in 1934 when it first transferred to the executive the power to set tariff levels. That issue was whether important powers over the national economy should be transferred to an executive that would bring a more international set of values to policymaking than would Congress itself.

A second problem dealt with interest groups. Just as Congress was reluctant to transfer power to the executive, so also were special interests reluctant to see national legislation from which they benefited made vulnerable to change. Unlike tariffs, where economic interests at least accept in principle that change might occur, NTM's are often regarded as a permanent economic right. Indeed, at the same time that Congress was being asked by the administration to make certain NTM's negotiable with foreign countries, it was being pressed by economic interests to apply more rigorously certain mechanisms like countervailing duties that would become subject to negotiation. Thus the proposal to negotiate NTM's brought forward deep-seated opposition from the protectionist lobbies in Washington, whose self-interest motivated them to encourage Congress to resist an apparent diminution of its powers to regulate international trade.

Yet another problem was diplomatic. Because of the sovereignty of Congress in international commerce, the U.S. system is not well structured to engage in international commercial diplomacy.[2] The problem is that either Congress must extend its authority to the executive, something it is reluctant to do, or the executive must negotiate an agreement abroad on the assumption that it will later win congressional approval. The latter is a dangerous diplomatic procedure, and the Kennedy Round demonstrated those dangers. In the Kennedy Round, the United States entered into negotiations and signed the international antidumping code of 1967, although it had not received specific authority from Congress to do so. In defending the action, the administration claimed the code it had negotiated was not inconsistent with relevant U.S. legislation, namely the U.S. Antidumping Act of 1921. To make matters worse, the administration also negotiated and offered concessions (subject to congressional approval) on the American Selling Price (ASP) system of customs valuation, even though it was forewarned by the U.S. Senate that it lacked legislative authority.[3] Following the Kennedy Round, Congress did not repeal the ASP, which angered the Europeans but did not cause negotiating losses, because foreign concessions tied to the ASP had been made contingent on congressional action. However, events were more embarrassing on the antidumping code. Many in Congress felt they had been bypassed in the matter of antidumping, and in retaliation Congress passed legislation authorizing the relevant judicial body, the U.S. Tariff Commission, to ignore the international code, something the Tariff Commission was more than prepared to do. As a result, several countries such as Canada felt they had been denied benefits they had paid for during the negotiation of the code.[4] The implication of this unhappy experience was that it would be necessary for the United States to demonstrate that it had a reliable method for assuring congressional support for its concessions on NTM's before it could expect other nations to negotiate with it seriously in the upcoming Tokyo Round.

The passage of the Trade Act of 1974 through the U.S. Congress was a torturous affair. This story has been well told and the relevant facts

[2] This is a statement that could equally be made about the Council of Ministers in the EC. Neither the EC nor the United States has as efficient a system for international commercial negotiation as has a unitary parliamentary government like Japan, or even a federal parliamentary system like Canada. This point is further elaborated in ch. 8.

[3] This warning was adopted by voice vote in the Senate on June 29, 1966. See Pastor, *Congress*, 120.

[4] Marks and Malmgren have noted: "The representatives of Canada at the 1974 meeting of the Committee on Antidumping Practices, for example, stated that Canada had failed to obtain from the United States all the concessions that it thought it had bought and paid for in negotiating the code. This view is shared by other governments" ("Negotiating Nontariff Distortions," 391).

will only be summarized briefly.[5] In April 1973, President Richard Nixon sent a trade bill to Congress requesting, among other things, negotiating authority to conduct the Tokyo Round. Work on this bill had already been slowed by the presidential election in 1972, but the administration hoped for quick action in the Congress along the lines of Kennedy's trade bill of 1962, which had taken Congress eight months to enact. The timing was bad for seeking trade legislation from Congress. The year 1972 had seen a record trade imbalance, and in 1973 relations between President Nixon and Congress were beginning to break down over the Watergate issue. To make matters worse, the president had requested that the trade bill include congressional authorization to extend MFN (most-favored nation) status to the Soviet Union, which would have followed up on an obligation the United States had undertaken in a trade agreement made with the Soviets the previous year. The MFN issue was politically sensitive, and some advisers had recommended against including this matter in the trade bill.

The trade bill went first to the House of Representatives. As expected, the House modified the president's request for blanket authority to negotiate NTM's, and it adopted a proposal by Senator Henry Jackson and Congressman Charles A. Vanik to make MFN status for the Soviets conditional on a determination by the U.S. president that that country did not deny its citizens freedom to emigrate.[6] The MFN issue slowed passage in the House, and it was not until December 1983 that the legislation was approved, and by a vote of 272 to 140. Significantly, labor had strongly opposed the bill, and this had encouraged a large group of usually liberal northern Democrats to vote against the measure.

The bill then went to the Senate. This body is traditionally more responsive to special economic interests (e.g., agricultural) and also more protective of congressional powers vis-à-vis the executive. The Senate further restricted the negotiating authority of the president, and it wrote in protection for weak industries like textiles and footwear. The main point of contention, however, was the Soviet MFN issue, and on this essentially extraneous issue the Senate was blocked for almost one year. The Administration (and particularly Secretary of State Henry Kissinger) was determined to preserve détente with the Soviets and to prevent the MFN issue from being tied to Soviet emigration. It threatened to veto the trade act if it included a conditional MFN clause. Sen-

[5] See particularly Destler, *Foreign Economic Policy*; and Paula Stern, *Water's Edge*.

[6] This action was particularly directed against Soviet restrictions on Jewish emigration to Israel.

ator Jackson was equally determined to force a change in Soviet emigration policies. Both men were prepared to put the Soviet issue ahead of the trade bill. A compromise on this matter was finally effected, which incidentally led the Soviets angrily to reject America's conditional offer of MFN status, and the bill was approved by an overwhelming majority. The legislation went to a conference committee to resolve differences between the House and Senate versions, and in most cases the more restrictive Senate version prevailed. Organized labor persisted in its uncompromising opposition to the legislation, but by this point it had become isolated. The bill was finally approved by Congress shortly before the Christmas recess, and was signed into law by President Gerald Ford on January 3, 1975.[7]

The legislation was entitled the "Trade Act of 1974." It included a number of items besides negotiating authority for the Tokyo Round, such as relief from injury caused by foreign competition or unfair trade practices, and generalized preferences for less-developed countries. Despite the fact that the legislation gave the president new powers to retaliate against foreign protectionism, the act was essentially liberal, and certainly more liberal than the protectionist Mills bill of 1970.[8] As for negotiating authority, the act was particularly innovative. It solved the problem of creating a negotating instrument that would be acceptable to both Congress and foreign governments, and it provided direction for the president in terms of negotiating desiderata, although it went less far in this direction than had the EC's Overall Approach document.

The basic thrust of the Trade Act was found in Title 1, which provided for "Negotiating and Other Authority." Consistent with past negotiations, the act gave the president authority to eliminate tariffs below 5 percent, and to reduce tariffs above 5 percent by up to 60 percent, in conjunction with commensurate actions by other countries. On NTM's, the act stated simply: "Whenever the President determines . . . [the existence of any barriers] . . . , the President . . . may enter into trade agreements with foreign countries or instrumentalities providing for the harmonization, reduction, or elimination of such barriers."[9] In substantive terms it is clear the act conferred sweeping powers on the

---

[7] President Ford replaced President Richard Nixon following the latter's resignation in August 1974 over the Watergate scandal.

[8] The judgment that the Trade Act of 1974 was liberal is shared by Pastor, *Congress*, and Destler, *Foreign Economic Policy*. Destler credits the difference between the 1970 and 1974 actions in Congress to: (i) the improved environment for American trade following the monetary actions of 1971, and (ii) strong leadership in the U.S. executive at a level below the presidency.

[9] U.S. Government, *Trade Act of 1974*, 5.

president. The limitations that accompanied these powers were procedural, and they were of two types. The first addressed the problem of Congress's sovereignty over foreign commercial policy; the second dealt with relations with interest groups.

The Trade Act met the congressional problem by providing special procedures for writing the enabling legislation for any prospective trade agreements, which Congress had to approve or disapprove as a whole without amendments to the legislation. Specifically, the Trade Act required the president to give Congress ninety days' notification before entering into any trade agreement, and to transmit following such an agreement a copy of the agreement, draft of an implementing bill, and "a statement of his reasons as to how the agreement serves the interests of United States commerce."[10] Congress then had sixty days to act on the legislation; it could not amend, table, or otherwise delay the bill. In practice, this procedure meant that the major provisions of the implementing bill would be known to Congress for some time, and that the relevant committees (the House Ways and Means Committee and the Senate Finance Committee) would be required to work closely with the special trade representative during the transmittal phase. In order to insure that such cooperation occurred, the Trade Act went further to empower both the House and Senate to select five members (not more than three from the same political party) to be accredited to the U.S. delegation to the trade negotiations. Additionally, the chairmen of Ways and Means and of Finance were authorized to designate members (and/or committee staff personnel) to be official advisers for the purpose of receiving continuous briefings by the U.S. trade representative. In sum, these procedures were designed to assure that Congress would be kept abreast of the negotiation during the Tokyo Round, in order to avoid the gulf that had opened up between the administration and Congress during the Kennedy Round.

The second procedural limitation dealt with interest groups. The potential risk for the United States in the Tokyo Round was that an agreement might shape up in Geneva that would be resisted by major domestic economic interests, with consequent pressure being brought on Congress to repudiate the settlement. The Trade Act handled this problem by creating a system of private-sector committees to supply advice and information for U.S. negotiators. In the first place, the act created an Advisory Committee for Trade Negotiations (ACTN) to provide overall policy advice. The ACTN was a presidentially appointed committee composed of forty-five members from all sections of the United

---

[10] Ibid., 6.

States, representing labor, industry, agriculture, small business, service industries, retailers, consumer interests, and the general public. It was to meet frequently in Washington under the chairmanship of the U.S. trade representative, and it would be convened in Geneva as well, where it was briefed by the GATT secretariat and negotiators from other nations. Second, at a level below the ACTN, the Trade Act called for the creation of a general policy advisory committee for industry, labor, and agriculture respectively, and for yet a third level of advisory committees to be established at the sectoral level. The president was charged with taking the initiative to insure that these committees were established. Thus, as a result of the Trade Act, a vast network of specialized committees was set up below the ACTN composed of individuals drawn from the private sector. For manufacturers, there was a general Industrial Policy Advisory Committee (IPAC) and twenty-seven specialized Industry Sector Advisory Committees (ISAC's), of which ISAC number 13, Hand Tools, Cutlery, and Tableware, is an example. Labor was represented by a Labor Policy Advisory Committee (LPAC), and six LSAC's; and agriculture, by an Agricultural Policy Advisory Committee (APAC) and eight ASAC's.

The Trade Act provided that the advisory committees would have access to confidential information and a capacity to make their advice meaningful, for the U.S. trade representative was obliged to "inform the Advisory Committees of failures to accept such advice or recommendations."[11] In fact, however, the act went much further than this. The ACTN (and each subsidiary advisory committee), was charged with providing, at the conclusion of the negotiation, an advisory opinion "as to whether and to what extent the Agreement promotes the economic interests of the United States and . . . provides for equity and reciprocity."[12] This arrangement created a right, even an obligation, for sectoral interests to pass judgment on the negotiation, which presumably Congress would take into account before passing the Tokyo Round results into law. There could be no doubt about the potential power this conferred on the advisory committees relative to the executive agencies conducting the negotiation. As one U.S. official privately commented in an interview, the advisory procedures virtually amounted to a report card on the conduct and substance of the negotiation, and even on the performance of individual executive agencies. With this mechanism in place, there was less likelihood that the U.S.

[11] Ibid., 21.
[12] Ibid., 20.

government could be charged with neglecting the concerns of special-interest groups in the economy.

There was a third procedural limitation included in the Trade Act, but this bore on Congress itself, and was designed to solve the diplomatic problem the United States had faced in negotiating trade issues with other nations. It was clear in framing the Trade Act that a method would have to be found to assure foreign governments that Congress would not accept, nor would it try to amend, an agreement that had already been worked out with U.S. negotiators. The method worked out was a compromise between what the executive thought was needed to deal with foreign governments and what the Congress was willing to accept in the way of prior limitation on its power. Specifically the compromise provided for an expedited procedure for implementing any legislation connected with a trade agreement, along with the stipulation that no amendments or delays to the legislation would be permitted. Many Senators were disturbed by these innovative procedures. Concern over the plan was perhaps best summed up by Senator Herman Talmadge of the Senate Finance Committee, who stated that this was simply "not the way we make laws."[13] In the end, however, it was a pragmatic matter. It was simply necessary for the United States to avoid a recurrence of the ASP issue, where congressional action was delayed indefinitely, or the antidumping matter, where Congress undid U.S. obligations to other nations. It was, after all, the United States that had initiated the Tokyo Round, and it was incumbent on the U.S. government to demonstrate that it had created a negotiating mechanism that was competent to address the issues it sought to negotiate. This was accomplished through legislation that effectively abridged customary congressional practice in the matter of regulating international commerce.

The grant of negotiating authority in Title 1 was the heart of the Trade Act insofar as the Tokyo Round was concerned. The act did not elaborate the substantive issues that were to come up in the subsequent negotiation,[14] and curiously it made no specific mention of agriculture, which presumably was intended to create the assumption that agriculture would be taken up in the talks in the same manner as industrial

[13] This plan for implementing an MTN agreement was taken from legislation dealing with internal administrative procedures, namely the Government Reorganization Acts of 1970. There was objection to using this mechanism to legislate substantive issues of foreign policy. For further discussion, see Marks and Malmgren, "Negotiating Nontariff Distortions," 339.

[14] An exception to this was the section on GATT revision, which raised some issues (such as a revision of Article 19) which were included in the Tokyo Round agenda.

products. Other sections in the act took up issues of U.S. trade policy not directly relevant to the Tokyo Round, such as trade-adjustment assistance or internal changes to the U.S. trade policy machinery. One title in the act dealt with "Relief from Unfair Trade Practices"; in it Congress expedited the procedures for levying U.S. countervailing duties in response to complaints from domestic industry that the Treasury Department was lax in administering the law. Also expedited were the escape-clause investigations conducted by the U.S. International Trade Commission. In response to the legislated changes, use of these protective mechanisms increased dramatically, which increased the incentive for other countries to negotiate changes in U.S. laws.[15] A further step in this direction was taken by a provision in the Trade Act which permitted the Treasury Department to waive countervailing duties for a period of four years (i.e., until January 3, 1979) if there was a "reasonable prospect that . . . successful trade agreements" would be reached that resolved the matter of countervailing duties with America's trading partners. This deadline, which was one year shorter than the five-year negotiating authority given to the administration, was to cause a crisis in the concluding period of the Tokyo Round.

New Issues before the Negotiation

The Tokyo Round negotiations got under way in Geneva in early 1974, despite the fact that U.S. negotiators were effectively acting without instructions. Regular meetings were held in most subject areas of the negotiation, with the emphasis being on gathering data and resolving definitional problems. From a technical standpoint, there was considerable momentum behind the negotiation. However, the aforementioned dispute between the United States and the EC over agriculture cast a pall over the negotiation that prevented delegates from making progress in any one area. Perhaps the blockage which prevented discussions from going deep on issues led to a lateral expansion of the negotiation into new areas, for in 1976 two new issues were brought into the Tokyo Round, namely government procurement and the "framework" negotiations inspired by the developing countries. The fact that these new issues were introduced demonstrates the extent to which the Tokyo Round had become a general forum for a debate on international trade policy.

[15] For example, Destler notes that the number of countervailing-duty investigations initiated by the Treasury Department rose from one in 1973 to thirty-eight in 1975, and that escape-clause investigations in the ITC went from two to thirteen (*Foreign Economic Policy*, 196).

Government Procurement

In July 1976, a subgroup was established to examine protectionism in government procurement. This was an unusual action, because government procurement was at that time on the agenda of the Organization for Economic Cooperation and Development (OECD), and in fact was the subject of a draft code worked out in that organization. The pressure to include this subject in the Tokyo Round came from several sources. For one thing, notifications relating to government procurement had surfaced in the GATT inventory of nontariff measures (see chapter 2) and had been collated by the GATT secretariat. Second, the developing countries pressed hard for the inclusion of the issue at the Tokyo Round on the grounds that they were not parties to the OECD discussions. This pressure was supported by the United States, which wanted action on government procurement and saw the move as a means to increase the tempo of the negotiation in this area. Finally, the issue was included because of its objective importance in international trade. Virtually all governments discriminate in favor of local producers in making purchases of goods and services. Since government disbursements amount to between one-quarter and one-half of the gross national products of most countries, this amounts to an enormous potential market that could be opened up for international trade. Indeed, in the calculations made following the conclusion of the Tokyo Round, the U.S. government estimated that the agreement reached in the government procurement code would open up a potential market of $20.7 billion among developed countries for American producers.[16] It was clear that negotiations in this area would be conducted for high stakes.

Protectionism in government procurement is a longstanding phenomenon, but it is a recent issue in international trade politics. Protectionism exists whenever a government discriminates in favor of local producers in procuring goods or services. The origin of such protectionism, as revealed in the GATT NTM inventory, is normally legislation, or ministerial or cabinet decrees, or administrative practice.[17] The motivations for this type of protectionism are usually to defend the balance of payments, to support economic activities vital to national defense, and, increasingly, simply to protect local producers from foreign competition.[18] In the history of government procurement, the U.S. Buy American Act of 1933 is a principal landmark and one of the most

[16] Anthony and Hagerty, "Government Procurement," 1341.
[17] "Government Procurement: Note by the Secretariat," GATT docs., MTN/NTM/W/16, August 5, 1975, 3–4.
[18] See Dam, The GATT, 200–02.

overt examples of a protectionist procurement policy.[19] This legislation has long been the target of complaints from America's trading partners, but despite its visibility it is unlikely that this legislation is more discriminatory than the administrative practices of many states, including some in the United States itself.

The most pervasive form of discrimination procurement is administrative practice. Such practice includes inviting bids on government contracts from only one supplier ("single tendering"), or soliciting bids on short notice with a minimum of publicity, or negotiating contracts with prespecified suppliers in lieu of opening contracts to public tender. Perhaps the most effective form of discriminating against foreign suppliers, as noted by Dam, is "the vesting of discretion in procurement officials to select among bidders on the basis of criteria other than price."[20] The essence of discriminatory administrative practice is that it can be carried out without publicity and without legislation, and hence it is difficult to observe it, let alone to measure its effects systematically. The result is that negotiations over government procurement typically involve a preliminary argument over the nature and extent of protectionism in various countries. For example, unlike the United States, France and Japan do not have legislation establishing protectionist government procurement policies, but internal research conducted by the U.S. government has held that administrative practice in both countries strongly favors domestic producers over foreign suppliers. Arguments over the exact nature of protectionism in the various countries points out another interesting problem in the negotiations over government procurement. In comparison with other areas like antidumping or customs valuation, where the complexity of national legislation could create a hindrance to international trade, government procurement was a conceptually simple area where the absence of formal rules made the prospects for trade liberalization more difficult. The task in negotiating government procurement was, even more than to deter discriminatory features already well established in national legislation, to introduce procedures into national legislation on government tendering that would compel equal treatment for foreign suppliers.

The General Agreement is essentially silent on the matter of government procurement; indeed it refers to government procurement only in Article 3.8, where it exempts "procurement by government agencies" from the general obligation of Article 3 to extend national treatment to

[19] For a useful background discussion of the act, see Pomeranz, "Government Procurement."

[20] Dam, The GATT, 204.

the products imported from other contracting parties. Formal international discussions on government procurement started in 1962, when Belgium and the United Kingdom brought a formal complaint to the OECD against the U.S. Buy American Act. A working party of the OECD Trade Committee was constituted to hear the complaint, but its report was subsequently deflected by U.S. pressure into a general review of government procurement in member countries. The matter was followed up with several actions in the OECD. In 1966, the OECD secretariat published a summary of government procurement practices, and in the following year it produced a brief draft text on guidelines for government procurement. In 1969, the United States submitted a draft document of its own. From then until the matter was transferred to the Tokyo Round in 1976, the issue of government procurement was under discussion in the OECD. This lengthy discussion essentially uncovered the political problems and resolved some terminological difficulties of the subject, but the major trading powers were unable to reach agreement on the matter in isolation from other areas of international trade.

The Tokyo Round inherited in 1970 a draft code from the OECD that had already structured the task of constructing a liberalization of government procurement. The draft code contained a statement of principle to the effect that "signatory governments shall base their purchasing policies . . . on the principle of non-discrimination against foreign products or suppliers."[21] It further specified procedures that were to be followed in awarding procurement contracts. The draft code included provisions for surveillance of the performance of signatory countries, and it outlined a series of approaches for dispute settlement under the code. An important section of the draft code was to be "derogations and/or escape clauses," which would specify conditions under which departures from code procedures would be permitted. This entire section was bracketed and no specific provisions were included under it.[22] Indeed many of the paragraphs in the twenty-page document contained square brackets, indicating there was much work to be done to complete the code.

The issues remaining for negotiation were difficult, and they tended to split the EC and the United States. For example, the latter pressed to eliminate the single-tender procedure, and it sought ex post publicity of contract awards, both of which were resisted by the EC. Other issues at

---

[21] "Draft OECD Instrument on Government Purchasing Policies, Procedures and Practices: Note Received from the OECD Secretariat," GATT docs., MTN/NTM/W/81, January 28, 1977, 4.

[22] In negotiated texts, square brackets are used to indicate sections which are controversial and on which no agreement has been reached.

stake included the threshold value of the contracts above which the code would apply, and the list of public purchasing entities in the several countries which would be included under code procedures. In both cases, the United States pressed for a wider as opposed to a narrower application of the prospective code. The government procurement code was an important desideratum for the United States at the Tokyo Round. As a staff report of the House Ways and Means Committee states; "The United States considers government procurement, along with product standards and subsidies, to be its top priority NTB's for resolution."[23]

The Framework Group

A second issue to be added to the Tokyo Round in 1976 was a proposal to change generally the structure of GATT obligations respecting the developing countries. The proposal was initiated by Ambassador George A. Maciel of Brazil and was widely supported by the developing countries. It led to the establishment of a working group in November 1976 which subsequently became known as the Framework Group.[24]

The intention of all parties in launching the Tokyo Round was to accommodate the differences between the developed and developing countries, and especially to make GATT as an organization more responsive to the economic needs of the latter. A strategy to accomplish this, as seen from developing-country perspectives, involved several steps. First, there was an attempt to engage negotiations on products of special concern to developing countries, such as the talks on primary products. Second, the deveoping countries pursued a particularistic approach in trying to secure "special and differential" treatment in each of the codes negotiated at the Tokyo Round and as well in the tariff negotiation.[25] And finally, the developing countries initiated with the Brazilian proposal a general effort to change the structure of GATT legal obligations to improve the trading position of the economically weaker countries. The main objective of this approach was to create a continuing legal obligation of developed countries to extend preferential

[23] U.S. House of Representatives, *Background and Status*, 31.

[24] The group took its name from one of the stated objectives of the Tokyo Declaration of 1973, namely to work toward "the improvement of the international framework for the conduct of world trade."

[25] The phrase "special and differential" (or shortened to "s and d") was an example of negotiation jargon that represented the manner in which the developed countries had committed themselves to treat the developing countries at the Tokyo Round. The origin of the phrase lies in the repeated references in the Tokyo Declaration to the "special" concerns of developing countries and their need for "differential" treatment.

treatment to the developing countries, in lieu of the present system which made such treatment subject to a waiver from normal GATT obligations of nondiscrimination. Furthermore this approach would have relieved the developing countries of some of the obligations they themselves faced in the General Agreement.

The motivations behind the strategy of the developing countries at the Tokyo Round were a product of longstanding frustration with GATT. The developing countries have historically viewed GATT as an outgrowth of the interests of the mainly Western, developed countries. This is an accurate perception on the whole. As an organization, GATT promotes the principles of reciprocity, nondiscrimination, and trade liberalism, and it looks to the competitive protectionism of the 1930s as the major evil to avoid. On the other hand, the developing countries promote the principles of differential treatment, preferences, and trade protectionism, and they seek more to escape their own underdevelopment than to create a liberal world trade regime. The developing countries are especially motivated by economic theories that call for trade protectionism to achieve goals of import substitution and export promotion, theories which in turn have historical roots in the mercantile theories of national development of the previous century.[26] Such theories are the antithesis of the theories of free trade, either current or classical, which in the main have served as a guiding beacon for GATT. Thus the conflict between the developed and developing countries in GATT, which in the diplomatic world sometimes gets carried to the point of caricature, is in the intellectual world born of profound differences about how national governments should handle international trade.[27] These differences create a perpetually uneasy relationship in GATT between the developed and developing countries, which is all the more irritating given that neither side can afford to ignore the other. The developing countries need whatever advantages can be taken from the developed nations within the framework of the General Agreement, while the developed countries need the more numerous developing nations to create a sense of universality for the GATT.

In 1958, GATT received a report (the Haberler report) which sharply called into question the trade policies of the developed countries vis-à-

[26] For example, List, *National System*.

[27] Legal scholar Kenneth Dam uses the term caricature in describing Article 18 (Government Assistance to Economic Development) of the GATT. Elsewhere, in describing GATT documentation dealing with developing countries, he speaks of "the elegant but indefinite style which has tended to characterize the work of those international organizations where the appearance of action has too often been substituted for action itself" (*The GATT*, 227, 238).

vis the developing nations.[28] This report documented numerous cases where developed countries maintained damaging restrictions against the traditional primary-product exports of the developing nations. It further illuminated the common practice of developed countries of increasing the duties charged on imported goods commensurate with the increased processing involved in making the goods. Even where the absolute level of duties was low, this practice produced very high effective rates on increased processing, and consequently it deterred the development of more-labor-intensive processing activities in poorer countries.[29] The significance of analyses like this was to undercut the notion fundamental in GATT that international trade is an engine of economic development. The Haberler report was quickly followed up by the establishment of a program for trade expansion in GATT, and by the creation of a committee (Committee III) charged with a responsibility for trade policy affecting developing countries. In the years since 1958, the special problem of economic underdevelopment has remained a major diplomatic concern in GATT. Committee III, and its successor the Committee on Trade and Development, produced a steady stream of analysis of interest to developing countries. In 1965, GATT took the important symbolic step of adding several articles (Part IV) on trade and development to the General Agreement.[30] Beyond diplomatic activity, however, there was little in the way of hard legal or economic gains by the developing countries, which was perhaps emphasized by the disappointment developing countries felt over the results of the Kennedy Round. The reason for the lack of real progress has been in part the unwillingness of developed countries to make painful concessions on products of great interest to developing countries, such as textiles; and in part the basic conflict between the developed and developing countries over the role of trade liberalism in economic development.

The major gains by the developing countries in their collective economic bargaining with the developed countries have come outside the area of the GATT. In 1963, the first United Nations Conference on Trade and Development (UNCTAD) was held. Not unlike the GATT, it subsequently became a permanent international organization. UNCTAD was

[28] GATT, *Trends* (Haberler report). The panel consisted of four economists with international reputations, and its findings were widely respected for their objectivity.

[29] This argument can easily be appreciated with a simple example. If an unprocessed good at $1/unit enters duty free, while the same good in a semiprocessed form at $1.25/unit enters at 10 percent *ad valorem* (or 12.5¢), then the effective tariff on the value added through increased processing is 50 percent.

[30] Part IV includes three articles, 36 to 38. Of these articles, Dam has noted "how few concrete commitments and how few qualifications of other provisions of the General Agreement are actually involved" (*The GATT*, 237–38).

essentially controlled by and served the interests of the developing countries. It took primary responsibility in the negotiation of commodity agreements, which insofar as they seek to control quantity and price are inconsistent with GATT principles of liberal trade. By 1971, a series of preference schemes for developing-country exports known as the Generalized System of Preferences (GSP) had been negotiated under UNCTAD. These schemes were applied unilaterally by developed countries, the aim being to allow certain qualifying products from developing countries duty-free entry. Typically quotas were set for each product, after which the ordinary MFN tariff would apply. The GSP schemes were inconsistent with Article 1 of the GATT requiring nondiscrimination, and hence a waiver was needed for GATT contracting parties to enter the arrangement. In 1966, Australia had applied for and received a waiver for a preference system, and then in 1971 a general waiver was extended for GSP schemes.

The GSP schemes suffered from a number of drawbacks. They were extended unilaterally and hence lacked uniformity. They were not permanent, but could be withdrawn by the nation granting them. Some countries applied the schemes discriminatorily, for example the United States, which excludes countries on the basis of political criteria like whether the recipient aids or abets international terrorism.[31] Despite these shortcomings, the GSP was a start toward establishing the principle of general preferential treatment for developing-country exports. What the developing countries sought in the Tokyo Round was to ground this principle as a basic right within the General Agreement.

The proposals put forward by Ambassador Maciel in 1976 gave concrete expression to the longstanding complaints of the developing countries about the GATT system. The proposals came in five parts. First, Brazil argued that for developing countries to participate in GATT fully they must be offered additional benefits in trade, and the means to achieve this was "to establish certain exceptions to the MFN clause."[32] To this end, Brazil proposed that the GATT should provide a "standing legal basis for GSP," that is, that GSP should be integrated into the General Agreement on a permanent basis and backed by sanctions to assure its effectiveness. The proposal further sought to make preferential treatment irrevocable, or subject to compensation if withdrawn, and nondiscriminatory, which would have made illegal the U.S. practice of withholding preferential treatment from certain developing countries on the basis of political criteria. The Brazilian proposal did not ensure

[31] Koumins, "Group 'Framework,' " 317.
[32] "Statement by the Representative of Brazil, H. E. Ambassador George A. Maciel, on 21 February 1977," *GATT* docs., MTN/FR/W/1, February 21, 1977, 2.

that preferences would be given; clearly, these would have to be negotiated much as individual tariff concessions are negotiated. What the proposal would have done was to put preferences on roughly the same legal footing as tariff concessions within the GATT, namely to remove their provisional status and the need to obtain waivers to apply them.

The remaining four parts of the Brazilian proposal put forward a number of amendments to the General Agreement which would have relieved developing countries of certain obligations and would have created additional obligations for developed countries toward developing countries. For example, the second part would have allowed greater flexibility to developing countries in the use of safeguarding measures for balance-of-payments purposes, while the third part would have revised Article 18 to permit greater use of safeguards for development purposes. The fourth part dealt with procedures for consultation, dispute settlement, and surveillance, and *inter alia* would have required "prior notification to the Contracting Parties of all government decisions which might adversely affect the trade interests of developing countries."[33] Finally, the last part would have rewritten the reciprocity provision of Article 36 to recognize nonreciprocity "as a *right* of developing countries rather than as an objective of developed countries."[34] The last provision would of course have reinforced the position of the developing countries on the MFN issue, as spelled out in part one of the Brazilian proposal.

The Brazilian proposals determined the agenda for the Framework Group. It was clear that the proposals had set the stage for a searching examination of GATT's role in economic development, as viewed by the developing countries themselves. The response from the developed countries was not long in coming. The U.S. representative to the Framework Group took the position that some of the Brazilian proposals would gravely weaken the MFN principle, and stated; "My government does not, however, expect to relegate the most-favoured-nation principle to some residual role."[35] For its part, the EC emphasized the need for balance between rights and obligations in any contractual agreement, and its representative stated; ". . . even if a balance is not feasible in each case, it does not seem possible to increase the rights on all sides without also and in parallel increasing the obligations. Everyone must contribute according to his capacity."[36] Both delegations were worried

[33] Ibid., 15.

[34] Koumins, "Group 'Framework,'" 321.

[35] "Statement of United States Representative on 21 February 1977," GATT docs., MTN/FR/W/2, March 1, 1977, 2.

[36] "Statement by the Representative of the EC on 21 February 1977," GATT docs., MTN, FR/W/4, March 8, 1977, 1.

about a further problem which subsequently became known as the "graduation" issue, namely: When does a developing country stop being a developing country for the purpose of GATT preferential treatment? As the U.S. delegate put it:

> In this light it is my Government's view that since the purpose of special and more favourable treatment for developing countries in the trading system is to assist in achieving development objectives, justification for such treatment ceases as each development objective is met. Thus . . . developing countries should be prepared over time to accept increasing obligations under the trading system, i.e., progressively to forgo that special treatment.[37]

The graduation issue became one of the most difficult questions faced by the Framework Group, because it raised the profound problem of defining the concept of "developing country" for the purpose of attributing limiting rights and obligations in GATT.[38] Furthermore, that the problem was intensely political can be quickly appreciated by the fact that Brazil, the leader of the developing countries at the Tokyo Round, would probably not qualify under some objective criteria for the status of developing country. Thus it was that the framework negotiation launched an inquiry into international economic relationships that went further than a dispute over GATT technicalities might at first blush appear to go.

THE PROBLEM OF AGRICULTURE

The main reason for the lack of progress in the Tokyo Round through mid-1977 was agriculture. Trade in temperate agricultural products has traditionally been a difficult problem in the history of GATT relations. Agricultural production has fared poorly in most countries, par-

---

[37] "Statement of United States Representative on 21 February 1977," GATT docs., MTN/FR/W/2, March 1, 1977, 6.

[38] On this point an experienced observer has offered the following advice: "It would be a step along the road of feasibility if an acceptable definition of 'developing country,' in terms which were relevant to the issues involved, could be found. With the best will in the world it is difficult to envisage much prospect of this. We wrestled with the problem in the OECD High Level Group on Preferences over a decade ago and gave it up: and since then I have seen nothing which has seemed likely to be more successful. Our pusillanimous conclusion at that time was to fall back on 'self election' to the status, with somewhat sanctimonious hopes that those who elected themselves into eligibility for generalised tariff preferences would recognise the moment when it was right and proper to elect themselves out. Nothing has happened to justify those hopes. Thus it is still difficult to envisage any kind of blanket exception, or derogation, from either the whole general body of GATT obligation . . . or from particular obligations" (Golt, *Developing Countries*, 28).

146

ticularly in comparison to industrial production, and virtually all countries have resorted to protectionism in this sector. From a negotiating standpoint, agriculture is especially problematic because it is the area in which the interests of the two major trading powers, the United States and the EC, are most sharply divided. In GATT negotiations, disputes over agriculture have taken on ideological proportions which in turn have become symbolic of issues that go beyond agriculture itself. To appreciate agriculture as a negotiating problem in GATT, it is useful to review the performance of this sector in terms of production and international trade.

As described earlier, the period from the early 1950s to the late 1970s has witnessed continuing strong worldwide economic growth, averaging about 5 percent per annum, with an even stronger annual rise of 7 percent in international trade. Such growth created favorable economic conditions for trade liberalization, which greatly facilitated the postwar efforts in GATT to reduce barriers to international commerce. However, agriculture has largely been an exception to this scenario. In comparison with industrial production, agriculture everywhere has suffered uneven growth, declining employment, and falling prices in the postwar period. For example, in the period from 1950–54 to 1977, total world production of all agricultural and nonagricultural goods more than tripled in volume, while agriculture alone has grown by only 75 to 80 percent. In terms of trade volumes, total world trade has grown by five times over the same period, while the increase in agricultural trade alone has been only threefold.[39] The result has been a decline in agriculture's contribution to total world production and trade, that is, from 1950, when agricultural trade accounted for approximately 34 percent of total world trade, to 1976, when it accounted for approximately 14 percent of total trade.

The economic conditions associated with the decline in agriculture have become characteristic of the farming sector in most countries of the world. Seasonal variations in supply and demand have produced uncertainty and instability in farm incomes. Chronic excesses of supply over demand of most commodities have led to a secular downturn in farm prices. Falling prices have resulted in lower incomes and losses of farm employment, with a consequent movement of population from rural to urban areas.[40] These conditions have proven to be politically intolerable in all countries, and the general response of governments

[39] Houck, "U.S. Agricultural Trade," 266.

[40] For example, an OECD study noted that "In almost all O.E.C.D. countries, the active agricultural population has been falling in recent years, as a result primarily of the attraction of higher earnings in other sectors" (OECD, *Low Incomes in Agriculture: Problems and Policies*, Paris, 1964, 27).

has been to regulate production and support prices and incomes in the agricultural sector. The tendency toward regulation of agriculture, which is undoubtedly a response to depressed economic conditions, has nevertheless been exaggerated by two factors. One is that agriculture tends to be viewed as more a social than an economic problem because of the implications of agricultural production for the distribution of people over land. Depressed conditions in the agricultural sector have historically led to an influx of unemployed farm workers into urban areas, and as cities became overcrowded there was an increasing tendency to view agricultural support programs as a social imperative. A second factor promoting support for agriculture is that in many countries agriculture has been politically well positioned to look after its own interests. Agriculture is typically overrepresented in the electoral politics of democratic countries, and, not unrelated, the bureaucratic machinery for handling agricultural policy has been well developed and vigorous in most national governments. Furthermore, agricultural interest groups have generally enjoyed the reputation of being one of the more effective lobbies in the area of economics and trade affairs. Thus the combination of constituency representation, strong government machinery, and effective political pressure has insured that agriculture plays a dominant role in the economic policymaking of most trading nations.

From the standpoint of international trade, agriculture represents a problem with deep historical roots. Agricultural protectionism became firmly established in central Europe in the late nineteenth century as a response to falling grain prices, which in turn resulted from expanding production in the New World. A later movement to protect farm products occurred during the depression of the 1930s. The 1930s left most nations with a protectionist policy on agricultural trade, which for the most part was a logical extension into the international arena of policies designed to support agricultural production and prices at the domestic level. Yet another major effort toward agricultural protectionism has occurred recently in Europe as part of the efforts of the EC to integrate farm-support policies in the member countries. About the same time as the EC was embarking on this effort, the U.S. government was beginning to appreciate the growing importance of agricultural exports in its overall trade position. The confluence of these two events set the stage for what has since become the most profound confrontation between the major trading powers in GATT, and hence the most dangerous issue for GATT itself. In many respects, the issue symbolizes the different concerns of importing nations and exporting nations in international trade.

The establishment of a common approach to agriculture was essential to the commitment of EC members to economic integration. From the outset, it was recognized that a customs union could not be achieved in Europe unless agriculture were included, but that this in turn would require the EC to coordinate and centralize the agricultural support programs of the various members. The necessary coordination was achieved through the gradual adoption of the Common Agricultural Policy (CAP). The mechanisms of the CAP vary for different products, but essentially consist of a series of internal prices designed to support EC farm incomes, and external variable levies designed to protect EC agricultural production from cheaper foreign imports.[41] First, a target price, set annually by the Commission, reflects the desired price level for a given commodity. Second, an intervention price, set 5 to 10 percent below the target price, represents a floor price at which the EC will guarantee to purchase stocks from producers. Third, a threshold price, set somewhere between the target and intervention prices, represents the minimum price at which imports can be sold on EC markets. The threshold price is maintained by a variable levy (i.e., the duty needed to raise actual import prices to threshold prices) which can be set on a day-to-day basis to insure that import prices do not undercut domestic production. Protection is thus absolute for Community suppliers, and foreign imports are limited to those products that cannot be supplied in any given period by domestic producers. The final major element of the CAP is the export subsidy (or restitution payment). Unlike prices, agricultural production is not controlled in the EC, and as a result the operation of intervention prices has produced large surpluses of some commodities. To reduce these surpluses the Community has provided subsidies to EC farmers to allow them to sell their higher-priced products without a loss on international markets. The costs of this program are regarded as the "responsibility of the Community," and have been largely borne by the budget of the EC.

The CAP was initiated in 1962, and over the succeeding years it gradually deepened and enlarged its protection of European agriculture. During the same period, Europe's main trading partner—the United States—moved in an opposite direction. The United States entered the decade of the 1960s with a protectionist regime on agriculture that was little different from that found in most Western countries. This regime was characterized by price supports, large government surpluses, and

---

[41] CAP regulations were first established in 1962 for grains, poultry, eggs, pork, and fruits and vegetables. In succeeding years, regulations followed for other products: e.g., beef and rice in 1964, sugar in 1967, and tobacco, wine, and fish in the early 1970s.

export subsidies. Previously the U.S. government had begun to encourage commercial sales abroad, and after 1960 it moved to reduce the system of price controls on major products. By the early 1970s, it was clear the United States had an enormous comparative advantage in many agricultural products.[42] It therefore moved toward a policy of free trade as a means of maintaining farm production (and incomes) without the problem of increasing domestic surpluses. The strong export position of the United States is clearly borne out by data on production and exports over the past three decades. Since the early 1950s, the volume of U.S. agricultural output has expanded by only 54 percent while exports have nearly quadrupled in volume. In the 1970s alone, volume increased twofold. By the mid-1970s, exports had come to constitute approximately one-fourth of the cash receipts of U.S. farmers, as compared with about 10 percent in the mid-1950s. From the standpoint of international trade, the U.S. share of total world agricultural exports grew from 12 percent to over 16 percent.[43] It is evident that international trade and U.S. agriculture are more important to each other than they were previously.

The actions of the EC in protecting agriculture under the CAP probably hurt the development of U.S. exports of agricultural products. For example, at the beginning of the Tokyo Round the U.S. government reported that U.S. agricultural exports subject to levies to the six EC nations for the years 1970–72 were down by 20 percent from the years 1965–67, which were the last three years before the EC achieved a complete internal market for most variable-levy products.[44] The report further indicated that the enlargement of the EC scheduled for 1973 would make further inroads into U.S. exports, which has in fact been the case.[45] It is important, however, to put the picture of declining U.S. agricultural exports into perspective. The United States has traditionally had a substantial surplus on agricultural trade with the EC (e.g., in 1975 it was $4.5 billion), and over the above-mentioned period from 1965–

[42] For example, in 1971 Peter G. Peterson, President Nixon's assistant for international economic affairs, wrote; "In the international division of labor, the U.S. has many comparative advantages, but the most obvious are in agriculture, management, capital goods, and advanced technology" (*United States*, 30).

[43] Houck, "U.S. Agricultural Trade," 268.

[44] "The Common Agricultural Policy of the European Community," U.S. Government, *Executive Branch GATT Studies*, 164.

[45] For example, the report stated; "It is expected, for example, that the enlarged Community will no longer be a net importer of grains within 10 years" (ibid., 165). A more recent study concluded that "For all cereals, the [EC's self-sufficiency] ratio has risen from 86 per cent in 1968/69 to 98 per cent in 1979/80 and to an estimated 105 per cent in 1980/81" (Anjaria et al., *Trade Policy*. 42).

67 to 1970–72, total U.S. agricultural exports to the EC increased by 22 percent. The apparent discrepancy is accounted for by the fact that U.S. trade has risen strikingly in products like oil seeds (e.g., soybeans) and oil cake that are not subject to duties, while it has fallen in products like grain and meat, which are subject to variable levies.

To sum up, the relationship between the United States and the EC in agricultural trade has been one where the U.S. government has been deeply aggrieved by the movement of the EC toward greater self-sufficiency.[46] On the other side, the EC Commission has felt vindicated in its policy by the fact that the EC remains the world's largest importer of agricultural products.[47] The result is that agriculture has been one of the most contentious issues of international economic negotiations since the 1960s, and it played a central role in the Kennedy Round, in the monetary negotiations of 1971, and in the Tokyo Round. The issue was still on the table as of the GATT ministerial meeting of November 1982, about which more will be said in chapter 9.

Agriculture has had a difficult history in GATT itself. The General Agreement does not say much about agriculture specifically, reflecting in theory the assumption that trade in agriculture would be treated essentially like trade in other goods. However, several articles provide exceptional status for agricultural products, which indicates that the drafters of the GATT were well aware of the unique position of agriculture in international trade. For example, Article 11 permitted quantitative restrictions on imports of agricultural products if the importing government was applying production-control policies to its domestic agricultural output. Similarly, Article 16 permitted wider scope for subsidies on primary (including agricultural) products, and in GATT practice the balance-of-payments exception of Article 12 came to have

[46] For example, Peterson has stated: "By any measure, the Community's policy has displaced imports, increased self-sufficiency, and forced exports onto world markets at distress prices. This system is the essence of mercantilism, forcing more efficient farmers in other countries to bear the costs which the Community itself ought to pay for internally" (*United States*, 21).

[47] The EC has also from time to time voiced suspicion about American motives on agriculture, represented in the following analysis in Warley, "Western Trade," 322: "America's enthusiasm for a liberal trading regime for farm products is not only a late conversion but is also highly selective. It focuses primarily on those commodities in which the United States is an exporter, and more especially on those in which it has a clear comparative advantage, notably wheat, feedgrains, oilseeds and meals, citrus fruits, poultry, and tobacco. For commodities in which it has no comparative advantage or is clearly uncompetitive, its agricultural policies have been as protectionist, and conditions of access to the US market as restrictive, as have been those of Western Europe or Japan. These commodities include dairy products, rice, sugar, cotton, manufacturing grades of beef, mutton and lamb, and wool."

wider application in connection with agricultural trade than for other exchanges. However, despite the provisions made for the exceptional nature of agriculture, protectionism in agriculture has been much deeper than foreseen in the General Agreement, and it has been a threat to the liberal trade regime promoted by the GATT. The purpose of the GATT since its inception has been to reduce all restrictions on trade, and especially to eliminate quantitative restrictions (QR's) in favor of other less harmful impediments to economic intercourse. What has occurred, however, is an apparent increase in agricultural protectionism over time, and a heavy reliance on quotas and other nontariff measures in lieu of the tariffs that are more in keeping with the GATT philosophy. In the early 1950s, internal surveys in GATT showed that practically all countries relied on nontariff measures, especially QR's, to protect their domestic agricultural producers. For some products, such as wheat, butter, and sugar, the protectionism was extensive. In the early 1960s, a newly created GATT committee on agriculture (Committee II) documented a similar story regarding protectionism on agricultural products. In most cases, such protection existed in apparent conflict with the obligations of the General Agreement. It is this situation that perhaps justifies Kenneth Dam's conclusion that the record of GATT on temperate agricultural commodities is "one of failure."[48]

The GATT position on agriculture has been complicated by the policies of the United States itself. The U.S. executive has been a major force behind trade liberalism in GATT, but on agriculture the United States is seriously compromised, which in turn has led to a weakening of GATT authority in this area. The original GATT articles on agriculture were in large measure written to be consistent with U.S. farm-support legislation existing in 1947.[49] In 1950, however, Congress imposed severe quotas on dairy products, and in 1951 it directed the administration to apply external quotas to other farm products regardless of the international obligations the United States had contracted under the GATT. These actions put the United States in violation of the GATT, and led to a successful retaliatory action by the Dutch under the provisions of Article 23, and as well to a succession of rebukes recorded by the contracting parties in the Council of GATT. In 1954, the United States

---

[48] The GATT, 257.

[49] For example, Article II provided an exception to the general prohibition on QR's in cases of agricultural restrictions which operate as part of a program "to restrict the quantities of the like domestic product permitted to be marketed or produced." This clause took account of the procedures of the U.S. Agricultural Adjustment Act of 1933 and had little application elsewhere, as few nations other than the United States have tried to restrict agricultural production.

sought to invoke the waiver provisions of Article 25 to legalize its position under the GATT. The following year the United States received an open-ended waiver that applied not only to existing programs but also to others that might be invoked in succeeding years. The political and legal impact of this action has been substantial, despite the fact that the United States has not on balance pursued a protectionist line on agriculture. The 1955 waiver has not been revoked by GATT or ever relinquished by the United States, and hence it has the effect of removing U.S. agricultural policy from the rigors of the GATT. In the words of T. K. Warley, the waiver "harmed the case the United States had been making for liberalization of the trade-restricting practices of other countries," and it put the United States "in the van of those who treated agriculture as subject to different trade rules and outside the accepted codes of international behaviour."[50] Even more important, the waiver left other nations with the impression that the United States was essentially hypocritical in advancing its policies on international trade. That this impression was caused by an internal struggle between the U.S. executive and Congress over agricultural trade policy, and by the independent power of the legislature in the U.S. system, perhaps moderated but did not remove the sense of grievance held by America's partners in GATT.

Agriculture has come to play an increasingly important role in the trade negotiations conducted under the GATT, particularly as the United States came to recognize its comparative advantage in this area. In the Dillon Round of 1960–62, there were extensive discussions of the impact of the EC's agricultural policy on products on which tariffs had previously been bound by the various EC members. Essentially little action was taken, although EC members did accord the United States certain future negotiating rights against the Community, in accepting which the United States also tacitly accepted the principle of the EC's agricultural policy. The rights of the United States against EC members subsequently became an issue in the unfortunate "chicken war" of 1962–63. This dispute arose because West Germany raised duties on poultry as part of its obligations under the CAP, thereby withdrawing a prior tariff concession of which the United States was the principal beneficiary. The U.S. government brought diplomatic pressure to turn back the German action, and when this failed it pursued retaliatory measures under the General Agreement. Eventually the United States withdrew concessions on a series of products (e.g., potato starch, brandy, and pickup trucks) in which it imported from the EC a dollar volume

---

[50] "Western Trade," 347.

equal to its West German poultry exports. This action may have given satisfaction to the frustrated U.S. executive, but it did not slow the development of the CAP, nor did it provide any compensatory benefit to U.S. poultry producers.

The Kennedy Round in the mid-1960s was the first major attempt to negotiate a liberalization of trade in agricultural products. The United States entered this negotiation with the demand that agriculture should be treated the same as trade in nonagricultural products, namely that nontariff restrictions should be converted to *ad valorem* duties, and that the latter should be bound and gradually reduced through GATT negotiations. The American position was completely unacceptable to the EC. The European negotiators held that governments everywhere intervened in agricultural production, and that this intervention was so profound that it made any notion of a free world market in agriculture meaningless. The EC insisted that agriculture should be negotiated separately from nonagricultural products. It proposed a plan (the *"montant de soutien"* plan) whereby a nation would measure the overall protection it gave to agricultural products through various methods, and would then negotiate to bind this protection against further increase. Obviously this plan did not entail substantial change in the EC's agricultural policy, the protection of which had been a major goal of EC negotiators at the Kennedy Round.

The *montant de soutien* proposal proved unacceptable to the Americans as a point of departure. The United States was committed to a reduction in existing protectionism, and the EC proposal would not have accomplished this goal at all. The U.S. negotiators were not, as the Europeans feared, seeking per se to dismantle the CAP, although in practice it is difficult to envisage how European protectionism could significantly be reduced without making fundamental changes in the CAP. The result was that the Kennedy Round met with little success in agriculture. The various parties did agree to exchange some tariff concessions on agricultural products, but the value of these was limited. The United States did not secure the improved access to export markets it had hoped to achieve. The widespread feeling in the United States was that "The results of the Kennedy Round (1964–67) proved disappointing insofar as agriculture was concerned."[51]

By the end of the Kennedy Round, it was clear that agriculture, more than any other area, had uncovered philosophical differences between the United States and the European Community. To be sure, there were

---

[51] "The Adequacy of GATT Provisions Dealing with Agriculture," U.S. Government, *Executive Branch GATT Studies*, 35.

sharp differences of economic interest, owing to the fact that the United States had a large and growing agricultural export surplus with the Community. However, the differences went much deeper than this. At the level of principle, the U.S. position on agriculture is not far from the free-trade position it has pressed since the earliest days of the GATT. These principles never received an unreserved welcome in Europe, where it was always assumed that the requirements of the international trade system would be subordinated to national economic policies. These philosophical differences became evident in the agricultural negotiation at the Kennedy Round and were equally evident in the preparations for the Tokyo Round. The following summary, put forward in a U.S. congressional briefing document early in the Tokyo Round, provides a clear and perhaps prophetic perspective on these differences:

> What appeared to many as differences over procedure reflected long-standing substantive differences between the EC and the U.S. in their objectives and approach to negotiations on agriculture. The EC emphasizes the importance of trade expansion through greater market and price stability achieved primarily by negotiation of international commodity agreements on major agricultural products. Its approach would preserve the principles and mechanisms of existing national agriculture policies, on the grounds that they reflect special domestic, economic, social, and political conditions in each country.
>
> The U.S. emphasizes the need for trade expansion and liberalization by achieving more open market access by reducing tariff and nontariff barriers and eliminating distortions from national policies which reduce the most efficient production and use of worldwide agricultural resources. The U.S. also stresses the need for balanced progress and results in the MTN on both agriculture and industry and opposes moves for separate negotiations in these two areas.[52]

IMPASSE AND RESOLUTION, 1974–1977

As mentioned previously, the Tokyo Round made little headway during the years 1974–77. No doubt some of the difficulty could be found in the tariff negotiation, where the task of devising a negotiating approach resurrected an old argument between U.S. and EC negotiators that went back to the early days of the Kennedy Round. However, the real cause for the blockage lay in the different approaches taken by the

[52] U.S. House of Representatives, *Background and Status*, 25.

United States and the Community to agriculture, which had a wide-ranging impact on almost all areas of the overall negotiation.

Negotiations on Agriculture

The United States and the European Community entered the Tokyo Round with basic positions that were little changed in the main from where they ended in the Kennedy Round. As is often the case, when fundamentally conflicting positions get translated into specific negotiating objections, a situation is created where the negotiating partners are unable to agree on the procedures for negotiating the problem. Such a situation occurred in the Tokyo Round. For its part, the EC started from the premise that the CAP was inviolable, and that neither its principles nor its mechanisms could be subject to negotiation in the Tokyo Round. The EC negotiators further insisted that agriculture had a unique position in international trade, and this led them to demand a separate negotiating group for agricultural products, which the Americans accepted. Finally, the EC put as much if not more emphasis on the stabilization of international agricultural markets as it did on the expansion of these markets. The last objective led the Community to propose international commodity agreements for the major agricultural products (i.e. grains and dairy products), and for other products to seek to negotiate codes of good conduct between exporters and importers that would ensure the orderly management of international trade.[53]

The negotiating objectives of the United States differed from those of the Community on all the major issues. Most of all, the U.S. government sought to negotiate agriculture identically with other products, which would have meant that trade restrictions on agriculture would be subjected to the same disciplines being negotiated in the nonagricultural area. This objective reflected both the export interests of the United States and the economic ideology of the U.S. government. A second objective of the U.S. government was the elimination of export subsidies on agriculture. Again, this objective was sought for reasons both of interest and ideology, for these subsidies hurt U.S. exports to third parties and reduced prospects of developing a more liberalized world trade in agriculture. With this objective, the United States put itself foursquare in opposition to one of the major mechanisms of the agricultural policy of the EC. Finally, the United States sought an expansion of the world market in agriculture even more than a stabilization

---

[53] The code approach was generally referred to in the vocabulary of EC negotiators as establishing "concerted disciplines." See Harris, "EEC Trade Relations," 8–9.

of that market, and it was specifically opposed to market organization schemes such as commodity agreements and the like.

The negotiation on agriculture started slowly. At the insistence of the EC, a negotiating group for agriculture was confirmed by the Trade Negotiation Committee in February 1975, but discussions immediately focused on the competence of the group. The EC wanted the group to be the exclusive forum for agricultural negotiations, while the U.S. government sought to negotiate agricultural restrictions in the various groups dealing with tariffs and nontariff measures. A temporary compromise was reached on this issue by May 1975, at which time Group "Agriculture" set up three subgroups to negotiate three major product areas: grains, meat, and dairy products. This represented a concession by the United States, which had opposed extending a mandate to negotiate to these subgroups.[54]

The compromise of May 1975 was short-lived, and the problem of the proper forum for agricultural negotiations came up again. Ostensibly the issue was procedural, but the crux of the matter was clearly the EC's claim for the uniqueness of agriculture and agricultural trade restrictions. The United States took the view that restrictions on trade in agricultural products were first and foremost restrictions on international trade. Hence all restrictions on agriculture, whether they were tariffs, subsidies, or whatever, should be handled primarily in those negotiating groups responsible for dealing with those subjects. For example, it was unacceptable to the United States to negotiate agricultural tariffs in Group Agriculture, when another forum, the Tariff Group, would be discussing tariffs on all other products. Such procedures would curtail the scope for tradeoffs in the tariff negotiation and, not incidentally, remove a sector where the U.S. government expected to make gains. For its part, the EC was insistent that the negotiation of agricultural restrictions should remain principally within the special structures created for agriculture. The Community was unwilling to be put in a position where it might be called upon to trade off agricultural and nonagricultural concessions, which might have involved negotiat-

[54] Ibid., 14. The main lines of controversy between the United States and the Community continued in the subgroups. Regarding Subgroup "Grains," a major issue was whether to transfer the negotiation to the International Wheat Council (IWC) in London, which the United States supported and the EC opposed. A further issue was the EC's proposal for floor and ceiling prices for grain in international trade, which the Americans opposed. In Subgroups "Meat" and "Dairy Products," the EC tabled a series of proposals aimed at establishing "concerted disciplines" in these sectors. The United States, which was opposed in principle to sector negotiations in agriculture, did not offer specific proposals in these areas.

ing away some of the principles or mechanisms of the CAP. The insistence of EC negotiators on separate procedures for agriculture was a logical preliminary step given their mandate to avoid any negotiation of the Community's agricultural policy, and it was a position on which they remained firm. U.S. negotiators found this position unacceptable, and, with the exception of essentially superficial efforts to bridge the differences, the negotiation on agriculture rested in a state of blockage until the breakthrough of July 1977.

The blockage in agriculture effectively stopped work at the Tokyo Round. It was obvious no headway could be made on agriculture itself, and the procedural dispute prevented the U.S. and EC delegations from making progress in other areas. Most seriously affected were the negotiations on subsidies and countervailing duties, where the EC was unwilling to negotiate subsidies with agriculture included, and the United States was unwilling to negotiate without agriculture included. A further blockage occurred in the standards negotiation, where the United States sought unsuccessfully to insert the problem of standards on agricultural products. The impasse between the United States and the Community was complete, and together their combined preponderance at the Tokyo Round insured that there was little scope for other nations to take initiatives. The issue that divided the two major powers was profoundly important to each, and events outside the negotiation appeared to confirm and even magnify that importance. In the trade statistics of 1974, the United States posted a surplus of $11.8 billion on agricultural trade, which went a long distance toward offsetting a deficit of $14.8 billion on nonagricultural products, the latter of which included the effects of the 1973 quadrupling of oil prices. On the Community side, the internal divisions over energy and monetary policies put into even sharper focus the fact that the CAP was one of the few common policies the EC had managed to achieve. In neither case could the position on agriculture be easily compromised.

Negotiations on Tariffs

The negotiations on tariffs shared with the agriculture sector some of the responsibility for the early slow progress at the Tokyo Round, although fortunately the division was not as deep on tariffs as on agriculture. The main problem in the tariff negotiation was one of approach, a state of affairs which had also plagued the Kennedy Round. As mentioned earlier, the participants in the Kennedy Round had agreed to take an across-the-board approach to negotiating tariff cuts (in lieu of tabling item-by-item offers), but there were sharp differences between the U.S. proposal for linear reductions and the harmonization approach pursued by the EC. The Tokyo Round produced a rerun of this old argument, which in retrospect was one of the more predictable events of the negotiations. When nations choose to take a general as opposed to a piecemeal approach to the negotiation of a complex issue, it is to be expected that they will haggle for a long time over how to approach the substance of the negotiation.

The preparations for the tariff negotiation were long drawn out. By 1971, the GATT secretariat had succeeded in putting the trade data of the major trading nations on computer tape. This was an enormous technical achievement. In the history of trade relations, one of the greatest problems has been to achieve a common classification of trade data across nations to facilitate negotiation and the exchange of concessions. This problem was largely overcome in the postwar development of two systems of trade classification: the Standard International Trade Classification (SITC) and the Brussels Tariff Nomenclature (BTN).[55] A further step was to design a computerized data bank of trade statistics, which would have obvious advantages from the standpoint of storage, retrieval, and analysis of information. This data bank was part of the GATT Tariff Study that had been initiated at the close of the Kennedy Round. Of this study, the GATT noted in its annual report on its activities that "For the first time, in this GATT tariff study, the full facts on the tariff structure of each of the major trading countries, together with trade statistics that make it possible to assess the importance of each tariff item, have been recorded on computer tape in full detail and subjected to thorough analysis."[56]

The Tariff Group faced and overcame a series of preliminary negotiating problems, including the matter of the base year(s) used in calculating trade statistics, and the unit of account to be used in representing the value of trade flows. The former problem, which was important because national trade flows fluctuated widely following the Kennedy Round, was settled by allowing a nation making an offer to choose its own base date, leaving other nations to evaluate the offer as they wished. On the latter problem, it was decided that the U.S. dollar would be used as the unit of account for the negotiation, despite a passing effort by the EC to substitute an international unit such as the SDR for the dollar. The U.S. dollar had been used in the Kennedy Round, and it was widely supported because it was the reference unit most fre-

[55] The SITC is generally used for analytical purposes, while the BTN is used by customs offices for the application of duties. For background on the development of these classificatory systems, see Ray, "Internationalization of Economic Analysis," esp. 411–15.

[56] GATT Activities in 1972, Geneva: GATT, 1973, 10.

quently encountered by importers and exporters in actual trade. The success in settling these issues however soon isolated the fundamental problem of the overall approach to be taken to the tariff negotiation. It was obvious that a general, or formula, approach would be taken to tariff-cutting, but what remained in dispute was how much harmonization such a formula would provide, and how much it would be directed toward the interests of the developing countries.[57]

There were essentially three points of view regarding the approach to the tariff negotiation. The first favored the linear approach, and was most clearly represented in a proposal tabled by the United States on March 24, 1976. The proposal was to cut tariffs across the board by an amount equal to one and a half times the amount of the tariff plus 50 percent, up to a maximum cut of 60 percent, which was the limit of the U.S. authority specified in the Trade Act of 1974.[58] It was obvious this proposal made a gesture toward the notion of harmonization, at least for tariffs that were originally below 6.67 percent, but it did not promise a greater-than-proportional reduction of the higher duties in America's tariff structure. These of course were the exact duties the Europeans and others wanted a tariff formula to address. As the EC delegation commented in a critique of the American proposal: "The United States quite rightly stresses that some duties—not all duties—remain especially high and inhibit trade. These are the duties which should be tackled first, by cutting them substantially and proportionately more than the low duties."[59]

[57] The various terms used in tariff negotiations can cause difficulties. The terms *general* or *formula* or *across-the-board* approach will refer here to an opening offer that is meant to apply to all tariffs (less exceptions) in a nation's tariff structure. An example of a general approach would be "all tariffs cut in half." Such an approach is only effective as a negotiating device if it has wide support. By convention, the term *linear* approach means a general approach in which all nations initially table equal cuts, with the amount of the cut to be specified. The example above could also be called a linear approach. *Harmonization* essentially means cutting high tariffs more than low tariffs, with the result that the tariff structures of different nations become more identical, or harmonized. An example of a harmonization approach would be "all tariffs cut by the amount of the tariff." Proposals for harmonization often employ a tariff-cutting equation; hence this approach is often called a formula approach. The essential division on this issue is between nations with high, or disparate, tariffs (e.g., the United States), which prefer equal or linear cuts, and nations with low, or similar, tariffs (e.g., the EC), which prefer harmonization.

[58] The formula for this proposal was: $y = 1.5x + 50$. This meant that a 5 percent tariff would be cut by $7.5 + 50$, or 57.5 percent. For all tariffs above 6.67 per cent, the proposal specified a flat 60 percent cut.

[59] "Statement made by the Delegation of the Commission of the European Communities at the Group 'Tariffs' Meeting, March 1976," GATT docs., MTN/TAR/W/20, March 26, 1976, 1. The EC representative further noted that the American proposal

A second perspective was advanced by the EC itself. Operating on the principle "the higher the duty, the greater the reduction," the EC negotiators presented a well-orchestrated proposal that called for cutting each tariff by its own value over a succession of four cuts.[60] This proposal would have reduced an original tariff of 50 percent to 12.91 percent, while a tariff of 10 percent would fall to only 6.95 percent, obviously achieving the goal of harmonization. Because of the exaggerated effect of this proposal on tariffs over 50 percent, the EC further proposed that 13 percent (rounded from 12.91) should serve as a final value for all tariffs of 50 percent or greater. The EC initiative drew an immediate critique from Canada, which claimed that it relied too heavily on the concept of harmonization. The Canadians acknowledged the "presentational advantages" of the proposal because of its simplicity, but argued that what really mattered about tariffs was their trade-distorting potential; and that ostensibly moderate tariffs could easily have a more pernicious impact than nominally higher duties. At its base, the Canadian critique was motivated by the suspicion that the EC proposal was carefully crafted to avoid any real reduction in the Community's level of protection. As the Canadian delegate expressed it; "Our view can be stated very simply; such a formula would require us to make substantial and meaningful tariff reductions on the exports of industrial products from the European Communities to Canada, and in return for which we would get virtually nothing."[61]

A third approach to the tariff negotiation came from the developing countries. The main preoccupation of these countries was the protection and improvement of the GSP. They sought an a priori commitment from the developed countries for preferential tariff reductions, and they resisted the argument advanced by the latter that preferential treatment could only be taken up on an item-by-item basis.[62] The developing

---

would leave the EC with "virtually no duties above 8 per cent," while the United States would have a "high proportion beyond 8 per cent, with duties of up to 20 per cent" (p. 3).

[60] This proposal was represented by the formula $y = x$ four times, where x is the initial duty and y is the reduction. This proposal would have reduced a 20 percent tariff to 10.28 percent through the following four stages: (1) 20% less (20% of 20%, or 4%) equals 16%; (2) 16% less (16% of 16%, or 2.56%) equals 13.44%; (3) etc.; (4) etc. equals 10.28%. Finally, it should be underscored that the EC intended this proposal to apply to industrial products alone.

[61] "Statement Made by the Canadian Delegation at the Group 'Tariffs' Meeting, July 1976," GATT docs., MTN/TAR/W/31, July 21, 1976, 2.

[62] For example, note the following penetrating point by Brazil: "We find it hard to accept that products must be indicated before such [preferential] measures can be agreed upon. If that were the case, why is it not necessary to indicate possible exceptions lists

countries also pressed for a system that would provide for the binding of preferential rates on developing-country exports, in order to allow the latter to plan their investment and production programs with greater security. Most of all, however, the developing countries sought to protect the GSP from what they saw as an erosion produced by a general worldwide lowering of tariff levels. Clearly, if all tariffs were reduced, the margin of preference that developing countries might have enjoyed under various national GSP schemes would disappear. The response of the developing countries was to resist a further downward movement of tariffs by calling for exceptions on products in which they had an interest.[63] Thus the developing countries had a profound conflict of interests with the developed countries in the tariff negotiation. Where the latter wanted universality and as deep cuts as possible, the former, in the pursuit of preferential treatment, sought to retard the movement toward a general liberalization of tariffs. In this direct clash of interests, eventually the developing countries' approach to the tariff negotiation was essentially ignored. In the fall of 1976, the Malaysian delegation voiced what was a common refrain among the developing countries: "We have now five formulas before us and more to come perhaps. This delegation had taken a look at them but found them not consistent with our economic needs. . . . In addition this delegation is of the view that none of the tariff-cutting formulae so far proposed have taken into account the special needs of developing countries."[64]

The proposals by the United States and the Community stimulated additional suggestions from several other countries. Because of the statistical nature of the subject, it was possible for a nation to make endless permutations to the tariff formula in order to advantage its particular trading structure. In such negotiating situations, it is commonplace that some participants will attempt to propose a winning compromise solution. One such effort at compromise was a formula tabled by the Swiss delegation on October 12, 1976. This formula took the form of

---

before a global formula can be agreed upon?" ("Special Procedures for Developing Countries: Statement Made by the Delegation of Brazil at the Meeting of Group 'Tariffs,' March 1976," GATT docs., MTN/TAR/W/22, April 1, 1976, 3).

[63] For example, India noted: "In so far as the erosion of the Generalized System of Preferences is concerned, we can provide for several remedies. These can take the form of *less deep than formula cuts* or in some cases the *exclusion*, altogether, of some products from the purview of the general formula" ("Special Procedures for Developing Countries: Statement Made by the Delegation of India at the Meeting of Group 'Tariffs,' March 1976," GATT docs., MTN/TAR/W/23, April 2, 1976, 1; italics in original).

[64] "Tariff-Cutting Formula: Statement Made by the Malaysian Delegation at the Group 'Tariffs' Meeting, October 1976," GATT docs., MTN/TAR/W/41, October 22, 1976, 1.

an equation, namely $z = 14x \div (14 + x)$, where x was the original tariff and z represented the new duty (not the percentage of reduction).[65] The Swiss claimed that their proposal met the primary criteria for an acceptable formula; that is, it provided both for liberalization and harmonization, and it could be universally applied by nations with different tariff structures.

It was clear the Swiss proposal had two important advantages. The first advantage was the simplicity of the formula, which was intentional and was exploited by the Swiss delegation. Negotiating formulas are usually more successful if they are readily understandable without great effort, and this maxim carries double force in tariff negotiations, where the subject itself possesses inherent complexity. In the potential confusion of competing formulas and voluminous data, the Swiss formula was simple and they ably defended it as such. In their words, it involved "three simple operations—one multiplication, one addition, and one division."[66] The second advantage of the Swiss proposal, which was less easily calculated, flowed from the fact that the formula was condemned in equal proportion by both the U.S. and EC negotiators. The Americans argued that three-quarters of all items carrying tariffs were dutiable at rates of 15 percent or less, and that the Swiss formula did not reduce duties sufficiently in the range of moderate duties. For their part, the Europeans argued that high duties were precisely those which had the most restrictive effect on trade, and that the Swiss proposal did not insure that these would be brought down to a reasonable level.

Following the activity of 1976, the negotiation on the tariff formula was caught up in the general dispute over agriculture, and little further progress was made. The United States maintained its position that agricultural tariffs should be included in any tariff-cutting formula, while the European Community was equally adamant that such tariffs could

[65] "Tariff Cutting Formula: Proposal by Switzerland," GATT docs., MTN/TAR/W/34, October 12, 1976, 1. The effect of this proposal was to cut initial duties of 5, 10, 15, and 20 percent by approximately 26, 41, 52, and 59 percent respectively. For initial duties of over 20 percent, the formula, if applied, would produce a cut of over 60 percent.

[66] "Tariff-Cutting Formula: Statement Made by the Swiss Delegation at the Group 'Tariffs' Meeting, October 1976," GATT docs., MTN/TAR/W/37, November 1, 1976. One might have assumed that a formula that possessed as many desirable qualities as the Swiss formula, in addition to being operationally simple, would have been the product of an intense analytical effort. Apparently this was not the case. The story is that an official from the Swiss customs service hit on the concept during a business lunch, and quickly committed the idea to paper on the back of a napkin. The idea subsequently caught on in the Swiss delegation. This episode points out the often unorthodox origin of creative ideas in complicated negotiations.

only be discussed in the Agriculture Group. There was no meeting of minds between the Americans and the Europeans on the tariff formula, but in the event this did not matter, since the dispute on agriculture overshadowed the tariff negotiation. It became clear that a breakthrough on the agriculture issue would be necessary before progress could be made on tariffs.

Breakthrough, 1977

There is never any certainty that international negotiations will reach an agreement. Risk of breakdown is inherent in the process. This is because there always exist certain kinds of issues that are fatal to the negotiation process, that is, issues of a fundamental nature over which the participants would rather terminate the negotiation itself than be seen to compromise. The normal term for such issues is nonnegotiable, but since parties often use the term nonnegotiable in their initial posturing with each other, it is likely it does not carry as precise a meaning as the term fatal. In the beginning phases of the Tokyo Round, agriculture got framed as a fatal issue. For the Europeans, negotiating agriculture was mainly a matter of defending the CAP, and they saw, not without cause, the American position as an attack on this policy. It was clear from their position that they wanted the CAP more than they wanted a successful negotiation at the Tokyo Round. For the Americans, negotiating agriculture was largely a question of achieving visible reductions in European protectionism, without which they doubted whether they could sell the final result to Congress. When positions are as tightly drawn as this, the only way a negotiation can proceed is by a redefinition of the issue or by a change of position by one or more of the parties. If this is to occur at all, it is usually an action taken at high political levels.

Political events in 1975–76 were not conducive to settling the blockage on agriculture at the Tokyo Round. The year 1976 was an election year in the United States, and in Germany and Japan as well. Elections left greater power to the bureaucrats, and in the United States this expanded the role of the Department of Agriculture, who were hawks on the subject of agricultural negotiations with the EC. Further complicating the dispute was the fact that some senior trade officials in the Ford administration took a hard line on agriculture, notably Special Trade Representative Frederick B. Dent and his deputy, Clayton K. Yeutter, formerly assistant secretary of agriculture. In this situation the election of the Democratic administration of Jimmy Carter in November 1976 created an important sea-change in U.S. trade policy. First, the Democrats have been somewhat less concerned about EC agricultural subsidies than the Republicans, perhaps because the Democrats themselves have traditionally been more interventionist in the domestic economy.[67] Second, the Carter administration initially took a more multilateral approach to world politics than its predecessor, which in trade politics became translated into a concern for the progress of the Tokyo Round. And finally, President Carter appointed a high-level management team on the trade side, headed by the selection as special trade representative of Robert Strauss, a colorful and experienced Washington politico.

The Carter administration raised the priority of the Tokyo Round for the U.S. government. During the London economic summit of May 1977, President Carter reached agreement with six other heads of government to bring the Tokyo Round negotiation to a successful conclusion. This agreement galvanized action in Washington. In early July the president dispatched a group of trade negotiators, including Strauss, on a brief visit to various European capitals. At the conclusion of this tour, a widely publicized meeting was held in Brussels on July 11 between Strauss and EC commissioners Wilhelm Haferkamp, Finn Gundelach, and Etienne Davignon. The meeting concluded with a press conference by Strauss and Haferkamp at which a timetable was announced for a rapid completion of the Tokyo Round negotiation, including the negotiation on agriculture.[68] Strauss himself described the event as "the most significant day in the history of the Tokyo Round." It was obvious that a breakthrough on agriculture had been achieved. It is useful to try to unravel this event, as a counterpoint to the bureaucratic-level negotiations that had characterized the Tokyo Round thus far.

It was frequently repeated in the world press that Robert Strauss had "breathed life" into the Tokyo Round negotiation. This may have made for vivid journalism, but reality, even at high levels, is more prosaic than that. Strauss went to Europe with one demand: a timetable for the completion of the negotiation. The U.S. government had decided it

---

[67] It is difficult to assess the importance of this factor, but it may have been decisive. For example, one official in the U.S. trade bureaucracy expressed the view that had Gerald Ford won the presidential election of 1976 there probably would not have been a Tokyo Round agreement.

[68] The timetable had four phases, and went roughly as follows: Phase I, a tariff plan, including a formula and specific instructions on agricultural tariffs; Phase II, tabling of offers/ requests for agricultural tariffs, noncode NTM's, and nonformula countries; Phase III, tabling of texts for all NTM codes; and Phase IV, tabling of all exceptions lists and item-by-item offers in the tariff negotiation. These four phases were to be completed by January 15, 1978 (David Egli, "GATT Agriculture Deadline Set," *Financial Times*, July 28, 1977).

wanted the Tokyo Round, the President had thrown his weight behind it, and now action was clearly needed. What Strauss gave to get a time-table was an easing of the American demand on agriculture, which appeared clear from the remarks at the Strauss–Haferkamp press conference. In response to a question asking whether the United States accepted that agriculture would be dealt with separately from industrial issues, Strauss said:

> There is a full recognition first, as I said, that we're not going, nor should we, attempt to upset any structural agricultural policies of the EEC. Number two, there is a full commitment on our part that agriculture, with its different social and economic aspects, will be negotiated in parallel with the industrial negotiations. Now obviously they won't be in the same room, because they're treated differently, and they will be concluded simultaneously.[69]

The position Strauss enunciated in Brussels was a fundamental change from the posture of the United States for the previous two years of the negotiation. As it was later summarized in the *MTN Studies* produced by the U.S. government; "In July of 1977, Ambassador Strauss agreed to drop the U.S. insistence that agriculture be negotiated along with industry on the condition that there would be a 'substantial result for agriculture' in the MTN."[70] It is improbable this position change was worked out in Brussels, for Strauss was there for less than one working day in all. More likely, it was worked out on the American side before Strauss left Washington, and communicated in advance to the EC at the working level.

Events after July confirmed that the U.S. government had changed its position on agriculture. On July 27, Group Agriculture adopted an offer/request procedure for handling individual agricultural products which was an obvious departure from the formula or code procedures being applied elsewhere in the negotiation on industrial tariffs.[71] And

---

[69] "Transcript of Ambassador Strauss Press Conference in Brussels," mimeographed, GATT Public Information Office, July 11, 1977, 5. Strauss went on to make a third point, namely that if the United States did not "achieve agricultural progress and reform . . . there is no point in our negotiating an agreement. It wouldn't pass the Congress." Strauss made the same three points in an interview in Washington, D.C., two weeks later, but the order of his points was exactly reversed! See "Tokyo Round Is in 'Open Negotiating Posture': Strauss," mimeographed, GATT Public Information Office, July 24, 1977, 3.

[70] U.S. Senate, *MTN Studies*, vol. 1, *Results for U.S. Agriculture*, 15.

[71] This procedure was confirmed by a press statement by U.S. Deputy Trade Representative Alan W. Wolff which read: "I am extremely gratified at the adoption today by Group Agriculture of a procedure for negotiating on agricultural products. . . . Participating countries agreed to submit lists of requests regarding tariff and non-tariff meas-

in September 1977, following another meeting between Strauss and the European leaders, an agreement was reached that the Swiss formula would be applied with reference to industrial tariffs exclusively. The question is: How did these changes come about? The answer is essentially that the offensive against European agricultural policies was held as a nearly theological position of the Ford administration and that this position changed with the election of Jimmy Carter. Strauss carried this changed position to the European leaders in July 1977, and it produced a dramatic effect on the stalled Tokyo Round negotiation. The position change was in effect an American concession—that is, a demand dropped—and of course it takes no real skill in itself to give a concession in a negotiation. Instead the skill was in the manner in which it was done, and this skill was demonstrated by both parties in the negotiation. With the help of the Europeans, the U.S. concession on agriculture was presented to the public (and to respective governments as well) more as a compromise than as a concession, for it was "exchanged" for a timetable and a renewed commitment to the Tokyo Round negotiation. As might be expected, the timetable was given much more play in public interviews on both sides than was the U.S. concession on agriculture. This allowed the Americans to take credit for the new sense of momentum that had been achieved, an opportunity that was not lost on the U.S. side. Indeed, the public-relations aspect of this issue approached sheer artistry, for the impression created for the U.S. public was that a lone Texan had gone to the Old World and shaken the Europeans into accepting an American call to action.[72]

---

ures affecting agricultural products by November 1, 1977, and accepted January 15, 1978, for the submission of offers" (U.S. Press Statement on Agriculture Group Meeting, Geneva, mimeographed, GATT Public Information Office, July 27, 1977).

[72] For example, in answer to a question from U.S. journalist Peter Dreyer suggesting that Strauss's July visit essentially produced only an agreement "on a time for clearing the decks for action," Strauss replied: ". . . I don't accept the premise of your question. I think we have agreed on a hell of a lot more than a time frame, sometime when we're going to begin action. I think we took more action today in a period of seven hours than has been taken in a long time; and my colleagues will agree with me on that" ("Tokyo Round Is in 'Open Negotiating Posture': Strauss," mimeographed, GATT Public Information Office, July 24, 1977, 4).

· 5 ·

MIDDLE PHASE, 1977–1978:
THE BONN SUMMIT RUN-UP

The meeting between Robert Strauss and the EC leaders in July 1977 launched the Tokyo Round into a period of intense activity. The negotiation proceeded on a decentralized basis, with the various subject areas of the Tokyo Round being handled in small groups of specialized personnel. There was little overlap among the different areas at this stage, and the results of the negotiation process were lumpy, with some areas reporting more progress than others. A major effort of stocktaking was made immediately prior to the Bonn economic summit of July 1978, in an effort to demonstrate progress to the seven chief executives gathered for that meeting. The Bonn summit created an interim deadline for the Tokyo Round, and thus the period from July 1977 to July 1978 constituted a natural phase in the development of the negotiation.

With some exceptions such as agriculture, most separate areas of the negotiation reported considerable progress during the 1977–78 period. Specific offers and withdrawals were tabled in the tariff negotiation. In some nontariff areas, such as the negotiations on standards (i.e., technical barriers to trade) and government procurement, draft codes were drawn up and advanced to a fairly high level of agreement. In other areas such as subsidy/countervail and customs valuation, major political breakthroughs were made in the definition of the negotiating problem. The analysis that follows will give special attention to the negotiations on subsidy/countervail and customs valuation. For one thing, with the possible exception of customs valuations in the United States, these negotiations presented difficult political problems for many actors at the Tokyo Round. Second, they occasioned a substantial rethinking of trade policies by governments and in some cases a restructuring of bureaucratic procedures as well. Finally, from the standpoint of process, these two negotiations appeared to be initiated and carried out by one of the major participants—the United States on subsidy/countervail, and the European Community on customs valuation—and the techniques used to accumulate support were essentially similar in both cases.

Movement on Subsidy/Countervail and Customs Valuation

Subsidy/Countervail

It is useful to recall where matters stood on subsidy/countervail at the beginning of the Tokyo Round. The negotiation centered on two articles in the General Agreement, namely Article 6 (Antidumping and Countervailing Duties) and Article 16 (Subsidies). Article 6 was straightforward. It defined countervailing duties (see chapter 3) and provided a series of restrictions for their use. Two of these restrictions figured in the Tokyo Round, namely the requirement that "material injury" to competing domestic industry be demonstrated before the imposition of countervailing duties, and the prohibition against using countervailing duties to offset a rebate of taxes on "consumption" given to the exporter by the government in the exporting country. The most important issue was material injury, and on this issue a considerable irony existed in GATT procedures. The United States was the only nation that had ever consistently applied countervailing duties, but because its legislation on countervail predated the GATT, it was effectively exempt from the international rules it had helped to negotiate. On the matter of subsidies, things were more complex. Article 16 required nations maintaining subsidies that increased exports to "notify" their GATT partners and to "discuss" the possibility of limiting the subsidy. This procedure was simply ineffective. In 1955, the GATT members added to Article 16 section B, which prohibited export subsidies, but the ban was qualified in a manner that greatly reduced its effectiveness. In 1960, GATT introduced a list of specific practices that were to be considered export subsidies for the purpose of the section B prohibition. This list included subsidies on nonprimary products; in general, the GATT provided very little restraint on subsidies on primary products. It likewise provided almost no restraint on production or domestic subsidies as opposed to export subsidies. On this point, it was clear by the 1970s that domestic subsidies were widely used by GATT members, and these practices were attacked, especially by the United States, as having a distorting effect on international trade.

To summarize, it could be said at the start of the Tokyo Round that the GATT law on countervailing duties was strong but irrelevant. It was strong because it clearly defined the practice in question, and it placed clear and reasonably operational restraints on that practice. It was irrelevant because the only nation that applied the practice was exempt from the principal restraint contained in the GATT. On subsidies, the situation was reversed: the GATT law was relevant but weak. It was relevant because it bore on commonplace practices of nations which actually accepted the law, but it was weak because it was ill defined and was largely ineffective in restraining national practices. The subsidy/countervail negotiation took on the trappings of a contest between the United States and the rest of GATT, with the EC acting as the principal negotiating agent for the latter. The negotiating task for the EC was to induce the United States to accept an international definition of injury (i.e., material injury) into its countervail legislation. The negotiating task for the Americans was to introduce discipline into the use of subsidies by the EC and other nations. Insofar as such discipline might limit the agricultural export subsidies of the EC, the United States found allies for its position among agricultural-exporting nations like New Zealand, Australia, and Canada.

The negotiation began with the United States pressing the EC and other nations on subsidies. As mentioned earlier, a point of departure for the Americans was that subsidies on agriculture should be negotiated within the subsidies/countervail subgroup and be subject to the same discipline as subsidies on other products. Beyond this, the U.S. negotiators worked to develop a position that would take account of the different types and effects of foreign subsidies. There were two types of subsidies at issue: export subsidies, of which the restitution payments provided under the CAP (Common Agricultural Policy) to exporting EC farmers are an example; and domestic (or production) subsidies, of which Canadian regional-expansion grants and emergency assistance to British steel manufacturers are examples.[1] The United States was essentially alone in seeking to place strict limits on the use of the latter subsidies. Regarding effects of subsidies, the U.S. government argued that subsidies produced three undesirable effects on international trade: first, an import-substitution effect in the market of the subsidizing nation; second, a direct export-promotion effect in the markets of foreign countries, where subsidized exports competed with domestic industries;[2] and third, an indirect export-promotion effect in the markets of "third" countries, where subsidized exports competed with the exports of other nations. GATT rules were minimal, especially on the third-country-market issue, and the United States above all sought recognition of the fact that exporting nations could be deeply affected by the subsidizing practices of their trading partners.

---

[1] These two examples represent what Ohlin has characterized as "positive" and "defensive" subsidies. See "Subsidies," 23.

[2] One should note that domestic subsidies can have export-promotion effects as well as can export subsidies, which are of course designed for that purpose.

The initial U.S. position was an attempt to create a link between countervailing duties and subsidies, and as well between countervailing duties and rebates of indirect taxes.[3] This had not been done in Articles 6 and 16 of the General Agreement, because most nations felt subsidies were a legitimate tool and hence they were reluctant to approve the use of countervailing duties against these policies. The U.S. position was summarized in what became known as the "traffic-light" approach to subsidy/countervail, which sought to categorize subsidies in three groups.[4] The first group would consist of prohibited practices, against which it was assumed injured nations could countervail without the need to demonstrate injury. The second group would include enumerated practices that were permissible, but against which injured nations could countervail following a demonstration of material injury. The third group would include practices expressly permitted, and against which countervail would be prohibited. The basic philosophy of the traffic-light approach was the effort to declare certain subsidy practices illegal, the accompanying assumption being that retaliatory measures like countervail could be taken without justification. This philosophy

---

[3] The rebate of indirect taxes (i.e., sales or consumption taxes, as opposed to direct taxes such as income or corporation taxes) was a high-profile issue in the early stages of the Tokyo Round. In most countries, indirect taxes are a primary revenue source, while the United States relies mainly on direct taxes. Nations typically rebate indirect taxes (e.g., value-added taxes—VAT) to domestic producers for goods that are exported, whereas the rebate of direct taxes would be widely considered as GATT practice as an unacceptable form of subsidization. Furthermore nations which rely on indirect taxes often levy a border tax on imports equal to what the tax would have been had the goods been produced locally. There has been general agreement that these practices work to the disadvantage of U.S. exporters.

The U.S. attempt to negotiate indirect-tax rebates and border taxes in connection with countervailing duties got nowhere in the Tokyo Round. For the EC and others, it was a nonnegotiable issue because it would have required nothing less of national governments than to alter their domestic tax structures fundamentally in order to accommodate trade with one other country. The matter was effectively put to rest by a ruling of the U.S. Supreme Court in the Zenith case in June 1978. The Zenith Corporation had requested the Court to rule that indirect-tax rebates on imported electronic products constituted a foreign subsidy for the purpose of U.S. countervail legislation, which would have required that countervailing duties he levied on these products. The Court rejected this interpretation. Had the case gone the other way, the implications would have been enormous, and according to a published estimate of U.S. Treasury officials it would effectively have increased U.S. protectionism by more than it had been reduced during the entire history of the GATT. See Dean A. DeRosa et al., "Zenith Case."

[4] It was suggested that the inspiration behind the traffic-light label came from the customs procedure at the Geneva airport, where passengers with nothing to declare pass through a corridor marked prominently with a green circle while others proceed through a corridor marked in red.

angered the Europeans, who felt the Americans were perpetuating a greater illegality by retaining countervail legislation that did not conform to the Article 6 requirement of the GATT that material injury be demonstrated in countervail proceedings. Without wishing to push the analysis too far, one could see the dispute in terms of a profound difference over the appropriateness of self-help, retaliatory measures (i.e., vigilantism) in a commercial legal system where there was minimal agreement on what constitutes illegal action, and minimal enforcement against those actions that are considered illegal. This was one of those procedural issues which overshadow the substantive aspects of the problem, and which had to be resolved before any headway could be made on an international code on subsidy/countervail.

Negotiation on the traffic-light approach quickly degenerated into a doctrinaire exchange. Typically the United States would negotiate from a long document which reflected the interagency process in Washington, and which left little room for maneuver. For example, the departments of Agriculture and Commerce both wanted strict controls on foreign subsidies, while for the Department of Labor nothing that could be achieved on the subsidies side would be worth putting a material-injury provision into U.S. countervail law. This approach failed to create any point of departure. The basic problem was that both sides were strictly limited by their domestic processes. U.S. negotiators were limited by the unwillingness of the Congress to accept an internationally negotiated definition of material injury (already demonstrated in connection with the antidumping code of the Kennedy Round), while EC negotiators were limited by the fact that member governments, and not the EC itself, insisted on the right to use subsidies as a tool of national economic policy. Positions were so deeply entrenched that by 1976 senior officials on both sides were recommending that the issue be dropped from the Tokyo Round entirely.

It is often the case in negotiation that changes in position are preceded by changes in personnel. In the wake of the U.S. election of 1976, subsidy/countervail on the American side was assigned to two appointed officials in the office of the U.S. trade representative (USTR), namely John Greenwald and Richard Rivers. On the EC side, the negotiation was assigned to Peter Klein and Alistaire Sutton, both EC career officials. From late spring 1977 onwards, the negotiation was run mainly on the basis of a direct Washington-Brussels exchange, and there was relatively little control exercised by the principal negotiating teams located in Geneva. The negotiation proceeded on a less-doctrinaire level than previously. On the EC side, there was a gradual acceptance of the fact that subsidies were an international as well as a domestic concern, while on the American side it was recognized that the United States itself had relied on subsidies in its national policy.[5] Furthermore, and particularly on the American side, the negotiation sought to avoid the internal interagency process that had built rigidities into the previous negotiation. The negotiation focused on a dialogue with the external partner at the cost of internal backstopping, and though this can be a risky procedure, it did lead to a fuller exploration of the problems in the external negotiation.[6]

The negotiations after 1977 were largely carried by the American side. In a major initiative, the United States agreed in principle to work from existing GATT rules on subsidy/countervail, which carried the implication of moving toward an international definition of material injury. The United States also dropped the traffic-light approach that rested on the notion of defining prohibited categories of subsidies. Negotiation on this basis quickly isolated the irreducible minimum for both partners. On the American side, this was the need to demonstrate that the Europeans were willing to accept increased international surveillance and discipline on the use of subsidies, while on the European side it was simply a matter of having the Americans accept a material-injury clause in their countervail legislation. These two demands eventually formed the basic quid pro quo of the subsidy/countervail negotiation. In terms of practical bottom-line negotiation, it narrowed down to a tradeoff between an injury test for the EC and an expanded listing of export subsidies and something on domestic subsidies for the United States. Once the negotiating partners had agreed to take these concrete steps, they were able to chart a course for the negotiation of the entire code.

Much of the conceptual negotiation of the subsidy/countervail agreement took place over the summer and fall of 1977. From all accounts, the process was exhausting, with the negotiators participating in successive rounds of consultation with each other and with other officials in their own bureaucracy, thus effectively serving as conduits between their domestic bureaucracies and the foreign negotiating partner. The process was largely exploratory and oral, with little in the way of for-

[5] For a list of U.S. subsidy practices, see Cooper, "U.S. Policies."

[6] A theoretical discussion of how far to proceed in the external negotiation without reference to internal constraints can be found in Walton and McKersie, *Labor Negotiations*. In this case, the fact that the main constraints regarding the definition of subsidies appeared to come from bureaucratic actors and not from direct constituency pressures may have given the U.S. negotiators some running room to deal with the external negotiation. National bureaucracies can be powerful forces in international negotiations, but in the last analysis they are less obdurate than strong constituency pressures.

mal position papers. Indeed there was an attempt to avoid any early commitment of views to paper, especially a paper that might be reviewed in interagency meetings in the United States or by various member governments in the EC. In December 1977, the two teams drew up a two-page document that summarized their evolving agreement, which was circulated by their delegations under formal GATT auspices.[7] The paper was heavily bracketed, which meant it left much to be negotiated between the United States and the Community; and it was manifestly brief, which meant it could not cover all concerns in the interagency process on either side. On the latter ground, the paper reportedly had difficulty in getting clearance from Washington. However, the paper did record a measure of agreement sufficient to raise the level of the negotiation, in terms of bring into the negotiating process both more issues and more nations. The paper committed the parties to recognizing that subsidies can "threaten serious prejudice to the trade interests of any other contracting party [in home or other country markets]," and it stated that "an updated illustrative list of [nonprimary] export subsidies should be developed."[8] The paper also stated that "Agreement should be sought whereby a [meaningful] test of injury [under] [in accordance with] Article VI would be applied in connection with the imposition of countervailing duties."[9] The December paper broke the deadlock that had existed since the outset of the subsidy/countervail negotiation. The agreement between the United States and the Community did not ensure success, but certainly without that agreement there would have been no point in continuing the negotiation.

The next step in the negotiation was to bring other nations into the process. It is probably inherent in a multilateral negotiation where two nations are as preponderant as the U.S. and the EC that issues on which these two parties disagree must first be negotiated between themselves. To have it otherwise would be to risk confrontation, and would be a style more reflective of bipolar alliance politics than of multilateral negotiation. If the goal is a negotiated agreement, and if each of the two majors has the capacity to prevent that agreement, then the early flow of decision-making probably should occur between the majors at the

---

[7] "Subsidies/Countervailing Duties: Outline of an Approach," GATT docs., MTN/INF/ 13, December 23, 1977. This document is reproduced in Rivers and Greenwald, "Negotiation of a Code," 1466–69.

[8] Ibid., 1467. The first set of brackets marks an EC reservation; the second, my addition.

[9] Ibid., 1469. The bracket around "meaningful" reflected a U.S. reservation. For the rest, the U.S. preferred "under," and the EC preferred "in accordance with."

expense of other nations at the negotiation. Furthermore the incipient agreement would probably be presented to the other nations not in one step, but gradually, in a manner that slowly sought adherents to an evolving accord. This process in fact occurred, and what seems from hindsight a matter of logic was indeed pursued with deliberate care by the U.S. and EC negotiators. Nations were invited to join the informal US/EC discussions on subsidy/countervail on the basis of their preferential contribution to the potential agreement. In most cases, a nation's trading position was the determining factor, but in some cases personal negotiating skills were also important. In the first dimension, Japan was included, while the second brought in Canada, whose ambassador, Rodney Grey, had long experience in trade negotiation and had negotiated the antidumping code in the Kennedy Round. The Nordic countries were added for reasons of trading interests with the Europeans, and for balance in the informal subsidy/countervail group.[10] Later, when the developing countries were added, the invitation went first to major nations such as Brazil, Mexico, and India. In this manner, the negotiation developed in a pyramidal pattern, from top to bottom, adding new delegations to the process, and accommodating, insofar as possible, the new concerns brought by the additional players.

Following the US/EC December paper, a five-party group was established in the subsidy/countervail negotiation, comprising the United States, the EC, Japan, Canada, and the Nordics. The group initially worked from the US/EC paper and previous GATT documentation.[11] The inclusion of new parties in the informal negotiation brought some changes in the negotiating agenda. For example, one of the major concerns of Canada, as well as the EC, was to induce the United States to drop certain tax legislation known as DISC (domestic international sales corporation), which permitted exporting corporations to defer corporate profits tax and thereby effectively created interest-free loans from the government for exporting activities. The Canadians and Europeans claimed that this tax provision operated as an export subsidy, and their claim was substantiated in a report of a GATT panel in Novem-

[10] One interviewee commented that an early group included the United States, the EC, Canada, and Japan, but that the EC had pressed for inclusion of the Nordics to balance the negotiating situation ("their hinterland to compensate for America's hinterland, Canada"). The reference to hinterland was tongue-in-cheek, but the lesson that can be learned about the need for balance in negotiation is quite serious.

[11] For example, the Canadian delegation had previously circulated a draft code which contained some useful ideas on multilateral dispute settlement, namely "Subsidies and Countervailing Duties: Draft Code Prepared by the Delegation of Canada," GATT docs., MTN/NTM/W/80, January 19, 1977.

ber 1976.[12] The United States, which undertook the DISC to equalize tax treatment on exporting activities with that on foreign investment, responded that the DISC served simply to provide the same tax-relief benefits to U.S. exporters as did tax legislation in other nations. On this point, the United States drew support from three GATT panel reports which held that certain income-tax practices of France, Belgium, and the Netherlands constituted subsidies on exports.[13] Because of the political sensitivities involved, none of the reports were accepted by the GATT Council.

The issue of tax policy ended in a standoff that extended through the Tokyo Round. It was suggested that the Carter administration may have been prepared to drop the DISC, but this move was flatly unacceptable to Congress on the grounds that the DISC was part of a broader legislative effort to tax U.S. companies on their overseas earnings (and thereby prevent those companies from sheltering profits by locating in low-tax jurisdictions known as tax havens). In the negotiation, the United States took the position that it would drop the DISC when the European nations changed their tax practices, which was tantamount to stonewalling the issue. Without doubt, the issue was a difficult one, and one U.S. negotiator admitted taking more "grief" on this matter than on any other subject in the subsidy/countervail negotiation. This entire story points out the importance of national tax legislation for international trade.[14]

Negotiations in the five-party group continued throughout the spring of 1978. Under the pressure of the Bonn summit scheduled for mid-July 1978, the group managed to draft a twenty four page "Outline of an Arrangement" that was circulated by GATT on July 10, 1978.[15] The draft began the long process of putting into legal language the basic political agreement that had been reached in the US/EC paper. It is of course impossible and probably pointless to assess exactly how far along the Outline had brought the negotiation, although the negotiators who were pressed by the Bonn summit to demonstrate progress cited the written accord as evidence of a signal achievement. What can be said is that the Outline achieved a conceptual structure that was es-

[12] "United States Tax Legislation (DISC): Report of the Panel Presented to the Council of Representatives on November 12, 1976," BISD Twenty-third Supplement, January 1977, 98–114.

[13] "Income Tax Practices Maintained by France [Belgium, Netherlands]: Report[s] . . . on November 12, 1976," ibid., 114–47.

[14] For further information, see Hufbauer, "Subsidy Issues," and Grey, Trade Policy, esp. ch. 7, "Subsidies, Taxation and Countervail."

[15] GATT docs., MTN/NTM/W/168, July 10, 1978.

sentially maintained in the final agreement, and it included about half the volume of words found in the latter. The section on countervailing measures was fairly complete, and although it was heavily bracketed, it dealt in some detail with the difficult issue of "determination of injury." Specifically the section included an unbracketed footnote which committed the United States to a "material-injury" definition of injury, viz., "Under this Arrangement the term 'injury' shall, unless otherwise specified, be taken to mean material injury to a domestic industry."[16] On the matter of subsidies, however, the Outline appeared to be less complete. There was only a very brief section on domestic subsidies, and instead of an actual list of export subsidies there was only a statement that such a list would be constructed later from the 1960 indicative list.[17]

From this document, one can get a sense of the negotiating strategy the United States and EC followed throughout the subsidy/countervail negotiation, which corresponded fairly closely to the traditional posture of these two parties in GATT negotiations. The Outline appeared to suggest that the United States was making a minimum (albeit conditional) offer on countervailing measures, in an attempt to encourage a forthcoming position on subsidies from the Europeans and others. However, on subsidies, the text of the Outline indicates that the EC took a more minimal position, certainly in comparison with the final code. Taken in sum, the text appeared to confirm an interpretation that was drawn from interviews with the participants themselves, namely that the United States extended itself to make an attractive offer on the countervail side, and then used this offer as leverage in the late months of the negotiation to encourage a more forthcoming position on subsidies from the European Community.

Customs Valuation

The negotiation of the code on customs valuation had interesting similarities to, and differences from, that on subsidy/countervail. Both negotiations proceeded first between the United States and the Community, and then extended to the other Tokyo Round participants in the

---

[16] Ibid., 3.
[17] Curiously the Outline did contain a completely bracketed illustrative list of internal (i.e., domestic) subsidies, with the added notation that "some" delegations felt such a list to be neither practicable nor desirable. This list was later dropped and did not appear in the final code. A list of internal subsidies would have been an extremely sensitive subject, and it was likely included in the interim document to assist the American negotiators with their internal negotiation.

pyramidal way already described. Both negotiations proceeded in a straightforward manner between the U.S. and EC negotiators themselves, especially once the two sides decided to put aside absolutist positions in favor of reaching an accord. Both negotiations created difficulties in the internal politics of the U.S. and EC, but in this dimension the effects were unbalanced. Subsidy/countervail was immensely difficult in the United States, especially late in the negotiation, but in the EC it encountered fewer bureaucratic or legal problems, and certainly less doctrinaire debate. On the other hand, customs valuation was more difficult in Europe, and especially in the middle period of the Tokyo Round, when the EC and its member countries worked out the organizational implications of a fundamental shift in the European approach to customs valuation. Finally, as for the process of negotiation itself, the two negotiations bore the intriguing similarity that the negotiating partner that seemed under greatest pressure to change internally appeared to carry the initiative in the external negotiation.

The situation as the negotiation on customs valuation got under way was that most trading nations (over one hundred) applied the Brussels Definition of Value (BDV), and of that number about thirty countries, including EC members, were members of the Customs Cooperation Council (CCC). The United States and Canada stood conspicuously apart from this group, and each maintained a separate system of valuation. There was considerable pressure within GATT to "harmonize" valuation systems, which translated into a demand that the United States and Canada accept the BDV. Indeed an *ad referendum* text (see chapter 3) on customs valuation had been developed prior to the Tokyo Round which was based substantially on the BDV. The United States and Canada refused to consider a change, however, and argued that their systems were satisfactory. There the matter rested. There was some suggestion that the United States might contemplate change when a U.S. Tariff Commission study in 1972 supported a modified version of the BDV, but this was quickly opposed by the American Importers Association (AIA). The latter claimed that the BDV was inherently too loose a system to achieve the goal of harmonizing the valuation systems of different nations.[18] This position was subsequently vindicated in the ensuing negotiation.

The EC took the lead in championing the BDV system. The differences between the Europeans and the North American nations were partly

[18] The AIA report states: "The BDV . . . standards, focused on what would be or should be, instead of what is, are too loose and leave so much leeway as to defeat uniformity." For further reference to this document, which is on file at the offices of *Law and Policy in International Business*, see Sherman, "Customs Valuation Code," 122.

philosophical, and partly a reflection of commercial interests. The BVD was based on a *notional* concept of valuation, that is, a price at which goods ought to be sold under a specified set of circumstances. The notional concept was not based on a reference to any real price (such as the invoice price of traded goods), but simply specified a set of procedures for arriving at the price at which the goods should be valued. The notional concept was a single, uniformly applicable standard for valuation, which was intended to create uniformity in the actual valuations arrived at by the customs services of various nations. In practice, the notional concept created much less uniformity than its proponents claimed. Even in Europe, where nations generally applied the BDV in a neutral (i.e., nonprotectionistic) manner, there were cases where identical products coming from outside Europe had received differences in valuation of up to 80 percent between various EC members. Elsewhere, where the BDV was more clearly used to protect local producers, the values assigned according to the notional concept could be uplifted by a large amount over the selling price of the goods. For example, Japan, a BDV country, followed the practice of adding advertising costs to the first importations of a new product. This practice added a crippling cost to products being introduced in the Japanese market, and because advertising costs are difficult to calculate in advance, it also added considerable uncertainty for the exporter as well.

The valuation procedures of the American and Canadian systems were based on a *positive* concept, that is, the price at which imported goods or like goods are in fact sold under specified conditions. In both systems, the valuation process began with a reference to real prices. In the United States, the main referent was the export value of the product, which meant the wholesale price of the product at the time of exportation to the United States. For Canada, the basic referent was the "fair market value" of the imported goods in the market of the exporting country. The differences between the notional and positive concepts of valuation reflect broader differences in legal thinking, and comparisons could be made of the rational approach of civil law versus the empirical approach of common law, or even the distinction in philosophy of the ideal versus the real.[19] Such differences of course permitted ample scope for doctrinaire argument during the negotiation. In practice, however, the importance of the philosophical distinction tended to blur. Either system allowed for adjustments from a basic reference point, and consequently either system could be neutral or used

[19] It is perhaps ironic that the BDV grew out of the practices of the British customs office, the very nation where the concept of common law originated.

179

as an instrument of protectionism through "aggressive valuation." It was therefore necessary for nations to look at actual national practice to determine their interests in the customs valuation negotiation.

The United States and Canada had relatively few export concerns on customs valuation, particularly with the EC. The average EC industrial tariff was already low (about 7 percent) by the start of the Tokyo Round, which itself reduced the economic impact of adjustments in valuation. On the whole, valuation in EC countries was neutral, although there were occasional problems of price uplifts,[20] and as a result U.S. exporters brought little pressure on the U.S. government to seek change. The same was not true of EC exporters, however. Both the American and Canadian systems were essentially protectionist, and U.S. procedures were complex and anachronistic as well. European exporters brought pressure on the EC to demand reform of these systems, and particularly reform of certain highly visible procedures such as the aforementioned ASP method of valuation.

The valuation system foreigners faced in exporting to the United States was indeed stupefying in its complexity. Prior to the Tokyo Round, the basic U.S. customs law was contained in section 402 of the United States Tariff Act of 1930. It provided for five methods of valuation, ranked in order of preference.[21] The basic law was amended by the improbably entitled Customs Simplification Act of 1956, which provided for four more methods of valuation, again ranked in descending order of application.[22] The definitions applied in the 1950 act were not always compatible with the 1930 legislation; hence section 402 of the 1956 act became known as the "new law" and a redesignated section 402a of the 1930 legislation was referred to as the "old law." It was determined that certain articles under the new law would be valued

[20] The main problem from uplifts (i.e., overvaluations) was the inconsistent treatment imported goods could receive in different countries in the EC. A similar problem could occur from undervaluation, where customs officers in ports competing for import trade might be encouraged to shave import valuations in order to attract business.

[21] These were (including approximate definitions) as follows: Foreign Value (price in market of exporting country); Export Value (actual export price of "freely offered" goods); United States Value (price of comparable imported products in United States); Cost of Production (estimated cost of production plus profit of goods in exporting country); and American Selling Price (price of comparable goods in domestic production in the United States, used only for specific named products). Customs officers typically worked down through the list of definitions until value could be determined, with the understanding that Foreign or Export values were used interchangeably depending on which produced higher values.

[22] These were: Export Value, United States Value, Constructed Value (similar to costs of production), and American Selling Price.

180

at only 95 percent or less of their value under the old law, and therefore Congress included in the 1950 act a "final list" of named products that were to be valued under the old law.[23] This action thus gave the United States nine separate methods of valuation. The system was based on a positive philosophy, which should have reduced uncertainty, but in fact the number of different valuation methods along with their attendant complicated definitions made the system impossible to administer consistently. One immediate problem was that it was often necessary for the exporter to get a low-level technical decision before it was clear what legislation would be applicable. For example, the final list included "machines, macaroni-making, having as an essential feature an electrical element or device." Presumably an exporter of spaghetti machines would have had to seek a customs ruling before it was clear whether old-law or new-law procedures would be relevant.

The Canadian valuation system was much simpler than the American. The standard of valuation was based on the "fair market value" at which the exported goods (or like goods) sold in the market of the exporting country. This approach explicitly rejected the export value (i.e., invoice price of exports) as basis for valuation. The Canadian valuation system was largely a product of its economic relationship with the United States, in which the Canadian market is approximately one-tenth the size of the United States but receives from the latter about two-thirds of its imports. In this situation, goods that constitute remnants or discontinued lines in the U.S. market have often been exported to Canada at bargain prices in sufficient numbers to swamp the smaller Canadian market.[24] The "fair market value" criterion was designed to address this problem. In addition, two other valuation methods were intended to achieve the same goal. In the event that Canadian customs could not determine fair market value, it could examine the "costs of production plus profit" in the exporting country to make a valuation on imported goods. Finally, in situations where the first two valuation methods were inadequate or were deemed impracticable by the Canadian government, the Customs Act of 1970 provided that "the value for duty shall be determined in such manner as the Minister [of Fi-

---

[23] The final list was twelve pages long, and products could not be added to or deleted from the list without new congressional legislation. See *Valuations of Imports: Final List Published by the Secretary of the Treasury Pursuant to Section 6(a), Public Law 927, 84th Congress* (T.D. 54521), Washington: GPO, January 20, 1958.

[24] A further problem in the Canadian-American context is trade between related parties, especially the trade between U.S. multinationals and their subsidiaries in Canada. In such cases, invoice prices may not be an accurate reflection of the value of traded goods. This issue subsequently became a major issue in the negotiation on customs valuation.

nance] decides."[25] The significant aspect of this method is that it invested political authorities at the highest level with discretionary power over the day-to-day matters of customs valuations.

The EC complaints against the U.S. and Canadian customs systems centered on the protectionist nature of these systems. In the United States, the protectionism of the final list and the ASP valuation method was obvious. In Canada, the protection afforded by the valuation system was arguably deeper, but because it was subtle it was a matter of some dispute. The EC pointed to the unwillingness of Canada to accept the invoice price of exports as prima facie evidence of protectionism. Furthermore the EC attacked the ministerial prescription in Canadian law, and pointed out that it had led to policy decisions such as applying a 23 percent uplift on the value of Italian shoes, or holding the value of remnant textile goods to between 5 and 10 percent of their original premium-goods price, thus preventing legitimate trade in less-valuable products. The Canadian response was to argue that invoice prices in foreign trade were inherently inaccurate, and that Canada employed the valuations system in a "neutral" manner to offset the predatory pricing practices of the larger exporters to it.

In retrospect, it is clear that Canada sought to use the valuation system in order to handle the problem of dumping, that is, the export of goods at prices lower than those in the exporting country. Employing valuation procedures to accomplish an antidumping policy made good sense economically, since both policies bear on the selling price of traded goods in the importing country's market. From the standpoint of politics, however, the practice was controversial. Antidumping is a formal process in which the exporter has certain procedural rights. Valuation, certainly as practiced through ministerial prescription, gave no such guarantee of procedural fairness to exporters. The EC complained about the Canadian ministerial prescription on the grounds that it maximized uncertainty for exporters, and that it created an interventionist posture by government in the pricing practices of private companies in international trade.

To sum up, the EC took a principled position of government neutrality in customs valuation, and in practice approached neutrality as much as its BDV system would allow. The Americans also supported a neutral system in theory, but in practice operated a chaotic and protectionist system. Among the major trading nations, only the Canadians supported an interventionist position in principle.

The negotiation of customs valuation at the Tokyo Round started up

[25] Government of Canada, Customs Act (Revised, 1970), section 39(d).

during 1975–76 on the basis of the *ad referendum* text previously prepared in GATT (see chapter 3). The discussion over this period was one
of principle, and it generally went nowhere. The EC pressed the importance of achieving customs uniformity under a modified BDV system,
which by then had approximately one hundred members. In this effort,
the EC received strong encouragement from the customs services of its
member governments, as well as from the CCC.[26] Above all, the EC stuck
to the notional concept of valuation, which was the basis of the BDV
system. For example, a proposed code which the EC tabled in December
1976, began with the following familiar notional terminology: "*Article
I* (1) Subject to . . . these Rules . . . , the customs value of goods shall,
notwithstanding any invoice or affidavit to the contrary, be the price
which such goods would fetch, on the date such goods were sold, on a
sale for export between an unrelated buyer and seller."[27] This notional
terminology remained unacceptable to the United States and Canada.
The American negotiators fully agreed on the need to reform the U.S.
customs system, but disagreed that a notionally based BDV could serve
as a basis for a uniform or neutral international standard. Much of the
U.S. opposition to the BDV came from the attendance by American observers at meetings of the Valuation Committee of the CCC, where technical problems of valuation procedures were candidly aired between
the member countries. It was obvious from the meetings that the notional concept of valuation presented inherent problems of inconsistency, and that these problems could likely get worse with wider ad-
herence to the BDV.

During 1976, events occurred in the EC which changed the direction
of the negotiation. The principal negotiators for the EC on customs valuation, Henri Chumas and Michael Mullins, recognized that the EC
had insufficient understanding of the U.S. and Canadian customs systems to negotiate a successful compromise. Consequently Mullins was
dispatched on a four-week study tour to Washington and Ottawa,
where he worked with the full cooperation of American and Canadian
authorities. The results of the trip confirmed EC suspicions about the
protectionism of the U.S. and Canadian procedures. However, the results also confirmed a point American negotiators had long been mak-

---

[26] For example, the CCC forwarded a document to the GATT recommending *inter alia*
that if the latter was indeed working toward a common valuation system, the solution
would be for GATT contracting parties to accept the CCC's Convention on Valuation. See
"Customs Matters: Communication from the Customs Co-operation Council," GATT
docs., MTN/NTM/W/17, August 26, 1975.

[27] "GATT MTN—Customs Valuation," EC Commission, GUD/1283/76–E (Document
no. 215-CVC), December 8, 1976.

ing about the U.S. system, namely that in its administration the system was more conducive to consistency and uniformity than the BDV, even if in practice it had been flawed by political intervention. Particularly appealing was the export-value criterion of valuation, which was a positive concept that in fact served as the valuation method for most U.S. imports. Also appealing was the hierarchy of valuation methods in U.S. law, which ordered the choices of customs officers, in contrast to the free scope to determine value they were given under the BDV.

The U.S. study led to a period of internal debate in the EC and its member governments. The EC negotiators felt that a proposal organized around the positive concept could be a basis for compromise with the United States, but the prospect of selling this internally seemed remote. The first problem was one of sheer inertia, plus the symbolic problem of the appearance of Europe and the rest of the world changing its customs procedures to please the Americans. Second, the CCC and the customs services in some EC member countries resisted any change from the notional system which would diminish their bureaucratic authority over the valuation process. Third, the customs service was organizationally more powerful in some EC governments (e.g., Denmark and West Germany) than in others, which translated into political resistance within the EC structures themselves. Apart from the symbolic issue of how to deal with the Americans, the crux of the argument within the EC was a division between officials oriented toward commerce and those oriented toward customs and finance. The former were responsive to export interests and wanted a neutral valuation method. The latter were more responsive to import interests and were more concerned with the capacity of the valuation system to provide import protection and revenue.

The structure of interests within the Community led the EC negotiators to travel to the EC member countries to inform trade ministries and major exporters of their concerns in the customs valuation negotiation. Customs valuation is regarded by most people, no doubt for good reason, as an esoteric subject, and it was necessary to convince many officials and businessmen that it was an important issue of commercial policy. Eventually a coalition was built that came to support an international reform of customs procedures.[28] In building the support for

[28] The argument used by the EC officials was outlined as follows in one of the many internal mimeographed documents on this subject: "In defining Community objectives it is important to consider the overall economic context in which they are being defined. The internal Customs Union, free trade agreements, preferential agreements and GSP [generalized system of preferences] produce a situation where something less than 25% of imports into the Community will be subject to customs duties. Our average industrial

reform, EC officials themselves were motivated by a concern that is often just beneath the surface in negotiations between the EC and external parties, namely the impact of the negotiation on the competence of the EC Commission itself. Customs services were attached to EC member governments, and the greater control they had over questions of valuation meant the less coordination and uniformity within the EC itself. It was in the EC Commission's interest vis-à-vis the national customs services to take the lead in reforming the system. It was further in the Commission's interest vis-à-vis the CCC to reform the customs system in the context of a negotiation within the GATT, rather than to seek reform through a harmonization of national policies within the CCC. In sum, the EC negotiators saw the negotiation with the United States over customs valuation as a means of expanding the Commission's own competence over valuation procedures in the Community, and also as a means of reducing the influence of member governments and a competitor international organization in matters involving trade relations between the EC and other countries.

The period of internal debate led to the preparation of parallel draft valuation codes within the EC. These were presented for decision at an ad hoc meeting of the 113 Committee held in September 1977.[29] One document began with the familiar notional form ("... the customs value shall be the price which a buyer ... would pay") and went on to include many elements of the BDV procedures.[30] The second document adopted the positive form ("... the price paid ... shall be accepted as the basis for determining the customs value"), and it went on to incorporate the hierarchy of customs procedures that the EC negotiators had found appealing in the U.S. system.[31] With two drafts before it, the 113 Committee was able to conduct a more precise examination of the matter than had been possible previously. The meeting came to the consen-

---

tariff is in the region of 7% and this is likely to be significantly reduced as a result of the Tokyo Round. The economic effect of the adjustment of import values is therefore, in general, marginal. On the other hand, Community exports are often subject to high tariffs, sometimes associated with protectionist valuation systems, where valuation adjustments can have considerable economic significance. For these reasons, export considerations should take precedence over import considerations in the customs valuation field" ("GATT MTN—Customs Valuation—Objectives and Strategy," Commission of the European Communities, Administration of the Customs Union, Brussels, January 26, 1977, 1).

[29] The EC's 113 Committee is described in ch. 6.

[30] "Valuation Rules: Value of Goods for the Purposes of Levying Ad Valorem Duties of Custom," EC Commission, GUD/804/77-E (Document no. 236-CVC), undated, 1.

[31] "Valuation Rules: Value of Goods for the Purposes of Levying Ad Valorem Duties of Custom," EC Commission, GUD/805/77-E (Document no. 237-CVC), undated, 1.

sus that the positive form was clearer and more precise, and therefore better. It was simplicity that carried the argument; or, in the words of one EC official, the appeal of the formula of "what did you *pay* for the blasted thing, not what the thing ought to have cost." From some accounts the 113 decision was an unexpected result, but most agreed it was a major turning point in the customs valuation negotiation.

The EC further refined its draft, then presented a revised proposal to GATT on November 8, 1977.[32] In an accompanying communication, the EC representative candidly outlined the considerable importance the EC attached to customs valuation in the Tokyo Round. The statement underscored the fact that the EC had accepted the positive approach with a defined hierarchy, and in so doing had based its proposal "on what we believe to be good features of the United States valuation system."[33] The EC presented its proposal "with a great deal of humility" as "a draft which could provide the starting point for these negotiations," but it also did not fail to emphasize the distance it felt it had gone to advance the negotiation. As the EC representative put it:

> As I said at the beginning of my statement we have opted for a positive approach. Those of you who know our valuation system and who know the Brussels definition will recognize that the adoption of a positive system would represent a fundamental change for the European Community. This would be a very big concession of the part of the Community made in the interest of the success of these negotiations.[34]

The EC commenced negotiations on its new proposals with the American team negotiating customs valuation, principally Geneva-based Douglas Newkirk (who had overall responsibility for code negotiations) and Bruce Wilson in Washington. The U.S. negotiators were receptive to the EC draft. Indeed they had little reason not to be, for the EC proposal accomplished things both sides wanted. First, both sides wanted a system that could be applied uniformly, and the fact that the EC adopted the positive approach vindicated what the Americans had been saying for some time about their own procedures. Second, both sides wanted reform of the chaotic elements in the U.S. system, and the new system promised to achieve that. Finally, both sides wanted to drop the protective aspects of the U.S. system, especially ASP

[32] "Customs Valuation," GATT docs., MTN/NTM/W/122, November 8, 1977.
[33] "Statement Made by the Commission of the European Communities at the Meeting of the Sub-Group of 15 November 1977," GATT docs., MTN/NTM/W/126, November 21, 1977, 3.
[34] Ibid., 7.

and the final list. This was always the major political sine qua non on the EC side, and it was even an important desideratum of the U.S. administration.[35] What had caused the problem was the demand by the American negotiators that they be "paid" something for dropping the ASP and final list, in order that they would have a more reciprocal package to present to Congress. The demand for payment had angered the Europeans, who hardly felt that a party violating GATT law through the stratagem of a grandfather clause should be compensated for ending the illegality. The EC concession (or initiative, if one prefers) succeeded in turning a difficult zero-sum problem of bargaining into a much broader debate over reform in which both parties had common interests. The EC initiative redefined the nature of the problem, which is a classic formula in the literature on negotiation and conflict resolution.[36]

The tabling of a revised position by the EC was more welcome to the United States than to the other major nations involved in the customs valuation negotiation. The Japanese, who had recently adopted the BDV, felt it was a better system and in any case were unenthusiastic about making a further change. The Nordics were initially noncommittal, not having been party to the internal debates in the EC. The Canadians strongly opposed the EC proposal. The EC draft did not allow for valuation in reference to the domestic market of the exporting country, which was the cornerstone of the Canadian system. Furthermore the Canadian delegation argued that the EC proposal did not pay sufficient attention to the problems of valuation in trade between related parties, which were a particular problem in smaller countries where a large proportion of trade might be accounted for by subsidiaries of foreign multinational firms. On the first point, Canada was completely isolated in the informal group of the Big Five, as the others sought to base valuation procedures on a more neutral or "business-oriented" approach and therefore found the Canadian approach too interventionist. The second point raised by the Canadian delegation

---

[35] As Saul Sherman put it, "Thus, the Valuation Code was designed largely to give ASP a decent burial" ("Customs Valuation Code," 124).

[36] The EC initiative was an important instance of cooperative solutions in bargaining, and might be interpreted by four different negotiation theories as follows: first, as an example of creative problem solving versus selection among given possibilities, as described by Sawyer and Guetzkow, "Bargaining and Negotiation"; second, as an example of "debates" as opposed to "fights," as described by Rapoport, *Fights, Games and Debates*; third, as an example of integrative bargaining versus distributive bargaining, as analyzed by Walton and McKersie, *Labor Negotiations*; and fourth, as an example of negotiation over common interests instead of negotiation over positions, as outlined by Fisher and Ury, *Getting to Yes*.

subsequently became the subject of long negotiation, in part because of its relevance for the developing countries. The Canadian position on the related-party issue was that invoice prices in trade between related parties were unreliable in principle, and that a valuation system should provide an adjustment to achieve neutral or fair pricing of imports. Both the Europeans and Americans resisted this argument; particularly, the former maintained that the Canadian valuation system was simply protectionist, and they resented the argument that the fourth-largest trading entity in GATT should get special treatment on customs valuation as a "small" country.

The developing countries were not privy to the bilateral discussions between the EC and the United States, nor to the negotiations within the Big Five. The negotiation expanded in a pyramidal fashion on customs valuation much as it had on subsidy/countervail. In part, pyramidal negotiation was a response to the need to organize multilateral negotiation on a very complicated and technical subject. However, on customs valuation the pyramidal process was convenient, because the developing countries had very different interests from the major countries, except possibly Canada. As a group, the developing countries sought a more interventionist and protectionist system than was acceptable to the majors. First, like the Canadians, the developing countries were concerned with related-party trade and the effects of import dependence on larger developed countries. Second, in much developing-country trade, cheating on customs declarations is simply taken for granted, and thus governments feel the need to exercise maximum discretion in establishing values on imported goods. Finally, and most important, many developing countries rely on tariffs to produce government revenue, and hence undervaluation of imports through cheating could result in financial losses for the government. This fact gradually drew finance ministries in the capitals of developing countries into the customs valuation negotiation, which had previously been under the direction of trade representatives in Geneva. The involvement of their finance ministries in turn reinforced the opposition of the developing countries to a neutral or business-oriented valuation approach.

As the negotiation moved into the spring of 1978, the developing countries were on the fringes of the main negotiation on customs valuation, and in fact were actively exploring the possibility of negotiating a separate code. However, work on the main customs valuation code progressed rapidly. The Nordics accepted the EC lead, and after some difficult negotiations on specific issues (e.g., advertising costs), the Japanese accepted the EC draft as well. By the time of the Bonn summit in July 1978, only the Canadians and the developing countries were outside the evolving code, and the code was reported as being politically "tied up" among the EC, Japan, and the United States.[37]

OTHER CODE NEGOTIATIONS

Government Procurement

Negotiation of the code on government procurement provided an interesting counterpoint to the negotiations on subsidy/countervail and customs valuation. Unlike the latter, it fully engaged all countries, including the developing countries, from its first appearance on the Tokyo Round agenda. This probably occurred because the GATT work on government procurement essentially proceeded from a partially completed draft code received from the OECD in 1976, in which the major industrialized countries had already defined the principal issues for negotiation.

The transfer of the government-procurement negotiation from the OECD reflected the constellation of interests that subsequently influenced the negotiation within GATT. Within the OECD, the draft government-procurement code had been negotiated between the individual countries of Western Europe and North America, plus Japan. At the same time, the EC Commission was working on a directive on procurement which sought to achieve greater liberalization of procurement policies within the Nine.[38] Progress in the OECD negotiation had been slow, reflecting the conservative attitudes of European governments toward opening the procurement process to international competition. The United States and Canada, both motivated by perceived export interests, supported the move to the Tokyo Round on the ground that the larger negotiating forum would provide greater opportunities for tradeoffs and eventual settlement. Some European nations, particularly France, strongly resisted the transfer. The EC Commission itself supported the move, and for two reasons. First, the Commission had a larger margin for maneuver in GATT than it had in the OECD in part because control over the issue shifted away from procurement specialists

[37] For example, "Three codes—dealing respectively with customs valuation, government procurement, and standards and technical regulations, have undergone major progress and are now politically 'tied up' even if some technical details remain to be negotiated. (However, Canada, it is noted in the text, did not take part in the negotiation on customs valuation)" ("Tokyo Round: Big Three Reach 'Framework of Understanding,'" *European Report* [EC Commission newsletter], no. 523, July 15, 1978).

[38] This directive was approved by the EC Council in December 1976. It was the third EC directive on government procurement, two previous directives having been issued in 1965. See Pomeranz, "Government Procurement," 1274–75.

within the member governments of the Nine and toward the more ex-port-oriented 113 Committee of the EC. Second, the greater prospect of settlement at the Tokyo Round opened the door for the Commission to use action at the GATT level to help it set policy on government pro-curement within the EC. While the views of the EC Commission ad-vanced the prospects for the shift from the OECD, the issue finally turned on the developing countries' strong insistence that government procurement be negotiated at the Tokyo Round, a position which was consistent with the Tokyo Declaration of 1973.

It is often the case that substance shapes the process in international negotiation. Such was the case in the government-procurement nego-tiation at the Tokyo Round. The task for the negotiators fell logically into two parts. First, it was necessary to reach agreement on the rules that would govern procurement practices in the signatory countries. This task was similar to that faced in the other code negotiations, and it emphasized the skills of multilateral consensus building and legal drafting. Second, it was necessary to decide which agencies (i.e., enti-ties) of the signatory governments the rules would apply to, since it was obvious no nation was prepared to allow the full range of its govern-ment expenditure for goods to be subject to international competition. The task in the second phase was similar to an item-by-item tariff ne-gotiation (or a poker game), where the participants placed items on or withdrew them from the bargaining table in an effort to wangle an at-tractive offer from the other partners. The positions nations took in the second phase obviously bore some relationship to the rules that were negotiated in the procurement code, and indeed some of the rules (such as the threshold value of the contracts to which the code would apply) were not finalized until late in the negotiation. Nevertheless the nego-tiation essentially proceeded in two stages: the first focused on the code itself and extended to about mid-1978, and the second concerned the entities to be covered by the code and lasted for the remainder of the Tokyo Round negotiation.

The Tokyo Round negotiation on government procurement began in earnest in January 1977 with the tabling of the draft OECD instrument. This text became much altered in the subsequent negotiation, although its basic working definitions and itemized breakdown of the tendering process were maintained in the final code.[39] The debate on the OECD text stimulated a number of proposals from national governments,

[39] For example, the OECD instrument generated the basic distinction between open tendering procedures, under which all interested suppliers could submit a tender, and se-lective tendering procedures, under which those suppliers invited to do so could submit a tender.

which were compiled by the GATT secretariat and presented in a draft integrated text in December 1977.[40] The form of this text was remarkably consistent with the form of the final code concluded some sixteen months later.[41] Again the draft integrated text brought forth additional proposals, and under the pressure of the Bonn summit "deadline" of July 1978 the key articles were revised by the joint efforts of a number of delegations. By this point, the square bracketing in the various code articles was greatly reduced, and it was obvious a successful result could be achieved. As if to confirm this, in July 1978 the United States, Japan, and several other countries tabled offers on entities to be covered by the code, which started the second phase of the negotiation.

Negotiation of the government-procurement code was formally carried out by the MTN subgroup responsible for this area. The subgroup met regularly, was chaired by Mr. Robin Tooker of the GATT secretariat, and was usually attended by about fifty to seventy delegations. The negotiation process was relatively open, and the subgroup took up written or oral proposals made by any nation. A smaller, informally selected group of around eighteen to twenty delegations met occasionally to take up various aspects of the code, and as well there were regular meetings of the developed countries (the Big Five plus Switzerland) and the developing countries. The GATT secretariat was invited to be present at these meeting below the subgroup level. Reports on the results of various meetings were circulated internally, and in general information flowed freely up and down the hierarchy of negotiating committees.

Despite the multilateral format of the government-procurement negotiation, the major negotiating problems arose in the bilateral relationship between the United States and the Community. The EC entered the government-procurement negotiations with two major concerns: one was to avoid making commitments to international tendering in the areas of energy, transportation, and telecommunications; and the second was to press for the adoption in GATT of the same procurement principles that had been developed internally within the EC.[42] The for-

[40] "Draft Integrated Text for Negotiation on Government Procurement: Note by the Secretariat," GATT docs., MTN/NTM/W/133, December 15, 1977.

[41] The draft text was heavily bracketed, but in the important article "Tendering Procedures" (Article 5 in the final code), the subheadings remained the same and most of the numbered points within the subheadings were also maintained. For example, under the sensitive subheading "Use of Single Tendering," six of the seven points of the earlier draft were essentially maintained in the final code, although the order of presentation was considerably altered.

[42] Two other EC goals were to secure export benefits for EC suppliers and to negotiate special treatment for developing countries, but these goals were clearly secondary to the first two.

191

mer concern would be taken up in the second phase of the procurement negotiation, but the latter applied to the drafting of the code itself. On the U.S. side, the greatest concerns were to maximize the scope and coverage of the code and to achieve greater transparency (i.e., public visibility) in the procurement practices of other countries, and particularly the Nine. The latter concern was motivated by the perception among American negotiators that U.S. procurement procedures were more open, and therefore fairer and more competitive, than those of the European countries. The U.S. concern over transparency carried important practical implications for the procurement negotiation, but it also had a symbolic dimension in the implicit demand that other countries should adopt what amounted to American procedures on procurement. This of course is no more than what the EC was doing in seeking to have GATT adopt its own internal procedures on procurement. The behavior on both sides was entirely typical, and it recurred frequently in the Tokyo Round. When nations meet to create a single international practice out of diverse national practices, it is to be expected they will seek wherever they can to extend their national procedures into the international arena.

The bilateral negotiation between the U.S. and the EC was essentially resolved by a tradeoff in which the Americans accepted the EC lead on outlining tendering procedures, and the EC accepted a greater measure of transparency than its member governments were comfortable with. Transparency was written into the code in several places. The code required signatories to publish information about procurement laws, regulations, and intended purchases, and it detailed the procedures whereby tender documentation is to be provided to suppliers. It defined and limited the extent to which "single tending" would be permitted. Finally, the code required entities to provide an explanation to an unsuccessful tenderer as to why the bid was unsuccessful, along with the name of the winning tenderer. The latter point was strongly resisted by the EC negotiators, who were concerned that providing such information would encourage collusion between suppliers on future contracts, and thereby subvert the competitive process that greater transparency was intended to create. This dispute was difficult to resolve, and it became the subject of a mediating effort by the Canadians, whose own position was between those of the Americans and the Europeans. In the end a compromise was worked out on the wording, but the EC essentially accepted the principle of providing full information to all suppliers who tendered on government contracts.

In the period up to July 1978, the developing countries had participated more in the government-procurement negotiation than they had in either the subsidy/countervail or customs valuation negotiations. As a result, the draft government-procurement code contained a relatively strong article on special and differential (s and D) treatment for developing countries. The article provided for reduced coverage of the code in the developing countries, while developed countries were encouraged to include entities that would purchase products from developing-country suppliers. The article had allowed developing countries to negotiate exceptions to the general obligation to extend "national treatment" to suppliers from developed countries, and it called on developed countries to provide technical assistance to developing countries in the field of government procurement. These various s and D provisions went some distance to satisfy the demands of the developing countries for exceptional treatment, but they obviously did not create far-reaching, or costly, commitments on the part of the developed countries. Of course the developing countries had proposed such commitments, but these proposals had made no headway in the negotiation.[43]

The absence of a pyramidal process in the government-procurement negotiation led the developing countries to be more favorably disposed toward this code, and largely to exempt it from the criticism they voiced about the Tokyo Round at the time of the Bonn summit. There were several reasons why developed/developing-country relations proceeded with less difficulty in this area. As already mentioned, the issue had been negotiated in the OECD prior to coming to GATT, and hence the developed countries had already structured the debate. Once it arrived in GATT, the negotiation was conducted openly, and consequently the GATT secretariat was able to play a prominent role in facilitating the negotiation process. Included in this role was the task of assuring that all nations, including the developing countries, were kept abreast of developments in the negotiation. Finally, the substance of the negotiation itself insured that the inherent conflict between the developed and developing nations could be "fractionated" over the whole span of the negotiation.[44] The negotiation on government procurement divided fairly naturally into two stages, the construction of the code itself and the decision as to which government entities were to be placed under the

[43] For example, Nigeria had proposed that "Direct favour to developing countries could be achieved by reserving a percentage of government purchases exclusively for developing countries (25 per cent)" ("Communication from the Delegation of Nigeria," GATT docs., MTN/NTM/W/128, December 5, 1977, 1).

[44] Fisher, *International Conflict*, has advanced the concept of fractionating conflict as a mechanism for resolving conflicts. This research would suggest that the technique is dependent on the substance of the negotiation.

code. The developed countries could easily give special treatment to the developing countries in the second stage, by extending the benefits of the code fully to those developing countries that in turn included only a few entities under the code. Thus the substance of the negotiation allowed the rules to be applied more in a gradual manner than in an all-or-nothing fashion, which reduced conflict over the rules themselves. As a result, the developing countries were able to negotiate more liberal rules than they otherwise might have done (particularly because they also had important export interests at stake), and the developed countries were more able to make concessions on important issues such as national treatment.

Standards

A draft code on technical barriers to trade, that is, standards, had been completed in GATT prior to the Tokyo Declaration of 1973 (see chapter 3). There had been pressure from the Americans to conclude the negotiation independently of the Tokyo Round, but the Europeans had resisted this, probably in order to use the standards negotiation as a bargaining chip in higher-priority areas such as customs valuation. Consequently, the standards negotiation was effectively put on hold throughout the early period of the Tokyo round negotiation. In the middle period, 1975–77, when the overall negotiation was bogged down on the agricultural problem, some progress was made on the definitions to be used in the draft code. Throughout this period, the Nordics made a persistent effort to incorporate in the GATT code definitions respecting standards already developed in Europe.[45] It will be recalled that the United States particularly had resisted moving to what the Europeans had claimed were "international" definitions. In the end, the United States conceded the point, and the draft code went through considerable definitional change over this period. This movement was encouraging, given the political impasse that existed in the Tokyo Round at that time. By the time of the breakthrough in mid-1977, the draft code had an agreed structure that was very similar to the code that was

[45] These definitions were developed by the Economic Commission for Europe (ECE) and the International Standards Organization (ISO). An example of the different definitions is that where the GATT code spoke of "quality assurance" systems, the nearest ECE/ISO equivalent was "certification" systems; it was argued that the former were misleading, since no guarantee of quality was given, but only one of conformity to different standards. See "The Applicability of the ECE/ISO Definitions for the Proposed Standards Code: Note by the Secretariat," GATT docs., MTN/NTM/W/18, September 17, 1975. This document reviewed a study of the ECE/ISO definitions prepared by M. K. Bergholm of Finland.

finally signed in 1979, with the important exception of a section on dispute settlement and provisions for special treatment for developing countries.[46]

The basic point of agreement among the various nations negotiating the standards code was to refrain from using standards as obstacles to trade. This commitment, which eventually became included in Article 2.1 of the final code, was important because it put trade concerns (and, more important, trade policymakers) into areas that were previously the exclusive domain of technical certification bodies.[47] Another important commitment was to accept the results of international testings and certification procedures, which has successfully been done in EFTA countries, and, even more important, to accept international standards as a basis for domestic regulations and standards.[48] A third area of agreement dealt with the fundamentals of standardization procedures; it called upon authorities to set standards in terms of performance criteria instead of design or descriptive characteristics. For example, this would require that safety standards in a power lawnmower would be specified in terms of the tested capability of the machine to be operated without injury, rather than in terms of compliance with a requirement that the machine have a particular foot guard that might have been designed by some manufacturer to prevent injury. This agreement would promote much more flexibility in meeting technical specifications, which is important from the perspective of permitting manufacturers in one country to meet the standards applied in another. Finally, national governments agreed to provide an "inquiry point" for foreign producers seeking information about technical regulations, standards, or certification procedures. This requirement was analogous to those in the government procurement code that required governments to take positive action to provide information about internal procedures to prospective exporters in other countries. This was a matter that had been vigorously pursued by the United States, and it was generally part of an effort by that nation to introduce what U.S. negotiators referred to as "sunshine procedures" into the internal trade-related practices of GATT members.

[46] "Draft Code of Conduct for Preventing Technical Barriers to Trade," GATT docs., MTN/NTM/W/94, May 20, 1977.

[47] The officials in these bodies were whimsically referred to by trade negotiators as "green-eyeshade people"; that is, officials whose main job was to examine products and ensure compliance with specified standards.

[48] This obligation was included in Article 2.2 of the final code, and has been described by R. W. Middleton, former assistant secretary general of the ISO, as "probably the most fundamental obligation in the Code." See "GATT Standards Code," 215.

The standards negotiation was a technical affair conducted outside the limelight of the Tokyo Round. The subject was highly specialized, and even the most technical negotiations did not deal with standards themselves, but only with a set of general obligations nations should assume when setting standards. The standards negotiation was conducted mainly in Geneva, and in a patient step-by-step manner in which a draft code would be written up, subjected to criticism and proposals in negotiation sessions, and then redrafted and circulated as a basis for subsequent meetings. The GATT staff, particularly Mr. Peter Williams, played an important role in the process of codifying and distributing the various alterations made to the draft code. Perhaps because it was so technical, the standards negotiation was relatively immune to political difficulties elsewhere in the Tokyo Round. For example, over the period April 1975, to March 1978, there were six separate draft codes promulgated by the GATT secretariat, and four of these were negotiated and drawn up during the 1975–77 impasse at the Tokyo Round.

From the standpoint of the process itself, the standards negotiation was a polar opposite to the negotiation on subsidy/countervail. The subsidy/countervail negotiation was a difficult, highly politicized, and even symbolic negotiation, while that on standards was much easier, more technical, and nonpolitical. The differences between these two negotiating areas were not only a matter of substance, but also a matter of history as well. Subsidy/countervail was a longstanding issue in GATT, and positions on this issue had become entrenched in the bureaucracies of different nations, particularly in the United States and Europe. Standards was a much newer subject, and consequently it did not present the same problem in terms of vested governmental or private interest. The main problem in the subsidy/countervail negotiation was to move actors on the domestic side off positions they had held for many years, while on standards the main task was to work out a new regime for a trade problem that was hardly even mentioned in the General Agreement. Yet another difference was the locus of the two negotiations. The standards negotiation was conducted within GATT at Geneva, while the subsidy/countervail negotiation, especially for the crucial major powers, was conducted from Washington and Brussels. A comparison of these two negotiations suggests that the more difficult politically a negotiation beomes, the more important the internal negotiation becomes relative to the negotiation with external parties, and consequently the greater likelihood that the negotiation will be run from a position close to home.

The standards negotiation was less politicized than other areas, but it was not without its political difficulties. The provisions for developing countries in the standards code presented problems, but the most contentious issue was the insistence by the EC that the code did not place the same obligations on nations with federal structures as it did on those with unitary governments. Specifically the difference lay in the fact that in federal systems some standards and certification processes might fall under the jurisdiction of regional governments which were not under any legal obligation to comply with an international code signed by a national government. This problem was further complicated in countries like the United States where many standards are set by autonomous agencies acting in the private sector. The issue of compliance of countries with federal structures was a longstanding controversy in the standards negotiation, and it was not resolved at the time of the Bonn summit of 1978. Generally the EC insisted that federal countries should use their "best endeavors" to ensure compliance, but how they were to do this was unresolved.[49] The problem eventually became linked to the dispute-settlement clause in the code, and was not resolved until near the conclusion of the overall negotiation. The irony was that the code which produced the least-polemical debate throughout the Tokyo Round was in the end one of the last to be settled politically.

Safeguards

There was relatively little negotiating activity in the safeguards area over the period 1974–78. The safeguards negotiation, it will be recalled, was largely a matter of revising Article 19 of the GATT to make it relevant to current trade practices. This article had provided procedures for nations to impose restriction on particular products in emergency situations, but these procedures were being ignored in favor of more informal export-restraint agreements (i.e., VER's—voluntary export restraints—and OMA's—orderly marketing arrangements) being reached between exporting and importing nations. The safeguards negotiation raised the question of how Article 19 could be revised to include the latter agreements, and it explored specific problems such as time limits for safeguard actions, and whether such actions should be

[49] The concern of the EC was how to operationalize "best endeavors," particularly when a nation might claim that it had invoked "best endeavors" simply by sending a routine letter to a certifying body, and also what redress other nations might have if failed "best endeavors" became a subject of contention. See 'Proposal of the European Communities for the Draft Code for Preventing Technical Barriers to Trade," GATT docs., MTN/NTM/W/135, January 13, 1978.

nondiscriminatory and taken under the aegis of GATT surveillance. Because they were often the target of export-restraint agreements, the developing countries were especially interested in the safeguards negotiation, and several (namely Brazil, Mexico, Nigeria, and Pakistan) brought forward proposals for discussion during the 1976–77 period. Generally these proposals sought to exclude developing countries from safeguarding measures taken by developed countries, and to insure that safeguarding actions would not be targeted selectively against particular countries.

The EC delegation had entered the safeguards negotiation with a mandate to seek change in the Article 19 system. The position of the EC, which could be traced to the analysis presented in the OECD Rey report of 1972, is that import disturbances were often caused by the exports of only one or two nations, and that to take nondiscriminatory safeguard action would only extend the disturbance to the entire trading system. This analysis became translated into a political imperative by the Council of Ministers of the EC, and in its early instructions to EC negotiators on nontariff measures it included a demand that the principle of selectivity (i.e., discriminatory application) be negotiated into a reformed safeguards procedure in the GATT.[50] The EC delegation formulated its negotiating position from this demand. First, the EC sought to rewrite Article 19 and to clarify its requirements regarding the definition of serious injury and market disturbance, the notification of safeguarding actions, and the limits of GATT surveillance over safeguards. Particularly the EC sought to create a workable system that would encourage nations to terminate the increasing use of informal (and illegal) export-restraint agreements. Second, the EC delegation sought to include a provision for selective safeguards in a revised system. The EC took the position that the language of Article 19 was not clear on the point of whether safeguarding action must be nondiscriminatory, even though in practice such actions had always been so considered. In any case, the issue for the EC turned on contemporary realities which suggested that at base the safeguards issue was an accumulation of very specific problems. For example, the EC delegation presented the argument that the problem could be as specific as a sudden fivefold increase of a particular product from a particular nation in one year, and that

[50] The demand to achieve selectivity in safeguards was one of three major political demands set by the EC Council on nontariff measures. The other two were the insertion of a material-injury clause in U.S. countervail legislation, and a customs valuation code that would terminate the American Selling Price (ASP) in the United States. In successive reviews of these demands, the Council resisted any modification of its position, which thus constituted a very tight mandate for EC negotiators.

for such a specific subject one needed a selective and nondiscriminatory instrument.

The pressure from the EC eventually led to the tabling of a draft integrated text on safeguards in June 1978.[51] The draft was supported by several developed countries, including the United States. The draft was heavily bracketed, and while the EC regarded it as a step forward, it was questionable whether the draft had raised more problems than it had settled.[52] The draft did provide for the principle of selectivity, but only after stating that "In general, safeguard measures . . . shall be applied on a global basis without discrimination." This limited the use of selectivity to what the draft described as "unusual and exceptional circumstances."[53] The draft formed the basis for an intensive negotiation on safeguards that commenced in the fall of 1978. Negotiations were largely between the developed and the developing countries, although there continued to be considerable disagreement among the developed countries themselves. For example, although the United States and the EC shared the problem of being vulnerable to sudden increases in exports from low-cost suppliers, the United States was far more sympathetic to the developing countries' position on selectivity. For one thing, the U.S. government was in conflict: Congress could have accepted selectivity easily, but the administration, particularly the State Department, was much more committed to the principle of nondiscrimination and, in the words of one participant, was reluctant "to go back on thirty years of GATT history." Furthermore the United States was politically closer than the EC to the nations leading the developing countries in the safeguards negotiation, which made it more difficult for the U.S. delegation to take a hard line on selectivity. As a result, the United States gravitated toward the middle ground between the EC and the de-

---

[51] "Draft Integrated Text on Safeguards," GATT docs., MTN/INF/26, June 21, 1978.

[52] For example, Merciai has commented; ". . . it was clear that disagreements on selectivity, adjustment assistance, determination of injury, and multilateral surveillance, prevented OECD countries from adopting a common position on these primordial issues" ("Safeguard Measures," 58).

[53] The following provision on selectivity indicates how heavily qualified the issue was in the draft text: "In unusual and exceptional circumstances where it is clearly established that serious injury or threat thereof, as described in Chapter 1, exists and is caused by sharp and substantial increase of imports from one or a limited number of countries and the effects of imports from other sources are regarded as being negligible, and where imports causing serious injury can be clearly distinguished from other imports of a particular product, an importing signatory may by agreement with the exporting signatory pursuant to the subsequent paragraphs, apply safeguard measures limited to imports or threat thereof, provided such measures are applied equitably. "Draft Integrated Text on Safeguards," GATT docs., MTN/INF/26, June 21, 1978).

veloping countries, and in the end was prepared to weaken the commitment on selectivity more than proved acceptable to the EC.

The developing countries were united against the integrated draft of June 1978 largely on account of opposition to the selectivity principle. Unlike some other issues, the selectivity issue found developing-country delegations generally under tight instructions from their capitals and their margin for compromise narrow. The representatives of developing countries attacked the selectivity principle on many fronts, ranging from the economic argument that it penalized the most efficient producers to the political argument that it put smaller developing countries in a disadvantaged position vis-à-vis large developed importers.[54] However, their ultimate objection to selectivity was that it would deny the few benefits that existed for developing countries under the GATT principle of nondiscrimination. In the framework negotiation and elsewhere, the developing countries had sought relief from the principle of nondiscrimination in the name of economic development, only to have the developed countries insist on the principle qua principle. In the safeguards negotiation, the developed countries appeared to be prepared to depart from this principle when it served their immediate trading interests, and moreover to do so in a manner that would jeopardize the interests of those developing countries that managed to compete successfully in the liberal GATT system. The position taken by the developed countries appeared hypocritical to the developing countries, and it was simply not acceptable in the governments of the latter.

Progress in the Tariff Negotiation

The code negotiations on nontariff measures were the innovative part of the Tokyo Round. In the tariff negotiation, the Tokyo Round reverted to a familiar form of trade bargaining that was reminiscent of GATT negotiations since the late 1940s. As had also occurred in the Kennedy Round, there was a lengthy prenegotiation in the Tokyo Round over the approach to take to the negotiation. This discussion had got caught up in the general dispute between the United States and the European Community over the role of agriculture in the negotiation, with the result that little headway had been made in the tariff negotiation over the period 1974–77.

In July 1977 Robert Strauss and Wilhelm Haferkamp negotiated a temporary settlement of the agriculture problem and succeeded in set-

[54] A list of some of the arguments against selectivity is presented in Price, "Surplus Capacity," 312.

ting a timetable for the completion of the negotiation.[55] This agreement helped break the impasse in other areas of the negotiation, notably tariffs. Consistent with the timetable, Strauss met again in Brussels with the EC leaders in September 1977 and reached a settlement on the approach to the tariff negotiation. The two parties agreed to apply the Swiss formula, namely $z = 14x \div (14 + x)$, in tabling their tariff offers, although it was accepted that the EC would apply the less-demanding constant 16 in their calculations. If applied without exceptions, the Swiss formula would reduce the average tariff level of the major developed countries by about 40 percent. This formula was eventually accepted by most developed nations in the tariff negotiation, although the Canadians rejected it and in the end applied their own formula. Finally, the September meeting between the U.S. and EC leaders produced a tentative agreement to phase in tariff cuts over an eight-year period. This staging period was subsequently accepted by the other participants in the tariff negotiation.

With the tariff-cutting formula in place, the negotiation followed the familiar pattern of tabling of initial offers (less exceptions), withdrawing from or adding to original offers, and bargaining over specific products or sectors in the offers of various nations. The major concerns of the participants in this kind of negotiation are the depth of tariff cuts offered, the types of products on which tariffs are cut, and the trade volumes associated with these products. Nations generally seek maximum tariff cuts on the products they export to their partners, and particularly on products that are considered to be "high quality"; that is, products in which the labor or technology content is high or where demand elasticities or competitive patterns are such that a reduction in the tariff will likely increase exports. Of course on such products (e.g., textiles and apparel) importing nations often have the most difficulty in reducing tariffs. Nations further seek tariff reductions on products in which trade volumes have already been established with importing countries, since the benefit from the reduction is then actual and not merely potential. As a result, tariff reductions are not usually expressed as simple percentages, but rather are weighted in terms of the trade volume of the importing country. The weighting permits a comparison of benefits exchanged between products where the tariff reductions and import volumes may be different; e.g., a 10 percent tariff cut on $30 million of trade might be equivalent to a 20 percent cut on $15 million of trade. Thus the two variables—tariff reductions and import volumes—form the basis of the general formulas that nations use to eval-

[55] The timetable is included in ch. 4, n. 68.

uate a tariff negotiation that includes many different products or product sectors.[56] These variables produce a quantitative assessment of tariff reductions, and "while they do not convey much information that is economically useful,"[57] they can be used to compare the performance of different nations in trade negotiations. As for the third variable—the inclusion of "quality" products in a tariff offer—it is usually regarded by trade negotiators as a nonquantitative and therefore subjective method of assessing national performance.[58]

The fact that trade volumes enter the picture in exchanging benefits in trade negotiation has important implications for the bargaining process. In offering concessions, nations usually propose tariff reductions to the "principal supplier" (i.e., the largest exporter) of a particular product. Conversely, in seeking concessions on their own exports, nations usually concentrate their efforts on the largest importers of their goods. This creates the tendency for nations with the largest trade flows to get the most action in tariff negotiations, while nations with smaller trade flows often find they have few interests with other small trading nations, and their interests with larger countries are overwhelmed by other large traders. Thus the logic of multilateral tariff negotiation dictates that a general agreement must be initiated between the largest trading partners. Only after an incipient agreement is under way are smaller traders able to negotiate their interests on products in which there is multilateral trade.[59] In practice, the logic of the situation led the United States and the European Community to take the lead in the tariff negotiation, while nations the size of Canada and smaller were often dependent on the outcome of negotiations between the majors. The position of Japan was roughly intermediate: there were numerous areas where the Japanese were the largest traders with the majors.

[56] In the Tokyo Round, some nations used a reduction in duty collected instead of the tariff reduction itself to calculate weighted average reductions over sectors or groupings of products. In theory there is no difference between the two variables, although the latter is regarded as more accurate for computational purposes.

[57] Robert M. Stern, "Evaluating Alternative Formulae," 54.

[58] Methods do exist for more fully quantifying the effects of tariff changes on trade and employment, but such methods were regarded by negotiators as overly precise (and insufficiently "political") for use in actual negotiation. See generally Cline et al., *Trade Negotiations*.

[59] There are some advantages in being a small trader, however, as tariff reductions negotiated between larger countries are extended to all countries through the provisions of Article 1 of the GATT requiring nondiscriminatory treatment of international trade. Small countries therefore have the possibility of receiving unreciprocated concessions, known as most-favored-nation (MFN) benefits.

Preparations for the tariff negotiation began in earnest after the summer of 1977. The deadline for tabling opening offers was set for January 1978, which meant a demanding schedule for all nations and particularly the larger traders like the EC and the United States.[60] The preparations in many countries were extensive and generally fell in two stages. First, lengthy consultations were held with import-competing interests which allowed negotiators to assess their limits in making tariff concessions to other countries, while similar meetings with exporters permitted them to determine what demands to make of other countries in the way of tariff reductions. The process generated an enormous amount of industry-specific information which needed to be assimilated and aggregated for general presentation. Second, strategy sessions were held to develop an external position vis-à-vis the principal trading partners. This stage necessitated careful analysis of the data gained from domestic interests, and particularly of how such data could be combined into an effective position in a competitive negotiating situation. In the United States, the preparatory stages were conducted largely by an interagency process within the trade bureaucracy, which was directed by the Trade Policy Staff Committee in the office of the U.S. trade representative. Congress was relatively uninvolved, having already given a mandate on tariffs to the executive in the Trade Act of 1974. In the EC, however, the tariff offer was the subject of high politics, and the EC offer was the subject of "lengthy discussions" at a Council of Ministers meeting in mid-January 1978.[61] Immediately afterward, on January 23, 1978, Ambassadors Strauss, Haferkamp, and Ushiba of Japan met in Geneva to present offers on industrial tariffs and other matters.

All three parties nominally followed the Swiss formula in tabling their tariff offers. Since the average pre–Tokyo Round tariff (on dutiable items) in these parties was in the 9 to 11 percent range,[62] this offer would have led to an average tariff cut of approximately 40 percent. All parties, of course, excepted certain products from their original formula offers. In making the offer, the United States presented a maxi-

[60] This tight scheduling was one of many examples of how Robert Strauss and other political leaders used the technique of deadline setting to maintain momentum in the negotiation. For example, U.S. officials initially thought that the deadline was unrealistic and that it revealed Strauss's inexperience in trade matters, but they nevertheless kept to the schedule.

[61] "Nine Agree Negotiating Stance," *European Report*, January 17, 1978. The discussions were largely occasioned by the French delegates, who later insisted that they had received assurances that overall average tariff reductions would not exceed 35 percent. However, the offer initially tabled by the EC was greater than that amount.

[62] Cline et al., *Trade Negotiations*, 10.

malist position in order to induce a favorable position from its partners. This strategy had the additional advantage that the political heat
from domestic interests would be taken early rather than late in the negotiation when other issues would be at stake. The United States proposed the concept of "no net exceptions" in its original offer, and it offered a larger-than-formula cut in some areas to balance out its
exceptions in other areas. Also the United States used the coefficient 14
in the tariff formula, which produced deeper cuts than the value of 16
employed by the EC, and for which U.S. negotiators expected to secure
compensating credit. As for the Japanese, they had tabled an offer consistent with the formula, but it was based on the formal GATT-bound
tariff rates existing in 1972, and not on the lower rates that had been
effectively applied by the Japanese after 1972. This stratagem had the
effect of reducing Japan's offer to its partners below the 40 percent
level.

The EC reacted adversely to the offers of Japan and the United States.
The U.S. offer had made less-than-formula cuts on a number of high-
tariff products of interest to the EC, particularly products in textiles,
chemicals, and ceramics. In return, the United States had offered larger-
than-formula cuts on products on which the tariff was already low,
thus partially defeating the principle of harmonization. This was part
of a general stratagem by the United States to withhold concessions on
"quality" products where pressures from domestic interests might be
intense, and to offer instead what trade negotiators might irreverently
describe as "garbage concessions."[63] The ploy was unsuccessful. The
EC protested against the U.S. offer, and in April withdrew from its offer
a number of products that were especially important in US/EC bilateral
trade. Included were products in sectors such as paper, chemicals, fer-
tilizers, and electronic goods. In June, the Council of Ministers instructed the EC Commission to prepare a further list of withdrawals if
the American offer were not improved. The intention of the EC was
clearly to induce the United States to increase its offers, but U.S. negotiators had gone about as far as they could with their initial offer on
sensitive products. Most of the original U.S. exceptions were never restored to formula cuts, with the result that the final tariff package on
both sides was smaller than the formula would have produced. In retrospect, it is doubtful whether, if the Americans had been prepared to
restore formula cuts on all products, the Europeans could have

[63] In the calculation of weighted average tariff reductions, a tariff cut on a product with
a low tariff and high import volume can be worth more than an equivalent cut on a product with a high tariff but lower import volume. The latter, however, would likely to be a
more valuable concession in trade terms.

matched them, since there was resistance in Council of the EC to average tariff reductions beyond 35 percent. Thus there appears to have been some element of bluff in the original EC tariff offer.[64]

The Japanese tariff offer was likewise protested against by the Europeans, who were joined by the Americans. The EC negotiators calculated that the Japanese offer amounted to an average reduction on EC exports alone of only 18 percent, and they accordingly shaped their April withdrawals to include products of interest to Japan. The Japanese negotiators indicated that further offers would be forthcoming, but these did not sufficiently materialize by July and consequently the Europeans considered adding automobiles to their exception list.[65] As for the Canadians, they had found the original U.S. offer to the EC very beneficial in terms of Canada/U.S. bilateral trade. This was because the United States, in an effort to give larger-than-formula cuts on low-tariff items, had proposed generous concessions on many semimanufactures where the Canadians had export interests. This offer encouraged the Canadians, for whom U.S. trade accounts for over 70 percent of Canadian exports, to make a maximum offer in return. The Canadian negotiators had particularly sought to win U.S. concessions on petrochemical products, but the United States had larger trade volumes in this sector with the Europeans than with the Canadians, and the former were generally unreceptive to reciprocal tariff reductions. Consequently the United States had little scope for negotiation with Canada in this area.

By mid-1978, most nations participating in the tariff negotiation had tabled offers of one sort or another. The negotiation then proceeded, as tariff negotiations usually do, to break down into a series of discussions on particular sectors and even products of interest to various trading nations. Although a tariff-cutting formula is a valuable aggregating device, in fact most negotiation occurs over a narrow range of sensitive issues as negotiators try to make reciprocal adjustments in their offers to promote a general balance in their respective positions. It was this tedious stage of probing and haggling over specific problem areas that the tariff negotiation entered in the second half of 1978.

THE BONN SUMMIT RUN-UP

Like most large bureaucratic endeavors, the Tokyo Round tended to operate at two levels. The first was the technical or line level where

[64] For example, the *Economist* noted, "Few but Europeans suggest these concessions were very sincerely offered in the first place" (June 17, 1978, 87).

[65] Reginald Dale, "Tariff Offer Pressure on Japan," *Financial Times*, July 12, 1978.

most of the work of the negotiation was accomplished. It was at this level that the precise wordings of the various agreements and codes were worked out, and where specific exchanges of concessions were proposed, discussed, and acted upon. Negotiations at this level tended to be very precise in terms of the substance of the negotiation, but they were far more inexact with respect to the timetable for the talks. One could have gained the impression that arguments at the technical level could go on for all eternity unless restrained by an outside force.

The second level of the negotiation was political, where most of the overall direction of the negotiation was determined. It was at this level where the most difficult problems were resolved, and where the time-table for the negotiation was established. Negotiations at this level tended to be precise about setting deadlines for the various tasks of the Tokyo Round, but they were much more inexact about the substance of what was to be accomplished. The impression one could have gained about negotiations at the political level is that almost anything that looked politically salable to enough people would be acceptable, as long as it could be settled within a given time frame.

The technical level was characterized above all by bargaining, or a continuing exchange of proposals and fact finding which went on without much attention to the problem of closure. The political level was characterized above all by decisionmaking, that is, an attempt to resolve outstanding issues without engaging in new factual analysis. Both levels were necessary at the Tokyo Round. However, the political level operated with much greater visibility, thus giving an incomplete picture of what really happened at the negotiation.[66]

The technical level has been the subject of most of the preceding analysis of the Tokyo Round. This included the drafting of NTM (non-tariff measure) codes and the tabling of specific offers and exceptions lists in the tariff negotiation. The technical level also included efforts in national capitals to put together a consensus among domestic interests that would permit issues to be negotiated in the external arena.[67] The political level of the Tokyo Round was conducted in a series of high-level meetings that largely began with the appointment of Robert Strauss as the United States trade representative. Prior to Strauss's ap-

[66] The differences between the two levels of negotiation were expressed in colorful terms by a practitioner at the political level: "If anybody wants to close the deal, you can line them up and we'll sign up. I am a closer, not a negotiator" (transcript of press conference of Ambassador Robert Strauss, Geneva: U.S. Delegation, mimeographed, July 13, 1978, 5).

[67] The negotiation procedures *within* national capitals (i.e., the internal negotiation) is the focus of ch. 8.

pointment, there was little overall direction of the negotiation, either from the Europeans, who had not initiated the Tokyo Round in the first place and who were concerned with internal EC problems, or from the Americans, who were distracted by a presidential election. A further important impetus at the political level was the meetings between heads of government in the London economic summit of May 1977 and the Bonn economic summit of July 1978. The former expressed high-level commitment to the Tokyo Round, and gave Strauss a mandate, indeed an excuse, to work out the resolution of the problem in agriculture that had blocked the negotiations through mid-1977. The latter served as a review mechanism for the Tokyo Round that was crucial in setting an interim deadline for the work accomplished through mid-1978.

The meetings held by Strauss were usually bilateral or multilateral encounters with the leading political representatives of the Big Four, particularly Wilhelm Haferkamp, the European Community's vice-president for external affairs; Nobohiko Ushiba, Japan's minister for external economic affairs; and Jake Warren, Canadian coordinator for trade negotiations. Two such meetings in July and September 1977 have been described; other meetings included a January 1978 session to table tariff offers and an April 1978 meeting devoted to problems in subsidy/countervail and agriculture.[68] The effect of these meetings was, in the words of one participant, "to rachet difficult issues up to a level where they could be acted upon through political tradeoffs." These meetings were an exercise in political dealing, which was a style Strauss knew and fostered. As a high-ranking Canadian was later to remark prior to a difficult meeting with the Americans, he was pleased to see that Strauss would attend because he "preferred to be leaned on by someone with class."

The meetings at the senior level helped to bring what might have been a distant, highly technical exercise in international policymaking closer to the political concerns of the respective nations in the Tokyo Round. They were crucial to the success of the endeavor, because of the complex and arcane nature of negotiation. These meetings were not without costs, however, as they were an irritant to negotiators at the technical level, who were often unsure of what had been decided or how to interpret in technical terms the more loosely worded political

[68] See "Trade Chiefs Seek to End Geneva Deadlock," *Times*, April 5, 1978. In addition to meetings between Strauss and his counterparts, there were also bilateral US/EC meetings at the next-lower level which helped to structure the issues between these two delegations. For example, an important stocktaking meeting was held in late December 1977 between Ambassador Alonzo MacDonald, U.S. head of delegation, and Sir Roy Denman, director general for external affairs in the Commission of the EC.

formulations that were worked out between senior figures. On the other hand, what was clear from the senior-level meetings were the expectations governments had for the progress of work at the lower level. Thus, in the April 1978 meeting between Strauss, Haferkamp, and Ushiba, a decision was taken to conduct a major review of Tokyo Round negotiation prior to the Bonn summit, with the aim of bringing the major political bargaining to an end before July. This deadline proved to be completely unrealistic, but the commitment itself created a fresh political impetus to what had been a lagging effort at the technical level.

Following the April meeting, there was a concerted attempt to negotiate a final package before the July 15 deadline. The main issues on which progress had been made, as reported by the press in mid-June, were safeguards, government procurement, standards, and customs valuation.[69] The major outstanding issues were reported to be subsidy/countervail, tariffs, and the negotiations in agriculture. Regarding the first, the press was probably reflecting more the political sensitivities of the subsidy/countervail issue than the actual progress in the negotiation, since by mid-1978 the important breakthrough had already occurred in the drafting of this code. However, on tariffs and agriculture the press was completely accurate. Because of the interlocking nature of tariff concessions, a tariff negotiation is not done until it is done, and by mid-1978 the respective parties had hardly begun to work out even the general lines along which a multilateral deal could be struck. As for agriculture, the United States in the person of Robert Strauss had become increasingly insistent since late 1977 that the overall negotiation was not making sufficient progress on agriculture, and that some tangible commitment by the EC would be needed in order to sell the Tokyo Round accords to the U.S. Congress.[70]

The working deadlines for the Bonn run-up were to have texts on safeguards and subsidy/countervail ready by June 30, and to resolve remaining differences on government procurement, customs valuation, and standards by July 5. In reality, things did not go as smoothly as had

---

[69] "Business Brief: GATT's Trade Talks," *Economist*, June 17, 1978, 86–87. The *Economist*'s piece was consistent with other reports, and was essentially correct in its judgment on government procurement, standards, and customs valuation. On safeguards however there was considerable discord, even in the EC itself, which was split (Germany and Denmark opposing) on the issue of selective safeguards. See "Community Negotiators Get Final Instructions," *European Report*, no. 519 (July 1, 1978), 1.

[70] As per the agreement of July 1977, the negotiations on agriculture proceeded independently of other issues in the negotiation, and were conducted in four areas: grains, dairy products, meat, and general access. See ch. 7.

been planned. Around July 10 Ambassador MacDonald from the United States and Director General Denman of the EC established themselves in an office in Geneva and proceeded to receive reports from the various task groups in the negotiation. The process went on for two days. Mostly the reporting involved U.S. and EC negotiators, who reported together by negotiating group, but it also included reports from the delegates of other countries such as Japan and Canada which had participated in the code negotiations. Where the reports seemed inadequate, the negotiators were asked to make a further effort on the spot to come up with a joint statement that would reflect some progress toward agreement. At the end of this period, a draft memo was composed by Denman and MacDonald, which was discussed and revised in an all-night session that included representatives from a number of developed countries. The next evening, after an hour's sleep, the principal political figures left for Bonn to report to the economic summit.

The result of the Bonn run-up was a nine-page memorandum of understanding which the developed nations circulated widely at the Tokyo Round.[71] The memo was a bland document; it attracted criticism from the press. In some measure, the vagueness of the memo stemmed from the inherent difficulty of giving a meaningful interim report on a tariff negotiation, and from the fact that the code negotiations were entirely too complicated to be sensibly summarized in a brief public document. While the document itself may have been evasive, the accompanying statements of the leaders who worked on it were not circumspect at all. The normally cautious press office in the EC announced that "Des progrès significatifs et substantiels ont été accomplis," although it did add that important issues remained to be settled.[72] The Americans were less guarded. The U.S. press release described it as "truly a remarkable achievement," and in a subsequent press interview Robert Strauss refused to be dissuaded from his optimism by a skeptical press. For example, in answer to a British journalist's question on whether U.S. domestically controlled oil prices constituted a flagrant subsidy, Strauss replied:

> I am not interested in the negative today and I am not interested in specifics in that area. . . . I am before you to say that I think dramatic progress has been made toward solutions of the world's

[71] "Statement by Several Delegations on Current Status of Tokyo Round Negotiation," GATT docs., MTN/INF/33, July 14, 1978.

[72] "Un Accord cadre sur les principaux éléments d'un paquet final pour le Tokyo Round," Communautés Européennes, Information à la Presse du Bureau de Genève, July 13, 1978.

trading problem. .... I am particularly pleased on the eve of this summit, that President Carter, who has taken political scars in our country for maintaining a positive trade posture, has kept us in a very tenacious posture in terms of taking on the forces of protectionism. I think that when we greet him and brief him this evening, he will be very pleased with the progress report that we give him. I think we are assured that this is a major, I repeat, major trade round.[73]

The memo of understanding, and even more the process that led to it, constituted an important watershed in the Tokyo Round. The memo was well received at the summit, and it led to a further commitment at the highest level to complete the negotiation.[74] The Bonn summit itself was an important meeting, and it has been characterized as "a textbook case of international policy coordination."[75] It is therefore not surprising that a high-level meeting where cooperation was directly manifested should put considerable pressure on negotiations below that level to produce agreement. The Bonn summit created pressures that bore on political leaders responsible for the Tokyo Round, just as those leaders had in turn put pressure on the negotiators who directly carried out the technical work of the negotiation. One sees in the relationships between these different international meetings a hierarchical form of management, where negotiations at a higher level are used to manage and direct negotiations at lower levels. The Tokyo Round experience may have demonstrated one valuable aspect of summits that has been missing in the largely critical commentaries on this process, namely the capacity of summit meetings to manage other important negotiations being conducted in the international arena.[76]

The Bonn run-up was important to the success of the Tokyo Round, but it had a major drawback in that it worsened the rift between developed and developing countries at the negotiation. The process of pyramidal negotiation has already been commented upon, that is, where

[73] Strauss press conference (see n. 66), 5.

[74] The text of the Bonn summit stated: "At last year's Downing Street Summit we rejected a protectionist course for world trade. We agreed to give a new impetus to the Tokyo Round. Our negotiators have fulfilled that commitment. Today we charge them in cooperation with the other participants to resolve the outstanding issues and to conclude successfully the detailed negotiations by December 15, 1978" (text of the declaration at the Bonn summit, *New York Times*, July 18, 1978, D-12).

[75] Putnam and Bayne, *Hanging Together*, 80.

[76] This analysis would suggest summit meetings complement the work of other international organizations and do not compete with them, as suggested by Schaetzel and Malmgren, "Talking Heads."

the negotiation in a multilateral scenario commences between the largest nations and spreads progressively downward to smaller nations after a basic quid pro quo has been established. This process tended to occur most when the United States and the European Community had a profound but not unbridgeable conflict, as in the negotiations on subsidy/countervail or customs valuation, and it had the effect of excluding the developing countries from negotiations in these areas. This had created considerable disillusionment among the developing countries well prior to the Bonn summit. The negotiation immediately prior to the summit only served to increase this disillusionment. During the Bonn run-up, the U.S. and EC negotiators were under great pressure to demonstrate interim results, and neither they nor the other developed countries wanted to jeopardize the tightly scheduled negotiation by including the developing countries. Thus the latter had no hand in shaping the memorandum of understanding and were consequently unwilling to accept it as a basis for future negotiation.[77] This incident deepened the sense of alienation that had already come about among many developing countries, and it caused the developed countries to place a much higher priority on the concerns of developing countries when the negotiations resumed after the summit.

[77] For example, *Le Monde* quoted the following warning from Ambassador Peter Tomic of Yugoslavia: "Il sera difficile, a-t-il dit, pour les pays non consultés par les Grands de revenir sur les décisions prises par ceux ci. . . . Mais nous pensons quand même que les conclusions auxquelles ils vont aboutir devraient être le point de départ et non le point d'arrivée pour la discussion multilaterale" (*Le Monde*, July 13, 1978).

· 6 ·

END PHASE, 1978–1979:
COMPLETION OF THE CODES

It is often said that negotiations move in phases over time.[1] If this is the case, it is necessary for the analyst to distinguish clearly between one phase and the next. In the Tokyo Round, this task is made easy by the fact that the Bonn summit served as a natural watershed in the negotiation. Prior to Bonn, the work of the negotiation had advanced from an exchange of general exploratory proposals to the drafting of specific clauses of the various codes. Disagreements over wording were haggled over and resolved at the technical level insofar as possible, and in this manner a package deal was slowly built. In some cases, such as subsidy/ countervail and customs valuation, the process had required that a political breakthrough be made, after which subsequent negotiation took the form of filling in the details related to the agreement.[2] In other cases, such as the standards code, negotiation proceeded essentially on a step-by-step basis from the inception of the issue. The Bonn summit provided an opportunity for the major participants to take stock of the Tokyo Round, and it was used to create a deadline for the negotiation.[3] The act of publicly setting a deadline created expectations that later increased the pressures on governments and on the negotiators themselves to reach a final settlement.

In viewing negotiations as progressing in phases, one can further distinguish between the behaviors of one phase versus those of another. Again the Tokyo Round case is felicitous, since the Bonn summit appeared to separate a final decisionmaking phase from an earlier middle period when the various parts of the negotiation were taking shape. The most salient characteristic of the middle phase of the Tokyo Round was incremental bargaining, that is, the process of resolving on an incremental basis those issues that could be settled, and postponing the more important or controversial issues for later in the negotiation. The use of square brackets was symbolic of this incremental process. As mentioned earlier, square brackets are used in a negotiated text to sig-

[1] See Winham, "Practitioners' Views."

[2] For an analysis of this type of negotiation process, see Zartman and Berman, *Practical Negotiator*, esp. 9–16.

[3] Reginald Dale, "World Trade Reform by Year-End, Say Industrial Nations," *Financial Times*, July 14, 1978.

212

nify disputed portions of the document, and these brackets are usually removed in a step-by-step process as the parties move toward general agreement. The more difficult issues remain in brackets, and often they are settled only through an act of political will that resolves fundamental points of principle and of procedure. Typically such decisions are taken up at a higher political level as the negotiation reaches its concluding phase. At this point, there is a need to reach a decision, for the parties cannot continue to negotiate indefinitely. Perhaps the crux of this process can be expressed by reference to the model of negotiation proposed by Fred Iklé.[4] Iklé advanced the notion that parties to a negotiation faced a continual threefold choice during the negotiation; that is, to accept available offers, break off the negotiation, or continue negotiating. In the concluding phase of a negotiation, the third choice becomes progressively less viable for the parties, and they must take decisions that they may have been avoiding up to that point. Thus the behavior of the end phase is essentially that of decisionmaking, in contrast to decision-deferring behavior that may have characterized the parties' approach to difficult issues earlier in the negotiation.

In the Tokyo Round, the negotiation entered its decisionmaking phase in the early fall of 1978 following the Bonn summit. At this point, the negotiation had been going on for five years and there was a strong desire on all sides to finish it. It was widely expected that the major decisions could be taken in time for a Christmas deadline, but this expectation proved to be too optimistic. Unforeseen difficulties were confronted in several areas of the negotiation; but by far the most serious involved an action by the U.S. Congress on countervailing duties. This issue created an impasse and hence a crisis in the Tokyo Round, and is estimated to have slowed the conclusion of the negotiation by about two months. This chapter will take up the countervail-waiver crisis in the context of a general analysis of the conclusion of the code negotiations at the Tokyo Round. Also included in this chapter are a discussion of the aborted safeguard code, and the negotiations on agriculture. Chapter 7 will take up the tariff negotiation, the framework agreements, and bilateral agreements, notably the wine-gallon issue.

SUBSIDY/COUNTERVAIL

Countervail-Waiver Crisis

The Tokyo Round talks resumed in Geneva in mid-September after a two-month summer recess. Work recommenced at the technical level in

[4] See *How Nations Negotiate.*

213

most of the committees and subgroups at the negotiation. A December deadline was still regarded as feasible by most major delegations, although it was thought that agriculture might cause difficulties with the schedule. In part, the problem on agriculture was related to the position of the French at the Tokyo Round. The French had opposed the memorandum of understanding drawn up prior to the Bonn summit on the matter of agriculture and subsidies, and in subsequent discussions in the EC Council they had continued their opposition to the use of this document as a basis for agreement in the Tokyo Round. Their opposition was largely motivated by the fear that specific U.S. demands in agriculture, together with American insistence on greater discipline on the use of export subsidies, would hit French agricultural interests harder than those of most other EC members. In addition, the French took a principled position supporting both agricultural export subsidies within the EC and production subsidies within individual member states of the EC. On the export subsidies, the French had widespread support in the EC. On production subsidies, opinion within the EC varied sharply, with the Germans favoring the least intervention possible from government, while other nations, such as the British under the Labour government, supported the more statist policy of the French. The upshot was that for reasons of interest and political-economic philosophy France and the United States were frequently at odds in the Tokyo Round. The issues on which their contentions were the sharpest, such as agriculture and subsidies, tended to become crisis points in the negotiation.

The crisis in the subsidy/countervail negotiation had its genesis in the negotiating mandate extended by Congress in the Trade Act of 1974. It will be recalled that in this legislation Congress obliged the administration to collect countervailing duties on foreign imports that were deemed to be subsidized, but it waived these duties for a four-year period ending January 3, 1979, in order to allow time for an international code to be negotiated which would govern both subsidies and countervailing duties.[5] The products deemed to be subsidized amounted to about $500 million of U.S. imports, and were mostly agricultural products exported from the EC. The purpose of Congress in creating the waiver had been to put pressure on the negotiators to reach an acceptable resolution of the subsidy/countervail issue, both by offering the waiver as an inducement to bargain and by fixing a termination date as an incentive to create action. The ploy was a classic example of the use of the carrot and stick in international trade negotiation. In the event,

[5] See ch. 4.

however, the timing of the waiver was such that it was to take effect at a delicate point in the negotiation, and it created the appearance of the EC and other nations negotiating under the threat of a penalty to be unilaterally administered by the United States. The EC refused to be put in such a position. In late September, Vice-President Haferkamp of the EC wrote Robert Strauss a stern letter warning that the termination of the waiver and the collection of countervailing duties would precipitate a "commercial war of considerable dimensions" between the EC and the United States. The EC, he added, was not in a position to conclude the Tokyo Round negotiation with the risk of such a war hanging in the balance.[6] Haferkamp asked Strauss to secure an extension of the waiver.

Haferkamp's letter received an immediate response from the American side. In the same week it was received, Strauss withdrew several key negotiators from Geneva and commenced a major effort to secure congressional action to extend the waiver. The issue was viewed in Washington, as in Brussels, as the most serious obstacle to the completion of the Tokyo Round. The argument Strauss made to the congressional trade leadership was that the threat of countervail action put the EC in an invidious position in the negotiation, and that moreover such action would hurt most of those EC members, such as the Dutch and the Danes, who were relatively supportive of U.S. trading interests.[7] The effort by the administration succeeded in getting a countervail waiver attached to two separate pieces of legislation, each of which passed the Senate and the House of Representatives, but the congressional session ended before the legislation could be finalized. The effort thus ended in failure, with the result that U.S. law required the collection of countervailing duties to commence on January 3, 1979. The administration made a passing attempt to attribute the failure to the vagaries of the U.S. legislative process, but the fact remained that many congressmen had dug in their heels on the issue. This latter fact was noted in Europe,

---

[6] Haferkamp's letter states: "Ni M. Gundelach (le commissaire chargé des affaires agricoles), ni moi-même pensons qu'il serait réaliste de soumettre aux Etats membres une décision politique à laquelle nous serons tous autant que nous sommes confrontés dans la phase ultime de la négociation si dans le même temps il devient clair qu'en raison de la législation américaine une guerre commerciale risque d'éclater dans quelques semaines" (Philippe Lemaitre, "Les Négociations du GATT sont menacées par un nouveau différend entre les Etats-Unis et la C.E.E.," Le Monde, September 21, 1978).

[7] For example, about 40 percent of the trade to be countervailed consisted of canned hams, dairy products, and butter cookies from Denmark. The products made up approximately 70 percent of Denmark's exports to the United States, and the subsidies involved resulted from the politically sensitive payments of the EC's common agricultural policy.

where it was now taken for granted that the negotiations could not be completed by the December deadline.

The reaction of the U.S. administration to the setback in Congress was to proceed in two directions. First, an effort was made to analyze the state of opinion in Congress. Instrumental in this effort was a letter from Congressmen Charles Vanik and William Steiger from the House Subcommittee on Trade outlining what they felt was the "lesson of the last few weeks for all of us." The letter explained:

> We believe this lesson is that we should not attempt to extend the waiver unless it is done in the context of obtaining international agreement on a code of discipline over subsidies and countervailing duties which meets U.S. objectives, and, more importantly, in the context of domestic implementation of such an agreement.[8]

The significance of this lesson is that it portrayed, no doubt accurately, the Congress as unwilling to remove the threat of countervailing duties before it had achieved its negotiating objectives in the subsidy/countervail negotiation. The position of Congress, together with the stand taken by the EC, thus appeared to create a complete impasse on the countervail issue. To ensure that European governments understood the domestic pressures the U.S. administration was up against, the U.S. delegation in Geneva widely circulated the text of the Vanik-Steiger letter. There was some suggestion afterward that the letter had been solicited by Strauss as a negotiating ploy against the EC, but, even if true, this did not change what was regarded as an essentially accurate description of the mood of Congress in the waning months of 1978.

A second direction by the U.S. administration was to limit the effects of the countervail legislation through executive action. A plan was put forward by the Treasury Department whereby the countervailing duties would be deferred in favor of a bond to be posted by importers. In the event of a general agreement in the subsidy/countervail negotiation, subsequent legislation would then rescind retroactively the duties that had been applied (but not collected) since January 3. Strauss proposed this plan to the Europeans in a round of high-level meetings in early November. For the EC, the reasons for supporting the plan were that the U.S. administration had worked visibly, even ostentatiously, for the extension of the waiver, and there was reason to believe that American trade officials were as distressed as the Europeans over congressional inaction. Furthermore the duties were indeed small in comparison to

---

[8] "Text of Vanik Letter on Countervailing Duties," *U.S. Mission Daily Bulletin*, October 19, 1978.

the EC's overall exports to the United States. On the down side, however, the American plan did not dilute one bit the legal obligations imposed by the U.S. countervail legislation, and it left the United States free to collect the back duties if a subsequent negotiated agreement was not satisfactory to Congress.

The decision was difficult, and it split the EC's Council of Ministers. The British view was that the countervail issue was simply not serious enough to stand in the way of a general agreement. The French, however, took a much harder line, and refused to consent to a continuation of the negotiation under the plan offered by Strauss.[9] France was unable to attract any support for its position, and in the end the Council agreed to complete the negotiation but to withhold final approval until the waiver was reinstated by Congress. France continued to oppose a settlement before the end of 1978, and its general reserve about the completion of the whole negotiation created a significant impediment in the bilateral negotiations between the EC and the United States.

The countervail-waiver affair demonstrated the importance of the political level of negotiation at the Tokyo Round. The precise wording of the various MTN codes was usually negotiated at the technical level, but it was the political level that was responsible for trouble-shooting and for maintaining the momentum of the negotiation. Maintaining momentum in a negotiation often involves maintaining the trust of the other side and, consequently, maintaining also the other side's will to negotiate. If trust is broken, then the will to negotiate will be shaken and the negotiation itself will be jeopardized. In the Tokyo Round, one could find no better example of the need for trust in negotiation than the countervail-waiver affair, for the EC eventually agreed to negotiate under the threat of an American threat that was legally in place, even if it was politically suspended for the duration of the negotiation. It took an extraordinary effort by the United States at the highest political level to convince the Europeans that they should negotiate in the shadow of a potential American reprisal. If there is one thing that negotiators anywhere instinctively seek to avoid, it is to bargain under the threat of a reprisal from a negotiating partner. The U.S. administration was unable to remove the threat which Congress had created, and hence its only hope was to convince the Europeans that the United States would not use that threat to extract advantage during the negotiation. The credit for accomplishing this went largely to Robert Strauss, and it was one

[9] Foreign Minister Jean-François Deniau stated that concluding the Tokyo Round before the waiver was extended "is exactly the mechanism of negotiation which I cannot accept" ("Tokyo Round: Uncertain Prospects for Early Conclusions Following French Hard-Line at EEC Council," *European Report*, no. 552, November 25, 1978).

reason why, in European capitals as well as Washington, he was widely credited with being instrumental to the success of the Tokyo Round.

Within the politics of trust and mistrust that are part of any negotiation, the hawks on one side inevitably play to the hawks on the other. In the United States the hawks on subsidy/countervail largely lay in Congress. It was Congress that in the first place designed the countervail waiver as a mechanism to put pressure on America's trading partners late in the negotiation. On the EC side, the hawks on subsidy/countervail were the French, and, not surprisingly, they were the ones who took greatest offense at the stern measures put in place by the U.S. Congress. In negotiation, the politics of maintaining trust is largely a matter of managing the hawks on both sides. Strauss was able to earn the trust of the European leaders because he convinced them that the evolving agreement on subsidy/countervail would be acceptable to even the most hawkish elements in the Congress. On the European side, the hawkish elements in the EC were managed by obfuscation, which is a time-honored technique for negotiating consensus in situations of sharp conflict. The French were opposed to concluding the negotiation with the Americans in December under the threat of a countervail waiver, and therefore the Council of the EC invented a fine distinction between concluding the negotiation and signing an agreement. The French were unhappy with this resolution and continued to press for a suspension of the negotiation. The arrangement left the Americans themselves in considerable uncertainty about whether the French would be able to cause a delicate compromise to become unhinged in the Council.[10] Perhaps the distress on the American side was inevitable, since it is often the case in negotiation that actions taken to increase the pressure on a negotiating partner rebound to increase the pressure on one's own position as well.

In the end, the countervail-waiver incident produced nothing more than a few weeks of political complications in what was already a technically complex negotiation. It made no lasting impact on the negotiation or on its results. From the vantage of hindsight, however, what the incident did demonstrate was the value of the subsidy/countervail agreement itself. Critics of the subsidy/countervail agreement could rightfully argue that the code was hardly a revolutionary document, but this argument fails to account for the distance some nations had to

[10] For example: "News of this continued French opposition . . . has led to anxiety in Washington, where chief U.S. negotiator Robert Strauss termed it 'the biggest problem' facing the Tokyo Round. . . . American trade negotiators are understood to be infuriated at the French position" ("Tokyo Round: EEC Council Meets Amid International Anxiety," *European Report*, no. 558, December 15, 1978).

go to negotiate the subject at all. The countervail-waiver incident showed how intently some elements in Europe were determined to promote the use of subsidies as legitimate tools of national and international economic policy, while at the same time demonstrating how deeply some elements in the United States opposed their use. Such deeply held convictions could have got out of control, and the whole incident demonstrated how easily nations might have got into a trade war over the issue. The incident also demonstrated how much the EC had at stake in negotiating the agreement, which undoubtedly was a factor behind Strauss's ability to persuade the EC not to disrupt the negotiation on account of the countervail waiver. The main problem for the EC (and the U.S. administration as well) was that Congress had not come to terms with subsidy practices that are pursued in most countries of the world, and that it viewed contervailing duties as a general policy tool to offset objectionable foreign practices rather than as a limited mechanism to protect specific U.S. interests. The introduction of an injury clause in U.S. countervail legislation, which the American negotiators were offering, promised to create a major change in the U.S. approach to foreign subsidies. The countervail-waiver incident had showed what could happen if that change did not occur. By persisting in a negotiation under difficult circumstances, the EC managed to achieve a new arrangement in which there would be much less likelihood of fundamental conflict with the United States over subsidy policy.

Completion of the Subsidy/Countervail Code

The work at the technical level on the subsidy/countervail code continued throughout the political controversy over the countervail waiver. The various delegations worked from the "Outline of an Arrangement" document that had been completed for the Bonn summit.[11] This document provided a structure for subsequent discussion; the main tasks remaining for the fall of 1978 were to remove the reservations expressed by various delegations, and to fill in the operational details needed to make the document meaningful. Work progressed quickly, and an agreement in principle on a subsidy/countervail code was reached on December 19, 1978, among the major participants at the Tokyo Round.[12]

[11] See ch. 5, p. 209.

[12] Reginald Dale, "Agreement on Subsidies Aids Geneva Trade Talks," *Financial Times*, December 19, 1978. See also "Subsidies/Countervailing Measures: Outline of an Arrangement," GATT docs., MTN/NTM/W/210, December 19, 1978.

During the fall of 1978 several major issues were encountered in the negotiation. The first was subsidies. The U.S. offer on an injury test had been forthcoming in the pre-Bonn document, which left the United States in a position to demand reciprocal movement on subsidies in the subsequent bargaining. Specifically the U.S. delegation pressed to include in the code a listing of internal (i.e., domestic) subsidies for the purpose of identifying potentially injurious practices. An illustrative list of internal subsidies proved unacceptable to the EC and other countries (although a brief enumeration of examples of subsidies was included in Article 11.3 of the subsidy/countervail code), and in the end the United States settled for a provision that granted injured countries the right of consultation and dispute-settlement procedures with nations applying subsidies of any type. This was the first time the GATT provided the right to take action against domestic subsidies, and it promised to give injured nations increased political access to subsidizing nations in the future. Given that the subsidies/countervail code did not substantially curtail domestic subsidy practices, this provision was characterized by U.S. negotiators Rivers and Greenwald as "a remedy without a corresponding obligation."[13] As a legal and negotiating mechanism, this provision clearly transferred the difficult issue of domestic subsidies to future relations.

On agricultural export subsidies, American negotiators sought to constrain the use of export subsidies on agricultural products through tightening the rather loose rule in Article 16.3 of the GATT that such subsidies may not result in "more than an equitable share of world export trade in that product." Specifically the rules were tightened to take account of the potential of subsidized exports to "displace" the trade of other exporters in third-country markets, which gave agricultural exporters in North America and elsewhere something of a legal handle against the agricultural subsidy programs of the EC. Finally, on non-agricultural export subsidies, the United States obtained an expansion of the list of prohibited practices already included in the General Agreement, which was of greatest importance vis-à-vis the trade practices of the more advanced of the developing countries.

The second major issue involved countervailing duties. In the draft drawn up prior to the Bonn summit, the United States had agreed in principle to introduce a national injury test into its countervail legislation. This agreement, which was the major concession that it made in the negotiation, was later to cause a major struggle in Washington over efforts to secure congressional approval of the Tokyo Round accords.

[13] Rivers and Greenwald, "Negotiation of a Code," 1466–69.

In the external negotiation, the fall of 1978 was spent in tightening the wording of the code with respect to the procedures for determining injury. The EC had insisted that the United States accede to the antidumping code which had been negotiated during the Kennedy Round but not accepted by the United States because of the unwillingness of Congress to subscribe to the internationally negotiated procedure for determining injury.[14] U.S. negotiators accepted the antidumping code, and this, plus the need to harmonize national practices for determining injury in antidumping and countervailing cases, necessitated a rewriting of the antidumping code. One of the major problems in this task was the stringent test of injury contained in the code, namely the requirement that dumped imports be "demonstrably the principal cause" of material injury to a domestic industry. U.S. negotiators argued that this test created a standard impossible to meet, and on this point eventually won support from the EC and the Canadians. Instead of the principal-cause formula, the negotiators settled on a series of objective criteria that had to be examined by domestic authorities in order to reach a determination of injury. These criteria included "all relevant economic factors," and the code further specified that the link between injury and imports be demonstrated and that any injury caused by other factors (such as general recession) could not be attributed to imports.

A third major issue in the subsidies negotiation concerned the developing countries. The developing countries had started out in the negotiation by defending the need for less-developed economies to make use of government subsidies. They sought special and differential treatment on subsidies, which initially was translated into the expectation that developed countries should refrain completely from using countervail procedures against the products from developing countries, while developing countries themselves had no restraints placed on their use of subsidies. The developing countries had a major advantage in this exchange in that they had not signed the 1960 Declaration on Export Subsidies, whereby the industrialized nations had committed themselves not to use export subsidies on nonprimary products. The developing countries felt that if they participated in the subsidy/countervail code they should not be expected to incur additional obligations as a result. On the other hand, developed nations such as the United States and Canada felt strongly that the larger developing countries should be prepared to accept gradually the basic GATT prohibition against nonprimary export subsidies. Indeed the United States was prepared to push this matter quite some distance. During the negotiation, the

[14] See ch. 9.

221

United States took several countervail actions against Brazilian products. U.S. negotiators made it clear to Brazil that the eventual price of exporting to the United States would be to begin to dismantle its large program of export subsidies. The fact that Brazil and other developing countries had growing exports to the United States gave the latter leverage to force the developing countries to bargain.[15]

The negotiations between the developed and developing countries were difficult and dragged on through March 1979. The result of the negotiation was a compromise that could be interpreted by either side as a victory. In the developing countries' favor, the code eventually accepted "that in developing countries, governments may play a large role in promoting economic growth and development,"[16] and it obliged signatories to "recognize that subsidies are an integral part of economic development programmes of developing countries."[17] To put these prescriptions into practice, the code reduced slightly the right of developed countries to pursue complaints about domestic subsidies employed by developing countries, save in instances where such subsidies nullified previous tariff concessions or constituted material injury in importing countries.

The most important concession the code made to developing countries was to exempt them from the general obligation of Article 9 to refrain from applying export subsidies on nonprimary products. However, this concession had an important qualifier in that developing countries were obliged to "endeavor" to reduce or eliminate such subsidies where they were inconsistent with the developing country's competitive or development needs.[18] This qualifier provided grounds for the developed countries to press for an eventual dismantling of export-subsidy programs in the more industrialized developing countries, and hence it incorporated the principle of graduation in the subsidy/countervail code. In other areas, the developing countries also accepted similar obligations to the developed countries. For example, there was no distinction made between developing and developed countries regarding the provisions on dispute settlement or on export subsidies on primary products, and on countervailing duties the material-injury provisions of the code applied equally to any subsidized imports regardless of the development status of their country of origin. In sum, the sub-

---

[15] See Rivers and Greenwald, "Negotiation of a Code," 1480–81. This leverage was later used to induce developing countries to sign the subsidies code.

[16] GATT, *Agreement on Articles VI, XVI and XXIII* (Subsidy/countervail), Article 14.7.

[17] Ibid., Article 14.1.

[18] Ibid., Article 14.5.

sidy/countervail code seemed to go some distance toward moderating the extreme positions taken at the outset of the negotiation, particularly the demand by the developing countries for the unrestrained right to use export subsidies in government development programs, and the insistence by the United States on the unfettered right to attack such programs through countervail procedures.

The issues involving the developing countries were among the last matters to be settled in Geneva over the subsidy/countervail code. However, well before these issues had been resolved, the major action of the negotiation, certainly as far as the United States was concerned, had shifted to an internal struggle in Washington. The code provisions on material injury proved unacceptable to important sectors of Congress, and the issue threatened for a time to cause the entire subsidy/countervail agreement to come unstuck. This matter will be returned to in chapter 9.

SUCCESSFUL CODE NEGOTIATIONS

Customs Valuation Code

The customs valuation negotiation was well advanced at the time of the Bonn summit. The major differences of approach between the United States and the Community had been resolved, and a workable draft was completed by June 1978. On reflection, the customs valuation negotiation was one of the most intellectually interesting of the Tokyo Round, which is perhaps a curious statement to make about a subject that is usually characterized by wearying technical detail. At base, the customs valuation negotiation dealt with price, or the economic value assigned to commodities, which is a fundamental philosophical and practical subject in the discipline of economics. The main arguments in the customs valuation negotiation had proceeded along two lines. The first line dealt with how value would be established: whether it would proceed empirically from real prices existing in the market place or ideally from a concept of price existing in someone's mind. The former was represented in the positive systems of the Americans and Canadians, while the latter was reflected in the Brussels Definition of Value (BDV) of the European nations. In settling on the transaction value as a basis for customs valuation, the evolving code resolved the first argument in favor of the North American approach to valuation. The transaction value was defined in the code as "the price actually paid or payable for the goods" (i.e., invoice price), subject to certain adjustments for actual costs such as brokerage fees, proceeds from resale, and so forth. The code thus obliged customs officials in principle to base valuation on real prices and costs existing on actual trading relations.

The second line of argument dealt with who would establish the value of commodities exchanged in international trade—the business person in setting invoice prices or the government official in making adjustments to those prices. Prima facie, by settling on the transaction value as the basis for valuation the code settled this issue in favor of the former, although this point remains a matter of interpretation of the code.[19] Use of the transaction price for valuation will probably give businesses greater opportunity to vary prices in their trading strategy without interference from customs officials. Such opportunity will undoubtedly aid business planning. Transaction-price valuation will also provide some advantage to firms that are powerful enough to influence prices, as in the case of a large importer that can obtain a low price for large shipments from a foreign supplier, thus paying both lower price and lower duty for the goods.[20] Conversely, use of the transaction price would reduce the capacity of customs officials to adjust values on traded goods for reasons of either protectionism or other government policy. It was on this point that Canada and the developing countries disagreed most with the evolving code.

Negotiation of the customs valuation code after July 1978 involved largely the objections raised by the Canadian and developing-country representatives, and dragged on well into 1979. Prior to these objections being fully engaged, however, an important issue was settled between the U.S. and the EC regarding the hierarchy of valuation methods. The draft code had provided for a series of five methods of determining value, with each succeeding method(s) to be used only if the preceding method(s) could not be applied. The first method was of course the transaction value of the goods in question; the remaining four were the transaction value of identical goods, the transaction value of similar goods, the deducted value of the traded goods, and the computed value of the goods.[21] The issue arose over the last two meth-

---

[19] For example, Sherman, "Customs Valuation Code," 132, writes, "Transaction value is the invoice price of the particular shipment, subject only to a few possible adjustments and only a few possible grounds for using alternative bases of valuation." On the other hand, former ambassador Rodney Grey of Canada, *Trade Policy*, 42, writes, "The key concept of the agreement is thus the 'transaction price' rather than the stated invoice price. Much of the agreement is therefore concerned with rules about what to add to, and what to subtract from, the stated invoice price to arrive at the real price for the transaction and about what standard a transaction price should be compared to for transactions between related companies."

[20] Sherman, "Customs Valuation Code," 136.

[21] The deducted method was based on the resale price of imported goods, from which

ods. The United States objected to the flexibility the deducted method gave to customs officers, while the Europeans, particularly the Germans, objected to the fact that the computed method opened up possibilities for customs officials in one country to inquire about production practices and pricing in other countries. The German concern was that the computed method could be used to sanction a form of industrial spying. The US/EC problem was resolved by allowing importers to specify the order of application of the final two valuation methods, and by providing guarantees that foreign companies could not be compelled by any government to provide information for customs investigation. Paradoxically, however, this solution only worsened relations between the U.S. and EC on the one hand and the developing countries on the other, as the latter would have preferred to leave the choice between the last two valuation methods to government officials and not to importers. Thus it seems in multilateral negotiations that the solution to one problem often creates another.

The position of Canada on the customs valuation code had from the outset of the negotiations varied from indifference to opposition. As mentioned previously, Canada took a more interventionist approach to customs valuation than the other developed countries, and used as a basis for valuing imported goods the "fair market price" of those goods in the exporting country.[22] This method necessitated customs investigations in the markets of exporting countries, which was less onerous than it sounds, since about 70 percent of Canadian imports came from the United States. The rationale of the system was the belief that "there is a good deal of dumping by countries exporting to Canada,"[23] which in turn was believed to be caused by the large proportion of related-party trade in Canadian imports. The Canadian government took the position that invoice prices in trade between related parties were often distorted; or, to put it another way, if the parties were in a position to manipulate prices, then indeed the prices would be manipulated. There were, of course, empirical examples to support this assumption. However, there was an equally strong argument on the other side that a relationship between parties did not produce distorted prices in interna-

commissions, profits, taxes, and other expenses would be deducted. The computed method was based on an assessment of the general costs of production in the exporting country.

[22] For an example, an EC study had observed about the Canadian system, "The fundamental concept of Canadian customs valuation is that the value for duty may not be less than the fair market value in the country of export" ("Canadian Valuation System," EC Commission, GUD/1222/76-E [Annex V, GUD/3], undated, 8).

[23] Grey, *Trade Policy*, 38.

tional trade, namely that the need for accurate internal accounting in multinational firms created pressure for rational pricing in the trade between different subsidiaries of the firm. A further argument was that multinational firms usually face higher tax rates than tariff duties in foreign countries, and it would be improbable that a foreign firm would undervalue its exports to avoid a small duty only to increase profits in a subsidiary which were subject to a higher rate of taxation. These arguments were unconvincing to the Canadian delegation, which continued to resist a valuation system based on invoice prices, and particularly regarding trade between related parties. On this point, the Canadians generally received support from the developing countries, many of which also faced the problem of related-party trade in their own trade structures.

The Canadian position on customs valuation was complicated by strong pressures from domestic industry. Rightly or wrongly, the Canadian valuation system was widely perceived as affording important protection to domestic industry. This perception was probably enhanced by the aforementioned ministerial prerogative over valuation, which gave industrial leaders political access that would be lost in a system based on invoice prices. Furthermore, customs valuation was perceived in Canada more as a part of the tariff system than as a nontariff measure. In tariffs, the Canadian government had already taken a decision to pursue a formula cut in the negotiation, which had been strongly resisted by Canadian business. Acceptance of the customs valuation code appeared to be a further step in the same direction, and the government was very wary of taking that step. In the words of one Canadian official, ". . . the Federal Government was just very nervous about this matter." Thus internal pressure, which influenced the government, plus the conviction on the part of Canadian negotiators that the customs valuation code did not serve unique Canadian interests, led to the unwillingness of Canada to accept the direction forged by the EC and the United States.

The results of the customs valuation negotiation were not favorable to Canadian interests. Regarding trade between related parties, the final code took the position that a relationship between the buyer and seller "shall not in itself be grounds for regarding the transaction value as unacceptable."[24] This placed the burden of proof on importing countries to demonstrate that any relationship that existed distorted the price of imported goods. The code also specifically prohibited the use of prices in the exporting country as a criterion for valuation, which

---

[24] GATT, *Agreement on Article VII* (Customs valuation), Article 1.2(a).

had been the basis for the Canadian "fair market value" approach.[25] Because its interests were so thoroughly divergent from the major countries on customs valuation, Canada did not put much effort into the negotiation in this area, and it is possible the government might have intended to abstain entirely from the agreement. However, late in the negotiation the U.S. administration decided it would be wise to have Canadian participation in the customs valuation code in order to make the agreement salable to Congress, and it put pressure on Canada to sign the agreement. Since the United States had made a generous tariff offer to Canada, it was in a position to exact a price if the Canadians refused to accede to the code.

The Canadians decided to sign the agreement but under a reservation that would allow for a time lapse before the code applied fully to Canada. During this period, Canada intended to convert any protection that might have been provided under existing valuation procedures to increased tariff protection. This procedure was similar to that followed by the United States for products previously protected under the ASP (American Selling Price) and final-list systems, but in pursuing this option Canada appeared to be taking a line inconsistent with its earlier argument that its valuation system was not protectionist. The reservation to the customs valuation code made by Canada was an acceptable basis for concluding the negotiation, but it could well cause problems in Canada's future relations with its trading partners. The Canadian government will be under strong pressure from domestic interests to make substantial increases in tariff protection, but if it does this it will encounter sharp protests from its trading partners, and particularly the Europeans. So it is that problems not fully resolved in international negotiations often cause difficulties at a later date.

With regard to the developing countries, their strategy was one of collective resistance to the direction taken by the majors in the customs valuation negotiation. The interests of the developing countries on customs matters varied sharply from those of the developed countries on a number of points. First, many developing countries such as India relied on customs duties as a major source of government revenue, which raised the stakes of the negotiation well beyond what they were for developed countries. Second, developing countries used protective tariffs

[25] The code states in Article 7.2(c), "No customs value shall be determined . . . on the basis of the price of goods on the domestic market of the country of exportation." This provision reflected the hostility nations felt toward customs officers in one jurisdiction seeking in other jurisdictions information on which to base customs valuations. Indeed Canadian officials themselves admitted that the practice was not popular and had caused diplomatic incidents.

as an important aspect of development policy, and hence they viewed valuation for duty as a more important concern than did developed countries, where the tariff on many items might be low enough to be inconsequential. Third, customs services in developing countries lacked the administrative capacity of those in developed countries, and hence they felt less able to employ valuation methods that required them to gather market information in other countries or to examine the circumstances of related-party trade. Finally, developing countries faced a larger problem with fraudulent invoices than did the developed countries. The case of Indonesia is illustrative. Trade in Indonesia is largely conducted by individuals of Chinese extraction. The resulting ethnic differences between traders and government officials lead to mutual suspicions and to a climate in which the latter find it impossible to trust trade invoices, or to assume that anything approaching an open "freely offered" market exists even between unrelated parties. In such situations, governments become extremely reluctant to put the burden on customs officers to detect deviations from a fair-market transaction value. Instead governments prefer a more discretionary, flexible, and ultimately more interventionist system.

Following the Bonn summit, the developing countries mobilized their efforts to make changes in the draft customs valuation code. These efforts were led by the Indian delegation, and were assisted by the Customs Cooperation Council (CCC), which saw its own role in the negotiation after June 1976 as helping to achieve a universal customs system. The CCC had been stung by the EC decision to drop the BDV system of valuation, which had been subscribed to by over one hundred nations. It thereafter sought to help the developing countries make amendments to the draft code which would incidentally expand the role of customs officials in valuation procedures. Not surprisingly, the EC and U.S. delegations found the CCC's involvement unhelpful to the negotiation.

In September, India proposed an alternative draft valuation code. It accepted transaction value (i.e., the price actually paid) as the basis for valuation, but subject to the provision that "The customs administration of the country of import is satisfied on the basis of the 'general price level' or *otherwise* that such value represents the price in a sale in the ordinary course of trade under fully competitive conditions, the price being the sole consideration for the sale."[26] This provision greatly reduced the commitment to the declared invoice price in transactions,

[26] "Customs Valuation: Draft Valuation Code," GATT docs., MTN/NTM/W/188, September 18, 1978, 1 (italics in original).

and expanded the scope for customs officers to determine value on the basis of very general guidelines. The Indian draft was unacceptable to the developed countries, and there ensued an intense effort to find a compromise between the developed and developing countries in order to avoid concluding the negotiation with two separate codes. By February 1979, differences had narrowed considerably, but positions had also hardened, and a further draft was circulated by "several developing countries."[27] The February draft revealed that the developing countries had come a considerable distance in the effort to achieve a single universal code. The draft dropped any reference to valuation based on a "general price level," and instead focused on several amendments to the developed countries' draft that increased the burden on importers (especially related parties) to demonstrate that transaction values were consistent with fair market prices. The draft also added a section on special and differential treatment that would delay the application of the completed code to developing countries by ten years, and that created an obligation by developed countries to provide technical assistance to developing countries.

The February draft proved unacceptable to the developed countries. Further small revisions were made, but the matter ended, and the customs valuation negotiation concluded without a general agreement. The draft code acceptable to the developed countries, and the revisions of the developing countries thereto, were both forwarded from the negotiating subgroup on customs valuation to the GATT membership. Negotiations on the customs valuation code were to continue in GATT throughout the summer and fall of 1979, but when the Tokyo Round officially concluded in April 1979 it was clear that the main negotiation had not succeeded in bridging the gap between the developed and developing countries on this issue.

Government-Procurement Code

The negotiation on government procurement produced a near-final draft of a code at the time of the Bonn summit in July 1978.[28] The general rules for tendering procedures were specified, the provisions for settling disputes were agreed to, and an extensive section of special and differential treatment for developing countries was included. Most of the negotiation after July dealt with the entities to be included under the code, and it proceeded on an offer-and-request basis. As for the code

[27] "Customs Valuation," GATT docs., MTN/NTM/W/222, February 28, 1979.
[28] "Government Procurement: Draft Integrated Text," GATT docs., MTN/NTM/W/174, July 17, 1978.

itself, only a few problems remained after Bonn. One was an attempt by the EC, resisted by the United States and Canada, to extend the dispute-settlement provisions of the code to smaller government contracts not otherwise expected to be covered under the code. This move was resisted because of the fear that the EC might thus take advantage of more open tendering procedures in North America. Another issue concerned especially the developing countries and was resolved only late in the negotiation. The July draft code had contained a bracketed phrase prohibiting entities from making procurement contracts conditional on the supplier licensing its technology with the government. Furthermore the draft required entities to refrain from awarding contracts on the basis of offsets or similar conditions. The developing countries argued both procedures could be an important form of technology transfer, and that the provision of technology might be an important reason for entities in developing countries to procure goods from foreign suppliers. The Canadians, who employ similar offsets and conditions in matters of foreign investment, supported the position of the developing countries and argued for greater flexibility in the code. This pressure was effective in the end and the code was modified. The final wording cautioned parties that the licensing of technology should not "normally" be used as a basis for awarding contracts, and that offsets should be limited to a reasonable proportion of the contract value.

The major issue faced in the procurement code after the Bonn summit was the threshold value of contracts to be subject to the provisions of the agreement. The issue was difficult, and mainly involved a dispute between the EC and the rest. The EC negotiators wanted a high threshold value because they felt the transparency provisions of the code would become too burdensome for contracts of lower value. The United States, Japan, and Canada all took an export-oriented approach to the code and argued for a lower figure. The developing countries also supported a lower figure because their suppliers were more likely to be able to provide procurements in the lower range. By late January 1979, the issue was moving toward settlement, and the EC eventually accepted the figure sought by the United States and the rest, namely $150,000 SDR (special drawing rights), or about U.S. $190,000.

The offer/request phase of the government-procurement negotiation started in July 1978 with the tabling of lists of entities by the United States, Japan, and the Nordic countries. Other nations followed shortly thereafter. Initial discussions focused on general exclusions to the list of entities. For example, no nation was prepared to place entities in its defense establishment under the code, although nonmilitary material procured by these entities was readily included. Three product types, namely heavy electrical equipment, transportation equipment, and telecommunications equipment, were generally excluded, and most nations refused to put entities that purchased such equipment in the agreement. Following a discussion of exclusions, nations exchanged lists of positive offers. For defense-related procurement, specific goods were identified; for nondefense matters, whole entities were named. It was recognized that lists could be considerably shorter for developing countries and that they could exclude certain products purchased by nondefense entities, an exclusion not permitted to developed countries. The actual negotiation of the positive lists quickly became decentralized, as nations with particular export interests took up their concerns with other countries on a bilateral or plurilateral basis. In this fashion the negotiations proceeded like a traditional request/offer negotiation in GATT, in which principal suppliers would deal with the major importers of specific products.

The positive lists were initially evaluated on the gross purchasing power of the entities included on the lists. By this criterion, the U.S. offer was $16 billion, the EC offer was about $10 billion, and the offer of Japan was approximately $3.5 billion. The Japanese offer was well below what would have been expected given Japan's GNP, and Japan came under pressure from U.S. and EC negotiators to raise its offer. By January 1979, the EC had increased its offer slightly to $10.5 billion, and the United States had withdrawn portions of its offer to a level of $12.5 billion, a level considered roughly reciprocal with the EC. The Japanese had not moved, which left their position considerably exposed. The United States demanded that Japan increase its offer to about $7 to $8 billion, and particularly it insisted that the Japanese offer include the state-owned telephone monopoly Nippon Telephone and Telegraph Company (NTT), which alone was responsible for procurements of over $3 billion. This demand triggered an unpleasant bilateral trade dispute which extended beyond the conclusion of the Tokyo Round.[29]

The reasons that motivated the United States to single out NTT were twofold. First, American negotiators perceived that the United States had the capacity to export telecommunications equipment to the Japanese, but was prevented from doing so by the admittedly protectionist policies of NTT. As a result, the United States, which had a comparative advantage in telecommunications equipment, had a sharply growing deficit with Japan. Thus the imbalance on these products only exacerbated the more general bilateral deficit the United States ran with the

---

[29] A detailed study of this dispute has been presented in Curran, "The NTT Case."

Japanese. A second concern was the nature of the products involved. Telecommunications was viewed as a high-quality industry because of its deployment of high technology, and there was deep concern in the United States that Japan was using protectionism to gain a position of strength in a significant industry of the future. For their part, the Japanese resisted the American demands and pointed out that no nation had submitted entities procuring telecommunications equipment for inclusion in the government-procurement agreement. This argument did not deter U.S. officials, who were more influenced in this case by bilateral trade figures than by multilateral negotiating procedures. The Americans pressed the case in a series of high-level bilateral meetings that extended through 1979 and 1980. The Tokyo Round deadline passed without a resolution of the issue, but in early June 1979, immediately preceding a summit meeting between President Carter and Prime Minister Ohira, the two sides reached a procedural resolution of the problem.[30] Further meetings produced a final settlement by December 1980, at which time Japan agreed to place more than $8 billion of procurement under the code, of which $3.3 billion would include NTT purchases. Although it was more extreme than most, this whole incident points out the capacity for multilateral negotiation to trigger disputes (and agreements) between individual parties to the negotiation. In this manner, multilateral talks tend to subsume much of the substance of ordinary bilateral trade policy during the period the negotiation is in progress.

The negotiations over procurement entities between the remaining nations were completed by April 1979 and the code on government procurement was adopted by twenty-one nations participating at the Tokyo Round. The agreement was widely touted by its proponents as making the largest contribution to the new-export potential of the Tokyo Round agreements. However, in this dimension it was clear the code was just a beginning. In the United States, for example, the procurement of federal government totals around $50 billion, while the agreement subjected only about $12.5 billion to international tendering procedures under the code.[31] For the developing countries, the code

---

[30] This agreement, termed an "agreement to agree," provided for reciprocal treatment between Japan and the United States on telecommunications equipment. Specifically it laid out a negotiation schedule, and declared that Japanese firms would be banned from the U.S. procurement market if an agreement were not reached. See ibid., 231.

[31] Anthony and Hagerty, "Government Procurement," 1318. Anthony and Hagerty survey findings on the effect the code will have on U.S. industry, and conclude that it "will spur growth for some U.S. industry sectors while damaging others," with the latter being statistically insignificant from a broad perspective (p. 1341).

represented a considerable export opportunity purchased at a reasonable price. The entity lists of the four developing-country signatories were not extensive,[32] but suppliers in these countries will have full access to the entities listed in the developed countries.

Standards Code

Like the procurement code, the standards code was a new issue in GATT. The negotiation of standards at the Tokyo Round above all represented the insertion of trade concerns into a field that deals with other matters, such as the protection of health and safety, and the consistency and uniformity of manufactured products. Much of the negotiation was an effort to induce domestic standards-setting bodies to accept the proposition that foreign concerns were relevant to their own work. There was basic agreement on this proposition at the Tokyo Round, and hence the negotiation went fairly easily between national delegations. The internal negotiations were more difficult, since national certification bodies were reluctant to have trade policy intrude on their work. Then, too, both government agencies and certification bodies in some countries felt that national standards were often superior to international standards, and they resisted what appeared to be a dilution of the former. This attitude was especially prevalent in the United States, where there was fear that the standards code might be used by domestic manufacturers to avoid complying with U.S. legislation. The task for the negotiators in the domestic arena was to ensure that international trade would be taken into account on standards, while at the same time alleviating fears that international political pressure would interfere with domestic technical decisionmaking.

The standards negotiation was a long process conducted mainly at the staff level. By the Bonn summit, a near-completed code had been drafted. The main outstanding issues were the aforementioned dispute between the EC and countries with a federal structure over different levels of obligation, and the matter of special and differential treatment for the developing countries. On the first, it will be recalled that an impasse in the negotiation was reached over the inability of federal governments to ensure compliance with the standards code of agencies operating in the private sector or at the level of regional governments. This problem created an imbalance between the negotiating partners and therefore was a genuine quandary. The countries with federal

---

[32] For example, Jamaica's list was limited to a single entity, namely Jamaica Building Materials, a division of the Jamaica State Trading Company. See U.S. Government, *Message from the President*, 145.

structures simply did not have the jurisdictional competence to force agencies at the regional level to comply, even though they were morally obliged to use their "best endeavors."[33] On the other hand, EC members with unitary governments could not accept a binding commitment on their part in exchange for a lesser obligation. The United States had proposed that the quandary could be resolved by building Article 22 of GATT into the code. This article provides for consultation, and obliges all parties to "accord sympathetic consideration to" the representations made by other parties under the General Agreement. The EC negotiators objected, saying the language of Article 22 was so vague that it was worthless, while the Americans responded that if it had been part of the GATT for thirty years it must be valuable. Such was the state of the discussion over levels of obligation in the last few months of the Tokyo Round.

The issue was finally resolved through a formula often employed in deadlocked negotiations, namely a declaration of what the parties would like to take place, coupled with a mechanism that permits the parties to take up the hard decisions in their future relations. The declaration entailed the obligation, frequently repeated throughout the standards code, that "Parties shall take such reasonable measures as may be available to them to ensure that local government bodies and non-governmental bodies within their territories . . . comply [with the operational provisions of the code]."[34] The mechanism that was employed was dispute settlement, which could be invoked in cases where the obligation above was not met and another party's "trade interests are significantly affected."[35] The standards negotiation thus resolved the problem by putting it off. In all of the codes negotiated at the Tokyo Round, dispute-settlement procedures were incorporated as a means to resolve the inevitable problems that will arise in adjusting to new obligations. There was no clearer example than the standards code of the use of the dispute-settlement mechanism to encourage nations to undertake those obligations in the first place.

With regard to the developing countries, the code eventually included a chapter providing for special and differential treatment for de-

---

[33] See ch. 5, n. 49, and accompanying text.

[34] GATT, *Agreement on Technical Barriers* (Standards), Article 3.1. Earlier drafts of this article had called upon parties "to use all reasonable means within their power" to ensure compliance, but this stronger language, which had been in the draft code until December 1978, was diluted when the dispute-settlement provisions were added. See "Technical Barriers to Trade: Revision," GATT docs., MTN/NTM/W/192/Rev 2, December 19, 1978, Article 2.9.

[35] GATT, *Agreement on Technical Barriers*, Article 14.24.

veloping countries. It was a difficult section to write and the work fell largely to Peter Williams of the GATT secretariat. On the one hand, the developing countries resisted the move toward international standards on the grounds that such standards would be beyond the technical competence of their manufacturing. On the other hand, there were limitations to how far developed countries could go in granting exceptions on regulatory procedures that might deal with matters of safety, health, environmental protection, or even product quality. In the end, the code instructed parties in several places to take account of the special needs of developing countries with regard to standards and technical regulations, but the wording was hortatory and did not spell out any precise actions developed countries were to take. Perhaps the most meaningful s and D provision of the code was the obligation of parties to provide technical assistance to developing countries on matters of standards. Such assistance would be designed to help developing countries establish regulatory bodies and to acquire methods at the production level whereby technical regulations could be met. In general, the thrust of the standards code was one more of attempting to bring developing countries up to an international level set by the developed countries than of making accommodations to conditions now existing in the economies of developing countries.

Import Licensing and Quantitative Restrictions

The negotiations on import licensing and quantitative restrictions (QR's) had a lower profile at the Tokyo Round than most other issues. The reasons were that import licensing was not a particularly difficult problem, either conceptually or politically, and a basic similarity of views was fairly easily achieved, and, second, that QR's were essentially a nonnegotiable area where views on most issues were so far apart that there was no point in negotiating. In 1975, the negotiations on import licensing and quantitative restrictions were folded together under the negotiating subgroup "Quantitative Restrictions."[36] At that time two separate codes were already in existence regarding import licensing. Negotiations on QR's made no headway during the 1975–77 period, and in July 1977 a decision was taken to negotiate QR's bilaterally and plurilaterally under the request/offer procedures being used for miscellaneous noncode issues. This decision effectively terminated efforts to reach agreement on a multilateral code on quantitative restrictions. As

[36] Import-licensing procedures are administratively necessary to apply quantitative restrictions; hence these two matters were brought together in the same negotiating group.

a result, the work of the subgroup was directed toward completing a code on licensing.

The negotiations on licensing itself proceeded slowly, in part because of the general stalemate during the early period which resulted from the impasse over agriculture. Then, too, negotiation went slowly because the United States had taken a strong position against automatic licensing systems of all types, on the grounds that these were simply annoying trade barriers which had no justifiable use in national commercial policies. U.S. opposition effectively blocked the negotiation on import licensing, since few developed nations wanted to contest the United States on an issue of minor importance, while the developing countries were quite willing to accept deadlock on the matter. In the spring of 1977, and as part of movement elsewhere in the negotiation on subsidies and agriculture, the United States appeared ready to moderate its opposition to automatic licensing. A series of meetings on import licensing were held between developed countries at the U.S. mission in Geneva, and over the summer these meetings were expanded to include key developing countries. By November 1977, when a formal meeting of Subgroup "Quantitative Restrictions" was held, the United States had accepted the use of automatic licensing procedures for the purpose of monitoring trade flows. This was a significant turning point in the import-licensing negotiation.

The next formal meeting of the subgroup was held in September 1978. In the interim, informal plurilateral meetings were held which moved the negotiation along. In July 1978, the GATT secretariat produced a single draft negotiating text at the request of various national delegations.[37] This text, compiled by Mr. Stuart Robinson, integrated the proposals for automatic and nonautomatic licensing procedures, and served as a basis for the subsequent negotiation. Further definitional clarity in the distinction between automatic and nonautomatic licensing was added in two proposals contributed by the Mexican delegation.[38] A further revision of the draft code was undertaken by the secretariat in December 1978, and the final version was concluded in the early months of the following year. Overall the last eighteen months of the negotiation of the import licensing code were characterized by wide consensus among all parties as well as by a technical and nonpolitical approach to the bargaining itself. One issue that might have created difficulties was whether the code would apply to agriculture, a

[37] GATT, *Tokyo Round*, 84.
[38] "Import Licensing System," GATT docs., MTN/NTM/W/170/Rev 1 and 171/Rev 1, September 4, 1978.

point which was sensitive for the EC. In the end, the EC made no demand for the exclusion of agriculture, with the result that the code applies to agricultural as well as nonagricultural products.

The basic consensus underlying the code on import licensing was that licensing procedures should be "neutral in application and administered in a fair and equitable manner."[39] The purpose was to separate administrative import procedures from other overt protectionist measures, and to insure that the former did not become covert protectionism through administrative delays or other forms of bureaucratic harassment. For automatic licensing systems, the code obliged parties to grant import licenses within ten working days of application, and to insure that licensing procedures did not restrict imports. For nonautomatic systems, the parties agreed that licensing procedures should not have restrictive effects beyond those restrictions (e.g., QR's) they were intended to administer. The code was universal and was meant to apply to all nations alike. This meant there could be little in the way of special and differential treatment for developing countries. The code did grant favorable treatment to developing countries in several minor instances, such as the obligation to provide import statistics to trading partners,[40] but in general the code made no distinction between developing and developed countries. From the standpoint of the negotiating process, it would appear that the developing countries accepted the basic noninterventionist premise of the import-licensing code, and that their success in securing the inclusion of automatic licensing provided sufficient reason for them to allow the code to go forward.

Code on Civil Aircraft

The Tokyo Round created a momentum behind the effort to find international solutions to trade problems. One indication of this was that new issues continued to be introduced as the multilateral negotiation moved along. One such issue was trade in civil aircraft. The inclusion of civil aircraft was an example of the application of the sector approach in trade negotiation, whereby it was envisaged that all trade barriers—tariff and nontariff—would be negotiated together within a given sector. The sector approach had been proposed earlier by Canada in the tariff negotiation, and whereas it gathered no support in that arena, it did attract the major powers as a method for handling aviation.[41]

---

[39] GATT, *Agreement on Import Licensing Procedures*, Article 1.3.

[40] Ibid., Article 3(b)(iv).

[41] The sector approach as originally proposed by Canada was intended to be a mech-

The rationale for the sector approach flowed very much from the nature of the aircraft industry. The industry is an extreme form of oligopoly, with a few major producers operating on a world scale. Sales of the final product are relatively few in number, and the product itself is enormously sophisticated and hence expensive. Furthermore the industry is intimately related to the military and defense needs of national governments. These characteristics encourage intervention by governments at all levels of the industry, from basic research and construction through to procurement of the final product. The result is that trade in aircraft is not trade in the Ricardian sense, and prima facie it is difficult to regulate such trade under the normal rules of the GATT. The industry appeared to call for special treatment, and this, plus the fact that there was concern over the ground rules for international exchanges in the industry, provided the impetus for the sectoral negotiation on trade in civil aircraft.

The aircraft negotiation was initiated by the Americans. The United States has a commanding position in the civil aircraft industry, producing some 85 percent of the world's commercial jet aircraft and over 95 percent of the world's general aviation aircraft (both figures exclude the Soviet Union). In 1978, when the aircraft code was negotiated, U.S. aerospace exports (including aircraft and parts) were $10 billion and imports were only $943 million. Despite the American lead, however, the U.S. industry was not sanguine about developments in aircraft trade during the 1970s. For one thing, a successful competitor, Airbus Industries, had been launched in 1969 as a partnership of European aerospace firms with the backing of government money for development and initial production. Government funding allowed Airbus to build inventory of wide-bodied A-300 commercial jets, a practice not normally followed in commercial aircraft construction, which positioned the company well for sales in the late 1970s and early 1980s. A further problem was that the U.S. industry saw European governments as prepared to use a full range of nontariff measures to insure growth of the European industry, including subsidies, export credits, and influence over the purchasing decisions of national airlines.

---

anism for negotiating all tariff and nontariff barriers in selected commodity areas, and particularly including goods at different levels of processing. An obvious prospect for a sector approach would be nonferrous metals, which could include products ranging from semiprocessed ores to fully processed metal goods. The sector approach was appealing to resource producers and hence to developing countries. However, it was not attractive to the major negotiating parties, largely on the grounds that it would not provide a sufficient basis for reciprocity, and consequently it was not pursued in the negotiation. For further information, see GATT, *Tokyo Round*, 88–89.

On the European side, there was also an incentive to negotiate. Despite its strong export surplus on trade in aircraft, the United States maintained a tariff of 5 percent in the aircraft sector. The tariff bulked quite large in absolute terms, and had amounted to duties of over $1 million per plane for a sale of twenty-three A-300's to Eastern Airlines in 1977. A further concern in the EC was U.S. government support for defense-related aviation research, which had the effect of underwriting development costs for comparable civilian aircraft. For example, research on engine performance and airframe construction for the B-1 bomber could easily be translated to large civilian carriers. The Europeans were sufficiently concerned about this matter to prepare a lengthy confidential report on disguised subsidies in the U.S. aircraft industry, which was intended to counter U.S. charges over the use of government subsidies in Europe.

Negotiation of the aircraft code was launched at the Bonn summit, where the major developed countries committed themselves to achieve the maximum freedom of trade possible in commercial aircraft. By the fall of 1978, the United States had proposed a working draft which called for the elimination (without staging) of all customs duties on aircrafts and parts, and which provided for disciplines on the various forms of government intervention in the industry. As might be expected, the negotiation focused on the latter issue. The objective of the Americans was to establish that the aircraft industry should operate on a basis of commercial competition, while the aim of some other governments was to maintain the use of government policy as a mechanism to insure equitable balance in the industry. The result of the negotiation was a compromise between these two positions. The United States prevailed on the principle of commercial competition,[42] and it obtained several concessions on nontariff measures. For example, the aircraft code made the provisions of the standards and subsidies codes applicable to aircraft trade, and on matters of procurement it restricted the right of signatories to oblige their airlines to discriminate against suppliers from other countries. Specifically, signatories accepted discipline over the use of obligatory subcontracts, generally known as offsets; and they agreed to avoid using inducements, either threats or incentives, to influence procurement decisions.[43] On the matter of export fi-

---

[42] The preamble to the code makes reference to the desire of the signatories to have their civil aircraft activities "operate on a commercially competitive basis" (GATT, *Agreement on Civil Aircraft*, 5).

[43] The clause on inducements was important, for there were examples reported during the Tokyo Round negotiation of both incentives (e.g., offers of landing rights for foreign airlines in return for purchases of equipment) and threats (e.g., threats to reduce imports

nancing, the United States was unable to secure agreement to reduce the role of governments in extending credits to foreign purchasers of commercial aircraft. During the Tokyo Round, an agreement on export financing had been negotiated in the OECD (the "Standstill Agreement" of 1975), and there was no willingness to extend the rather weak terms of this agreement in the aircraft negotiation in 1978.

The aircraft code essentially represented a tradeoff between the U.S. desire to regulate the use by other nations of nontariff measures in aircraft trade and other countries' wish to eliminate tariffs in the U.S. market, which remains the largest national market for commercial aircraft. The lead in the negotiation came largely from the U.S. industry itself, which was clearly ascendant in world production, but which was beginning to face serious and even damaging competition from foreign producers.[44] In the face of foreign competition, the U.S. took a liberal direction which reaffirmed the principle of competitive free trade in the industry. Without doubt, this posture was dictated by enlightened self-interest, for the commercial aircraft industry is such that all companies require an international market to achieve the volumes needed to justify investment in development and production of a product. Nevertheless industries under foreign pressure do not always take a liberal course, even if it is beneficial. The U.S. industry took advantage of the momentum of the Tokyo Round to establish a more liberal regime on trade in civilian aircraft than might have evolved without the stimulus of a major multilateral negotiation.

FAILURE IN THE SAFEGUARDS NEGOTIATION

The failure to revise and modernize Article 19 on safeguarding measures was the major setback of the Tokyo Round. The safeguards issue has historically been a difficult one in GATT, and traditional differences could not be bridged even under the pressure of a multilateral negotiation. Nations ended the Tokyo Round with perhaps a better understanding of where they stood on safeguards but no further ahead in terms of concrete guidelines for commercial policy.

The facts of the failed negotiation can be recounted simply. In June 1978, a draft text of a safeguards code was drawn up as part of the pre-

---

of another product if purchases of aircraft equipment were not undertaken). See Piper, "Unique Sectoral Agreement," 226.

[44] This competition increased in the early 1980s. See Thomas C. Haynes, "The Make or Break Sales for Boeing," *New York Times*, June 6, 1982; and James Sarazen, "La Grande Bataille des constructeurs d'avions: Boeing et des autres," *Le Monde*, March 10, 1983.

liminaries to the Bonn summit. The EC had initiated this draft, and the developing countries had opposed it. The June draft served as the basis for negotiation during the fall of 1978. By December, a new draft was drawn up.[45] Again the new draft was heavily bracketed, and there were frequent footnotes indicating reservations by one or more delegations. Additionally the chapter "Nature of Safeguard Action," which in the June draft had outlined a selective safeguarding procedure, was completely absent from the December draft. As a result, the December draft represented hardly any advance over the earlier version. Negotiations intensified after January, but by March 1979 it was clear the effort to conclude by an April deadline would be unsuccessful. In April, the GATT secretariat, at the request of the safeguards negotiating group, prepared a working draft intended to serve as a basis for further consultations within GATT.[46] This document summarized the most prominent positions achieved in the negotiation, but obviously it did not commit any nation, nor did it advance the negotiation appreciably. National delegations agreed to make a last-ditch, post–Tokyo Round attempt to conclude a safeguards code, but this effort, which lasted through July 1979, also failed to bridge the gap on the crucial question of selectivity. After July, the safeguards code was a dead letter as far as the Tokyo Round was concerned.

The safeguards negotiation foundered on the issue of selectivity, but in fact the entire subject constituted a minefield in relations between the GATT members. Selectivity was the terrain on which the delegations chose to fight, mainly because EC negotiators were operating with unyielding instructions from their Council of Ministers to obtain selectivity as part of a reform of Article 19 of the GATT. However, there were other issues that could easily have caused breakdown. For example, one issue was the definition of injury. The concept of safeguards implies a protective action taken in response to injury from an excess of imports, but there was no agreement on how to reform the loosely worded concept "serious injury" in Article 19. The developed countries, making use of legal constructions such as "market disruption" formulated in the history of textile negotiations, focused on price as the major determinant of injury.[47] The developing countries resisted a unicausal definition of injury and insisted that factors such as "technology, power and spread of marketing organizations, publicity . . . and also changes

---

[45] "Draft Integrated Text on Safeguards (Circulated at the Request of Certain Delegations)," GATT docs., MTN/INF/26, June 21, 1978.

[46] "Safeguards: Note by the Secretariat," GATT docs., MTN/SG/W/47, April 11, 1979.

[47] See Dam, *The GATT*, 298–99.

in consumer tastes" should be taken into account.[48] Among other things, inclusion of these factors would make injury more difficult to determine, a fact which would reduce the incidence of safeguards actions against products from developing countries.

A second critical issue was adjustment assistance. A basic position of the developing countries in situations where their products became more competitive than those from developed countries was that "the appropriate remedy [was] adjustment assistance and not import relief."[49] This position led the developing countries to demand that any code that provided for safeguarding action to limit imports from developing countries should also require policies to achieve structural adjustment in developed countries as well. This demand was resisted by the developed countries, which tended to blame the "aggressive exporting practices" of the developing countries themselves for creating the conditions that made safeguarding policies necessary in the first place. Third, the developed and developing countries argued over the role of multilateral surveillance over safeguard actions, with the latter predictably demanding maximum control by international mechanisms over national safeguarding policies. This matter became bound up with the question of selectivity, and as such it received a thorough examination in the negotiation.

In addition to the issues above, there were two other subjects that could have created difficulties on safeguards, although they were not extensively discussed in the negotiation. One was the perennial question of special and differential treatment for developing countries. A demand from the developing countries for differential treatment likely would have arisen along the lines that developed countries ought not to apply safeguarding measures at all to the exports of developing countries. This demand would have confronted the obvious fact that, as judged from practice, most developed countries considered the developing countries to be the principal targets of safeguarding actions. Indeed, without the prospect of "destabilizing" exports from the developing countries, it is probable the issue of safeguards could have been resolved among the developed nations. A second issue was so-called voluntary export restraints (VER's). One of the main reasons for negotiating safeguards at the Tokyo Round was the increasing (and extralegal) use of VER's, and yet VER's were not prominent in the negotia-

[48] "Safeguards (Circulated at the Request of Certain Developing Countries)," GATT docs., MTN/INF/17, February 6, 1978, 2.
[49] Ibid., 1.

tion.[50] It would seem that the Tokyo Round negotiators decided to resolve the selectivity problem before tackling these other difficult issues. As a result, the negotiators avoided the enormous problem of defining VER's for the purpose of controlling their use, and particularly defining whether the "voluntary" aspects of VER's removed them from the domain of national policies which could be subject to a multilateral GATT code.[51] Yet another result of focusing on selectivity was that the EC, which was unbending on the subject, became essentially isolated in the safeguards negotiation. This might have changed had the negotiation shifted to VER's. The United States has made extensive use of VER's in its trade relations with Japan and the developing countries, and it is doubtful whether the U.S. government would have accepted substantial limitations on its capacity to make such agreements. It is probable that negotiation of the VER issue would have entailed a greater confrontation between the United States and the developing countries than occurred over the selectivity issue.[52]

In the end, selectivity was a fatal issue in the safeguards negotiation, but there was considerable movement on this issue throughout the negotiation. The developing countries began the Tokyo Round united and wholly opposed to the principle of discriminatory application of safeguarding measures. This principle was important in both symbolic and practical terms. It was eventually dropped, however, in favor of selective safeguards which could be undertaken either in agreement with the exporting party(ies) involved, or subject to the surveillance of an international body. Specifically, the developing countries were prepared to accept the provisions of the secretariat draft of April 1979, which permitted selective safeguards where serious injury (or threat) exists, and "where unusual and exceptional unforeseen circumstances are clearly established by the importing Party."[53] Such measures would require the agreement of the exporting party(ies), or would have to be

---

[50] For example, the April draft compiled by the secretariat states only that "It is for consideration how any rules on the use of export restraint measures should be formulated." See "Safeguards: Note by the Secretariat," GATT docs., MTN/SG/W/47, April 11, 1979, 32.

[51] On the matter of defining VER's, see ch. 3, especially the discussion of safeguards.

[52] There is a strong argument in the United States that VER's deflect the pressure for more stringent controls such as legislated quotas. Indeed this argument was used by the Reagan administration in 1981 to defend its "consultations" with Japan which resulted in a VER on automobiles. On the other side, however, there is some sympathy in the U.S. government for international rules to restrict the use of VER's, in order to reduce the pressure on Washington from lobbies seeking protection through these measures.

[53] "Safeguards: Note by the Secretariat," GATT docs., MTN/SG/W/47, April 11, 1979, 10.

approved by a committee on safeguard measures to be set up under the code. Thus a relationship was established between selectivity and surveillance. It was a formula that was acceptable to the United States, Japan, and Canada, but it was rejected by the European Community. The EC would have accepted posthoc surveillance of actions that had already been determined by the importing nation, but it could not accept an obligation to submit an action to prior review and approval by an international organ. For the EC, the obligation constituted a derogation of economic sovereignty. This was the point on which the issue turned.

Most important issues of international economic policy eventually raise issues of economic sovereignty, and it is usually the large actors that are least willing to bend domestic procedures to international norms. Certainly an example of this proposition could be seen in the difficulty with which the United States moved toward acceptance of an international definition of material injury in antidumping and countervailing duties. On the selectivity issue, it was the EC and not the United States that found it difficult to accept an international consensus. The United States was arguably as well served by selectivity as the EC, but it was prepared to accept that selectivity could be limited by a surveillance mechanism that in practice would nearly have prevented the application of selective safeguards. One reason for this position was that the U.S. delegation wanted the developing countries "on board" the safeguard negotiation (and the Tokyo Round generally) more than it wanted selectivity. For the EC delegation, this was an incongruous position, since the developing countries were not expected to sign the safeguards code anyway.

A second reason behind the U.S. position was that the United States did not expect that a safeguards code would put an end to VER's or other orderly marketing arrangements (OMA's) negotiated on a bilateral basis with individual exporters. These were the principal safety valves by which the United States had arrived at an uneasy accommodation with sharply increasing exports from Japan and the developing countries. A final reason for the U.S. position, and perhaps the most important, was related to the statutory nature of U.S. domestic trade policy. The American approach to safeguarding measures had been to proceed with a determination of injury by a quasi-judicial body of the U.S. government, following which import restrictions could be undertaken to reduce the injury. The system was open, and accessible to testimony from all sides. For American negotiators, it was the transparency, even more than the resulting policy, that made the system commendable. The U.S. system was not unlike that being proposed in the safeguards negotiation under the guise of international surveillance. The safeguards code would have set up a quasi-judicial international body, and nations seeking to apply selective safeguards would have been expected to present a case before that body. This was an international system U.S. negotiators felt comfortable with because it replicated U.S. domestic procedures.[54]

For the Europeans, the selectivity issue was much more difficult. For one thing, selectivity was sought after as a goal in its own right. The concept of selectivity originated with the British Board of Trade, where it was viewed as a reasonable mechanism to create orderly change in the international economic system. The idea was attractive to the EC members (less so to the Germans and Danes) because it promised to promote stability in the international trade and, not incidentally, to provide protection for European industries threatened by competition from developing countries exports. The British government under the leadership of Prime Minister Margaret Thatcher later changed its position on selectivity, but by that time other EC members, particularly the French, had become committed to the idea. Second, the link between selectivity and surveillance, which was necessary to sell selectivity to the developing countries, made matters worse for the EC. The quasi-legal nature of the surveillance mechanism in the safeguards code was antithetical to the system of administrative guidance that more nearly characterized the approach of European governments and the EC itself to trade policy. For the Europeans, it was far more important that the system operate on clearly defined criteria than that it operate on the basis of openness. As one EC official stated, "The fact that a system produces a thousand pages of open testimony doesn't make it a good system."[55]

Beyond the immediate problem of politics, selectivity raised constitutional difficulties for the EC. Normally it is assumed the EC operates like a nation-state in international trade negotiations, but in fact it is

[54] It is interesting to speculate about what might have happened had the negotiation ever turned to a detailed examination of the procedures for determining injury. The United States might have had much more difficulty with safeguards, because U.S. domestic definitions of injury have been more lenient than international definitions.

[55] As the EC delegation stated formally: "It is well-known that our existing procedures do not incorporate requirements for public investigation and equally that we are not convinced that such procedures necessarily lead to more defensible decisions. Indeed, the existence of a public forum can sometimes contribute in itself to an increase in political pressures on a government making it more rather than less difficult to avoid taking some action. We consider that it is much more important to have a clearer basis for action in terms of better defined criteria than to enforce any particular procedures for decision making" ("Statement by Representative of European Communities on 27 October 1976," GATT docs., MTN/SG/W/18, November 16, 1976, 6).

politically weaker than a single nation. The safeguards negotiation revealed this weakness. At the time of the Tokyo Round, the EC was a collection of nine separate national economies. Foreign imports do not impact evenly on this system; hence, any attempt to take safeguarding actions in response to demands from one quarter is likely to be met with countervailing pressure from another. Such countervailing pressure makes the EC a cumbersome system internally, and creates pressure to handle policy through informal mechanisms of administrative guidance because formal mechanisms of policy making are prone to immobility. In the safeguards negotiation, the EC was unwilling to become involved in an open, judicial system at the international level that it could not have operated at the internal level without putting the fragile EC system under intolerable strain. In this negotiation, one saw the limits that a domestic system can impose on the movement toward a more internationalized system. The limits were not so much the protectionism of the European Community as its political weakness.

There are different ways a negotiation can break down. One way is for the parties to lose patience with each other and then to differ on an issue that has perhaps symbolic but not much practical importance. The near-deadlock in the Kennedy Round over the American Selling Price in chemicals was an example of this form of breakdown. The breakdown on safeguards at the Tokyo Round was not of this sort. Safeguards was a substantive and not a procedural problem, or, in terms that negotiators would use, it was a real and not a phony issue. It went to the heart of the GATT system of legal obligations, and it reflected the profound problems of the contemporary world economy.

As an economic issue, safeguards touched on the problem of integrating the developing countries into an international economic system dominated by the developed countries. This is the central economic problem of our time, and it is an enormously painful one. In the longer run, it will entail a struggle over redistribution of productive capacity and economic wealth in the world. In the near run, however, the problem is a matter of who will pay for free trade. Free trade is not free, for there are costs of adjustment that must be borne if a system is to enjoy the benefits of greater efficiency brought by unrestricted commerce. The safeguards negotiation dealt with conflicting views over the rate at which that adjustment would be made, and the extent to which economically weak sectors in powerful countries would be shielded from making any adjustment at all. This is an economic problem that will continue to be the focus of negotiations in GATT and other international economic institutions.

As a legal problem, Article 19 and the matter of safeguards have long been a difficult problem within the GATT, because in principle they have involved the release of a GATT member from the obligations it incurred pursuant to the General Agreement. In addition, the selective application of safeguards entailed a further release from obligations, since it violated the longstanding customary principle of nondiscrimination in the use of safeguard measures. It should not be surprising that selective safeguards was a difficult issue to negotiate, since members in any system of legal obligations rarely make it easy for other participants to circumvent the requirements of the system. This explains why the application of selective safeguards became hedged in with limitations pertaining to international surveillance, which in the end jeopardized its acceptance by one of the two actors that effectively had veto power at the Tokyo Round.

Finally, as a political problem, selective safeguards raised the question of who adjusts to whom in the context of today's changing world economy. The argument of the EC in proposing selective safeguards was that this method was a judicious response to the instability produced by the rapid and uneven growth of exports from the newly industrializing developing countries. Selective safeguards were defended as a means to promote orderly change and stability in the international economic system, particularly because they focused corrective policy on the countries causing the disturbance. Of course this argument is correct from the standpoint of system theory, for stability is always best maintained when a regulating mechanism can be pinpointed on a disturbing force without affecting other interactions within the system. What this argument does not take account of, however, is that developing countries are less well served by stability than they are by rapid changes in traditional trading patterns. In its essence, the effort to negotiate selective safeguards was motivated by a desire to force developing-countries exporters to adjust to a pace of change that would not create dislocation in competing industries in the developed countries. This was a demand that the developing countries not surprisingly resisted.

AGRICULTURE

It will be recalled that the negotiations on agriculture had been the scene of a major impasse between the United States and the European Community during the early part of the Tokyo Round. That impasse was broken by a meeting in July 1977 between Robert Strauss and several European Commissioners, at which time the Americans agreed to negotiate agriculture separately from the other issues in the Tokyo

Round. Following this meeting, multilateral negotiations resumed in the three subgroups within Group "Agriculture," namely meat, dairy products, and grain. Additionally, bilateral negotiations began on an offer/request basis between individual countries over specific products. The results of these several negotiations were two "arrangements" and a series of individual bilateral agreements. These results were perhaps impressive in view of the traditional difficulties of negotiating any agreements on agriculture in the GATT context, but they were far less significant than the accomplishments posted in the code negotiations or in the negotiations on industrial tariffs.

Bilateral Agreements

Major bilateral agreements consisting of tariff and quota changes on agricultural products were reached between the four principal actors at the Tokyo Round. In addition some thirty other nations concluded lesser agreements. The major bilateral deal was of course between the EC and the United States, and it had political importance for the overall progress of the Tokyo Round. As part of the agreement of 1977, the United States agreed to negotiate agriculture separately from other matters on the condition that a "substantial result for agriculture" would be reached at the Tokyo Round.[56] The U.S. negotiators followed up the 1977 agreement with a list of specific agriculture demands on the Community on which it was claimed the United States needed some action if the Tokyo Round accords were to be sold to Congress. The list became known as the Strauss list, and it enjoyed a certain notoriety during the negotiation. The list included politically important products such as rice, tobacco, citrus fruits, prunes, and beef.[57]

The EC countered the Strauss list with its own requests in agriculture, namely: concessions in dairy products, an area in which the United

---

[56] U.S. Senate, *MTN Studies*, vol. 1, *Results for U.S. Agriculture*, 15.

[57] The Strauss list was one of those negotiation artifacts that get established partly through the help of an imaginative press, but in this case the behavior of the principals may have given credence to the idea. At one point, Robert Strauss was host at a dinner meeting at the Intercontinental Hotel in Geneva for the late Finn Gundelach, EC commissioner for agriculture. This was an important meeting: Strauss prepared for it; he wanted a lot from Gundelach. At the dinner, the men discussed a number of issues and then came down to the agricultural products Strauss wanted. Gundelach professed to be a little uncertain as to exactly what Strauss wanted. Strauss took out his pen and wrote out a list of products on the tablecloth. This greatly exercised the maître d'. He was used to barbaric North American behavior, but this was too much. He accosted Strauss, who took out his wallet, bought the tablecloth on the spot, and gave it to an EC official. A trade negotiator later commented, 'It was a very expensive tablecloth.'

States did not have a comparative advantage over Europe; elimination of discriminatory barriers against certain EC products such as cognac that were erected during the "chicken war" of the mid-1960s; and elimination of the wine-gallon method of taxing alcoholic beverages, which is analyzed at length in chapter 7. Further EC requests were more symbolic, and included the demand that the United States reduce the intensity of its opposition to Common Agricultural Policy (CAP) subsidies and that it participate in negotiations to establish a world framework for agriculture, and specifically the multilateral negotiations under way in the meat, dairy products, and grains sectors. The demand regarding CAP subsidies was a matter for the subsidy/countervail negotiation, and was effectively settled with the conclusion of a code in this area. The demand regarding multilateral negotiations touched on an important principle for the EC. The EC negotiators viewed the United States as resisting international efforts to organize agricultural markets, or even to encourage market surveillance under the aegis of a multilateral agreement. The EC had long sought to involve the United States in such activities, and it used the prospect of product concessions in bilateral negotiations as a bargaining chip to promote this aim.

The US/EC bilateral negotiations resulted in an exchange of concessions that were valued at $168 million on the EC side and $106 million for the United States.[58] The main concession by the United States was an increase in the quota of foreign cheese. It was estimated that this increase would depress U.S. milk prices by about 5.4¢ per hundredweight through lost domestic production, which at the 1978 level of production of 122 billion pounds of milk would mean a concession of some $66 million.[59] On the EC side, the principal concession was high-quality (i.e., "hotel") beef, on which the Community opened a new tariff line with a quota of 10,000 metric tons (22.1 million pounds). At $3 per pound, this concession was valued at $66 million in new trade. There was some suggestion that cheese and beef were traded off between the United States and the Community, which was a sensitive matter during the negotiation because of the disadvantaged groups on both sides. It would seem that the equivalence of the concession on either side supports the argument that these two products were negotiated as a single exchange.

---

[58] U.S. Senate, *MTN Studies*, vol. 2, *Tokyo-Geneva Round: Its Relation to U.S. Agriculture*, 64. The figure for the U.S. concession does not include the elimination of the wine-gallon assessment, which the Europeans included in the agricultural negotiations. Inclusion of this item, which was valued at $60 million for the EC, brought the overall U.S. concessions to $166 million.

[59] Houck, "U.S. Agricultural Trade," 287.

The remainder of the U.S. agricultural package proposed to the EC included a number of lesser concessions such as tariff changes on lamb, wool, barley, and some dairy products. On the EC side, the concessions were economically more significant, and certainly were more difficult to achieve in political terms. The EC agricultural concessions did not entail any significant changes to the CAP, but they were nevertheless difficult because of the balance of interests within the EC. Many of the U.S. demands bore heavily on the Italians and to a lesser extent the French, while the benefits of U.S. concessions were enjoyed mainly by the British. In some cases, such as almonds, which are grown in southern Italy, the EC refused to make any concession at all.[60] In other cases, such as tobacco and rice, the EC offset external concessions with changes in internal restitution procedures which indemnified domestic producers whose interests were affected. For example, prunes were grown in a region represented by a senior political figure in France, which made concessions on this product very difficult to engineer. Prior to settling this problem externally, an EC official visited the prune growers and worked out a deal whereby those producers would receive benefits from changes in EC restitution procedures equivalent to what they would lose on concessions to the Americans. Although hardly consistent with the philosophy of trade liberalization, these maneuvers at least helped to spread internally the costs of benefits given to external producers.

Regarding agricultural agreements made by other countries, Japan offered major concessions valued at $215 million in new trade to the United States, with the latter responding with concessions mainly outside the area of agriculture. The package offered by Japan consisted of a series of tariff reductions and quota increases on a wide range of American exports, including citrus fruits and juices, high-quality beef, and pork. Not included in the calculation of new trade was a Japanese decision to bind soybean imports at "free" (i.e., no tariff), an action that could lead to substantial future growth in U.S. exports (valued at $770 million in 1976). As reported by Houck, many observers placed a high value on this concession, since a similar concession by the EC in the Dillon Round of 1962 had facilitated the subsequent rapid growth of U.S. soybean exports to Europe.[61] The negotiation between the Japanese and the EC yielded disappointing results. The Japanese were less forthcoming toward the Europeans than toward the Americans on ag-

[60] One other area in which the EC refused concessions was citrus fruits, because such concessions would have affected Greece and Spain and would have burdened the EC's Mediterranean policy.

[61] Houck, "U.S. Agricultural Trade," 282.

riculture, which was consistent with the basic difficulties Japan and the EC had in dealing on industrial tariffs (see chapter 7) and other issues of bilateral trade. The EC had hoped to gain numerous concessions from Japan on agriculture in order to reduce its bilateral trade deficit, but the Japanese had made few requests of the Europeans in the agricultural sector, and the Europeans were not prepared to address the concessions the Japanese did want, such as an end to discriminatory treatment of Japanese industrial exports. The EC pressed Japan hard for a removal of those domestic taxes that hurt European exports of alcoholic beverages, but the Japanese considered these to be internal measures and were unwilling to negotiate them.

Canada was also a major player in the agricultural negotiation, and it concluded a significant bilateral agreement with the United States and the Community. Canada has a widely varied agricultural trade with the United States, which is hindered but not appreciably distorted by the trade restrictions applied by the two countries. In keeping with this varied trade, Canada made a wide range of offers on American exports which included tariff reductions, bindings, and quota increases. The United States reciprocated with similar offers. An accord was reached between the two countries which was estimated by the United States to be worth $156 million in new trade, which, to put it in perspective, could be compared with the $168 million the United States received from the EC and the $23 million it received from all other countries combined (less Japan).[62] With regard to the EC, the Canadians concluded a substantial reciprocal agreement on cheese, and they undertook to reduce discriminatory taxation by Canadian provincial governments of European exports of alcoholic beverages. In return, Canada received tariff reductions on some fishery products, as well as on berries, whiskey, and maple syrup.

The Big Four accounted for most of the volume of trade covered by agricultural concessions at the Tokyo Round. Other nations which were important in the agricultural negotiations included Australia, New Zealand, Brazil, Argentina, and Mexico. The first two nations concluded a long and sometimes difficult negotiation with the EC, which concluded in agreements that may start a movement toward substantially liberalized trade between these parties. The difficulties in agricultural negotiations between Australia, New Zealand, and the EC stem from the fact that the only agricultural products the Community can export to these countries are processed foodstuffs, whereas they

---

[62] U.S. Senate, *MTN Studies*, vol. 2, *Tokyo-Geneva Round: Its Relation to U.S. Agriculture*, 65.

seek to protect the processing component in agricultural production because of the employment it provides. In the Tokyo Round, agreements were struck between these parties which promised to lead to further cooperation in the future. The EC described these agreements as essentially modest, but of "considerable political importance."[63]

Multilateral Agreements

The multilateral negotiations in Group "Agriculture" yielded two agreements, namely the Arrangement regarding Bovine Meat (i.e., beef and veal) and the International Dairy Arrangement. Both agreements were designed mainly to increase the exchange of information among the signatories, and they had little economic effect on actual trade. Specifically the agreements provided for international councils to meet regularly and collect information on world trade in meat and dairy products respectively. These councils were also empowered to evaluate problems of production and trade and to make policy recommendations to participating governments. The latter power was intended to give the councils a rudimentary capability to serve as a forum for consultation and mediation of trade disputes over meat or dairy products. Additionally the Dairy Arrangement provided for a series of minimum export prices for milk and various dairy products. These prices were set well below market and support prices in the major trading nations, and indeed below the point at which even the most efficient producers could profit. The main function of these export prices is to serve as a protection against distress selling and to prevent nations from subsidizing sales below the prices stipulated in the agreement.

A third multilateral agreement was attempted on grains. Initially work on grains started in a subgroup of Group "Agriculture" at the Tokyo Round. However, a parallel negotiation on wheat was started in the London-based International Wheat Council (IWC) in 1975, which later came under the auspices of UNCTAD's Integrated Commodity Program inaugurated in 1976. By 1977 the GATT negotiation on grains had been subsumed under the IWC, the purpose being to replace the International Wheat Agreement, which was due to run out in 1979. The basic goal of the Wheat Conference (as it became known) was to organize world trade in wheat in order to prevent the wide price fluctuations that are commonly experienced in commodity markets. Such a goal is difficult to negotiate, for it pits the interests of importers directly against those of exporters. The Wheat Conference failed to reach this

---

[63] Commission, *GATT Multilateral Negotiations*, 75.

goal, and in this failure it clearly revealed the difficulties inherent in negotiating commodity agreements.

There is a long tradition of cooperation between nations that import and export wheat. International agreements on wheat have been in force continuously since 1949. Through 1968, these agreements contained provisions that regulated maximum and minimum prices, although the policies of the dominant suppliers like the United States and Canada of holding surplus stocks and restraining production probably had more effect on price than the agreements themselves. After 1968, increased world production depressed prices, and exporters were not sufficiently disciplined to maintain any agreed international price. For most of the period since 1949, surplus rather than deficit has been the main difficulty motivating international action, although large Soviet purchases in the mid-1960s created an uncharacteristic worldwide shortage of wheat. The period leading up to the Wheat Conference was similarly one of scarcity and high prices, and hence the concern was equally for the food needs of importers, especially developing countries, as well as the need for exporters of stable earnings.

The aim of any commodity agreement is to stabilize markets. This is typically done through the creation of a reserve stock, with an agreement on the price at which the stock is acquired and released. As might be expected, exporters usually seek high acquisition and release prices, while importers seek lower prices. In the Wheat Conference, the main actors were the United States, which led the negotiation for the grain exporters, and the European Community, which for most of the negotiation served as spokesman for the importers. Near the end of the negotiation, the developing countries assumed a major role in the talks. The fact that their interests were not sufficiently represented until late in the game contributed to the breakdown of the conference.

By December 1978, the positions of the principals at the seventy-nation Wheat Conference were clarified. The United States wanted an acquisition price of $145 per ton with a total world reserve stock of thirty million tons. The EC proposed a figure of $115 per ton and a reserve stock of fifteen million tons. Both sides were roughly agreed that the "ceiling" or release price should be around $200 per ton. The minimum price of $145 per ton approximately reflected U.S. production costs; higher-cost producers such as Canada and Australia sought an even higher level. As for the reserve stock, the United States proposed that it be held in agreed shares by importers and exporters alike. It was perhaps curious that a major exporting country like the United States would press for large reserve stocks, since larger stocks usually provide greater insurance to importers against rising prices. The reason is that the commitment to hold reserve stocks would have absorbed most of the EC's surplus of wheat, which the EC normally cleared through the operation of CAP export subsidies, to the great distress of American farmers. For its part, the EC, which has not had a tradition of stockpiling wheat, argued for a smaller reserve and a lower acquisition price in order to make holding reserves a more temporary phenomenon. In the U.S. and EC positions on reserve stocks, one sees again the tendency of nations to propose solutions in the international arena that reflect policies already in force in their own domestic systems.[64]

A compromise on the matter of acquisition price was reached early in the new year between the United States and the Community. The two delegations agreed on a two-stage acquisition price whereby half the agreed reserves would be purchased when the price fell to $140 a ton, with the other half purchased if the price went to $125. The division of the reserves remained at issue, however, and became the subject of further efforts at compromise. In an effort to break the impasse, the Swiss chairman of the conference, Arthur Dunkel, secured pledges from the various delegations of prospective national contributions to the wheat reserves. This exercise produced pledges of around twenty-two million tons, which, together with a general understanding on the acquisition and release prices, would probably have been sufficient to produce an agreement between the United States and the Community.[65] At this point, the main action shifted from a US/EC exchange to a more multilateral negotiation involving especially the developing countries.

The main issues for the developing countries were "special provisions" and the price range. On the former, the developing countries sought exemptions from the obligations to maintain reserve stock, but the United States and other developed nations rejected this idea on the grounds that development aid should be considered separately from the establishment of a commercial agreement. On the latter, the developing countries generally sought a lower price range than that agreed between the U.S. and EC delegations, although the developing countries were divided on this matter. India and Pakistan accepted the US/EC range, but other "hardliners" like Iraq, Brazil, and Yugoslavia insisted

[64] Price and market control were also at issue between the United States and the Community. The EC argued that the cost of larger reserves was too great for importers to bear, particularly developing countries. However, the United States maintained that thirty million tons would be needed to control prices, given that world production could vary by as much as sixty-five million tons per year. See Ian Guest, "US Blamed for Impasse in Wheat Negotiations," *Guardian*, February 8, 1979.

[65] Brij Khindaria, "Compromise Saves Wheat Conference from Breakdown," *Financial Times*, February 10, 1979.

on a price range of $130 to $160 per ton. In the end, the differences between the developed and the developing countries simply could not be bridged. Nor was the difference simply between these two groups, for, as the U.S. delegation noted, the US/EC compromise was not entirely settled on the matter of reserve size, nor had other important countries like Japan ever agreed formally to the compromise.[66] The Wheat Conference concluded with an understanding that the existing agreement should continue; it provided for consultation but not market stabilization. Also continued was the existing arrangement on food aid. In view of this disappointing result, the link between the London Wheat Conference and the Tokyo Round in Geneva was quietly dropped.

In sum, the Tokyo Round did not produce a substantial result in the area of multilateral agricultural negotiations. To be sure, some accomplishments were posted. The Wheat Conference was a bold initiative, and it moved some distance in structuring the issues between importers and exporters and between developed and developing countries before it collapsed. The meat and dairy-products arrangements will provide for multilateral consultation and information gathering, both of which are valuable and a necessary prerequisite to international policymaking. Finally, agriculture was affected by some of the multilateral codes negotiated at the Tokyo Round, for example, the standards code, which applies to agriculture as well as nonagricultural products. However that may be, a final judgment of the Tokyo Round must be that it did not significantly advance international policy with regard to agricultural trade. The participating nations ended the Tokyo Round about as far apart on agricultural trade policy as they were at the beginning of the negotiation.

[66] Alan Spence and Douglas Martin, "Wheat Council Envoys to Try to Salvage Talks on World Pact at March 20 Meeting," *Wall Street Journal*, March 1, 1979.

7

END PHASE, 1978–1979:
TARIFFS, WINE GALLONS, AND OTHER MATTERS

Conclusion of the Tariff Negotiation

Like the code negotiations at the Tokyo Round, the tariff negotiation was a compartmentalized affair. The tariff negotiation had its own specialists and to some extent its own timetable. Offers had been tabled by the Big Three early in 1978, and some negotiation had occurred between them during the spring of that year. By the time of the Bonn summit, most nations participating in the tariff negotiation had tabled specific negotiating offers. For some countries, particularly the developed nations, offers were based on formula reductions; for the developing countries, offers were made on an item-by-item basis.

Once offers were tabled, efforts to achieve a general settlement lay mainly in the negotiations between the major nations, especially the United States and the European Community. The reason is that, as explained earlier, influence in a tariff negotiation is a direct function of the size of a nation's trade. Nations with smaller trade flows simply are not in a position to offer many concessions to other countries and hence have little standing in a negotiation where the modus operandi is reciprocal exchange. Thus the tariff negotiation emphasized the discrepancy between the developing and developed countries even more than occurred in the code negotiations, where at least in principle developing countries had a stake as GATT members in the trade rules that were negotiated for the system. As a historical note, the fact that GATT negotiations have traditionally been tariff negotiations has probably increased the tendency of developing countries to regard GATT as a rich man's club.

There are two opposing ideal strategies in the approach to tariff negotiation. One is to make a minimum offer with the expectation that it will be enhanced during the bargaining; the other is to make a maximum offer with the prospect that it will be reduced if one's negotiating partners are not forthcoming. In the history of GATT negotiations, the former strategy was reflected in the item-by-item approach taken to multilateral tariff negotiations until the 1960s. The latter strategy was more characteristic of the across-the-board or formula approach taken to tariff cutting in the Kennedy and Tokyo rounds. The choice of the latter strategy has been well vindicated in GATT practice, for it is clear that a formula approach gets more on the table at the start of the negotiation, and as a result leads to a deeper settlement at the end. The disadvantage of the formula approach is that it creates a more cantankerous negotiation. In the formula approach, nations tend to settle on as liberal a formula as possible, on the assumption that exceptions will be made for sensitive sectors when offers are actually tabled. However, exceptions by one country can lead to exceptions by others, which in turn can lead to withdrawals of offers already previously tabled, and so on. As a result, the negotiating play in the maximum-offer strategy tends to be over withdrawals of existing offers, rather than over additions of new offers (often known as "sweeteners") which might occur in a minimum-offer strategy.

In the psychology of negotiation, as in life generally, there is a tendency to "bank" the offers a negotiating partner has put on the table even when those offers are tabled on an *ad referendum* basis. Withdrawals of those offers violate the expectations that negotiators develop about their situation, and consequently they can be more damaging to a negotiating relationship than if an offer had never been made in the first place. Thus the method chosen for the Tokyo Round tariff negotiation foreordained the negotiators to experience a certain amount of disappointment and even rancor.

Following the Bonn summit, the tariff negotiation settled down into a series of bilateral and plurilateral meetings as the participating nations sought to exchange specific concessions with their principal trading partners. Progress was not good, especially between the major countries. The EC offer, which at the time of the Bonn summit had been for about a 33 percent weighted overall reduction, was reduced to about 31 percent by further withdrawals. These withdrawals hit particularly at the exports of the United States and Japan. On November 30, 1978, the Americans retaliated with withdrawals of their own which affected products in the chemicals, steel, and textile sectors. Prior to these withdrawals, the U.S. offer had been for a 49 percent weighted overall reduction. This figure was impressive in aggregate terms, but it was achieved largely through making greater-than-formula cuts on products with low tariffs, and consequently it did not promote the goal of tariff harmonization that EC negotiators were committed to. The November 30 withdrawals by the United States were described in an internal EC Commission document as having a "severe impact on the quality of the U.S. offer," and the document went on to note that the offer left some 42 percent of EC exports to the United States subject to duties of 15 percent or greater.[1] In retaliation for the

[1] The document is reported in John Robinson, "Outline of the Final EEC Negotiating

U.S. action, the EC circulated a list of further possible withdrawals on textiles.

One of the sources of difficulty in the tariff negotiation was that the attention of senior U.S. negotiators lay elsewhere. One distracting issue was the countervail waiver, which arose in the context of the subsidy/countervail negotiation. Another distraction was related more directly to the tariff negotiation. On September 29, with little warning, the U.S. Senate passed a resolution prohibiting the United States from offering concessions on textile and apparel tariffs during the Tokyo Round negotiation. The resolution was sponsored by Senator Ernest Hollings of South Carolina and was attached as an amendment to a bill authorizing funds for the Export-Import Bank. The resolution received the cosponsorship of fifty senators. The administration took the position that the resolution would have a "devastating" effect on the negotiation if it were not reversed, and it mobilized to fight the measure when the bill went to the House-Senate conference committee. Even more important than the resolution itself was the apparent rise of protectionist sentiment in the Senate. Such sentiment was especially worrisome from the standpoint of winning subsequent Senate approval for the Tokyo Round as a whole.

The administration took three actions to counter the Hollings initiative. First, it successfully lobbied to get the resolution attached to an inconsequential piece of legislation that could easily be vetoed by the president. Second, on November 11, President Carter vetoed the legislation, on the grounds that the loss of U.S. export markets through probable retaliation from America's trading partners would be too high a price for the nation to pay. However, in his statement accompanying the veto, the president promised, "I am determined to assist the beleaguered textile industry."[2] Third, the administration immediately entered into negotiations with the textile industry to establish a program to fulfill the president's promise. The result of these negotiations emerged some three months later in a white paper that carried the title "Administration Textile Program."[3] In this program, the administration pledged to ensure that the growth of textile and apparel imports into the United States would be held to levels that would not dis-

---

Position for the Tokyo Round's Closing Phase," *European Report*, no. 557, December 13, 1978.

[2] "Carter Vetoes MTN-Threatening Textile Legislation," *U.S. Mission Daily Bulletin*, November 15, 1978.

[3] A text of the white paper was transmitted on February 16, 1979, from Robert Strauss to Charles Vanik, chairman of the House Subcommittee on Trade. The document is included in U.S. Government, *Background Material*, 4–15.

rupt the American industry. This entailed a closer monitoring of textile imports on a category-by-category basis and a promise to negotiate tougher bilateral agreements with major exporters under the Multifibre Arrangement (MFA). Finally, the administration reaffirmed its existing policy of excluding textiles and apparel from coverage under the Government Procurement Code, and it promised full support for a major new export-expansion program by the industry.

The administration textile program was a leading example of a strategy that Strauss and the administration used to deal with powerful domestic critics of the Tokyo Round, namely to negotiate less-stringent side agreements with those groups powerful enough to threaten the eventual success of the overall negotiation. In the textile case, the strategy had an immediate payoff, and it was widely assumed that the textile program was the price the administration had to pay to get Congress to approve the countervail waiver. The administration's strategy was the essence of pragmatism; it was colorfully defended by Strauss in the following terms: "You feed the sharks a little this and a little that, and you get the canoe to shore."[4] The strategy was of course not without its critics. The free-trade bar in Washington bitterly resented the concessions made to protectionist sentiment, and the EC negotiators were distressed to see the United States increasing import restrictions in a sector where tariffs were already too high and should come down. However, the opposition from the EC was moderated by the fact that the program did not hurt Community interests. The program was largely aimed at exporters in advanced developing countries like Hong Kong and Brazil, and their opposition to the stiffer import controls did not carry enough weight to deter the U.S. action.

U.S./EC Bilateral Negotiations

The bilateral negotiation between the United States and the European Community was the key to establishing a substantial result in the tariff negotiation. This negotiation was mainly conducted in a series of meetings during the fall of 1978 under the direction of James McNamara for the United States and Jacques Dugimont for the EC. By December, it was generally recognized that the US/EC tariff negotiation was lagging. This was not unusual, as distributive bargaining such as is found in tariff negotiations often tends to go down to the wire as parties delay concessions until the last moment. In mid-December, a high-level meeting was held to chart the direction for an eventual settlement. This

[4] Quotation paraphrased; received by word of mouth.

meeting was the first of three high-level encounters between December and March 1979 that were needed to conclude things between the Americans and the Community. Following the third meeting, the two majors quickly settled outstanding issues with other parties, particularly Canada, the non-EC European nations, and the developing countries. The major exception to this scenario was the bilateral negotiation between the United States and Japan, which had essentially been concluded in December 1978.

The December meeting between the United States and the Community was intended to revise the basis on which these parties exchanged offers in the more troublesome sectors, such as textiles, chemicals, and paper. In chemicals, the negotiation had become extremely complicated, and hence difficult. Many chemical products in the United States carried specific duties (e.g., 10¢ per pound) rather than *ad valorem* rates. The U.S. industry pressed to have these converted to *ad valorem* tariffs because inflation had reduced the protection provided by specific rates. Such a move was generally welcomed because it was consistent with tariff reform. However, it required the United States to fix customs valuations on the products in question, since valuation was not needed when specific duties were applied. The United States and its partners quickly fell into disagreement over what would be the appropriate *ad valorem* equivalent (AVE) of the various specific duties on chemical products.[5] In addition, the United States sought to negotiate an increase in AVE's for the chemical products previously covered under the ASP (American Selling Price) and final list, since these valuation procedures were being phased out as a result of the customs valuation negotiation. This U.S. move was stimulated by the concern of the American industry that it would be taking a double loss of protection from the Tokyo Round in comparison with the European counterparts. As might be expected, the EC resisted this American demand because it promised to undercut the value of negotiating an end to the ASP, for which EC negotiators felt that they had already paid full value in the customs valuation negotiation itself.

The December meeting had an important organizational impact on the tariff negotiation. The meeting made little overall progress, in spite of having been attended by senior negotiators on both sides. Following the meeting, Alonzo MacDonald asked William Kelly, senior trade official on the American side and chairman of the Washington-based

[5] For example, Grey notes that the U.S. International Trade Commission initially calculated the AVE on methyl alcohol to be 37.5 percent, while the Canadian government had calculated it to be 14 percent (*Trade Policy*, 32).

Trade Policy Staff Committee (TPSC), to take charge of the tariff negotiation. This plan was quickly approved by Ambassadors Strauss and Wolff. MacDonald then proposed that the EC upgrade their side of the negotiation as well, with the result that the tariff negotiation was assigned to Fernand Braun, director-general of the recently expanded department DG-III (Internal Market and Industrial Affairs). This move by the EC was comparable to that of the Americans, since Braun was a ranking official in the Commission and his directorate was one of the most influential in the EC's structure. An added advantage on the EC side was that the move engaged Commissioner Etienne Davignon in the tariff negotiation, and thus increased the circle of influential Europeans who might be expected to defend any ultimate agreement. A move is often made to increase the seniority of officials in difficult situations in negotiation, and it proved to be a successful stratagem in the Tokyo Round tariff negotiation. Negotiators at lower levels often have greater responsibility for defending a nation's weak positions than for creating new positions that will permit agreement. As a result, it is easy for them to come to loggerheads with an opposing party, and an impasse ensues. If such an impasse is to be overcome, raising the level of the negotiation and providing fresh instructions to a new negotiator is one of the classic procedures for moving toward consensus in international negotiation.

Following the reassignment, Kelly moved to Geneva with about fifteen to twenty members of the TPSC. This put the tariff negotiation on the same basis as some of the code negotiations, where task-oriented teams of individuals were occasionally dispatched to negotiate specific matters in the Tokyo Round. In this case, the team was a large one drawn from several different agencies, in response to the enormous amount of material covered in the tariff negotiation. Once in Geneva, the U.S. team did not return to Washington until after the negotiation was completed. The intention was to have most U.S. tariff analysis and decisionmaking after January 1979 taken in Geneva and to reduce the need for interagency consultation in Washington to a minimum. The advantage that accrued to the United States by opening the tariff negotiation with a maximum position, a point which has been referred to earlier, was again noticed in the flexibility the U.S. delegation possessed in the last weeks of the negotiation. Most of the heat on tariffs coming from interest groups and from Congress had been taken early, and the administration consequently had less need to interact with domestic lobbies at the end than might otherwise have been expected. Had a strategy of maximum opening position not been followed, it is much less likely that the TPSC could have been moved to Geneva to conclude the negotiation.

261

The next major meeting between the United States and the Community occurred in New York in mid-January.[6] Again the meeting involved individuals of ambassadorial rank—Alonzo MacDonald on the American side and Roy Denman for the Europeans—and it was intended to forge a compromise on the most difficult outstanding items. The U.S. side came prepared to make final decisions, hoping to conclude all the major issues at the meeting. On the EC side, the New York meeting was taken less seriously, and was described by one participant more as an "armed reconnaissance" than as a concluding session. The EC negotiators did not have as much leeway to conclude as the Americans, and were required to submit any settlement reached at New York to their Council of Ministers for approval. They were consequently unwilling to conclude issues save on a tentative or *ad referendum* basis.

The agenda for the January meeting included the same troublesome sectors that had bedeviled previous negotiations: textiles, chemicals, and paper. In an effort to force a conclusion to the negotiation, the United States advanced what it described as a close-out offer in textiles and chemicals. Among other things, this offer included greater-than-formula offers on some sixty-six products of special interest to France and Italy, since on balance Britain and Germany appeared to fare better from U.S. offers than other EC members. For its part, the EC offered concessions in a number of areas, including electronics and paper. The parties were able to conclude an *ad referendum* agreement on this basis. In general, both sides operated at the limit of their instructions in drawing up the January package. This was especially the case with the EC offers, which were expressly contingent on approval of the Council, due to meet shortly.

In the event, the January package was not acceptable to the Council of Ministers. The Council particularly objected to the U.S. textile offer, which it felt effectively removed textile tariffs from the harmonization formula. On this matter, the Council was under considerable pressure from the European textile industry, which made representations to the effect that a substantial gap existed between average textile tariffs in

---

[6] It might seem incongruous that a major meeting would be held in New York shortly after the U.S. team moved to Geneva. This incident vividly points out the extent to which negotiation in the Tokyo Round had become internationalized geographically. High-level meetings tended to be held where the people who had to attend the meetings happened to be, with the result that such meetings were often held in any one of several major European or North American cities. This reflects the fact that in modern negotiation, travel is rapid and the funds for transcontinental travel are a less scarce commodity than the time of senior officials.

Europe and the United States.[7] To indicate how far apart the two sides were on textiles, the U.S. delegation was quietly relieved when the January package fell apart, because it was felt too much had been given on textiles. It was reported that Robert Strauss was doubtful about the New York agreement, and that he felt the deal would have created problems with the industry and with eventual congressional approval.

The post-January period offered the parties an opportunity to review their positions. The New York agreement on chemicals stuck for the most part, but there was some U.S. backsliding on the matter of ASP conversions that angered the EC. Specifically the United States served notice that it intended to increase duties on a number of existing and future chemical products that were not at the time covered by the ASP, and hence subject to duty revision. This move would have effectively nullified Tokyo Round tariff cuts on these products, or, as Mr. Haferkamp wrote to Mr. Strauss, ". . . it would take us eight years to get back to the status quo."[8] Other products that were disputed were paper goods, only this time the Americans were in the position of demandeur. Paper is an important export of the United States, but there was a danger that established markets in the EC would be lost to Scandinavian producers through the effects of an EC/EFTA agreement unless the external tariff of the EC could be brought down. The U.S. paper industry was very supportive of the Tokyo Round, and in a memo to the EC Robert Strauss noted that a reduction in EC duties on paper was "an essential element for me in putting together a winning political coalition."[9]

One area that underwent substantial revision after the New York meeting was textiles. The textile resolution in the Congress had left the U.S. administration extremely sensitive about carrying through any substantial reduction in the textile sector. Following the January meeting in New York, U.S. negotiators operated on the basis of instructions that they could cut textile tariffs on an average of 5 to 6 percent deeper than comparable EC reductions, but that they could not make the deeper reductions implied in the Swiss formula. The five- to six-point spread took account of the higher initial level of U.S. tariffs and was

---

[7] These averages were 14.4 percent (weighted by imports) for the EC and 23.9 percent for the United States. The EC did not have any tariffs over 20 percent, while 58 percent of the U.S. textile tariffs were over this figure. See "Textiles: Industry's Anxiety over Tokyo Round," *European Report*, 15 December 1978.

[8] "Tokyo Round: EEC Maintains Tough Position against U.S.A., Japan," *European Report*, January 26, 1979.

[9] John Robinson, "Memos Bare Difficulties in U.S.: Europe Trade Talks," *International Herald Tribune*, January 25, 1979.

simply a political calculation of what would be marginally acceptable to the industry and its political backers in Washington.

The instructions on textiles left the U.S. delegation with the interesting problem of translating a political demand into an operational negotiating tactic. The United States solved this problem by proposing to the Europeans that both parties reduce textile tariffs by 60 percent of what the Swiss formula would have required. This would have resulted in an average cut of about 32 percent on textile products for the United States and about 27.5 percent for the Community. The U.S. proposal, which in effect was a linear cut based on a formula, was simply a stratagem that managed to incorporate U.S. unilateral instructions into a generally applicable procedure both parties could use. The U.S. delegation called it the elevator concept, because a figure higher than 60 percent would increase the spread (i.e., depth of cut) between the United States and the Community, and a figure under 60 percent would narrow the spread. For the United States, the elevator concept effectively isolated textiles from the rest of the tariff negotiation, which was necessary because textiles were, in the words of one U.S. negotiator, "the one thing that could kill us in Congress." For the EC, the elevator concept created some incentive to deepen tariff cuts as much as possible, because this would increase the harmonization between U.S. and EC textile tariffs. The EC negotiators never explicitly accepted the elevator concept, but it nevertheless became a useful bargaining mechanism in later negotiation.

At the end of any negotiation, there is a natural tendency for the parties to link and to trade off the major outstanding issues. There was some suggestion that this occurred in the bargaining following the New York meeting. The tradeoff involved European concessions on paper in exchange for U.S. concessions on chemicals, with both sides offering a bit more on textiles, especially the United States on woolen products.[10] Of course, any such tradeoff across sectors would make sense from a bargaining perspective, since negotiators instinctively try to link concessions in a manner that leaves both sides feeling they got a fair exchange. Also, a cross-sectoral linkage is defensible from the perspective of economic rationality, since tradeoffs usually involve a reduction of protection in a high-cost industry for expanded trade opportunities in a low-cost industry. However, cross-sectoral tradeoffs are not easily defended in political terms, which is why GATT negotiations have generally produced compensated tariff reductions more easily within sec-

[10] Brij Khindaria, "U.S.-EEC Progress on Chemicals Boosts Hope for GATT Tariff Pact," *Financial Times*, February 20, 1979.

tors than they have across sectors.[11] Cross-sector tradeoffs produce winners and losers from the standpoint of the industries involved, while tradeoffs within sectors provide offsetting winnings and losses to the same industries. The losers in a cross-sectoral deal are hardly in a position to be comforted by the gains made elsewhere, and they almost always fight harder to forestall loss than the potential winners do to achieve gains. In the concluding period of the Tokyo Round tariff negotiation, industries occasionally mobilized to prevent concessions being made in their areas. In some cases, their demands were particularly insistent, which resulted in enormous pressure being brought to bear on the last decisions of the negotiation.[12]

Pressure in a negotiation creates the appearance of high stakes. In turn, the appearance of high stakes creates a certain tension in the negotiation process. Negotiators seek to convince their constituencies that they are serving their interests, and one way to do this is to hold back on concessions until the last possible moment. This of course is not a permanent solution, for eventually issues must be decided and not deferred. In an effort to decide, the U.S. and EC negotiators scheduled a final meeting on tariffs at the end of February 1979. The political pressure surrounding this meeting, even more than the objective economic importance of the decisions that were to be made, imparted a sense of drama to the occasion.[13]

The meeting was chaired by William Kelly for the United States and Fernand Braun for the Community. Both were obliged to conclude the negotiation. The pressure on Kelly came from the U.S. administration, which wanted the tariff negotiation finalized as quickly as possible in order not to jeopardize negotiations already under way with Congress.

---

[11] A similar observation has been made by Hufbauer and Chilas: "GATT negotiations very much favor intra-industry over inter-industry specialization" ("Specialization by Industrial Countries: Extent and Consequences" in Giersch [ed.], *International Division*, 6).

[12] The following excerpt provides a glimpse of this pressure in one industry: "The European paper and board industry is to make a last ditch effort this week to prevent the U.S. from obtaining tariff reductions which it is claimed could lead to the closure of mills in the Common Market countries" (Rex Wilkinson, "Threat to European Papermakers," *Financial Times*, March 7, 1979).

[13] One should not generalize that the concluding issues have more subjective than objective importance, but this nevertheless is a common phenomenon. For example, in the negotiation over paper the final battle was fueled by the unrelenting demand by the United States (backed by the equally unrelenting pressure of Industry Sector Advisory Committee #4 and its persistent chairwoman, Irene Meister) that the EC cut its tariff on Kraft paper to 6 percent, while on the other side the European industry demanded with equal intensity that the reduction not go below 8 percent. The difference separating the parties was only 2 percent, a small figure which has been overwhelmed by changes in exchange rates since the Tokyo Round.

The demands on Braun were even more immediate. The EC commissioners responsible for handling the Tokyo Round wanted to bring the entire agreement before only one meeting of the Council of Ministers, which was scheduled for March 6, 1979. In the bargaining that ensued, both Kelly and Braun played a waiting game with each other. It was an occasion to employ the classic competitive strategy of withholding agreement until the last possible moment, and thereby risking breakdown, in order to wring maximum concessions from the other side.[14]

In tariff negotiations, which are intensely competitive, and complicated as well, parties usually develop a rationale for the positions they put forward. The aforementioned concept of an "elevator" served as such a rationale in the bargaining over textile tariffs. In broadest terms, the customary rationale in tariff negotiations is reciprocity, and this concept creates a means of exchange which underlies the bargaining relationship.[15] In more specific terms, the way reciprocity gets put into practice is through a calculation of balance in the concessions that are being exchanged. This calculation of balance is quantitative, and it produces numerical measures that allow negotiators to evaluate the equivalence of the concessions offered by each side. As mentioned earlier, these measures were generated from two variables: the reduction of a tariff, measured by the amount that the duty collected on a given volume of trade (e.g., 1976 imports) would be reduced; and the trade volumes themselves, which were used to weight the percentage cuts on tariffs.[16] Normally such quantitative measures would be calculated by computer, especially if the purpose was to calculate an average weighted reduction over a large number of tariff reductions from different sectors. However, at the end of a negotiation there is usually movement on only a few products, and balance is hence calculated over fewer items. At this point in the Tokyo Round, the computer was no longer used, and, in one participant's words, the final meeting ended up being a series of "long battles fought with hand calculators."

When balance becomes a goal in a tariff negotiation, certain distortions creep into the process of exchanging concessions. Normally nations follow an incremental strategy in requesting and offering tariff

[14] A neat way to portray this strategy is the game of chicken, which has been analyzed in the literature on international bargaining. See Schelling, *Arms and Influence*, esp. 116–25.

[15] Former trade negotiator John Evans has noted, "When a negotiator invokes his right to reciprocity, he is speaking a language that both he and his fellow bargainers understand" (*Kennedy Round*, 23).

[16] Evans speaks of these variables (i.e., "trade coverage times depth of tariff cut") as creating a "time honored yardstick" that has served in the past to approximate a negotiating balance (*ibid.*, 314–15).

concessions. This is because concessions must be authorized at home, and such authorization requires enormous effort in terms of domestic politics. At the end of a negotiation, however, negotiators often have certain latitude in their instructions in some areas, and this, plus the desire to achieve an overall balance of offers, can lead to sharp discontinuities. For example, the United States still had a number of greater-than-formula offers on the table at the February/March meeting, and it also had offered to cut the U.S. tariff on trucks from 25 to 17 percent contingent on the EC lowering its own tariff on trucks to 17 percent as well. On the former, the EC refused to give the Americans bargaining credit for the greater-than-formula offers, and on the latter it was unable to reduce its own tariff on trucks below 21 percent. In the end, the United States withdrew suddenly both its greater-than-formula offers and its offer on trucks in order to achieve a balanced settlement. As one participant said of the greater-than-formula offers, "They all came off the table in about three and a half minutes . . . along with the trucks."

On its side, the EC also engaged in some last-minute juggling. As one example, the EC offered to reduce its tariff on semiconductors from 17 to 16 percent, although the United States had requested the tariff be lowered to 10 or 12 percent. The United States refused bargaining credit for this offer because the large trade volumes associated with the product would have made the tariff cut worth more on the aggregate balance than the cut was worth in trade terms. As a result, the EC withdrew the offer entirely. One sees in these examples that the rationale of balance used in tariff bargaining is not entirely rational from the standpoint of economic policymaking. The examples point out the limitations of making commercial policy through international negotiation.

The February/March meeting between Kelly and Braun produced an agreement between the United States and the Community to cut tariffs over eight years on industrial products by about 35 percent on each other's trade. For the United States, this will reduce the average EC tariff on U.S. goods from 7.2 to 5.7 percent, sufficient to insure that preferential access within the Community will play a smaller role in purchasing decisions. For the Community, the agreement will go some distance toward achieving the EC goal of tariff harmonization. The proportion of U.S. imports from the EC subject to duties over 20 percent will fall from 4.8 to 1.2 percent, or, in real terms, the number of tariff headings in the U.S. Tariff Schedule (TSUS) over 20 percent will drop from 757 to 185. Similarly the proportion of duties over 10 percent is scheduled to fall from 16.3 to 6.0 percent.[17]

[17] These figures were taken from U.S. Government, *Results of Industrial Tariff Negotiations*; and Commission, *GATT Multilateral Trade Negotiations*.

The US/EC bilateral agreement on tariffs was included in the Commission's presentation on the Tokyo Round to the March 5 meeting of the Council of Ministers. Both Commissioners Davignon and Haferkamp strongly pressed the Council to accept the package. For its part, the Council was prepared to approve the results of the code negotiations, but the French had reservations regarding the results of the tariff negotiation. With some support from Italy, Ireland, and the United Kingdom, the French argued that the EC had paid too much in tariff and other concessions for the U.S. agreement to eliminate the ASP and its duties on aircraft.[18] These U.S. actions, the French argued, constituted a removal of anomalies only and should not have been the subject of compensating benefit from the EC. The French reservation succeeded in delaying EC approval of the EC/US tariff negotiation until a Council meeting early in April. The delay created anxiety, but it did not change appreciably the results reached in the Kelly-Braun meeting.

Other Bilateral Negotiations

In terms of size, the next most significant sets of tariff negotiations were between the two majors and the remaining developed countries. Throughout the last half of 1978, the United States and Japan conducted a bilateral tariff negotiation which was largely centered in Washington, D.C. This negotiation was not as formalized as the US/EC tariff talks and mainly consisted of occasional meetings between Ambassador Ushiba of Japan and Ambassadors Strauss and Wolff of the United States. The negotiation was relatively low-key and it reached a conclusion in December 1978, well before the other principal bilateral talks were concluded. The results of these talks continued a trend that had been started in the Kennedy Round, namely the dismantling of Japan's extensive postwar protectionism in the context of multilateral trade negotiations. The Tokyo Round was conducted in the context of an increasingly strong Japanese industrial and trade performance, and the results of bilateral negotiations with the United States reflected this fact. Both parties made tariff reductions sufficient to lower their respective post–Tokyo Round average tariffs to about 4.5 percent on each other's trade. However, to achieve these levels the Japanese made reductions in effective tariff rates of about 47 percent on average, or about half again greater than the average reduction of 32 percent by the Americans. In addition, Japan took significant action on some priority

[18] See "Tokyo Round: Commission to Seek Further Advantages in Closing Weeks of Talks," *European Report*, March 6, 1979.

268

products of concern to U.S. manufacturers, such as reductions of over 50 percent on computer mainframes, color film, and integrated circuits. The Tokyo Round achieved a remarkable harmonization of the U.S. and Japanese industrial tariff structures. The significance for the United States can be seen in the fact that the Tokyo Round will leave Japan with no industrial duties of greater than 10 percent on U.S. exports, which will affect over $1 billion of U.S. trade that previously entered Japan at rates of 10 percent or higher.

The bilateral tariff negotiation between Japan and the EC was less successful. It was a difficult and frustrating negotiation for both parties. By June 1978, the Japanese had made an offer of about a 48 percent average reduction on the legal tariff on EC exports, which translated into a 25 percent reduction on effective rates. However, this offer related mainly to duty items and products on which the EC was not the principal supplier, and hence it was not particularly attractive to the Community. The EC demanded a qualitative improvement on products of interest to European exporters, especially leather goods, processed farm products, and textiles. This demand was particularly intense because of the large trade surplus the Japanese held with the Community. The Japanese response to the EC demands was to remain firm on its June offer. Ambassador Ushiba explained to the Community negotiators that the Japanese delegation had no authority to offer further cuts, and indicated that one reason was the negative reaction in Japan to various discriminatory quantitative restrictions applied against Japanese exports by the EC and its member governments.[19] There was little movement in the EC/Japan tariff negotiation after June 1978 except for a gradual retrenchment on the European side. In the end, an agreement was finally reached by mid-March 1979. Japan's offer on EC exports remained approximately 25 percent, while the EC finally settled on an average reduction on Japanese exports of 22 percent. No action was taken to increase the quality of the Japanese offer to the Community. The overall result was less satisfactory than in the U.S./Japanese negotiation, and it produced less harmonization between average EC and Japanese tariff levels.

Negotiations between Canada and the majors were concluded following the completion of a US/EC bilateral deal. In many respects, Canada pursued the traditional strategy of a smaller country at the Tokyo Round. Canada is not the principal supplier of most products it trades with the majors; hence it is not in a position to be a principal negotiator

[19] Guy de Jonquieres, "EEC and Japan Fail to Agree on GATT Tariff Cuts," *Financial Times*, January 25, 1979.

with these parties. The disadvantage of this position is that Canada is limited in the extent to which it can secure benefits for its exporters, but it is advantaged in that through the operation of MFN procedures it can obtain the benefits that accrue from tariff reductions between the majors without needing to reciprocate. Thus the bargaining situation in a multilateral tariff negotiation predisposes a smaller country toward a passive strategy, quite independently of the underlying commercial policy of that country. Canada followed such a passive strategy in the Kennedy Round of the 1960s, to the occasional annoyance of American and European negotiators.[20] Similarly in the Tokyo Round, Canada was initially reluctant to accept a formula approach to the tariff negotiation, and then applied its own formula rather than the generally agreed Swiss formula. With regard to actual bargaining, Canadian agreements with the two majors were among the last tariff deals to be completed, although this may have been due largely to the reluctance of the majors to deal with Canada before they had reached a bilateral agreement between themselves.

The main tariff negotiation for the Canadians came with the United States, which accounts for over two-thirds of Canadian foreign trade. The negotiation began with a high initial offer by the United States on Canadian products, which was a residue of bilateral US/EC bargaining. This offer led the Americans to demand a generous offer in return. One target of U.S. attention was the Canadian machinery program, a protectionist policy which was part of the broader effort of the Canadian government to promote domestic secondary manufacturing. Under the machinery program, Canada levied a 15 percent tariff on all machinery imports, but remitted the duty to importers if the machinery was not made in Canada. This program created high protection for Canadian manufacturers and as well uncertainty for U.S. exporters, since the introduction of a new machinery product by a Canadian manufacturer could cause the effective tariff on that product to go from nil to 15 percent. On the Canadian side, a request was made by Ottawa to improve access for Canadian petrochemical producers, which were an important offshoot of the oil and gas industry in western Canada. On the latter request, the U.S. government found its position complicated by a larger volume of petrochemical trade with the EC and by a domestic industry that strongly resisted any lowering of U.S. tariffs.

[20] This annoyance was frequently expressed in terms of Canada's not having accepted the "obligations" of Kennedy Round participants, viz.: "Canada, by refusing to accept the obligations of other industrial countries, and in particular the linear approach to tariff reduction, restricted its role principally to commercial interests with the United States and a few major commodities" (Preeg, *Traders and Diplomats*, 263).

The result of the U.S./Canadian tariff negotiation was that the United States agreed to an average reduction of 44 percent on products of interest to Canada, while Canada lowered tariffs on U.S. exports by an average of 35 percent of applied rates, or 43 percent of bound rates.[21] This agreement had the effect of harmonizing tariffs between the United States and Canada. Prior to the Tokyo Round, the average U.S. tariff on Canadian exports was 5.2 percent, which will fall to 2.9 percent in the post–Tokyo Round period. The average Canadian tariff (applied) on U.S. goods prior to the Tokyo Round was 11.9 percent, and this will go to 7.7 percent. The United States achieved an important concession respecting the Canadian machinery program, in that Canada agreed to keep a constant proportion of machinery goods free of duty, which meant that if a product became dutiable under the program, another product of equivalent import value would go off the duty list. Additionally Canada agreed to maintain duty-free status on about one-fourth of its machinery imports, irrespective of whether they were made in Canada. Finally, with regard to petrochemicals, a protracted effort by the Canadian negotiators was unable to improve the U.S. offer, and both sides settled on what was generally regarded as an unsatisfactory outcome.[22]

The bilateral negotiation between the EC and Canada proved more difficult than that between Canada and the United States. The reason for this was best summarized in the observation of an EC participant: "We tend to ask the impossible of each other." Canada was especially interested in eliminating low EC duties on its exports of nonferrous metals and forestry products, but on the former Canada was not the principal supplier to the EC and on the latter the Canadian request conflicted with the relations between the EC and its Scandinavian trading partners. Another request by Canada was on exports of Canadian fish products, but here the Canadian interests conflicted sharply with those of the United Kingdom. On the other side, the Europeans especially sought a reduction of Canadian tariffs on textiles, furniture, and footwear. These products have traditionally been difficult for Canada in international trade, not the least because liberalization in these areas would disproportionately affect manufacturing interests in the province of Quebec. In the agreement eventually reached between the two parties, Canada offered an average reduction of 31 percent to the EC, while the EC offered an average cut of about 30 percent vis-à-vis Ca-

[21] Like Japan, Canada maintained two rates of duty on many products, a legal rate bound in the GATT and a lower rate that was actually in use.
[22] For further information, see Grey, *Trade Policy*, esp. ch. 4, "Petrochemicals."

nadian exports. The EC benefited especially from the Canadian liberalization of the machinery program, while Canada realized an advantage from EC concessions on paper goods. However, on the sensitive products in their bilateral trade neither party was able to offer significant concessions to the other. In one case, namely fishery products, the discussions initiated in the Tokyo Round were taken up in an extended sectoral negotiation between Canada and the Community.[23]

Comparisons with the Kennedy Round

The tariff negotiation concluded in the Tokyo Round invites comparisons with the Kennedy Round of the 1960s, which was itself primarily a tariff negotiation. In terms of the outcome, the two negotiations were roughly equivalent, since both achieved approximately a 35 percent average weighted tariff reduction on the imports of developed countries. However, the process of negotiating these two multilateral agreements was quite different. In terms of the future of international commercial policy, the differences on process may be more significant than the similarities on substance.

One difference between the negotiations was structural. The Kennedy Round had four to five major actors (commonly referred to as the bridge club), and essentially all of the action of the negotiation occurred within this group. In the Tokyo Round, the major actors were fewer and economic power was more concentrated, but curiously this appeared to expand rather than contract the number of negotiating relationships as the United States and the Community sought to conclude bilateral agreements with other nations. There was no role for a small directorate of developed countries in the Tokyo Round tariff negotiation, even though meetings of these countries were occasionally held. Additionally the role of the developing countries altered the structure of the Tokyo Round. In contrast to the Kennedy Round, where the developing countries were wholly marginal participants, the delegations from these countries took a more active role in the Tokyo Round. As one senior GATT official said of the Tokyo Round tariff negotiation, ". . . this time we had twenty-one developing countries which have done something!" Of course, the actions of the developing-country delegations were not extensive, because as smaller participants they faced a strategic situation much like the Canadians', which fostered a some-

---

[23] In this negotiation, Canada used its capacity to regulate EC fishing in the Canadian exclusive economic zone as a bargaining chip to seek greater access for fishery products in the EC. For further information, see Barry, "Canada–European Community Fisheries Agreement."

what more passive attitude toward bargaining initiatives. Then, too, the developing countries were badly divided in their approach to tariffs at the Tokyo Round. Some, like the Latin American nations, pressed hard for preferential tariff cuts from developed countries. However, this was resisted by the African nations on the grounds that this would undercut the preferential access many countries already enjoyed through association with the EC. Division in the developing-country ranks reduced the impact of their participation in the Tokyo Round tariff negotiation, but they were no longer as marginal as they had been in the Kennedy Round. In this sense, the Tokyo Round was a more multilateral negotiation than its predecessor.

Yet another difference between the Kennedy and Tokyo Rounds was functional. The tariff negotiation was the major part of the Kennedy Round, whereas it was only one aspect of the Tokyo Round, and not a large one at that. The Tokyo Round accomplished as much as the Kennedy Round (admittedly at a lower level of tariffs) with far less manpower and concentrated effort on the part of the participating nations. There appears to have been a step-level improvement in the efficiency of the negotiation process. One reason for this is that the Tokyo Round negotiators had better control of data they were working with, which reduced the complexity of their negotiating problem. In large measure, this was due to the GATT tariff study of the early 1970s, which put tariff data into computer-readable form. The results of this study vastly simplified the problem of storage and recall of information, and it facilitated the calculation of simplified measures of reciprocity, such as weighted average reductions, over large volumes of tariff changes. The upshot was that negotiators in the Tokyo Round knew faster the implications of their specific moves for their overall position, and hence were better able to avoid irrelevant argument, whether between or within delegations. Another reason why the Tokyo Round appeared more efficient was that the respective nations had more control over their domestic processes. Multilateral trade negotiations like the Tokyo and Kennedy rounds have an impact on an enormous number of internal interests within nation-states, and these must be organized if the negotiation is to go smoothly. The most important single difference in negotiating tariffs between the Kennedy and Tokyo rounds was the extent of organization of the domestic process in the latter negotiation (see chapter 8). In the Tokyo Round, negotiators had a better idea of what their constituents wanted, and they were better organized to deal with those demands. As a result, they were able to exchange commitments with other nations more rapidly, and with less uncertainty and unnecessary haggling.

273

A final difference between the two negotiations was style. In the Kennedy Round, negotiating teams went to Geneva and stayed there. Civil servants became professional negotiators, and they reported back to their capitals in traditional diplomatic style. In the words of one experienced U.S. bureaucrat, ". . . a transatlantic trip was a special event." In the Tokyo Round, the situation was much more fluid. There was far more movement between national capitals and the negotiating site in the Tokyo Round than in the previous negotiation. If the style of the Kennedy Round could have been called "fixed-piece negotiation," the style of the Tokyo Round might be called "contingent negotiation," where the relevant people from national capitals or elsewhere gravitated to a problem as needed, and where meetings involving such people were scheduled as necessary. It was said by old hands in the GATT secretariat that the negotiators at the Kennedy Round were professionals but that many at the Tokyo Round were amateurs, with the implication that the latter were less familiar with trade diplomacy as it has evolved in the GATT. This may have been true, but one should not overlook those things that the more peripatetic negotiators at the Tokyo Round were professional at, namely their own national commercial policies and the domestic constraints that would have to be overcome to change those policies. This was perhaps the most important expertise that could be brought to the negotiation, especially a negotiation that was as preoccupied as the Tokyo Round with negotiating policies that could be "sold" at home.

The Framework Negotiation and the Developing Countries

In spite of the fact that they are conducted multilaterally, trade negotiations emphasize independent behavior more than group activity. The Tokyo Round was not like, for example, the United Nations Conference on the Law of the Sea (UNCLOS), where nations readily formed informal groups to pursue common interests. Such UNCLOS groups were often geographical (the Landlocked States) or economic (Landbased Mineral Producers) and occasionally political (the Like-Minded States).[24] These informal groups were as much part of the UNCLOS negotiating process as were the formal groups that were established to handle the work of the negotiation. In the Tokyo Round, there was no similar pattern of informal group activity, for both objective and subjective reasons. The objective reason is that in trade negotiations na-

---

[24] William Wertenbaker, "A Reporter at Large (Law of the Sea Conference—Part I)," *New Yorker*, August 1, 1983, 38–65, 50.

tions formulate their negotiating positions primarily on the basis of economic interests, and these are usually not similar over a large number of nations. Where common interests are held (e.g., exporters of temperate agricultural products), there may be some attempt to coordinate negotiating strategies, but these common interests are usually not profound enough in comparison with other concerns to lead to enduring alliance patterns on the UNCLOS model. The subjective reason for less group activity at the Tokyo Round was that the political climate was less ideological at that negotiation than it was at the UNCLOS. The Law of the Sea Conference was conducted for the avowedly ideological purpose of creating a new international regime for the world's oceans that would provide, among other things, for the "common heritage of mankind." The Tokyo Round, by contrast, had the more prosaic goal of achieving "the expansion and ever-greater liberalization of world trade." Ideology tends to make nations seek political alliances, even sometimes in the face of conflicting objective interests, and it keeps nations together in alliances even after objective interests may have grown apart. Such ideology has never been part of the trade negotiations conducted under the GATT, and as a result the negotiating style has reflected a more independent behavior based on individual national interest.

The principal exception to the generalization above has been the developing countries. Since the mid-1950s, the developing nations have attempted to pursue their interests as a group, either in trade negotiations or in the routine operations of GATT. At the Kennedy Round, the developing countries pressed as a group for nonreciprocal concessions from developed countries. At the Tokyo Round, the developing countries again coalesced to pursue essentially three objectives. One was to negotiate "special and differential treatment" for developing countries in the various codes concluded at the Tokyo Round. The second was to secure specific concessions on products of particular interest to developing countries. A third objective was to change the basic rules and structure of GATT in a direction more amenable to developing-country interests.

The developing countries recorded some successes in negotiating special and differential treatment, and several codes (e.g., subsidies/countervail) contain clauses that will be economically significant. As for the second objective, specific preferences were sought by developing countries on a bilateral basis in the negotiations on industrial tariffs, agriculture, and tropical products. In the tariff negotiation, the results were mixed. Nations made MFN (most-favored nation) tariff cuts that will be worth about $1.7 billion in new trade for developing countries, but against this must be set the loss from GSP (generalized system of preferences) margins, estimated at nearly $2.1 billion.[25] This represents a net trade loss of $400 million, although it should be emphasized that MFN benefits constitute a permanent gain in comparison to GSP preferences, which are extended unilaterally and may be revoked by the grantor. As for tropical products, it will be recalled (see chapter 3) that negotiations in this area proceeded on a request/offer basis in essentially two stages: first, the period 1975–77, when developed countries responded to as many requests as possible on a unilateral, nonreciprocal basis; and the period after 1977, when the specific requests of developing countries were handled in the tariff and agricultural negotiations on the same basis as those of developed countries. In terms of the aggregate results, Group "Tropical Products" established a list of 4,400 dutiable items on which developing countries had made requests for concessions from developed countries. Of this number, MFN concessions and GSP contributions were made on 2,930 items. Approximately 940 benefits were made in the 1975–77 period, with the remaining number resulting from the procedures adopted after 1977.

The third objective of the developing countries was taken up in the framework negotiation. The framework negotiation was initiated by a series of proposals put forward in 1976 by Ambassador George A. Maciel of Brazil (see chapter 4). The crux of these proposals was to change the rules of the GATT in a direction that would favor the developing countries, principally through making exceptions to the MFN principle and the concept of reciprocity. The Brazilian proposals constituted a legal challenge to the GATT, and they reflected the view of the developing countries that it was the larger, developed countries that most frequently violated the rules of the GATT. Curiously the United States was particularly interested in the Brazilian proposals, which could be easily integrated into that nation's own legalistic and contractual approach to the GATT.[26] The U.S. delegation saw in the framework negotiation an opportunity to raise its own concerns about the increasing divergence between GATT rules and actual trading practices. Beyond GATT law however, the framework negotiation was grounded on some very practical issues of economics and politics. The developing countries argued that before they could use scarce resources to make investments to expand their export trade, they had to be confident that such trade would in fact materialize. This could not be done without a stable system of preferences, since developing countries could not compete with industrialized nations on an equal footing. The political argument that

[25] UNCTAD V, *Multilateral Trade*, 14–15.
[26] U.S. Senate, *MTN Studies*, vol. 6, pt. 4 (Group "Framework"), 144–45.

flowed from this position was that in order to integrate the developing countries more fully into GATT, GATT would first have to provide a more attractive situation for those countries. It has been said that GATT is a unique mixture of law, economics, and politics. If so, one could not find a better example than the framework negotiation of the interplay among these three factors.

The result of the framework negotiations was a package of four agreements. These agreements essentially modified GATT procedures and not national practices, and therefore did not require the signatories to follow through with domestic implementing legislation. The first agreement carried the lengthy title "Differential and More Favourable Treatment: Reciprocity and Fuller Participation of Developing Countries." This agreement provided an "enabling clause" which allowed, but did not require, contracting parties to accord preferential treatment to developing countries despite the MFN requirement of Article 1 of the GATT. In return, developing countries accepted a form of graduation whereby they indicated that their capacity to make negotiated concessions "would improve with the progressive development of their economies."[27] The agreement went some distance to accommodate the objectives of the developing countries by building preferential treatment into the legal structure of GATT. However, it did not create an obligation to extend preferences, which was a disappointment from the developing-country perspective. Furthermore the price of the enabling clause was the graduation clause, which many developing countries had opposed on the grounds that it left the developed countries with the capacity to determine at what point preferences would be withdrawn.

The second agreement was a "Declaration on Trade Measures Taken for Balance-of-Payments Purposes," and it was one of the concerns that the developed countries inserted in the framework negotiation. The agreement grew out of an attempt to plug a loophole in GATT law regarding the use of quantitative restrictions (QR's). As explained earlier, the philosophy of the GATT is against QR's, and the use of these measures is specifically prohibited in Article 7. However, an exception to this prohibition was established in cases where nations required temporary trade restraints to ameliorate balance-of-payments difficulties.[28] In what now appears as a historical anomaly, the GATT not only authorized QR's for balance-of-payments crises, but it also prohibited the use of qualitative trade restrictions such as tariff surcharges. The

[27] GATT, *Agreement Relating to the Framework*, Article 7.7.
[28] GATT Article 7 provided that a "Contracting Party, in order to safeguard its external financial position and its balance of payments, may restrict the quantity or value of merchandise permitted to be imported."

reason is that in the early postwar period, when there was a shortage of competitive goods at any price, market-directed restrictions such as tariff surcharges would have been insufficient to correct a payments disequilibrium. It was felt that more severe measures such as QR's would be needed, and furthermore that QR's would less endanger the movement toward tariff liberalization than would the use of tariff surcharges. The upshot is that as recently as the late 1970s, the only trade measures that the GATT sanctioned in time of balance-of-payments difficulties were those widely felt to be most disruptive of the international trading system.

In practice, the GATT rules respecting balance-of-payments measures have been ignored, and in recent years nations have frequently resorted to tariff surcharges or deposit schemes to relieve temporarily a payments crisis.[29] The use of non-QR's may have reflected a desirable pragmatism by the contracting parties, but it also created a disturbing gulf between practice and the law. Furthermore the GATT articles which authorized QR's also placed restrictions on their use, which presumably did not pertain to non-QR's that were illegal in the first place. The balance-of-payments agreement did not legalize non-QR's per se, but it did ensure that any restraints on QR's would also apply to the use of "all restrictive import measures taken for balance-of-payments purposes."[30] Furthermore the agreement made improvements in the process of consultation and review for QR's as well as non-QR measures. In sum, the agreement made the GATT more consistent with modern economic circumstances, which will perhaps make the GATT more relevant as a legal document. It reflected an adjustment of law to policy, and as a result will not have much impact on national practice.

The third agreement, entitled "Safeguard Action for Development Purposes," contained a concession for developing countries. The agreement modified Article 18, which itself was adopted in 1955 and gave developing countries the right to take trade measures to assist in the development of particular industries. Article 18 was subject to certain limitations, including consultations with affected parties and approval of GATT, which made the application of protective measures a cumbersome process. The safeguard agreement allowed greater flexibility and shorter delays to developing countries in taking action under Article

---

[29] For example, the United States employed a 15 percent tariff surcharge during its payments crisis of 1971, and specifically justified its position on the grounds that a surcharge was more easily dismantled, less discriminatory, and more compatible with a competitive approach than quantitative restrictions. See *Department of State Bulletin*, vol. 65 (1971), 305–07.

[30] GATT, *Agreement Relating to the Framework*, 8.

18. The agreement made Article 18 easier to use, but it did not change the basic requirements that an Article 18 action be nondiscriminatory and that adequate compensation be offered affected parties. As a result, it is unlikely that the agreement will result in a substantially greater use of Article 18 by developing countries.[31]

The fourth agreement was the "Understanding regarding Notification, Consultation, Dispute Settlement and Surveillance." This agreement was intended to elaborate Articles 22 (Consultation) and 23 (Nullification or Impairment), which in turn were the cornerstone of the GATT nonadjudicatory informal processes of dispute settlement. The understanding included the obligation to notify member countries whenever any country adopts a trade measure that affects the operation of the General Agreement. This provision was originally proposed by Brazil in a narrower form, but subsequent negotiation broadened it and also, from the perspective of the developing countries, weakened it.[32] The main achievement of the understanding was that it codified and reaffirmed customary GATT practice regarding the use of panels in dispute settlement. Panels are an important mechanism for resolving trade disputes and for maintaining the commitment of the contracting parties to a liberal trading regime. It was hoped that negotiating an agreement that spelled out and tightened customary dispute-settlement procedures would mean a renewed commitment to those procedures.

The framework negotiation included an attempt to negotiate an agreement regulating the use of export restrictions. Such practices are not as prevalent in international trade as are import restrictions, but they are often employed for purposes such as avoiding shortages and price rises in exporting countries (e.g., U.S. export controls on wheat) and for developing domestic processing industries (e.g., Canadian restrictions on the export of unprocessed logs).[33] The participants failed to make any headway on this subject at the Tokyo Round, and the matter was left for subsequent negotiation within GATT. A text on export restrictions was produced in the final working papers of the framework negotiation, but it simply cataloged existing GATT provisions on export

[31] Koumins, "Group 'Framework,' " 328.

[32] The original proposal was summarized in the following terms: "Current procedures should . . . provide for prior notifications of decisions which affect the trade interests of a developing country." See "Inventory of the Main Elements That Have Been the Subject of Suggestions: Note by the Secretariat," GATT docs., MTN/FR/W/15, January 12, 1978, 5.

[33] For a listing of export-restraint measures, see Bergsten, "Completing the GATT," esp. 109–14.

restrictions, which are scattered throughout various articles of the General Agreement.[34]

It is difficult to assess the outcome of the framework negotiation. For countries such as the United States which take a legalistic approach to the GATT, the negotiation was a success in that it regularized preferential treatment for developing countries, reaffirmed panel and dispute-settlement procedures, and removed certain legal anomalies regarding balance-of-payments measures. For the EC, these accomplishments were less important or necessary. For the developing countries, which largely initiated the framework negotiation, the results were decidedly mixed. The developing countries did accomplish an important goal of establishing preferential treatment as a permanent exception to the normal GATT requirement of nondiscrimination. This was an important legal change to the GATT, and it makes the General Agreement less hostile to the concept of preferential treatment. However, this change did not create a corresponding obligation on developed countries to extend preferences, nor did it change the developed countries' rights to withdraw preferential treatment. It is unlikely that the change in GATT law will have much impact on international behavior, since the practical limit on the use of preferences is political will and not the legal restraints of the GATT. In the end, the developing countries stood largely aloof from the framework agreements, as they did from most of the MTN codes, and only Argentina signed the agreements at the close of the Tokyo Round. As for a summary judgment of the framework results, it is likely that the report of UNCTAD on the Tokyo Round which described the framework agreements as "frustrating and incomplete" would represent the view of most developing countries at the negotiation.[35]

CASE STUDY: THE U.S. WINE-GALLON CONCESSION (HOW THE "BIGGEST CHIP" IN THE TOKYO ROUND WAS NEGOTIATED)

The Tokyo Round was a multilateral negotiation, but there were many bilateral or small plurilateral negotiations conducted within its general framework. In some cases, issues that were ostensibly multilateral, such

---

[34] See "Group 'Framework': Note by the Acting Chairman of Group—Revision," GATT docs., MTN/FR/W/20/Rev 2, March 30, 1979, 5/1 to 5/12.

[35] UNCTAD V, *Multilateral Trade*, 34. The report also noted that the framework negotiations "probably demonstrate the futility of attempting to reform the international trading rules from within the GATT system itself." This reflects a longstanding position of UNCTAD toward GATT.

as industrial tariffs or agricultural products, were effectively negotiated on a bilateral basis. In other cases, the multilateral code negotiations gave rise to bilateral issues, such as the Japan/U.S. negotiation over NTT, which arose in the context of the government-procurement code. Finally, there were some issues that involved only two or a few countries, and which were taken up in the Tokyo Round because the momentum of that negotiation created an opportunity to resolve a wide range of outstanding trade problems. Among the issues in the third category, the U.S. wine-gallon tax stands out. It was a longstanding trade problem, and the resolution of this problem constituted one of the most important deals of the Tokyo Round negotiation.

When Carl von Clausewitz wrote his classic work on military strategy, he indicated he would not entertain any abstruse or complicated definition of war. Clausewitz simply defined war as a *duel*. Admittedly it was a duel writ large, and there were many complicating factors that arose in both the design and the execution of warfare. But at its base war was a duel, and the means of war was violence.[36] Now if the student of negotiation were to be led by Clausewitz's admirable brevity, he might define international negotiation as a *deal*. Granted, it is a deal writ large, and there are complexities in modern negotiation that defy any easy comprehension of the subject. But negotiation is at base a process of arranging a deal, and the means of negotiation is quid pro quo. This essence was clearly revealed in the wine gallon concession in the Tokyo Round negotiation. However else one might have described it, one would have had to call the wine-gallon concession a deal.

There is an argument as to whether the wine-gallon concession was an important event in the Tokyo Round at all, let alone whether it was the biggest bargaining chip, as it has been characterized here. In objective terms, it was a very small trade issue, and it was completely dwarfed, for example, by the government-procurement code, which had the potential to open up a market of some $20 billion. The wine-gallon issue had a low profile in the international negotiation at Geneva, and it was improbable that even the most knowledgeable GATT staffers were fully informed on the matter. The wine-gallon concession was not the largest trade concession made by the United States at the Tokyo Round, particularly when compared to the overall benefits exchanged in the tariff negotiation. Certainly the notion that the wine-gallon concession was the "biggest chip" would be questioned by many people, and especially those who might have an interest in minimizing the issue. And yet the concession did represent an annual windfall gain

[36] Clausewitz, *On War*, Book One, ch. 1.2, 101.

281

to foreign producers of $100 to $120 million per year, and it commenced in one stroke on January 1, 1980, when the law providing for U.S. taxation of spirits was changed. Unlike most tariff concessions that were phased in gradually over eight years, the wine-gallon concession created a sudden, substantial gain, and was therefore a very prominent benefit. And finally, because it created a bottleneck near the end of an important negotiation, resolving the wine-gallon issue contributed an enormous amount to the momentum of the negotiation. From the perspective of the *process* of the negotiation, one could easily have viewed the wine-gallon concession as a major event that helped secure a successful conclusion to the negotiation.

For the student of international trade, the wine-gallon issue is an important case study because it gives a glimpse into the difficulties nontariff measures create in trade liberalization. Unlike tariffs, nontariff measures often arise for reasons other than trade protection, and they are hard to negotiate because they involve nontrading interests. Nontariff measures frequently become embedded in national legislation, thereby creating vested interests within both the private sector and the government bureaucracy which resist any change from the status quo. The wine-gallon concession accurately reflected these more general problems of negotiating nontariff measures, and thus it presents a snapshot of the area in which the Tokyo Round made its greatest contribution to international trade.

Definitions and Background

The term wine gallon refers to a method of assessing taxes on distilled spirits. Prior to 1980, there were two such methods employed in the United States: proof gallon and wine gallon. Proof gallon was normally used for bulk spirits, and was defined as the alcoholic equivalent of one gallon of spirits at 100 proof (i.e., 50 percent alcohol). The tax in 1979 on one proof gallon was $10.50. The important aspect of the proof-gallon method is that the tax calculation was variable depending on volume and proof. Hence if spirits were assessed in bulk at a proof other than 100, they would be assessed according to the actual amount of alcohol in those spirits (e.g., tax on one gallon of 150-proof spirits would be $15.75; and on two gallons of 50-proof spirits, $10.50). By contrast, the tax law defined wine gallon, a method which was normally reserved for bottled spirits, as one gallon of spirits regardless of proof. In 1979, the tax on one wine gallon was $10.50, the same amount as the tax on one proof gallon.

The pre-1980 methods become clear when related to the process of producing spirits. Drinkable spirits were normally distilled at well over

100 proof and became subject to tax in the United States when they were made. Distillers posted bonds on their produce, and then normally removed their spirits from bond and paid taxes (according to the proof-gallon method) prior to bottling. The spirits were then cut with water, bottled, and sold. Spirits entering the United States in bulk were handled according to the same procedures, that is, taxed at high proof while in bulk, then diluted, bottled, and distributed to wholesalers.

The wine-gallon method of assessment was designed to be used on bottled spirits, particularly spirits that had been bottled while in bonded premises. This method was used for some prestige domestic products (e.g., "bottled-in-bond") and on all bottled imported spirits as well. The U.S. tax procedures provided a distinct advantage for domestic over foreign distillers. As an example, the 1979 method might produce taxes on bulk spirits at 160 proof of $16.80 per gallon, which when the spirits were cut to drinkable liquor at 80 proof would produce an effective tax of $8.40 per gallon. By contrast, the tax on one gallon of bottled liquor at 80 proof was $10.50 per gallon according to the wine-gallon method; that is, it was taxed as if it were 100 proof. The result was that producers (mainly foreign) required to use the wine-gallon method paid more for each gallon of liquor sold, and in practice suffered a tax disadvantage of about 15 to 18 percent.

The operation of the U.S. tax procedures for spirits created protection for the domestic industry. More important, it discriminated against foreign bottling, and tended to shift bottling to the United States. This was significant because bottling was the most lucrative part of the business and provided the greatest employment benefits. Furthermore it invoked the greatest prestige, in an industry where prestige is an increasingly salient marketing factor. The wine-gallon method was bitterly resisted by foreign producers and the branch plants of foreign producers in the United States, such as the American subsidiaries of the Canadian firms of Hiram Walker, Seagrams, and Schenley. The foreign producers derided the U.S. law and claimed it was an improper use of the taxing authority: it was a tax on water, they said. The domestic industry, largely the bourbon producers, called it a tax on foreign labor, and they regarded it as a proper and legitimate use of national taxing powers.

One might be excused for assuming that the wine-gallon method was the ingenious creation of a protectionist Congress seeking to shelter the domestic industry from foreign competition. In reality, this was not at all how it had come about. Nontariff barriers like the wine-gallon method often arise for reasons unrelated to trade protection and only come to impact on foreign trade later on, at which point they create benefits for domestic interests and become very resistant to change. In the present case, the wine-gallon method originated shortly after the Civil War and was part of a much broader program of regulation of the liquor industry.

During the Civil War, the federal government imposed taxes on a number of activities. These taxes were increased as the war continued and the federal government became more desperate for revenue. The liquor industry provides a good example of the process. In August of 1862, the federal excise tax on distilled spirits was 20¢ a gallon. In March 1864, it was increased threefold to 60¢ a gallon. By July 1864, it had increased to $1.50 a gallon, and it further increased by January 1865 to $2.00 a gallon. The total increase was tenfold in less than three years. With respect to revenues, the government's return on the spirits tax climbed in around $28 million in 1864 as the tax rate rose. In 1865, after the sharp tax increases leading to $2.00 per gallon, the revenues dropped to $16 million. This gave rise to what a U.S. comptroller general's study of tax reform in the liquor industry has called "the 1860 theory on the economy of taxation," which goes roughly as follows: as the tax rate becomes proportionately higher compared to the cost of the commodity taxed, the inducement to evade the tax becomes too powerful to resist.[37] Evasion, of course, is precisely what happened following the tax increases during the Civil War. Illegal distilleries flourished. In the large cities in the United States, bootleg whiskey sold quite profitably at around $1.50 a gallon without taxation. Obviously if taxes were to increase the price to $3.50 per gallon, one could not be honest and survive economically; hence few made any attempt at the former. The government was unable to prevent the illegal operations during the Civil War.

Following the Civil War, the government passed laws to stop tax evasion by the liquor industry. Without much overstatement, these laws proceeded essentially from the principle that anyone who distilled spirits was probably a crook and had to be treated suspiciously by the government. The government introduced the concept of joint custody, which meant distillers notified the government when they were going to distill spirits, and then they were required to store the product in facilities controlled by government inspectors. Bonds were posted to cover stored spirits. A series of seals were installed on crucial spigots which could be opened only by authorized government officials, and revenue officers made routine on-site inspections to insure that the seals were unbroken. Before the spirits were removed from bond, govern-

[37] U.S. Government, *Alcohol and Tobacco*, 6.

ment officers gauged (they were called "gaugers") the amount of alcohol in the spirits and levied taxes according to the proof-gallon method.

Into this system was introduced the wine-gallon method for taxing bottled spirits. The proof-gallon method, which required measurement of alcoholic content, was the normal way the government taxed spirits. Government officers obviously could not test the alcoholic content of spirits already bottled for consumption without destroying the bottle and its contents. Therefore the law provided for the wine-gallon assessment, which effectively assumed the alcoholic content of bottled spirits to be 100 proof, no doubt a reasonable round figure to use at the time. The wine-gallon method was not heavily used in the early period, since most tax assessments were made on bulk spirits and the level of imported spirits was low.

For those who may have been apprehensive about the future of the federal government's taxing powers, the story of the U.S. liquor industry has a happy ending. By 1869, the federal government had gained control over illegal operations. By 1875, federal taxes on spirits had rebounded to roughly $52 million per annum. The fact that the distilled-spirits industry contributed enormously to the federal treasury—indeed nearly half of total revenues—explains why the government went to such extraordinary lengths to protect its sources of revenue.

Since 1875, there has been an enormous modernization in the distilled-spirits industry. From many small distillers, the industry has shrunk to fewer and larger operations. These distillers have a modern business structure, and their record keeping, which in past years was purposefully nonexistent, is now clearly adequate for taxation purposes. However, government regulations and procedures remained essentially unchanged from the late 1860s. Various attempts were made over the years to reform the tax system, especially since the system had become inefficient for government and costly to the industry. For example, regulations required government inspectors to supervise openings and closings of spigots in the distilling process, a task which by the 1970s had become a charade and was referred to tongue-in-cheek in the comptroller general's report as an "unfulling job." However, the procedures were retained, largely for two reasons. One was the reluctance of the Bureau of Alcohol, Tobacco, and Firearms in the Treasury Department to accept a diminution of its bureaucratic responsibilities. The second reason was political pressure from the industry. The industry supported the archaic regulatory system because the wine-gallon method, which was part and parcel of the old system, had become very important over the years in terms of protecting domestic distillers from foreign competition. The industry was unwilling to have any reform that would have included throwing out the wine gallon as an anachronism, and thus efforts at reform were effectively stalemated.

External Negotiation

The wine gallon has a rich history in the international negotiations conducted under the GATT system. It has been raised in virtually every trade negotiation since GATT was formed. It has been widely perceived as contrary to the spirit of the GATT. The U.K. government, speaking for the Scottish distillers, was particularly opposed to the wine gallon, and the intensity of its opposition appeared to mount as time went by until it became not only an issue of substance but also an issue of principle and fair play. The United States, however, was unable to negotiate the wine-gallon issue. Because it was a tax law, Congress had to give prior approval for any negotiation on the wine gallon, and pressure from the domestic liquor industry removed any possibility that this might occur. This changed in the Trade Act of 1974 when Congress gave a general authorization to the administration to negotiate nontariff measures, which presumably included the wine-gallon taxation procedures. As a result, officials in the trade bureaucracy in Washington began gearing up after the authorization of the 1974 act to negotiate the wine gallon and other issues with foreign governments. The way they handled this provides a glimpse of the preparatory phase of international negotiations.

In the first place, U.S. trade officials evaluated the wine gallon as a potential concession. If we give up the wine gallon, what value are other nations getting, and who receives the benefits? The Treasury Department valued the wine-gallon concession roughly as a windfall of approximately $110 million of avoidable tax for foreign producers. That $110 million was divided roughly as follows: $60 million would go to EC exporters, largely Scottish distillers and French winemakers; $40 million to Canadian exporters, largely the spirits industry; and $10 million to less-developed countries, particularly Jamaica and Mexico. These figures dictated that the main deal would come with the Europeans. Second, trade officials calculated possible tradeoffs for the concession. If we give up the wine gallon, what do we get? The Americans expected that EC negotiators would probably make an offer on industrial products rather than in their more sensitive agricultural sector. However, the U.S. negotiators knew they would be under pressure from Congress to get something in agriculture, and they hoped that the wine gallon would be a valuable bargaining chip to this end. Now the problem became one of definition of the situation. The United States had always treated alcohol as an industrial product in its tariff schedules and in its external negotiations with foreign countries. Furthermore, the domestic regulation of the issue was handled by the Department of Commerce and not by the Department of Agriculture. The problem was that if Commerce was left in control of the issue, it would probably demand a tradeoff in the industrial products area, which was its mandate, and not in agriculture, which was more important for bringing Congress on board in the negotiation. Thus the trade bureaucrats faced the trick of guiding the issue into an agricultural negotiation. The United States did this essentially by accepting the EC formula that called for a separation between industrial and agricultural product. This was a substantial change overall in the U.S. position, since as an agricultural exporter the United States hoped to see these two sectors negotiated together, with equivalent cuts made in both areas, whereas the EC, being protectionistic in agriculture, had refused to do this. The United States accepted the EC position that agriculture was separate from the industrial sector, and it further accepted the EC definition of agricultural products, which included spirits in EC agricultural tariff schedules. This move reportedly surprised the EC negotiators, but it helped to define the issue in the terms of a potential tradeoff on the agricultural side.

The U.S. trade bureaucrats next established a shopping list of agricultural products with the EC, which became known as the Strauss list of agricultural products. Tobacco was on the list, and it was politically well chosen, considering that tobacco is grown in roughly the same area where bourbon is produced, and if one is going to hurt the bourbon industry one might at least try to help the tobacco industry in the same area. This calculation may have helped somewhat in Kentucky. It probably also helped in Connecticut, where an important domestic distiller (Heublein) existed side-by-side with tobacco interests, and in a state that was represented in the Senate by the chairman of the Senate Finance Committee, Abraham Ribicoff. In addition to tobacco, the United States went after grapes, citrus, beef, poultry, prunes, almonds, and rice. These were essentially the Strauss products.

In the subsequent negotiations, the United States got something on most of these products. Both sides accepted the propriety of exchanging agricultural benefits for the wine-gallon concession (which itself had been defined as an agricultural issue), and documents issued by both the United States and the EC were explicit about the nature of the tradeoff.[38] The concessions on the EC side may have been open, but they

---

[38] See particularly U.S. Government, ACTN Report, 16; and Commission, GATT Multilateral Trade Negotiations, AGRI. III.2, 70–71.

were nevertheless painful concessions to give. The benefits from the wine gallon tended to go to distillers in Scotland and winemakers in France, while the costs of the EC agricultural concessions tended to fall disproportionately on the Italians. This required internal adjustments through the EC restitution scheme.

Next came the bargaining with Canada, and here the question of tradeoffs becomes very interesting. In this case, unlike the US/EC deal, where the tradeoffs were made explicit, the U.S. and Canadian governments released very little specific information about any exchanges involved in the wine-gallon concession. Even observers and lobbyists very close to the Tokyo Round felt that they were uninformed about this aspect of the negotiations, as is evident in the remarks in April 1979 of Mr. Leo Vernon, a representative of Publicker Industries, Inc.:

> During the course of these negotiations, we were told that unless Canada were to come up with something in the way of an offer, a reciprocal offer, they won't get any relief. Yet, most recently, I have been advised that Canada has offered nothing in any reciprocal form. Yet, I am troubled that the elimination of the wine gallon, made a statutory matter, will cause Canada to get a tremendous windfall, just without giving us anything.[39]

Two factors had initially motivated the Americans in their negotiation with Canada. The first was that Canada received fewer benefits in national trade terms from the wine-gallon concession than the EC and therefore was of secondary importance to U.S. negotiating efforts. If the Canadian government had not been prepared to offer anything for the wine-gallon concession, it is possible that Canada could have gotten a windfall benefit, but it is more likely the United States would have converted the wine-gallon protection to some other kind of protection on Canadian exports. Therefore it was important for Canada to appear relatively forthcoming to benefit directly from the concession and, even more important, to facilitate a US/EC deal that would be beneficial to Canada.

Second, the main interests of the United States in negotiating with Canada were not in the agricultural area, as had been the case with the EC, but rather in the industrial products area, and specifically the Canadian machinery program. The Canadian tariff on machinery products was high (15 percent), but the duty would be collected and retained only if a Canadian company made the product in question. On products that were not made in Canada, the duties would be remitted

---

[39] U.S. Government, *Hearings on Wine Gallon/Proof Gallon*, 73.

to the importer. The problem was that this scheme gave the Canadian government administrative discretion to retain the duty whenever a Canadian firm began production of a machinery product, thus creating an effective tariff increase from nil to 15 percent for foreign exporters. The United States wanted lower tariffs on machinery across the board, and it particularly wanted to dismantle the discretionary machinery program. U.S. negotiators hoped to use the wine gallon to pry loose concessions in this area.

Whether any direct exchange was worked out that involved the wine gallon is a matter of conflicting evidence. Some individuals interviewed in connection with this research have suggested that specific concessions were given by Canada in exchange for the wine gallon, that these concessions were very sensitive, and that Canadian and American negotiators agreed to keep this matter confidential. Whether such an agreement was struck is unknown, but what is clear is that public officials were disinclined to discuss the issue. Late in the negotiation, the Canadian Broadcasting Corporation called the U.S. trade representative's office to inquire about what Canada was giving up for the wine-gallon concession, and was told the issue was under the jurisdiction of the Treasury Department. A call to Treasury produced the information that the matter was being handled at the White House. The CBC phoned the White House, and there got the story that the wine gallon was being negotiated by the trade representatives office! There is no doubt that the term "bureaucratic runaround" was well known long before the Tokyo Round, but it is likely the Washington trade bureaucracy gave the term a new meaning for a few CBC journalists.

Most Canadian officials discussed the wine gallon with an openness that belied the suggestion that the issue was ever treated confidentially at all. The wine gallon was put into the much broader context of the give-and-take of the overall trade negotiation. It was suggested that in successful negotiations nations have to make many deals and that these quickly become woven into a package deal which cannot possibly be unraveled to determine exactly which concession was exchanged for what. Into this broader scenario, the wine gallon was incorporated as an admittedly valuable U.S. concession, which was reciprocated with equally valuable benefits in the overall range of Canadian offers to the United States.

Whatever the testimony of public officials, the objective evidence would suggest a tradeoff between the wine gallon and the machinery sector. In the first place, the final report of the U.S. Advisory Committee for Trade Negotiations (ACTN) made clear that the Canadian concession for the wine gallon came in the industrial-products area.[40] The dollar value of the concession was put at $76 million in the ACTN report, but likely a more accurate statement can be found in the court deposition of Robert Strauss, then U.S. trade representative, in connection with a suit brought by the domestic liquor industry in an attempt to stop the wine-gallon concession. Strauss stated:

> In return [for the wine gallon], the United States has received tariff offers from the EC on U.S. agricultural exports valued at over $1 billion per year, and concessions from Canada that could impact $1.5 to $2.0 billion per year in U.S. exports to Canada. The estimated EC revenue loss is $65–75 million per year; the estimated Canadian revenue loss could be as high as $71 million.[41]

This statement would suggest that the United States calculated fairly closely what it thought it was giving and receiving in the wine-gallon concession.

A second shard of evidence can be found in the changes to the Canadian tariff schedule which occurred as a result of the Tokyo Round. The tariffs on most line items were reduced according to the formula cuts negotiated in the Tokyo Round. These provided, for example, that an original tariff of 15 percent would fall to about 9 percent. However, on three line items in the machinery area, namely 42700–6, 7, and 8, tariffs were reduced from 15 percent to zero; that is, free entry. Furthermore, unlike most items attracting tariff reductions in the Tokyo Round, which were phased in over eight years, the items above were marked with an asterisk and qualified with the words "concessions to be implemented in one step on January 1, 1980." This date was the same date the U.S. legislation which eliminated the wine-gallon assessment procedures entered into force.

Further investigation determined that the tariff-line items above did not exist prior to the Tokyo Round, but were created to take effect on January 1, 1980. Item 42700-7 included a wide range of metalworking machines, and item 42700-8 was made up of a number of dishwasher parts. Item 42700-6, however, grouped together a vast and apparently unrelated assortment of machinery products, ranging from self-pro-

[40] The report states: "The United States also received concessions from Canada which will benefit U.S. industrial exports and will result in an annual Canadian revenue loss that could be as high as $76 million in return for the wine-gallon concession" U.S. Government, ACTN *Report*, 16.

[41] U.S. District Court for the District of Columbia, *American Distilling Company et al.* vs. *Jimmy Carter et al.* (Civil Action no. 77-C-11), declaration of Ambassador Robert A. Strauss, April 2, 1979.

pelled crawler machines with blades (i.e., bulldozers) and textile-industry machines to popcorn, fish-skinning, and toothbrush-making machines and countertop electric dishwashers. The total 1980 imports in the three tariff items, mostly coming from the United States, were as follows: 42700-6, $441 million; 42700-7, $137 million; and 42700-8, $4 million.[42] The total imports from the United States in these three items came to $477 million. Since these products were legally dutiable, the potential revenue loss for Canada from the tariff falling from 15 percent to free could be argued to be 15 percent of $477 million, or $71.5 million. This amount is almost exactly the figure Ambassador Strauss claimed the Canadians had conceded in return for the wine gallon.

The suggestion that an explicit exchange had been worked out with Canada on the wine gallon seemed plausible to some individuals in the United States. One longtime observer of trade negotiations commented: "Governments just don't give away these kinds of benefits for nothing: there had to be a deal." However, the evidence suggesting a relationship between the wine-gallon and machinery concessions was dismissed as simply coincidental by Canadian bureaucrats. Most intriguing was testimony on the American side that confirmed the Canadian position. A knowledgeable observer in Washington flatly rejected the notion of explicit linkage on the wine gallon, and described it as an example of overprecisionism that occasionally creeps into the business of negotiation. Some government bureaucrats, it was claimed, were trained to calculate things down to the last nickel, and thus develop elaborate theories about what items should be traded off for each other. In practice, however, such theories about linkages are rarely realistic or useful, and good negotiators usually ignore these theories in favor of letting each side define the situation for itself. Using this logic, the argument continued, it would be both implausible that the wine gallon was exchanged for specific concessions from Canada and plausible that there would be theories that just such an exchange had taken place.

What this conflicting testimony indicates is that establishing trade-offs or linkages in negotiation is really a delicate step, despite the textbook rule that negotiators should quickly move to create a quid pro quo between the parties. Normally trade negotiators try to strike deals within comparable categories, that is, to make offers in the same areas where they are receiving benefits, in order to avoid advantaging one industry at the cost of another. However, this would have been difficult

---

[42] Trade data provided orally from Statistics Canada, Ottawa. These data are public, but not published.

to do in the wine-gallon case, since the Canadian federal government had very little it could give American producers in the spirits industry. Hence it probably was necessary in practice to exchange benefits across categories. But one might expect difficulties in carrying this out, since disadvantaged parties are rarely able to appreciate the need for any exchange from which they do not benefit. Then, too, there is the question of propriety that tradeoffs often raise. Tradeoffs require negotiators to make comparisons of relative value between different things, and such comparisons can easily appear repugnant to a domestic constituency. Perhaps the best example of this problem in recent history was the unfortunate linking by the U.S. government of Japanese textile concessions with the offer to return Okinawa to Japanese sovereignty. In the present case, the difficulties were much less severe, but had there been an explicit linkage between the wine-gallon and machinery interests, it might have led to questions in Canada about the propriety of providing benefits for a multinational liquor industry at the cost of future growth in an important domestic manufacturing sector.

It is possible that if there was a tradeoff over the wine gallon, both the U.S. and Canadian governments would prefer to say as little about the arrangement as possible. For the Canadians, of course, there is the appearance of a liquor industry so strong that it could encourage Ottawa to begin dismantling, on an apparently haphazard basis, an entrenched program of protection in an important area of secondary manufacturing.[43] The fact that Ottawa was probably ill advised to commence the program in the first place only adds a touch of irony to the enterprise. For the United States, the results are deeply ironic. It is doubtful, given political realities, that the Canadian government ever could have given the Americans a benefit equivalent to the wine-gallon concession, and in one sense it clearly did not do so. The machinery products that were grouped in tariff items 42700(6–8) were uniformly products that were not made in Canada, and on which the duties were never retained by the Canadian government. Indeed some products made by Canadian firms were originally defined into the tariff items above, but, as a Canadian appliance manufacturer confirmed, they were quickly dropped by the government following a letter of protest. The result is that the 42700(6–8) machinery concession did not reduce effective protectionism by Canada at all, even though it did reduce Canada's flexibility to protect in the future (which arguably may be

[43] On this point, one individual commented, "Seagrams and Hiram Walker are the two largest liquor companies in the world. One can see how much clout they have in Washington, and they're not even American. One would assume they had a lot of influence in Ottawa."

more important in the long run). Most of all, the concession did not produce an actual revenue loss of $71 million by the Canadian government such as could be stacked up against the revenue lost by the U.S. government in favor of the Canadian liquor industry. Whether the Canadian concession ever could have produced a revenue loss of $71 million, as claimed by Ambassador Strauss, seems highly conjectural.

Internal Negotiation

As much as the wine gallon was a negotiation between nations, it was an internal negotiation between various commercial and bureaucratic interests in the United States. The American spirits industry was very intense about the wine-gallon issue. However, the industry was divided. The three largest producers in the United States are Seagrams, Hiram Walker, and Schenley, and they are all American subsidiaries of Canadian multinational firms. As foreign firms, these subsidiaries had a strong interest in having the wine gallon eliminated. The American portion of the industry, particularly the bourbon producers, felt equally strongly about having the wine gallon retained. As a result of these differences, the ISAC which dealt with the spirits industry was divided, which left the bureaucracy with considerably more leeway to handle the issue than it might otherwise have had.

The U.S. trade representative's office recognized that it had a serious problem in the wine-gallon issue, and so a brief hearing was scheduled with representatives from the liquor industry in late March 1979. The hearing provided a very interesting picture of the concerns of the American industry. In the first place, the domestic side of the industry was clearly declining, particularly the bourbon producers. The reason for this was more changing taste than competition from imports. For some years, American consumers have been shifting away from heavier whiskies such as bourbon to lighter drinks such as Scotch, rum, and gin. As one representative from the industry put it, the United States was shifting from its traditional habit of being a red-whiskey country. The result was falling sales and depressed conditions for domestic distillers.

Second, it was clear the domestic industry had taken the advantages provided by the wine gallon to go into bottling in an attempt to retain profitability. For example, one spokesman claimed that the industry was surviving by diversifying its product mix, and specifically by bottling Scotch and Canadian whiskies in the United States. This, it was pointed out, created valuable spinoff business in the bottlemaking, packaging, and transportation industries, all of which would be threatened if the wine-gallon procedures were repealed. In the third place, the domestic industry contended that if the wine gallon was as much of a trade barrier as its opponents claimed, then it certainly was not doing the job adequately. It was pointed out that over the preceding forty years Scotch whiskey distillers had increased their sales in the United States by tenfold, and Canadian distillers by sixfold. In the same period, American whiskey production had declined to one-third its former level. Hence clearly the wine gallon could not be said to be a trade barrier. Repealing the wine gallon would only hurt an industry that was already suffering, and would give a further advantage to those who had the advantage already.

A fourth argument dealt with the windfall gains that would accrue to foreign industry from the wine-gallon repeal. The greatest fear of the domestic distillers was that foreign producers would use their tax savings to increase advertisement and thereby exacerbate the trend away from American whiskey that was already occurring. Advertisement was the main concern because in the liquor business advertisement creates prestige, and prestige creates sales. The concern over advertisement was put in very personal terms. One representative stated, "We don't want the Government to step in and hand the winners in this competition another $4.00 a case and say: Go out and bang them over the head again in the slick magazines or any place you like."[44] Moreover the concern over advertisement was well founded, for the representatives of the multinational companies were candid about their intention to increase advertisement with their wine-gallon windfall.

Finally, the domestic industry was concerned about jobs. It is safe to say that employment was the most contentious of the issues raised in the wine-gallon hearings. Estimates of the number of American jobs that would be lost through wine-gallon repeal ranged across the waterfront, from a high of 25,000 referred to in a one-page letter of March 19, 1979, from former Teamsters president Frank Fitzsimmons to Ambassador Strauss, to a low of "no negative effect" by industry supporters of the wine-gallon repeal. In between was a study commissioned by Hiram Walker and conducted by Professor Roger Stobaugh of Harvard University that concluded that on the perhaps 1,800 persons employed in bottling bulk imports in the United States the impact of the wine-gallon repeal would be "very small." Two classified government studies estimated higher figures, with the total of the higher study being "under 5,000." Finally, one exasperated counsel counted the bottles made per worker in the United States, counted the number of bottles (narrow-neck only) involved in a shift from the wine-gallon method, concluded

---

[44] Leo Vernon in U.S. Government, *Hearings on Wine Gallon/Proof Gallon*, 119.

that 439 jobs were affected, and then doubled the figure to 800 on the grounds that as a lawyer he might be accused of not being knowledgeable about the bottling business. One might conclude from the wine-gallon case that economic debate reaches its heights of emotion and depths of precision when assessing the impact of changed political structures on levels of employment.

If the hearings with the trade representative's office were intended to placate the domestic liquor industry, they clearly did not achieve this purpose. A subsequent meeting was held in Robert Strauss's office with representatives of twenty-five domestic companies, and by all accounts it was a very difficult meeting. The representatives claimed they were not given timely notification of pending wine-gallon changes, as required in the Trade Act of 1974. They complained about the advisory process which gave as much influence to multinational industries as it did to American producers. They threatened a court action to obtain a temporary restraining order preventing the U.S. government from proceeding with the wine-gallon concession. The representatives alleged certain connections between the multinational liquor industry and the Democratic party, which angered Strauss. What followed is murky. Suffice it to say Strauss observed that he had been sued by better people, and he challenged the companies to sue. They did. But they had no case and they lost quickly.

It is uncommon in diplomatic history for a sovereign's representative to be hauled into court by constituents for the conduct of his diplomatic function. No doubt this is a peculiarity of the American system, which generally is not well constructed for the exigencies of external diplomacy. Whatever its value for the principals, the court action had value for the analyst in that it revealed through court depositions the sworn testimony of the trade representative's office about the importance of the wine-gallon concession. For example, in a legal statement that began "I am the United States Special Representative for Trade Negotiation" Ambassador Strauss declared:

> The willingness of the United States to include in its package of concessions a change in the wine gallon assessment method was critical to our ability to obtain valuable concessions from other countries on items of interest to the United States. . . . For these reasons, wine gallon is a critical element in the overall agreement we are seeking to reach. . . . An injunction against the execution or implementation of such an agreement [on wine gallon] would have serious and perhaps disastrous, consequences for the essential success of the negotiations. . . . If this happens the United States could

well lose an opportunity to build a new and better approach to international trade.[45]

The court depositions of Strauss and others confirmed information received in interviews with U.S. officials about the importance of the wine gallon to the Tokyo Round. These officials had indicated that the wine gallon was crucial in getting agricultural benefits from the EC, which in turn were crucial in getting the support of the farm block in Congress. Without this support, congressional approval of the Tokyo Round results was indeed dubious. As for the EC side in this equation, European interviewees confirmed that the wine gallon was "absolutely necessary" in getting the support of the U.K. government, and therefore of the Council of Ministers of the EC, for the Tokyo Round negotiation. For the bureaucrats in the European Commission, the concessions on the Strauss list of agricultural products were an acceptable price to pay for the wine gallon, which had become effectively a sine qua non demand in EC negotiations.

Following the lawsuit, the wine-gallon issue went to the Hill, and specifically to the Finance Committee in the Senate. There it immediately ran into problems. The domestic industry had by this point accepted wine-gallon repeal as a fait accompli, and now the issue became one of seeking compensating gain. The issue was put in these terms: the government had decided through wine-gallon repeal to give $110 million to foreign producers; now what was the government prepared to do for the domestic firms? Since the Finance Committee was chaired by Senator Abraham Ribicoff of Connecticut, who represented the state in which the American distiller Heublein is located, it is not surprising that the concerns of the domestic distillers were given careful attention.

What was done to compensate the domestic firms was effectively to rewrite U.S. tax legislation concerning assessment procedures on distilled spirits. With assistance from the trade bureaucracy, congressional staffers first removed the system of on-site government inspectors that had been part of revenue enforcement procedures since the 1860s. This freed the industry from the need to mesh distillery operations with the hourly schedules of government inspectors, and saved approximately $20–25 million. Second, the new system provided for assessments on bottled rather than bulk spirits, which allowed the companies to avoid paying taxes on spillage and produced an annual saving estimated at $20 million. Implicit in this arrangement was that the tax assessment would be based on the distiller's business records and audits rather than on the physical presence of government inspectors. Third, a rec-

[45] *American Distilling Company*, Declaration of Ambassador Strauss, April 2, 1979.

tification tax levied on U.S. (but not foreign) blending activities was dropped, with a saving to the industry of about $20 million; and several other procedural regulations were eliminated. These reforms were all consistent with those which had been proposed in the earlier comptroller general's report on the liquor industry (see note 37 above), but which had not been politically acceptable because of their implications for the wine-gallon assessment method. When the wine gallon was removed through external pressure, it unlocked the process of internal reform that was long overdue. One could not find a better example of a more general phenomenon than one saw in the Tokyo Round, namely the capacity of external negotiation to generate reform in internal systems.

Up to this point, the industry and the government were both happy with the reform. But the domestic producers calculated: $110 million went to foreigners, $60–65 million went to the domestic industry. It was hardly equitable. What the domestic companies really wanted was an extension of their tax deadline to help cover the shortfall that could accrue between the incidence of taxation and the payment from wholesalers. There was some justification to this demand, since the customs procedures for handling foreign-made spirits usually resulted in a smaller gap between taxation and sale of product for foreign distillers. However, tax deferral was not at all implied in tax reform, and the U.S. Office of Management and Budgeting (OMB) was vigorously opposed to the proposal. For OMB bureaucrats, tax deferral was tantamount to giving away the shop: it effectively provided a working-capital loan by the U.S. Treasury to domestic industry, and it created an enormous question of principle and precedent. The opposition of the OMB created a bottleneck in the efforts to rewrite the tax laws on spirits along lines that would be acceptable to the domestic industry and its influential Senate supporters.

The trade representative's office supported the domestic industry on this issue, but it could not buck the OMB. The matter landed on Robert Strauss's desk, and it was his handling of problems like this one that have led many to claim that his participation was essential to the completion of the Tokyo Round. Strauss took the issue to the president. Reportedly the president indicated that a general trade agreement was the highest national priority, and told Strauss that whatever he could sell to the Senate was acceptable to the White House. The domestic industry got a fifteen-day deferral. The issue must have been painful, as one can discern from the Ways and Means report on the Trade Act of 1979: "The Administration indicated very strongly that this proposal [i.e., tax deferral] was a quid pro quo as a result of the unique circumstances in this area and that it does not favor the use of the deferral in this case as a precedent for any other area."[46]

The tax deferral concluded the wine-gallon negotiation. The wine gallon itself was repealed by the Trade Act of 1979. To the end, it was regarded by some in the Washington trade bureaucracy as one of the more dramatic struggles of the Tokyo Round. It was described as the linchpin of the negotiation even by those who admitted to being puzzled about how it had come off. As one participant told the Ways and Means Trade Subcommittee:

> We were told that the elimination of wine gallon was the linchpin of the negotiation with the Common Market. . . . We found it somewhat surprising that by the simple expedient of offering the better part of $120 million a year to two Canadian distillers who also own whiskey plants in Scotland and to a handful of Scottish distillers we were able to persuade the rest of Europe to increase its purchases of U.S. beef, poultry, rice, fruit and tobacco. Another surprising aspect of these negotiations is that the Canadian Government has not offered the United States any real concession notwithstanding our generosity to their distillers.
>
> Nevertheless I must acknowledge the possibility that this committee will accept the linchpin theory.[47]

Conclusion

The wine gallon could be said to be the biggest chip, or the linchpin, of the Tokyo Round when assessed by its contribution to the negotiating process. How it became the linchpin was surely more the work of happenstance than design. Often in complex negotiations, so many concessions are exchanged that the attention of negotiators turns more to the management of the negotiating situation than to careful calculation of benefits from any particular exchange.[48] Such did not seem to be the case with the wine-gallon concession. Within a large negotiation the purpose of which broadly was to modernize and liberalize the rules governing the international trading system, the wine gallon stood out as a primitive bargain that had to be struck before other, more important matters could be settled. The wine gallon was a curious artifact of

[46] U.S. House of Representatives, *Trade Agreements Act of 1979*, 169.

[47] Statement of Leo Vernon on behalf of the Independent American Whiskey Association (U.S. House of Representatives, *Multilateral Trade Negotiations*, 284).

[48] Winham, "Negotiation."

the negotiation process. It approached as close to a Clausewitzian ideal *deal* as one is likely to find in modern international negotiation.

The wine gallon points out the tendency of government regulation to create vested interests in the economic system. The wine-gallon negotiation was similar to some other areas of the Tokyo Round in that what was being negotiated were proposals for new government regulations that would overthrow past government regulations that domestic interests had become familiar with and had found could be worked to their advantage. The wine gallon in its inception of course had little to do with international trade. It was an issue of tax enforcement, not protectionism, and it came to have significant protective effects only much later in its existence. There was a tendency for the domestic industry in the United States to regard the wine gallon as an immutable part of the economic landscape, and the fact that it had been around for over a century made this a not-implausible expectation. Until the very end, the domestic industry made its investment plans on the assumption that the wine-gallon assessment methods would be continued, and the possibility that the government might change these procedures was bitterly resisted. Thus it is that in solving one problem, governments often create others. In this vein, it is interesting to speculate which of the various arrangements that were negotiated in the course of wine-gallon reform might itself become the subject of some future negotiation designed to liberate the world economy from inappropriate government regulation.

The wine-gallon affair presents an interesting case study of the political influence of transnational business. The Trade Act of 1974 required the U.S. government to consult with ISAC's in formulating Tokyo Round policy. Because they constituted over 50 percent of U.S. spirits production, the firms of Seagrams and Hiram Walker were represented on the relevant committee, namely ISAC #1, Food and Kindred Products, and hence they effectively nullified the opposition of the domestic producers coming from this quarter. There was no doubt that the trade representative's office took the advisory process seriously, and it is reasonable to assume that had the committee not been split, the trade representative would have been very reluctant to recommend wine-gallon repeal to the Congress.

The American producers complained bitterly about the influence of foreign firms on American policy, which they viewed as illegitimate. Their position was best summarized by Leo Vernon:

> One final thing on the question of whether the Canadian companies are American companies. That is true. They employ a lot of

American labor. They have a lot of American capital, but the fact of the matter is that the parent company is in Canada. When the parent company is in Canada and everything operating in the United States is a wholly owned subsidiary then any increase in their wealth is for Canada. . . . So, when they say they represent most of the domestic industry or a great portion, they enjoy the benefits of American industry sales. But it doesn't change their nationality.[49]

The sentiments expressed by Vernon were subsequently included in the lawsuit brought by the domestic industry as an accusation that ISAC #1 had been improperly constituted. The trade representative's response, expressed in a motion to dismiss the lawsuit of the domestic companies, was stated as follows:

In view of the fact that some 50 percent of distilled spirits production is accounted for by foreign-owned companies, it would appear not only consistent with [the Trade Act] but also perfectly appropriate to include in a sector advisory committee on "food and kindred productions" a person employed by a multinational company producing in the United States.[50]

Obviously the trade representative's viewpoint prevailed. As a result of its inclusion on the ISAC, the foreign industry gained access to the bureaucratic process that shaped the outcome of the wine-gallon issue. In the activities of the two Canadian giants during the Tokyo Round one could not find a more clear-cut example of the capacity of multinational corporations to influence the domestic policymaking of a host country.[51]

The wine-gallon story produced more than its share of irony. The outcome did not inspire a glow of satisfied conviction that economic justice had been done, nor did the process offer a spectacle of governments working nobly in pursuit of the public interest. As in much of real life, it was hard to know whom to cheer for in the wine-gallon story. But the greatest irony came in placing the whole episode in the

---

[49] Leo Vernon in U.S. Government, *Hearings on Wine Gallon/Proof Gallon*, 74.

[50] *American Distilling Company*, memorandum of defendants in opposition to plaintiff's application for temporary restraining order, April 21, 1979, 25.

[51] For some, this influence had sinister connotations, as indicated by the following testimony: "I don't believe that wine gallon/proof gallon is only [a matter of] the 120 million or the return of Scotch and Canadian whiskies to countries of origin. I feel that is only the tip of the iceberg. I believe this is a calculated, well-orchestrated, long-range takeover of the American distilling business by foreign interest. That is my personal opinion" (comments of Marshall Berkowitz, American Distilling Company, in U.S. Government, *Hearings on Wine Gallon/Proof Gallon*, 117).

perspective of the purposes of the Tokyo Round. The main purpose of the Tokyo Round was ostensibly to liberalize trade from tariffs and other nontariff measures. According to economic theory, tariffs and other barriers constitute a tax on trade, thereby creating economic inefficiencies and raising the price of the goods to consumers. If trade barriers were removed, one would assume that the prices of products would fall somewhat. The wine gallon is a useful test of this theory, since it represented a large, identifiable, and immediate windfall for producers. Thus it is that one might ask what the foreign producers would do with their tax savings from the wine-gallon concession, and whether these savings would be passed on to the consumer.

This question was asked in the hearings with the liquor industry representatives in March 1979. It is sobering to discover that one of the main uses the liquor industry would make of the windfall was to counter what it saw as the alarming tendency of Americans to drink less. In testimony, trade officials were told that the per capita consumption of spirits in the United States was "vastly less than it was at the time of the founding of this nation." In addition, if one took the top twenty-five wine-consuming nations, the country was not on the list; that is, ". . . the United States does not rate within the top 25 nations." "Marketing support," that is, advertisement and promotion, was seen as a priority by the industry in order to increase the sales of products that had not moved for several years. One representative, talking about a hypothetical case of a stagnant whiskey market, offered the following analysis:

> One would think that there might be wisdom in the participants in that business in spending more money trying to tell the consumer why their product is good. If they were to go about this they would bring additional jobs in the media and associated businesses for as long as they spent additional moneys which once started are very difficult to arrest.[52]

There were no references to jobs (other than advertising jobs) in connection with how the windfall moneys might be spent, even though the potential loss of jobs was one of the most emotional arguments raised by the domestic opponents of the wine-gallon concession. This apparently puzzled trade officials, as evidenced by the following query:

> What you have said here is nothing is really going to happen in terms of employment. We are going to have the same number of people bottling in the bulk as before. . . .

[52] Remarks by James D. N. Ford, Hiram Walker and Sons, Inc., ibid., 55.

There must be some kind of economic effect that is likely to result from this.[53]

But the answer essentially dealt with advertisement, and not job creation or diversion. If in the long run the repeal of the wine gallon were
to lead to a shift in American jobs to foreign countries, it was not apparent from the stated intentions of the producers who stood to gain
from the action.

Finally comes the question of the consumer. The answer to what
would be done with the money produced a listing of priorities by one
company representative. It started with the general concern for "facing
up to inflationary increases and losses in dollar value." Mentioned second were "adjustments to the level of marketing activity" (i.e., advertisement). In third place was "satisfying the thirst of the Internal Revenue Service." Fourth, some might go to the shareholders. And in the
fifth place, stated simply: "Some may finish up going directly to the
consumer."[54]

By way of a postscript, I called a whiskey importer in Boston to ask
about the effects of the wine-gallon concession. The company's representative was fully informed about the wine-gallon repeal, and he knew
it would create a windfall for foreign exporters. I asked him about the
price effects of the wine-gallon repeal, since it represented an immediate savings on production costs for the producer: did he expect, say, the
price of Scotch to go down? There was a long silence. "Did you say you
were from a university?" he asked finally. "Everybody knows Scotch is
only going one way."

CONCLUSION OF THE TOKYO ROUND

The Tokyo Round officially concluded in Geneva on April 12, 1979. In
an understated ceremony, a covering procès-verbal was signed along
with a series of agreements embodying the texts of the nontariff-meas-
ure codes and tariff concessions. Additional agreements negotiated bilaterally were not attached to the procès-verbal. The accords were
signed immediately by twelve nations, including all the industrialized
countries that participated in the Tokyo Round. Also included were
Hungary and Argentina, the latter being the only developing countries
to accept the agreements.

The signing ceremony was a tentative and disappointing conclusion
to a major negotiation that had been under way for some six years. In

[53] Remarks by William B. Kelly, Jr., Trade Policy Staff Committee, USTR, ibid., 55.
[54] James Ford, ibid., 47.

comparison with the dramatic and well-publicized conclusion of the Kennedy Round in 1967, the end of the Tokyo Round was a little-heralded event. One reason for this is that the Tokyo Round required national action to ratify the results of the negotiation, and even before the various agreements were completed in Geneva the decisionmaking action had already shifted to the domestic arenas of the major participants, and particularly to the United States. One indicator of this was that Robert Strauss was already too involved in the political effort to assure congressional approval of the agreements to attend the Geneva ceremony. A second reason for the quiet denouement of the Tokyo Round was that there were a number of political and legal issues still in contention when the negotiation was officially concluded. This created an air of uncertainty and made the issue of whether or not the negotiation was concluded itself a matter of debate among the participating nations.

The major political difficulty in concluding the Tokyo Round was the opposition of the developing countries. This opposition was a product of several specific disputes and of a more generalized belief that the overall benefits of the accords were not sufficiently in the interests of developing countries to warrant their acceptance. Safeguards was the primary area of contention, and it became an issue that was too important to drop and yet was incapable of resolution. Much of the delay over this issue centered on the EC delegation, which was under instruction to secure a safeguards code and yet was unable to accept the code without a selectivity provision that was unacceptable to the developing countries. Another specific problem was customs valuation. Differences between the developed and developing countries over the treatment of parent-subsidiary relations in customs matters remained unresolved at the close of the negotiation, and this among other issues had motivated the developing countries to draw up a separate code of customs valuation. A final problem was the aforementioned differences in approach to the framework negotiation. Once it was clear the leading developing countries would not sign the Tokyo Round agreements, pressure developed among these delegations to postpone any decision on the Tokyo Round until the UNCTAD meeting scheduled for May 1979.[55] This pressure was reinforced by the subsequent release of a report from the UNCTAD secretariat that criticized the Tokyo Round agreements for perpetuating a trading system that worked to the disadvantage of the developing countries.

[55] Brij Khindaria, "Tokyo Round: Third World Boycotts Signature," *Financial Times*, April 20, 1979.

There were other political problems at the close of the Tokyo Round besides the relations between developing and developed countries. For one thing, the negotiations between Japan and the two major countries did not end decisively, and enough issues were left unresolved so as to create an atmosphere of uncertainty. The problem was especially acute between Japan and the EC. The Japanese delegation went on record in mid-April noting their regret at the failure of individual EC members to reduce discriminatory quantitative restrictions against Japan, a matter which Japan regarded as unfinished business remaining from the negotiation.[56] The Japanese statement was seen as an effort to counter sharp criticism flowing from the EC that Japan had not been forthcoming in the tariff negotiation, nor had it addressed the major problem of its nontariff measures. On the U.S. side, Japan also had several unresolved items, notably the particular arrangements under which NTT would be included in the government-procurement code. The issue was not settled until later in the year, and at a higher level than the Tokyo Round negotiations. A further problem in concluding the Tokyo Round was the political differences between the United States and the EC over the meaning of the April 12 signing ceremony. The United States had insisted that the signing of the procès-verbal constituted a formal conclusion of the Tokyo Round. The EC, however, took the position that the negotiation remained well short of being finished. At issue was the matter of congressional approval of the Trade Act of 1979, which would constitute U.S. ratification of the Tokyo Round accords. By insisting the April 12 signing was not the end of the negotiation, the EC delegation sought to insure itself against overconfidence on the American side and against overreaction in Europe should the agreement become unraveled. The EC reaction was understandable given that Congress had previously failed to approve trade agreements negotiated by the administration, and this reaction contributed to the uncertainty surrounding the conclusion of the Tokyo Round.

Further complicating the conclusion of the negotiation was the legal uncertainty created by the Tokyo Round accords. The main problem was the legal relationship of the various codes to the GATT itself. The GATT was a legal agreement to which eighty-nine nations (in 1979) were contracting parties, but the codes were signed by far fewer than the whole GATT membership. A question arose whether the codes could be considered part of the GATT and, if so, whether they should be ratified by a GATT organ, such as the Council. Further uncertainty flowed

[56] "Japanese See Tokyo Round as Unfinished Business," *European Report*, April 21, 1979.

from the operational differences between the codes and the GATT. For example, the Tokyo Round codes were intended to apply only between the signatory countries, but the basic thrust in Article 1 of the GATT was toward the nondiscriminatory, multilateral application of trade regulations. Another example was the potential conflict between the dispute-settlement mechanism of GATT and the various committees established under the codes to serve the same purpose. Finally, there were some difficulties with the Tokyo Round package itself, such as the fact that there were two conflicting codes on customs valuation, one produced by the developed and one by the developing countries. These various legal uncertainties gave to those nations hesitant to sign on economic grounds further reason not to accede to the Tokyo Round accords at the April signing.

Following the conclusion of the Tokyo Round in April, the action of the negotiation shifted to the GATT Council and to the internal machinery of the various participating governments. In the former arena, the GATT members negotiated informally over the summer of 1979, in preparation for major decisions to be made on the legal aspects of the Tokyo Round agreements in a GATT Council meeting set for November 1979. In the latter arena, the Tokyo Round participants, particularly the United States, prepared the domestic legislation needed to implement the agreements reached in Geneva. It is generally the case that the internal decisionmaking that attends international negotiation is especially important at the beginning and end of a negotiation; that is, when nations draw up their opening positions and when they decide to accept or reject a settlement. In the Tokyo Round, the latter was demonstrated by the process of internalization of the negotiation, which began gradually after January 1979 and became complete by the April signing ceremony.

8

INTERNAL DECISIONMAKING IN THE
MAJOR PARTICIPANTS

Most of the action of the Tokyo Round occurred in Geneva. In classic diplomatic fashion, representatives were sent from participating governments. In this manner, the external negotiation took on an institutional reality that bore some analogy to the lawmaking process of a modern parliament. However, unlike individuals who are the constituents of a national parliament, the constituents of the Tokyo Round were nation-states which possessed a complicated decisionmaking structure in their own right. For any individual nation at the Tokyo Round, the negotiation in Geneva was only half the problem, for behind that interaction was an internal intragovernmental process needed to support the external negotiation. The internal process often took on the form of a negotiation itself, since conflicting positions had to be accommodated before instructions could be sent to negotiators in the field. Thus the Tokyo Round became a negotiation conducted on two fronts: external and internal. The external negotiation was characterized by discussions between national representatives, and it was the arena where negotiators tried to get the best deal they could for their country from the other participating nations. The internal negotiation was characterized by discussions between government bureaucracies, legislators, and interest groups, and it was the arena where decisions were reached about how much the nation could accommodate the interests of other nations. All nations that participated seriously at the Tokyo Round experienced difficulties from time to time in managing their internal negotiations.

In a large multilateral negotiation, it is impossible to follow the internal negotiation in all countries. This chapter will instead describe the internal procedures of the Big Four (the United States, the European Community, Japan, and Canada), which because of the scope of their commercial activities presented some of the most complicated problems of internal organization. In the following account it will be clear, first, that all four faced certain common problems, such as the need to maintain communication with domestic interest groups or the need to create an interagency decision process that would uniquely service the external negotiation. Second, it will be seen that the four nations had certain shared similarities and differences in their internal response to the Tokyo Round negotiation. For example, the internal process was much more politicized by interest-group activities in the United States than in Japan, with the EC and Canada falling roughly between these two poles. A further difference is that the United States and Canada set up important ad hoc procedures to manage the internal negotiation, while Japan and the EC essentially expanded decision procedures that were already in place. Third, it will be observed that individual national characteristics affected the decisionmaking performance of the various nations in the internal negotiation. These characteristics—such as the sector advisory committees in the United States, the admixture of national governmental representatives and international civil servants in the EC and the influence of regional governments (i.e., provinces) in Canada—ultimately created a uniqueness in the negotiating behavior of the several countries at the Tokyo Round.

THE UNITED STATES

The structure of U.S. policymaking in the Tokyo Round was laid down in the Trade Act of 1974. This legislation has been described in chapter 4, but the main points can be quickly reviewed. The Trade Act gave the president authority to conduct a trade negotiation, and significantly it extended this authority to the negotiation of nontariff measures as well as tariffs. Second, the act spelled out the procedures whereby Congress would implement the results of the negotiation in U.S. law, and it provided for limitations on traditional congressional legislative practices. Finally, and most innovatively, the act established an elaborate machinery of advisory committees designed to integrate the private sector into the decisionmaking process. From a historical perspective, the act continued the movement the United States had taken since the 1930s toward a decreasing politicization of international trade and an increasing role for the executive in trade policy.

In U.S. politics, it is one thing to have a structure for making foreign policy, but it is another thing to make it work. Particularly when Congress is involved in foreign policy, the act of getting policy enacted is often tortuous. This appeared to be the case with the legislation to implement the Tokyo Round. At the start of 1979, few Washington observers thought the Tokyo Round legislation would clear Congress without a fight. The reason was that the American economy was in trouble, and Congress, itself more protectionist than it was in the early 1970s, was expected to be buffeted by constituency pressures to maintain protection for ailing U.S. industries. Congress, it was thought, would either vote down the agreements or would insist on changes that would have to be renegotiated abroad at great risk to the entire negotiation. Surprisingly this did not occur. Instead on July 11, 1979, the House of Representatives voted to approve the Tokyo Round agreements by an overwhelming margin of 395 to 7. Shortly afterward, the Senate followed suit with an equally lopsided 90-to-4 vote. The votes scarcely caused a stir in Washington. Indeed passage went so simply that one could have been tempted to conclude that Congress had lost interest in trade and the U.S. economy.

There was a tendency to assume that congressional approval of the Tokyo Round agreements was simply a product of Robert Strauss's legendary skill in handling Congress. Certainly that skill did exist. Strauss's subordinates described him as "the only man in America who could sell a bad deal to Congress." Yet it was wrong, and unreasonably demeaning to congressmen, to say that Congress was charmed out of its role of safeguarding the national economic interest by a slick politician. What convinced Congress it should support the treaty was an immensely sophisticated process of constituency relations that effectively convinced the people who bring pressure on congressmen. The process appeared simple because the essence of technical sophistication is apparent simplicity of movement, a point Robert Pirsig has made about motorcycle mechanics that is equally appropriate to human systems of government.[1] When Robert Strauss took over as the president's trade representative, he became a key player in an already existing system of executive-legislative-constituency relations that had been created by Congress itself in the Trade Act of 1974. That system was easily as important as the political personalities that made it work. The Trade Act paved the way for a new kind of constituency involvement in U.S. economic diplomacy. That involvement made extraordinary political demands on government, which in the Tokyo Round case were matched by the political energies of Strauss and his associates.

It will be recalled that the Trade Act created a vast network of private-sector advisory committees (SAC's) to represent constituents' interests in the negotiation. Initiative for establishing these committees was mandated to the president. Even before the Trade Act was passed the executive moved to establish the advisory process. For example, over the period June–September 1973, the Department of Commerce held a series of briefings for some six hundred representatives of companies concerned with trade. The representatives were grouped into committees based on Standard Industrial Classification (SIC) codes. The grouping was done mainly on the basis of common sense; as one

[1] Pirsig, *Zen.*

Commerce official said, "We tried to avoid putting radios in with steel." The figure of twenty-seven Industry Sector Advisory Committees (ISAC's) was arrived at and was itself a compromise: more committees would have been too many for government officials to service, while fewer would have aggregated too many diverse activities in one group. Even the name sector committee grew by evolution: they were originally called technical committees, but industry officials complained this implied a low-level operation and was not consistent with the senior-management personnel who served on the committees.

By most accounts, the SAC system worked rather well, but there is no doubt that it created a lot of work. For example, in the year 1978 there were 141 ISAC meetings, about 200 visits by advisory-committee members to a special trade-documents collection maintained by the Department of Commerce, and a series of briefing tours in Geneva with on-site negotiating teams. Comparable activity occurred in the Agricultural and Labor Advisory Committees. In addition, government personnel helped prepare the reports of the advisory committees, which then ostensibly became part of the pressures on the U.S. government. For example, each ISAC was expected to produce a sector report (ISAR) which would later be compiled into an overall report from the constituency advisory process. Commerce officials helped their ISAC's by compiling a briefing book (i.e., "brown book") for each sector detailing the sector's trade, employment, and production position, as well as foreign and domestic protection applicable to the sector. The brown books helped the representatives from industry to assess what they needed and what they could justify, and the constituency process overall helped both the constituents and government officials to establish priorities in the negotiation.

The various sector reports were accumulated into a final report by the presidentially appointed Advisory Committee on Trade Negotiations (ACTN). As mentioned in chapter 4, the ACTN report constituted in effect a report card on the Tokyo Round agreements. Had the results of the negotiations flunked this test, it is doubtful whether Congress would have approved the agreements. In retrospect, it is clear that the agreements passed with flying colors. When the ACTN transmitted its report in June 1979, prominently under the heading "Evaluation of the MTN Agreements" was recorded the following warm endorsement of the Tokyo Round accords:

> Thus, in evaluating the MTN results, a primary test is the extent to which the objectives and purposes set forth by the Congress in the Trade Act of 1974 have been realized. Recognizing that any ne-

309

gotiation of an international nature is a process of accommodation and adjustment among the several negotiating parties in order to reach agreement, it is the conclusion of the ACTN *that the agreements which have been completed reflect a faithful and largely successful effort on the part of the President and his Special Representative for Trade Negotiations to give effect to the instructions set forth in the Trade Act of 1974.*[2]

The ACTN report made it clear why Congress overwhelmingly supported the Tokyo Round agreements. The Tokyo Round was an exercise in diplomacy, and the Trade Act was, at bottom, a sovereign's instructions to its negotiator. Identified in those instructions were the constituents whose interests were to be served, and included was a procedure whereby those constituents could report back to the sovereign on the conduct of the negotiation. In terms of U.S. politics, the Trade Act forced the executive to deal with the constituents who bring the pressure on Congress during trade negotiations. Once the constituents had reported that the negotiation served their interests, it was unlikely that Congress would reject the agreements.

While the system of constituency relations was the key to congressional approval of the Tokyo Round accords, the relations established between Congress and the executive also contributed substantially to a successful outcome. The Trade Act of 1974 had required the president to give Congress a ninety-day notification before submitting trade agreements for enactment, after which Congress had sixty days to pass or reject the agreements without amendment. Furthermore the act had provided the right to selected congressmen to receive regular briefings from the executive and to participate as accredited delegates in the negotiations themselves. These procedures constituted important new departures in U.S. commercial diplomacy, and they produced an opportunity for, but not necessarily a guarantee of, closer-than-normal cooperation between Congress and the executive.

On January 4, 1979, President Carter formally notified Congress of his intent to submit the Tokyo Round agreements for approval. This was followed by an intense period of internal negotiations.[3] These negotiations, which mainly took the form of informal committee sessions, were closed to the public because the external negotiation was still being conducted in Geneva. On the executive side, the lead was taken by the Office of the Special Representative for Trade Negotiations, but

---

[2] U.S. Government, ACTN *Report*, 2 (emphasis in original).

[3] These negotiations have been recorded in greater detail in Destler and Graham, "United States Congress."

other agencies from the departments of State, Treasury, Agriculture, and Labor also participated in the sessions. The two committees principally involved in Congress were the Senate Finance Committee and the Subcommittee on International Trade of the House Ways and Means Committee. Throughout these sessions, the greatest concern of the administration was that Congress would force a revision in U.S. commitments already negotiated in Geneva. In only one case did this occur. The congressional scrutiny revealed that the U.S. offer on government procurement had undercut previous bidding advantages that had been extended by law to businesses owned by blacks and other minority groups. The proponents of minority business were unwilling to yield on the matter, and in the end the administration was forced to make adjustments in its offers and to remove agencies purchasing from minority businesses from the list of entities included under the government-procurement code.

The last and most difficult issue to be settled in the internal negotiation between Congress and the executive was the material-injury clause. It has been asserted that there is a Shakespearean richness and deviousness to the rhetoric of foreign economic policymaking in Washington,[4] which is an assertion easily sustained by the material-injury case. On the face of it, the facts of the case were straightforward. Prior to 1979, U.S. law provided for two injury tests in connection with international trade. One bore on escape-clause procedures, and required that to warrant protection imports be a substantial cause of serious injury. The other test arose under the Antidumping Act of 1921 (as amended), and this simply required that imports be a cause of injury. Of course, there was no injury test at all in U.S. countervailing-duty legislation. At issue before the Congress was the need to incorporate into U.S. antidumping and countervailing-duty legislation the term "material injury" that had been negotiated in the relevant codes in Geneva. What made this task difficult was that U.S. law defined, albeit weakly, what is meant by injury, whereas the international codes did not go that far. Representatives of the domestic industry argued passionately that the term injury should continue to be defined weakly in U.S. law, while the administration argued equally persistently for the insertion of the term material injury, which implied a stronger definition. The Senate Finance Committee was sympathetic to domestic industry and was the scene of the major battle. In the end, the committee accepted the term material injury, but only at the price of writing into law the definition of material injury as "harm which is not inconsequential, immaterial or

---

[4] Malmgren, "The United States," 37.

unimportant."[5] Simply on the face of it, such silly language conveys the extent to which the debate had become theological.

When debate becomes theological in commercial diplomacy, it usually reveals more about the values of the parties than about the economic realities of the issues. It could have been said that the debate over material injury was itself an exchange of little real consequence. The proportion of trade which is involved in antidumping or countervailing actions is on the margin of U.S. trade flows, and the cases where a determination of material injury was the deciding factor were even more marginal. Then, too, the determination of injury in actual trade cases rests with the International Trade Commission (ITC), and it was understood that administrative practice would govern the operational application of an injury test even more than the words that Congress wrote into the legislation.[6] Of course, it could be argued that a minimal legal definition of injury would make countervailing and antidumping actions easier to obtain, which was a real issue on which domestic producers and some congressmen were on opposite sides from the administration and foreign governments. But apart from this, the argument was mostly one of symbols. For domestic producers, the wrong was committed when foreign governments subsidized or foreign producers dumped.[7] The idea of having to prove injury was as objectionable as a homeowner having to prove injury in order to have a burglar convicted. In Congress, this position could not be easily dismissed, because U.S. law did after all define both dumping and subsidies as unfair trade practices against which U.S. producers had a right of redress. Thus the issue was carried on for several weeks in the Senate Finance Committee. It was the last round in what was arguably the most difficult issue of the Tokyo Round.

The SAC system, and the unique legislative procedures provided in the Trade Act of 1974, had the effect of reducing certain aspects of congressional involvement with the Tokyo Round. The reason was that

[5] U.S. Government, *Trade Agreements Act of 1979*, sect. 101, adding to the Tariff Act of 1930, new sec. 771(7).

[6] For example, the doctrine of *de minimis* injury, which was an important mechanism for applying an injury test, arose from administrative practice in the ITC. See Marks, "American Law."

[7] This position was clearly expressed by Samuel H. Washburn of the National Cattlemen's Association: "Products that are produced or marketed under a government subsidy and are exported in competition with domestic products which are produced without subsidies or governmental regulations (except those for standardization, health and sanitation) constituted a prima facie case of injury to domestic producers and the United States should immediately impose countervailing duties to the extent of that subsidy" (U.S. Government, *Comparison of Recommendations*, 11).

Congress is probably ill equipped to legislate effectively on the kinds of issues that are raised in multilateral trade negotiations. The issues raised in the Tokyo Round were technical and complex, and often required a range of specialized knowledge that could go beyond the reasonable grasp of most congressmen or their staffs. An even greater problem is that the issues involved the different policy structures that different nations use to control foreign trade. A recurring problem in commercial diplomacy is that nations erect different bureaucratic procedures to handle essentially similar problems. Congress can be expected to be familiar with American procedures on matters of commerce, but it is unlikely to know much about the procedures followed in other countries. When the task is to adjust legislation on trade to the domestic legislation of other nations, there is a greater need for expertise on trade itself than Congress might be expected to possess.

Congress is also ill equipped to cope with the politics of some issues of foreign trade. The last decade has seen a rise of single-issue constituencies which have made domestic policymaking more difficult. These constituencies are especially troublesome when the task is to balance American interests against those of foreign nations. The power of special-interest groups is that they are usually well informed and well organized, and are willing to evaluate a complicated policy on the basis of a single concern. It takes information and organization to counter the demands of such constituencies and to put their demands into the broader perspective of the national interest. Congress simply does not have the analytical capability or organization in the policy area of international trade to cope with all the specialized demands that can be made in this area.

In the Trade Act of 1974, Congress effectively removed itself from a major role in representing constituents in connection with the Tokyo Round. Congress created a structure for policymaking and constituency representation, and then delegated these tasks to the executive trade bureaucracy and to the constituents themselves. By establishing the SAC system, Congress effectively forced the bureaucracy, which has the capacity to understand trade, to deal with the constituents; and it likewise forced the constituents to deal with the bureaucracy, which incidentally gave them a broader understanding of American trade problems. Congress left itself the task of assessing the results of the process. The congressional role was a judicial one more than it was legislative.

Because it curtailed the power of Congress to amend the Tokyo Round agreements, the Trade Act helped to remove Congress as an object of constituency pressure. That Congress would have chosen this procedure may seem startling to those who automatically assume Con-

313

gress to be "protectionist" on foreign trade, but further reflection may suggest that such protectionism as Congress does exhibit occurs more by force of constituency demands than by exercise of choice. The Trade Act gave congressmen the capacity to assess foreign trade policy from the basis of broader criteria than they might otherwise have been able to apply. The act gave Congress the capacity to take on a steering role, which, as Karl Deutsch reminds us, is the essential element in the definition of government.[8] If one wanted a modern analogy to the role of Congress, it would be in the controlling function that modern conglomerates exercise over their subsidiaries. The essence of such control is that functions are delegated, performance criteria are specified, and a mechanism is put in place for monitoring the results of the process. From the standpoint of cybernetic theory, Congress's role in the Tokyo Round demonstrated the capacity of a democratic organization to adapt to environmental complexity, and to establish new patterns of politics while maintaining control of the process. From the standpoint of practical politics, the process was significant because it worked reasonably well.

A further observation about U.S. participation in the Tokyo Round deals more with the bureaucracy than with Congress. In a fundamental sense, the Trade Act bureaucratized the process of maintaining relations between constituency groups and government during the Tokyo Round. In the first place, Congress delegated the task of liaising with constituency groups to the trade bureaucracy of the executive, and particularly to the special trade representative. More important, however, Congress bureaucratized the constituency groups themselves. The number of interests that must be served in a large-scale trade negotiation is so vast that it is difficult to get a handle on the problem. The Trade Act helped solve this problem by organizing constituency groups into SAC's. The SAC system reflected the principles of hierarchy and specialization that are found in bureaucratic structures generally; and it was a practical application of Simon's argument that "hierarchy . . . is one of the central structural schemes that the architect of complexity uses."[9] The SAC system created information channels and legitimized a structure through which advice could be put forward to government. It allowed government, and the specialized interests themselves, to aggregate and balance the various factions in a more orderly way than would normally be done through congressional lobbying alone.[10] The struc-

---

[8] Deutsch, *Nerves of Government*, ch. 11.

[9] "Architecture of Complexity," 87.

[10] On this point, the Tokyo Round process was strikingly different from the process described by Schattschneider in the Smoot-Hawley tariff case. Schattschneider writes: "The Committee [House Committee on Ways and Means] heard only those who came

ture of the SAC system increased both the power and the responsibility of constituency groups in the Tokyo Round. It is unlikely that Congress would have supported the Tokyo Round agreements had the ACTN strongly opposed them, but then it was also unlikely that the ACTN's advice would have been unrepresentative of the broader interests of U.S. economic groups.

In delegating the task of constituency relations to the executive, Congress took advantage of the capacity of governmental bureaucracy to take the initiative in dealing with constituents. One usually assumes that the flow of information and pressure is from interest groups to Congress. The Tokyo Round demonstrated that this flow could move in the opposite direction. The Trade Act required the special trade representative (STR) and other government agencies to initiate meetings with constituency groups, and to coordinate the task of maintaining political communications with the representatives of important interests. The SAC system was a valuable asset for this risk. The same system that organized the sectoral interests and gave them influence in government also structured the task of the executive in dealing with those interests. In the words of one government official, "The SAC system gave STR a series of targets to shoot at." The STR and other agencies responded by initiating communications to find out what constituency concerns were, and then reporting back to those same constituents about the progress of the negotiation. The main reason the executive was successful in selling the Tokyo Round to constituency groups is the work that was put in (one STR official described the continuous meetings with constituency groups as "exhausting"), but the SAC system itself ensured that the effort spent would be coordinated and well organized, and that potential trouble spots could be identified quickly.

There is a natural tendency for those in charge of policymaking to ignore constituency groups and to assume such groups will look after their own interests. Such an assumption can be dangerous because it encourages policymakers to interpret silence as compliance, or even political support. By comparison, the SAC system developed something new in constituency relations. The Trade Act made the SAC's crucially important to the executive, with the result that the executive took the initiative to find out what the constituency groups wanted. By seeking this information, and then by accommodating preferences wherever possible, the executive gave the SAC's a stake in the evolving Tokyo

---

freely and made no great effort to identify clearly those whom it heard. It did not assume responsibility for a systematic canvass of opinion covering all economic interests in the nation, but set up instead a free private enterprise in pressure politics which administered itself. . . . the committee took no jurisdiction over any part of the process of organizing pressures carried on beyond the confines of the committee room" (*Politics*, 30–31).

Round agreements, and made compliance in the ultimate result more probable. One STR officer unceremoniously referred to the process in the following terms: "When you let a dog piss all over a fire hydrant, he thinks he owns it." This of course is a well-understood principle of cooptation, but the executive carried the principle one step further. By taking the initiative to communicate with constituency groups, it effectively carried the hydrants to the dogs.

The special trade representative and other executive agencies had some advantages in dealing with constituency groups that are not normally available to Congress. For one thing, the Trade Act required the executive to initiate communications with the SAC's, which meant that communications with constituency groups generally occurred in an environment defined by trade officials and not by the constituents themselves. This gave the trade officials some capacity to help shape the kinds of demands that would be made on the government. Second, and more important, was the amount of expertise and information the trade bureaucracy had about matters of international trade. Trade is an exceptionally technical field, and in technical fields the power to make policy is essentially conferred through the ability to gather and analyze information. One of the advantages of special-interest lobbies in dealing with Congress is that the lobbies have more knowledge about their sphere of activities than is available to congressmen, and hence congressmen feel obliged to rely on the policy judgments presented by lobbies. In the Tokyo Round case, the special interests were required to deal with bureaucrats who were specialists in the issues under consideration. The bureaucracy had the capacity to evaluate the implications of the policy recommendations coming from the private sector, with the result that those recommendations could be less self-serving and politicized than they otherwise might have been.

Third and finally, the trade bureaucracy was more able than Congress might have been to balance the demands of interest groups against each other. Trade negotiations require a balancing of many diverse interests, both within and across national lines. The main lines of cleavage are the differences between those industries seeking foreign markets and who are free traders versus those competing against foreign imports and who are protectionist. In this internationalized brokering of interests, access to the external negotiation increased the capacity to balance interests internally. The greater the access that government agencies dealing with constituency groups had to the external negotiation, the greater the likelihood that they could trade off interests internally to reduce the more extreme demands of some groups. Extreme demands on other countries in trade negotiations almost always involve a "payment" in return. Because the STR, working through the SAC system, could transmit back to the internal constituency what the costs might be of taking certain extreme positions, it helped to keep such positions from being taken in the first place.

The system created by the Trade Act obviously satisfied the constituents of U.S. trade policy. The ACTN report spoke of the "vastly improved partnership between the Congress, the Executive and the private sector in the United States,"[11] and the report recommended the continuance of the arrangement. This is a recommendation the executive should clearly support, for while the system satisfied constituency groups it also increased the executive's control over the internal negotiation that occurred during the Tokyo Round. The Trade Act created channels that provided legitimate access to the executive for constituency groups. But structures that create legitimate access also discourage illegitimate access, and one of the main effects of establishing channels of access was to contain and rationalize the lobbying process that was bound to occur throughout the Tokyo Round.

To sum up, the Tokyo Round experience demonstrated that channels of access could be two-way streets: access to the executive by the private sector could also mean access to the private sector by the executive. In comparison to Congress, which is the normal arena of interest-group activity, the executive was better able to confront constituency groups with a coordinated plan of its own for trade policy. In this situation, bureaucracy was a more active form of government than the legislature. It is customary in classic thinking about government to assume that bureaucracy inhibits initiative, but in fact, because of its superior capacity to gather, organize, and analyze information, bureaucracy is the instrument of the initiative in contemporary large-scale government. It takes coordination and control of the different·factions in a democracy to achieve new departures in public policy. The Trade Act facilitated such control in the Tokyo Round by obliging constituency groups to deal with the executive, which was the more powerful branch of government on trade matters, and not the legislature, which would have been more easily influenced by the particular demands of specialized interests.

THE EUROPEAN COMMUNITY

Multilateral trade negotiations in GATT created pressures to establish internal diplomatic mechanisms in the European Community just as they had done in the United States. The reasons, however, were somewhat different. In the United States, the domestic system was not well

---

[11] U.S. Government, ACTN *Report*, 4.

suited to modern commercial diplomacy, and the difficulties with the system became apparent in the Kennedy Round. Criticism of U.S. performance led to the procedural changes mandated by the Trade Act of 1974, which altered the form of executive-congressional-constituency relations in U.S. internal processes. In the EC, by contrast, the pressure to establish internal diplomatic mechanisms arose because the EC was an international organization seeking to conduct external negotiations on behalf of its member states. The pressure to create an internal process arose in the Kennedy Round of the 1960s, which was the first large-scale external negotiation joined by the EC. The Commission of the EC responded to the stimulus on the Kennedy Round by establishing the institutions and internal procedures needed to represent the Community. The new arrangement served reasonably well in the Kennedy Round, and it was essentially duplicated in the Tokyo Round.

It will be recalled from chapter 2 that the Kennedy Round was very important to the Commission. The negotiation was widely seen as a test of internal cohesion for the Europe of the Six and, as a corollary, a test of the Commission's capacity to take action in the name of the Six. Such a capacity was in no sense well established by the 1960s. The Commission, which is the internal executive body of the EC, is required to obtain approval for its actions from the Council of Ministers, the organ of sovereign control by EC member governments. The Treaty of Rome, which created the European Economic Community, gave the Commission the power to initiate but not to decide. Included in its power under Article 111 was the right to represent the Community in external negotiations.[12] Such legal competence, however, was not a guarantee of political or bureaucratic competence. In fact, the Commission was given little real discretion to negotiate until about 1966, and member governments conducted their external economic relations through a combination of direct bilateral contacts and some multilateral representations under the auspices of the Commission. It was not until after the walkout by France in 1965–66, which brought to a head issues of internal constitutional arrangements, that the Council had sufficient unity to authorize the Commission to negotiate seriously on behalf of the member governments.

The task for the EC in developing a negotiating mechanism was to

---

[12] These powers were spelled out as follows: "The Commission presents to the Council recommendations with a view to tariff negotiations with third countries on the common customs tariff. The Council authorizes the Commission to open the negotiations. The Commission conducts these negotiations in consultation with a special committee appointed by the Council to assist it in the task, and in the framework of directives which the Council may address to it" (Treaty of Rome, Article 111.2).

establish an external negotiating team, and to create a practical internal procedure to analyze the substance of the negotiation and to represent the interests of the member governments. Establishment of the negotiating team was largely left to the Commission, with the result that the members of the team were drawn from the Commission on the basis of individual and personal competence. On this matter, the EC operated much as any national government. For the internal procedures, the lead was taken from Article 111, which called for the Commission to conduct negotiations "in consultation with a special Committee appointed by the Council to assist it in this task." Such a committee was constituted in the Kennedy Round and became known as the "Article 111 Committee." Its function was similar to an interagency committee that might backstop a negotiation in any national government, but nevertheless it had unique features owing to the supranational character of the EC.

The functions of the Article 111 Committee were both political and bureaucratic. It was composed of senior civil servants (or their assistants) drawn mainly from the economic and financial ministries of the EC members. This structure was designed to represent the interests of the members in an external negotiation. For most working negotiations, the committee was divided into subcommittees of more junior officials and/or specialists in various matters of international economic policy. These working procedures provided the committee with the analytical capabilities to follow and make recommendations on the technical developments in negotiation. The Article 111 Committee was an advisory body; it could not take decisions respecting the substance of a negotiation, a power that resided only in the Council. However, because the committee included national representatives, its recommendations on most issues were regarded as a preview of Council positions, and therefore such recommendations were often definitive. In the development of the Article 111 procedures in the Kennedy Round, it is clear that the Council of Ministers expected the Commission to report regularly to the Article 111 Committee, and that this was one of the conditions on which the Council expanded the Commission's capacity to conduct and conclude that negotiation.[13]

One of the crucial concerns in trade negotiations is the representation of internal domestic interests. In most countries, constituent interests are strong enough so that cooperative policies cannot be pursued externally without some measure of internal support. During the Ken-

[13] For further discussion of these conditions, see Coombes, *Politics and Bureaucracy*, 193.

nedy Round, the Commission had worked closely on sensitive issues such as tariff exceptions lists with the representatives of Community-wide industrial groups. These groups, such as the Union des Industries de la Communauté Européenne and the Comité des Organisations Pro-fessionelles Agricoles, had become well established in Brussels prior to the start of the negotiation in order to provide constituent input into Community policy. The Commission itself encouraged the formation of these groups by refusing to deal with national interest groups. In part, this refusal was simply expedient, since dealing with six (and later nine) separate national interest groups would have presented an im-possible task for the understaffed Commission. However, the Commis-sion's policy was also symbolic, for it took on the view that the for-mation of transnational interest groups would encourage the process of European integration.

Group interests were considered by the Commission during the Ken-nedy Round mainly at the level of the subcommittees of the Article 111 Committee. Contact between interest group and bureaucrats was in-formal and intensive, especially during the early stages in the consid-eration of any new issue. More formal contacts were established through special consultative committees. Generally most interaction occurred at the technical level, and if influence was wielded by interest groups it was more likely to be accomplished through the provision of information, or the analysis of policy alternatives, than through the mobilization of political pressure as seen in the U.S. Congress. As pol-icy considerations moved upward in the Commission, interest groups tended to have less access to Community policymakers and conse-quently they had less influence over the decisions that affected the out-come of the Kennedy Round. In the European Community, when pol-icy issues get forwarded from the Commission to the Council, they are normally taken up first in the Committee of Permanent Representatives (COREPER), a body established through customary practice designed to prepare the agenda for the Council. Generally interventions by interest groups were not welcome at the level of the COREPER or beyond, with the result that private groups had little direct influence over the final brokering of issues at the Kennedy Round.

Although precise measures do not exist for these matters, it is prob-able that interest groups played a weaker role in the European Com-munity during the Kennedy Round than they did in the United States. There are several reasons for this. For one thing, the fact that interest groups in the EC are organized along transnational lines tends to in-crease the internal conflict within groups and as a result weakens the impact groups can make on EC institutions. Of course a similar phenomenon could exist in wholly national interest groups,[14] but the probability of division is greater when groups aggregate interests from different national systems. A second reason is that interest groups in the EC had access mainly to bureaucratic institutions (namely the Commission), whereas comparable groups in the United States had access to a mixture of bureaucratic and representative democratic institutions (namely the federal bureaucracy and Congress). For reasons that have been elaborated in the previous pages, it is probable that representative institutions like the Congress are more easily influenced by constituency interests than is a bureaucracy. Finally, the European interest groups in the Kennedy Round faced competing pressures from other concerns as policymaking rose to the highest political levels in the Community, namely the need to resolve differences as between the member governments of the EC in order to create unified Community policy on issues before the negotiation. The basic cleavage in the Council was along national and, to some extent, regional lines. Unless the concerns of constituency groups were congruent with the interests of member governments, such concerns were likely to take second priority. In some cases, national interest groups that were ineffective at the Community level sought to bring pressure on their own governments, but this tactic again encountered the competing pressure of the need for member governments to accommodate to the interests of other EC members in maintaining a common front in the Kennedy Round negotiation.

The Commission adopted a unique internal negotiating style during the Kennedy Round, which was a blend of European bureaucratic processes adapted to the requirements of making policy in a supranational organization. The Commission is a quasi-governmental bureaucracy, but it is also a supranational organization that must prepare policy acceptable to sovereign member governments. The latter feature has led to the creation of unique bodies in the Commission like the COREPER and the Article 111 Committee, which are designed to integrate national representatives into the working procedures of the EC Commission. The involvement of national representatives has been regarded as an essential feature of the Commission's operations since the formation of this organization. In 1963, five years after the Treaty of Rome established the EEC, Lindberg wrote of the "continuous involvement of the governments of the Member States in every stage of Community decision-making," which he noted was legally mandated in the Treaty of

---

[14] An example of this phenomenon could be seen in the operation of the U.S. liquor industry on the wine-gallon issue, as discussed in the previous chapter.

Rome and was carried out in the day-to-day operations of the Commission.[15] Such "continuous involvement" was put into practice through a consensual decisionmaking process in which policies were cleared with member governments before decisions were taken by the Council. Policy issues moved upward and downward in the hierarchy as they were formulated in the Commission and Council, which has been labeled in more recent writings the "elevator" technique.[16] The process was cumbersome, and it put a premium on achieving political accommodation within the bureaucratic machinery of the Commission before issues were finally submitted to the Council. Nevertheless in the Kennedy Round the process worked fairly well, and it was suggested that the negotiation machinery of the EC was more efficient at the end of that negotiation than was that of the United States.[17]

The internal negotiation process established for the Kennedy Round was continued in the Tokyo Round. The Article 111 Committee was redesignated the "113 Committee" to be consistent with the renumbered articles of the Treaty of Rome, and its functions were enhanced. The essential machinery by which the EC prosecuted the Tokyo Round included the members of the negotiating team (principally located in Geneva), the 113 Committee, COREPER, and the Council. The 113 Committee was the cornerstone of this structure. In keeping with the decentralized nature of the Tokyo Round, with its separate negotiations on the various codes, the 113 Committee expanded as needed to include experts drawn from the member governments on the various subjects before the negotiation. The 113 Committee met at different levels and intervals, more frequently (up to twice per week) at the technical level, and about once per month at the level of directors general. As in the Kennedy Round, decisionmaking functioned slowly, and consensus was emphasized through the consideration and balancing of national viewpoints early in the development of policy in the EC bureaucracy. The 113 Committee was the point of departure for the reconciliation of different national positions, and most conflicts be-

---

[15] *Political Dynamics*, 52. Coombes has described this process with the word *engrenage*, meaning meshing or interlocking; or a mechanism that involves the Commission's "engaging national ministries and, particularly, civil servants in the decision-making process of the Community" (*Politics and Bureaucracy*, 86).

[16] See Denton and Peeters, "European Community," 196.

[17] For example, Coombes noted; "To many observers the Commission team seemed to be acting in a more responsible and consistent manner than some of the national delegations at Geneva, particularly that of the U.S.A. The U.S. negotiators not only took constant trips back and forth to Washington for renewed instructions, but the composition of the negotiating team had to be continually changed in response to changes of political winds at home" (*Politics and Bureaucracy*, 195).

tween member states were brokered at this level. Where disagreements persisted, issues would be sent to the Council for a broader perspective, but this occurred more often to resolve a point on which civil servants had become dug in than to reconcile fundamental conflicts of national interest. As in the Kennedy Round, some observers and participants characterized the EC internal negotiating process in the Tokyo Round as essentially more harmonious and consensual than that found in the United States, where greater internal conflict resulted either from institutional competition between the executive and Congress due to the separation of powers, or from the competitive "bureaucratic politics" culture that characterizes decisionmaking in the U.S. government.[18]

Although it did not fall prey to the same difficulties as the U.S. system, the EC was nevertheless a conflicted negotiating partner in the Tokyo Round. In part, this resulted from its sheer size. Large actors aggregate many economic interests, and as a result find it more difficult to achieve policy cohesion than smaller powers. What Richard Gardner has said about the United States would apply equally to the EC, namely: "Any country with a widely dispersed and heterogeneous population would find it difficult to form an integrated and consistent foreign economic policy."[19] A further problem was that the Council of the EC required consensus—in other words, unanimity—on the part of member governments to proceed in the negotiation. Consensus was often difficult to achieve, and even at the best of times it was a slow process. The bureaucratic process of *engrenage* (see note 15 above) enormously improved the process of consensus building, but this did not alter the basic necessity for members to reach agreement. Because of this necessity, the EC is essentially a weak negotiating partner in multilateral trade negotiations, despite its position as a superpower in the world economy.[20] The EC shares with the United States the inability "to form a government," which is a capability enjoyed by parliamentary democracies like Japan and Canada, and which expands a nation's potential in external negotiations.[21]

[18] See generally Allison, *Essence of Decision*.

[19] *Sterling-Dollar Diplomacy*, 3.

[20] Ralf Dahrendorf has made a similar observation: "There is an almost absurd disproportion between the expectations of the European Community's partners in the world, and the instruments which the Community has at its disposal in order to respond to these expectations" ("External Relations," 65).

[21] John Holmes has made a similar observation: "One problem Canada faces in international economic policy is that it must deal with the United States and the European Community, and neither has a Government" (remarks at the Anglo-Canadian Colloquium, Dalhousie University, May 14–15, 1984). See also the insightful critique of U.S. treatymaking procedures in Cutler, "To Form a Government."

The main problem in the EC negotiating mechanism is its potential for rigidity and immobilism. The EC system works well at the administrative level, but only when there is consensus at the political level, such as existed at the end of the Kennedy Round negotiation. The problem is that achieving a consensus among a group of sovereign nations requires balancing and trading off of many issues. In the effort to reach a collective negotiating mandate, issues become linked and simplified as well, and what results are rigid and simplistic negotiating instructions that are often unsuitable to the fluid and complex world of the negotiation. Positions on individual issues cannot be easily reconsidered without violating the understandings on which the original agreement was achieved.[22] Such problems plagued the EC at the Tokyo Round in the negotiation on safeguards. The original position of the Council on safeguards was to revise Article 19 of the GATT to permit GATT members to apply safeguards selectively. Because of the lack of policy consensus in the Council, the EC was unable to change its negotiating mandate sufficiently to permit its negotiators to accept a renegotiated code, or even to adopt positions that would have put more pressure on other parties, notably the Americans. The failed safeguards code underscored the limitations of the EC in multilateral trade negotiations.

JAPAN

In many respects, Japan was representative of most national governments that negotiated the Tokyo Round. As Trezise and Suzuki have noted, "Japan's postwar political system on the face of it is anything but unusual, mysterious, or specially adapted to the performance of economic or other miracles."[23] What is true of Japan's political system is also true of its diplomatic machinery. Unlike the United States with its separation of powers at the federal level, Japan has a parliamentary structure that has enjoyed majority government under the Liberal Democratic party (LDP) since the mid-1950s. The parliamentary structure has ensured that the Japanese government could ratify without difficulty the results of agreements reached in external negotiations, a fact which increased the efficiency of its economic diplomacy. In contrast to Canada, another parliamentary democracy, Japan is a unitary and not a federal state, and thus it avoided the internal complication of dealing with subgovernments that have some influence over external negotia-

[22] On this point, Arild Underdal has noted, "When a coalition, that is supported by its members, has succeeded—after great difficulties—in reaching a joint decision, that decision is likely to be very hard to modify or change" ("Multinational Negotiation," 179).
[23] "Economic Growth in Japan," 757.

tions. Finally, Japan is a nation-state with a homogeneous society, and it thereby avoided the complexity that different national groupings created in the EC. Thus, from the standpoint of structure, Japan had the potential to maximize its position in the external negotiation by virtue of avoiding the worst of the cleavages that bedeviled its major negotiating partners.

Many observers have taken the view that economic foreign policy is a matter of bureaucratic governance in Japan.[24] This was also the case in the Tokyo Round, as noted by Fukui:

> The structure of decision making in the Japanese government that emerged during the Tokyo Round negotiations was essentially "routine" as opposed to "critical." Even politically sensitive problems were, with few exceptions, contained and resolved within the government bureaucracy. Politicians and interest group leaders were extensively involved in several key areas, but they acted mostly through routine bureaucratic channels.[25]

While the organs of the bureaucracy may have been especially powerful, they were nevertheless similar to those found in most Western democracies, and to those in Canada in particular. In the Tokyo Round, four government departments were largely responsible for the preparation and decisionmaking associated with the negotiation. These were the ministries of Foreign Affairs, Finance, International Trade and Industry (MITI) and Agriculture and Forestry.

The Ministry of Foreign Affairs (MFA), as its name suggests, had a general responsibility for the conduct of Japan's foreign economic policy.[26] Its main concern was the diplomatic aspects of that policy. The MFA was especially charged with the conduct of multilateral economic relations, and hence GATT negotiations such as the Tokyo Round expanded its role beyond what would be expected in normal bilateral relations. The ministry was sensitive to the political dimension of Japan's economic relations with other countries, and it often took an internationalist line in internal policy debates. This, plus the fact that the MFA lacked a domestic constituency and its officers were trained as gener-

[24] For example, Trezise and Suzuki have written, "As in Europe, officials in Japan receive from the public and even from politicians a degree of deference that is not usually accorded civil servants in the United States. In a cabinet government, with ministers regularly moving in and out, these officials by custom and necessity exercise substantial responsibility for forming and carrying out national policies" (ibid., 784).

[25] "GATT Tokyo Round," 80.

[26] The following description of Japanese policymaking institutions borrows from Fukui's account (ibid., 80–113).

alists rather than specialists in economic foreign policy, weakened the influence of the ministry in domestic politicking. In these various aspects, the MFA bore a resemblance to the Department of External Affairs (DEA) in Canada; the foreign-office character that weakened the MFA in its internal relations with the major economic ministries in Japan had the same effect on the DEA in Canada. In both countries, the principal internal function of the foreign ministry during the Tokyo Round was more to coordinate the interagency process than to provide substantive instructions for the negotiators.[27]

The Ministry of Finance operated from a position of strength in the internal negotiations that backstopped the Tokyo Round. The ministry enjoyed a historic preeminence within the government bureaucracy that long preceded the postwar restructuring of the Japanese government. This preeminence came especially from the ministry's control of the government budget, which conferred on it a general responsibility over all economic policymaking. As well, Finance had exclusive control of international monetary matters, and it exercised with the Bank of Japan close supervision over internal operations of banking and financial institutions. Such powers gave Finance a considerable mandate over international trade. The position the ministry took on international trade was that, unlike the "special-interest" ministries (such as MITI or Agriculture and Fisheries—see below), it represented the collective interest of the entire nation, and consequently it pursued with vigor an independent position in interministry negotiations. The viewpoint of the ministry on trade liberalization fell somewhere between the MFA and the special-interest ministries. Finance took a liberal internationalist position on most issues, although on matters that had implications for government revenues, such as the negotiations on customs valuation, it could be expected to take a conservative line. Again in most particulars, the Ministry of Finance in Japan is very similar to the Department of Finance in Canada, both in its position within the government bureaucracy and in its response to external trade negotiations. If anything, the department in Canada may be more influential, owing to its undisputed statutory responsibility for the Canadian tariff.[28]

Japan's Ministry of International Trade and Industry is a government department which has received considerable international attention.[29] During the postwar period, MITI exercised strong leadership over the direction of Japanese trade policy, employing a range of export

[27] See the account by Protheroe, who comments on "DEA's concern for coordination" (*Imports and Politics*, 80).
[28] Ibid., 73.
[29] For example, Johnson, "MITI."

incentives and restrictive import-licensing practices to maximize the contribution of international trade to Japanese economic growth. By the mid-1970s, the extent of MITI's control over trade had greatly attenuated, but a close relationship persisted between the ministry and Japanese industry. The ministry represents an example of a patron-client relationship between a government bureaucracy and industry, and it is organized into sector bureaus to better represent and service the various sectors of the Japanese economy. As a result, MITI is a large, sprawling, and internally conflicted ministry, and considerable effort was expended in the Tokyo Round to coordinate MITI's positions internally prior to interagency decisions with other government bodies. The general trade orientation of MITI tended to vary as a reflection of the different positions taken by the industrial sectors under its aegis, but in general the orientation of the ministry was more protectionist than that of either Finance or the MFA. By way of comparison, MITI was remarkably similar in structure to the Canadian Department of Industry, Trade, and Commerce (ITC), although the latter never exercised the direction over Canadian trade and development that MITI did in Japan.[30] The two organs functioned similarly during the Tokyo Round, which is to say they took a generally liberal posture toward the negotiation, but they provided a voice for protectionism in government bureaucracy for those client industries that were under severe pressure from foreign competition. In Japan, this included industrial sectors such as coal, leather, and textiles, while in Canada it included textiles, footware, and electronics.

The Ministry of Agriculture and Forestry (MAF) operated as an avowedly client department in the Tokyo Round, as it does in Japanese economic policy more generally. The entire agricultural sector is a weak area in the Japanese economy, and it is critically dependent on government for protection from more efficient foreign competition. Various programs providing for tariff and quota protection are maintained by the ministry, and there is strong internal resistance to reducing this protection. To make matters worse, agriculture is deeply politicized in Japan, and any efforts to liberalize agricultural trade meet with sharp resistance from members of the Japanese parliament (Dietmen). The result is that the MAF took a straightforward position of opposition to any agricultural concessions by Japan in the Tokyo Round, and it resorted to the politics of delay and resistance in the interagency

[30] The ITC was created in 1975 and was an amalgam of the old Trade and Commerce Department and the Department of Industry, in existence since 1963. It was dismantled in 1982; its trade and commerce functions were absorbed by the DEA, and its industry mandate went to the newly created Department of Regional Industrial Expansion.

discussions in Tokyo. As with the other ministries, there were certain similarities that could be noted between the MAF and the Canadian Department of Agriculture. Both these departments were characterized by a patron-client relationship with agricultural producers, which led to a representational style of behavior in interagency negotiations. Both also sought to demand and justify barriers against foreign products in order to protect the domestic agricultural support programs they were responsible for maintaining. Perhaps the greatest difference between these two agencies stemmed from the objective differences between the agricultural sectors in the two countries. Japan has no strength in agriculture, while Canada has a mixture of internationally competitive product groups, such as grains, along with weaker groups that are heavily protected, such as dairy, poultry, and wine. As a result, the Agriculture Department in Canada has a mixed orientation toward trade liberalization, and in this regard its position is conflicted much like that of MITI or ITC.

Negotiations within the Japanese government on Tokyo Round issues tended to occur at two levels: first, as an interagency process between the various ministries of the bureaucracy, and second, as a political interaction that involved senior members of the Japanese cabinet and their immediate staffs. The interagency process itself operated on four levels, from the regular informal exchanges at the level of deputy division directors or below to the more ordered weekly meetings at the bureau director's level, which were chaired by a deputy vice-minister from the MFA.[31] The most important interaction between ministries occurred one step below bureau directors at the level of division chiefs.[32] The division chiefs' meetings kept abreast of the unfolding negotiation in Geneva, and on most matters instructions were sent directly from these meetings to the Japanese negotiating team. The style of decisionmaking in these meetings was informal and friendly, and indeed this attitude is typical of decisionmaking throughout the Japanese bureaucracy. Decisions were taken on the basis of unanimity, and it was accepted that no one ministry could impose its views on another. In this process, conflicts were resolved by mutual persuasion rather than by more definitive procedures based on majoritarian principles or hierarchical command. The unanimity rule made decisionmaking in the Japanese bureaucracy slow, inflexible, and indecisive, but it increased

---

[31] See Fukui, "GATT Tokyo Round," 114–20.

[32] Fukui notes: "Division chiefs are the linchpins of decision making in every ministry of the Japanese government. They are the representatives of their ministries when they negotiate with one another" (ibid., 114).

commitment to the decisions taken and thereby facilitated the implementation of policy.

As the work picked up in the Tokyo Round, Japan needed a more efficient internal process for servicing the negotiation, and particularly one that could handle the more politicized problems that were encountered. In December 1977, Prime Minister Fukuda Takeo created a new cabinet position of minister for external economic affairs, with principal responsibility for handling the Tokyo Round negotiation. Former Vice-Minister of the MFA Ushiba Nobuhiko, a senior bureaucrat with a reputation for effectiveness, was named to this post. Mr. Ushiba was in effect an "old boy" from the bureaucracy, and he was well connected to deal with the powerful bureaucrats from the line ministries. At the cabinet level, Ushiba in principle shared jurisdiction over Tokyo Round matters with the ministers from other trade-related ministries, but in practice he had full support from Prime Minister Fukuda. The most sensitive political problems were handled by the prime minister himself, particularly at the end of the negotiation when there was not enough time, as one interviewee put it, to let issues "percolate" up through the bureaucracy.[33] The prime minister was assisted in Tokyo Round matters by a small group of senior bureaucrats seconded to the prime minister's office (PMO) from the line ministries. This ad hoc arrangement was a further attempt to manage the domestic, political side of the negotiation, in order to leave Ushiba relatively free to pursue a final settlement in the external negotiation.

Most issues in the Tokyo Round were handled by the bureaucracy in Japan, but some, like citrus fruit and beef, were played almost wholly at the political level. On these issues, Ushiba was disadvantaged by his background in the bureaucracy. The pressures on citrus fruit and beef came from constituency groups, but they were enormously magnified by the actions of LDP Dietmen (backbenchers) who had far more influence in protecting local economic interests than the theory of parliamentary government would suggest they should have had. The protection of products like beef was an emotional issue in Japan, and, in the words of one Japanese interviewee, "It was not an issue characterized by rational decisionmaking from the standpoint of the national interest." Issues of this kind encountered enormous rigidities in the decisionmaking process, and where concessions were made they tended to come from the top and to be justified as a necessary accommodation to

---

[33] The term percolate is a useful shorthand description of the Japanese *ringisei* system, where decisions are made on the basis of a document (*ringisho*) that has been drafted at a lower level and successively cleared at higher levels in an administrative organization. See Tsuji, "Decision-Making."

irresistible foreign pressure. Such decision procedures, which clearly violated norms of consensus, were known in Japan as "black ship" tactics, a reference to the accommodations made to Western seafaring traders in an earlier age.

There are several conclusions that can be drawn from Japan's participation in the Tokyo Round. The first is that even in a well-run parliamentary democracy where both the political and bureaucratic machinery was structured to conduct diplomacy efficiently, there was a need to set up an ad hoc political structure near the top to prosecute the negotiation. The normal decisionmaking procedure in Japan is "bureaucratic governance," which is a norm that on trade matters would apply to most other nations as well. However, large multilateral trade negotiations are not a normal event. Fukui has made a useful distinction between routine and controversial situations in Japanese decisionmaking, and he suggests that "In routine cases, relatively more ministry bureaucrats and relatively fewer outsiders participate, whereas in controversial cases the opposite tends to be true."[34] The Tokyo Round case provides some evidence for his proposition for, in Japan as elsewhere, the negotiation created pressures that could not be contained within the bureaucratic procedures normally employed in making trade policy. Although not to the same extent as the United States or Canada, Japan responded to these pressures by establishing a special ministerial position to provide overall management of the negotiation.

A second observation concerns the often-misunderstood role of consensus in Japanese negotiation and decisionmaking. It is true that the Japanese exhibit a confrontation-avoidance style of negotiation with foreign diplomats. For example, Henry Kissinger has noted that "The typical Japanese leader is impelled by his culture to avoid explicitness in dealing with foreign counterparts—at nearly all costs."[35] This style puts great emphasis on the prenegotiation phase of diplomacy, in which parties might seek to achieve a common understanding of the problem without taking precise positions. The Japanese tend to exhibit a similar behavior in internal negotiations, practicing a style of decisionmaking that avoids early commitment or tests of strength over formally stated positions. As a result, achieving consensus requires much hard work, and it is a slow process. Because consensus is a goal of Japanese decisionmaking, there is a tendency for foreigners to confuse consensus with cohesiveness, and to assume that any system that produces the former would necessarily reflect the latter. Such assumptions are

[34] "Japanese Foreign Ministry," 9.
[35] *Years of Upheaval*, 738.

most easily drawn from a focus on U.S. politics, where the "bureaucratic politics" model leads the analyst to expect that differences in preferences among bureaucratic actors typically result in a lack of consensus on policy decisions. However, in Japan, in the words of one trade official, "Consensus is a result and not the process," and there is a tendency for bureaucrats to subscribe to a decision publicly after fighting their battles privately. In the Tokyo Round, there were issues which occasioned serious struggles in the Japanese government, and which evoked the "combative pluralism" which students of Japanese diplomacy have claimed typifies internal decisionmaking.[36] Both the internal and the external decisionmaking styles in Japanese diplomacy ultimately had a bearing on the Japanese performance at the Tokyo Round. Success in multilateral negotiation is often a matter of seizing the initiative at the outset, coupled with an ability to react quickly to changing positions as the negotiation proceeds. In neither dimension does the Japanese system perform very well. In contrast to the United States in the Tokyo Round, Japan had a government structure that was well suited to the conduct of economic diplomacy, but the practice of decisionmaking in Japan offset that advantage.

A third observation from the Tokyo Round bears on the capacity of the Japanese government to make economic policy for the nation. In contrast to the United States, it is commonplace to describe Japan as having an interventionist government that has broad powers over the major economic interests in the society. In addition, it is assumed there is little differentiation between state and society in Japan, with the result that government policy is less controversial and more easily implemented than in the United States.[37] Were these assumptions correct, one would expect the Japanese government to be relatively unconstrained in its ability to offer concessions in its trade negotiations with other nations. This clearly did not describe Japan's position in the Tokyo Round, for, to take but one example, the Japanese government was as constrained in the negotiations on agriculture as was the U.S. government on textiles, if not more so. It is often assumed that there exists an identity of interest in Japan between an interventionist government and major industrial or economic groups, an assumption which is captured in the phrase "Japan, Inc." Some students have warned, however, that the assumption of "Japan, Inc." is out of step with developments

---

[36] Blaker, "Japanese Tactical Style," 99.

[37] See Katzenstein, "Conclusion," 899 (volume also published as *Between Power and Plenty: Foreign Economic Policies of Advanced Industrial States*, Madison: University of Wisconsin Press, 1978).

in Japan since the mid-1960s.[38] As just one indicator, Japan's performance during the Tokyo Round appears to confirm the appropriateness
of this warning.

CANADA

The differences in culture mask similarities between Canada and Japan
in the Tokyo Round negotiation. Both nations are parliamentary democracies with majority governments. Both nations have a strong government bureaucracy for making international economic policy, and,
as has been noted, there were remarkable similarities between the individual departments (ministries) in the two countries. Both countries
had a roughly comparable position in the external negotiation, namely
that of being an important nation whose cooperation was needed in
multilateral agreements, but not a superpower that could make or
break those agreements. However, an important difference is that Canada went much farther than Japan in creating an exceptional mechanism for managing the internal negotiation. This mechanism was the
Canadian coordinator for trade negotiations (CCTN), and in function it
served the same need in the Canadian system that the SAC process did
in the American system. The development of this ad hoc procedure was
brought about by the internal political complications of the Canadian
system, particularly the federal structure of the country; and by the extent to which the Tokyo Round brought pressure on Canada to make
changes in a historic trade policy.

Canada's longstanding commercial objectives formed the setting for
its participation in the Tokyo Round. These objectives were twofold.
As a producer of primary products and semiprocessed goods, Canada
has pursued internationalist policies designed to encourage a healthy
export trade.[39] On the other hand, Canada has been a relatively protectionist nation in terms of imports, particularly imports of industrial
and finished products, in an effort to develop the manufacturing sector
of the Canadian economy. This policy has longstanding political roots.
The National Policy of 1879 led initially to protectionism in three important developing industries (textiles, iron and steel, and agricultural
machinery), and it served not only as an economic policy to promote
industrial development but also as a political policy to promote an
East-West market and hence to encourage Canadian identity. Protec-

[38] See Hugh Patrick and Henry Rosovsky, "Japan's Economic Performance: An Overview," in Patrick and Rosovsky (eds.), *Asia's New Giant*, 1–61.

[39] Canada has also vigorously supported institutions designed to liberalize trade. See
Barber, "Canadian Tariff Policy."

tionism inherent in the National Policy has been a controversial element in Canadian domestic politics, since both the less-industrialized western and eastern provinces traditionally favored a low-tariff approach to manufactured imports.

By the 1960s, Canadian protection of secondary industry was under severe criticism from both within and without. The manufacturing sector in Western economies was becoming increasingly important, and hence protectionism in this sector made a significant impact on trading partners. Furthermore criticism of trade policy increased within Canada, and focused on the need to improve the competitiveness and technological capability of Canadian firms.[40] Canada's participation in the Kennedy Round of the 1960s did not create a substantial departure in its trade policy. It will be recalled that the Kennedy Round introduced a linear approach to tariff reductions in an effort to increase the reductions achieved at the negotiation. Canada, as well as South Africa, Australia, and New Zealand, did not accept this approach to the negotiation, on the grounds that it was not suitable for nations with a special economic or trade structure. Canada contended that its exports were largely primary products, on which tariffs were low, while its imports were industrial products, on which tariffs much higher in all countries. Hence, if Canada accepted a formula approach, especially a 50 percent linear cut, it would arguably extend more benefits than it received.[41] Instead, Canada pursued essentially an item-by-item approach with its major trading partners, with the objective of achieving, as outlined in the GATT memorandum of understanding of May 21, 1963, "a balance of advantages based on trade concessions by them of equal value."

The subsequent performance of Canada in the Kennedy Round is a matter of some controversy. While Canadian negotiators have defended Canada's performance as generous, it is undeniable that Canada's major trading partners, particularly the United States and the EEC, have been sharply critical of Canada's performance. There is some justification for the belief that Canada received a better-than-even bargain

[40] For example, Eric W. Kierans has stated: "It is my belief that a policy of tariff protection of secondary industry will not serve Canada in the 1960s. . . . tariff protection will not give us the important benefits that technology can bring. . . . Commercial policy in the sixties must seek to foster the growth of those industries that can compete in world markets. This is a fundamental change from a policy which has, since 1879, attempted to protect industry from external pressures" ("Wanted—A New Commercial Policy," *Canadian Chartered Accountant* 80 [1962], 372–77, 375–76). For a more recent expression of the same viewpoint, see Government of Canada, *Looking Outward*.

[41] The opposite view, largely put forward by the Europeans, was that Canada was a fully industrialized and mature economy, and should be treated like other Western nations.

at the Kennedy Round. For one thing, sources in Canada have raised this point explicitly.[42] Second, it is obvious that by the customary measures nations have evolved to assess trade negotiations, Canada's performance fell short of those of other major trading nations as the Kennedy Round. This point has been admitted by David Slater in an article which nevertheless went on to defend the Canadian position at the Kennedy Round:

> Reckoning by the "common method" of measuring tariffs, Canada's cuts do not cover as large a fraction of her imports as has been indicated for the U.S., EEC and selected EFTA areas, and the *average* degree of cut looks somewhat smaller. Only about one-half of Canada's dutiable trade appears to come under the knife, compared with about two-thirds for the countries considered earlier. The average cut on all negotiated items seems to be about 24%. Thus, in these terms, Canada's overall tariff cuts appear about half as large as those of the major negotiators.[43]

The Tokyo Round increased the pressure on Canada to reassess its commercial policies. After 1977, when the Swiss formula had been accepted as an approach to the tariff negotiation, there was considerable external pressure on Canada to table offers consistent with the agreed formula. The fact that Canada was known to rely more on tariffs than on nontariff measures to protect domestic industry served to increase this pressure. Internally however the Canadian government was under pressure from domestic industry not to accept a formula approach at the Tokyo Round, but rather to pursue a policy similar to that taken in the Kennedy Round. For example, the Canadian Manufacturers' Association stated in a submission that "We do not favour the adoption of general tariff cutting formulae in the negotiations. Any attempt to reduce an entire tariff structure to a few simple numbers would not be helpful and might be damaging."[44] The decision to accept the formula was a difficult one for the Canadian government, and it was taken only

[42] For example, Norman Vickery has noted: "Canadian negotiators managed the remarkable tour de force. . . . over three billion in Canadian exports stand to benefit . . . while Canada has agreed to reduce on some two and a half billion on imports. Nearly half Canada's present dutiable imports remained untouched" (address to the Annual Convention of the Institute of Associate Executives, Ottawa, August 18, 1967; cited in Evans, *Kennedy Round*, 287).

[43] David W. Slater, "Canada in the Kennedy Round," *Canadian Banker* 74 (1967), 5–17, 7 (emphasis in original).

[44] Canadian Manufacturers' Association, *Submission of the Canadian Manufacturers' Association to the Canadian Trade and Tariffs Committee with respect to the GATT Negotiations*, August 1974, 30.

after extensive consultation with industrial groups and provincial governments. It was reached after a series of meetings of an ad hoc cabinet committee on the MTN, attended variously by up to twenty ministers and high-ranking civil servants. The decision was announced on January 19, 1978, in a press statement released jointly by the ministers of External Affairs, Finance, and Industry, Trade, and Commerce. The Canadian position at Geneva gradually reflected the government's decision, and by April 1978 Canada had tabled a "line-by-line" description and assessment of its offer.

Canada's decision to accept the Swiss formula was an example of policymaking, but in a curious sense it was not an example of decision-making. The distinction between the two relates to the nature of interdependence in the modern world. The real issue for Canada in the tariff negotiation was not one of deciding whether to go alone in the negotiation, but rather one of managing a decision that was widely recognized in the Canadian government as being inevitable. Given Canada's interests in international trade, and given that Canada's interests are interdependent with the interests of other nations, there was little real choice about whether Canada would become committed to the formula procedures in the Tokyo Round. Instead the real issue was how to manage what was a necessary accommodation to a multilateral trading system. This is a problem that all nations, and especially medium and smaller powers, continually face in multilateral negotiations. In this case, it is useful to go back and reconstruct how the Canadian government organized itself to manage a substantial change in its trade policy.

Concurrently with the meeting of ministers in Tokyo in 1973, the Canadian government established an interdepartmental Canadian Trade and Tariffs Committee (CTTC) "to meet the government's wish to have an appropriate mechanism to receive the views of and to maintain liaison with all interested parties in Canada with respect to Canada's participation in the [Tokyo Round]."[45] The CTTC was designed to receive briefs principally from industry, and it represented a significant advance in terms of input and feedback mechanisms over what had existed between government and industry in the Kennedy Round. The CTTC was also intended to provide liaison between the federal and provincial governments. By 1973, it was recognized by the federal government that the provincial governments were playing a larger role in Canadian public policymaking, and it was reasonable to assume they would demand participation in the economic decisions of the Tokyo Round. Certainly it was probable that the provinces would demand a

[45] Government of Canada, *Review of Developments*, 1.

larger role than they had played in the Kennedy Round, when, in the words of one federal official, "They got told when everyone else got told." Then, too, the subject material of the Tokyo Round demanded greater provincial involvement. Much of the Tokyo Round dealt with nontariff measures (NTM's), for example liquor-procurement practices which are provincial in origin. It was unlikely that the federal government could participate fully in the code negotiations without continuous consultation with provincial governments.

The CTTC operated after 1973 as a formal information conduit principally between industry and government. It called for information from exporting companies on restrictions they faced in foreign markets, and from importing companies on the likely effects of changes in Canadian tariff or nontariff restrictions. The CTTC mechanism was an active part of the Canadian negotiation process; by August 1977, by its own reckoning, it had received nearly four hundred briefs and supplementary submissions, and it had held over seventy oral consultations with companies, associations, and other groups. The CTTC procedure was another testimonial to the importance of information in modern international negotiation. Trade negotiations are complex, and the data needed to support a nation's position abroad are not normally available to its government. Consequently an "information task force" approach is often needed, first, to secure information on a vertical basis and get it up to the top level of government, and, second, to disseminate information on a horizontal basis among the decisionmaking units of government. The CTTC appears to have been successful in these tasks, and throughout the negotiation it served as a point of departure for securing information on company positions.

The original view of the federal government had been that the CTTC would be a vehicle for communication with the provincial governments as well as with industry. In this area, the CTTC procedures were apparently inadequate from the very outset. The CTTC did receive briefs from most provinces, and held numerous meetings particularly on NTM questions such as subsidies, government-procurement practices, and standards. However, it is questionable how seriously provincial governments took such interaction. One provincial civil servant stated that "We were supposed to be dealing with the CTTC, but this was always a dead letter. We always sent stuff duplicate to Finance and ITC. The CTTC had no power, and no influence." Indeed this statement was confirmed by the fact that provincial governments themselves demanded a larger role in the negotiation, with the result that an ad hoc federal-provincial committee of deputy ministers was set up in 1975. Communication between federal and provincial governments was both more political and more continuous than the CTTC could accommodate. In effect, the CTTC was intended to contain the lobbying process between the federal government and its constituents. It provided for an information-gathering function, but it did not contain the lobbying efforts of interested parties, and especially that of provincial governments.

By the early months of 1977, the pace of the Tokyo Round had quickened and it was obvious that substantial bureaucratic changes were needed. The pressure for change came from four distinct areas of the policy process. First, there was a need to improve the efficiency of communication and decisionmaking between the government and the negotiating team in Geneva. This is a pressure that all nations experienced during the Tokyo Round; it led to structural changes in other countries as well, notably Japan. Second, it was necessary to improve the coordination within the federal bureaucracy itself, particularly on a working level. Shortly after 1973, an interdepartmental Trade Negotiations Coordinating Committee (TNCC) had been set up in Ottawa at the level of department deputy ministers. The TNCC was similar in form to the interdepartmental liaison maintained during the Kennedy Round, but it was little used in the Tokyo Round and became essentially inoperative after 1977.[46] Third, it was necessary to coordinate the federal bureaucracy with the federal cabinet. The Tokyo Round, as foreign negotiations often do, raised problems that cut across the established structures of national governments, and made normal channels between bureaucracy and political leadership less useful than they would normally be. It was known that the federal cabinet would expect to play an active role in the Tokyo Round, and hence an efficient structure would be needed to input data to ministers. Finally, and most important, there was a need to upgrade communications with provincial bureaucracies and, to a lesser extent, industry. The upgrading of relations with the provinces was in large measure a defensive reaction on the part of the federal government. The provinces (particularly Quebec, Ontario, and the western provinces) were energized by their concern over the Tokyo Round to begin to conduct their own studies to determine the advantage of alternative proposals. Coordination between the federal government and provinces was needed to permit Ottawa to take fullest advantage of the information and analysis coming from

[46] One official interviewed late in 1977 described the TNCC as ". . . now out of the picture. It was too oriented to the MTN, and not to the wider picture." The inference was that the TNCC was too oriented to the external negotiation and unable to generate the domestic political and analytical preparatory work needed to support the Canadian position at the Tokyo Round.

provincial bureaucracies, and to keep track of any serious differences that might develop in the Canadian position overall.

As a result of these pressures, the CCTN was established on August 1, 1977. The position was staffed by J. H. Warren, then serving as Ambassador to the United States, and previously head of Canada's delegation to the Kennedy Round. The office of the coordinator was authorized a small staff (approximately five persons initially), which was chosen by Warren on secondment from the federal bureaucracy. In terms of formal responsibilities, the office of the coordinator became a secretariat for the ad hoc Cabinet Committee on the MTN, which was chaired by Deputy Prime Minister Allan MacEachen and which had effective political control over the preparation of the Canadian negotiating position. The coordinator also took over the chair of the Federal-Provincial Committee at the deputy-minister level, and cochaired the newly established Interdepartmental Committee on Trade and Industrial Policy. The latter committee was formed at the deputy-minister level with the mandate to deal with the wider problems of economic adjustment that the Tokyo Round would trigger. Finally, the coordinator took over the task of providing instructions to the negotiating team in Geneva. The establishment of the coordinator had been strongly supported by the negotiating team, in order to secure an effective mandate for continued Canadian efforts in Geneva. As one interviewee stated: "[Ambassador Rodney] Grey of Canada insisted the CCTN was necessary. It represented the first senior person appointed with full responsibility for trade in Ottawa. . . . the external negotiation was the only thing working well before the summer of 1977."

The CCTN's role of being a conduit between the cabinet and the negotiating team as well as a secretariat to the ad hoc cabinet committee gave it a political (or decisionmaking) role which made it preeminent among the bureaucratic units dealing with the Tokyo Round. Its political role in turn made it a focal point for information and/or attempts to influence coming from provincial governments, industry, and other areas in the federal bureaucracy, while, conversely, its information-gathering capabilities increased its political importance. The CCTN altered the role of the federal bureaucracy in trade negotiation, notably the departments of Finance and ITC. These departments continued to conduct the analysis necessary to support Canada's negotiating position, but they engaged much less in the function of political communication. In the words of one official, "It [the CCTN] took away the interplay with industry. We now very seldom get requests from industry to explain what's going on. The PR aspect of the job has shifted completely. We used to do this."

While the CCTN reduced the role of the principal federal departments in the trade negotiation, it increased the role of the provinces. The structure of the CCTN alone increased the importance of the provinces because it provided a focal point for provincial bureaucracies to penetrate an otherwise decentralized federal bureaucratic structure.[47] Consider the case of exceptions lists. Lists of exceptions to general tariff reductions are highly sensitive information in trade negotiations, and in Canada they are customarily fabricated at the highest level of the federal government under conditions of budgetary secrecy. During the late fall of 1977, interested provincial governments submitted exceptions lists to the CCTN, which fact in itself reflects the importance of the provinces in the process. The exceptions lists were treated as extremely confidential information in the CCTN,[48] and they were compared with independent analyses produced by the Department of Finance. This comparative procedure itself provided the possibility for provincial influence, although it did not guarantee it. Further possibilities for influence were provided in the communications triggered by the exceptions lists. The exceptions lists became a focal point in subsequent internal negotiations, and, in the words of a federal official, ". . . by the time the Canadian offer was in place in Geneva, those lists had been massaged on both sides. . . . there were many reinterpretations."

Along with the United States, Canada made more changes to its political system to negotiate the Tokyo Round than did either Japan or the EC. It is useful to examine the functional impact that these changes had. In the United States, the major change was the SAC system, and it increased the role of the private sector in U.S. trade policy. In Canada, the CCTN was the major change, and it increased the role of the provinces in Canadian trade policy. In these changes, one sees the tendency of large external negotiations to expose the building blocks of which nations are constituted. In America, these building blocks are corporatist in nature, and consist, for example, of industrial groups, labor unions, business associations, and the various institutions of government that often speak for specialized interests. The corporatist nature of the United States led Canadian negotiators, surveying the chaos in their neighbor's house during the Tokyo Round, to say, "At least we don't have the Chamber of Commerce coming to Geneva to tell us how to

---

[47] One provincial official stated, "When you send [the federal government] a package of proposals, it gets divided up, and you can't find it again. . . . it gets lost, it's not put together again. Warren's shop opened up more channels of communication than possible under the old system."

[48] An interviewee indicated that the lists were circulated no lower than the level of assistant deputy minister, and that a total of about six people in Ottawa saw them.

run the negotiation." In Canada, on the other hand, the constituent parts tend to be provinces. For reasons of history and personal loyalties, Canada aggregates its political life more on a territorial basis than on other criteria. This led American negotiators, surveying the chaos in *their* neighbor's house, to say, "At least we don't have state governors coming to Geneva to tell us how to run the negotiation."

With regard to Canada, it is a commonplace to observe that the provinces are part of Canadian political life. However, the trend toward provincial involvement in trade policy may be increasing, as demonstrated by the Tokyo Round case. When the Tokyo Round began, the federal government treated the provinces as constituents. By the time major decisions had been made, the provinces had been upgraded to the role of joint policymakers, and they appeared to be on a par in this capacity with the major federal departments in Ottawa. Similarly the direction of policy coordination changed over the period of the Tokyo Round. The early negotiating structures were designed primarily to coordinate the activities of the federal government, but these became less useful than structures that represented provincial interests more fully. What started out as horizontal coordination tended to become vertical coordination as the negotiation progressed.

One conclusion regarding federal-provincial relations from the Tokyo Round is that the increased federal responsiveness to the provincial governments was more a matter of bureaucracy than of politics. Provincial ministers were relatively uninvolved with the Tokyo Round. This is because trade is a federal responsibility, and there were good political reasons for provincial politicians not to take responsibility for any more than they had to. But this was not true of the provincial bureaucracies. Trade is a technical subject in which provincial bureaucracies have become increasingly involved in recent years. Furthermore they have expanded their power by developing an independent capacity to gather and analyze information. The real power of the provinces lay in the capacity of provincial bureaucracies to gather the data and to conduct the analyses necessary to determine provincial interests. Where provincial bureaucracies were able to determine inadequacies in the approach of the federal government, there was created a compelling case for information exchange between these governments, and for possible provincial influence. However, like the SAC case in the United States, one should not assume influence is all one way. In the Tokyo Round, greater involvement by the provinces gave federal officials the opportunity to communicate the real problems Canada had in the external negotiation, and particularly the difficulty of securing favorable deals from its larger trading partners. Such communication helped to

340

reduce the stridency of some provincial demands, and helped to get provincial support for a balanced Canadian position.

While the internal negotiating structures that evolved in Canada and the United States had functional similarities, there were important differences in the style of internal politicking in the two countries. Curiously, while the Canadian and American societies resemble each other in most respects, politics in Canada during the Tokyo Round was more reminiscent of the "bureaucratic governance" style of the Japanese than the open confrontational style of the Americans. The Tokyo Round caused both Canada and the United States to "open up" the policy process. Whereas in the United States this led to a widespread inclusion of private-sector actors, in Canada it mainly meant the inclusion of governmental actors below the federal level, and in addition some involvement of large-scale actors from the private sector. In the United States, those actors seeking to influence public policy were often motivated to demand specific actions from government, or to put precise limits on what the government could do in external negotiations. In comparison, in Canada much of the domestic political activity resulted from institutional actors who previously had not been involved in trade policy demanding to have "an input into the policy process." Exactly what was meant by an "input into the political process" was not always very clear, even, curiously, to the individuals making such a demand. What this demand usually translated into was some assurance by the person making an input that his concerns were being understood at the decisionmaking levels of government, and, occasionally, that these concerns could serve as the basis for further communication. The words most often used by interviewees to describe what was sought were "two-way communication" and "dialogue."[49]

In Canada, the concern for input into the political process generally did not extend to the setting of performance tests to assess the effects of such inputs. This of course could have been done. Tariffs are a quantitative and hence measurable issue, and it would have been possible, by demanding to know what positions had been put on the bargaining table in Geneva, to assess whether an individual making an input had influenced the final outcome. However, the process did not work this way. Nonfederal actors mainly wanted to feel assured that their concerns had been understood; once that was accomplished, actual poli-

[49] On this point, there was no question that the CCTN met the expectations of its important constituents. For example, an Ontario provincial official stated flatly; "I really do think that Jake Warren is carrying on a meaningful dialogue." And a spokesman from industry, comparing the Tokyo Round with the Kennedy Round, stated, "The communication process this time is *much* better."

cymaking was left to the federal government, essentially because it was felt to be most rational to do it that way. This may not seem striking, but politics does not always work this way, and not in the United States where inputs to the policy process are usually more intense, politicized, and divisive than they are in Canada. On the matter of the style of constituency involvement, Canada appeared more like Japan than like the United States, a fact due more to the uniqueness of the U.S. style than to any intrinsic similarity between the Canadian and Japanese political cultures.

CONCLUSION

The preceding account demonstrates that domestic policymaking was important to the Tokyo Round negotiations. It is simply the case that the Tokyo Round engaged domestic politics more than trade negotiations have ever done in the past. Whether the Tokyo Round will be a model for future commercial diplomacy is not now clear, but there are reasons to believe it could be. One reason is that commercial diplomacy is currently in the process of accommodating to the interdependence of modern international life. Interdependence means more than simply adjusting to the fact that nations must rely on each other for needed goods and services. A truer gauge of interdependence is at what point a nation must reorient its domestic priorities and processes to take account of foreign interests. Such a reorientation took place in the Tokyo Round, and by definition it engaged domestic policymaking within the parties participating in that negotiation.

An important reason why domestic politics was inserted into the Tokyo Round is that more policymaking is occurring at the international level than in previous eras. Henry Kissinger has written that diplomacy is "the art of restraining the exercise of power,"[50] which is an accurate description of the peacekeeping sort of diplomacy that arose out of the traditional nation-state system. However, diplomacy today is exercised over a much broader range of governmental functions than just maintaining international security, and much of that diplomacy cuts deeper into the fabric of domestic policy than it did previously. For example, commercial policy was historically one of the great mobilizing issues of domestic party strife, and even in contemporary times one would hardly expect commercial policy to be free of domestic politics, regardless of whether the policymaking was done at the national or international level. What is more visible about the conduct of international af-

[50] *World Restored*, 2.

fairs today is the politicization of the diplomatic function, but this is only a symptom of the real change that is occurring. The real change is a shift in decisionmaking from national to international structures, and toward the creation of what is in effect international legislation. This was made clear in the report on the Tokyo Round by the U.S. Advisory Committee on Trade Negotiations: "These codes and agreements therefore constitute a kind of legislation—at the international level—whose results will only be seen through its application and interpretation over time."[51] The Tokyo Round was thus an experiment in a direction that nations have been moving for some time, namely an extension of international decisionmaking coupled with a greater responsiveness to domestic politics. In such an experiment, success abroad cannot be had without success at home.[52]

The international politics inherited from the European nation-state system has been preoccupied with an effort to maintain a separation between foreign and domestic diplomacy. This has been facilitated by the types of issues dealt with in both areas. International politics dealt with great issues of war and peace. These were considered fitting subjects for diplomacy, and other matters, especially the management of domestic economies, were regarded as the prerogatives of domestic policy. Nations jealously guarded the right of "domestic jurisdiction," and built this concept prominently into the Charter of the United Nations. Today the international agenda has expanded. Nations regularly take up issues through diplomatic negotiations that only a few decades ago would have been exclusively matters of domestic policymaking. The rhetoric of domestic jurisdiction is less important in international politics than it once was, and in some areas, such as international trade policy, it no longer has any absolute meaning whatsoever. The expanding international agenda has profoundly changed the task of statesmanship in the modern age. Formerly the test of statesmanship was the ability to manage external relations in order to protect the capacity of the domestic system for independent initiatives. Nations conducted diplomacy using the currency of power, and the mechanism of control was the balance-of-power system. The technology of the twentieth century has increasingly immobilized the exercise of military power in ex-

[51] U.S. Government, ACTN *Report*, 3.

[52] John Midgley has made a similar observation: "For ten years now, the United States has been experimenting with the re-design of its foreign policy and its diplomatic methods to effect the changes that have been happening both in the world scene and in the American situation. The experiments continue. Even a thoroughly reformed foreign policy will require a more successful conduct of domestic government as a condition of its success" ("Linkage Revisited," *New York Times*, April 4, 1979, op-ed page.

343

ternal relations, and in this new condition the protection of domestic jurisdiction became less necessary. Nations seem more preoccupied today with the making of policy at the international level than they are in the protection of domestic jurisdiction. An important test of statesmanship has now become the ability to manage domestic politics in order to protect the capacity of the external system for independent initiatives.

An important requirement of diplomacy today is for internal control over domestic politics in order to conduct negotiations abroad. This need has not traditionally been an issue of diplomatic theory. The concern for control over domestic pressures has more antecedents in the theory of democratic government than in the theory of international diplomacy. One example from U.S. politics is the Federalist Papers. These papers were written by three men seeking to convince their compatriots that they should ratify the United States Constitution, a broader and stronger form of government than existed in America immediately after independence. The writers of the Federalist Papers were seeking the creation of a government with sufficient control over its constituents to govern effectively, just as negotiators in the Tokyo Round sought to create internal mechanisms with sufficient control over domestic constituents to negotiate effectively. The writers of the Federalist Papers were seeking to avoid the uncertainty and chaos of a narrower conception of government that did not have sufficient control to raise taxes, regulate commerce, or enforce its own laws. By analogy, Tokyo Round negotiators were seeking to avoid the uncertainty and chaos produced by a particularistic versus a more general approach to international trade.

It is not surprising that theory related to the development of the U.S. Constitution should be relevant to modern international diplomacy. The concerns that motivated the authors of the Federalist Papers to support the adoption of the U.S. Constitution bear some similarities to the values that inspired the Tokyo Round, for both cases represented an attempt to expand the functions of centralized government to encompass a wider system. Fairness and orderliness were sought in both the Federalist case and in the Tokyo Round, and the greatest threats to achieving these were governments that responded too readily to narrowly based demands from their constituents. There are some functions today, such as the regulation of commerce between nations, that can only be handled effectively outside the nation-state, just as the regulation of commerce between the American states could be handled effectively only by a strong federal government. Through an extension of the negotiation process, international diplomacy today is becoming a means for conducting policy at a broader level than the nation-state. Some of this diplomacy is constitutional in nature (as was clear in the Tokyo Round agreements which provided mechanisms for future consultations), and thus the analogy to the extension of government that occurred in American history is appropriate.

A central concern of James Madison's memorable contribution to the Federalist Papers was the control of faction. This concern has its counterpart in today's world of diplomacy in the problem of the management of domestic constituencies. Madison argued that factions were dangerous in a democracy because they prevented the realization of the public good, and thus were responsible for confusion, instability and, most important, injustice. Because factions were a natural outgrowth of political liberty ("liberty is to faction what air is to fire"), it was necessary for government to control their effects without removing their causes. In framing the government, said Madison, ". . . you must first enable the government to control the governed; and in the next place oblige it to control itself."[53] The control of faction, he claimed, lay in the republican principle: specifically in the delegation of government to a small number of citizens elected by the rest, and then in the extension of government over a greater number of citizens. The former created some detachment from the process of governing, while the latter diluted the claims of special interests in the broader concerns of a larger group.

Madison's republican principle has considerable relevance to controlling the pressures that bear on trade policy, as is clear from a reading of Schattschneider's account of the Smoot-Hawley tariff of 1930. Schattschneider described the potential for powerful economic interests to wield oligarchic power in the legislative process, which was due as much as anything to the differential effort that interests invest in promoting their particular concerns.[54] The remedy for the oligarchic power of interest groups was a government process that could balance the forces acting on government and allow government to "play one off against the other."[55] In the Tokyo Round, the SAC mechanism in the

[53] The Federalist, no. 51, in Commager (ed.), Selections, 86.

[54] As Schattschneider put it; ". . . the activity of economic groups in the tariff revision of 1929 was variable, in part, because they were not equally well informed of the event" (Politics, 212). As a result: "Unsupervised conduct in pressure politics means that the few will control the process at the expense of the many" (p. 287). Schattschneider described the economic pressure politics that resulted from this process as "oligarchic" and "anti-democratic." This is an interesting formulation, since the usual criticism of the Smoot-Hawley process is that it created an "excess" of democracy, but not that it was fundamentally undemocratic in nature.

[55] Ibid., 288.

United States was an extension both of Madison's republican principle and Schattschneider's balance-of-forces approach. The mechanism expanded the U.S. government's capacity to deal with constituency groups, although curiously it was put into practice by the bureaucracy rather than by the legislature, as Madison had intended. The task of negotiating the Tokyo Round was delegated to a small number of government officers who were responsible for protecting the interests of groups in a community, and the process of consulting with constituents was extended widely through the SAC system in order to receive a fair representation of all interests. The SAC's, by bringing constituent groups into the government process, helped the government to control the groups. The SAC system was a modern example of the Madisonian principle of republican government (which is no less valid for being circular): the government controls the people, but the people control the government.

Control of faction, or domestic interest groups, is a general problem of democratic government, but it is a special preoccupation of the American system. Students of comparative government from de Tocqueville onward have noted the tendency of the American society to form into associations to represent their interests to government.[56] Not accidentally, the U.S. government is organized in a manner that facilitates the representation of private interests to government. For example, Schattschneider himself noted that "It may be said of the American form of government that it places a premium on pressures and facilitates the expression of interests that could not gain recognition under another constitutional system."[57] However, because constituency pressures may be less intrusive in other systems than in the United States, it is wrong to conclude that control of internal pressures is any less problematic. The four largest actors in the Tokyo Round were all democracies, and democratic government everywhere presents its own problems of management. In a democratic system, policy is based essentially on the consent of the governed. In practice, this means that government policy must be nonarbitrary and must be convincing to those who are in a position to resist. For a democratic system to have the capacity to control its internal policymaking, it must have the ca-

[56] A more recent expression of this same notion has been advanced by Peter Katzenstein, who draws a distinction between a society-centered United States and a state-centered France. See "International Relations," esp. 15.

[57] Schattschneider further elaborated: "One of the consequences of the system of separation of powers has been to give the individual member of Congress an unprecedented initiative in legislation and to relax party discipline in Congress. The system has in this way given an unusual opening to pressures upon the members" (*Politics*, 291–92).

pacity to convince its influential constituents that the policy change is in their interest. The capacity for control is achieved in any democratic system through internal bargaining between those who would make changes to policy and those who would resist those changes. In the Tokyo Round, the process of internal bargaining was universal, but the form differed with the structure of the system in which the bargaining took place.

To raise the issue of control in negotiation leads to the question of what it is that must be controlled. Here the difference between the parties' internal negotiating behavior becomes important. In the Tokyo Round, there were three kinds of pressures arising in the domestic arena that the parties sought to control, but these pressures were not important in equal proportion to the four parties. These pressures arose from economic interest groups, such as the Canadian Manufacturers' Association and the U.S. textile industry; or from domestic bureaucratic institutions, such as the European-based Customs Cooperation Council and the MITI of Japan; or finally, from internal governments, such as national governments in the EC and provincial and state governments in Canada and the United States. In the United States, interest groups appeared to bring the most influential pressures, while internal governments brought the least. Domestic bureaucracies occupied the second ranking. In the EC, this ranking was reversed: the national governments of the Community were the source of the greatest pressure on EC external diplomacy, while the least amount of pressure, in relative terms, came from interest groups. In Japan, the most influential pressures appeared to come from the government bureaucracy, with interest groups in the second ranking. Internal government pressures were essentially nonexistent in Japanese trade negotiation. Finally, Canada presented a profile similar to the EC's: internal governments generated the most influential pressures, followed next by the organizations of the federal government bureaucracy and last by interest groups. Thus presented in approximate comparative terms were the pressures that negotiators from the various parties sought to control in order to negotiate the Tokyo Round. The need for control was the same, although differences in the form of the pressure gave rise to different negotiating strategies in the four systems.

Different pressures also led to different negotiating priorities. Territorial units, whether they were nation-states or provinces, received more attention from EC and Canadian negotiators than they did from negotiators from the United States and Japan. Similarly interest groups made a greater impact on U.S. government officials than they did on officials from the other three systems.[58] But the similarity of the problem the four parties faced, namely how to achieve control over domesic policymaking in order to arrive at a common position in the external negotiation, led to a functional equivalence of structures from one party to the next. In the United States, the SAC mechanism was established to manage constituency pressures that were uniquely American. There was nothing else quite like this mechanism, yet it functioned like the CCTN in Canada, which was created to manage the important pressures faced in that system. Then, too, the process of *engrenage* in the European Community, which was more like the Canadian than the American arrangement but nevertheless different from either, was the mechanism that functioned in that system to manage the most threatening of its internal pressures. Finally, parliamentary bureaucracy, coupled with an ad hoc steering mechanism at the top, was the arrangement Japan used to manage the pressures that the Tokyo Round created in that system. What proved similar about the four systems were the functions performed by the mechanisms that were set up to gain a capacity to make difficult decisions in a major external negotiation.

It is interesting to speculate what might have happened had the four major Tokyo Round participants not been able to establish effective machinery to control the internal negotiation. Clearly this is ultimately an unanswerable question, but nevertheless the Canadian case does shed some light on the matter. The CCTN was set up for the Tokyo Round, and there had been no counterpart to this mechanism in the Kennedy Round. In that earlier negotiation, the government did not have a way to carry on political communication with its influential constituents that was as effective as the CCTN. Now it is true that Canada did not make difficult departures in trade policy during the Kennedy Round, and hence the need for political communication may not have been acute. However, had there been the political will at the last minute to make far-reaching decisions on trade policy, one doubts whether the government would have had internal support. Without a mechanism to bargain effectively with its important constituents, the government might well have lacked the confidence to press ahead. And without the CCTN in the Tokyo Round, or its equivalent in other actors, Canada or the other major parties might not have been prepared to conclude the Tokyo Round agreements.

[58] A vignette from an interview underscored these differences. One EC official noted that negotiators for the EC would never disclose their line-by-line negotiating positions with constituent groups, as did American negotiators, because "European governments would not want to appear to be unduly influenced by lobbies."

The need for control is a normal preoccupation in all international negotiations, but it has a particular importance in trade negotiation. Loss of control in commercial negotiations between nations has often meant the surrender of wider, general interests to narrower, particular concerns. One could not find a better example of this phenomenon during the Tokyo Round than the statement of Japan's agricultural minister, Sakurauchi Yoshio, that liberalization of agricultural imports was "beyond my control."[59] In the past, loss of government control over economic foreign policy has led to even more striking occasions of the triumph of protectionism over a more liberal approach to trade. For example, in the policymaking that led to the Smoot-Hawley tariff in the United States, Schattschneider found that loss of governmental control over economic interests was the main contributing factor to the passage of this extremely protectionist trade legislation. Indeed his book was an attempt to insure that that incident was not repeated, for, in his words; "The philosophy of the attempt made in these pages is that the forces that are brought to bear on democratic government are not wholly beyond conscious control."[60] This is a philosophy that has also motivated my own research, and that apparently motivated as well many negotiators at the Tokyo Round.

[59] Fukui, "GATT Tokyo Round," 110.
[60] *Politics*, 292–93.

· 9 ·

EXPLANATION OF PROCESS AND RESULTS

The end of a negotiation in international relations rarely brings an end to the problems that brought about the negotiation in the first place. There are few areas of international relations, and especially not international trade, where major problems are of the once-and-for-all variety. Relationships in the international system are continuing, and so are the problems. Major negotiations like the Tokyo Round are not so much intended to settle problems as they are to provide an opportunity for a concentrated examination of the most vexing aspects of continuing relations. Of course, negotiators try to resolve the problems their nations face, either minimally through developing a new awareness of the other side's perceptions, or maximally through forging new agreements that will end certain points of conflict. But even when the maximum is attained, and a new, concrete, and apparently meaningful agreement is struck, there is a relativity to the affair that exasperates those who seek black-and-white solutions to life's problems. Even in cases where the wording of agreements is robust (which is often not the case), they must still be carried out in practice, and it is well known in diplomacy that those who draft agreements often postpone the most insoluble problems for those who must administer the agreements in the future.

The agreements reached at the Tokyo Round were intended to affect the behavior of government officials who make trade policy in the signatory countries, and thereby ultimately to affect the legal, political, and to some extent economic environment of those who actually engage in international trade. But the environment of international trade has a momentum of its own. International agreements are just one of the factors that affect the vast day-to-day operations of that environment. Then, too, the pressures that make it difficult to strike international agreements in the first place are still there when those agreements must be administered. Thus it is appropriate to ask, just as with new legislation within a nation-state, what effect the agreements will have on the system they are intended to influence. Because the system which the Tokyo Round sought to influence is large and because the accords themselves are not backed up by a single sovereign authority, their impact could be expected to be weaker and less easily demonstrable than the impact made by most national legislation.

Chapters 9 and 10 will attempt to evaluate and put in perspective the Tokyo Round accords. The first task will be to pick up the threads of the story after the spring of 1979 to examine how the various agreements were concluded and integrated into the GATT system. The focus will be on the implementation process, and on the substantive issue of the effect those agreements are likely to have on the international trading system. To what extent will the agreements ameliorate the trading problems of the 1970s for which they were created? Second, the process itself of the Tokyo Round negotiation will be evaluated. The Tokyo Round was a rich experience in multilateral negotiation, with an especially wide variety of negotiating behaviors, and important lessons about the negotiation process can be learned from studying it. Such lessons obviously concern the diplomatic process, but they are not confined to this, since ultimately process can never wholly be divorced from substance. For example, in the history of international trade in this century, liberal policies have been related to international negotiation, whereas protectionist policies have been related to individual national action. The lesson of the 1930s is that it can take but one nation to close down the international trading system, but it takes many acting cooperatively to open it. To respond to the challenges of maintaining an open world trade system, it is necessary to analyze and perfect those processes that help to produce it.

A third task of evaluation is to assess certain theories of the causes of liberal responses in the international trading system. The Tokyo Round was a signal occurrence in recent trade history, and it was clearly intended by those who negotiated it to be a liberalizing influence on trade relationships. The Tokyo Round negotiation can be used to better understand the trading system and the factors which lead to liberal responses in that system. Finally, in Chapter 10, the Tokyo Round will be evaluated from the perspective of the future, that is, in light of the trading problems that will be faced in the 1980s and beyond. The Tokyo Round was intended to revitalize GATT; in effect, to make a constitutional change in the multilateral system of international trade management. One can ask how well this constitutional change equipped GATT to manage international trade relationships in the coming years.

IMPLEMENTATION OF THE TOKYO ROUND AGREEMENTS

The Tokyo Round concluded in April 1979 with the signing of a procès-verbal, but this conclusion did not end the negotiation. Most of the codes were in final form by the April signing, but there were important exceptions. The most obvious exception was the failed safeguards code, on which intense discussions continued throughout the summer months of 1979. However, positions were locked in along the lines already described, and the best that could be salvaged was an agreement to constitute a committee to continue the negotiation in the future. Other exceptions included the customs valuation code and the revised antidumping code, where continuing disagreements between the developing and developed countries held up final approval of these agreements. In noncode areas, there was considerable further work, largely of a technical nature, to prepare the tariff agreements for final approval. Protocols containing formal schedules of concessions were drawn up and opened for acceptance in July and in November of 1979. The later agreement (i.e., supplementary protocol) included the results of further negotiations that improved the benefits to developing countries. Finally, discussions continued on the establishment of a multilateral consultative framework in agriculture, which had been recommended at the time of the signing of the procès-verbal in April. No agreement was reached on a formal mechanism, and in the end the best face that could be put on the matter was that "No country, however, disagreed that improved international co-operation in the agricultural sector was necessary and desirable."[1]

It will be recalled that the procès-verbal had included two texts on customs valuation, one complete text supported by most developed countries, and another containing revisions which the developing countries sought to have incorporated in the main text. The main points at issue continued to be trade between related parties, which reflected the general unease of the developing countries in dealing with transnational corporations. A principal concern of the developing countries was to retain sufficient regulatory flexibility in their customs procedures to offset any trading advantages that might accrue to exporters and importers that were related. Another concern was to provide customs officers with sufficient authority to examine the information presented to them for customs purposes. These concerns prompted the developing countries to propose a protocol to the customs valuation code that would ease the general requirement of accepting the transaction price as the primary basis for valuation. Among other things, the protocol deleted Article 1.2(b)(iv) of the code, under which customs officers were obliged to accept a transaction price if an importer could demonstrate that the price on that product closely approximated equivalent prices in sales between unrelated parties. Furthermore, it permitted developing-country signatories to disallow the

[1] GATT, *Supplementary Report*, 12.

importer's right to choose alternative valuation methods under Article 4 of the code. The protocol also elaborated the rights of customs officers to examine the truthfulness of any document presented for valuation purposes. The thrust of these changes was to increase the authority of customs administrators over what the code had originally provided, and in some cases to give developing countries certain specific advantages in applying the code. The protocol was intensely negotiated during the fall of 1979, and agreement was finally reached. The attachment of the protocol to the customs valuation code ended the threat of a fundamental split between the developing and developed countries in this area.

A second code which was renegotiated after April was the revised antidumping code. The original antidumping code had been negotiated at the Kennedy Round and entered into force on July 1, 1968. Its purpose was essentially to interpret the provisions of Article 6 of the GATT in order to insure greater uniformity of antidumping procedures among signatory nations. The United States was not included among the signatories to this code. Congress had objected sharply to the differences between the code and U.S. law on the degree of injury required for a finding of dumping (the code required "material injury"), and consequently refused to ratify the agreement. In the Tokyo Round, the main task for the negotiators was to revise the existing antidumping code to be consistent with the code on subsidy/countervail, particularly as to specifics on the determination of injury and on price undertakings between exporters and importing countries. A further task that motivated especially the Europeans and Canadians was to insure that the United States brought its antidumping legislation into line with the revised code, particularly through the insertion of a material-injury test.[2]

The revised code was completed and included in the procès-verbal of April 1979. However, a problem arose when the developing countries tabled a reservation to the code on the matter of determining "normal" prices for products exported by developing countries. Dumping is the selling of goods in foreign markets at prices below fair market value in the exporting country. To assess antidumping duties, an importing country must determine a normal price in the exporting country, which is then compared with the traded price in the importing country. The developing countries as a bloc argued that because of small domestic markets and other factors, prices in developing countries could not form a realistic basis for developed countries' dumping calculations. The developing countries pressed this position in the post-April nego-

[2] See generally Lorenzen, "Anti-Dumping Agreement."

tiations, and won an addendum to the revised code that permitted a determination of dumping in the case of developing countries to be based on export prices to third countries, rather than being based on normal domestic prices. A further addendum was negotiated that allowed developing countries to receive on a case-by-case basis exceptions to the administrative requirements that bore on antidumping investigations. On the basis of these addenda, the developing countries withdrew their reservations and the revised antidumping code received GATT approval in November 1979.[3]

The final act of the Tokyo Round negotiation occurred at a session of the contracting parties on November 28, 1979. The task for this meeting was to integrate the Tokyo Round results, which included eleven major international agreements,[4] in the structure of the GATT. The problem was that, of the eleven agreements, only two (the tariff protocols and the framework agreements) were inherently part of the GATT structure. The remaining nine agreements were all separate treaties which, theoretically at least, could exist independently of the GATT.[5] The negotiation followed this legal procedure in order to avoid conference rules that might require all agreements to be approved by consensus or by two-thirds of all GATT contracting parties. In legal terms, the codes were to take effect between the signatories to the agreements, which then opened the possibility that a limited number of GATT members could agree to interpret and apply GATT law in a manner that affected the interests of remaining members. These legal rules had made possible the aforementioned pyramidal style of negotiation at the Tokyo Round, whereby negotiations were initiated by the major nations and flowed downward to include other nations only after important decisions had been made and compromises had been struck. This style of negotiation caused resentment, particularly among the developing countries which were most frequently excluded from the process. In the judgment of a former GATT official, this style was a larger factor in causing the developing countries to voice objections to the Tokyo Round than was the substantive result of the negotiation.[6] Thus the problem for the GATT session of November 1979 was both legal and political: how to integrate the Tokyo Round accords into the GATT legal framework in the context of a political process that had left the majority of the GATT membership frustrated and alienated.

[3] The full title of the code was "Agreement on Implementation of Article VI of the General Agreement on Tariffs and Trade."

[4] The eleven agreements are listed and marked by asterisks (*) in the bibliography.

[5] See Jackson, "GATT Machinery," 172.

[6] See Patterson, "European Community," 232.

The legal problem was even more profound than it appeared on the surface. It is well recognized that the GATT rests on the foundation of the Article 1 obligation to extend unconditional MFN (most-favored nation) treatment to all members. In practice, this foundation has been weakened by the establishment of various bilateral and/or preference arrangements under GATT, until by the 1970s the GATT norm could be more precisely described as conditional MFN treatment. The Tokyo Round codes extended this trend toward conditionality in MFN treatment. Although individual nations could apply the codes unconditionally to all members, in fact the codes themselves specify that participation in the organs set up under the codes was limited to the signatories to the agreement. Nonsignatories were thus denied the benefits of the agreements, among which could be the capacity to participate in decisions that could reinterpret the GATT and therefore affect their legal rights under the General Agreement. Furthermore in two cases—the government-procurement and subsidy/countervail codes—the substantive benefits of the agreements were intended to apply only to signatories. For example, the access to government tendering which was extended in the former code was available only to firms in other signatory countries, while on the latter code nations like the United States made the injury test in countervail procedures contingent on the acceptance by other countries of the code's disciplines on subsidies. It is debatable whether the movement toward conditional MFN treatment was sound policy for the GATT system as a whole, but it was undeniable that this policy created a legal problem in rendering the Tokyo Round codes consistent with the General Agreement.[7]

The concerns of those GATT contracting parties which did not initially sign the Tokyo Round accords (principally the developing countries) were addressed in the GATT session of November 1979. In a tense environment, the members adopted a decision which took note of the Tokyo Round accords and which also reaffirmed the legal and procedural rights of GATT members vis-à-vis the codes.[8] Furthermore, the decision insured the right of nonsignatories to participate in the various code committees in an observer capacity. The latter point was a clear victory for the developing countries; it had been resisted by the developed countries on the grounds that it would diminish the confidentiality and efficiency of committee procedures. With this decision, the To-

[7] See Hufbauer et al., "GATT Codes."

[8] The decision is reproduced in Annex 7 of GATT, *Supplementary Report.* It stated that the "existing rights and benefits under the GATT of contracting parties not being parties to these [Tokyo Round] Agreements . . . are not affected by these Agreements" (p. 47).

kyo Round was officially concluded by the GATT, and attention turned to implementing the various code agreements.

Implementation of the Tokyo Round results went forward on three levels. First, there was the purely organizational task of carrying out the procedural requirements of the codes. All codes entered into effect by January 1981, and each required that a committee of signatories be established, along with rules of procedure, to put the code machinery into operation. These tasks occupied national representatives and GATT staffers through the end of 1980. By early 1981, all code committees had held at least one meeting and had resolved issues such as the future work program and the arrangements for participation of observers. In most cases, the initial meetings were spent in reviewing plans for gathering information from signatory governments and in simply setting up the committee machinery at the GATT level.

At a second level, the codes were implemented by monitoring the different national procedures for putting the codes into practice. By the end of 1982, forty nations had signed one or more of the Tokyo Round agreements, including twelve developing countries.[9] In most cases, implementation was straightforward, but the procedure could raise difficult issues. The question of whether a nation had accepted the legal obligations of an agreement was usually not at issue, since this was a legal act that was communicated formally to GATT. However, uncertainty could exist over the extent to which a code was directly applied in the domestic law of a signatory country. Another question dealt with the administrative machinery to administer the code. Some agreements like the government-procurement code required that countries applying the code take administrative action to make their acceptance meaningful, such as providing foreign contractors with information on tendering procedures. The code committees monitored the progress of such administrative procedures to insure that code implementation was consistent in the various countries.

At a third level, the Tokyo Round agreements called for the establishment of dispute-settlement procedures. It has been estimated that the Tokyo Round increased the juridical competence of GATT about fourfold or more,[10] and much of this has been in the area of dispute settlement. Each of the Tokyo Round agreements (bar the tariff and framework agreements) contains a dispute-settlement mechanism, ranging from a simple commitment to consult, as found in the bovine-meat agreement, to the formal mechanism for adjudication contained

[9] *GATT Activities in 1982*, Geneva: GATT, 1983, 86–87.
[10] Jackson "GATT Machinery," 165.

in the subsidy/countervail code. These procedures potentially overlap with each other, and they certainly overlap with existing dispute-settlement procedures of GATT. This creates the possibility for disputants to seek out those arenas ("forum shopping") where they have the best opportunity for success. The code dispute-settlement procedures have not been heavily used; through 1982 there were only two cases completed, both, significantly, involving complaints by the United States against EC agricultural subsidies. There has been a tendency in dispute-settlement procedures to continue old arguments that were aired earlier in the Tokyo Round, and the Committee on Subsidies and Countervailing Measures has not been noticeably more effective in defining the limits of permissible subsidies than was the earlier negotiation. The same has also been true in other areas. For example, the United States attempted to bring a case against the United Kingdom on the grounds that a processing requirement for chilling chicken did not apply equally to U.S. and British producers, with resulting injury to U.S. exports. The United States tried to raise this issue under the standards code, but received a ruling that standards could apply only to a product itself and not to productive "processes." This ruling rebuffed a U.S. attempt to expand the competence of the code, although the United States subsequently successfully raised the dispute under Article 3 (National Treatment) of the General Agreement itself.[11]

The crucial test of the success of the Tokyo Round agreements will not come on the establishment of international diplomatic procedures, however important or necessary these procedures may be. Rather the test will be on the effect of the agreements on national trade policies, and ultimately on trading behavior between nations. How the codes are working in this realm is difficult to say, and it is probably too early to advance a balanced assessment. However, some indications are available in the work that has taken place since the agreements came into effect.

The codes that were technical in nature, namely customs valuation, standards, and import licensing, have all been brought into force with a minimum of difficulty and appear to be operating effectively. In customs valuation, the technical adjustments within customs services were done promptly after the Tokyo Round ended, and it is estimated that over 90 percent of all valuations for customs purposes in signatory countries are now made on the basis of transaction prices. As Sidney Golt has noted in an assessment of the Tokyo Round, there have been

[11] "EEC/United States: Imports of Poultry into the United Kingdom from the United States," *GATT Activities in 1980* Geneva: GATT, 1981, 50–51.

few complaints about the operations of the code from traders, who would have been adversely affected had the code not worked well. The same thing can be said for the standards code, although here the procedures are more complex and will take longer to put fully into practice. What has been achieved to this point is greater transparency regarding the technical regulations that are applied within signatory governments, and this will give exporters a clearer picture of the government and nongovernment rules that affect their commercial activities. Finally, with regard to the import-licensing code, work has gone ahead in approving the transparency of licensing procedures, and particularly on getting the signatories to provide information through official publications to traders regarding the current status of quota allocations of products subject to licensing requirements. There have been complaints by the Europeans against the Japanese in this area, but these claims probably lack sufficient substance to warrant formal dispute-settlement procedures.

In the areas where the Tokyo Round made little headway, namely agriculture and safeguards, little progress has likewise been made since the end of the negotiation. The agreements on bovine meat and dairy products were weak to begin with, and while the signatories to these agreements have carried out the information exchanges and other endeavors that were called for, little effort has been made to deepen cooperation on agricultural matters. Indeed agriculture was one of the main subjects under examination at the 1982 GATT ministerial session, but even this concentrated attention produced no additional significant undertakings on agriculture by GATT members.[12] Regarding safeguards, a GATT committee continued to collect information through notifications of the various safeguarding measures taken by members, but no further progress has been made toward a common approach to the matter. One official characterized the post–Tokyo Round position on the safeguards code as "dead in the water," and indicated that the best nations could do was to seek stopgap measures in this area.

The two most important agreements in the Tokyo Round were the codes on government procurement and subsidy/countervail, the former being important for economic reasons and the latter for political reasons. Worthwhile progress has been made on the government-procurement code, particularly on national-government implementation of measures designed to increase transparency and to improve the flow of information to foreigners bidding on government contracts. For ex-

[12] For a brief review of the 1982 GATT ministerial meeting, see Graham, "Global Trade", and Winham, "New Trade World."

ample, in Canada, where foreign officials and businessmen have complained about a secretive procurement process, the government has advertised an additional $1 million in government contracts in the official *Canada Gazette*, and it has released a six-volume supply policy manual hitherto unavailable to the public.[13] For Japan and the United States, continuing efforts to negotiate a telecommunications agreement that would implement the procurement opportunities offered by the government-procurement code finally bore fruit in late 1980. As part of this telecommunications agreement, Japan agreed to open to foreign bidding all of the telecommunications procurement of the Nippon Telephone and Telegraph Corporation (NTT), which was valued at over $3 billion.[14] U.S. officials have commented privately that the Japanese have been scrupulous in carrying out this agreement and have provided seminars and orientation tours for U.S. companies on effective marketing techniques in Japan. It is still too early to get a clear picture of the results of this and other government initiatives in the procurement field in terms of new orders for foreign bidders. Business behavior is slow to change in the aggregate. However, procurement remains the largest opportunity for liberalized trade that was initiated by the Tokyo Round, and it is apparent that governments are moving to exploit the potential created by the new code.

The subsidy/countervail code has the reputation of being the least effective of the Tokyo Round codes.[15] This is due in part to the attention that has focused on certain disputes over this code between the United States and its trading partners. In the first place, the United States has used the threat of countervailing duties to persuade developing nations to subscribe to the subsidy/countervail code. These efforts themselves have received attention. In addition, the fact that they have been applied inconsistently, thus opening the United States to counterpressure, has further increased the publicity. For example, the United States accepted Pakistan's accession to the code and in turn accepted the obligation not to countervail against Pakistan's exports without first applying an injury test, on the basis of a weak commitment by Pakistan to eliminate its subsidies. In the case of India, the United States demanded

---

[13] Fred Harrison, "Doors Open to Foreign Suppliers," *Financial Post*, April 4, 1981.

[14] Mike Tharp, "US in Tentative Accord on Japan Procurement," *New York Times*, December 6, 1980.

[15] For example, Deputy Director General William B. Kelly of GATT has stated that the code on subsidies and countervailing measures is not working well and therefore has received most public attention, ("Satisfactory Implementation of Most Tokyo Round Agreements" [summary of remarks by William B. Kelly], *GATT Focus*, no. 27 [January–February 1984], 2).

a stronger commitment on subsidies.[16] Concurrently with this action, the United States also initiated countervailing duties on subsidized industrial fasteners (nuts and bolts) coming from India. India responded by commencing formal dispute proceedings against the United States, on the ground that the conditional application of its subsidy/countervail code obligation violated the code and Article 1 of the GATT. Before the dispute was heard, the United States and India resolved their difference and India dropped formal proceedings. With regard to other disputes involving the subsidy/countervail code, it was noted earlier that the United States has initiated several complaints against EC agricultural subsidies, two of which have been formally heard in the dispute-settlement procedures of the subsidy/countervail code. These cases raised the same kinds of jurisdictional and definitional problems that were present when the code was first written, and which led to the code's relatively weak obligation on subsidies. The dispute-settlement process has not resolved these problems, but has instead contributed to pessimism over this aspect of the Tokyo Round results.[17]

It is clear that subsidies will continue to be a problem in international trade. Recent OECD statistics indicate that the United States resorts to government subsidies substantially less than other industrial nations, and as a result has an objective reason to feel aggrieved by the trade-distorting aspects of these practices.[18] How to resolve this discrepancy between the United States and its trading partners is not immediately obvious. While it might be politically satisfying to some if the United States were to conform to international practice on this matter, the fact

[16] See Michael T. Kaufman, "U.S.-India Trade Talks Fail on Tariff Issue," *New York Times*, August 27, 1980, and Clyde H. Farnsworth, "Panel to Hear U.S.-India Trade Dispute," *New York Times*, November 3, 1980. The U.S. demands on India were prompted by commitments made to Congress during the passage of the Trade Act of 1979 to use the threat of countervailing duties as a bargaining chip to reduce subsidies in developing countries. Regarding the different treatment of India and Pakistan, U.S. officials claimed that India's greater industrial capacity warranted different treatment, but it was widely suggested that the Carter administration had treated Pakistan more leniently because of foreign-policy considerations having to do with the situation in Afghanistan.

[17] In May and June of 1983, the Committee on Subsidies and Countervailing Measures considered reports of panels on pasta products and wheat flour brought by the United States against the European Community. On the first, the majority of the panel found the subsidies in question to be inconsistent with the subsidy/countervail code; on the second, the panel could not determine whether subsidies had resulted in the EC "having more than an equitable share" of world trade in that product. The subsequent discussion in the committee reached no conclusion on what further action should be taken pursuant to the two reports. See "Subsidies and Countervailing Measures," *GATT Focus*, no. 22 (June–July 1983), 4.

[18] Hufbauer, "Subsidy Issues," esp. 328–32.

is that economic pressures and the probability of trade disputes would increase were it to do so.[19] There is an argument that the economic costs of subsidies will begin to weaken the commitment of governments to these practices, but any such change would be long in coming and would not remove at all the political reasons why governments find it necessary to subsidize. There is little to be expected short of continued division of opinion over subsidies, and the important question is to what extent GATT and the subsidy/countervail code procedures will be able to manage those divisions. On this matter, GATT practice may offer some hope. Trade in steel products has been a longstanding problem between the United States and the European Community, and in the early 1980s U.S. complaints about European subsidies in this industry have become increasingly strident. Although GATT has not been formally involved in this controversy, one meeting was held at GATT on this issue during the summer of 1982. The meeting was a serious, unemotional discussion of what constitutes a subsidy under the subsidy/countervail code and on what grounds such subsidies could be countervailed, and it was, in the words of one official, "one of the best meetings I ever attended in my life." It is obviously hard to assess in precise terms the value of such meetings (although the same official noted that subsequent to the meeting the United States reduced by half its calculation of countervailing duties), but nevertheless one assumes that such meetings have a positive value in resolving conflicting views over the long run. In this sense, the subsidy/countervail code may be an important political mechanism in the contemporary unsettled trade world, even if it has not been successful to date in influencing government behavior on subsidy practices.

At this point, the analysis comes back around to the question posed for this section: How well did the Tokyo Round negotiation settle the trade problems of the 1970s? The answer, as it often is in diplomacy, is mixed. First, the Tokyo Round removed certain elements of U.S. trade law which were anomalies when measured against common international practice, and therefore were irritants to America's trading partners. These elements included the American Selling Price, the lack of an injury test in countervail and antidumping procedures, and the wine-gallon method of assessing liquor taxes. The world trading system is substantially more stable and more resilient politically without these ir-

[19] This has already happened, for a GATT panel has been established to hear an EC complaint against U.S. sales of wheat flour to Egypt at subsidized terms. See *GATT Focus*, no. 22, 4.

ritants, and the United States is hardly worse off economically without them. In the future, it may be the turn of other parties to rid the system of irritants; the agricultural export subsidies of the EC may be the place to start. Second, on multilateral agricultural arrangements and safeguards, the Tokyo Round essentially failed. Both were important failures. Agriculture is the area of most intense controversy between the developed nations in the trading system, and, like the Balkans at the turn of this century, it is the place in the system where conflict could most easily touch off a much wider war. In a similar fashion, safeguards is the area of most intense conflict between the developing and the developed countries in the international trade system. This issue will have to be resolved if ever the developing countries are to be fully integrated into GATT.

Third, on subsidies, the Tokyo Round made institutional and political progress at the international level, but it did not influence the behavior of governmental actors in the international trade system. The institutional mechanisms of the subsidy/countervail code will likely provide a diplomatic means to remove some of the heat from this trade irritant in the future, and it may have some influence on governmental behavior in the longer run. Fourth, the Tokyo Round was an overt attempt by the GATT members to create a more liberal and open trading system. This attempt was achieved essentially in the tariff negotiation, in some bilateral agreements, in the code on civil aircraft, and in the code on government procurement. The last code obviously has the greatest potential for international trade liberalization. It will take persistent administrative action at the national level to achieve this potential, and this action is ongoing. Fifth, in addition to creating freer trade, the Tokyo Round was also an overt attempt to create a system of fair trade, which means a reduction in the scope for arbitrary government constraints on international trade. To an important extent, the codes on customs valuation, technical barriers to trade (standards), and import licensing, as well as the transparency provisions of the government-procurement code, accomplished this objective. Uncertainty and unpredictability are inherent in the economics of international trade, but the problem is compounded when traders confront uncertainty from political factors as well. Without a measure of predictability, business cannot plan, and international trade is thereby reduced. The Tokyo Round codes will help to increase the predictability and stability of the political environment within which trade is conducted.

Finally, the Tokyo Round must be assessed in terms of the absence of negatives, for it was an exercise in damage limitation. The Tokyo Round was initiated in the context of the U.S. emergency monetary measures of 1971, and it was a means for the United States and the European countries to extricate themselves from the untenable situation caused by those measures. Without that possibility, there easily could have been a trade war. But that is not all. Added to the monetary confrontation between the Americans and the Europeans were the oil shocks and severe recession of the mid-1970s. These events alone could have produced intolerable pressures in the international trade system. It is well known that multilateral trade negotiations are an important deterrent to national protectionist measures; in retrospect, there is little doubt that the Tokyo Round offered a rationale for governments to avoid taking protectionist actions during the 1970s. The irony is that, while the economic crises of the 1970s made it a bad time to negotiate trade, the trade negotiation made it a good time to have a crisis. The upheavals of the 1970s were not as damaging to international trade or the GATT system as they could have been, and in all probability the main reason was the existence of the Tokyo Round negotiation.

THE TOKYO ROUND AND THE PROCESS OF NEGOTIATION

Negotiation and International Trade

Since 1934, the trade policy of the Western nations has increasingly been made through international negotiation. In that year, the United States commenced the Reciprocal Trade Agreements Program. This program involved the negotiation of a large number of bilateral trade agreements, which were then extended multilaterally under the MFN procedure. In 1947, this process was formalized and expanded with the signing of the General Agreement. The GATT itself was a result of negotiation, and in turn it promoted multilateral tariff negotiation as a major instrument of trade policy. The Tokyo Round continued this trend, and advanced it by developing the capacity to negotiate NTM's (nontariff measures). In this continuous upward trend in the use of international negotiation, there are two questions that can be asked by way of taking stock of this process: What influence has the use of negotiation had on international trade policy; and what influence has international trade had on international negotiation? In short, what is the interaction between substance and process?

In examining these questions, it is useful to bear two things in mind. First, international negotiation in the postwar period has been associated in the main with liberal trade policy, and protectionism has been associated with unilateral national action. The demands for protectionist policy have been generated at the grassroots level, and their appeal has tended to be emotional and nationalist. The demands for liberal policy have been generated at the national level, and their appeal has tended to be analytical and internationalist. A second point is that although there are strong historical and even logical reasons why liberal trade policy should be associated with negotiation, it is not an inevitable relationship. Liberal policy could be made unilaterally (indeed many economists would recommend this), or it could be made through cooperative processes other than formal negotiation, such as participation in supranational bureaucracy or in judicial proceedings like dispute settlement. Negotiation is only one method and it may not be the best one for some purposes.

One effect of the use of negotiation is to put extraordinary emphasis on reciprocity in the conduct of trade policy. Reciprocity is normally a good thing, and a concern for reciprocity can help avoid the enormous damage to the international trading system that can occur when nations act only on the basis of narrow self-interest. However, a policy of strict reciprocity can be threatening to a liberal trade order because it ultimately strikes at the concept of comparative advantage.[20] Even with the best of intentions, reciprocity can introduce distortions and lack of coherence into trade policy. For example, it was noted in chapter 7 that the pursuit of reciprocal exchanges by means of necessarily artificial tariff-cutting formulas occasionally led to sharp discontinuities in tariff negotiations. In the code negotiations, reciprocity led negotiators to demand payment for the actions they took, regardless of whether those actions were more beneficial to the initiator or to the supposed recipients. An unfortunate result of an emphasis on reciprocity is that it better facilitates making trade policy between parties that are equal than between those that are unequal. Thus in the Tokyo Round, the U.S. demand that it be paid for dropping the American Selling Price or the wine-gallon assessment could be accommodated by the EC, but there was less scope to accommodate the demand of the developing countries for special and differential treatment within the negotiation. In the past, negotiation has been important in promoting a stable world trading order. However, with its emphasis on reciprocity, negotiation may be a less useful tool in the future for managing problems like graduation between the developed and developing countries, or for integrating the developing countries fully into the world trading system.

A second effect of negotiation has been to move nations toward a

[20] For a discussion of the policy of reciprocity as it was proposed in the U.S. Congress in the early 1980s, see Cline, "Reciprocity."

rule-oriented rather than a power-oriented international trade policy.[21] International trade can be manipulated, especially by large countries, to increase national power.[22] Fortunately the present trading system is sufficiently developed along the lines of rule-based cooperative interaction to avoid the worst excesses of power-based economic diplomacy. However, the rules produced through negotiation create their own problems. In a political system, rules are intended to produce order, certainty, and simplicity. However, when large multilateral negotiations are held to establish rules, there is pressure from the momentum of the process to agree on something, but the sheer number of parties and multiplicity of interests make it difficult to produce results that are orderly, certain, or simple. Many diverse interests must be accommodated, with the result that political documents or treaties that flow from such negotiations are often conflicted or confusing. A solution may be to give greater scope for customary practice to reform the rules of the international trading system at the expense of formal, rule-writing multilateral negotiations. In short, it may be desirable to disaggregate some aspects of the process of making changes to the GATT. It is possible a more active dispute-settlement process flowing from the Tokyo Round accords might be able to accomplish this function.

On the other side of the equation, the negotiation of trade has also had an effect on international negotiation processes. Trade, along with war, has been an engine of diplomacy throughout history,[23] and one can see in modern commercial diplomacy the capacity of trade to make changes, and even improvements, in diplomatic methods. For example, it should be recalled from chapter 2 that at the end of the Kennedy Round NTM's were regarded as too difficult to negotiate. Whatever else, the Tokyo Round demonstrated the capacity of international negotiation to handle, eventually, issues of great complexity.

Negotiation of trade, as opposed to political issues, has moved diplomacy in the direction of the management of technical issues. This has reduced, but obviously not eliminated, the importance of cultural and other emotional concerns such as nationalism in negotiation, and it has increased the importance of bureaucracy, delegation management, and information handling. It has historically been common to describe negotiation as a process of psychological manipulation, and indeed Anwar Sadat, former president of Egypt, reinforced this viewpoint by describing Middle East negotiations as "70 percent psychological."

---

[21] These terms are borrowed from Jackson, "GATT-MTN System," who speaks of rule-oriented versus power-oriented trade diplomacy (esp. p. 27).

[22] See especially Hirschmann, *National Power*, esp. ch. 2.

[23] This argument is developed in Numelin, *Beginnings of Diplomacy*.

However, this probably would not describe most trade negotiations, where the emphasis is more on the organizational component than on the psychological. Symbolic issues and psychological barriers do find their way into trade negotiations, but they tend to stick out as anomalies rather than blending in as an ordinary part of the process.

Trade has promoted the non-conflictual aspects of negotiation and also multilateral negotiation, and the two are probably correlated. Nonconflictual negotiation, that is, where violent conflict is not an obvious alternative to the diplomatic process, is the norm in most trade negotiations. In the trade negotiations conducted under GATT, nations cannot improve their bargaining position by threatening hostilities; usually the greatest threat available to the parties is to refuse to cooperate, or possibly to withdraw a concession previously given. Trade also promotes multilateral negotiation because the relative absence of conflict permits the rise of multipolar interests, something that is not possible when conflict is more intense. As conflict increases in a situation, it tends to bilateralize relationships, a proposition which can immediately be appreciated in the difficulty of conceiving of a multipolar war. There can be a clear linkage between negotiation and conflict, such that under some circumstances one can almost serve as a substitute for the other in the achievement of national goals. Harold Nicolson appreciated this linkage when he elaborated the "warrior" theory of diplomacy, that is, diplomatic behavior that "regards diplomacy as war by another means."[24] But such a linkage seems less plausible in the case of multilateral negotiation. If there were to be analogies made between multilateral negotiation like the Tokyo Round and other forms of political behavior, they would be directed more toward processes occurring within nation-states than between nation-states. Thus trade has helped move international negotiation away from its traditional close relationship with coercive diplomacy and more in the direction of the policymaking process found in the institutions of parliamentary democracy.

An important goal of the Tokyo Round was to maintain control over the international trading system, and to build a cooperative structure that would contain competitive actions by individual nations. The task was the management of a relationship, even more than the distribution of specific benefits. Now managing relationships is not an exclusive concern of modern trade negotiations, and one can see aspects of this concern evident in negotiations such as SALT, which were bilateral talks over security matters and consequently very different from the Tokyo

[24] *Diplomacy*, 25.

Round. Yet management objectives (that is, the establishment of general rules of conduct) appear to be increasingly important in trade negotiation today, at the expense of processes that simply distribute benefits to parties or resolve differences between them. Thus trade has tended to add an institution-building, or regime-building, aspect to international negotiation to balance the more traditional role it has had in conflict resolution and mediation.[25]

Comparisons across Issue Areas

The Tokyo Round presented a rich laboratory for studying negotiating behavior. There were eleven formal multilateral agreements negotiated at the Tokyo Round, and each was negotiated separately, usually by separate persons. In addition, there were numerous bilateral or plurilateral agreements negotiated, of which the deal on the wine-gallon tax method was the most prominent. In this enormous diversity of negotiating behavior, one has an opportunity for comparative analysis that is not available in most case studies of international negotiation.

What obvious differences in negotiation process were observed at the Tokyo Round? One was the difference between negotiation over words, as was usually found in the code negotiations, and negotiation over numbers, which was found in the bargaining over tariffs or the wine-gallon tax method. Because numbers are usually more precise than words, they led to a negotiating style that emphasized strict reciprocity in terms of items exchanged. Whether that reciprocity was meaningful in broader terms appeared to be a separate question. By comparison, words admit of greater nuance than numbers, and therefore they promoted a bargaining style that was more flexible and more exploratory. In terms of the literature on negotiation, the differences between negotiation over numbers and over words have been ably captured in the theory of distributive versus integrative bargaining advanced by Walton and McKersie.[26] One conclusion that these authors reach is that negotiation is usually intense and agreement difficult in distributive situations, a finding that would be confirmed by this research.

The code negotiations prompted another variation in the negotiating process, namely the difference between multilateral negotiations of a

[25] There is an apparent similarity between negotiations on issues like trade and the establishment of cooperative international regimes, which are defined in part as rules and decisionmaking procedures around which actors' expectations can converge. See Keohane, *After Hegemony*, esp. ch. 5.
[26] *Labor Negotiations*.

common document and bilateral negotiations on the basis of individual requests and offers. The latter negotiations occurred on agricultural products, in the tariff negotiation, and in the negotiations over the entities to be included by individual nations under the government-procurement code. Bilateral negotiations tended to be characterized by a cagey search for one quid pro quo after another, and they were often a slower and more deliberate process than the code negotiations. By contrast, the multilateral code negotiations put a greater premium on early initiative and later flexibility. They were more difficult to organize and conduct than bilateral negotiations, and unlike the latter they tended to place more emphasis on organizational management than on the strategic calculation of cost and benefit.

A third bargaining variation noted in the Tokyo Round involved the process of reaching agreement. Agreement in negotiation has often been portrayed as a process of concession and convergence, where parties move in a reciprocal step-by-step fashion from opening positions to concluding settlement. This process is gradual and essentially orderly, and it puts a premium on modification of the other party's utilities through persuasion and timely concession.[27] An alternative view is that parties reach agreement by negotiating a formula that reconciles their major differences and which then serves as a framework for later incorporating the details of the agreement.[28] By way of shorthand, the former process is known as concession/convergence; the latter as formula/detail. In the Tokyo Round, as already noted, there were examples of both of these processes. The most clear-cut example of concession/convergence was the negotiation of the standards code, which proceeded step by step on the basis of innumerable technical drafts which gradually incorporated the various positions of the parties and closed the gap between them. The most clear-cut example of formula/detail was the negotiation of the subsidies/countervail code, in which a major tradeoff and breakthrough were achieved between U.S. and EC negotiators, after which further details of the agreement were worked out in subsequent exchanges between the two major parties and the other participants in that negotiation. Other Tokyo Round negotiations exhibited the characteristics of both these ideal-type bargaining models. For example, the import-licensing code and the framework agreements essentially proceeded on the basis of an orderly progression of negotiating drafts, while the customs valuation code essentially re-

[27] The analysis by Iklé and Leites, "Political Negotiation," is a good example of the concession-and-convergence approach.
[28] See Zartman and Berman, *Practical Negotiator*, esp. 9–15.

quired a major reformulating initiative by the EC which then served as a formula around which parties could coalesce and find agreement.

Having identified some differences that occurred in the Tokyo Round negotiating process, the next question is: What accounts for these differences? The answer appears to lie not in the negotiating process itself, but rather in the substance of what was being negotiated, and possibly in the importance that the parties attached to that substance. For example, the process of tariff negotiation, which has some unique aspects, was largely determined by the fact that tariffs are quantifiable, comparable, aggregatable, and negotiable between dyads in an otherwise multilateral situation. Were these substantive characteristics to change, the process of negotiating tariffs would likely change as well. The code negotiations proceeded differently from the tariff negotiation largely because they involved bargaining over oral undertakings; and they proceeded differently from bilateral negotiations because they involved issues of multilateral concern, on which alliance behavior could take place. In both cases, the difference was mainly one of substance. Finally, in the negotiation on the government procurement code, the process changed entirely within the same negotiation because of the discontinuities in the substance under discussion.

The processes by which agreement was reached on the various codes also differed because of the substance being negotiated. In the subsidy/countervail code, there was an enormous substantive dispute between the United States and the European Community over the use of subsidies and countervailing duties; until some basic compromise could be reached, it was impossible to proceed on the wording of a general agreement. On standards, however, there was no comparable issue of substance on which the parties were likely to have profound difficulties. Hence the substance itself helped lead to an orderly and low-keyed negotiation. These various examples remind the analyst that what is being negotiated is an important determinant of how it is negotiated. This fact places an important limitation on the capacity of theorists to establish general propositions about negotiation that are at the same time meaningful for specific situations of negotiation.[29]

In the discussion of differences in the patterns of negotiation that occurred at the Tokyo Round, one should not overlook the similarities that existed in the various arenas. One issue that came up repeatedly

[29] Further discussion of this point can be found in Lord McCarthy's critique of the attempt by Roger Fisher and William Ury to develop a general model of negotiation. See William McCarthy, "The Role of Power and Principle in *Getting to Yes*," *Negotiation Journal* 1, no. 1 (January 1985), 59–66. See also Fisher's rebuttal ("Beyond *Yes*") in the same volume.

was the importance that definitions had in shaping the negotiation process. The act of giving names to political or economic constructs is usually not value-free, and the definitions that are associated can have operational implications for the parties that use them. Negotiations are often struggles over whose values will prevail, and what operational obligations the parties will have toward one another; and hence questions of definition are likely to be among the most pervasive and bitterly fought issues in the whole process. For example, how one defined a developing country for legal and operational purposes was faced in the debate over graduation, and it was never fully resolved during the negotiation. Nations had difficulty defining domestic as opposed to export subsidies, and indeed the subsidy code goes only a short distance on this critical matter. The U.S. Congress tied itself in knots trying to define material injury. Nations eventually failed to give an operational definition to quantitative restrictions, and had to give up altogether the attempt to negotiate a code in this area. Finally, the whole subject of customs valuation was a matter of how, and by whom, economic value would be defined for traded goods. In the context of these difficulties in achieving operational definitions, the establishment of the inventory of NTM's, discussed in chapter 2, was indeed a signal accomplishment. The inventory was an organizational accomplishment, but at a more profound level it was a linguistic, and therefore a political, accomplishment. The inventory helped change the debate from a discussion of undifferentiated and therefore unactionable NTM's to an examination of specific types of NTM's, on which action could be, and later was, undertaken.

Definitions were at once a petty and yet a profound part of the Tokyo Round negotiating process. One could not have understood that process without dealing with this issue, just as one cannot appreciate much of political behavior without taking account of cognitive perception, or, more simply, the "definition of the situation."[30] The current literature on perception in political behavior is voluminous, but it is indeed an ancient subject of political commentary. Perhaps the most lasting reminder of the importance of this subject to the process of governing comes from the ancient philosopher Confucius, who was asked: "If the Prince of Wei were waiting for the Master to administer his government, what would you place first on your agenda?" The answer was as follows:

[30] The phrase "definition of the situation" comes from a pioneering but now dated analysis of foreign policymaking, namely Snyder, Bruck, and Sapin (eds.), *Foreign Policy Decision Making*. For a more recent analysis of perception in international relations, see Jervis, *Perception and Misperception*.

Of indispensable importance would be to render all designations
accurately. . . . If the designations are not accurate, language will
not be clear. If language is not clear, duties will not be carried out.
. . . Hence when Great Man has given something a name it may
with all certainty be expressed in language; when he expresses it,
it may with certainty be set in operation.[31]

External and Internal Negotiation

Other generalizations that can be gleaned from the Tokyo Round negotiation deal in part with the external negotiating process between nations and the internal process within nations. At the outset, one should
keep in mind that the multilateral aspect of the Tokyo Round had enormous impact on the bargaining process. The essence of multilateral negotiation is that what other parties do between themselves affects one's
own position with each of them, and hence ultimately affects one's own
interests. It is in this sense that GATT tariff negotiations, which in fact
are usually conducted bilaterally between principal suppliers and principal consumers of specific products, are nevertheless multilateral negotiations. It should be obvious, given the definition of multilateral
used above, that the power or position of nations at a negotiation will
affect how much a multilateral negotiation in name will be a multilateral negotiation in fact. Nations are usually not equal in importance to
each other and hence not in their importance to a multilateral agreement. In the Tokyo Round, the preponderant trade positions of the European Community and the United States gave these parties enormous
influence over most agreements at the negotiation. This influence led to
a pyramidal style of multilateral negotiation, where issues would first
be negotiated bilaterally between the larger powers and then later multilateralized as the negotiations went on. It is hard to imagine how
things could have been otherwise, given what was negotiated at the Tokyo Round and given the importance of the United States and European Community to that subject.

One of the interesting features of the Tokyo Round was the tradeoffs, or linkages, established between different issues. Linkages can be
an important mechanism to promote agreement in negotiation.[32] They
are probably especially important at the beginning of a negotiation,
when they help the parties to achieve compromise and structure an incipient agreement; and at the end, when they help parties to wrap up

[31] Confucius, *Sayings*, 82–83.
[32] See Tollison and Willett, "Linkages in International Negotiations."

outstanding issues in a package deal. There were numerous examples of linkage in the Tokyo Round. Perhaps the most obvious were found in the subsidy/countervail code, in which some greater discipline over subsidies was traded off for an injury test in the United States; and in the customs-valuation code, where the EC gained a major benefit by the reform of U.S. practices, but paid for this benefit by rewriting European customs practices as well. There were other examples of a more competitive use of linkage tactics, such as the suggestion that the United States made tariff concessions to Canada contingent on Canada's participation in the customs valuation code. This sort of linkage is probably more common in international relations generally than in international negotiation.[33] The only time it would likely be successful in trade negotiations is when a nation had already made a significant concession to a negotiating partner. In this case, withdrawal of a concession previously offered can be an important tactic in getting a reciprocating benefit put on the bargaining table.

One of the main lessons of the Tokyo Round is that linkage or tradeoffs can be a delicate matter and hence difficult to carry through effectively. For example, there undoubtedly were linked concessions in the tariff negotiation, but these caused political difficulties for negotiators, who in turn did their best to disavow those linkages. Linkages create the impression at home that one group has paid for the benefits received by another group, which is difficult for democratic governments to justify. For similar reasons, Tokyo Round negotiators took the position that the individual code negotiations were "self-balancing," even though nations had obvious differential interests in the codes which would have made tradeoffs between them probable. In the wine-gallon case, the likely tradeoffs between U.S. concessions and those offered by other countries, particularly Canada, created major problems of "presentation" for the governments involved. From these and other examples in the text, one might be tempted to conclude that in recommending the use of linkages to facilitate agreement, negotiation theory is out of step with the practice of diplomacy. However, the problem might be better described as a gulf between substance and process. The Tokyo Round negotiation would suggest that, while the notion of linkage is a useful idea from the perspective of the substance of trade negotiation, the politics of dealing with the constituents of the negotiation process sharply limit the uses of overt linkage tactics.

With regard to other aspects of the external negotiation, it is useful

[33] For a discussion of linkage in international relations, including strategies of blackmailing and backscratching, see Oye, "Domain of Choice."

to recall that the Tokyo Round was not only a multilateral negotiation but also a complex and highly technical negotiation. Information and organization were very important in the negotiation process. In chapter 2, one saw how information handling and organization could affect the collective capacity of the negotiation to address the problem of nontariff measures. Similarly the ability to manage information affected the role played by individual nations in the negotiation process. In technical negotiations, power is conferred through the ability to analyze and process information.[34] And in complex negotiations, sound organization at the delegation level increases the capacity of individual nations to engage the issues of the negotiation.[35] In the Tokyo Round, the negotiating power derived from information handling and organization often created an advantage for the developed over the developing countries, but this advantage is unlikely to be permanent. A transfer of technology occurs more easily on negotiation methodology than on many other subjects in international life, and in this regard the Tokyo Round was an enormous learning experience for all nations, especially the developing countries, in the negotiation of economic codes of conduct.

The Tokyo Round produced several observations about the internal process that accompanied external negotiations. In chapter 8, the problem of maintaining control over domestic constituents (or factions, in the language of the *Federalist papers*) was identified as a major task for negotiators at the Tokyo Round. As the account makes clear, this is a problem faced especially by democratic governments. Democracy as a system of government is better designed to serve the needs of domestic society than to relate the needs of one society to those of another. Yet multilateral trade negotiations usually entail the meshing of one society's needs and governing procedures with those in other countries. The dilemma is that such a meshing requires in some degree the consent of affected domestic groups, but that such consent is not easy to engineer. One of the main challenges of the future for diplomats represent-

[34] This point has been made by O'Brien and Helleiner, "Political Economy of Information," 463, as follows: "It is the application of knowledge and organization, skill and planning in the use of information, whether produced or transmitted by ordinary or electronic means, which may be the most crucial factor in negotiating advantage; the capacity to synthesize information is itself based on innovation and is vital to negotiating power."

[35] For example, one effective delegation structure was exhibited by the U.S. delegation, which was organized on functional and geographical lines. Each member of delegation received both a functional tasking (e.g., tariffs) and geographical responsibilities (e.g., ASEAN nations). One U.S. official claimed enthusiastically, "We were so well organized that we had agreements with countries that other nations didn't even know were at the negotiation!"

ing democratic governments will be how to organize the democratic process internally so that the nation can make necessary accommodations to international life.

One tactic that occurred frequently at the Tokyo Round was for national delegations to base their negotiating proposals on their own domestic practices. For example, in the negotiation on import licensing the developed countries pressed for an end to automatic licensing partly because they no longer had a need for these administrative practices and had discontinued them. On government procurement, the United States tried to promote the policy of transparency, because it was an essential element in U.S. practice. In the customs valuation negotiation, the European Community initially proposed a system based on the BDV (Brussels Definition of Value), which originated among the European nations. In proposing the sector approach to tariff negotiations, Canada essentially put forward a negotiating procedure compatible with its own trade structure. In many of these cases, the reason why negotiators proposed their own national procedures was simply that they were familiar with them, and that they had an almost instinctive tendency to assume that the burden of change should fall on other parties in the negotiation. In other cases, there may have been a careful examination of alternatives in which a negotiator's own practices were sincerely judged to be the best and therefore worthy of being copied elsewhere. Regardless of the reason, however, negotiating behavior at the Tokyo Round was usually inwardly focused and self-interested, which is a common way to describe nation-state behavior in the international system.[36]

There were exceptions to the norm of inwardly focused negotiation behavior, namely those situations where the negotiation was used to generate reform in domestic procedures. In the wine-gallon case, for example, U.S. officials used the pressure of the external negotiation to make long-overdue changes in internal tax regulations. On the government-procurement code, EC negotiators took the opportunity afforded by the Tokyo Round to commence the process of changing the illiberal procurement practices of member governments. And in the customs valuation code, both U.S. and EC negotiators attempted a tradeoff that produced reform and improvement in both systems. In these examples, negotiators embraced international negotiation as a means of making reforms that would not have been possible otherwise. These were

---

[36] For example, Keohane, *After Hegemony*, frequently refers to nations as egoistic actors, i.e, having independent utility function, a term which is borrowed from the gaming literature. See also Axelrod, *Evolution of Cooperation*.

among the most enlightened uses of international negotiation at the Tokyo Round.

It is usually the case that the greatest difficulties in negotiation arise
at home.[37] This was generally true of the problem areas of the Tokyo
Round. In agriculture, it was largely the politics of individual European
governments and the institutions of the EC that made progress in that
negotiation impossible. In the United States, the Carter administration
was forced to negotiate a side arrangement with the textile lobby which
virtually eliminated any possibility of substantial reductions in high
textile tariffs. In Japan, liberalization of the agricultural sector was
largely beyond the capacity of the Japanese government. And on the
safeguard issue, the rigidity of internal positions in the EC prevented the
Community from accepting a compromise on the matter of selectivity,
which ended prospects for agreement on that code. In all these examples, the internal positions were tightly drawn, with no latitude for external negotiation or accommodation.

When national governments run into specific issues they just cannot
negotiate, often there are unique structural reasons that create weakness of government and therefore loss of negotiating resolve. Such reasons existed in the EC on the safeguard issue, analyzed in chapter 6.
Similarly in Japan, the role of agriculture in the ruling LDP party, or in
the United States, the role of the textile lobby in Congress, helped to
make these governments weak in the external negotiation of these issues. There is no obvious general explanation to account for these examples of weakness in negotiation. It seems that explanations of these
incidents must be disaggregated by issue area and related to the context
of specific situations.[38] Again this is an instance where the substance of
negotiation, and the particular patterns of constituency pressures that
are related to that substance, may be the most important factor in understanding the negotiation process.

GATT and UNCTAD Negotiations

The greatest problem of the world trading system is how to integrate
the developing countries fully into that system. This is a problem the
method of negotiation should be able to ameliorate. In the 1970s, there
were two major economic negotiations that occurred between the developed and developing countries (that is, the North and the South),

[37] For further discussion of this point, see Winham, "Practitioners' Views."

[38] This is a point that has been made more generally about research in international
relations. See Keohane and Nye, *Power and Independence*; and Stein, "Politics of Linkage."

namely the Tokyo Round and the negotiation over UNCTAD's Integrated Program for Commodities (IPC), which took place mainly in the period 1974–77. The latter negotiations were largely to establish a common fund for commodities, and thus to give substantive meaning to symbolic efforts to achieve a New International Economic Order. Neither negotiation was successful in bridging the gap between the North and South, although in fairness the Tokyo Round did produce some tangible benefits for developing countries and charted areas for future cooperation. In terms of results, of course, the two negotiations were very different. The Tokyo Round concluded a series of agreements which will help shape world trading behavior. The IPC negotiations concluded nothing.[39]

The negotiating process was very different in the two negotiations, particularly as it affected relations between the developed and developing countries. The Tokyo Round was mainly an economic negotiation between developed countries. The main actors were nations or quasi-national actors like the EC, and their importance in the negotiation was a reflection of their importance in international trade. Negotiations between the developed and developing countries followed the pyramidal pattern described earlier, where agreements were initiated by the major powers at the top and then gradually multilateralized through the inclusion of other parties in the discussions. The Tokyo Round reached tangible agreements, but the developing countries were not essential to the process and the accords did not directly address their perceived needs. In the UNCTAD's IPC negotiations, the interplay was more directly between the North and South. Negotiations were mainly conducted between groups, not between individual nations, and the effort of bargaining was largely expended in seeking consensus within groups at the cost of exploring and resolving disagreements between groups. The negotiations were over economic matters, but because the real issue was over decisionmaking in the international system, "the political [was] clearly prior to the economic."[40] The combination of a broad politicized agenda and an inflexible group process that militated toward tendentious statements of position removed all prospect of success from the endeavor.

Neither the GATT nor the UNCTAD negotiating process proved very satisfactory to the developing countries. The Tokyo Round reached meaningful agreements, but through the pyramidal negotiation it ex-

[39] Rothstein, *Global Bargaining*, 4, has stated, ". . . there is no conceivable way in which the negotiations I shall discuss could be described as successful."
[40] Ibid., 9.

cluded the developing countries from most major decisions. The IPC negotiation included the developing countries, but it did not reach agreements. In the future, neither process will likely be a good model for improving relations between the developed and developing countries. However, because the IPC's form was more politically acceptable to the developing countries, that negotiation is more likely to serve as a future model for the developing countries, as demonstrated by current demands for global negotiations on international economic cooperation between the North and South.[41] It is not certain that multilateral negotiations with the North will accomplish many of the goals the developing countries seek. The developing countries tend to make revolutionary demands on the developed countries, and negotiation is normally not an appropriate method to achieve revolutionary demands. However, on the assumption that some form of North-South negotiation is likely to be held in the future, it is appropriate to ask what lessons can be learned from the Tokyo Round experience.

The negotiation over the IPC was a politicized affair: there was almost no technical component to the process. The negotiation was conducted essentially at one level. By contrast, the Tokyo Round was conducted at two levels, the political and the technical. Both levels are necessary in multilateral economic negotiations. The political level determines what *can* be done: it sets timetables for the negotiation and controls the process. The technical level determines what *will* be done: it creates and structures the substance of the negotiation. Without the political level, a negotiation is directionless, but without a technical level, a negotiation is meaningless. Because creativity is usually exercised in relation to substance, it is often the task at the technical level to establish the analyses, or the reformulations, that will allow nations to reach agreement. Because judgment is usually exercised in relation to process, it is usually the task at the political level to put the substance of a negotiation into propositions that other negotiators can accept. Negotiators at the technical level invent substantive ideas, and they need originality. Negotiators at the political level resolve conflicts, and they need courage and conviction more than originality. The political level is vastly more visible in negotiation than the technical level, and hence it is possible to assume that courage and conviction are all that are necessary to conduct a negotiation. In the Tokyo Round, the tech-

[41] These demands are outlined in the reports of the Independent (Brandt) Commission, *North-South* and *Common Crisis*. The demands are also supported by a high-level study group in a report that nevertheless goes on to criticize some aspects of developing-country negotiating behaviors noted here, such as the conduct of group negotiation. See Commonwealth Group, *North-South Dialogue*, esp. p. 14.

nical level was indispensable to a successful conclusion, and it was particularly responsible for the preparation and implementation of the negotiation. In the IPC negotiation, concerns for preparation and implementation were conspicuously absent.[42] If North-South negotiations are to be repeated, the technical-level negotiations of the Tokyo Round should be examined for the relevance they may have for the problem of achieving reform in the international economic system. As Condliffe has wisely noted, achieving reform and change can only be accomplished through the mastery of technical detail.[43]

The IPC negotiation was an undifferentiated negotiation. Little attention was given to breaking the substantive material down into its constituent parts and then negotiating the details from the bottom up. The negotiation was carried on mainly at the level of principle, for example the principle that a common fund had to be established before specific agreements on individual commodities could be made. By contrast, the Tokyo Round was a differentiated and disaggregated negotiation. This pattern was established by the NTM inventory, which generated the substance of the negotiation and then broke it down into workable categories to which were attached task-oriented working groups of negotiators. The Tokyo Round moved forward on the promise of concrete accomplishment, and it gathered momentum from the bottom up. As it gathered momentum, it expanded its competence and took up new issues, and it accounted for much of the trade policy of the participating countries over the period of its existence. By contrast, the IPC negotiations contracted to an argument essentially over the pros and cons of the common fund, and the argument became, in Rothstein's words, "a protracted ideological—and at times virtually metaphysical—confrontation over an institution invested with powers and effects it was never likely to develop or manifest."[44] As a result, the IPC negotiation became isolated from the objective developments of North-South economic relations. In the end, the Tokyo Round was a more successful political process than the IPC negotiation, even between the developed and developing countries.

It has been previously noted that in negotiation there is an interplay between substance and process. The IPC negotiation elevated process

---

[42] For example, Rothstein, *Global Bargaining*, 145–46, states, "I believe that one of the most important things to understand about the commodity negotiations is that the issue of implementation was virtually *never* discussed" (italics in original).

[43] Condliffe, *Commerce*, states, "The lesson of the free-trade agitation is that enduring reform is the result of patient mastery of detailed issues, registered not merely in broad legislative acts but in practical procedures of administration" (p. 209).

[44] Rothstein, *Global Bargaining*, 97.

over substance. By contrast, the Tokyo Round was a negotiation of substance. There were negotiable issues on the agenda and those issues largely determined the process. The result is that the Tokyo Round presented a rich source of experience in different styles and content of international economic negotiation. As negotiations between the North and South become more focused on specific issues, this experience may become more valuable to developing countries than it now appears. As Rothstein has noted about the UNCTAD experience, "In an environment of conflict and uncertainty, separate systems with different but interlocking sets of rules may be more realistic than the quest for global rules."[45] This would seem to describe what was produced in the separate codes of the Tokyo Round.

Leadership and International Negotiations

One cannot analyze negotiating behavior in the Tokyo Round without reference to the behavior of individual leaders. Leadership was important to the Tokyo Round, as it is in trade liberalization generally, or indeed in any efforts to develop a more cooperative world society. The reason is that cooperation requires a long-run perspective, whereas the natural tendency in politics is to focus on the prospect of immediate gain. Cooperation requires a foreign policy based on enlightened self-interest, but nations often find it more expedient to base policy on narrow self-interest. Protectionism and conflict can occur by default in the international system, but liberalism and cooperation require the qualities of leadership. Such qualities were evidenced in the Tokyo Round in the collective leadership of the Commission of the EC and in the personalized leadership style of Ambassador Robert Strauss of the United States and in the skill and judgment found in the Brazilian leadership of the developing countries.

As noted above, the greatest problems in negotiation often lie in the home government. This is especially true in multilateral economic negotiations, because those negotiations have the potential to reform domestic structures. Because most of the crucial action in a negotiation is at home, leadership is even more important in the internal negotiation than in the external negotiation. Particularly in the United States, leadership in the domestic arena was demonstrated by Ambassador Strauss, just as he also demonstrated that ability in negotiations with other governments. It is useful to analyze his style, since it may be a style that will

[45] Ibid., 242.

become more important in an age of increasing economic interdependence.

Robert Strauss brought to the office of U.S. trade representative an irreverent manner and a thorough familiarity with Congress and American domestic politics. He had little background in international trade, however, and he did not conceal the fact. At his first meeting with USTR officials, he is reported to have said he knew so little about trade he was unsure how to spell it! Strauss did, however, bring to the job an attribute more valuable than substantive expertise: presidential attention. Strauss's close relationship with President Carter assured presidential concern for the Tokyo Round, which Strauss and senior USTR officials quickly used over the summer of 1977 to invigorate the lagging negotiation. Strauss personally had power abroad because of his standing in his own government. His diplomacy in the external negotiation had the inbuilt advantage that he was perceived as able to get action from a domestic system which was widely seen abroad (with the assistance of American negotiators) as difficult to control.

Strauss's influence on the domestic side of the Tokyo Round likewise proceeded from his reputation as a person able to get things done. As Elizabeth Drew wrote in a profile of Strauss, to be perceived as powerful in Washington is to be powerful.[46] However, political reputations usually rest on performance. By the time the Tokyo Round had ended, Strauss's performance as U.S. trade representative had done more for his reputation than his reputation had done for his capacity to do the job. When political leaders are successfully matched to a governing system, it is hard to separate individual talents from the normal workings of the system. In the case of the Tokyo Round, Robert Strauss was exceedingly well matched to the system in which he operated. It is an utterly fair account of his performance to say he made the U.S. system work.

Strauss saw more quickly than most the extent to which the constituency advisory system established by the Trade Act of 1974 could be used to promote congressional support for the Tokyo Round. The system allowed for the anticipation of problems with constituents; and Strauss used the system, as well as his personal contacts, to head off difficulties with constituents before they escalated into difficulties with Congress. Strauss foresaw the potential for an opposition coalition to the Tokyo Round and he went after the potential members of this coalition one by one. Strauss operated from the theory that one "neutralized" potential domestic opponents through a mixture of continuing

[46] Drew, "Profiles," 54.

communications, persuasion, and timely concession. The process was one of being continually alert to pressure and then responding to pressure and, if possible, eliminating it. The style paid off in the end, for it gave constituency groups the feeling that their interests had been taken into account.

Relations between Congress and a Strauss-led USTR were closer than normal, especially during the crucial six weeks of closed hearings during the spring of 1979. Few individuals can be as personally popular with Congress as Strauss, yet some of the tactics that gained him Congress's respect were utterly ordinary. Strauss insisted that congressional committees and their staffs be given complete information about the negotiation in Geneva. Likewise, he required that congressional trade advisers designated under the Trade Act be integrated fully into the overall negotiating effort, and his office took the initiative in scheduling such advisers into meetings with the constituency groups. At the end of the negotiation, Strauss demonstrated that he was prepared to concede several issues of keen importance to constituency groups and their congressional supporters. Admittedly, Strauss's last-minute concessions are a matter of judgment which have received some criticism, but the fact that they were put forward unquestionably improved Congress's predisposition toward the Tokyo Round agreements.

Strauss's personal skills were appropriate to the situation he found himself in. Much has been made of the fact that he was mainly interested in people and that he was a process person rather than being a substance person. Certainly Strauss's informal, voluble, manner, and on the other hand his lack of experience on trade issues, would tend to confirm this interpretation. But the truth is that Strauss was well prepared on those matters he chose to deal with, a fact Strauss himself confided to Drew ("The heart of the matter is, I know more about the substance than most of the people I work with").[47] It was the manner in which Strauss handled substance that gave the impression that he was unknowledgeable, and incidentally also gave him effectiveness. Strauss had above all a sense of priority about substance. He recognized that in negotiation most substance handles itself, which is another way of saying it is settled without major conflict. Strauss chose instead to deal in substance where it created conflict and therefore logjams in decision-making. Substance was thus chosen in relation to process. It was not the size of the issue but the contribution it made to negotiating momentum that gave importance to substance. Strauss's sense of priority in relation to the decision process of the Tokyo Round kept him where the

[47] Ibid., 88.

action was, which he no doubt found satisfying. But more important, a sense of priority allowed him to retain control of a vast and complicated process. The Tokyo Round could be described as a massive and complex political puzzle, and Strauss's ability to bring the pieces of the puzzle together was near-legendary. A sense of priority, both in terms of importance of issues and a timetable for their solution, helped to structure the puzzle and make it less overwhelming.

Another aspect of Strauss's reputation for being a nonsubstance person involved manipulation on his part (Strauss, like all good negotiators, was a manipulative, and empathetic, person). Strauss often claimed in negotiations with others that he was interested only in the politics and not in the substance of the issues under consideration. Whether this was true or not was a matter of conjecture among Strauss's subordinates. However, the impression it created was that of a mediatorial style of negotiation. Such a style emphasized the importance of Strauss's presence to any final settlement, at the cost of positions that he might have taken. This style may have been generally less appropriate in an external negotiation, where it is assumed negotiators will have positions they must defend against other nations. However, it was very useful in internal negotiations, where negotiators must try to accommodate the differences between what constituents demand and what foreign nations offer. Thus it is probable that a negotiating style Strauss felt comfortable with was especially suitable to the internal negotiation in the United States.

Different situations of diplomacy call for individuals with different talents. In the 1970s, two very different men served the United States in high diplomatic positions: Robert Strauss and Henry Kissinger. Both demonstrated that they are world-class negotiators. In their different styles, one can see alternative reflections of the international system.

Kissinger's diplomacy was based on the primacy of international politics over the domestic system. It emphasized history, rational design, and above all the intellectual ability to recognize the forces of the international system and to move with them. All diplomats seek control of the important aspects of the environment they operate within. Kissinger sought control of the external system, and the mechanism of control was the judicious use of national power. Kissinger's diplomacy was closed and secretive, and it sought arenas where interaction was limited to a few individuals. It was a style best suited to the sensitive issues of national security.

Strauss's diplomacy, by contrast, was based on the primacy of the domestic system over international politics. It was motivated by the diverse political pressures of the moment and it moved in relation to them in a trial-and-error fashion. It eschewed grand design. Its intellectual force was the capacity to find order in a vast array of competing demands. Strauss sought control of the domestic system, and the mechanism of control was bureaucracy and politicking. Strauss's diplomacy was open and it sought to expand the arena in which political decisions were debated. The style was best suited to ordinary issues of economic life.

Kissinger's style and his background were consistent with the traditions of diplomacy. Were the great diplomats of the past to observe the contemporary international system, they would see in Kissinger's diplomacy a familiar style. In Strauss, they would perceive an alien and even barbaric manner. One wonders what Prince Klemens von Metternich, minister of foreign affairs to Emperor Francis I of Austria, would have made of a man who has described his negotiating ability in the following terms: "I didn't just come into town on a wagon full of watermelons."[48] Strauss's background, his strength, and his style were not consistent with the classical conception of the job requirements of a diplomat. In itself, this is an interesting commentary on change in international relations.

THE TOKYO ROUND AND THEORIES OF POLITICAL ECONOMY

The analysis now reconsiders, in light of the Tokyo Round experience, the political-economic theories of trade regimes raised in chapter 1. It will be recalled from that earlier discussion that the main issue raised by these theories was how to account for the liberalness or openness of international trade regimes. It was argued in chapter 1 that because the Tokyo Round was a major event in recent trade history, it might serve as a rudimentary test for some of these theories.

A question that must be settled at the outset is whether the Tokyo Round negotiation was a liberal, or on the contrary a protectionist, experience in international trade. Clearly this is a matter of judgment on which opinion can differ. The view taken here is that the Tokyo Round did produce on balance a liberalizing effect on the international trade system. This conclusion is first of all substantiated by the weight of expert opinion.[49] Second, it appears to be the case objectively as

---

[48] John Kifner, "Strauss Meets in Israel with Begin, See a 'Long, Hard Pull' in Mideast," *New York Times*, July 2, 1979. The reference is to watermelon vendors in rural Texas, an image of poverty from Strauss's childhood that he sought to escape.

[49] Regarding such opinion, Bergsten and Cline, "Conclusion," 768, write of "the con-

well.[50] Third, the Tokyo Round was described as a liberalizing phenomenon by various leading governments and by GATT itself,[51] and in the case of the largest nation at the Tokyo Round this description was confirmed by a nongovernmental advisory committee constituted to pass judgment on the results of the negotiation.[52] There were sharply opposing assessments of the Tokyo Round, but these tended to focus on the strengthening of contingent protection in certain areas such as antidumping and countervailing duties, and not on the results in other areas of the negotiation.[53] To sum up, the conclusion reached here is that the Tokyo Round negotiation had a liberalizing impact on trade; thus the negotiation should provide some grounds for assessing various political-economic theories that account for liberalism in international trade.

The various factors used to account for trade liberalism were outlined in chapter 1. They are hegemonic dominance by a leading nation, interest-group processes, trade structures, and liberal values. One factor that will not be examined, although it is often related to policies of liberalism or protectionism, is the occurrence of world economic recession or depression. The reason for not considering this rather obvious factor is that recession is too cyclical and short-term a factor to be relevant to a negotiation effort that took place over a decade or longer. On the other hand, depression is too general or long-term a phenomenon

---

ventional wisdom that the Kennedy and Tokyo Rounds made net contributions to an open trading system."

[50] Of the major endeavors at the Tokyo Round, the tariff negotiation and the codes on government procurement and civil aircraft produced unequivocally liberalizing results. Additionally codes on subsidies and countervailing duties, customs valuation, and standards increased the predictability of trade, which in turn has a liberalizing effect.

[51] GATT described the Tokyo Round as "designed, not only to bring about the reduction or elimination of tariff and non-tariff barriers to trade, but also to shape the multilateral trading system and international trade relations well into the next decade" (GATT Tokyo Round, 1).

[52] The U.S. Trade Act of 1974 included as objectives the liberalizing tasks of the attainment of more open market access, and the reduction or elimination of devices which distort trade. The report of the Advisory Committee for Trade Negotiations (ACTN) emphasized that the Tokyo Round agreements reflected "a faithful and largely successful effort . . . to give effect to the instructions set forth in the Trade Act of 1974" (U.S. Government, ACTN Report, 2).

[53] The critical assessment of Rodney Grey, "U.S. Trade Practices," did juxtapose an apparent tightening of contingent protectionism in the Tokyo Round accords and the reduced resort to bound tariff rates, which were fixed and therefore less onerous to international trade. However, Grey's argument did not address areas where the Tokyo Round reduced contingent protectionism, such as the reduction of interventionist valuation practices or protectionist administrative practices in the standards and procurement areas.

to be relevant, and in any case did not occur during the Tokyo Round. If anything were to be learned from the Tokyo Round concerning the relationship between economic performance and trade policy, it would be that the Tokyo Round disconfirmed a normal expectation that economic downturn (e.g., the oil shock of 1973) produces protectionist policies. Probably protectionism was averted because the negotiation process itself provided a rationale for policymakers to deflect the demands for protectionist policies which occur during an economic downturn.

Impact of Hegemonic Stability

The theory of hegemonic stability would appear to be directly applicable to the Tokyo Round negotiation. The theory states essentially that open cooperative trading regimes are produced during periods of hegemonic dominance by a leading nation. It establishes a link between the economic power of the leading nation and the liberalism of the overall trading system. The theory explains fairly well the British-led liberalism of the nineteenth century, the illiberalism of the interwar period of the twentieth century, and the U.S.-dominated postwar period of the 1950s and 1960s. The theory predicts that as a hegemonic power declines, one would expect the international trading system to become less cooperative and less liberal.

By the time the Tokyo Round started, the United States had conclusively lost any position of hegemony in the trading system, and it was no longer the central player in the fixed-exchange monetary system created at Bretton Woods. It was substantially less preponderant in the international economic system overall as measured by key variables in trade, investment, and monetary reserves.[54] According to the theory of hegemonic stability, the Tokyo Round negotiation should have produced an uncooperative and illiberal result. The fact that this did not occur raises some serious questions about the capacity of this theory to interpret major events in the contemporary trading system. The failure of the theory to account for national behavior at the Tokyo Round is even more striking given that it was national behavior at another international economic conference (the World Economic Conference of 1933) that originally led Charles Kindleberger to argue for the need for "one stabilizer" in the international economy.[55]

In the last analysis, the theory of hegemonic stability is a theory

[54] See ch. 1, pp. 45-46.
[55] *World in Depression*, 305.

about system structure. In these terms, one could ask what kind of system was reflected in the Tokyo Round negotiation. This research has demonstrated that much of the Tokyo Round consisted of an interaction between the two preponderant parties at the negotiation: the European Community and the United States. Most agreements were negotiated between them or not at all, and, as the safeguards negotiation demonstrated, they had effective veto power over all major accords. In most cases, the negotiation process began between the two superpowers, and then spread only later to other parties. Leadership was clearly in evidence during the Tokyo Round, but it was exercised by two parties, not by a single hegemonic power. If one were to assume, as Kenneth Waltz has put it, that "the structure of a system is generated by the interactions of its principal parts,"[56] then the system that would best describe the Tokyo Round would be a harmonious bipolar system. Such a system differed from the more familiar conflictual bipolar structure found in the international political system in the fact that on most issues the leading powers were not separated by fundamental ideological cleavage.

It is probable that the harmonious bipolar structure of the Tokyo Round produced a more meaningful negotiation than would have taken place under conditions of hegemony. In previous GATT negotiations, particularly before the Kennedy Round, the preponderant position of the United States led to an artificial exchange of concessions and to a situation where most initiatives were expected to come from the United States. For their part, the Europeans made the willingness to negotiate a concession in its own right. In the Tokyo Round, however, the initiatives were more balanced between the Americans and the Europeans, which led to a fuller exchange of issues. The reason is that nations negotiate more seriously and over a greater range of issues with equals than with unequals.[57] The Tokyo Round demonstrated that as negotiating parties become more equal, the increasing importance of the smaller party to the larger will lead both to increase their demands on the other. More is put on the agenda, and the potential of external negotiation to achieve internal reform is expanded. It was the case that the Tokyo Round negotiated a much wider agenda than any trade negotiation had ever done previously. One reason was the aforementioned bureaucratic processes that made accessible more information about nontariff measures than was available in previous negotiations.

[56] *Theory*, 72.

[57] It is not the case that any bipolar arrangement will produce a wider agenda in negotiation, as is clear in the conflictual bipolar relationship between the United States and the Soviet Union.

The other reason, however, was the changed political-economic structure that encouraged the Americans and the Europeans to deal more seriously with each other than they had ever done before.[58]

The bipolar structure of the Tokyo Round had two other important consequences as well. First, the United States and the European countries have approached trade from different perspectives in the postwar era. The Americans have taken a more doctrinaire approach that emphasized free trade and legal commitments between nations, while the Europeans have taken a more pragmatic approach that emphasized the management of trade and the harmonization of trade policies between nations.[59] The Tokyo Round, with its greater emphasis on open trade rather than free trade, tended to bring the two sides closer together in terms of the values that underlie trade policy. Changes of this sort are subtle and tend to be subject to individual perception and interpretation. Nevertheless a common perception among U.S. negotiators was that where previously the United States might occasionally have sacrificed specific objective interests to keep intact the institutional values of GATT, at the Tokyo Round it was less willing to forego the tangible benefits for its conception of wider institutional values. As one U.S. official put it, "We came closer to the French approach to free trade; the thrust was open, managed trade, not free trade. We won more on specifics in this negotiation, but we gave away the concept."

A second consequence of the bipolar structure of the Tokyo Round was that it increased the natural tendency of the developed countries to ignore the developing countries in the negotiation. The effort to manage a bipolar arrangement is considerable, even when the parties are fundamentally similar in their organization and values. The two superpowers expended an uncommon effort in reaching bilateral agreement at the Tokyo Round, with the result that they tended to ignore the demands of other parties early in the negotiation and to resist them later on. In a bipolar arrangement, there is less incentive for the superpowers to service the interests of smaller powers than there would be for a hegemonial power in a unipolar system, a fact which may explain the greater interest of some developing countries in preferential relationships with the EC than in nonpreferential relationships under the GATT. Even as early as the Kennedy Round, the United States began focusing much of its attention in trade negotiations on the EC, which led one Ca-

---

[58] An example of this proposition could be seen in the negotiations over subsidy/countervail and customs valuation. The United States carried the initiative on the former and the EC on the latter; and, as noted in ch. 7, the party under the greatest internal pressure for change carried the initiative in the external negotiation.

[59] See generally Gardner, *Sterling-Dollar Diplomacy*.

nadian official to criticize privately the "tunnel vision of the U.S. with respect to the Common Market." By the time of the Tokyo Round, the structure of the international economic system had increased the importance of the United States and the European Community for each other. In systemic terms, this meant that successful relations between the United States and the Community on the one hand and the developing countries on the other would be an unnatural act, and from the standpoint of negotiation processes it widened a gulf that already existed in terms of substantive issues of economics.

The harmonious bipolar structure of the Tokyo Round effectively represented a new systemic arrangement in the international trade system. One of the important questions that can be asked about any new system is whether it will be stable and provide for political cooperation. This concern is analogous to the "key question" of Robert Keohane's extended analysis of the post-hegemonic international economic system, namely the problem of "how international cooperation can be maintained among capitalist states in the absence of hegemony."[60] As Keohane puts it: "How cooperation can take place without hegemony is an important and difficult question precisely because there is evidence that the decline of hegemony makes cooperation more difficult. Multilateral institutions must furnish some of the sense of certainty and confidence that a hegemony formerly provided."[61] It would seem that the process and results of the Tokyo Round have demonstrated that, in the trade system at least, bipolar cooperation has provided a sense of direction that Keohane argues was formerly provided by hegemonic U.S. leadership. Whether this new system will be stable in the near run depends importantly on the trade policies pursued by the United States and the Community in the next decade, and is a subject we will return to in the last chapter.

In examining the potential for stability of the post–Tokyo Round trade system, it is useful to borrow from the theory of international politics, for traditionally more analysis has been given to the structural aspects of political relations between nations than to economic relations between them. Curiously theorists of international politics have not been as enthusiastic about hegemony as theorists of international political economy. Perhaps the reason is that hegemony in politics smacks of imperialism, and it is usually not viewed as an acceptable arrangement for promoting cooperation or stability.[62] Alternatively, stability

---

[60] *After Hegemony*, 43.

[61] Ibid., 183.

[62] A common dictionary definition of hegemony is the dominant influence of a nation, while imperialism is more the practice or exercise of national dominance. One might con-

and cooperation are more normally seen as produced from a multipolar situation, and especially from the successful operation of a balance-of-power system such as was represented in the nineteenth-century Concert of Europe.[63] Another system that has been viewed as stable, if not necessarily cooperative, is a bipolar arrangement of power.[64] What these comparisons with political theory may suggest is that the cooperation in managing a stable and liberal trade regime, which is claimed to have been produced since 1945 by U.S. hegemony, may have been due less to the power of the hegemon and due more to the policies which it pursued. Of particular importance was the manner in which those policies interacted with the policies of the principal subordinate nations. In an interesting article that criticized the theory of British hegemony of the nineteenth century, Fred Lawson argued that the capacity of Great Britain to promote free trade throughout its empire was substantially affected by the policies of regional leaders in the imperialized territories.[65] In a similar point made about hegemony in the postwar period, Andrew Shonfield has queried whether the stability of the international economic system was due to U.S. hegemony or to leadership, which is a more subtle phenomenon that would take into account how the policies of the leader interacted with the interests of the followers.[66]

To sum up, it seems unlikely that a hegemonial system is an inherently stable or cooperative arrangement. The fact that U.S. hegemony

---

clude that hegemony could be natural or accidental while imperialism is purposive, but the difference appears to be narrow and may exist very much in the eye of the beholder. As for the popularity of imperialism as a form of system management, Waltz, *Theory*, 205, has noted: "Old-style imperialist countries were not warmly appreciated by most of their subjects, nor were the Japanese when they were assembling their 'Greater East Asian Co-Prosperity Sphere,' nor the Germans when they were building Hitler's new order."

[63] See generally Morgenthau, *Politics among Nations*.

[64] For example, in the 1960s Waltz, "International Structure," 229, wrote, ". . . the bipolar world of the past two decades has been highly stable." More recently he has noted, "With only two great powers, both can be expected to act to maintain the system" (*Theory*, 204).

[65] See "Hegemony Reassessed."

[66] Shonfield, "Overall View," 136, has summarized U.S. behavior in the postwar period as follows: "A detailed study of the epoch as a whole suggests that the U.S. approach to national interests was different, but not so very different, from that of other countries with which it was allied. What was more remarkable about its behaviour was that given its capacity to exercise hegemonial power, and its evident impulse to do so on occasion, it so readily accepted the constraints prescribed by the conventions of alliance politics." This point is confirmed by Stein, "Hegemon's Dilemma," 386, who states flatly, "Hegemons need followers in order to liberalize international exchanges."

has been associated with stability, cooperation, and trade liberalism in the postwar international economic system has been more a historical artifact than a result of the power distribution in the system. There is probably little reason to think that a first alternative to the hegemonial system, namely a bipolar system, would be any less stable or cooperative, and indeed the Tokyo Round provides some evidence for the co-operativeness of a bipolar system. If there is any point at which the distribution of economic power would affect system stability, it is likely the point at which a bipolar system begins to become multipolar. There is some certainty that the process of economic development will produce such a result in the future,[67] and there is little agreement in the political literature over which of the two systems has greater potential for cooperation.[68] Thus it is that the process of economic development will, in the coming years, produce challenging problems of political structure as well as economic accommodation for the international economic system.

Impact of Group Processes

A second theory would account for trade liberalism by reference to domestic political processes, particularly the actions (or inactions) of interest groups. One begins in assessing this theory with the self-evident fact that domestic politics and group activity clearly shape a nation's economic policies and hence affect its commitment to liberalized trade. The importance of domestic processes has been nicely established by Charles Kindleberger,[69] and the importance of interest-group activity within those domestic processes has been established by Richard Caves in a paper that compared that activity with other factors in the domestic arena such as electoral concerns or national economic strategies.[70] However, it has been difficult to develop any general theory of the effects of domestic processes or interest groups on international trade policy. The reason is that national policy processes are *sui generis*, and they are not always comparable; much less can they be rendered into general theoretical propositions. Kindleberger himself noted that there was no satisfactory theory of group behavior to explain national commercial policies, and a similar refrain, which applied expressly to international negotiations, has been struck more recently by Andrew Shon-

[67] See Organski, *World Politics*.
[68] For a useful comparison of these two systems, see Rosecrance, "Bipolarity."
[69] See "Group Behavior."
[70] See "Canada's Tariff."

field.[71] Consistent with these observations, this research on the Tokyo Round has not produced any generalizable theory about the effect of international political processes or group behavior in negotiation.

The internal process that existed in four parties to Tokyo Round negotiations was the subject of chapter 8. That chapter demonstrated that the impact of interest groups differed from one negotiating party to the next, depending on how the parties had organized themselves to conduct the negotiation, or depending to what extent group pressures were offset by other competing pressures coming from internal governments or bureaucratic actors. A further aspect that differentiated the impact of interest groups was issue area, since the political pressures tended to be greater in some areas, such as tariffs and subsidy/countervail, and lower in other areas, such as standards and customs valuation. Thus the subject matter of the negotiation, and the way it was perceived as important or unimportant in the domestic arena, added a further complication to the analysis of group processes. Apart from this, however, there was little out of the ordinary that could be said in a general sense about the operation of interest groups at the Tokyo Round, except perhaps to suggest that one might have expected groups to be more influential than they apparently were in the outcome of the negotiation.[72] It has been well understood since the Kennedy Round that large trade negotiations create a momentum for trade liberalization, and give policymakers a rationale that is absent in more normal times for balancing the demands for protectionism against the opportunity costs that such protectionism can have in other areas of the economy. Perhaps what this indicates about theories of group processes is that such theories are more useful in explaining protectionist actions taken by governments than liberalizing actions.

One general finding that could be gleaned from the domestic processes that attended the Tokyo Round was the capacity of domestic bureaucracies to resist trade liberalization. Examples of this phenomenon came up repeatedly, and across different governmental systems represented at the negotiation. In the negotiation on agriculture, the Commission of the EC defended its own institutional authority at the same time as it defended agricultural protectionism. In the U.S. Department of Commerce, Canada's Department of Industry, Trade, and Commerce, and Japan's MITI, officials could usually be counted on to speak

---

[71] Shonfield, "Overall View," 44, states, "There is thus no satisfactory general theory about the functioning of domestic economic interest groups as a constraint on international economic bargaining."

[72] This observation is consistent with the findings reported in Bauer et al., *American Business*, esp. ch. 28, "The Pressure Groups—A Summary."

for the interests of client import-competing industries. In Canada, the protectionism of the machinery program was stoutly defended by the officials who administered it. Japan's Ministry of Agriculture and Forestry stonewalled changes in that country's agricultural restrictions, and the U.S. Bureau of Alcohol, Tobacco, and Firearms fought against repeal of the wine-gallon tax. The Customs Cooperation Council in Europe similarly resisted reform of customs valuation procedures. There was almost no issue at the Tokyo Round which somewhere did not encounter a measure of bureaucratic resistance, and there was no nation free of this phenomenon. This finding should not be surprising, however. Policymaking in modern governments usually produces a certain amount of "bureaucratic politics." The Tokyo Round was an exercise in internationalized policymaking, and it produced an internationalized bureaucratic politics that cut across national boundaries.[73]

In modern trade negotiations, domestic government bureaucracies may eventually replace economic interest groups as a major source of protectionist pressure. The reason is that modern protectionist pressure is more than just a matter of private economic interests seeking relief from import competition. Modern protectionism consists also of attempts by government bureaucracies to provide advantages for domestic producers through a whole range of sophisticated programs. The government officials who design and administer such programs feel they serve their nations' interests, and the programs as well provide role and mission for government agencies, and on neither count can they be dispensed with easily. The face of trade protectionism is changing. Old-style trade protectionism directly protected the economic interests of specific import-competing industries. What modern trade protectionism often protects is "bureaucratic nationalism," that is, a bureaucratic conception of how the national economy should be managed and how it should relate to the international economy. In modern technical trade negotiations, the principal task is to mesh together different bureaucratic procedures found in different countries. This negotiation process produces winners and losers among government bureaucracies, and the losers can be expected to fight across national lines as much as they fight when similar battles occur internally.

The idea that pressure for protectionism might stem more from government bureaucracy than from economic interest groups would seem strange to many who have witnessed the overt, uncompromising, and even crass displays of political pressure that economic groups can mount on their own behalf. However, in the Tokyo Round the most

[73] Cf. Hopkins, "International Role."

blatant attempts to apply pressure tactics—for example, the U.S. liquor industry on the wine-gallon issue and the European pulp and paper producers on tariffs—did not stop concessions from being made. Usually in trade negotiations, the effective exercise of influence is more subtle than that represented in these examples. Effective influence depends largely on access, a point Schattschneider emphasized in his study of interest-group pressures on Congress, and in this dimension members of government bureaucracies have a natural advantage. Trade policies in most countries are made by bureaucratic officials, and when the time comes to change those policies, the officials responsible for administering them will attend the meetings, or the negotiating sessions, where changes to policies are considered. Most changes in government policymaking procedures require the compliance, if not the consent, of the agencies that are affected by the change. It would be unusual in most countries to change a major government program without hearing from the officials who administer that program, and in this manner officials are given what is normally denied to economic interest groups from the private sector, namely the right to participate in government decisionmaking on issues in which they have an interest. The right to take part in decisions creates the capacity to resist decisions. It should therefore not be surprising that decisions to change government policies and programs in international trade occur slowly and with great difficulty in most countries.

As we have seen, much of the Tokyo Round negotiation was over the process of reform of the international trade system. Paradoxically, while bureaucratic machinery is often the target of reform, bureaucratic machinery is also necessary to accomplish the process of reform. The problem is essentially that of the new and appropriate growing out of the old and inappropriate, and it is a problem of Hegelian proportions in the movement toward a more internationalized policymaking process in international trade. In a sense, the Tokyo Round renewed the reform process that started as far back as the Reciprocal Trade Agreements Act of 1934. To the extent that the Tokyo Round succeeds, it will continue the trend toward internationalized policymaking at the expense of exclusively national procedures.

Impact of Trade Structures

A third theory that has been advanced to account for trade liberalism refers to productive processes and the nature of goods exchanged in international trade. There are two variants of this theory, which were outlined in chapter 1. They are that trade liberalism is promoted by increasing volumes of intraindustry trade on the one hand, and by increases in intrafirm trade on the other. The relationship between trade structure and trade liberalism has not been adequately tested by this study, and to do so would have required a more precise and quantitative breakdown of the nature and flows of trade by industry, as well as the position taken by those industries with respect to the Tokyo Round. What can be said from a more general examination of this issue is that the theory received weak confirmation in the Tokyo Round, but with sufficient exceptions to make it an uncertain predictor of liberal behavior. As a variable, trade structure did not appear to be related to the code negotiations; but in the tariff negotiations, sectors such as automotive equipment where intraindustry trade was high were liberalized according to formula procedures without extensive exceptions. A similar result occurred in sectors such as nonelectrical machinery where the percentage of intrafirm trade is high. Textiles, on the other hand, is a sector where intraindustry trade is increasing, but this did not mitigate the extreme protectionism of the industry in the United States or Canada. Similarly, multinational firms predominate in the petrochemical sector, but this sector resisted the full liberalization implied by the Tokyo Round formula. It would seem that further work should be done on industry-specific conditions before trade structure is useful as a general explanatory factor in trade liberalization.[74]

One aspect which the Tokyo Round did underscore is the growing importance of direct foreign investment and intrafirm trade in international trade negotiations. Issues of foreign investment lay behind the related-parties issue in the customs valuation negotiation, and the concern over the effect of subsidies and countervailing duties on investment decisions made the negotiation of the subsidy/countervail code more problematic. Following the Tokyo Round, another investment-related issue—performance requirements—became a major agenda item at the 1982 GATT ministerial meeting.[75] Foreign investment is important in international trade because it has enormous potential to shape trade flows, and this is even more the case where nations pursue policies of export promotion. In this sense, direct foreign investment is a prior concern, and nations seeking to manipulate trade flows to their

---

[74] Trade structure should be compared with other industry-level variables as well, such as the labor share of value added, and existing levels of import penetration. See generally Baldwin, "United States Trade Policy."

[75] For general background on performance requirements, see *The Use of Investment Incentives and Performance Requirements by Foreign Governments*, Washington, D.C.: U.S. Department of Commerce, 1981, and *Performance Requirements*, Washington, D.C.: Labor-Industry Coalition for International Trade, 1981.

benefit will also attempt to control foreign investment. This is a problem which will likely be raised in any future multilateral negotiations under GATT.

Impact of Liberal Values

A fourth theory holds that the presence of a liberal trading regime is accounted for mainly by the underlying values of publics and governments toward the desirability of freer trade. The main issue is whether such values exist and, if they exist, whether they have been created by other factors, such as a hegemonial distribution of economic power. On the latter point, an argument has already been advanced that hegemony itself does not necessarily create a liberal orientation toward international trade. It is the former point, that is, whether liberal values were indeed present during the Tokyo Round negotiation, that will be assessed here. The presence of values in negotiation is normally not an easy thing to demonstrate, and conclusions along these lines are far from indisputable. Usually the evidence used to establish values is statements made by individuals or national representatives that express the objectives that motivated them in the negotiation. Such statements will be used here because they are the only evidence available, even though they only constitute circumstantial evidence at best.

An examination of values in the Tokyo Round should start by taking account of a historical shift that goes back to the 1930s in the approach taken to international trade policy by governments and publics alike. It was generally recognized that the protectionism that followed World War I had been damaging to all countries, and that the way to increase world welfare was progressively to remove national restrictions.[76] This view was embraced by the Roosevelt administration, and was expanded in the personal philosophy of Cordell Hull into a belief that open trade would create a peaceful world. In 1934, the United States passed the Reciprocal Trade Agreements Act and initiated the reciprocal trade program of negotiations to begin reducing the high tariff levels of the 1930s. The reciprocal trade program commenced a trend toward liberalism in trade policy that continued intact to the Tokyo Round. It benefited from the reaction to World War II that led people to desire a safer and more prosperous world. The Pan-Europeanism

---

[76] Grey, "U.S. Trade Practices," 246, has noted the commitment of the GATT contracting parties to the concepts of international specialization of production and trade, and has commented, "The strength with which this view was held derived from the pre-war experience that discriminatory policies and the widespread and competitive resource to devices for exporting unemployment, quickly made all much poorer."

that led to the Common Market was consistent with this trend. This liberal trend led to the generally successful formation and the subsequent performance of GATT, and it survived the collapse of the International Trade Organization and the resurgence of contingent protectionism in the 1970s. Throughout the postwar period, the liberal trend was supported by the reality of an average 7 percent annual growth in international trade volumes.

It is interesting to speculate what caused this trend toward liberalism. It is usually assumed that the trend started with governments, particularly the initiation of the reciprocal trade program by the U.S. government. While this may be the case, it could also be argued that the more important change was a gradual liberalizing of public attitudes toward international trade, which then created the scope for governments to translate attitudinal changes into policy. There are four factors that lead to this conclusion. First, there was the aforementioned fear of the protectionism of the interwar years, which publics as well as governments believed had contributed to the depressed condition of that period. Second, there was a reduction of nationalist fervor after World War II, which all but eliminated one of the main emotional causes of protectionist demands. The increasing internationalism of Western publics proved to be ideologically incompatible with protectionism, which had coexisted more easily with the isolationism and nationalism of an earlier period. Third, there was a general recognition that trade was growing in the postwar period; as the Curzons have noted, growing trade volumes themselves create their own momentum for trade liberalization.[77] A fourth factor was the decline in the politicization and the popularity of the tariff, which was the main policy tool of trade protectionism. This decline was most noticed in the United States, where according to Theodore Lowi the tariff became less a means to distribute the benefits of protection to domestic industries and more a means to regulate the domestic economy for international purposes.[78] For these reasons, public opinion on protectionism went through a transformation from roughly the mid-1930s to the mid-1950s, a transformation which supported the liberalization of trade policy over that period. By the 1960s, liberal attitudes were clearly ascendant in the public opinion of most Western countries.

The answer to why such a transformation in public attitudes occurred is admittedly speculative, but the fact that it occurred seems beyond doubt. The evidence from the United States at least can be found

[77] See "Management of Trade Relations," 154.
[78] See "American Business."

in the language with which constituents framed their demands for protectionist policies. From this language, one can discern which values predominated in the policy process. Writing in the early 1930s, Schattschneider noted that public testimony before Congress on the Smoot-Hawley tariff rarely dissented from the principle of protectionism, and that "many of the most passionate avowals of faith in the dogma of the protective tariff to be found anywhere in the record were made in the course of arguments against particular increases in the rate structure."[79] In other words, the opposition to protectionism was reduced to the position of arguing against tariff increases as an exception to a generally assumed policy of protectionism. Arguments of this type took a familiar and almost standardized form, as in Schattschneider's example of one Mr. Peter Fletcher, who began his argument against higher duties on flax with the following disclaimer: "The protectionist principle itself is not questioned, but. . . ."[80]

In the three decades that followed Schattschneider's writing, the ideological initiative passed from the protectionists to the liberal traders. This difference has been recorded in the following observation of Bauer, Pool, and Dexter about the language of trade politics in the mid-1950s: "It has become relatively rare for a protectionist spokesman to argue for protectionism in principle."[81] The authors state further: "More often than not one hears the advocate of protectionism begin his statement about as follows: 'Of course I am for increasing trade and believe in lowering trade barriers, but . . .' "[82] This change in language reveals that the tables had been turned, and that by the mid-1950s the liberal trade position had assumed the position of ideological orthodoxy. In the Tokyo Round, this orthodoxy was still unchallenged, and, as the following example from a published letter of Mr. Douglas A. Fraser, president of the United Auto Workers, demonstrates, the proponents of a more protectionist stance continued to defend their positions with arguments that did not oppose the principle of liberalized trade:

> The UAW still believes that expanded trade can be beneficial to the American people, both as workers and consumers. But this will take some adjustment in the implementation of the new trade policies. . . . If adequate guarantees are not forthcoming . . . the UAW

[79] See *Politics*, 141.
[80] Ibid., 143.
[81] *American Business*, 147.
[82] Ibid.

does not believe that our membership could be persuaded to support the trade package.

We continue to believe in the benefits of liberal trade. But we cannot support a policy that does not share those benefits fairly and equitably.[83]

One cannot measure precisely the impact that the differences between public opinion in the 1930s and the 1960s had on trade policymaking, but it was likely substantial. These differences turn on the matter of which policy is presumed right in principle, and which is to be applied in the absence of specific evidence to the contrary. In law, this would be a matter of which side had the burden of proof. In a complicated affair like trade policy, where there is rarely solid proof for any proposition that might be advanced, it means that decisionmaking in many situations would tend to produce policies that are in line with the predominant values. From Schattschneider's account, one can draw the conclusion that congressmen in 1930 operated from a perspective that is common in decisionmaking everywhere; namely when in doubt, apply the prevailing principles. Since there was enormous uncertainty surrounding tariff setting in 1930, it was by and large protectionist principles that got applied.

It is usually the case that arguments consistent with the predominant values received a warmer welcome and are subject to less resistance than those opposing conventional values. On this point, there is an interesting comparison between the descriptions of Schattschneider and of Bauer, Pool, and Dexter of the way interest-group lobbyists performed in the public arena. The former notes the "gentle, sympathetic, apologetic questions" that were asked by congressmen of the interest groups demanding protection,[84] and he concluded that such groups had great influence on congressional lawmaking. The latter emphasized the capacity of Congress to resist pressures, and state that in proportion to the other activities pursued by interest groups "direct lobbying was a very minor activity."[85] These authors concluded that "the groups did not appear to have the raw material of great power."[86] What had changed in the three decades was the public's attitudes about trade protectionism, which in turn changed how interest groups presented their demands on the political system, and how effective or pow-

[83] Letter to Hon. Charles Vanik, Chairman, House Subcommittee on Trade, reproduced in U.S. House of Representatives, *Multilateral Trade Negotiations*, 655–58.

[84] Schattschneider, *Politics*, 40.

[85] Bauer et al., *American Business*, 398. With regard to the activities of interest groups, the authors note, "We were further unprepared for the fact that most activities of pressure groups involved interaction with people on the same side."

[86] Ibid.

erful they might have appeared to an observer. It is easier to make and win a case before a friendly jury than before a hostile one. Thus the liberal values of the policy environment of the postwar period, which extended into the 1970s, made it easier to produce liberal results. These liberal values were in turn an important factor in explaining the liberal results produced by the Tokyo Round.

But what about, then, the positions of governments in the Tokyo Round? It is one thing to argue that the Tokyo Round negotiation was conducted in a milieu of liberal values, but it is another to assume that these values motivated governments as well. Again any evidence is circumstantial at best, and exists mainly in the statements that governments made justifying the policies they were proposing. Two examples can be found from the beginning and end of the negotiation, drawn from the American and European sides. In the United States, the commitments "to negotiate for a more open and equitable world trading system" and "to strengthen economic relations between the United States and foreign countries through open and non-discriminatory world trade" were included prominently in respectively the president's message transmitting a trade-reform bill to Congress in 1973 and in the statement of purposes in the act that Congress passed in 1975.[87] At the end of the negotiation, the same themes were repeated, first in the president's letter of transmittal which spoke of the ambitious effort "to revise the rules of international trade and to achieve a fairer, more open, world trading system"; and second in the statement of purposes in the act itself, which included the words "to foster the growth and maintenance of an open world trading system."[88]

Such statements were of course shared by other Tokyo Round participants and notably the European Community. For example, in the text of the "Overall Approach" which set out the Community's position at the beginning of the Tokyo Round, the EC stated:

> The Community is therefore convinced that international trade is a vital and increasingly important factor in its development. It hopes that the policy of liberalising trade will be continued.[89]

And again, at the end of the negotiation, in the document from the Commission recommending approval of the Tokyo Round accords, the assessment of the Tokyo Round was as follows:

[87] U.S. House of Representatives, "Message of the President" (1973), 101; and U.S. Government, *Trade Act of 1974*, 4.

[88] U.S. House of Representatives, *Message of the President* (1979), p. III; and U.S. Government, *Trade Agreements Act of 1979*, 5.

[89] Commission, "Overall Approach," 11.

Above all, the success of the Tokyo Round means that the major trading countries of the world have turned their backs on the protectionism which has threatened over the last few years and which would have engulfed the world even more virulently than in the early 1930's if these negotiations had failed.[90]

Thus, in statements such as these, the two major powers at the Tokyo Round clearly revealed the liberal orientations that motivated their behavior during the lengthy negotiation.

In the end, the most important factor in explaining the liberal results of the Tokyo Round was the environment of liberal values within which the negotiation was conducted. This factor was more important than a hegemonic distribution of economic power, for without the desire to produce liberal results in the leader and in other countries, power alone could not have done so. Liberal values were also more important than the activities of interest groups per se, since the success of those groups is dependent in the aggregate on the environment in which they operate. Finally, liberal values were more important than trade structure, which simply did not appear to be a prominent general explanation for the liberalism of the Tokyo Round. In sum, the nations participating in the Tokyo Round placed a high priority on maintaining a liberal, open trading regime, and in the main they were able to achieve this end. The Tokyo Round negotiation demonstrated at the international level the assertion about social achievement previously cited from the work of David McClelland, namely: "What each generation wanted above all, it got."[91]

Governments and individual negotiators at the Tokyo Round were motivated by the fundamental belief that life could be better through a policy of liberalism and international cooperation. This belief was pursued with sufficient determination to achieve a successful conclusion to the negotiation. As with any political or economic belief, the importance of the belief was not that it is rational, or that it is capable of being proven correct with empirical evidence, but rather that it is capable of sustaining political action. The importance of beliefs is often best revealed in time of adversity, which in the Tokyo Round might have been the uncertain days prior to the Bonn summit. In this period, Robert Strauss was asked in a press briefing whether or not the timing of the Tokyo Round concurrent with a world recession bothered him. His complete answer is a vivid testimony to the importance of beliefs in international economic negotiation:

[90] Commission, *GATT Multilateral Trade Negotiations*, pt. I (p. 5).
[91] *Achieving Society*, 437.

Everything bothers me, but it does not set me back. The timing when I left Jones County to try to get an education was in the middle of the 30's in the height of the depression. It bothered me but it did not stop me from leaving home and trying for something better, and that is the way I feel about this. That is a key point. I want to remind you that the first thing that was asked me a year ago when we started talking about making progress, was doesn't the timing convince you that you could not conceivably have any successful trade negotiations. Economies are fragile; there is inflation around the world; growth rates are failing to meet goals; nations are jockeying for positions with each other. Doesn't the timing disturb you? You can't make progress in a climate like this. My answer then was, and I don't want to be arrogant about it, that the timing is such that we cannot fail to make progress. And I say to you that the timing now is such and the conditions are such around the world that we cannot fail to make progress. I heard Franklin Roosevelt one day say before some of you were born that he thought a number of us had, what he termed in that classic line, a rendez-vous with destiny. I don't want to over-dramatize it, but I think negotiators have a bit of that in their hands. I think they are playing for real stakes that are going to affect people's lives in real ways where they eat better, where they dress better, where they live a bit better. *You have to believe that or you would not be here.* Maybe it's all hogwash and maybe I am a bit of a senile old fool; but for the present, I will stand on that statement.[92]

[92] U.S. Mission to GATT, Geneva, transcript of press conference of Ambassador Strauss, Geneva, July 13, 1978 (emphasis added).

· 10 ·

CONCLUSION: THE FUTURE OF THE
WORLD TRADING SYSTEM

In the half decade since the Tokyo Round, things have not gone well for
GATT or the world trading system. World recession deepened in the
early 1980s, and problems of debt and monetary exchanges worsened
international economic relationships. Public attitudes at the elite and
mass level seemed less supportive of liberalism. Certain illiberal practices were applied by national governments. All this has created concern over whether the liberal consensus of the postwar period can be
maintained. Such concern arises because it is widely recognized that the
world trading system is an inherently fragile system. It is a system
where relations are expected to be competitive, but where that competition is in turn kept within reasonable bounds by a series of self-imposed rules and norms of behavior. In such a system, if one transgresses
the norms there is danger of retaliation, and then further retaliation in
response. There are reasons for nations to protect their interests, and
therefore there is always a danger that the competition which is a legitimate part of the world trading system might degenerate into competitive protectionism, and then into full-scale retaliation such as occurred
in the early 1930s. In the last analysis, the international trade system is
a self-help system, and in this respect it is not much different from the
international security system. Even though peace may be the norm, the
potential for destructive conflict is never far away.

The greatest concern facing the world trading system in the mid-
1980s is how to maintain the liberal consensus that helped lead to the
Tokyo Round, and that could continue to promote an open and mutually beneficial international economy into the future. Not only is this
concern important because it affects economic prosperity or, in Robert
Strauss's words, how people are fed and how they are clothed, but it
also has the potential to affect the peace and good order of the international political system. In an earlier age when simple theories of international relations were perhaps more easily tolerated, Cordell Hull
advanced the notion that "unhampered trade dovetailed with peace,
high tariffs . . . with war."[1] More sophisticated analysis has since dismissed Hull's ideas, but one wonders if this dismissal may have been

---

[1] *Memoires*, 81.

too hasty.[2] In more recent times, particularly in economic relations between East and West, it has appeared that trade has been related to periods of cooperation and détente, and conversely that political tension has been related to economic sanctions and embargoes. Then, too, there are recent official statements that would seem to accept implicitly Hull's argument. For example, in the 1970s a U.S. president, in proposing trade-liberalizing legislation to the Congress, exhorted his compatriots with the following words:

> Increasingly in recent years, countries have come to see that the best way of advancing their own interests is by expanding peaceful contacts with other peoples. We have thus begun to erect a durable structure of peace in the world from which all nations can benefit and in which all nations have a stake.
>
> This structure of peace cannot be strong, however, unless it encompasses international economic affairs. . . .
>
> I urge the Congress to enact these proposals so that we can help move our country . . . into a new era in which trade among nations helps us to build a peaceful, more prosperous world.[3]

These words came from Richard Nixon, who of all postwar U.S. presidents had the most firmly established reputation for realpolitik in international affairs. Nixon's words confirm that the stakes are high as regards the maintenance of international economic relationships, because those relationships ultimately have a bearing on the preservation of peace in international affairs. The fact that the last great breakdown in the international economic system preceded a world war seems to underscore the point.

There are three overriding problems that the future will bring concerning the maintenance of liberalism in the international trading system. The first is that of accommodating current national practices that are inconsistent with the GATT-inspired concept of free trade, and that threaten to diminish the value of free trade as an organizing principle of foreign economic policy. A second problem is to contain economic

---

[2] See Buzan, "Economic Structure." See also Kindleberger, *Foreign Trade*, 239, who has said trade contributes to prosperity, but "It probably has little effect on the incidence of war." Kindleberger goes on to argue that close trade ties within countries have not prevented civil war. This is obviously true, and it is also the case that trade cannot prevent a war that arises for other reasons. In this sense, war is the dominant form of behavior, trade recessive. Nevertheless the prosperity brought by trade is itself an inducement to cooperation; and in the international system, which is much less integrated than domestic systems, trade has a different (and more important) role in establishing human contact and communication.

[3] U.S. House of Representatives, "Message of the President" (1973), 101, 113.

nationalism, which traditionally has been a fundamental source of instability in the world trading system. The third problem is to advance the techniques of system control within the international economic system commensurate with the extent to which we now rely on that system for our economic and political well-being.

The first problem—the conflict of current practices with GATT assumptions—has become increasingly apparent during the past decade. GATT is based on the desideratum of a free international market between independent private buyers and sellers. It assumes that trade in goods is to some extent separable from other international economic problems such as monetary exchanges or foreign investment. As a code of conduct, the GATT promotes nonintervention by governments in international trade, and it mandates, with a few exceptions, that whatever intervention is done be done on a nondiscriminatory basis. GATT seeks to prohibit quantitative trade restrictions and it promotes the use of tariffs for protection; tariffs in turn are to be mutually lowered through multilateral trade negotiations. The overriding goal of GATT is an open world trading system free of government restrictions.

Modern practices run counter to the GATT ideal in several particulars. First is the matter of negotiated protectionism. It was assumed under the General Agreement that negotiation would be a means to liberalize the system, but more recent experience has seen negotiation used to promote protectionism. Such negotiated protectionism has produced a large number of bilateral agreements, known as voluntary export restraints (VER's) or orderly marketing agreements (OMA's), which now substantially regulate trade in sectors such as textiles, consumer electronics, and automobiles. Other agreements have been multilateral, notably the multifibre agreement and its predecessors.[4] An important characteristic of these agreements is that they have made extensive use of quantitative restrictions, which are most inconsistent with the GATT ideal of a free market system. Another inconsistency is the discriminatory nature of negotiated protectionism, for the restrictions are borne by relatively few exporting nations. Finally, these agreements are inimical to the spirit of the GATT and to the essence of negotiation itself, for they are usually undertaken between the weak and the strong, and are obtained under an implicit threat by the stronger of sterner measures had the weak not complied. These negotiations, conducted outside GATT, raised doubts about the ability of the GATT system to address the most pressing problems of the world trading system.

Another practice concerns foreign investment. The main concern of

---

[4] For a review of these measures, see Bergsten and Cline, "Overview."

GATT has been international trade in goods, and the normal assumption is made that trade occurs in response to comparative advantage, assessed mainly in terms of factor costs and markets. Modern foreign investment calls these assumptions into question. International trade occurs increasingly between related parties, especially transnational corporations (TNC's) and their affiliates, which in itself raises doubts about the arm's-length nature of many international transactions. Furthermore, the matter of where affiliates are located has an important bearing on trade flows. The location of major foreign investments is usually negotiated between governments and TNC's, and motivations on both sides are often political. Host governments regularly provide investment incentives such as tax holidays or direct subsidies to attract foreign investment, and they often impose performance requirements to influence the economic behavior of firms that establish within their jurisdiction. For their part, firms have shown a capacity to adapt to host-government practices in their investment decisions,[5] and they have engaged in other investment patterns, such as a follow-the-leader pattern, that could produce trade flows different from those based on factor costs or market opportunities.[6] Finally, the principle of comparative advantage has likewise been subject to reinterpretation in light of modern investment practices. Comparative advantage traditionally depended on resource endowments or on slowly accumulating capital stocks, but today it depends more on major investment decisions or on the development of human capital through training in research. The process of acquiring a comparative advantage in a sector is more manipulatable than before, which gives countries greater capacity to influence their own trade patterns.[7] As a result, the composition of trade flows is becoming subject to the actions of government.[8] In GATT, it is assumed that the major action governments take regarding trade is to restrict it, and GATT rules attempt to regulate the manner in which governments can deploy those restrictions. Modern policies toward foreign investment give governments greater scope to create trade in the first place, and, except for the area of subsidies, GATT rules do not regulate this aspect of the problem.

[5] For example, Whitman, "Two Perspectives," 10, describes this as a strategy of "defensive investment."

[6] See Vernon, "Old Rules," 29.

[7] As Reich, "Beyond Free Trade," 782, has observed, "In a very real and immediate way, a nation *chooses* its comparative advantage."

[8] A good example of this is the Canada-U.S. automobile agreement, which has been instrumental in promoting a twentyfold increase in Canada's automobile exports since 1965. For further information, see Winham, "Canadian Automobile Industry."

Finally, there are a number of unrelated government practices that raise doubts about the GATT norm that national economies are composed of private economic actors relatively free of intervention by governments. Heading the list of these practices are the institutions and policies of the Japanese government, which are often referred to collectively as an industrial policy, and which have given that government unusual capacity to influence the direction of the Japanese economy. These institutions and policies restrict trade, but they are not readily amenable to reform through GATT rules.[9] Since most other countries of the world incorporate some elements of Japanese industrial policies in their own national practices, the problem of controlling their potential damage to the world trading system is a general one. A further issue is direct government activity in the economy, either through the operations of state enterprises or through state trading (which is common in sectors such as urban-mass-transit equipment or commodities) or through the practice of countertrade.[10] The reality created by these practices is a world in which trade is increasingly "managed" by governments.[11] Taken all together, these practices, plus those on foreign investment and negotiated protectionism, portray a world in which governments are more involved in national and international economic activity. While this involvement will not necessarily produce illiberal results, such an outcome is nevertheless probable if for no other reason than that governments exist principally to provide for the exclusive interests of their own nationals. At minimum, the increasing role of governments in the international economy will mean that, in the future, increasing diplomatic efforts will have to be expended to insure that the trade system operates in a manner perceived to be fair by its participants.

The second problem in maintaining a liberal consensus will be to contain economic nationalism. This indeed is not a novel problem, for a link between nationalism and protectionism exists in practice and in theory alike. The practice can be seen in the often-nationalistic appeals interest groups make for protectionism on their behalf, which are perhaps best summed up in the aforementioned words of a nineteenth-cen-

---

[9] See Saxonhouse, "Foreign Sales to Japan."

[10] Countertrade is defined by Banks, "Countertrade," 159, as "the explicit linking of import and export transactions between two traders; in short, barter." Banks notes that it occurs mostly in trade with Eastern bloc countries, and he argues that in itself it is unlikely ever to become a serious threat to the multilateral trading system.

[11] Brittan, "World Adjustment," 546, has estimated that some 40 percent of world trade was managed in 1980.

tury pamphleteer: "Free trade is in favour of the foreign."[12] In theory, the link has been established in the writing of Frederick List, and especially in the comparison List himself drew between his writings and those of the Classical School of Adam Smith or Jean-Baptiste Say.[13] List attacked the cosmopolitan views of the Classical School as reflecting a world that did not exist in reality. Reality for List was the nation, for, in his words, "between the individual and the whole human race there is the nation . . . [which is] an association having not only an entirely separate existence, but having an intelligence and an interest, particularly its own, a whole existing for itself."[14] Now in the modern age, List's nationalistic philosophy has been almost forgotten. Certainly the Classical School has been vastly more influential, in part because of World War II and the growing appeal of internationalism, and in part because of the appeal of the simple Ricardian notion that the world is economically better off if people are allowed to produce what they make most efficiently and trade freely to receive the rest. However, List was right in his structural analysis of the international economic system, for it is undeniable that we live in an age of nations and nationalism that is far from being ended. Furthermore, at the philosophical level, List's argument has considerable appeal, for it was not simply jingoism but rather was rooted in an analysis of how human civilization could achieve its greatest potential. List held that "As an individual acquires chiefly by the aid of the nation and in the bosom of the nation, intellectual culture, productive power, security and well-being, human civilization can only be conceived as possible by means of the civilization and development of nations."[15] This is an argument that would likely receive substantial support among the different peoples of the world today, even if the philosopher who wrote them is not widely regarded as an influential thinker. Thus two important philosophic strands form the intellectual roots of contending approaches to trade policy: the internationalism and concern for economic efficiency of the Classical School versus the nationalism of List's Historical School.

At the level of policy, List proposed a model of national development that progressed in five stages from a savage state to a fully developed agricultural, manufacturing, and commercial state. Transitions through the early stages were, in List's view, efficiently promoted by

---

[12] Phillips, *Protection and Free Trade*, 15.
[13] See List, *National System*.
[14] Ibid., 263.
[15] Ibid.

free trade.[16] However, to develop manufacturing industry, which was an essential ingredient of modern national life, protectionism was a necessary policy. For a nation already strong and industrially developed, free trade was the preferred policy, and in a remarkable display of foresight List predicted the development of a free-trade policy in England.[17] But List's prescription for industrial development and protectionism was directed to his native Germany, and it was eagerly received in the United States, both of which were underdeveloped economies of that era. For such underdeveloped economies, List's thesis was profoundly contrary to the theory of comparative advantage. As List put it,

> The [Classical] School mistakes completely the nature of economical relations between nations, in supposing that the exchange of agricultural products for manufactured products is just as useful to the civilization, prosperity, and generally to the social progress of such nations, as the establishment in their own territory of manufacturing industry.[18]

The developing countries today largely pursue policies that are consistent with List's philosophy. In an effort to promote national economic development, they have extended heavy protection to import-competing manufactures and have used a range of commercial and investment policies to stimulate manufactured exports. But List's ideas are followed not only in the developing countries. Highly developed nations are today under pressure to improve their commercial performance, and to do this are turning to a variety of government tools that will advantage their national producers in international competition. In the United States, where government intervention in the economy is less accepted than in most other countries, the use of government industrial policies to promote economic performance is controversial. On one side of this debate, Robert Reich has argued that the United States should abandon its ideological opposition to government intervention and assist American manufacturers to move toward

---

[16] List stated, "The transition from the savage to the pastoral, and from the pastoral to the agricultural state, as well as the first progress in agriculture, is very efficiently promoted by free intercourse among manufacturing and commercial nations" (ibid., 72).

[17] List stated, "England will take a course quite contrary to that she has heretofore pursued; instead of soliciting other nations to adopt free trade, whilst she maintains at home her rigorous prohibitive system, she will open to the world her own markets, without troubling herself with the protective system of others" (ibid., 276).

[18] Ibid., 267.

higher-value and therefore more competitive production.[19] Reich's argument is not protectionist, because he opposes subsidies and other government policies that retard economic adjustment, but it is a competitive argument based on the performance of national economies as units. As such, it is not far from the national strategy advanced by List, who claimed, in regard to the economic activity and wealth of a nation's citizens, that "nowhere have labour, economy, the spirit of invention, and the spirit of industrial enterprise, accomplished any thing great, where civil liberty, the institutions and laws, external policy, the internal government, and especially where national unity and power have not lent their support."[20]

The national competitiveness Reich has called for is an unavoidable response in the current troubled world economy, and such competition probably has the potential to make all countries better off. As Reich himself notes, "The American interest lies in promoting the rapid transformation of all nations' industrial bases toward high-value production, while discouraging zero-sum efforts to preserve the status-quo."[21] However, the real problem may yet be the ability to retain perspective and to control the excesses of nationalistic competition. The danger is that excessive nationalism in economic affairs inevitably becomes protectionist, and that those who are committed protectionists inevitably use nationalism to gain material ends. This is an old problem in the international economy, which will continue to test the capacity of national leaders to maintain a liberal system in the future.

The third problem in maintaining a liberal consensus into the future is to advance the techniques of economic organization and control at the international level. In the last analysis, the international economy is a very primitive system. Traditionally, national economies have operated as a system, but the international economy has operated as an occasional relationship. Most business decisions were made in reference to the national economy, and most government control was exercised there. Over time, governments came to exercise very substantial control over the internal economic system, for example, control over financial institutions, energy supply and pricing, business practices such as monopoly, and agricultural production and distribution. It is true that

[19] Reich, "Beyond Free Trade," 803, noted, "The United States must understand that government expenditure in the form of subsidies, loan guarantees and tax benefits designed to keep or lure high value-added emerging businesses within the United States, are no less legitimate investments in the education of America's labor force than are investments in the public schools."

[20] List, *National System*, 178.

[21] Reich, "Beyond Free Trade," 790.

an uncontrolled exchange (i.e., free trade) of goods and services existed in the internal system, but this was manageable because many other aspects of that system were controlled.

Now, at the international level, the economic system is becoming less an occasional relationship and more the primary area for much economic activity. However, the capacity for control of the international system has not kept pace with the growth in importance of that system for aggregate world economic activity. Nations attempt to maintain a liberal international trading system, but these attempts risk being rendered absurd by the free movement of other variables in the system. For example, a lengthy and arduous trade negotiation might produce a reduction in average tariffs from 10 to 5 percent, but fluctuation in the exchange rate can produce price changes up to three times that amount in a few months. As we have seen, much of the incentive to negotiate the Tokyo Round was to reduce the uncertainty in international trade that flowed from unilateral and (often) arbitrary government decision-making. The challenge in the future may be to reduce the uncertainty in international trade that comes from elsewhere in the international economy. Unless greater control can be exercised over the international economy as a whole, the liberal consensus that has existed on international trade may not be sustainable.

The problems of the immediate future appear to lie substantially in international monetary relations. In most of the postwar period, the fixed-exchange Bretton Woods system which maintained control over fluctuations of monetary values obtained. Following the breakdown of the Bretton Woods system, those values were eventually allowed to fluctuate freely. There is now a need for greater control over exchange-rate fluctuations, or the world will likely see greater control through protectionism in trade flows.[22] The Tokyo Round demonstrated how problems in the international monetary system gave impetus to a negotiation on international trade. Now it appears that problems in the international trade system have underscored the need for greater monetary cooperation. Were this to occur, it would require a closer coordination of macroeconomic policy between nations along the lines attempted in the annual economic summits of the seven major Western

---

[22] In a thoughtful article, Bressand, " 'Worldeconomy,' " has argued that the temporary coexistence of free-market regimes in trade, finance, and money creates a greater potential for change than the world economy can accommodate. He calls sensibly for a three-year interim stabilization agreement to stabilize exchange rates.

Further support for the need for greater monetary control is provided by Bergsten and Cline, "Overview," who demonstrate a relationship between exchange-rate misalignments and the direction of trade policy.

powers. Both monetary cooperation and macroeconomic coordination are extraordinarily difficult issues to bring up on the international scene, because they raise questions both of national economic sovereignty and of the proper role of government in the economy. If these are not dealt with, however, one of the costs may be the loss of the liberal consensus in the international trading system.

Related to this problem is the matter of the structure of the international trading system. As mentioned earlier, the rule of nondiscriminatory treatment was abridged in the GATT codes, and it has been even more fundamentally threatened in the establishment of preference arrangements such as the EC's relationship with selected developing countries under the Lomé agreements. These occurrences risk breaking what has been an undifferentiated system of legal relationships into several parts. It has been argued by proponents of liberalism that a distinction exists between liberal trading relations and nondiscriminatory relations, and that indeed an insistence on universal nondiscrimination (i.e., the most-favored-nation procedures of GATT) in international trade can slow progress toward further trade liberalization that might be made on a piecemeal basis.[23] This is undoubtedly true, but what is not taken account of is that preferential or discriminatory arrangements create a political structure wherein it is more difficult to pursue liberalism. Preferential arrangements introduce alliance considerations into trading relationships. Preferences and discrimination ultimately introduce into trade policy a search for pragmatic side deals and trade offs, which usually have inimical consequences for trading partners not party to the deal.[24] Preferential arrangements tend to break the association between free trade and internationalism, and it has been internationalist sentiments in the postwar world that have been one of the attitudinal bulwarks behind free trade. Preferential or discriminatory relationships present a structural threat to the system of liberal international trade that has been set up in the postwar international system, and the probability is that one cannot threaten the structure of a system without threatening as well the values that help maintain it.

To maintain a liberal consensus into the future, there will be a need to expand human control of the international economic system and, insofar as possible, to contain the threats to its universal character. This will have to be done through a process of international multilateral negotiations, which for want of anything better is the most effective tool

[23] This argument is currently widely held in the office of the U.S. trade representative.
[24] This point can be appreciated in Hull's discussion of a proposed cotton barter deal with Nazi Germany (*Memoires*, 370–74).

for managing major problems in a system of sovereign nation-states. The Tokyo Round, which was a negotiation designed to reform for the 1970s a trade system created in the 1940s, was just the first step in this process. Nations are now on the frontier of an exploration of multilateral negotiation, and international organization as well,[25] as a means of managing the international economy. This is an exploration that will proceed incrementally, and with occasional failures, but proceed it must if we are to develop a better way to manage world economic problems than we now have. At a time when the world could be said to be in a mess economically, it is also in a mess organizationally. The political structure of the world community is not suited to the problems it is now facing. The world is organized into nation-states, but, as Daniel Bell has noted, the nation-state is too big for the small problems and too small for the big problems. Managing the international economy is a big problem. New tools will have to be developed and refined to handle the task, and especially the tool of multilateral negotiation. In this sense, the development of new processes of management must proceed apace with new substantive economic policies at the international level.

The world needs new processes of managing the international economy to escape the problems of the 1980s as much as it needed new processes of management to escape the problems it faced in the 1930s. The 1930s saw a systemic change in the handling of problems like the tariff, namely from decisionmaking by unilateral national action to decisionmaking by bilateral negotiation. The change in the 1980s and beyond will have to be of a similar order, namely from decisionmaking by occasional multilateral cooperation to decisionmaking by a more profound process of multilateral management. If this change in decisionmaking processes does not occur—and it would be as profound a move for the 1980s as was the change of the 1930s for that decade—then it will be more difficult to maintain the liberal consensus that has helped to produce prosperity and peace for the past generation.

[25] See Jacobson, *Networks*, esp. ch. 16.

APPENDIX A

THE TOKYO DECLARATION

DECLARATION ISSUED AT THE END OF THE MINISTERIAL MEETING
HELD IN TOKYO, 12–14 SEPTEMBER 1973

1. The Ministers, having considered the report of the Preparatory Committee for the Trade Negotiations and having noted that a number of governments have decided to enter into comprehensive multilateral trade negotiations in the framework of GATT and that other governments have indicated their intention to make a decision as soon as possible, declare the negotiations officially open. Those governments which have decided to negotiate have notified the Director-General of GATT to this effect, and the Ministers agree that it will be open to any other government, through a notification to the Director-General, to participate in the negotiations. The Ministers hope that the negotiations will involve the active participation of as many countries as possible. They expect the negotiations to be engaged effectively as rapidly as possible, and that, to that end, the governments concerned will have such authority as may be required.[100]

2. The negotiations shall aim to:

–achieve the expansion and ever-greater liberalization of world trade and improvement in the standard of living and welfare of the people of the world, objectives which can be achieved, inter alia, through the progressive dismantling of obstacles to trade and the improvement of the international framework for the conduct of world trade.

–secure additional benefits for the international trade of developing countries so as to achieve a substantial increase in their foreign exchange earnings, the diversification of their exports, the acceleration of the rate of growth of their trade, taking into account their development needs, an improvement in the possibilities for these countries to participate in the expansion of world trade and a better balance as between developed and developing countries in the sharing of the advantages resulting from this expansion, through, in the largest possible measure, a substantial improvement in the conditions of access for the products of interest to the developing countries and, wherever appropriate, meas-

Taken from *GATT Activities in 1973*, Geneva: GATT, 1974, 5–10.

ures designed to attain stable, equitable and remunerative prices for primary products.

To this end, co-ordinated efforts shall be made to solve in an equitable way the trade problems of all participating countries, taking into account the specific trade problems of the developing countries.

3. To this end the negotiations should aim, inter alia, to:

(a) conduct negotiations on tariffs by employment of appropriate formulae of as general application as possible;

(b) reduce or eliminate non-tariff measures or, where this is not appropriate, to reduce or eliminate their trade restricting or distorting effects, and to bring such measures under more effective international discipline;

(c) include an examination of the possibilities for the co-ordinated reduction or elimination of all barriers to trade in selected sectors as complementary technique;

(d) include an examination of the adequacy of the multilateral safeguard system, considering particularly the modalities of application of Article XIX, with a view to furthering trade liberalization and preserving its results;

(e) include, as regards agriculture, an approach to negotiations which, while in line with the general objectives of the negotiations, should take account of the special characteristics and problems in this sector;

(f) treat tropical products as a special and priority sector.

4. The negotiations shall cover tariffs, non-tariff barriers and other measures which impede or distort international trade in both industrial and agricultural products, including tropical products and raw materials, whether in primary form or at any stage of processing including in particular products of export interest to developing countries and measures affecting their exports.

5. The negotiations shall be conducted on the basis of the principles of mutual advantage, mutual commitment and overall reciprocity, while observing the most-favoured-nation clause, and consistently with the provisions of the General Agreement relating to such negotiations. Participants shall jointly endeavour in the negotiations to achieve, by appropriate methods, an overall balance of advantage at the highest possible level. The developed countries do not expect reciprocity for commitments made by them in the negotiations to reduce or remove tariff and other barriers to the trade of developing countries, i.e., the developed countries do not expect the developing countries, in the course of the trade negotiations, to make contributions which are inconsistent with their individual development, financial and trade

needs. The Ministers recognize the need for special measures to be taken in the negotiations to assist the developing countries in their efforts to increase their export earnings and promote their economic development and, where appropriate, for priority attention to be given to products or areas of interest to developing countries. They also recognize the importance of maintaining and improving the Generalized System of Preferences. They further recognize the importance of the application of differential measures to developing countries in ways which will provide special and more favourable treatment for them in areas of the negotiation where this is feasible and appropriate.

6. The Ministers recognize that the particular situation and problems of the least developed among the developing countries shall be given special attention, and stress the need to ensure that these countries receive special treatment in the context of any general or specific measures taken in favour of the developing countries during the negotiations.

7. The policy of liberalizing world trade cannot be carried out successfully in the absence of parallel efforts to set up a monetary system which shields the world economy from the shocks and imbalances which have previously occurred. The Ministers will not lose sight of the fact that the efforts which are to be made in the trade field imply continuing efforts to maintain orderly conditions and to establish a durable and equitable monetary system.

The Ministers recognize equally that the new phase in the liberalization of trade which it is their intention to undertake should facilitate the orderly functioning of the monetary system.

The Ministers recognize that they should bear these considerations in mind both at the opening of and throughout the negotiations. Efforts in these two fields will thus be able to contribute effectively to an improvement of international economic relations, taking into account the special characteristics of the economies of the developing countries and their problems.

8. The negotiations shall be considered as one undertaking, the various elements of which shall move forward together.

9. Support is reaffirmed for the principles, rules and disciplines provided for under the General Agreement.[1] Considerations shall be given to improvements in the international framework for the conduct of world trade which might be desirable in the light of progress in the negotiations and, in this endeavour, care shall be taken to ensure that any

---

[1] This does not necessarily represent the views of representatives of countries not now parties to the General Agreement.

measures introduced as a result are consistent with the overall objectives and principles of the trade negotiations and particularly of trade liberalization.

10. A Trade Negotiations Committee is established, with authority, taking into account the present Declaration, inter alia:

(a) to elaborate and put into effect detailed trade negotiating plans and to establish appropriate negotiating procedures, including special procedures for the negotiations between developed and developing countries;

(b) to supervise the progress of the negotiations.

The Trade Negotiations Committee shall be open to participating governments.[2] The Trade Negotiations Committee shall hold its opening meeting not later than 1 November 1973.

11. The Ministers intend that the trade negotiations be concluded in 1975.

[2] Including the European Countries.

APPENDIX B

SUMMARY OF SIX "CODE" AGREEMENTS NEGOTIATED AT THE TOKYO ROUND

AGREEMENT ON GOVERNMENT PROCUREMENT

Relevant GATT Provisions

The GATT is essentially silent on government procurement, and therefore permits government entities to discriminate in procurement. Article 3 (National Treatment) states that its provisions do not apply to government agencies.

The Agreement

The purpose of this code is to "establish an agreed international framework of rights and obligations with respect to laws, regulations, procedures and practices regarding government procurement with a view to achieving greater liberalization and expansion of world trade"; to prevent discrimination against foreign suppliers or protection of domestic suppliers; to provide for transparency of laws; and to recognize that, "taking into account their balance-of-payments positions, developing countries may need to adopt agreed differential measures."

Article 1 provides that the agreement will apply under three conditions: The purchaser is a government entity subject to the agreement and listed in the annex; the procurement is for products (including services incidental to the purchase of the product); and the procurement contract is valued at SDR 150,000 (approximately U.S. $195,000 in 1979) or more. Article 2 obliges parties to extend national treatment and nondiscrimination to products and suppliers of other parties covered by the agreement. Article 3 (Special and Differential Treatment) provides that developing countries "may negotiate . . . mutually acceptable exclusions from the rules on national treatment with respect to certain entities of products." Developed countries are obliged to establish information centers to respond to reasonable requests for information from developing-country parties.

Article 4 establishes that technical specifications may not be used as barriers; specifications should be stated in terms of performance rather than design. Article 5 (Tendering) establishes norms for tendering pro-

417

cedures. The tendering process is to be as open as possible, although entities may avail themselves of provisions which permit selective and single tendering procedures. Selective tendering means the entity will qualify a potential supplier on its ability to fulfill the contracts, although the entity "shall not discriminate among foreign suppliers or between domestic and foreign suppliers." Single tendering, under which only one entity will be asked to submit a bid, will be carried out only under restricted circumstances, including: when tenders under open or selective means were not received, or were not judged acceptable; or when only one supplier can supply a particular contract for artistic or technological reasons. Article 5 also details requirements on the availability of information and the submission of tenders.

Article 8 provides: "Nothing in this agreement shall be construed to prevent any party from taking any actions or not disclosing any information which it considers necessary for the protection of its essential security interests." The agreement also provides for accession and withdrawal, the establishment of a Committee on Government Procurement (Article 7), consultation and enforcement (Article 9).

AGREEMENT ON IMPLEMENTATION OF ARTICLE 7 OF THE GENERAL AGREEMENT ON TARIFFS AND TRADE AND PROTOCOL (CUSTOMS VALUATION)

Relevant GATT Provisions

Article 2 (Schedules of Concessions) provides: "No contracting party shall alter its method of determining dutiable value or of converting currencies so as to impair the value of any concessions provided for in . . . this agreement." Article 7 (Valuation) states that value "should be based on actual value of imported merchandise on which duty is assessed, or like merchandise, and should not be based on the value of merchandise of national origin or on arbitrary or fictitious values." The actual value is the price at which like merchandise is sold or offered for sale, at a certain time or place, under fully competitive conditions. When the actual value was not ascertainable, valuation was to be based on the nearest "ascertainable equivalent of such value."

The Agreement

The purpose of this code is that customs value should "be based on simple and equitable criteria consistent with commercial practices and that valuation procedures should be of general application without distinction between sources of supply." Article 1 establishes that the transaction value, that is, the price actually paid for the goods when sold for export, is the preferred means of customs valuation.

Articles 2–6 delineate, in descending order, four other means of valuation if the transaction value cannot be determined under Article 1. In Article 2, "the customs value shall be the transaction value of identical goods sold for export to the same country of importation and exported at or about the same time as the goods being valued." If the value cannot be determined by this method, then Article 3 provides that valuation should be calculated on the transaction value of similar goods imported by the importing country.

If value cannot be determined by the three methods above, the importer may choose between the fourth and fifth methods; alternatively, the fourth method takes precedence. Article 5 provides that value be obtained according to the resale price of the goods less commissions or profits, cost of transport and insurance, and customs duties and taxes. Article 6 provides that value be established through computation of the cost of materials and fabrication or processing plus an amount for profits and general expenses.

Article 7 specifies that value shall not be determined by certain methods, including price of goods on the domestic market of the country of export. The code establishes two committees—a Committee on Customs Valuation and a Technical Committee on Customs Valuation—to resolve conflicts between parties. Article 21 provides for special and differential treatment for developing countries.

AGREEMENT ON TECHNICAL BARRIERS TO TRADE (STANDARDS)

Relevant GATT Provisions

The GATT contains few provisions on technical barriers to trade. Article 3 (National Treatment) states, inter alia, that internal quantitative regulation requiring the mixture, processing, or use of products in specified amounts or proportions "should not be applied to imported or domestic products so as to afford protection to domestic production."

The Agreement

The purpose of this code is "to ensure that technical regulations and standards, including packaging, marking and labelling requirements, and methods for certifying conformity with technical regulations and standards do not create unnecessary obstacles to international trade."

419

The agreement applies to both agricultural and industrial products. Article 2 provides that "Parties shall ensure that technical regulations and standards are not prepared, adopted or applied with a view to creating obstacles to international trade." Parties agree to use international standards which already exist and, wherever appropriate, to "specify technical regulations and standards in terms of performance rather than design or descriptive characteristics." Article 2 further requires signatories to publish information detailing the requirements of proposed or existing standards which have or are expected to have an impact on trade; and to notify and consult with other parties through the GATT secretariat.

Article 10 requires each party to establish an easily accessible inquiry point to provide information to interested parties on the subjects of technical regulations, standards, certification processes, and location of notices published pursuant to this agreement.

The agreement provides for the establishment of a Committee on Technical Barriers to Trade, "for the purpose of affording Parties the opportunity of consulting on matters relating to the operation of this Agreement." The agreement also provides for panels and working groups and contains rules for consultation and dispute settlement.

AGREEMENT ON IMPORT LICENSING PROCEDURES

Relevant GATT Provisions

Article 8 (Fees and Formalities) provides that fees and charges connected with, inter alia, import licensing, are to be "limited in amount to the approximate cost of services rendered and shall not represent an indirect protection to domestic products or a taxation of imports or exports for fiscal purposes." The parties "also recognize the need for minimizing the incidence and complexity of import and export formalities and for decreasing and simplifying import and export documentation requirements."

The Agreement

The purpose of this code is threefold: "To simplify, and bring transparency to, the administrative procedures and practices used in international trade"; "to ensure the fair and equitable application and administration of such procedures"; and "to provide for a consultative mechanism and the speedy, effective and equitable resolution of disputes."

420

To these ends, the five articles of the code outline general provisions for import licensing, "automatic" import licensing, "non-automatic" import licensing, and final provisions for consultation, dispute settlement, review, and amendment.

Article 1 provides that parties ensure that domestic import licensing procedures are in accordance with all relevant GATT provisions; rules relevant to licensing are to be published, application forms and procedures are to be as simple as possible, and procedures are to be administered in a fair and equitable manner. Article 1 also directs that applications for licenses shall not be refused for minor errors in documentation or for minor variations in value, quantity, or weight during shipping. Exceptions to these rules are permitted on the grounds of security or law enforcement.

Article 2 provides that automatic import licenses (import licenses for which approval of the application is freely granted, often used for administrative purposes such as the collection of statistics) are permitted insofar as they do not have any restrictive effects. A license may be maintained "as long as the circumstances which gave rise to its introduction prevail or as long as its underlying administrative purposes cannot be achieved in a more appropriate way."

Article 3 stipulates that nonautomatic import licenses, used in administering quotas and other import restrictions, are not to have restrictive effects on imports in addition to the effects of the restrictions themselves. Importers are required to make available all relevant information, and parties have a right to an explanation and an appeal.

Under Articles 4 and 5, a Committee on Import Licensing and a system for consultation and dispute settlement are set up to deal with problems arising between parties.

AGREEMENT ON IMPLEMENTATION OF ARTICLE 6 OF THE GENERAL AGREEMENT ON TARIFFS AND TRADE (ANTIDUMPING)

Relevant GATT Provisions

Article 6 (Antidumping) of the GATT defines dumping as a process "by which products of one country are introduced into the commerce of another country at less than the normal value of the products." Dumping is condemned "if it causes or threatens material injury to an established industry . . . or materially retards the establishment of a domestic industry." To prevent dumping, an antidumping duty may be levied "not greater in amount than the margin of dumping."

The Agreement

The purpose of the antidumping code is to bring relevant provisions of the antidumping code concluded at the end of the Kennedy Round into line with the provisions of the new code on subsidies and countervailing duties. The most important revisions concerned the determination of injury, price undertakings between exporters and importing countries, and procedures for imposing and collecting antidumping duties.

Article 3 provides that (material) injury be determined by the volume of the dumped imports and their effect on prices, and by the impact dumped imports have on domestic producers. Article 7 provides that antidumping proceedings may be suspended or terminated in the event the exporter raises prices or ceases to export at dumped prices.

Article 13 recognizes "that special regard must be given to the special situation of developing countries when considering the application of anti-dumping measures under this Code." Article 14 establishes a Committee on Antidumping Practices in order to "afford Parties the opportunity of consulting on any matters relating to the operation of the agreement." A statement of understanding affecting the interpretation of Article 13 is attached stating that the Committee on Antidumping Practices may grant time-limited exceptions to developing countries relating to the conduct of antidumping investigations.

AGREEMENT ON INTERPRETATION AND APPLICATION OF ARTICLES 6, 16, AND 23 OF THE GENERAL AGREEMENT ON TARIFFS AND TRADE (SUBSIDIES AND COUNTERVAILING DUTIES)

Relevant GATT Provisions

Article 16 (Subsidies) provides rules governing the use of subsidies. First, parties must notify the GATT if a subsidy will increase exports or decrease imports. Second, an injured party has the right to consult with the subsidizing state when "serious prejudice" is caused or threatened by a subsidy. Third, parties are to avoid granting export subsidies on primary products, specifically in cases where a party would acquire a "more than equitable share" of the world market. Finally, parties are not to introduce subsidies on nonprimary products which have the effect of lowering the export price below the domestic price.

Article 6 (Antidumping and Countervailing Duties) delineates two main conditions governing the imposition of countervailing duties. First, "no countervailing duty shall be levied . . . in excess of an amount equal to the estimated bounty or subsidy determined to have been granted, directly or indirectly, on the manufacture, production or export of such product." Second, a contracting party may impose a countervailing duty only if the effect of the dumping or subsidy is such as to "cause or threaten material injury to an established domestic industry."

The Agreement

The purpose of this code is to "ensure that the use of subsidies does not adversely affect or prejudice the interests of any signatory . . . and that countervailing measures do not unjustifiably impede international trade."

Subsidies are provided for in Part II (Articles 7–13). Article 8 notes that subsidies are used by governments to promote useful economic and social policies; however, parties agree they shall seek to avoid causing through subsidies harm or prejudice to the interests of the other parties. Export subsidies on nonprimary products are prohibited in Article 9, and an annex to the agreement provides an expanded list of prohibited export subsidies on manufactured goods. Article 10 further defines "equitable share of world trade" for export subsidies on primary products. Article 11 lists a number of subsidies other than export subsidies; it recognizes that these (domestic) subsidies can cause injury to other parties and declares parties shall seek to avoid causing such effects.

The code provides two broad means by which a state may respond to subsidies from another party. First, as outlined in Articles 1–6, an injured party may impose countervailing duties on the goods of another party following an investigation that has produced evidence on the existence of a subsidy, on the material injury produced by the subsidy, and on the causal link between subsidy and injury. The procedures for conducting an investigation and imposing duties are prescribed; provision is made for consultation between parties during this process. The code also permits an injured party to impose a "provisional measure" following a preliminary finding of subsidy. After final determination, the proceeds of this measure are either forfeited retroactively or are reimbursed.

Second, as is outlined in Articles 12 and 13, parties believing themselves to be injured by any subsidies may request consultations with the offending party. The latter is obliged to enter into consultations as quickly as possible. After thirty days, a Committee on Subsidies and Countervailing Measures, or a panel appointed by it, shall consider disputes which were not resolved to the mutual satisfaction of the disputants. Countermeasures can be authorized against an offending signatory; such a decision is taken by the committee, rather than the Council of GATT, under specified time restrictions.

Developing countries are excepted from the provisions of Article 9; however, they are obliged to eliminate export subsidies inconsistent with their "competitive and development needs."

SELECTED BIBLIOGRAPHY

The bibliography is selected from items cited in the footnotes. An item appearing here is referred to in the footnotes only by the author's name and short title. Items marked by an asterisk (*) are Tokyo Round agreements.

Allison, Graham T. *Essence of Decision: Explaining the Cuban Missile Crisis.* Boston: Little, Brown and Company, 1971.

Anjaria, Shailendra J., Zubair Igbal, Naheed Kirmani, and Lorenzo L. Perez. *Developments in International Trade Policy.* Occasional Papers, no. 16. Washington: International Monetary Fund, November 1982.

Anthony, David V., and Carol K. Hagerty. "Cautious Optimism as a Guide to Foreign Government Procurement." *Law and Policy in International Business* 11 (1979), pp. 1301–44.

Aron, Raymond. *The Imperial Republic: The United States and the World 1945-1973.* Translated by Frank Jellinek. Cambridge, Mass.: Winthrop Publishers, 1973.

Axelrod, Robert. *The Evolution of Cooperation.* New York: Basic Books, 1984.

Baldwin, Robert E. "The Political Economy of Postwar United States Trade Policy." In Robert E. Baldwin and J. David Richardson, eds., *International Trade and Finance: Readings*, pp. 64–77. 2d ed. Boston: Little, Brown and Company, 1981.

Banks, Gary. "The Economics and Politics of Countertrade." *World Economy* 6 (1983), pp. 159–82.

Barber, Clarence L. "Canadian Tariff Policy." *Canadian Journal of Economics and Political Science* 21 (1955), pp. 513–30.

Barry, Donald. "The Canada–European Community Long Term Fisheries Agreement: Internal Politics and Fisheries Diplomacy." Paper presented to the Annual Meeting of the Canadian Political Science Association, Vancouver, B.C., June 6–8, 1983.

Bauer, Raymond A., Ithiel de Dola Pool, and Lewis A. Dexter. *American Business and Public Policy.* 2d ed. Chicago: Aldine Atherton, 1972.

Bergsten, C. Fred. "Completing the GATT: Toward New International Rules to Govern Export Controls." In *Toward a New International Economic Order: Selected Papers of C. Fred Bergsten, 1972–1974*, pp. 107–56. Lexington, Mass.: Lexington Books, 1975.

———. "Crisis in U.S. Trade Policy." *Foreign Affairs* 49 (July 1971), pp. 619–35.

Bergsten, C. Fred, and William R. Cline. "Conclusion and Policy Implications." In Cline, ed., *Trade Policy*, pp. 747–78.

————. "Trade Policy in the 1980's: An Overview." In Cline, ed., *Trade Policy*, pp. 59–98.

Blaker, Michael K. "Push, Probe and Panic: The Japanese Tactical Style in International Negotiations." In Scalapino, ed., *Modern Japan*, pp. 55–101.

Bressand, Albert. "Mastering the 'Worldeconomy.' " *Foreign Affairs* 61, no. 4 (Spring, 1983), pp. 745–72.

Brittan, Samuel. "A Very Painful World Adjustment." *Foreign Affairs* 61, no. 3 (1982), pp. 541–68.

Burenstam Linder, Staffan. "How to Avoid a New International Economic Disorder." *World Economy* 3 (November 1980), pp. 275–84.

————. *An Essay on Trade and Transformation.* New York: John Wiley and Sons, 1961.

Buzan, Barry. "Economic Structure and International Security: The Limits of the Liberal Case." *International Organization* 38 (Autumn 1984), pp. 597–624.

Canada, Government of. *Review of Developments in the GATT Multilateral Trade Negotiations in Geneva.* Ottawa: CTTC, 1977.

————. *Looking Outward: A New Strategy for Canada.* Ottawa: Economic Council of Canada, 1975.

Caves, Richard E. "Economic Models of Political Choice: Canada's Tariff Structure." *Canadian Journal of Economics* 9 (1976), pp. 278–300.

Clausewitz, Carl von. *On War.* Edited by Anatol Rapoport. Harmondsworth: Penguin Books, 1968.

Cline, William R. "Reciprocity: A New Approach to World Trade Policy." In Cline, ed., *Trade Policy*, pp. 121–58.

Cline, William R., ed. *Trade Policy in the 1980s.* Washington: Institute for International Economics, 1983.

Cline, William R., Noboru Kawanabe, T.O.M. Kronsjo, and Thomas Williams. *Trade Negotiations in the Tokyo Round: A Quantitative Assessment.* Washington: Brookings Institution, 1978.

Commager, Henry S., ed. *Selections from "The Federalist."* New York: Appleton-Century-Crofts, 1949.

Commission of the European Communities. "Development of an Overall Approach to Trade in View of the Coming Multilateral Negotiations in GATT (Memorandum from the Commission to the Council Forwarded on 9 April and Amended on 22 May 1973)." *Bulletin of the European Commission*, Supplement, 2/73.

————. *GATT Multilateral Trade Negotiations: Final Report on the GATT MTN (Tokyo Round) and Proposal for Council Decision.* Brussels: Commission of the European Communities, COM (79) 514 final, October 8, 1979.

————. *Sixth General Report on the Activities of the Communities.* Brussels: EC, 1970.

Commonwealth Group of Experts. *The North-South Dialogue: Making It Work*. London: Commonwealth Secretariat, 1982.

Condliffe, J. B. *The Commerce of Nations*. New York: W. W. Norton and Company, 1950.

Confucius. *The Sayings of Confucius*. Translated by James R. Ware. New York: New American Library, Mentor Books, 1955.

Coombes, David. *Politics and Bureaucracy in the European Community: A Portrait of the Commission of the EEC*. London: George Allen and Unwin, 1970.

Cooper, Richard N. *The Economics of Interdependence*. New York: McGraw-Hill, 1968.

———. "U.S. Policies and Practices on Subsidies in International Trade." In Warnecke, ed., *International Trade*, pp. 107–22.

Curran, Timothy J. "Politics and High Technology: The NTT Case." In I. M. Destler and Hideo Sato, eds., *Coping with U.S.-Japanese Economic Conflicts*, pp. 185–241. Lexington, Mass.: Lexington Books, 1982.

Curzon, Gerard. "Crisis in the International Trading System." In Hugh Corbet and Robert Jackson, eds., *In Search of a New World Economic Order*, pp. 33–45. New York: John Wiley and Sons, 1974.

Curzon, Gerard, and Victoria Curzon. "The Management of Trade Relations in the GATT." In Shonfield, ed., *International Economic Relations*, pp. 141–283.

Cutler, Lloyd. "To Form a Government." *Foreign Affairs* 59 (Fall 1980), pp. 126–43.

Dahrendorf, Ralf. "External Relations of the European Community." In Hugh Corbet and Robert Jackson, eds., *In Search of a New World Economic Order*. New York: John Wiley and Sons, 1974.

Dam, Kenneth W. *The GATT: Law and International Economic Organization*. Chicago: University of Chicago Press, 1970.

Denton, Geoffrey, and Theo Peeters. "The European Community." In Wilfred Kohl, ed., *Economic Foreign Policies of Industrial States*, pp. 189–213. Lexington, Mass.: Lexington Books, 1977.

DeRosa, Dean A., J. Michael Finger, Stephen S. Golub, and William W. Nye. "What the 'Zenith Case' Might Have Meant." *Journal of World Trade Law* 13 (January–February 1979), pp. 47–54.

Destler, I. M. *Making Foreign Economic Policy*. Washington: Brookings Institution, 1980.

Destler, I. M., and Thomas R. Graham. "United States Congress and the Tokyo Round: Lessons of a Success Story." *World Economy* 3 (June 1980), pp. 53–70.

Deutsch, Karl W. *The Nerves of Government*. New York: Free Press, 1966.

de Vries, Tom. "Jamaica, or the Non-Reform of the International Monetary System." *Foreign Affairs* 54, no. 3 (April 1976), pp. 577–605.

Drew, Elizabeth. "Profiles (Robert S. Strauss)." *New Yorker*, 7 May 1979, pp. 50–129.

Economic Council of Canada. *Looking Outward: A New Trade Strategy for Canada*. Ottawa: Economic Council of Canada, 1975.

Evans, John W. *The Kennedy Round in American Trade Policy: The Twilight of the GATT*. Cambridge: Harvard University Press, 1971.

Finlayson, Jock, and Mark Zacher. "The GATT and the Regulation of Trade Barriers: Regime Dynamics and Functions." *International Organization* 35 (Autumn 1981), pp. 561–602.

Fisher, Roger. *International Conflict for Beginners*. New York: Harper and Row, 1969.

Fisher, Roger, and William Ury. *Getting to Yes: Negotiating Agreement without Giving In*. Boston: Houghton Mifflin, 1981.

France, Government of. *Les Prochaines Négociations commerciales: Avis et rapport sur le problème des échanges internationaux*. Paris: Conseil économique et social, May 1973.

Friedman, Milton. "Using the Free Market to Resolve the Balance-of-Payments Problem." In Benjamin J. Cohen, ed., *American Foreign Economic Policy: Essays and Comments*, pp. 87–98. New York: Harper and Row, 1968.

Fukui, Haruhiro. "The GATT Tokyo Round: The Bureaucratic Politics of Multilateral Diplomacy." In Michael Blaker, ed., *The Politics of Trade: U.S. and Japanese Policymaking for the GATT Negotiations*. Occasional Papers of the East Asian Institute. New York: Columbia University, 1978.

———. "Policy-Making in the Japanese Foreign Ministry." In Scalapino, ed., *Modern Japan*, pp. 3–35.

Galbraith, John Kenneth. *The New Industrial State*. Boston: Houghton Mifflin, 1967.

Gardner, Richard N. *Sterling-Dollar Diplomacy*. 2d ed. New York: McGraw-Hill, 1969.

*GATT. *Agreement on Government Procurement*. Geneva: GATT, 1979.

*———. *Agreement on Implementation of Article VI* (Antidumping). Geneva: GATT, 1979.

*———. *Agreement on Implementation of Article VII* (Customs valuation). Geneva: GATT, 1979.

*———. *Agreement on Import Licensing Procedures*. Geneva: GATT, 1979.

*———. *Agreement on Interpretation and Application of Articles VI, XVI and XXIII* (Subsidy/countervail). Geneva: GATT, 1979.

*———. *Agreement on Technical Barriers to Trade* (Standards) Geneva: GATT, 1979.

*———. *Agreement on Trade in Civil Aircraft*. Geneva: GATT, 1979.

*———. *Agreement relating to the Framework for the Conduct of International Trade*. Geneva: GATT, 1979.

*———. *Arrangement regarding Bovine Meat*. Geneva: GATT, 1979.

*———. *Geneva (1979) Protocol and Supplementary Protocol* (Tariffs). Geneva: GATT, 1979.

*———. *International Dairy Arrangement*. Geneva: GATT, 1979.

——. "The Tokyo Declaration." In *GATT Activities in 1973*. Geneva: GATT, 1974.

——. *The Tokyo Round of Multilateral Trade Negotiations* (report by the Director General of GATT). Geneva: GATT, April 1979.

——. *The Tokyo Round of Multilateral Trade Negotiations: Supplementary Report*. Geneva: GATT, 1980.

——. *Trends in International Trade* (Haberler report). Geneva: GATT, 1958.

Giersch, Herbert, ed. *The International Division of Labour: Problems and Perspectives*. Tübingen: J.C.B. Mohr, 1974.

——. *On the Economics of Intra-Industry Trade*. Tübingen: J.C.B. Mohr, Paul Siebeck, 1979.

Gilpin, Robert. *U.S. Power and the Multinational Corporation*. New York: Basic Books, 1975.

Golt, Sidney. *Developing Countries in the GATT System*. Thames Essays, no. 13. London: Trade Policy Research Centre, 1978.

——. *The GATT Negotiations, 1973–75: A Guide to the Issues*. British–North American Committee Publication. Montreal: C. D. Howe Research Institute, 1974.

Graham, Thomas R. "Global Trade: War and Peace." *Foreign Policy* no. 50 (Spring 1983), pp. 124–35.

Grey, Rodney de C. "A Note on U.S. Trade Practices." In Cline, ed., *Trade Policy*, pp. 243–57.

——. *Trade Policy in the 1980s: An Agenda for Canadian-U.S. Relations*. Montreal: C. D. Howe Institute, 1981.

Grubel, G., and P. J. Lloyd. *Intra-Industry Trade: The Theory and Measurement of International Trade in Differentiated Products*. New York: Halstead Press, 1975.

Haberler, Gottfried. "The International Monetary System after Jamaica and Manila." In John Adams, ed., *The Contemporary International Economy: A Reader*, pp. 218–40. New York: St. Martin's Press, 1979.

Harris, Simon. "EEC Trade Relations with the USA in Agricultural Products: Multilateral Tariff Negotiations." Occasional Papers no. 3. Ashford: Centre for European Agricultural Studies, Wye College, 1977.

Helleiner, Gerald K. *Intra-Firm Trade and the Developing Countries*. New York: St. Martin's Press, 1981.

Hirschman, Albert O. *National Power and the Structure of Foreign Trade*. Berkeley: University of California Press, 1969.

Hopkins, Raymond F. "The International Role of 'Domestic' Bureaucracy." *International Organization* 30 (1976), pp. 405–32.

Houck, James P. "U.S. Agricultural Trade and the Tokyo Round." *Law and Policy in International Business* 12 (1980), pp. 265–95.

Hudec, Robert E. *The GATT Legal System and World Trade Diplomacy*. New York: Praeger Publishers, 1975.

Hufbauer, Gary Clyde. "Subsidy Issues after the Tokyo Round." In Cline, ed., *Trade Policy*, pp. 327–61.

Hufbauer, Gary Clyde, and John C. Chilas. "Specialization by Industrial Countries: Extent and Consequences." In Giersch, ed., *The International Division*, pp. 3–38.

Hufbauer, Gary Clyde, J. Shelton Erb, and H. P. Starr. "The GATT Codes and the Unconditional Most-Favoured-Nation Principle." *Law and Policy in International Business* 12 (1980), pp. 59–93.

Hull, Cordell. *Memoires*. New York: Macmillan Company, 1948.

Iklé, Fred C. *How Nations Negotiate*. New York: Praeger Publishers, 1967.

Iklé, Fred C., and Nathan Leites. "Political Negotiation as a Process of Modifying Utilities." *Journal of Conflict Resolution* 6 (March 1962), pp. 19–28.

Independent Commission on International Development Issues (Brandt Commission). *Common Crisis North-South: Co-operation for World Recovery*. London: Pan Books, 1983.

———. *North South: A Program for Survival*. London: Pan Books, 1980.

International Monetary Fund. *Directory of Trade Yearbook, Part A*. Washington: IMF, 1979.

Jackson, John H. "The Birth of the GATT-MTN System: A Constitutional Appraisal." *Law and Policy in International Business* 12 (1980), pp. 21–58.

———. "GATT Machinery and the Tokyo Round Agreements." In Cline, ed., *Trade Policy*, pp. 159–87.

———. *World Trade and the Law of the GATT*. Indianapolis: Bobbs-Merrill Company, 1969.

Jacobson, Harold K. *Networks of Interdependence*. New York: Alfred A. Knopf, 1979.

Jervis, Robert. *Perception and Misperception in International Politics*. Princeton: Princeton University Press, 1976.

Johnson, Chalmers. "MITI and Japanese International Economic Policy." In Scalapino ed., *Modern Japan*, pp. 227–79.

Katzenstein, Peter J. "Conclusion: Domestic Structures and Strategies of Foreign Economic Policy." *International Organization* 31 (1977), pp. 879–920. Volume also published as *Between Power and Plenty: Foreign Economic Policies of Advanced Industrial States*. Madison: University of Wisconsin Press, 1978.

———. "International Relations and Domestic Structures: Foreign Economic Policies of Advanced Industrial States." *International Organization* 30 (Winter 1976), pp. 1–45.

Kennan, George F. *American Diplomacy 1900–1950*. Chicago: University of Chicago Press, 1951.

Keohane, Robert O. *After Hegemony: Cooperation and Discord in the World Political Economy*. Princeton: Princeton University Press, 1984.

———. "The Theory of Hegemonic Stability and Changes in International Regimes, 1967–1977." In Ole R. Holsti, Randolph M. Silverson, and Alexander L. George, eds., *Change in the International System*, pp. 131–62. Boulder, Colo.: Westview Press, 1980.

Keohane, Robert O., and Joseph S. Nye. *Power and Interdependence: World Politics in Transition*. Boston: Little, Brown and Company, 1977.

Kindleberger, Charles P. *Foreign Trade and the National Economy*. New Haven: Yale University Press, 1962.

———. "Group Behavior and International Trade." *Journal of Political Economy* 59 (1951), pp. 30–46.

———. *The World in Depression 1929–1939*. London: Allen Lane, Penguin Press, 1973.

Kissinger, Henry A. *American Foreign Policy: Three Essays*. New York: W. W. Norton and Company, 1969.

———. *A World Restored*. Boston: Houghton Mifflin, 1957.

———. *Years of Upheaval*. Boston: Little, Brown and Company, 1982.

Koumins, M. Richard. "Technical Analysis of the Group 'Framework.' " *Law and Policy in International Business* 12 (1980), pp. 299–334.

Krasner, Stephen D. "State Power and the Structure of International Trade." *World Politics* 28 (1976), pp. 317–47.

———. "The Tokyo Round: Particularistic Interests and Prospects for Stability in the Global Trading System." *International Studies Quarterly* 23 (December 1979), pp. 491–531.

Krause, Lawrence. "Trade Policy for the Seventies." *Columbia Journal of World Business* 6, no. 1 (January–February 1971), pp. 5–14.

Lawson, Fred H. "Hegemony and the Structure of International Trade Reassessed: A View from Arabia." *International Organization* 37 (Spring 1983), pp. 317–37.

Lindberg, Leon N. *The Political Dynamics of European Economic Integration*. Stanford: Stanford University Press, 1963.

Lipson, Charles. "The Transformation of Trade: The Sources and Effects of Regime Change." *International Organization* 36 (Spring 1982), pp. 417–52.

List, Frederick. *National System of Political Economy*. Translated by G. A. Matile. Philadelphia: J. B. Lippincott and Company, 1856.

Lorenzen, Shelley A. "Technical Analysis of the Anti-Dumping Agreement and the Trade Agreements Act." *Law and Policy in International Business* 2 (1979), pp. 1405–36.

Lowi, Theodore J. "American Business, Public Policy, Case Studies, and Political Theory." *World Politics* 16 (1963–64), pp. 677–715.

McClelland, David C. *The Achieving Society*. New York: D. Van Nostrand Company, 1961.

Maier, Charles S. "The Politics of Productivity: Foundations of American International Economic Policy after World War II." *International Organization* 31 (Autumn 1977), pp. 607–34.

Malmgren, Harald B. "Coming Trade Wars? Neomercantilism and Foreign Policy." *Foreign Policy* no. 3 (Winter 1970–71), pp. 115-43.

———. "The United States." In Wilfred Kohl, ed., *Economic Policies of the United States*. Lexington, Mass.: Lexington Books, 1977.

431

Marks, Matthew J. "American Law and Regulatory Trade Measures." *World Economy* 2 (February 1980), pp. 427–40.

Marks, Matthew J., and Harald B. Malmgren. "Negotiating Nontariff Distortions to Trade." *Law and Policy in International Business* 7 (April 1975), pp. 327–41.

Merciai, Patrizio. "Safeguard Measures in GATT." *Journal of World Trade Law* 15 (1981), pp. 41–65.

Middleton, R. W. "The GATT Standards Code." *Journal of World Trade Law* 14 (May–June 1980), pp. 201–19.

Morgenthau, Hans J. *Politics among Nations*. 5th ed. New York: Alfred A. Knopf, 1973.

Nicolson, Sir Harold. *Diplomacy*. 3d ed. London: Oxford University Press, 1963.

Numelin, Ragnar. *The Beginnings of Diplomacy: A Sociological Study of Intertribal and International Relations*. London: Oxford University Press, 1950.

O'Brien, Rita Cruise, and Gerald K. Helleiner. "The Political Economy of Information in a Changing International Economic Order." *International Organization* 34 (Autumn 1980), pp. 445–70.

Odell, John S. *U.S. International Monetary Policy*. Princeton: Princeton University Press, 1982.

OECD. *Policy Perspectives for International Trade and Economic Relations*. Report by the High Level Group on Trade and Related Problems to the Secretary General of OECD. Paris: OECD, 1972.

Ohlin, Goran. "Subsidies and Other Industrial Aids." In Warnecke, ed., *International Trade*, pp. 21–34.

Organski, A.F.K. *World Politics*. New York: Alfred A. Knopf, 1961.

Oye, Kenneth A. "The Domain of Choice: International Constraints and Carter Administration Foreign Policy." In Kenneth A. Oye, Donald Rothchild, and Robert J. Lieber, eds., *Eagle Entangled: U.S. Foreign Policy in a Complex World*. New York: Longman, 1979, pp. 3–33.

Pastor, Robert A. *Congress and the Politics of U.S. Foreign Economic Policy*. Berkeley: University of California Press, 1980.

Patrick, Hugh, and Henry Rosovsky, eds., *Asia's New Giant: How the Japanese Economy Works*. Washington: Brookings Institution, 1976.

Patterson, Gardner. "The European Community as a Threat to the System." In Cline, ed., *Trade Policy*, pp. 223–42.

Peterson, Peter G. *The United States in the Changing World Economy*. Vol. 1, *A Foreign Economic Perspective*. London: British–North American Research Association, 1971.

Phillips, Willard. *Proposition concerning Protection and Free Trade*. Boston: Charles C. Little and James C. Brown, 1850.

Piper, W. Stephen. "Unique Sectoral Agreement Establishes Free Trade Framework." *Law and Policy in International Business* 12 (1980), pp. 221–42.

Pirsig, Robert M. *Zen and the Art of Motorcycle Maintenance.* New York: Bantam Books, 1974.

Pomeranz, Morton. "Toward a New International Order in Government Procurement." *Law and Policy in International Business* 11 (1979), pp. 1264–300.

Preeg, Ernest H. *Traders and Diplomats: An Analysis of the Kennedy Round under the General Agreement on Tariffs and Trade.* Washington: Brookings Institution, 1970.

Price, Victoria Curzon. "Surplus Capacity and What the Tokyo Round Failed to Do." *World Economy* 2 (1979), pp. 305–18.

Protheroe, David R. *Imports and Politics: Trade Decision-Making in Canada, 1968–1979.* Montreal: Institute for Research on Public Policy, 1980.

Putnam, Robert D., and Nicholas Bayne. *Hanging Together: The Seven-Power Summits.* Cambridge: Harvard University Press, 1984.

Raiffa, Howard. *The Art and Science of Negotiation.* Cambridge: Harvard University Press, 1982.

Rapoport, Anatol. *Fights, Games and Debates.* Ann Arbor: University of Michigan Press, 1960.

Ray, George F. "The Internationalization of Economic Analysis." In Shonfield, ed., *International Economic Relations,* pp. 403–35.

Reich, Robert B. "Beyond Free Trade." *Foreign Affairs* 61, no. 4 (Spring, 1983), pp. 773–804.

Rivers, Richard R., and John D. Greenwald. "The Negotiation of a Code on Subsidies and Countervailing Measures: Bridging Fundamental Policy Differences." *Law and Policy in International Business* 2 (1979), pp. 1447–96.

Rosecrance, Richard N. "Bipolarity, Multipolarity, and the Future." *Journal of Conflict Resolution* 10 (1966), pp. 314–27.

Rothstein, Robert L. *Global Bargaining: UNCTAD and the Quest for a New International Economic Order.* Princeton: Princeton University Press, 1979.

Ruggie, John Gerard. "International Regimes, Transactions, and Change: Embedded Liberalism in the Postwar Economic Order." *International Organization* 36 (Spring 1982), pp. 379–415.

Sawyer, Jack, and Harold Guetzkow. "Bargaining and Negotiation in International Relations." In Harold C. Kelman, ed., *International Behavior.* New York: Holt, Rinehart and Winston, 1966.

Saxonhouse, Gary R. "The Micro- and Macroeconomics of Foreign Sales to Japan." In Cline, ed., *Trade Policy,* pp. 259–304.

Scalapino, Robert A., ed. *The Foreign Policy of Modern Japan.* Berkeley: University of California Press, 1977.

Schaetzel, J. Robert, and H. B. Malmgren. "Talking Heads." *Foreign Policy* no. 39 (Summer 1980), pp. 130–42.

Schattschneider, E. E. *Politics, Pressures and the Tariff.* New York: Prentice-Hall, 1935.

Schelling, Thomas C. *Arms and Influence*. New Haven: Yale University Press, 1966.

———. "National Security Considerations Affecting Trade Policy." In U.S. Government, *United States International Economic Policy in an Interdependent World*, vol. 1, pp. 723–37. Williams Commission Report. Washington: GPO, 1971.

Sebenius, James K. *Negotiating the Law of the Sea*. Cambridge: Harvard University Press, 1984.

Sherman, Saul L. "Reflections on the New Customs Valuation Code." *Law and Policy in International Business* 12 (1980), pp. 119–58.

Shonfield, Andrew. "International Economic Relations of the Western World: An Overall View." In Shonfield, ed., *International Economic Relations*, pp. 1–140.

Shonfield, Andrew, ed. *International Economic Relations of the Western World 1959-1971*. Vol. 1, *Politics and Trade*. London: Oxford University Press, 1976.

Simon, Herbert A. "The Architecture of Complexity." In Simon, *The Sciences of the Artificial*. Cambridge: MIT Press, 1969.

Snyder, Richard C., H. W. Bruck, and Burton Sapin, eds. *Foreign Policy Decision Making: An Approach to the Study of International Politics*. New York: Free Press, 1962.

Solomon, Robert. *The International Monetary System 1945–1976: An Insider's View*. New York: Harper and Row, 1977.

Stein, Arthur A. "The Hegemon's Dilemma: Great Britain, the United States, and the International Economic Order." *International Organization* 38 (Spring 1984), pp. 335–86.

———. "The Politics of Linkage." *World Politics* 33 (1980–81), pp. 62–81.

Stern, Paula. *Water's Edge: Domestic Politics and the Making of American Foreign Policy*. Westport, Conn.: Greenwood Press, 1979.

Stern, Robert M. "Evaluating Alternative Formulae for Reducing Industrial Tariffs." *Journal of World Trade Law* 10 (January–February 1976), pp. 50–64.

Stone, Frank. *Canada, the GATT and the International Trade System*. Montreal: Institute for Research on Public Policy, 1984.

Tasca, Henry J. *The Reciprocal Trade Policy of the United States*. New York: Russell and Russell, 1938.

Taussig, F. W. *Free Trade, the Tariff and Reciprocity*. New York: Macmillan Company, 1927.

Tollison, Robert D., and Thomas D. Willett. "An Economic Theory of Mutually Advantageous Issue Linkages in International Negotiations." *International Organization* 33 (Autumn 1979), pp. 425–49.

Trezise, Philip, and Yukio Suzuki. "Politics, Government and Economic Growth in Japan." In Hugh Patrick and Henry Rosovsky, eds., *Asia's New Giant: How the Japanese Economy Works*, pp. 753–811. Washington: Brookings Institution, 1976.

Tsuji, Kiyoaki. "Decision-Making in the Japanese Government: A Study of Ringisei." In Robert E. Ward, ed., *Political Development in Modern Japan*, pp. 457–75. Princeton: Princeton University Press, 1970.

U.N. Commission on Transnational Corporations. *Transnational Corporations in World Development: A Re-Examination*. New York: U.N. Publications, 1978.

UNCTAD V. *Multilateral Trade Negotiations: Evaluation and Further Recommendations Arising Therefrom*. U.N. Doc. TD/227, April 1979.

Underdal, Arild. "Multinational Negotiation Parties: The Case of the European Community." *Cooperation and Conflict* 8 (1973), pp. 173–82.

U.S. District Court for the District of Columbia. *The American Distilling Company et al.* vs. *Jimmy Carter et al.* (Civil Action no. 77-C-11).

U.S. Government. *Alcohol and Tobacco Excise Taxes: Laws and Audits Need Modernizing*. Report to the Joint Congressional Committee on Taxation by the Comptroller General of the United States, 1976.

————. *Economic Report of the President*. Washington: GPO, 1972.

————. *Executive Branch GATT Studies*. Compiled at the request of the Subcommittee on International Trade of the U.S. Senate Committee on Finance. Washington: GPO, 1974.

————. *Future United States Foreign Trade Policy*. Report to the president submitted by the special representative for trade negotiations, January 14, 1969. Washington: GPO, 1969.

————. *United States International Economic Policy in an Interdependent World*. Report to the president by the Commission on International Trade and Investment Policy (Williams Commission), July 1971. Washington: GPO, 1971.

————. *Trade Act of 1974*. Public Law 93-618. 93d Cong., 2d sess., January 3, 1975.

————. *Trade Agreements Act of 1979*. Public Law 96-39. 96th Cong., 1st sess., July 29, 1979.

————. Advisory Committee on Trade Negotiations. *Report to the President, the Congress and the Special Representative for Trade Negotiation*, June 1979.

————. Office of the Special Representative for Trade Negotiations. *1964–1967 Trade Conference: Report on United States Negotiations*. 2 vols. Washington: GPO, 1968.

————. *Results of the United States Industrial Tariff Negotiations with Other Major Developed Countries in the Multilateral Trade Negotiations*. Washington: GPO, 1979.

————. Trade Policy Staff Committee. *Hearings on Wine Gallon/Proof Gallon Methods of Taxing Distilled Spirits*, March 20, 1979. Mimeographed.

U.S. House of Representatives. *Message of the President of the United States Transmitting the Text of the Trade Agreements Negotiated in the Tokyo Round* . . . 96th Cong., 1st sess., June 19, 1979.

————. Committee on Ways and Means. *Comparison of Recommendations*

Received from Public Witnesses on Multilateral Trade Negotiators' Implementing Legislation: Hearings before the Subcommittee on Trade. 96th Cong., 1st sess., April 23–27, 1979.

————. *Multilateral Trade Negotiations: Hearings before the Subcommittee on Trade.* 96th Cong., 1st sess., April 23–27, 1979.

————. "Message of the President." In *Hearings on the Trade Reform Act of 1973.* 93d Cong., 1st session., May 9, 1973.

————. *Trade Agreements Act of 1979.* 96th Cong., 1st sess.

————. Subcommittee on Trade. *Background and Status of the Multilateral Trade Negotiations.* 94th Cong., 1st sess., February 4, 1975.

————. *Background Material on the Multifibre Arrangement (1979 Edition).* 96th Cong., 1st sess., April 2, 1979.

U.S. Senate. Committee on Finance. *The International Financial Crisis: Hearings before the Subcommittee on International Finance Resources,* 93d Cong., 1st sess., May 30–June 5, 1973.

————. *MTN Studies,* 6 vols. Report prepared for the Subcommittee on International Trade, Senate Committee on Finance. 96th Cong., 1st sess.

Vernon, Raymond. "International Investment and International Trade in the Product Cycle." *Quarterly Journal of Economics* 80 (May 1966), pp. 190–207.

————. "Old Rules and New Pledges: GATT in the World Trading System." Paper presented at 25th Anniversary of the Center for International Affairs, Harvard University, May 11, 1983.

Walton, R. E., and R. B. McKersie. *A Behavioral Theory of Labor Negotiations.* New York: McGraw-Hill, 1965.

Waltz, Kenneth N. "International Structure, National Force and the Balance of World Power." *Journal of International Affairs* 21 (1967), pp. 215–31.

————. *Theory of International Politics.* Reading, Mass.: Addison Wesley, 1979.

Warley, T. K. "Western Trade in Agricultural Products." In Shonfield, ed., *International Economic Relations,* pp. 287–402.

Warnecke, Steven J., ed. *International Trade and Industrial Policies.* New York: Holmes and Meier Publishers, 1978.

Webster, Daniel. "Speech upon the Tariff of 1824." In F. W. Taussig, ed., *State Papers and Speeches on the Tariff.* Cambridge: Harvard University Press, 1892. Reprinted Clifton, N.J.: Augustus M. Kelley Publishers, 1972.

Wertenberger, William. "A Reporter at Large (Law of the Sea Conference— Part I)." *New Yorker,* August 1, 1983, pp. 38–65.

Whitman, Marina vN. *International Trade and Investment: Two Perspectives.* Essays in International Finance, no. 143. Princeton: Department of Economics, Princeton University, 1981.

Winham, Gilbert R. "GATT and the New Trade World." *International Perspectives,* March–April 1983, pp. 3–5.

————. "Negotiation as a Management Process." *World Politics* 30 (October 1977), pp. 87–114.

————. "Practitioners' Views of International Negotiations." *World Politics* 32, no. 1 (October 1979), pp. 111–35.

————. "The Canadian Automobile Industry and Trade-Related Performance Requirements." *Journal of World Trade Law* 18 (November–December 1984), pp. 471–96.

Young, Oran R. "International Regimes: Problems of Concept Formation." *World Politics* 32 (April 1980), pp. 331–56.

Zartman, William I., and Maureen R. Berman. *The Practical Negotiator*. New Haven: Yale University Press, 1982.

INDEX

Abel, I. W., 53
ad referendum agreement, definition of, 64n
Advisory Committee for Trade Negotiations, U.S. (ACTN), 134, 309-310, 343, 384n
Afghanistan, 360n
Agricultural Adjustment Act (U.S.), 113, 152n
agriculture, 18, 100, 112, 146-55; negotiation of, 125-27, 156-58, 164-67, 208, 247-55; progress since Tokyo Round, 358; quantitative restrictions, 112; Strauss list of agricultural products, 248, 287; subsidies in, 119, 220. *See also* tropical products
Airbus Industries, 238
aircraft, civil, negotiation of, 237-40
Allison, Graham T., 323n
American Importers Association (AIA), 178
American Selling Price (ASP), 17, 38, 67 69, 70, 78, 82, 107-109, 180n, 186
Anjaria, Shailendra J. et al., 150n
Annecy negotiations (1949), 33
Anthony, David V., and Carol K. Hagerty, 138n, 232n
Antidumping Act of 1921 (U.S.), 311
antidumping code, 69, 73, 118, 131, 221; revised code, 353-54
Argentina, 251, 280, 302
Aron, Raymond, 23n
Arrangement regarding Bovine Meat, 252
Arrangement regarding International Trade in Textiles, 122-23n
Article 113 Committee/Article 111 Committee, 185, 319-22
Associated African and Malagasy States, 78
Australia, 121-22, 144, 170, 251, 253, 333
Austria, 383; Austria-Hungary, 40
Axelrod, Robert, 374n

Baldwin, Robert E., 394n
Banks, Gary, 406n
Barber, Clarence L., 332n
Barry, Donald, 272n
Bauer, Raymond A. et al., 10n, 34n, 39, 391n, 397n, 398n
Belgium, 140, 176
Bell, Daniel, 412
Bergholm, M. K., 194n
Bergsten, C. Fred, 9, 49n, 279n
Bergsten, C. Fred, and William R. Cline, 383-84n, 404n, 410n
Berkowitz, Marshall, 300n
Blaker, Michael K., 331n
Bonn Economic Summit, 168, 205-211, 212; memorandum of understanding, 209-210, 214
bracketing, square, use of, 140n, 212-13
Brandt, Willie, 25
Brandt Commission, 337n
Braun, Fernand, 261, 265-68
Brazil, 18, 106, 141, 144-46, 161-62n, 175, 198, 222, 231, 254, 259, 270
Bressand, Albert, 410n
Bretton Woods Agreement (1944), 3
British Board of Trade, 245
Brittan, Samuel, 406n
Brussels Convention on Valuation, 106
Brussels Definition of Value (BDV), 106, 108-109, 178-79, 223
Brussels Tariff Nomenclature system (BTN), 106, 159
Burenstam Linder, Staffan, 44n, 51n
Buy American Act (1933), 138, 140
Buzan, Barry, 403n

Canada, 65n, 79, 115, 131, 209, 237, 237-38n, 323, 324, 330, 394; agriculture, 251-53; antidumping, 69, 221; Canada-U.S. automobile agreement, 405n; Canadian coordinator for trade negotiations (CCTN), 332, 338-39, 341n; Canadian Trade and Tariffs

Canada (*cont.*)
  Committee (CTTC), 335-37; Customs
  Act of 1970, 181; customs valuation,
  106, 108n, 178-83, 187-89, 223-29;
  Department of External Affairs (DEA),
  326; Department of Finance, 326; Department of Industry, Trade and Commerce, 327; Department of Regional
  Economic Expansion, 117; government
  procurement, 189, 192, 229-30, 358-
  59; internal negotiation, 332-42, 347-
  48, 391-92; in Kennedy Round, 333-
  34; National Policy of 1879, 332; safeguards, 121-23, 224; subsidy/counter-
  vail, 117-18, 170, 175; tariffs, 161,
  201-202, 205, 260, 269-72, 372; voluntary export restraints, 123; wine gallon, 286, 288-94, 299-300
Canada-U.S. automobile agreement, 405n
Canadian Broadcasting Corporation
  (CBC), 289
Canadian coordinator for trade negotia-
  tions (CCTN), 332, 338-39, 341n
Canadian Manufacturers Association,
  334
Canadian Trade and Tariffs Committee
  (CTTC), 335-37
Carter, Jimmy, 164-65, 210, 232, 258,
  310, 380
Caves, Richard, 390n
Chevalier, Michel, 38
"chicken war," 153
Chumas, Henri, 183
Civil War (U.S.), 40, 284-85
classical school, 407-409
Clausewitz, Carl von, 281n
Cline, William R., 364n
Cline, William R. et al., 202n, 203n
Cobden, Richard, 41
Cobden-Chevalier treaty (1860), 39, 41-
  42
cold war, 29
Comité des Organisations Professionelles
  Agricoles, 320
Commager, Henry S., 345n
Committee of Permanent Representatives
  (COREPER), 320
Committee on Trade and Development
  (GATT), 125, 143

Common Agriculture Policy (CAP), 25,
  82, 95, 113, 115, 149-51, 215n
Common Market. *See* European Community
Concert of Europe, 389
Condliffe, J. B., 39n, 41n, 378n
Conference on Import and Export Prohi-
  bitions and Restrictions (1927), 35
Confucius, 371n
Connolly, John, 25
"contingent" protectionism, 45, 384n
Coombes, David, 77n, 319n, 322n
Cooper, Richard N., 8n, 27n, 51n, 173n
Corn Laws, 38, 41
countertrade, 406; definition of, 406n
countervailing duties (CVD's), countervail
  procedures. *See* subsidies and countervailing duties
countervail waiver crisis. *See* subsidies
  and countervailing duties
Curran, Timothy J., 231n
Curzon, Gerard, 31n, 34n
Curzon, Gerard, and Victoria Curzon,
  7n, 20n, 55-56n, 396n
Customs Act of 1970 (Canada), 181
Customs Cooperation Council (CCC), 99,
  106, 178, 183-84, 228
Customs Simplification Act (U.S.), 180
custom valuation, 54, 105-109; Brussels
  Definition of Value, definition of, 106;
  "final list," 181, 187; implementation
  of code, 357-58; negotiation of, 106-
  109, 177-89, 223-29, 352-53; no-
  tional/positive concepts of, 178-180
Cutler, Lloyd, 323n

Dahrendorf, Rolf, 323n
Dale, Reginald, 205n, 212n, 219n
Dam, Kenneth W., 19n, 31n, 67n, 82n,
  94n, 112n, 113n, 138n, 139n, 142n,
  143n, 152n, 241n
Davignon, Etienne, 165, 268
Declaration on Export Subsidies (1960),
  221
de Gaulle, Charles, 76
de Jonquieres, Guy, 269n
Deniau, Jean-François, 217n
Denman, Sir Roy, 207n, 209, 262

Denmark, 8, 48, 78, 79n, 184, 208n, 215n, 244
Dent, Frederick B., 164
Denton, Geoffrey, and Theo Peeters, 322n
depression: 1930s, 35-38, 45-46, 148; 1870s, 40, 48
DeRosa, Dean A. et al., 171n
Destler, I. M., 132n, 133n
Destler, I. M., and Thomas R. Graham, 310n
Deutsch, Karl, 314n
developing countries, 21, 83, 95-97, 133, 274-80, 303, 355-56, 408-409; agriculture, 254-55; antidumping, 353-54; customs valuation, 188-89, 227-29; definition of, 146n; government procurement, 192-94, 229-30, 230, 232-33; graduation of, 94, 146, 222-23, 277; import licensing, 109-111, 237; international negotiation, 375-79; pyramidal negotiation, 174-75, 188, 193-94, 210-11, 354; quantitative restrictions, 114; safeguards, 198-200, 241-47; "special and differential treatment," 8-9, 141-42; standards, 234-35; subsidy/countervail, 119, 221-23; tariff negotiations, 161-62, 272-73, 275; wheat conference, 254-55. See also Framework Agreement; Haberler Report; Lome Agreements; UNCTAD
de Vries, Tom, 6n
Dillon Round (1960-61), 33, 60, 153, 250
domestic international sales corporation tax (DISC), 175-76
Downing Street Summit, 210n
Drew, Elizabeth, 380n, 381n
Dreyer, H. Peter, 64n, 167n
Dugimont, Jacques, 259
Dunkel, Arthur, 254

East African Community, 78
Eastern Airlines, 239
Economic Commission for Europe (ECE), 99, 104, 194n
Egli, David, 165n
Egypt, 361n
Eisenhower, Dwight, 39

European Atomic Energy Community (Euratom), 3n
European Coal and Steel Community, 3n
European Community (EC), 8-9, 65n, 131n, 164-67, 304, 333; Article 113 Committee/Article 111 Committee, 185, 319-22; agriculture, 3-4, 18, 77, 82-83, 94-95, 148-51, 153-55, 156-58, 164-67, 248-55; aircraft, 238-40; Committee of Permanent Representatives, 320; Common Agriculture Policy (CAP), 25, 82, 95, 113, 115, 149-51, 215n; countervail waiver crisis, 214-19; customs valuation, 106-109, 177-89; Dillon Round, 60; elevator technique in EC decisionmaking, 322; government procurement, 140, 189-92, 229-31; history of, 3n, 34-35, 69-70, 76-84; import licensing, 237; internal negotiation, 317-24, 347-48, 391-92; leadership of, 385-90; main negotiating demands, 198n; Overall Approach, 79-84, 133, 399; quantitative restrictions, 115; role in international system, 11, 28-29; safeguards, 198-200, 208n, 240-47, 324; standards, 103-105, 194-97; subsidy/countervail, 16, 170-77, 213-23, 360n, 361n; tariffs, 158-64, 200-205, 257-72; wine gallon, 286-88, 296. See also Lome Agreements
European Customs Union Study Group, 106
European Economic Community (EEC). See European Community
European Free Trade Association (EFTA), 25
Europe of the Six, 69, 318. See also European Community
Evans, John W., 60n, 62n, 266n, 334n
export restrictions, 279-80

Farnsworth, Clyde, 360n
Federal Republic of Germany, 28, 57, 77-78, 164, 208n, 245; agriculture, 153, 213-14; customs valuation, 184, 225; foreign investment, 29; mark, 25; standards, negotiation of, 103; tariffs, 262
Federalist Papers, 344-46

Finland, 194n
Finlayson, Jock, and Mark Zacher, 20n
Fisher, Roger, 193n
Fisher, Roger, and William Ury, 187n, 369n
Fitzsimmons, Frank, 294
fixed-exchange system, 5-6, 22-27
Fletcher, Peter, 397
Ford, Gerald, 133, 165n
Ford, James D. N., 301n, 302n
Fordney-McCumber tariff of 1922 (U.S.), 37n
Framework Agreement, 18, 100, 141-46, 200, 274-80
France, 23, 27, 40, 48, 49, 57, 76-78, 93, 245, 318; agriculture, 78, 213-14, 250; franc, 25; government procurement, 139, 189; standards, negotiation of, 103; subsidy/countervail, 176, 213-19; tariffs, 203n, 262, 268; United States, relations with, 214, 218-19; wine gallon, 286, 288
Francis I, Emperor of Austria, 383
Fraser, Douglas A., 397
free trade, history of, 38-42, 55-56. See also international trade, developments in
Friedman, Milton, 7n
Fukui, Haruhiro, 325n, 328n, 330n, 349n

Galbraith, John Kenneth, 52n, 89n
Gardner, Richard, 31n, 323n, 387n
General Agreement on Tariffs and Trade (GATT); agriculture, 151-55; Committee on Trade and Development, 125, 143; customs valuation, 106-109; developing countries, 142-46, 256, 274-80; government procurement, 139-41; history of, 19-22, 33n, 39; influence of American values, 29-35; impact of Tokyo Round on, 9, 17, 57, 304-305, 355-56; inventory of nontariff measures, negotiations of, 84-90, 99, 102-103, 108, 109, 119, 138, 370, 378; memo of understanding (1963), 373; most favored nation treatment, 31, 62, 355; nondiscrimination, principle of, 20, 144, 200; program for trade expan-
sion, 143; program of work of 1967, 98; Protocol of Provisional Acceptance, 107, 112; quantitative restrictions, 72, 111-15, 120, 277-78; safeguards, 120-25, 197-200, 240-43, 246-47; standards, 102; subsidy/countervail, 116-19, 169-77, 219-23; tariffs, 17; Trade Negotiations Committee, 97-100, 124, 157; tropical products group, 125-27
Generalized System of Preferences (GSP), 144-45, 161
Geneva negotiations (1956), 33
Germany, 40, 48, 408. See also Federal Republic of Germany
Giersch, Herbert, 51n, 265n
Gilpin, Robert, 23n, 42n, 46n, 52n
Golt, Sidney, 83n, 93n, 146n, 357
government procurement, 138-41; negotiation of, 140-41, 189-94, 229-33; progress since Tokyo Round, 358-59
graduation of developing countries, 94, 146, 222-23, 277
Graham, Thomas R., 358n
Grass, Jennifer, 117n
Government Reorganization Acts of 1970 (U.S.), 136n
Great Britain. See United Kingdom
Greece, 250n
Greenwald, John, 172
Grey, Rodney, 45n, 175, 176n, 224n, 225n, 260n, 271n, 338, 384n, 395n
Group of 77, 94
Group of Ten, 26
group processes, impact on trade, 48-50, 390-93, 400
Grubel, G., and P. J. Lloyd, 51n
Guest, Ian, 254n
Gundelach, Finn, 165, 215n, 248n

Haberler, Gottfried, 6n, 142
Haberler Report, 142-43
Haferkamp, Wilhelm, 165, 200, 203, 207-208, 215, 263, 268
harmonization of tariffs, 8, 160n
Harris, Simon, 156n, 157n
Harrison, Fred, 359n
Haynes, Thomas C., 240n
hegemonic stability, theory of, 45-48, 385-90, 400

Helleiner, Gerald, 53-54n
Heublein Company, 287, 296
Hiram Walker Company, 283, 292n, 293, 294, 299, 301n
Hirschman, Albert O., 365n
historical school, 407-409
Holland. See Netherlands
Hollings, Ernest, 258
Holmes, John, 323n
Hong Kong, 123, 259
Hoover, Herbert, 36
Hopkins, Raymond F., 392n
Houck, James P., 147n, 150n, 249n, 250n
Hudec, Robert E., 71n
Hufbauer, Gary Clyde, 176n, 355n, 360n
Hufbauer, Gary Clyde, and John C. Chilas, 52n, 265n
Hull, Cordell, 4, 37-38n, 41, 395, 402n, 403, 411n
Hungary, 302

Iklé, Fred, 213n
Iklé, Fred, and Nathan Leites, 368n
import licensing, 109-111; definition of, 109; implementation of code, 357-58; negotiation of, 109-111, 235-37
India, 106, 162n, 175, 227-29, 251, 359-60
Indonesia, 228
Integrated Program for Commodities (UNCTAD), 127, 252, 375-79
International Conference on Customs Formalities, 1923, 105-106
International Convention relating to the Simplification of Customs Formalities, 105-106
International Dairy Arrangement, 252
international economic system: bipolar structure of, 385-90; economic nationalism in, 406-409; history of, 21, 35-42, 58-59; integration of developing countries, 246-47; liberal consensus in, 402-403, 411-12; nature of, 29; organization of, 409-411; protectionism in, 58-59, 404-406; reforms of, 6-8, 92-94. See also international trade, developments in; International Monetary Fund

International Grains Agreement (Kennedy Round), 60
International Monetary Fund (IMF): Bretton Woods Agreement, 3; fixed-rate system, 5-6, 22-27; international monetary relations, 3-8, 22-27, 410-412
International Standards Organization, 194n
International Trade Commission, U.S. (ITC), 121, 312
International Trade Organization (ITO), 19, 27, 33, 396
international trade, developments in, 58-59, 70-76; theories of liberalism and protectionism, 42-45, 383-84; "bureaucratic nationalism," 391-93; impact of hegemonic stability on, 45-48, 385-90, 400; impact of group processes on, 48-50, 390-93, 400; impact of liberal values on, 54-57, 395-401; impact of trade structures on, 50-54, 393-95. See also international economic system
International Wheat Agreement, 252
International Wheat Council (IWC), 157n, 252
investment, international, 52-54, 404-405
Iraq, 254
Ireland, 8, 78, 79n, 268
Israel, 132n
Italy, 40, 48, 250, 262, 268, 288

Jackson, Henry, 132-33
Jackson, John H., 10n, 39n, 71n, 102n, 106n, 113n, 121n, 354n, 356n, 365n
Jacobson, Harold K., 412n
Jamaica, 6, 7, 233n, 286
Japan, 24, 57, 65n, 71, 76, 79, 93, 123, 131n, 151n, 164, 209, 292, 304, 323, 349; agriculture, 18, 250-51; customs valuation, 179, 187-88; foreign investment, 29; government procurement, 139, 189, 191, 229-33, 359; industrial policy, 406; internal negotiation, 324-32, 337, 339, 342, 347-49, 391-92; Ministry of Agriculture and Forestry (MAF), 327; Ministry of Finance, 326; Ministry of International Trade and Industry (MITI), 326-327; Nippon Telephone and Telegraph Company, 231;

Japan (*cont.*)
    quantitative restrictions, 122; safe-
    guards, 244; subsidy/countervail, 175;
    tariffs, 202-205, 257, 260, 268-69,
    271n; voluntary export restraints, 123,
    243-44
Jervis, Robert, 370n
Johnson, Chalmers, 326n
Johnson, Lyndon B., 73

Katzenstein, Peter, 49n, 331n, 346n
Kaufman, Michael T., 360n
Kelly, William, 260-62, 265, 267-68,
    302n, 359n
Kennan, George, 32n
Kennedy, John F., 77, 129, 132
Kennedy Round, 17, 77-78, 84, 129-31,
    318, 333; agriculture, 60-61, 154-55;
    comparisons with Tokyo Round, 272-
    74; nontariff measures, 9, 61, 85; re-
    sults of, 34-35, 58, 60-70. *See also* anti-
    dumping code
Keohane, Robert O., 42-43n, 47n, 367n,
    374n, 388n
Keohane, Robert O., and Joseph S. Nye,
    375n
Khindaria, Brij, 254n, 264n, 303n
Kierans, Eric W., 333n
Kifner, John, 383n
Kindleberger, Charles, 3n, 36n, 45-46n,
    48-50, 55, 385n, 390, 403n
Kissinger, Henry, 88n, 132-33, 330n,
    342n, 382-83
Klein, Peter, 172
Korea, 71, 123
Koumins, M. Richard, 144n, 145n, 279n
Krasner, Steven, 27n, 28, 46n
Krause, Lawrence, 49n

Lawson, Fred, 389n
Lemaitre, Philippe, 215n
liberalism. *See* international trade, devel-
    opments in
licensing. *See* import licensing
Lindberg, Leon N., 321, 322n
Lipson, Charles, 44n, 47, 52n
List, Frederick, 142n, 407n, 408n, 409n
Lome Agreements, 411
London Economic Summit (1977), 207

Long, Olivier, 97
Long-Term Arrangement on Cotton Tex-
    tiles (LTA) (1962), 71
Lorenzen, Shelley A., 353n
Lowi, Theodore, 396n

McCarthy, William, 369n
McClelland, Charles, 55n, 400n
MacDonald, Alonzo, 207n, 209, 260-62
MacEachen, Allan, 338
Maciel, George A., 141, 144, 276
McNamara, James, 259
Madison, James, 345
Maier, Charles, 30n
Malaysia, 162
Malmgren, Harald B., 59n, 311n
market disruption, definition of, 71, 122-
    23n
Marks, Matthew J., 312n
Marks, Matthew J., and Harald B. Malm-
    gren, 131n, 136n
Marshall Plan, 27, 30
material injury. *See* subsidies and coun-
    tervailing duties
Meister, Irene, 265n
memorandum of understanding. *See un-
    der* Bonn Economic Summit
Merciai, Patrizio, 199n
Metternich, Klemens von, 383
Mexico, 39, 175, 198, 236, 251, 286
Michelin case, 117, 119n
Middleton, R. W., 195n
Midgley, John, 343n
Mills bill (U.S.) of 1970, 4, 133
Monnet, Jean, 32
"*montant de soutien*" plan, 154
Morgenthau, Hans J., 389n
most favored nation (MFN) treatment, 31,
    62, 132-33, 355
Mullins, Michael, 183

Napoleon, Louis, 38
National Cattlemen's Association, 312n
National Policy of 1879 (Canada), 332
negotiation: comparisons across issue
    areas, 367-71; comparisons of Tokyo
    and Kennedy Rounds, 272-74; conces-
    sion/convergence, 368; control of do-
    mestic politics, 344-49; definition of,

281; difficulties in, 375; formula/detail, 368; importance of definitions in, 369-71; "fractionating of conflict," 193; internal/external negotiation, 305, 306, 371-75; and international trade, 363-67; leadership and, 379-80; linkages or tradeoffs in, 66-67, 264-65, 291-92, 371-72; as a management process, 12-13, 210, 272-73; methods of, 62-67, 187n, 203n, 204, 233-34, 256-57; nature of, 58, 71, 84-85, 98-99, 128-29, 164, 174-75, 196-97, 212-13, 218-19, 246-47, 265, 312, 350, 374-75; political/technical levels of, 205-207, 217, 377-79; pyramidal, 174-75, 188, 193-94, 210-11, 354; sector approach, 237-38n; (importance of) substance in, 190, 193-94, 369; variations in style, GATT/UNCLOS, 274-75, GATT/UNCTAD, 375-379. *See also* bracketing; reciprocity
negotiated protectionism, 404
Netherlands (Holland), 40, 152, 176, 215; foreign investment, 29
Newkirk, Douglas, 186
New Zealand, 170, 251, 333
Nicolson, Harold, 366n
Nigeria, 193n, 198
Nippon Telephone and Telegraph Company (NTT), 231
Nixon, Richard M., 25, 59n, 74, 132, 133n, 403n
nontariff measures (NTM), 16, 68-69, 72-73, 76, 99-100, 130; wine-gallon concession, 280-302. *See also* General Agreement on Tariffs and Trade, inventory of nontariff measures
Norway, 78, 79n
notification process of gathering data, 86-88
Numelin, Ragnar, 12n, 365n
Nyhart, J. D., 89n

O'Brien, Rita Cruise, and Gerald K. Helleiner, 373n
Ohlin, Goran, 170n
oil crisis of 1973, 4, 8, 94, 128, 385
Okinawa, 292
orderly marketing arrangements (OMA), 123-24n

Organization for Economic Cooperation and Development (OECD), 22, 75, 138, 140, 146n, 147n, 189-90, 198, 240. *See also* Rey group
Organization for European Economic Cooperation (OEEC), 112
Organization of Petroleum Exporting Countries (OPEC), 8
Organski, A.F.K., 390n
Ottawa agreements of 1932, 37
Overall Approach, 79-84, 133, 399
Oye, Kenneth A., 372n

Pakistan, 198, 254, 359, 360n
Paris Treaty (1852), 3n
Pastor, Robert A., 131n, 133n
Patrick, Hugh, and Henry Rosovsky, 332n
Patterson, Gardner, 354n
Peterson, Peter G., 150n, 151n
Phillips, Willard, 407n
Piper, W. Stephen, 239-40n
Pirsig, Robert, 308n
political economy, theories of: classical school, 407-409; historical school, 407-409. *See also* international economic system; international trade
Pomfret, Morton, 139n, 189n
Pompidou, Georges, 25
Preeg, Ernest H., 34n, 35n, 60n, 129n, 270n
Price, Victoria Curzon, 123n, 200n
protectionism. *See* international trade, developments in
Protheroe, David R., 326n
Protocol of Provisional Acceptance (GATT), 107, 112
Publicker Industries, 288
Putnam, Robert D., and Nicholas Bayne, 210n

quantitative restrictions (QR's), 110, 111-15, 404; negotiation of, 113-15, 235-36, 277-78

Rapoport, Anatol, 187n
Ray, George F., 86n, 159n
recession of 1970s, 8

Reciprocal Trade Agreements Act of 1934 (RTA), 13, 35, 38-40, 56, 129, 363
reciprocity, definition of, 62; in tariff negotiations, 266-67; advantages/disadvantages, 364
Reform Act of 1832 (Britain), 41
regime, definition of, 42-43n
Reich, Robert, 405n, 409n
Rey, Jean, 75
Rey group, 75-76, 90, 198
Ribicoff, Abraham, 287, 296
Rivers, Richard, 172
Rivers, Richard R., and John D. Greenwald, 174n, 220n, 222n
Robinson, John, 257-58n, 263n
Robinson, Stuart, 236
Roosevelt, Franklin Delano, 36, 37, 395, 401
Rosecrance, Richard N., 390n
Roth, William R., 73
Rothstein, Robert L., 376n, 378n, 379n
Ruggie, John, 56n, 57

Sadat, Anwar, 365
safeguards, 83, 120-22; negotiation of, 123-25, 197-200, 240-47, 278-79; progress since Tokyo Round, 358; selectivity, 198n, 199n, 243-47
SALT negotiations, 10
Sarazen, James, 240
Sawyer, Jack, and Harold Guetzkow, 187n
Saxonhouse, Gary R., 406n
Say, Jean Baptiste, 407
Schaetzel, J. Robert, and H. B. Malmgren, 210n
Schattschneider, E. E., 13-14, 36n, 37n, 39, 314-15, 345n, 346n, 349n, 393, 397n, 398n
Schelling, Thomas C., 12n, 266n
Scheneley Company, 283, 293
Scotland, 286, 288
Seagrams Company, 283, 292, 299
Sebenius, James K., 89n
selectivity, 198n, 199n, 243-47
Semple, Robert B., Jr., 26n

Sherman, Saul, 178n, 187n, 224n
Shonfield, Andrew, 25n, 26n, 36n, 50-51n, 53n, 56n, 57, 389n, 391n
Simon, Herbert A., 314n
Slater, David, 334n
Smith, Adam, 407
Smith, Floyd E., 53
Smithsonian Agreement, 5, 15, 26, 78, 79n
Smoot-Hawley tariff, 4, 13-14, 35-39, 46, 314n, 345, 349, 397
Snyder, Richard C. et al., 370n
Solomon, Robert, 6n, 26n
South Africa, 333
sovereignty, national, impact of Tokyo Round on, 17
Spain, 250n
Spence, Alan, and Douglas Martin, 255n
standards, 101-105; definition of, 101, 194n; implementation of code, 357-58; negotiation of 101-105, 189n, 194-97, 233-35
Standard International Trade Classification, 159
Standstill Agreement (OECD), 240
Steiger, William, 216
Stein, Arthur A., 375n, 389n
Stern, Paula, 132n
Stern, Robert M., 202n
Stobaugh, Roger, 294
Strauss, Robert, 165-67, 168, 200, 203, 206-210, 247, 248n, 258n, 259, 400-401, 402; internal U.S. negotiations, 303, 308; leadership in Tokyo Round, 379-83; memorandum of understanding, 209-210; subsidy negotiations, 215-19; tariff negotiations, 200-201, 261, 263, 268; wine-gallon negotiations, 290-91, 294-97
Strauss list of agricultural products, 248, 287
subsidies and countervailing duties, 17, 54, 116-20, 213-23; countervail waiver crisis, 214-19; definitions, 116-17; implementation of subsidy/countervail code, 359-61; injury test, 117-18, 220-21; injury, definition of, 177; lists of subsidies, 168, 177; material injury, 169, 177, 311-12; negotiation of, 169-

77, 196, 208, 219-23; types and effects of subsidies, 170
Sutton, Alistaire, 172
Swiss formula. See tariffs
Switzerland, 40, 106, 191; foreign investment, 29; tariff negotiation, 162-63, 163n

Taiwan, 71, 123
Takeo, Fukuda, 326
Talmadge, Herman, 136
Tariff Act of 1930 (U.S.), 180, 312n
tariffs: harmonization, 8; definition of, 160n; elevator concept of negotiation, 264, 266; negotiation of, 17-18, 67, 158-64, 200-205, 208, 256-74; Swiss formula, 18, 201, 203-204; tariff study, GATT, 86
Tasca, Henry J., 4n, 37n
Taussig, F. W., 41n
technical barriers to trade. See standards
Tharp, Mike, 359n
Thatcher, Margaret, 245
Tokyo Declaration, 91, 92-100, 104-105, 141n, 190
Tokyo Round, beginning of, 15-16; bipolar structure of, 385-90, 128-29; conclusion of, 302-305, 351-55; deadlock and breakthrough (1977), 164-67; evaluation of, 361-63; explanations of, 400-401; and the GATT, 19-22; historical perspectives, 19-42; implementation of agreements, 356-61; and Kennedy Round, 67-70, 272-74; monetary relations, 3-8, 22-27, 410-12; problems faced at outset, 8-9; results of, 9-12, 16-18; trade policymaking, impact on, 10; and U.S. hegemony, 27-35. See also Tokyo Declaration
Tollison, Robert D., and Thomas D. Willett, 371n
Tomic, Peter, 211n
Tooker, Robin, 191
Torquay negotiation (1951), 33
trade, international. See international trade, developments in
Trade Act of 1974 (U.S.), 15, 77, 84, 128,

129-37, 160, 203, 214, 286, 295, 299, 307-308, 310, 313-14, 384n
Trade Agreements Act of 1979 (U.S.), 121, 298, 304
Trade Expansion Act of 1962, U.S. (TEA), 129
Trade Negotiation Committee (TNC), 97-100, 124, 157
trade structures, impact on trade. See international trade, developments in
Treaty of Rome (1958), 3n, 77, 121, 318
Trezise, Philip, and Yukio Suzuki, 324n, 325n
tropical products, 125-27, 276
Truman Declaration (1947), 27
Tsuji, Kiyoaki, 329n

Underdal, Arild, 324n
Union des Industries de la Communauté Européene, 320
Union of Soviet Socialist Republics (USSR), 10, 29, 84, 132-33, 238, 253
United Auto Workers, 397-98
United Kingdom (and Great Britain), 8, 27, 28, 33, 56, 65n, 76, 78, 79n, 140, 357; agriculture, 48, 213-14, 250; British Board of Trade, 245; Corn Laws, 38, 41; foreign investment, 29; free trade policy, 37-42, 407-408; hegemony of, 46-47; pound, devaluation of, 3; Reform Act of 1832, 41; standards, 103; subsidy/countervail, 170, 217; tariffs, 262, 268, 271; wine gallon, 286, 296
United Nations Conference on the Law of the Sea (UNCLOS), 89-90, 274-75
United Nations Conference on Trade and Development (UNCTAD), 22, 144, 280n, 303; Generalized System of Preferences, 144-45, 161; Integrated Program for Commodities (IPC), 127, 252, 375-79
United States, 65n, 76-77, 79, 93, 97, 164-67, 323n, 324, 330-31, 333, 408; administration textile program, 258; Advisory Committee on Trade Negotiations, 134, 309-310, 343, 384n; agri-

United States (*cont.*)
culture, 18, 30, 94-95, 136-37, 149-55,
156-58, 164-67, 208, 248-51, 253-55;
Agricultural Adjustment Act, 113,
152n; aircraft, 238-40; antidumping,
69, 131, 353; Antidumping Act of
1921, 311; Buy American Act (1933),
138, 140; Canada-U.S. automobile
agreement, 405n; Civil War, 40, 284-
85; Congress, role in Tokyo Round,
312-14; Customs Simplification Act,
180; customs valuation, 106-109, 177-
89, 223-29; deficit, 23-24; Dillon
Round, 60; dollar, 3, 5-6, 22-27, 28,
80-81, 92-93; domestic international
sales corportion tax (DISC), 175-76;
"final list" customs valuation system,
181, 187; Fordney-McCumber tariff of
1922, 37n; foreign investment, 29, 52-
54; France, relations with, 214, 218-
19; Generalized System of preferences,
144; government procurement, 139-40,
189-92, 229-33, 359; Government Reorganization Acts of 1970, 136n; hegemony of, postwar, 8, 11, 26-29, 46-
47, 389, 390; import licensing, 109-
111, 236; inflation in, 5; influence on
GATT, 29-33, 121n; interest groups,
130, 135-36, 347; internal negotiation,
307-317, 341-42, 347-48, 391-92; International Trade Commission, 121,
312; leadership of, 385-90; and liberalism, 56-57, 73, 399, 411n; Marshall
Plan, 27, 30; material injury, 311-12;
Mills bill, 4, 133; and protectionism,
39-40, 70-71, 74, 394, 408; quantitative restrictions, 113-15; Reciprocal
Trade Agreements Act of 1934, 13, 35,
38-40, 56, 129, 363; safeguards, 121-
23, 199-200, 244-45; sector advisory
committees, 135, 308-310, 314-17,
346; Smoot-Hawley tariff, 4, 13-14,
35-39, 46, 314n, 345, 349, 397; standards, 103-105, 194-96, 357; subsidy/
countervail, 16, 117-20, 137, 170-77,
213-23, 355, 359-61; Tariff Act of
1930, 180, 312n; tariff commission,
178; tariffs, 17-18, 20, 60-61, 158-64,
200-205, 256-72; tariff of 1824, 11;
Trade Act of 1974, 15, 77, 84, 128,
129-37, 160, 203, 214, 286, 295, 299,
307-308, 310, 313-14, 384n; Trade
Agreements Act of 1979, 121, 298,
304; Trade Expansion Act of 1962,
129; trade policy staff committee, 203;
Truman Declaration (1947), 27; Vietnam War, 23; voluntary export restraints, 4, 71-72, 113, 123, 242-43;
Watergate, 132, 133n; Williams Commission, 53, 59n, 74-76, 81, 90, 92;
wine-gallon concession, 280-302. *See
also* American Selling Price
Ury, William, 187n
Ushiba, Nobohiko, 203, 207-208, 268-
69, 329

Vanik, Charles A., 132, 216, 258n, 398n
variable levy (used by EC), 149
Vernon, Leo, 288n, 294n, 298n, 300n
Vernon, Raymond, 52n, 405n
Vickery, Norman, 334n
Vietnam War, 23
Viner, Jacob, 56
voluntary export restraints (voluntary
quotas) (VER), 4, 71-72, 115, 123, 242-
43

Wallace and Fay, 37n
Walton, R. E., and B. McKersie, 173n,
187n, 367n
Waltz, Kenneth, 386n, 389n
Warley, T. K., 151n, 153n
Warren, Jake, 207, 338, 339n, 341n
Washburn, Samuel H., 312n
Watergate, 132, 133n
Webster, Daniel, 11n
Wertenbaker, William, 274n
Western Alliance, 27, 57
West Germany. *See* Federal Republic of
Germany
Wheat Conference, 252-55
Whitman, Marina vN., 405n
Wilkinson, Rex, 265n
Williams, Albert L., 74
Williams, Peter, 196, 235

Williams Commission, 53, 59n, 74-76,
    81, 90, 92
Wilson, Bruce, 186
wine-gallon concession, 280-302
Winham, Gilbert R., 89n, 212n, 298n,
    358n, 375n, 405n
Wolff, Alan W., 166-67n, 261, 268
World Economic Conference of 1927, 35;
    of 1933, 36, 38, 385
Wyndham-White, Sir Eric, 15, 67, 70

Yeutter, Clayton K., 164
Yom Kippur War, 128
Yoshio, Sakurauchi, 349
Young, Oran, 42-43n
Yugoslavia, 211n, 254

Zartman, William I., and Maureen R.
    Berman, 212n, 368n
Zenith Case, 171n

Library of Congress Cataloging-in-Publication Data

Winham, Gilbert R.
International trade and the Tokyo round negotiation.
Bibliography: p.
Includes index.
1. Commercial policy.   2. Tokyo Round (1973-1979)
I. Title.
HF1412.W45   1986   382.9′1   86-9385
ISBN 0-691-07725-8
ISBN 0-691-02243-7 (pbk.)

Gilbert R. Winham is Professor of Political Science at
Dalhousie University in Halifax, Nova Scotia.